THE
MEDAL
YEARBOOK
2005

Edited by
James Mackay, MA, DLitt
John W. Mussell, FRGS
and
the Editorial Team of MEDAL NEWS

ISBN 1 870 192 66 4
(Hardback edition 1 870 192 67 2)

Published by
TOKEN PUBLISHING LIMITED

Orchard House, Duchy Road, Heathpark, Honiton, Devon EX14 1YD, UK
Telephone: 01404 46972   Fax: 01404 44788
e-mail: info@tokenpublishing.com   Website: www.tokenpublishing.com

USA distributor: Steve Johnson, Worldwide Militaria Exchange Inc., PO Box 745, Batavia, IL 60510
Canadian distributor: Eugene G. Ursual, PO Box 8096, Ottawa, Ontario, K1G 3H6

Printed in Great Britain by Haynes of Sparkford

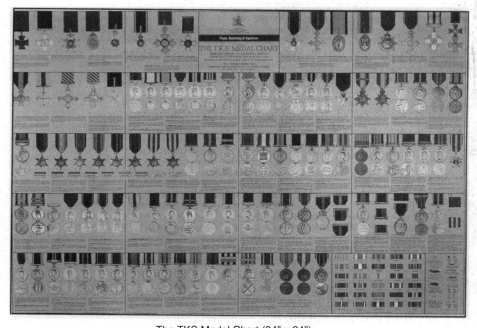

Contents

Index to advertisers

Preface

THIS is the eleventh annual edition of the MEDAL YEARBOOK and once again there have been a number of major changes, although essentially the book remains in the same format as the tenth edition. There are new useful sections added as well as a number of new medals, although after the deluge of new medals and decorations recorded last year the number chronicled for the first time in this edition is reduced. We are very pleased to record that the long-running campaign to secure an award that recognised the service of thousands of regulars and National Servicemen in the Canal Zone in the crucial years of 1951–54 has at long last been recognised by the issue of the General Service Medal with the clasp *Canal Zone*.

Inevitably the main news this year concerns the campaign medals and gallantry awards in respect of Operation Telic, more commonly known as the Second Gulf War. The proliferation of "international" awards for which British personnel are eligible in certain circumstances continues apace and these are duly itemised in the appropriate sections of this edition. This is something of a grey area, with British personnel entitled to wear the ribbon and medal in some cases but not in others. As in previous editions we list those medals in which British or Commonwealth personnel were involved, but omit others in which there was no British participation.

Several medals "on the fringe" have been added to this edition, both hitherto unrecorded unofficial medals and new issues which cater to ex-service personnel whose service was not recognised by an official award.

Now that the epic battle for the Canal Zone medal has been won the latest campaign for such recognition comes from veterans of the Arctic convoys who point out that their service in the Atlantic prior to engaging in this most hazardous operation was recognised by the Atlantic Star, and that naval personnel who subsequently spent a single day in the Mediterranean qualified for the Italy Star. If campaign stars should have been instituted for North Africa, Burma and the Pacific, the argument runs that the service in the Arctic certainly merited a comparable award. Ironically British veterans were subsequently awarded in 1985 a medal by the Soviet Union marking the 40th anniversary of the war. Apart from that, they have so far had to content themselves with the Arctic Campaign Medal instituted by Award Productions.

The review of the auction scene over the past year reveals that the market continues to surge ahead. If there have been far fewer Victoria Crosses under the hammer than in previous years this is an inevitable result of diminishing supplies of the coveted award in private hands. Incidentally it is interesting to note that several VCs have been donated to the appropriate museums by descendants and relatives who resisted the temptation to offer them for sale and let the museums raise the money to buy them.

What is probably more significant is the astonishing prices paid for medals which, not so long ago, would have been regarded as of little or no account. Not so long ago the Great War trio was frequently vandalised, the British War Medal being consigned to the melting pot on account of its precious metal content, and the 1914–15 Medal and Victory Medal dumped. How many "groups" exist today that are lacking the vital BWM? No one has ever attempted to assess the permanent loss incurred, but it is significant that complete trios are now fetching real money and in a few cases have even crossed the psychological four-figure barrier (e.g. awards to a casualty from the first day of the Somme serving in one of the units engaged in the heaviest fighting). It is significant that the man behind the medal has taken on increasing importance, and the collateral material associated with the medals has become of much greater value than was once the case.

We would like to thank all those who have sent us their comments and constructive criticism as well as furnishing details of new medals and further information regarding previously recorded ones. In particular we would like to thank the members of the Headquarters Land Command, Personnel Division, G. D. Aram, Peter Baker, Howard Chamberlain, Michael Charteris, Norman G. Gooding, Colin Hole, Peter Leek, Rear-Admiral J. A. L. Myers, Michael O'Brien, Lieutenant-Colonel N. W. Poulson, Brigadier Stuart Ryder, Allan Stanistreet, Lieutenant-Colonel Ashley Tinson, Jack V. Webb and John Wilson. Special thanks are also due to Captain C. Gauthier of the Honours and Awards Department of the Directorate of History and Heritage, Canada, for help with the Canadian entries and Peter Digby and the members of the Military Medal Society of South Africa for their invaluable help with the South Africa section.

We are also grateful to many dealers and professional numismatists for checking the prices of medals and miniatures in light of auction results and dealers' lists in the course of the past twelve months to enable us to keep the YEARBOOK up to date, particularly Phil Burman, Chris Dixon, Michael Kaplan, John Millensted and Gary Neate.

The YEAR at a glance

An at-a-glance resumé of the main events and occurrences that affected the medal hobby during the past twelve months as reported in MEDAL NEWS . . .

April 2003

From April 1 the Public Record Office and the Historical Manuscripts Commission amalgamate to form a new body entitled the National Archives.

June 2003

On June 11 the Prime Minister announces the award of the General Service Medal to veterans of the Canal Zone, 1951–54, with a clasp for Canal Zone.

The Wellington Museum at Apsley House, Hyde Park Corner (the residence of the Iron Duke), stages Waterloo Week (June 14–22) with an exhibition and series of talks.

The family of World War I hero Charles Hudson donate his VC, won at Asiago, Italy on June 15, 1918, to the Sherwood Foresters regimental museum in Nottingham. Brigadier Hudson retired in 1947 and died in 1959.

The deaths are announced of Paul Hilton who won the CMG as a sergeant-pilot at the age of 20 and Fusilier John Murray of the Royal Scots Fusiliers who earned his DCM at Derlyck, Belgium in September 1944.

The Royal Logistics Corps Museum at the Princess Royal Barracks, Deepcut, Camberley reopens after extensive refurbishment.

A memorial cairn is erected at Rosyth to commemorate the crews of two K-Class submarines sunk in the Firth of Forth in January 1918—85 years after the disaster when the two subs collided and sank, with the loss of 103 lives.

The Perth Mint, Western Australia, issued a series of bullion coins paying tribute to those who served in the five great conflicts of the 20th century (Boer, Korean and Vietnam wars as well as both world wars), the appropriate medal being reproduced on the obverse.

The National Service Memorial is unveiled at the National Arboretum, Alrewas. Staffordshire on June 29, National Service Day. The six-foot bronze and steel monument was sculpted by Ian Stewart CM and sponsored by Award Productions Limited.

The Bigbury Mint is commissioned to strike a special medal for the personnel involved in the production and dismantling of the Pershing and Cruise missiles.

The US Department of Defense announces the award of two new medals in the worldwide war on terrorism. The Global War on Terrorism Expeditionary Medal is awarded to personnel who took part in military operations against terrorism overseas on or after September 11, 2001 in Operation Enduring Freedom. The Global War on Terrorism Service Medal is granted for Operation Noble Eagle for homeland defence. Both bronze medals carry a design incorporating the American eagle.

At the annual Somme Day ceremony at the Cenotaph in Whitehall a 102-year-old veteran, William Stone, was on parade. Francis Murphy, the Northern Ireland Secretary, announces the grant of £400,000 to the Somme Association for the purchase of Thiepval Wood as a memorial.

July 2003

Bill Fevyer dies on July 2. A leading member of the OMRS for many years, he founded the Life Saving Awards Research Society in 1987.

John Darwent, who died on July 16 at the age of 77, traded in medals and militaria under the name "Soldiers of the Queen" and was a leading member of the OMRS. Having done his National Service in the Provost Corps he joined the Lancashire Constabulary and served as a detective for 25 years before becoming a full-time medal dealer.

The military historian Graham Maddocks dies on July 18 at the early age of 61.

The International Battlefield Conference staged at the National Army Museum over the weekend of July 19–20, entitled "Digging Up People" provides a wide range of lectures and discussion topics, from combat victims of the Bronze Age to archaeology of the 20th century.

The York Coin and Stamp Fair, held on July 25–26, included medals for the first time.

The two unique Atlantic Stars, the only ones awarded to an officer and a rating of the QRNS, go on display at the Wrens' Museum, Portsmouth.

Jeffrey Hoare, the Canadian auctioneer, sells the important World War II Canadian Memorial Cross of Major Sir Frederick Banting for $70,000. Banting was the co-discoverer of insulin, for which he was awarded the Nobel Prize in the 1920s. Previously he won the MC in September 1918.

The Royal Air Force Museum at Hendon gets a £7.4 million grant for major re-development.

At the Imperial War Museum's branch at Duxford the daughters of the late Wing Commander R. P. "Bee" Beaumont were presented with the Croix de Guerre by the Belgian authorities. It was a belated award recognising Beaumont's role in destroying some 638 V1 flying bombs while in command of the first wing of the Hawker Tempest V.

Judge Henry Pownall, twice President of the OMRS, dies on July 28.

Peter F. Ashford, a prominent member of the OMRS for many years, dies at Cheltenham on July 29.

The newly refurbished Museum of the Worcestershire Soldier opens at the City Museum and Art Gallery in Worcester.

The first awards of the new Royal Fleet Auxiliary Long Service & Good Conduct Medal are presented.

August 2003

On August 1 Ian Gordon Robertson, Director of the National Army Museum, dies at the early age of 60.

The Friends of the Royal Engineers Museum commence the task of publishing all the honours and awards of members of the Corps.

The death is announced of Sergeant George "Killer" Dring, MM and bar, at the age of 85, one of the ablest tank commanders in the Sherwood Rangers Yeomanry in World War II, and Ronald McKinley who won his CGM as a petty officer in the Royal Naval Commandos on D-Day.

Jeannie Robinson receives the Order of Merit of the OMRS from President Norman Gooding.

September 2003

New Zealand's Prime Minister, Helen Clark, presents the first NZ Operational Service Medals to the next of kin of 49 New Zealanders who lost their lives in military operations since 1945.

"The Horse in War" exhibition takes place on September 6–7 at Burton court opposite the National Army Museum in Chelsea.

Military historian John Urquhart organised a "Zulu Day" at the QEH Theatre, Bristol on September 7.

The Annual Convention of the Orders and Medals Research Society takes place at the New Connaught Rooms, London on September 20.

Harpers Wartime Research Media and Murphy's Register join forces and are re-launched at the OMRS Convention.

The Rev Bill Skelton dies at the age of 82. As a wartime navigator he won the DSO and bar and DFC and bar. After the war he entered holy orders and was an Anglican priest.

Edward Fedora, a Canadian medal collector, is arrested in an FBI "sting" for attempting to sell two Congressional Medals of Honor, from the Civil War and Spanish-American War respectively, and now faces five years in gaol and a fine of $250,000 for breaking Federal law that forbids the buying and selling of America's top gallantry award.

October 2003

The first part of the collection formed by the late Dr Arthur B. King sold at auction by Morton & Eden realises a total of £556,850 (not including the 15 per cent buyers' premium).

An exhibition and series of talks entitled "For Valour" takes place at the National Army Museum on October 4–5.

The National Army Museum stages a re-enactment of the battle of Salamanca on October 11–12.

The Royal Armouries at Fort Nelson, Fareham, inaugurate a militaria fair on October 12, coinciding with a re-enactment weekend by the Great War Society and the Brockhurst Artillery.

On October 14 Her Majesty the Queen opens the "Women at War" exhibition at the Imperial War Museum. Exhibits range from Mata Hari's stage costume to Princess Diana's body armour, touring the minefields of the Balkans.

An exhibition at the Imperial War Museum entitled "Women and War" opens on October 15 and continues till February 27, 2004.

The death is announced of Major John Edwards, GM at the age of 77. After war service in the Royal Marines and SAS he joined the Metropolitan Police and earned his George Medal in a road chase in November 1951. Shortly afterwards he rejoined the Armed Forces and served with distinction till his retirement in 1977. The death is also intimated of Wing Commander Peter Parrott, DFC and bar, AFC, who died recently at the age of 83.

The death is announced of 91 year-old Sidney Wiltshire, the oldest holder of the George Cross. He was originally awarded the Empire Gallantry Medal in 1930 but emigrated to New Zealand and exchanged his medal for the GC in 1944.

Admiral Sir Jonathan Band, Commander-in-Chief Fleet, attends the unveiling of a memorial to the Norwegian Campaign at Narvik.

A major part of the medal collection of the Queen's West Surrey regiment is stolen from Clandon Park, Surrey during the night of October 25. Thieves make off with about 1,000 medals and groups including gallantry awards.

November 2003

The National Army Museum holds a series of talks and activities on November 8–9 to explore the significance of Remembrance.

The Secretary of State for Defence, Geoff Hoon, announces on November 10 the erection of a memorial to more than 2,600 personnel killed in conflicts since 1945. The memorial will be located at the National Memorial Arboretum in Staffordshire.

Peter and Dee Helmore organise a "Weekend of Medals" at Banbury.

At a Warwick & Warwick sale on November 12 the gallantry group of Squadron Leader E.D. Parker is sold. It includes the DFC and GC, the latter exchanged in 1941 for the EGM awarded to Parker in August 1940. He was killed in action in 1943.

The death is announced of Alun Blackwell who won his DCM as a lance-corporal in Tunisia in 1941. He was twice captured while engaged on covert operations behind enemy lines and twice escaped before being recaptured and ended the war as a POW in Poland.

Imperial War Museum North stage an exhibition in Manchester entitled "Painting Caserta Red" based on the work of artist Hughie O'Donaghue.

Corporal Eddie Power, the oldest RAAF recipient of the MM in Vietnam, dies in Australia.

Veterans Minister Ivor Caplin presents the first Canal Zone medals to veterans at Wellington Barracks.

The new accommodation block at Vimy Barracks, Catterick is named in honour of Lance Corporal William Amey, VC, MM of the Royal Warwickshire Regiment. Amey survived the war and died in May 1940. He won his Victoria Cross at Landrecies, France on November 4, 1918.

December 2003

The Medal Society of Ireland holds its second annual auction on December 6 at the Teachers' Club, Parnell Square, Dublin.

Four generations of medals to the Buckle family come under the hammer at Morton & Eden's sale on December 11–12, ranging from the gold medal for the capture of Louisburg to World War I.

A "Victorian Soldier's Christmas" is the theme of a special event at the National Army Museum on December 14–15.

The new exhibition hall of the RAF Museum, Hendon is opened on December 17 by HRH the Duke of Edinburgh.

The death is announced of Captain "Tinker" Taylor at the age of 81. He won his MC with the Irish Guards in Normandy in August 1944. Major-General Peter Blunt, who also died recently at the age of 79, won the George Medal for his courageous action at a petrol spill in 1959.

The balance of the collection of naval medals formed by the late Captain Kenneth Douglas-Morris goes to the Royal Naval Museum, Portsmouth.

January 2004

The death is announced of Vice-admiral Sir Peter Berger aged 79, awarded the Distinguished Service Cross for his part in the Yangtze incident in 1949. He was badly wounded while navigating HMS *Amethyst* at the beginning of the bombardment, but gallantly carried on after the ship's captain was killed.

The Army Museum at Fremantle, Western Australia, receives the Victoria Cross won by Lieutenant William St Lucien Chase for outstanding bravery in Afghanistan, 1880.

Lieutenant-Colonel Jim Condon retires from his position as officer-in-charge of the Army Medal Office.

Sally Bosley launches a website www.regimentalbrooches.com specialising in the sale of fine quality brooches of the armed forces and their spouses.

February 2004

The Dublin Coin and Medal Fair takes place at the Royal Dublin Society over the weekend of February 21–22.

The auction held by Colonial Coins & Medals amd C.J. Medals of Brisbane on February 21 sees the George Cross group of Lt. Cdr. John Stuart Mould fetch $A444,000, a record price for any Australian group and a world record for a George Cross.

On February 23 the Ministry of Defence announces the issue of a campaign medal recognising service in Operation Telic (the Second Gulf War). Known as the Iraq Medal, it also has a clasp for those who served between March 19 and April 28, 2003.

The death is announced of Lieutenant-General Reg Lane at the age of 83. He commanded Canada's only Pathfinder squadron in World War II during which he won the DSO and DFC and bar.

March 2004

A new Internet auction site, www.wangled.com is inaugurated, with fees undercutting the giant eBay.

The National Archive institutes a website www.nationalarchivist.com to assist genealogists seeking details of relatives military service.

The review of the British Honours system, published by the Public Administration Select Committee, reveals that more than 300 prominent figures from the world of arts and entertainment declined honours since the end of World War II.

The death is intimated of Lieutenant-Colonel Mike Webb at the age of 82. He fought with 2 Commando and won the MC and bar.

Medal specialists TM Medals launch their website www.tmmedals.co.uk

Money from the National Lottery Fund is earmarked for a project called "Heroes Return" to enable World War II veterans to visit the battlefields of France, North Africa and the Far East.

The Ministry of Defence reveals details of the decorations awarded to servicemen engaged in Operation Barras, which freed six Royal Irish Regiment hostages in Sierra Leone in 2001.

A medal society for collectors in Singapore and Malaysia is inaugurated by Gerard Leong, marketing manager of Royal Insignia of Singapore.

At a ceremony in Australia House, London, Miss Nancy Wake, nicknamed the White Mouse by the Gestapo, is made a Companion of the Order of Australia, belatedly recognising her gallantry as a British secret agent in World War II. She is also the older of the George Medal and three Croix de Guerre. In addition she has the Médaille de la Resistance, the American Medal of Freedom and the insignia of a Chevalier of the Légion d'Honneur.

By the end of March the Army Medal Office has processed 26,878 applications for the Canal Zone award, but only 4,150 had actually been assessed.

April 2004

The Queen's Volunteer Reserves hold their inaugural dinner at the Officers' Mess. Inns of Court Signals Squadron, London.

The second OMRS North medal weekend takes place at Runcorn, Cheshire over the weekend of April 16–17.

A memorial to the Irishmen who fought in World War I is unveiled at Leighlinbridge, Co. Carlow, remembering the 470men from the county who served in action. They include Major James McCudden, VC, DSO, MC and bar and his two brothers Anthony and William. McCudden, the top-scoring Allied ace with 57 kills to his credit, was killed in a flying accident in March 1918.

On April 23 Framlingham College presents to the Imperial War Museum two Victoria Crosses won by former pupils during World War I. They were awarded to Lance-Corporal William Henry Hewitt of the 2nd South African Light Infantry and Lieutenant Gordon Muriel Flowerdew of Lord Strathcona's Horse. The to VCs join a third by a former pupil, that won by Lieutenant Augustus Agar, RN.

The death is announced of Brigadier Peter Jeffreys at the age of 93. He earned a DSO in Chindit operations in Burma and a bar while commanding the 1st Battalion, Durham Light Infantry in Korea. Other deaths intimated are those of Group-Captain John Peel aged 92, a Battle of Britain DFC, and Air Vice-Marshal

John Stacey aged 83, who led the attack to lay mines in Singapore harbour in March 1945, for which he won an immediate DSO.

May 2004

Tour operator King Harry's Cornwall organises a tour of the Normandy battlefields over the weekend of May 29–31.

The death is announced of Captain Henry St John Fancourt at the age of 103. He served as a midshipman at the battle of Jutland in 1916 He won the DSO in World War II during the ill-fated assault on Algiers harbour in November 1942.

Angela and Tony Kirk launch a new company, Honours and Awards, of Wolverhamton dedication to the restoration and display of medals.

The Imperial War Museum stages a month-long exhibition devoted to D-Day to mark the 60th anniversary.

The death is intimated of Rear-Admiral Roger Welby at the age of 97. He was in command of the little-known expeditionary force in France in 1940 to lay mines in the French rivers to delay the German advance and won the DSO as a result.

Sir Hayden Phillips, Permanent Secretary at the Department for Constitutional Affairs, is reviewing current arrangements for the award of honours, particularly concerning the lack of diversity and transparency in the awards system.

June 2004

A special memorial service takes place on June 6 at St Nicholas Church, HMS *Drake*, Devonport to commemorate the 64th anniversary of the sinking of the aircraft carrier *Glorious* and her escorts on June 8, 1940 in the Norwegian Sea with the loss of 1,531 lives.

The Birmingham Medal Society celebrates its 40th anniversary with a convention over the weekend of June 12–13 at the Allesley Hotel, Coventry.

The Nelson Society reveals plans to mark the bicentenary of the battle of Trafalgar in October 2005, including the production of replicas of the Flag Officers and Captains Gold Medals of 1794–1815 in gold, silver gilt and gilt bronze.

The death is announced of Lieutenant Commander Peter Williams at the age of 91. As commander of a gunboat, he ran agents arms, ammunition and vital supplies to Allied agents in occupied Europe in 1943–44. He was awarded the DSC for his exploits and in 1994, on the 50th anniversary of D-Day he was made a Chevalier of the Légion d'Honneur.

Her Majesty the Queen approves the establishment of specific campaign medals for members of the Australian Defence Force who have been deployed in Afghanistan and Iraq. The Governor-General of Australia authorises the Iraq clasp for the Humanitarian Overseas Service Medal.

Major Roy Gribble dies at the age of 85. He won the MC and bar serving with the Commandos in Burma.

July 2004

The National Army Museum stages a Battlefield Archaeology conference on July 24–25.

The Government announce the issue of a new lapel badge to be worn by former Servicemen of all ranks as part of the commemorative events associated with the 60th anniversary of World War II. The first one is presented to Lord Healey, a veteran of the Salerno landings.

Leslie Frost, OBE, Legion d'Honneur, the popular National Chairman of the Normandy Veterans Association, dies at the age of 84— just after his return from the Normandy Landings anniversary events in France.

The Life Saving Awards Research Society celebrate the 50th edition of their *Journal* which is dedicated to the memory of the late Bill Fevyer.

Market trends

In the period under review (mid–2003 to mid–2004) the pound sterling continued to rise against the dollar and the Euro. Although the disparity between sterling and the Euro was not so great the gap between the pound and the dollar tended to widen. At one point it looked as if the pound might reach the magic two-dollar barrier but even though this was short-lived the pound has generally been around the $1.85 mark in recent months. This has produced a noticeable drop in American participation in international auctions generally, although when the material on offer was exceptionally fine, this seemed to make no difference. However, there was no diminution in the activities of bidders from the Eurozone countries. In the same period the FTSE index of leading shares made a significant recovery, and despite some disappointing fluctuations over the year it has maintained a level well above the 4000 barrier. Disillusion with traditional savings and investments and a greater willingness to trust in "tangibles", the more fashionable term for alternative investments, has seen an upsurge right across the board in collectables of all kind. Inevitably medals have been swept up in this also, and this is reflected in the prices paid at auction for material which would hardly have merited a second glance a few short years ago.

Despite occasional warnings from banks and building societies, the house market has continued to boom, although it is significant that the grossly overheated London market has eased off while prices have shot ahead in previously unfashionable areas. Increases in interest rates by the Bank of England, dutifully followed by banks and building societies, seems to have had little impact in dampening down the housing market. Interest rates have not risen much in relative terms and so there is little incentive to savers. For this reason many people, encouraged by media coverage of sales and the current fashion for television programmes that cover everything from car-boot sales to the fine-art auctions, have been turning their attention to collectables. In many cases the spectacular and highly entertaining results obtained in these televised sales have stimulated people to rummage in the attic for grand-dad's war medals and these have come on to the market.

The core of this material fresh to the market belongs to World War I (with a substantial amount of Boer War medals for good measure). Even World War II groups have found their niche if supported by collateral material, although the opportunities for fabricating such groups which do not include at least one named medal should not be ignored.

During this period a number of fine collections, carefully built up over many years, came under the hammer. One may cite the collections of John Tamplin, Tony Mount and David Evans which added lustre to the DNW sale in September 2003. The first of these was as choice an assemblage of material as has been seen in the saleroom for some years while the others were excellent examples of collections devoted to medals and groups of particular regiments. The Richard Magor collection of Indian and African medals was one of the undoubted highlights of the year, but the most star-studded was the British and Commonwealth section of the collection formed by the late Dr. Arthur B. King of the USA, the American portion being disposed off by Siegel in New York. The important collection of Napoleonic and Crimean War medals formed by John Darwent of Blackburn formed the core of the DNW sale on April 2, 2004.

The health of the market is often measured by the blue chip items that pass through the saleroom but at that rarified level so many other factors and imponderables may be involved. For example, the excessively rare and probably unique GBE breast star worn by HRH Princess Mary, the Princess Royal was the undoubted star (no pun intended) of the Morton & Eden sale in May 2004 but it remained unsold. Despite this disappointment, however, it was a satisfactory sale with many items surpassing their estimates and sometimes handsomely so.

What is arguably a better barometer of the market is the performance of what, not so long ago, was dismissed as "bog standard stuff". The best example of this is provided by the Great War trio. Some of us can remember a time when the trio changed hands for a few shillings, and when the scrap value of silver rose, countless thousands of the British War Medals were consigned to the melting pot. Many of the 1914–15 and Victory medals that made up such groups were probably thrown away as of no account whatsoever, but this depredation accounts for the pairs of these medals that lie forlorn, with no hope of completion. Those Great War trios that are intact, however, have risen steadily in value in recent years, largely as a result of the efforts and shining example of the Orders and Medals Research Society which has opened our eyes to the potential for discovering the man behind the medals. It is the personal element of British campaign awards which gives them their unique advantage over comparable medals from other countries. A DCM group awarded to a casualty of the first day of the Somme sold for £2,900 at Baldwin's in April 2003 against an estimate of £1,700–£2,000, but already prices for the trio to first day Somme casualties, without a gallantry award, are approaching four figures. Several trios in the DNW sale of July 6, 2004, in fact sold well above £2,000 on account of the rather tenuous association of the recipient with someone famous. For example the trio to Captain Helenus Robertson, a comrade in arms of war poet Robert Graves sold for £2,645 (including premium), the trio to 2nd Lt Marsham-Townshend of the Scots Guards sold for £2,300 due to the fact that his father was a famous 19th century numismatist, while the trio to Lieut Leonard Mill made £1,610 because he was killed at Guillemont, the action in which Noel Chavasse won his first VC.

Highest Gallantry Awards

At the other end of the spectrum no fewer than five Victoria Crosses came up at auction during the period under review. At the Dix Noonan Webb sale on July 2, 2003 which broke the million pound barrier for the first time, the highlight was undoubtedly the Indian Mutiny VC group of three awarded to Colonel John Daunt of the Bengal Native Infantry (illustrated above), the jewel in the crown of the collection formed by Richard Magor. One of the finest collections of Indian and African campaign medals ever formed it grossed £770,971 (£886,617 with premium). When Magor purchased this VC group in 1973 he paid £2,000, an auction record at that time. On this occasion it sold for £110,000 (£126,500)—just £10,000 less than the current joint auction record for a VC.

The second VC group to hit the headlines was that awarded to Lance-Corporal Frederick William Holmes of the KOYLI for exceptional bravery under fire at Le Cateau in August 1914. Remarkably Holmes went right through the war, was commissioned in 1917 and retired in 1921 after service in Ireland during the Troubles. His group fetched £80,000, pretty well in line with the estimate of £70,000–£90,000.

Spink handled the third VC of the season, on November 5, 2003. This was part of the sensational 12-medal group to Daniel Beak of the Royal Naval Division at Gallipoli, along with a DSO, MC and bar and campaign medals for both world wars, ending as GOC Malta. Again, it sold in line with the estimate of £150,000–£180,000, selling for £155,000 (not counting the premium). A month later Morton & Eden conducted a relatively small sale, but what it lacked in quantity was compensated for in quality. The VC, Egypt Medal and Khedive's Star group

awarded to Warrant Officer Israel Harding during the bombardment of Alexandria in 1882 sold for £86,000. The finest of them all was the group to Sergeant Norman Jackson, RAF which sold at Spink on April 30, 2004 for the record price of £235,000 (including premium).

The differential between the Victoria Cross and its civil counterpart, the George Cross, is considerable despite the fact that it is much rarer. Only one George Cross came up for sale in England in this period, awarded posthumously for bravery during the London Blitz. Featured in the DNW sale of July 2003, it was estimated at £18,000–£20,000 but remained unsold. In the same sale the extraordinary George Medal and Bar group to Able Seaman W.H. Bevan for gallantry in bomb and mine disposal operations in Manchester in 1940 and for disarming a parachute bomb on the roof of the London Palladium in 1941, realised £22,000 (£25,300 with premium). The same auction saw a George Medal and Binney Medal awarded to the actor and writer Donald Smith for his part in fighting off a group of drunken youths on the rampage in Regents Park, London, sell for £3,450. On the other hand the George Cross group of eight to Lieutenant-Commander John Stuart Mould, awarded for defusing unexploded bombs during the Blitz, sold for A$444,000 in Brisbane on February 21, 2004, a world record price; so perhaps the George Cross is now beginning to get the recognition it deserves.

An extremely rare New Zealand Cross pair awarded to Private Thomas Adamson sold for £28,000 £32,000 with premium) in the same auction.

Other Decorations

DSO groups add interest to any auction and there were plenty of fine examples in this period. Prices, of course, vary widely, depending on the circumstances of the award (an immediate award for gallantry in action rating much more than a "service" award) and also the medals making up the rest of the group, not to mention the personal circumstances of the recipient. The DSO group of six to Lieutenant Edward Hardinge, whose decoration was one of the very first awarded in August 1914, sold for £20,700 at DNW in July 2003. A fine group of ten to Major-General B. F. Armstrong sold for £4,800 (not including premium) at Bosley's on June 11, 2003. Armstrong rose through the ranks, was commissioned and ended up as a major-general. Along the way he won his DSO for gallantry at Sidi Rezegh, was taken prisoner and later escaped from captivity.

The quirkiness of the market is best illustrated by the two Great War DSO groups at Bonhams on July 8, 2003. The first, estimated at £1,500–£2,000, was unsold while the second (estimated at £2,000–£3,000) to Lieutenant-Colonel Turnbull of the Gordon Highlanders was fiercely contested before being knocked down for £4,800.

Orders of Knighthood

Orders of knighthood are often problematical. Their rarity and intrinsic value (often incorporating precious stones) is to some extent offset by the fact that they usually represent rank and privilege rather than the reward of gallantry. On the one hand a dazzling group at Dix Noonan Webb on July 2, 2003 was the array of medals and decorations awarded to Sir Charles Hardinge, first Baron Hardinge of Penshurst

(1858–1944), Viceroy of India from 1910 to 1916, which included the Grand Commander of the Star of India. This sumptuous order sold for £36,000 (£41,400 with premium). On the other hand, the excessively rare and possibly unique diamond-studded breast star of Dame Grand Cross of the British Empire, second version, belonging to HRH Princess Mary, the Princess Royal which was the highlight of the Morton & Eden sale in May 2004, estimated at £15,000 –£20,000, remained unsold.

A first type Indian Order of Merit, first class, of which only 42 were ever awarded between 1837 and 1912, sold at DNW in July 2003 for £8,050, while a gold and enamel neck badge of the Order of Burma, of which only 24 were awarded, fetched £7,475 in the same auction, and £5,980 secured the Companion's breast badge of the Star of India awarded to Edward Clarke.

Campaign Medals

If the Victoria Crosses sold very much in line with pre-sale expectation, and gallantry awards of the second and third levels did relatively better, it is in the realm of campaign medals that they greatest percentage increases were recorded in this period.

At the very top of the pecking order are the gold medals and crosses from the Napoleonic Wars. An Army Gold Cross fetched £36,000 at Morton & Eden's sale on October 3, 2003, but a month later a seven clasp cross, accompanied by a breast star and other insignia awarded to Major-General Sir Denis Pack, fetched £100,000 at Spink. An Army Gold Cross and Army Small Gold Medal, accompanied by the insignia of the Bath, awarded to Colonel John Piper of the 4th Foot, realised £36,000 at the Morton & Eden sale in October 2003. In the same sale the Army Large Gold Medal for Java to Major-General F.A. Wetherall, fetched £22,000 and the same sum was paid for a gold Mysore Medal of 1791–2.

Waterloo medals come into the category of barometric pieces, whose performance at auction is a good guide to the state of the market in general. During this period there were plenty to choose from, most selling over the £1,000 mark which not so long ago would have been unthinkable, and in sales in 2004 some examples have doubled that sum and one medal, to Lieutenant John McDonald of the Royal Welch Fusiliers, sold for the staggering sum of £7,475 (including premium) at DNW's sale in April 2004.

Naval and Military GSMs of the Napoleonic period were not perhaps as plentiful as they have been in previous years (until the deluge in the Darwent sale), and this was reflected in the sums realised which continued to surge ahead. Not untypical was the Military GSM with three clasps accompanied by the Waterloo Medal (illustrated above right) which went for £5,400 against an estimate of £1,500–£2,000 at Bonhams in October. A nine-clasp Military GSM sold at DNW in April 2004 for £4,300, while a stupendous 12-clasp medal in the same sale realised £7,360. A Naval GSM with clasp *Terpsichore, 13 Octr 1796*, estimated at £2,000–£3,000, was bid all the way up to £24,000 at Bonhams in December 2003. In the same month a single-clasp medal for Trafalgar to Midshipman Robert Patton of HMS *Bellerophon* went for £18,000 at DNW,

the recipient being regarded as the senior ranking veteran, an admiral who died in 1882 at the age of 92. Almost as high a price was the £17,000 (£19,550 with premium) paid at DNW in April 2004 for the NGS with unique combination of three "North American" clasps.

However, the biggest surprise in this area came at the Thomson, Roddick & Medcalf sale at Carlisle on May 7 when two NGS medals awarded to shipmates (and possibly relatives) on HMS *Pincher* were featured. The first medal had the boat service clasp for *27th July 1809*—only of only two to this ship. The other medal had the only other clasp to this ship, plus four other clasps from *1st June 1794* to *Algiers* and including *Sylph 28th Sept. 1801* and *Trafalgar*. The first medal went to a dealer for £15,000—five times the upper estimate, but the second medal was a terrific battle between room bidders and four on the telephones, one of whom eventually secured it for £70,000, ten times the mid estimate and a new record for a NGS medal.

Campaign medals did extremely well right across the board at the DNW sale in July 2003, where the Magor collection was exceptionally strong in Mutiny medals. No fewer than a dozen Army of India singles came under the hammer and yielded some record results. A two-clasp medal to Captain Lucius Smith of the 6th Cavalry—one of only 21 Europeans to receive the rare *Seetabuldee & Nagpore* clasp, sold for £8,050. Among the Mutiny medals the best was a four-clasp award to Bombardier John Cook of the Bengal Artillery which yielded £2,900. A rare group of three to John Smith, a schoolboy volunteer at Lucknow, made £5,500.

A scarce Nile Expedition group in this sale, awarded to a private in the 94th regiment who was killed at Abu Klea, sold for £5,290. Runner-up was a Great War trio and plaque to Nursing Sister Alice Hallam who died in France in 1916. Estimated at £2,000–£2,500, this lot rose to £5,175, an astonishing result explained by the fact that plaques to ladies have usually survived without the associated medals. In the year of the 150th anniversary it was appropriate that the Crimean medals and groups in the Darwent sale should do so well. Top price in this section was the £14,000 paid for a fine Charge of the Light Brigade DCM and four-clasp medal along with long service medals.

There has been a definite hardening of the market

for Military Medal groups. The World War I trio with the MM has leaped ahead this year, but groups from World War II have performed even better. An outstanding example was the extremely rare Long Range Desert Group to Sergeant J.M. Lowenthal which sold for £10,925 at the DNW sale on September 19, 2003.

American collectors were conspicuously successful in securing a number of the better items in the Morton & Eden sale of October 2003, yet in the same sale the pair of Polar medals to Seaman Thomas Dunning of the United States Navy, together with the extremely rare Grinnell Medal presented by British residents of New York to American seamen who took part in the search for the ill-fated Franklin Expedition should sell for only £5,200 against an estimate of £6,000–£8,000.

Among the miscellaneous items may be mentioned the Women's Social and Political Union Medal with eight bars awarded to Mary "Slasher" Richardson which sold at DNW in December 2003 for £19,000; she earned her nickname for attacking the Velazquez masterpiece known as the *Rokeby Venus*.

Foreign Medals

Although the bulk of the material which passes through the British salerooms pertains to Britain and the Commonwealth, there is a not insubstantial quantity of foreign medals and decorations. Without the personal element which is such a strong feature of British awards, these items are somewhat problematical, sometimes selling very well, but often selling below estimate or failing to find an bidder. Among the lots which attracted keen bidding was an interesting Balkan Wars group at Bosley's in September 2003 which sold for £1,100 against an estimate of £300–£500. At Bonhams that July the biggest surprise was provided by a Silver Jubilee medal for Rama V, King of Siam, 1893 (illustrated above right), estimated at £250–£300, which was pursued all the way to £2,300.

A group of 15 awards to Major-General Anatoly Ivanovich Volodin, a Red Army air ace, the veteran of 397 combat sorties with 22 kills to his name, included Hero of the Soviet Union, the Orders of Lenin, Nevsky, the Patriotic War and three orders of the Red Banner as well as lesser decorations and campaign medals, sold for £2,760 at Spink in May 2003.

No survey of the past auction season would be complete without a reference to the extraordinary lots of medals, jewels, memorabilia and family archives relating to General Sir David Baird, GCB sold by DNW in September 2003. The star item was the jewelled sword of Tipu Sultan which sold for £172,500. Baird's General Officer's gold medal for Corunna sold for £52,900, a record price for a single medal of this type.

NB. Prices quoted above include the buyer's premium.

Medals and the Internet

The Internet revolution has touched almost every aspect of our lives in one way or another. One of the biggest areas of growth has been on-line ordering—electronic mail order if you like. At first this simply took the guise of catalogues, lists, etc., appearing on-line much as they would in paper form, i.e. a product is listed at a fixed price and customers are able to buy it for that. However, it wasn't long before somebody came up with the idea of on-line auctions: giving people the chance to pay more for an item to secure it should they so wish. So eBay was born and has gone on to become one of the success stories of the Internet. When all around "virtual" business models were failing, Ebay went from strength to strength and it wasn't long before the model was being copied in every collecting area and beyond.

Now you can buy or sell practically anything in a virtual auction, be it clothes, cars, concert tickets or, of course, collectables. Medals have become an obvious favourite and every day hundreds of orders, campaign medals and decorations are being listed on eBay and on the specialist sites that have been developed such as Speedbid.com and bid2u.com.

Another alternative, Bidwyze.com, has also been developed by Bosleys the Buckinghamshire auctioneers, but this differs slightly from the others inasmuch that it is more of a traditional sale but on-line. All items are vetted and guaranteed by Bosleys and the sales all last for a set duration. However, this article looks more at the "rolling sales" where items are unvetted and placed on-line by individuals although it should be noted that other internet sale rooms similar to Bidwyze are becoming increasingly popular

For those readers who aren't familiar with auction sites the process is a simple one. Just as with a real live auction, you "view" the objects for sale and, if you wish to have a go at buying, you register and place bids accordingly. You can be outbid at any time, but always get the chance to "have another go" should you so wish. Auctions are timed (in days) and at the end of that time the virtual hammer falls and the highest bidder secures the lot if the reserve price is met. Buyer and seller then contact each other via email, payment is made and, once the vendor is satisfied that all is in order, the goods are despatched. Of course, unlike a "regular" auction house that has built its reputation over time, you are generally dealing with individuals and must therefore take a great deal on trust. To counter this the "feedback" system has been devised to allow potential buyers (and sellers) to tell at a glance whether the person they are dealing with has a good track record or not. Inevitably there are occasional disputes, with fakes being sold as originals, items not as described, etc., but in general those organising these auctions are keen to stamp out any such goings-on and will bar the rogue traders pretty quickly. If in doubt a look at the vendor profile will tell you all you need to know—if time after time unhappy buyers report that a paryicular seller deals in fakes then it's best to steer clear!

Internet auctions have undoubtedly opened up the medal world: now anyone can become a dealer. As a consequence buying has become simple—collectors keen to get as much as they can for their unwanted items and "overs" are often by-passing the traditional route of dealer or auction with the necessary charges and mark-ups (after all, dealers do need to make a living too you know!). Collectors are selling pieces on-line that they might otherwise have held on to. Buyers, who often don't care whether they buy from a dealer or "direct" from the collector, just so long as the price is right, are reaping the benefit as singles and groups that might otherwise have never surfaced are seeing the light of day.

However, as with everything, there is another side—and, as anyone who has ever bought on-line will know, there can be occasions when even the most innocuous-looking medals fetch astronomical sums. Ordinary WWI Pairs selling for £100+, "Standard" QSAs fetching five times what they would normally and gallantry groups going through the roof. The reason such sums are reached is easy to work out —the Internet is open to all with access and unlike a dealer's list or a "traditional" medal auction, buyers who would, in the past, never have considered medals as a purchase are now suddenly taking an interest.

Instead of just medal collectors buying, we now also have a whole raft of other people happy to part with money for mementoes that bear their name or have a connection with their town, county, etc. Where once medal collecting was the preserve solely of those with an interest in the hobby, now others who would never consider themselves collectors are paying big money simply to own something that might once have belonged to a member of their family or someone who once lived in their street.

For example take the fictitious case of a simple 1914/15 trio to a Private Darroll who was killed with the Devon Regiment but whose parents lived in Willoughby Street, Nottingham—the city where he was born and enlisted although he himself lived in Wyndham Avenue, Exeter. Not only do you have the Devon Regiment collectors interested but if you get an eBay bidder living in Willoughby Street, Nottingham, another living in Wyndham Avenue, Exeter and a third whose surname is Darroll then suddenly you have a very interesting auction. Of course this has always been the case, and in auction houses up and down the country phenomenal prices have been fetched when two or more bidders have had personal interests in an item—the difference now is that potentially millions of people are able to bid, and with those odds you can guarantee that there will be one or two buyers whose interests will clash. In a room of 300 people the chances that two come from Exeter or Nottingham are slim—with the internet those chances get a lot bigger.

So it is that the internet salerooms can give us a somewhat distorted view of things and lead us to believe that prices are climbing even higher than they actually are. The specialist medal sites aren't too bad: they generally attract medal collectors rather than the general public and thus the problem of "name collectors" or "town collectors" doesn't come up that often. But with the more obviously public sites some astounding results can be attained—which is great if you're the seller, but not so good if you are the poor soul trying to pick up that trio you've been after for years when you're up against a bidder with the same surname as the recipient!

That all said, bargains can be picked up. If you're quick the "buy it now" options (usually put on for a quick sale) can prove lucrative (the vendor being more interested in hard cash now than potentially more later on) and even in the full-on auctions it is certainly possible to get your hands on something others might have missed. It is easily possible to place what seems like a ridiculously low bid early, only to find you in fact get your prize as no one has bid against you. It is also equally possible to "snipe" an existing bid at the last minute, thus securing your purchase without giving the other bidder a chance to "retaliate". How you bid is up to you, but what is certain is that like any other auction anything is possible and, if used carefully and sensibly, Internet auctions can be as much fun as the "real thing" and are an excellent way of adding to your collection without ever leaving the comfort of your own home. They have a place in our hobby now and cannot be ignored, nor should they be. But just how big a part they are to play remains to be seen and only time will tell.

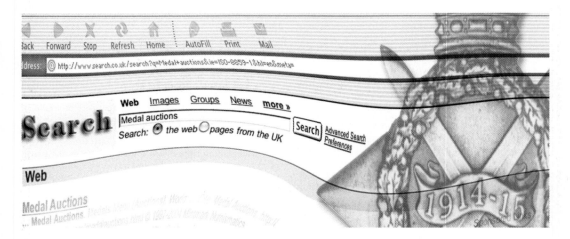

Caveat **Emptor**

Medal collecting has more than its fair share of pitfalls to trap the unwary, although the exercise of commonsense will often save you from wasting your money on a worthless fake. Your best guarantee always is to buy only from reputable dealers who will promptly refund your money should your purchase prove to be not quite what it seems. The problem arises when you buy medals from general antique shops, street market stalls, car-boot sales, swap-meets and collectors' fairs. Despite the Trades Descriptions Act and other legislation to protect the consumer, in practice it is very difficult, time-consuming and costly to gain restitution through the courts. Indeed, the situation is exacerbated by the rapid growth of on-line selling, where such phrases as "sold as is" or "not sure if this is genuine or not" are unlikely to inspire confidence. The only saving grace of on-line buying is that it is usually possible to download a high-resolution image of the medal and this can then be enlarged to study the finer details more carefully. It is one thing to study a medal critically in the comfort of your own home with all the necessary tools and reference works at your elbow, and quite another matter to spot a fake or outright forgery while browsing in a dealer's stock. But a little care and a better idea of the potential problems may prevent you from making a costly mistake. If you are offered a medal or group for sale at a bargain price, the alarm bells should be ringing loud and clear.

After we touched on this problem in editorials in MEDAL NEWS (February and March 2003), it appeared that we had touched a raw nerve. We were astonished at the wide spectrum of reaction from readers, ranging from the rather negative "nothing can be done so why bother" or "let the beginner learn from his mistakes" to tales of woe from readers who were duped in the past. One thing came out loud and clear; the scale of forgery and faking of medals is far larger and more widespread than we had imagined. There is also a large grey area concerning "copies" of medals required for museum exhibits or perhaps as replacements for genuinely lost medals to complete groups. There is actually a very small requirement for such "museum quality" replicas and we support the views of the Orders and Medals Research Society which does not countenance the sale, advertisement or display of such material. Occasional features now appear in MEDAL NEWS under the title of "On Guard" as different medals and decorations are put under the spotlight and the subtle differences between the genuine and the false are clearly set out.

OUTRIGHT FORGERY

The traditional method of producing an outright forgery of a medal was to make moulds from a genuine example and then take casts from it. The most obvious telltale sign of forgery is the metal itself, for forgers seldom took the trouble to get exactly the right composition of alloy. A good example of this is the forgery of the India General Service Medal of 1854 which has a leaden appearance and a peculiarly soapy texture to the touch. On checking the diameter of the suspect medals, using callipers and a half-millimetre scale, it will invariably be found that the diameter is slightly smaller than the genuine medal. This is due to the fact that the plaster used in the mould shrinks slightly as it dries, with the result that any cast will be that bit smaller and thinner than the genuine article.

Whether the alloy is suspect or not, you should always make a point of checking the precise dimensions of medals, suspension bars and clasps. Both the thickness and diameter of medals should be measured as accurately as possible, the latter being checked at several points (for a reason which will become obvious later).

Apart from alloy and dimensions, the other telltale sign of forgery is the surface condition. Is every detail of the design sharp, or is there evidence of blurring? There are quite fundamental differences in the techniques of production between a genuinely struck medal and a cast forgery. The latter will usually show some signs of microscopic surface pitting, caused by tiny air bubbles in the molten metal as it cools down. Some forgeries we have examined are actually unbelievably crude, and the wonder is that anyone could be deceived by them—but they frequently are!

These forgeries were produced in simple sand moulds which, although lacking the shrinkage factor inherent in plaster moulds, have a grainy quality. Sometimes the forger will attempt to remove this grainy characteristic as well as other surface blemishes, by chasing, an ancient technique of metal workers which involves filing and scraping with fine chisels and burins. This technique inevitably leaves very fine marks which are absent in genuinely struck medals. Casts also exhibit fine lines on the rim, where the two halves of the mould join, and although they are invariably filed off this often leaves a slight ridge, often visible by holding the medal with the rim to the light and rotating it slowly. Always examine the surface of medals with a good magnifier, at least ten times magnification, for these telltale blemishes to be readily apparent.

In recent years, as the value of medals has soared, forgers have been taking infinitely greater pains, even going to the length of having new dies made (by hubbing from a genuine original) and then striking them. Such struck forgeries are more difficult to detect, but usually there is some subtle difference in the design which betrays their true character. The Air Crew Europe Star, for example, has been a frequent target of the forger, and several counterfeits of varying quality have been recorded. These range from the easily detectable type, with three pearls instead of five on the central arch of the crown, to a very accurate design albeit slightly thinner than the genuine star and having the points noticeably rounded instead of cut square. For a very detailed study of the various copies of this rarest and most sought after of all the World War II campaign stars, see the On Guard feature in the June–July 2004 issue of *MEDAL NEWS* by Ian R. Hartley and Paul Firth.

Unfortunately with today's computer-aided technology, forgeries are becoming more and more difficult to detect but hopefully the same technology will help us to combat the problem by making simple methods of detection available to everyone. Fortunately, once it is known that a forgery of a particular medal exists it isn't long before the differences between it and the original are noted and passed on from collector to collector. *MEDAL NEWS*, the Orders & Medals Research Society (OMRS) and the Orders & Medals Society of America (OMSA), as well as certain dealers and others frequently and regularly publish information on how to spot fakes and forgeries and it is vital that the collector keeps up with developments.

COPIES

Under this heading come all manner of reproductions and imitations, which are often much harder to detect, especially if their provenance leads you to believe them to be genuine. It was not uncommon in years gone by, when the wearing of medals was much more frequent than it is today, for generals, admirals, ambassadors and other high officials to have a second set of medals mounted for everyday wear. These copies were often produced by the very firms who held the government contracts to manufacture the originals, and they were struck from the same dies, using the same materials. In this case, however, as a precaution, these medals were clearly marked COPY. Where this was stamped in incuse lettering there was little fear of erasure, but where raised capitals were employed these could be filed off. Again, it is advisable to check medals for any evidence of file-marks or erasure on the rim or in the field.

This problem becomes especially acute where gallantry medals and decorations are concerned. It has sometimes been the case that the recipient of a gallantry medal has been compelled, through straitened circumstances, to sell the decoration while retaining the campaign medals which made up the rest of the group. Subsequently he obtains an official copy or duplicate medal to complete the set, and in the fullness of time this group comes on the market. In extreme cases the copy decoration may even be detached from the group

and sold separately. Thus we have instances of gallantry awards appearing to sell twice over, when in fact only one was the genuine original and the second one was the replacement. This is a potential minefield, for there are also other reasons for replacement medals supplied by the official contractors for legitimate reasons.

Gallantry awards, notably the Victoria Cross, have been replaced due to accidental loss or theft, and have then been worn just as proudly by the recipient. At the end of the day, however, the status of these replacements is lower than that of the original medals, and is usually reflected in the market value. The question of status is something of a grey area which only the individual collector can decide for himself.

Campaign and general service medals, issued to serving soldiers to replace those lost or stolen, are clearly marked REPLACEMENT at the time of issue and, as such, are not highly regarded by dealers or collectors. Unfortunately there have been numerous examples in recent years of these replacements having their true identity concealed by erasure. Be on your guard against such medals which appear to have been filed, rubbed or disfigured along the rim where the naming is found, as this could imply that the word has been removed for fraudulent purposes.

FAKES

These are genuine medals which have been tampered with in some way in order to convert a common (and relatively cheap) item into a rarity commanding a greatly enhanced price. Fakery is much harder to detect than forgery and each case has to be examined on its individual merits. The biggest problem is concerned with renaming, and we give a few pointers to look out for.

One common practice is to take a perfectly genuine medal and replace a common campaign clasp by one which is rare. Apart from the fact that the substitute will probably be an out and out forgery, detectable from the factors outlined above, a high-powered magnifier will usually show up evidence of tampering with the rivets securing the clasp to the medal. This in itself is not proof positive of substitution, for clasps can work loose for various reasons; but any sign of tampering with the rivets, or their replacement, should put you immediately on your guard. Examine the rivets closely for signs of file marks, soldering or any other form of tampering.

The chief ploy to improve the value of a medal, however, stems from the British practice of naming campaign medals to their recipients. This has given rise to a form of faking in which a medal named to someone in a plentiful regiment, or to a non-combatant, has had the original name erased by careful filing, and a new name, rank, number and regiment substituted. Some of these fakes were relatively crude in that the original name might be left intact and only the regiment altered, but as medal rolls and regimental muster rolls became more widely available to collectors and military historians, fakers were forced to give closer attention to adding the name of a serviceman who would theoretically have been awarded such a medal.

This is where a careful measurement of the diameter from several angles, is vital. Medals should be perfectly round and regular, so that any variation in diameter measured from different points will almost certainly indicate that the rim has been slightly shaved to remove the original impressed lettering. In some cases the original lettering may have been raised; filing this off may not materially affect the diameter, but the substitution of incuse or engraved lettering may be dead giveaway It is very important, therefore, to study the detailed catalogues of individual medals, and compare the method of naming with that found on your specimen. Even this is not always foolproof, for replacement medals issued to serving soldiers to make up for lost medals may be named in a manner which differed from the original issue. 19th century campaign medals were not always marked as clearly as they are nowadays to indicate that they were replacements, but the use of different lettering may provide a clue.

Of course, renaming or altering a medal in some ways has not always been done to fool the collector; serving personnel have been guilty of such practices over the years for a variety of reasons!

Any aspect of a medal which appears to differ from the norm should immediately put the collector on his guard. However, it is only fair to point out that many long-running general service medals differed in some subtle way in the fastenings of the clasps over a long period. In this case it is necessary to become fully acquainted with the different styles, including different shapes and sizes of rivets, types of solder and even twisted wire—all of which have been used quite legitimately at various times for the same medal.

Similarly differences in the lettering and numerals inscribed on campaign clasps may not betray the handiwork of the forger or faker, for such subtle variations may merely denote that the clasps were the work of one of the Royal Mint's sub-contractors, for example, India General Service Medals may be found with clasps manufactured at the branch mint in Calcutta, rather than in London. Once again, it is necessary for the collector to study all the available literature in his chosen field and thoroughly familiarise himself with the variants which may quite legitimately arise, as well as the difference between genuine and fake which have been recorded over the years.

RENAMING

Trying to determine whether a medal is correctly named is a problem that every collector has to face at some time or another. When checking for evidence of renaming always examine the medal with the aid of a magnifying glass. It is useful to bear in mind the following points:

1. Generally speaking, it is easier to re-name engraved medals than those that bear impressed namings. An engraved medal is relatively quick and easy to re-name as it is necessary to remove less metal to erase the original naming. To re-name a medal with an impressed naming requires special tools which are not easy to obtain. Nevertheless, it should be pointed out that many of the most notorious cases of re-naming (especially with more expensive medals), done with the intention to deceive, have involved impressed medals.

2. Always consider whether the style of naming is correct for the particular medal under consideration, also for the particular clasp(s) concerned and for the regiment, etc. Sometimes medals issued for the same campaign are named in different styles depending on the unit involved and the clasp(s). A good example of this is the India General Service medal 1854–95.

Such information can be acquired in part from books and articles, but this can be inaccurate or not sufficiently specialised. The best way to acquire knowledge is by examining as many medals as possible. Always take full advantage of medal fairs, auction viewings, visits to dealers' premises and any opportunity to look at friends' medal collections to enhance your knowledge.

3. Before a medal can be re-named, the original naming must be removed and you can usually see some evidence of this, such as in the form of file marks.

Figure 1 shows the results of an attempt to remove a recipient's name from a medal—notice the many scratch marks caused by the file. Unless the removal of the original naming has been done extremely

Figure 1

carefully the edge of the medal may have a rounded appearance, instead of being square and flat.

Figure 2 shows a renamed medal with edge view silhouette. See how rounded the edge is when compared with the flat edge of a correctly named medal in Figure 3.

Figure 2

Figure 3

4. If the suspender on the medal is assumed to be the 12 o'clock position, the naming on most medals appears on the edge between 9 o'clock and 3 o'clock. When the original naming is removed this thins down the rim between these two points. This is well illustrated in Figures 4 and 5. The former shows a re-named medal with a thin rim where the naming has been removed

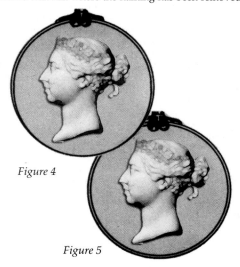

Figure 4

Figure 5

and the latter shows a correct medal with an even rim all round. The removal of the original naming will also reduce the size of the medal and this can be checked by using either a micrometer or a vernier calliper. The diameter of the medal should be measured across the 9 o'clock to 3 o'clock position and then across the 1 o'clock to 7 o'clock position. If the medal is not renamed, the two measurements should be the same. A suspect medal can also be checked for size against a known genuine medal, although it should be noted that a random check of ten similar medals will show some variations in size.

5. Traces of an original naming may be visible under the new naming. Figures 6, 7 and 8 show examples of this. In Figure 6, traces are seen under the new naming and also beyond the end of it. Figure 7 shows the outline of an impressed letter A under the new S and also shows traces of file marks. Figure 8 has a small impressed T appearing between the L and A of the new naming.

To recap, always check a medal for the following points:

    a. Is it named in the correct style?
    b. Does the edge show file marks?
    c. Is the edge flat?
    d. Is the rim thinned at any point?
    e. Is the diameter the same all round?
    f. Are there traces of the original naming?
    g. Has the medal been checked in all respects with a known correct medal?

A term which often appears in auction catalogues and dealers' lists is "officially corrected" or simply "corrected". Normally these expressions refer to instances where a single letter in the naming has been corrected by the issuing authority or by the recipient in order to rectify spelling mistakes, etc. Figures 9 and 10 show examples of "official" corrections. In both cases, traces of file marks can be seen and the corrected letter is impressed more heavily than the other letters.

Examples of privately corrected errors can be seen in Figures 11 and 12, where the new letters have been engraved rather than impressed and so do not match the rest of the naming. Traces of file marks are also visible. Figure 13 shows an example of a correction as an "addition" due to the recipient's name being incorrectly spelt. It is corrected by the addition of the letter E, which is engraved and hence does not match the rest of the impressed naming. The engraved full-stop after the K can just be seen beneath the new E. Figure 14 shows a Naval General Service medal of 1793–1840, where the recipient has had his original rank removed and his later rank of "Lieut" added. Again, this is engraved and does not match the rest of the naming, which is correctly impressed. Once more, notice the traces of file marks and the original impressed full-stop some way beyond the "Lieut". Corrections of this type were necessary because of human error and hence cannot really be classified as re-namings.

Why do re-named medals exist on the market? The majority were not produced to deceive medal collectors,

Figure 6

Figure 7

Figure 8

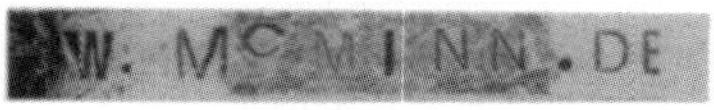

Figure 9

Figure 10

Figure 11

Figure 12

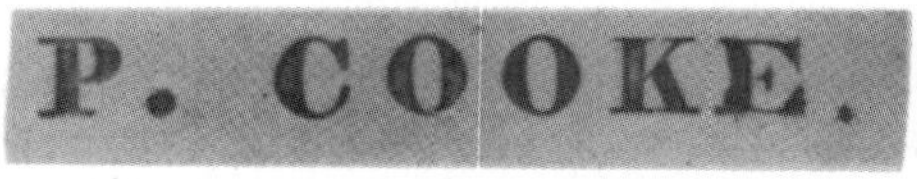

Figure 13

Figure 14

but are the result of officers and men losing their own medals and having to find replacements. The obvious and easiest remedy was to buy someone else's medals and have them renamed. Servicemen out to impress their friends and family were not above adding an extra medal to their rows and what better proof of entitlement than to see that the medal had their name on it. Many such medals were re-named by local jewellers.

Most collectors shun re-named medals and they are not usually offered for sale. Unfortunately, an "official" correction mars the appeal of a medal and hence affects its value. Nevertheless, some medals are very skilfully re-named with the sole intention of deceiving the unwary collector and dealer. This is especially the case with rare and expensive items. The best advice is to use the check list above and then, if still in doubt, consult a competent authority or recognised expert.

Operational honours

Following the Review of Operational Awards in 1993, a custom was established of publishing two Operational lists each year, one in the Spring and one in the Autumn. Beginning with this issue, the *Medal Yearbook* is to publish the Autumn list of the previous year, and the Spring list of the *Medal Yearbook* date. Exceptionally, a "Special Iraq Honours supplement" was published in 2003—this has been included. At level 4, only the names of recipients awarded commendations for bravery will be published, and those recognised "in connection with" operations are excluded.

The *LONDON GAZETTE*
OF MONDAY SEPTEMBER 29, 2003.
SUPPLEMENT No. 2

NORTHERN IRELAND
OBE
Lieutenant Colonel William CAMPBELL. The Royal Irish Regiment.
Lieutenant Colonel Hames HOCKENHULL, MBE, Intelligence Corps.

MBE
Colour Sergeant William REID, Royal Marines
Captain Paul COLLISTER, The Cheshire Regiment.
Warrant Officer Class 1 Ralph GRAY, The Royal Anglian Regiment.
Major David ORR EWING, The Black Watch
Warrant Officer Class Paul PLOWMAN, The Princess of Wales's Royal Regiment.
Corporal Irene VAUGHAN, The Royal Irish Regiment.
Squadron Leader Michele CROSSMAN, Royal Air Force.

QGM
Warrant Officer Class 2 Nigel BRADLEY, The Royal Irish Regiment.
Corporal Jonathan HOLLINGSWORTH, The Parachute Regiment.
Staff Sergeant Stephen PARKER, The Royal Logistic Corps.

QCB
Corporal Paul McINTOSH, Royal Marines.
Lance Corporal Matthew BALL, Royal Army Veterinary Corps.
Corporal Jason BOWDEN, Intelligence Corps.
Lance Corporal Graeme CARR, The Parachute Regiment.
Sergeant Ian MacLACHLAN, The Royal Highland Fusiliers.
Sergeant Colin NUFER, The Royal Green Jackets.
Warrant Officer Class 2 Roger PEARSON, The Royal Logistic Corps.
Warrant Officer Class 1 Robert PRICE, QCM, Army Physical Training Corps.
Sergeant Jeremy SMITH, The Royal Anglian Regiment.

FORMER YUGOSLAVIA
MBE
Corporal Justin GRATTAN, The Staffordshire Regiment.
Corporal Eric WIND, The Royal Scots.

AFGHANISTAN
MBE
Sergeant Richard POWELL, Adjutant General's Corps (Royal Military Police).

THE GULF
MBE
Squadron Leader Joanna KHAN, Royal Air Force.

DFC
Flight Lieutenant James HEALD, Royal Air Forcer.

SIERRA LEONE
MBE
Major Mark EDKINS, The Devonshire and Dorset Regiment.

OBE
Lieutenant Colonel Thomas BARNWELL, Royal Marines Reserve.
Colonel Timothy WATTS, Late Royal Corps of Signals.

LATE PUBLICATIONS

SIERRA LEONE
MBE
Major Thomas McMURTRIE, The Light Infantry.
Squadron Leader John GLADSTON, Royal Air Force.

DSO
Major General John HOLMES, OBE, MC, late Scots Guards.

MC
Warrant Officer Class 2 Harry BARTLETT, The Parachute Regiment.
Major James CHISWELL, The Parachute Regiment.
Captain Evan FUERY, The Parachute Regiment.

DFC
Captain Allan MOYES, Army Air Corps.
Flight Lieutenant Timothy BURGESS, Royal Air Force
Squadron leader Ian MacFARLANE, Royal Air Force.
Flight Lieutenant Jonathan PRIEST, Royal Air Force.
Flight Lieutenant Paul SHEPHERD, Royal Air Force.

Mention in Despatches
Colour Sergeant Alexander GIBB, Royal Marines.
Colour Sergeant Tobias HARRIS, The Parachute Regiment.
Colour Sergeant Alexander REID, The Parachute Regiment.
Squadron Leader Richard MASON, Royal Air Force.
Flight Lieutenant Richard WHIPP, Royal Air Force.

AFGHANISTAN
CBE
Lieutenant Colonel Richard PICKUP, Royal Marines.

MBE
Captain Nigel SOMERVILLE, Royal Marines.
Sergeant (Acting Colour Sergeant) David TROTTER, The Parachute Regiment.

MC
Colour Sergeant Stuart BROWN, Royal Marines.
Colour Sergeant Michael BELL, The Parachute Regiment.
Colour Sergeant Scott DAVIDSON, The Parachute Regiment.
Major Edward Eaton THORNE, The Royal Anglian Regiment.
Major Richard WILLIAMS, MBE, The Parachute Regiment.

DFC
Squadron Leader John GLADSTON, MBE, Royal Air Force.
Flight Lieutenant Ian HOPCROFT, Royal Air force.
Flight Lieutenant Philip ROBINSON, Royal Air Force.

Mention in Despatches
Sergeant Paul McGOUGH, Royal Marines.
Colour Sergeant Simon CLARK, The Parachute Regiment.
Staff Sergeant Gordon DUNCAN, Royal Regiment of Artillery.
Lance Corporal Kenneth McMILLAN, The Parachute Regiment.

Corporal Andrew MILLER, The Parachute Regiment.
Sergeant Sean McNIFF, The Royal Green Jackets.
Captain James RODDIS, The Black Watch.
Sergeant Shane TAYLOR, Royal Australian Infantry.
Flight Lieutenant Stephen BETHELL, Royal Air Force.

NON CAMPAIGN AWARDS
AFC
Flight Lieutenant Kevin BERRY, Royal Air Force.
Sergeant Neil HARRISON, Royal Air Force.

Queen's Commendation for Bravery
Air Engineering Mechanic Gene KELLEY, Royal Navy.
Leading Airman (Aircraft Handler) Kevin LATCHAM, Royal Navy.
Lance Corporal Ryan DAVIES, The Princess of Wales's Royal Regiment.
Private Simon POLAND, The Princess of Wales's Royal Regiment.
Private Stuart DUFF, The Princess of Wales's Royal Regiment.
Lance Corporal Benedict JOHNSON, The Princess of Wales's Royal Regiment.
Sergeant Stephen BRIGGS, Royal Air Force.
Corporal Stuart WEYMAN, Royal Air Force.
Corporal David TOLLEY, Royal Air Force.

Queen's Commendation for Bravery in the Air
Sergeant Timothy GILBERT, Royal Air Force.

The *LONDON GAZETTE*
OF THURSDAY, OCTOBER 30, 2003.
SUPPLEMENT No. 1

IRAQ
George Cross
Trooper Christopher FINNEY, The Blues and Royals.

KCB
Air Marshal Brian BURRIDGE, CBE, ADC, Royal Air Force.

CMG
Brigadier (Acting Major General) Albert WHITLEY, CBE, Late Corps of Royal Engineers.

CBE
Brigadier James DUTTON,
Captain Alan Massey, Royal Navy.
Colonel Patrick MARRIOTT, OBE, late The Queen's Royal Lancers.
Wing Commander (Acting Group Captain) Simon DOBB, OBE, Royal Air Force
Air Commodore Christopher NICKOLS, Royal Air Force

OBE
Commander Paul BURKE, Royal Navy
Commander Martin EWENCE, Royal Navy.
Lieutenant Colonel (Acting Colonel) Francis HOWES, Royal Marines.
Commander Kenneth KEBLE, Royal Navy.
Commander Dawn KENNEY, Queen Alexandra's Royal Naval Nursing Service Reserve.
Commander Simon TATE, Royal Navy.
Captain Robert ALLAN, Royal Fleet Auxiliary.
Captain Ross FERRIS, Royal Fleet Auxiliary.

CBE
The Reverend Tudor BOTWOOD, Royal Navy.
Sergeant Simon DACK, Royal Marines.
Lieutenant Commander Alastair GIBSON, Royal Navy.
Major Justin HOLT, Royal Marines.
Lieutenant Peter LAUGHTON, Royal Navy.
Major Dominic MAY, Royal Marines.
Lieutenant Commander Malcolm McKENZIE, Royal Navy.
Major Ian O'DONNELL, Royal Marines.
Warrant Officer (Master At Arms) Alexander Thomas SHARPE.
Lieutenant Commander Andrew SWAIN, Royal Navy.
Lieutenant Colonel Nicholas ASHMORE, Royal Regiment of Artillery.

Lieutenant Colonel Timothy COLLINS, The Royal Irish Regiment.
Lieutenant Colonel Duncan FRANCIS, Royal Regiment of Artillery.
Lieutenant Colonel Peter JONES, MBE, The Royal Logistic Corps.
Lieutenant Colonel Rory MAXWELL, MBE, The Royal Logistic Corps.
Lieutenant Colonel David PATERSON, The Royal Regiment of Fusiliers.
Lieutenant Colonel Christopher POPE, Corps of Royal Engineers.
Lieutenant Colonel John SHANAHAN, MBE, Corps of Royal Engineers.
Lieutenant Colonel Christopher TICKELL, MBE, Corps of Royal Engineers.
Lieutenant Colonel Simon WOLSEY, Royal Regiment of Artillery.

MBE
Major Philip ARNOLD, The Royal Logistic corps.
Major Nigel ASTLEY, The Royal Logistic Corps.
Signaller John BENTLEY, Royal Corps of Signals
Major William BRACE, BEM, The Queen's Dragoon Guards.
Captain (Acting Major) Mark BUDDEN, Corps of Royal Engineers.
Major Douglas CHALMERS, The Royal Irish Regiment.
Captain Alan DURRANT, Royal Regiment of Artillery.
Major Nicholas ELLIOTT, Corps of Royal Engineers.
Second Lieutenant Jennifer EVANS, Corps of Royal Engineers.
Captain Susan EVERINGTON, Queen Alexandra's Royal Army Nursing Corps, Territorial Army.
Corporal Craig FILMER, The Royal Logistic corps.
Corporal John FLEMING, Corps of Royal Electrical and Mechanical Engineers.
Captain Andrew FORBES, Royal Corps of Signals.
Captain Anton FOULGER, Royal Army Medical Corps.
Warrant Officer Class 2 Philip HARTLEY, Adjutant General's Corps (Staff and personnel Support Branch).
Captain David McGINNIS, Corps of Royal Engineers.
Warrant Officer Class 1 Alan McKENNA, Corps of Royal Engineers.
Major Peter MacMULLEN, Irish Guards.
Warrant Officer Class 2 John MULHERAN, The Royal Regiment of Fusiliers.

Major Samuel PAMBAKIAN, Royal Army Medical Corps.
Major Christopher PARKER, The Princess of Wales's Royal Regiment.
Warrant officer Class 2 Michael PETERS, The King's Regiment.
Captain (Acting Major) Kay ROBERTS, Adjutant General's Corps (Royal Military Police).
Staff Sergeant Paul SIMPSON, The Royal Logistic Corps.
Colour Sergeant Robert THOMAS, The Parachute Regiment.
Major Mark TILLEY, Corps of Royal Engineers.
Warrant Officer Class 2 Christopher UNDERHILL, Corps of Royal Engineers.
Warrant Officer Class 1 Stephen WELSH, Adjutant General's Corps (Royal Military police).
Major John WHITE, Corps of Royal Engineers.
Captain Michael WILLIAMSON, The Black Watch.
Flight Lieutenant Mohammed AHMED, Royal Air Force.
Squadron Leader Graham KYTE, Royal Air Force.
Corporal Jason LEWIS, Royal Air Force.
Flight Lieutenant Trevor RUTHERFORD, Royal Air Force.
Chief Technician Richard THORNHILL, Royal Air Force.
Squadron Leader Dominic TORIATI, Royal Air Force.
Squadron Leader Paul WEBSTER, Royal Air Force.
Squadron Leader Stephen WILCOCK, Royal Air Force.

DSO
Colonel Gordon MESSENGER, OBE, Royal Marines
Brigadier Graham BINNS, CBE, MC, late the Prince of Wales's Own Regiment of Yorkshire.
Major General Robin BRIMS, CBE, late The Light Infantry.
Lieutenant Colonel Michael RIDDELL-WEBSTER, The Black Watch.
Major Richard Taylor, The Life Guards
Wing Commander Stuart ATHA, Royal Air Force.
Wing commander Ian TEAKLE, OBE, Royal Air Force.

CGC
Marine Justin THOMAS, Royal marines.

DSC
Lieutenant Commander Philip IRELAND, Royal Navy.

MC
Corporal David BERESFORD, Royal Marines.
Marine Gareth THOMAS, Royal Marines.
Corporal Peter WATTS, Royal Marines.
Sergeant Nathan BELL, The Parachute Regiment.
Guardsman Anton BRANCHFLOWER, Irish Guards.
Lieutenant Charles CAMPBELL, The Royal Regiment of Fusiliers.
Corporal Craig COMBER, Corps of Royal Electrical and Mechanical Engineers.
Lieutenant Simon FAREBROTHER, The Queen's Dragoon Guards.
Lieutenant Christopher HEAD, The Royal Regiment of Fusiliers.
Sergeant Mark HELEY, Corps of Royal Engineers.
Captain Grant INGLETON, Royal Regiment of Artillery.
Staff Sergeant Richard JOHNSON, Corps of Royal Engineers.
Lance Corporal Peter LAING, The Black Watch.
Lieutenant Daniel O'CONNELL, Irish Guards
Second Lieutenant Thomas ORDE-POWLETT, Irish Guards.
Lieutenant Toby RIDER, Corps of Royal Engineers.
Corporal John ROSE, The Black Watch.
Major Henry Francis SUGDEN, Queens' Dragoon Guards.

DFC
Lieutenant (Acting Lieutenant Commander) James NEWTON, Royal Navy.
Staff Sergeant Rupert BANFIELD, Army Air Corps.
Captain Richard CUTHILL, Army Air Corps.
Squadron Leader Stephen CARR, Royal Air Force.
Squadron Leader David KNOWLES, Royal Air Force.
Flight Lieutenant Scott MORLEY, Royal Air Force.
Squadron Leader Harvy SMYTH, Royal Air Force.
Flight Lieutenant Andrew TURK, Royal Air Force.
Squadron Leader John TURNER, Royal Air Force.
Squadron Leader Ian WALTON, Royal Air Force.

CGC
Lance Corporal of Horse Michael FLYNN, The Blues & Royals.

AFC
Wing Commander Kevin HAVELOCK, Royal Air Force.
Flight Lieutenant Nicholas IRELAND, Royal Air Force.

ARRC
Lieutenant Julian DESPRES, Queen Alexandra's Royal Naval Army Nursing Corps.

QGM
Corporal John HISCOCK, Royal Marines.
Captain timothy GOULD, the Royal Logistic Corps.
Sergeant Andrew SINDALL, Corps of Royal Engineers.

Mention in Despatches (Posthumous)
Lieutenant Anthony KING, Royal Navy.
Lance Corporal Barry STEPHEN, The Black Watch.
Fusilier Kelan TURRINGTON, The Royal Regiment of Fusiliers.

Mention in Despatches
Captain Alan BARNWELL, Royal Marines.
Lieutenant Jason BLACKWELL, Royal Navy.
Corporal Jack BROUGHTON, Royal Marines.
Captain The Honourable Michael COCHRANE, OBE, Royal Navy.
Marine Andrew COLLEN, Royal Marines.
Petty Officer (Diver) Anthony DIXON.
Sergeant Stephen EATON, Royal Marines.
Lieutenant Commander Graham FINN, Royal Navy.
Commander Guy ROBINSON, Royal Navy.
Corporal Robert STOREY, Royal Marines.
Medical Assistant Mark SUMNER.
Colour Sergeant Gary PATTERSON, Royal Marines.
Sergeant Ross TELFORD, Royal Marines.
Marine John Thompson, Royal Marines.
Corporal James Twycross, Royal Marines.
Flight Lieutenant Robert CHEVLI, Royal Air Force.
Flight Lieutenant Steven CLARKE, Royal Air Force.
Flight Lieutenant Marcus DOYLE, Royal Air Force.
Flight Lieutenant Jennifer EAYRS, Royal Air Force.
Squadron Leader Scott HAMMOND, Royal Air Force.
Flight Sergeant Ian JACKSON, Royal Air Force.
Flight Lieutenant Shaun KIMBERLEY, Royal Air Force.
Squadron Leader James LINTER, Royal Air Force.
Flight Lieutenant Andrew ROBINS, Royal Air Force.
Squadron Leader Paul SMITH, Royal Air Force.

Queen's Commendation for Bravery
Warrant Officer Class 1 Douglas BEATTIE, The Royal Irish Regiment.
Corporal Carl LEWIN, The Queen's Royal Lancers.
Corporal (Acting Sergeant) Stephen McGRATH, Adjutant General's Corps (Royal Military Police).
Corporal Robert NUNN, Adjutant General's Corps (Royal Military Police).
Senior Aircraftman Christian TOBIN, Royal Air Force.

DECORATIONS CONFERRED BY THE PRESIDENT OF THE UNITED STATES OF AMERICA.

Legion of Merit
(Degree of Officer)
Commodore Andrew MILLER,
Rear Admiral David SNELSON.
Brigadier Adrian BRADSHAW, OBE, late The King's Royal Hussars.
Air Vice Marshall Glenn TORPY, CBE, DSO, Royal Air Force.
Air Commodore Andrew WALTON, CBE, Royal Air Force.

Legion of Merit
(Degree of Legionnaire)
Captain Nicholas LAMBERT, Royal Navy.

Bronze Star
Captain Mark ANDERSON, Royal Navy.
Captain The Honourable Michael COCHRANE, OBE, Royal Navy.
Captain Jeffrey GABLE, Adjutant General's Corps (Royal Military Police), Territorial Army.
Major Alistair MACK, Adjutant General's Corps (Education and Training Services Branch).
Group Captain Stephen FORWARD, Royal Air Force.
Group Captain Stephen HILLIER, DFC, Royal Air Force.

The *LONDON GAZETTE*
OF THURSDAY APRIL 22, 2004.
SUPPLEMENT No. 1

NORTHERN IRELAND
MBE
Sergeant Brian ALLAN, Royal Marines.
Captain Ivor BAIGENT, Intelligence Corps.
Lance Corporal Matthew BATES, The Prince of Wales's
Own Regiment of Yorkshire.
Major Christopher JOB, The King's Regiment.
Major Charles MACFARLANE, The Argyll and Sutherland
Highlanders.
Staff Sergeant (Acting Warrant Officer Class 2) Simon
METCALFE, Royal Corps of Signals.
Staff Sergeant Andrew MOORE, Intelligence Corps.

CBE
Brigadier James BUCKNALL, MBE, late Coldstream
Guards.

OBE
Lieutenant Colonel Stephen PADGETT, The Prince of
Wales's Own Regiment of Yorkshire.

QGM
Colour Sergeant Steven JOHNSON, The Green Howards.

Queen's Commendation for Bravery
Warrant Officer Class 2 Garth THOMPSON, Intelligence
Corps.

FORMER YUGOSLAVIA
MBE
Major Quentin NAYLOR, The Royal Gurkha Rifles.
Major Rupert SHAW, The Royal Green Jackets.
Major Jonathan PROBERT, The Royal Logistic Corps.

AFGHANISTAN
CBE
Colonel Richard DAVIS, MBE, late Corps of Royal
Engineers.

MBE
Colour Sergeant Martin GRAY, The Royal Anglian
Regiment.

Queen's Commendation for Bravery.
Major Bruce DOWN, The Royal Anglian Regiment.

IRAQ
CMG
Major General Frederick VIGGERS, MBE, late Royal
Regiment of Artillery.

CBE
Brigadier William MOORE, late Royal Regiment of Artillery.

OBE
Lieutenant Colonel John BEVAN, MBE, The Royal Logistic
Corps.
Lieutenant Colonel Duncan BRUCE, MBE, The Duke of
Wellington's Regiment.
Lieutenant Colonel John CASTLE, The King's Own Scottish
Borderers.
Lieutenant Colonel Ciaran GRIFFIN, The King's Regiment.
Lieutenant Colonel Timothy Gareth KIDWELL, Royal
Regiment of Artillery.

MBE
Major Andrew ALDERSON, The Queen's Own Yeomanry
Territorial Army.
Major Nadine HERON, Adjutant General's Corps (Royal
Military Police).
Major Edward MELOTTE, Irish Guards.
Major Mark ROBINSON, The Duke of Wellington's
Regiment.

DSO
Major General Graeme LAMB, CMG, OBE, late Queen's
Own Highlanders.
Lieutenant Colonel Jorge MENDONCA, MBE, The Queen's
Lancashire Regiment.

GCG
Corporal Shaun JARDINE, The king's Own Scottish
Borderers.
Sergeant Gordon ROBERTSON, The Parachute Regiment.

RRC
Lieutenant Colonel Caroline WHITTAKER, TD, Queen
alexandra's Royal Army Nursing Corps, Territorial
Army.

MC
Corporal of Horse Glynn BELL, The Blues and Royals.
Corporal Anthony CURRIE, The King's Own Scottish
Borderers.
Kingsman Michael DAVISON, The King's and Cheshire
Regiment, Territorial Army.
Major James HOLLISTER, The King's Regiment.
Warrant Officer Class 2 Darren LEIGH, The Queen's
Lancashire Regiment.

GM
Warrant Officer Class 1 Nicholas PETTIT, QGM, Corps of
Royal Engineers.

QGM
Staff Sergeant Anthony WYLES, Corps of Royal Engineers,
Territorial Army.

Mention in Despatches
Lance Corporal Marcus CLARKE, Corps of Royal engineers.
Warrant Officer Class 2 Mark CUNLIFFE, Corps of Royal
Engineers.
Corporal John DOLMAN, The Parachute Regiment.
Second Lieutenant Glen ESPIE, The King's Own Scottish
Borderers.
Private David FRAME, The King's Own Scottish Borderers.
Corporal (Local Sergeant) James HASLAM, The King's
Own Scottish Borderers.
Lance Corporal Barry JOLLY, Corps or Royal Engineers.
Lieutenant Ross KENNEDY, The Parachute Regiment.
Corporal Darren KIMBER, The King's Own Scottish
Borderers.
Lance Corporal Philip LAW, Corps of Royal Engineers.
Lance Corporal Mark LAWRIE, The King's Own Scottish
Borderers.
Lance Bombardier (Acting Bombardier) Jamie McMILLAN,
Royal Regiment of Artillery.
Corporal Eammon Thomas MUIRHEAD, The King's own
Scottish Borderers.
Second Lieutenant Michael PEEL, The Queen's Lancashire
Regiment.
Major Andrew PULLAN, the King's Regiment.
Private Gary Francis SMITH, The Lancastrian and
Cumbrian Volunteers, Territorial Army.
Lieutenant Charles SPEERS, The Blues and Royals.
Kingsman Paul VANDEN, The King's Regiment.
Lance Corporal Craig WEIR, The Black Watch.

Queen's Commendation for Bravery.
Gunner Martin BOAKES, Royal Regiment of Artillery,
Territorial Army.
Corporal Scot LARNER, Corps of Royal Engineers.

DEMOCRATIC REPUBLIC OF THE CONGO
MBE
Major Simon HIGGENS, Corps of Royal Engineers.

IN THE FIELD
MBE
Sergeant Wayne HUNT, Royal Marines.

LATE PUBLICATIONS

IRAQ
OBE
Lieutenant Colonel Mark CHARLETON-SMITH, MBE, Irish
Guards

MC
Captain James STENNER, Welsh Guards (since deceased).

**DECORATIONS CONFERRED BY THE PRESIDENT OF
THE UNITED STATES OF AMERICA.**

Legion of Merit (Degree of Officer)
Air Commodore Peter RUDDOCK, CBE, Royal Air Force.

Bronze Star Medal
Major Nicholas GEE, Royal Regiment of Artillery.
Major John WHITE, Corps of Royal Electrical and
Mechanical Engineers.
Major James LODEN, The Parachute Regiment.

US Air Medal
Captain Davis WILKINS, Army Air Corps.
Squadron Leader Richard WALLER, Royal Air Force.

Wearing awards

The wearing of Orders, Decorations and Medals is a complex subject too complicated to cover in a publication such as this. However, there a number of questions that collectors frequently ask, so we have attempted to deal with these as fully as possible.

Full-size Awards Mounted for Wear

Orders, decorations and medals are worn on the left breast in a line suspended from a single brooch mount or a rectangular frame (court mounted), the latter gives a firmer grip which occasions less damage than medals hanging more loosely from a brooch. The brooch/frame is covered by the medal ribbons. The most senior medal (see the following Order of Precedence) is furthest from the left shoulder. The obverse of the medals should show (this will usually be the sovereign's head, coat of arms, cypher, etc.).

If more than five medals are worn (three for the Navy), they should not be suspended side by side, but overlapped, the senior medal and ribbon is the one to be positioned so it can be seen completely. Medals should be lined up straight by the bottom rim/point, the length of ribbon should be one and a quarter inches (33mm) from the top of the mount to the first clasp or the suspension, which ever is appropriate (one and three quarters (45mm) for the Navy). Where the awards differ in size then a ribbon adjustment will be necessary to ensure a straight line.

Mentions-in-Despatches emblems should be worn on the relevant campaign medal, for example on the Victory Medal for the First World War and the War Medal 1939–45 for the Second World War. Where a recipient has no relevant campaign medal, the MID emblem is worn directly on the coat after any medal ribbons, or if no ribbons then in the position of a single ribbon.

There are a number of awards for which the sovereign has granted permission that they be worn on the right breast:

Royal Humane Society Medals
Stanhope Gold Medal
Royal National Lifeboat Institution Medal
Order of St John of Jerusalem Life Saving Medal.

Foreign Orders, Decorations and Medals

The British sovereign's subjects are not permitted to accept and wear the orders, decorations and medals of a foreign country of which the sovereign is not head of state. Application can be made for wear and permission is of two types: (a) restricted, that is instructions are given as to the exact occasions on which the award(s) may be worn; (b) unrestricted which allows the item(s) to be worn on all occasions according to the Order of Precedence, that is, generally speaking, arranged after British awards by date—first orders, then decorations, followed by medals (there are exceptions for the members of the armed services serving in an overseas force and receive that country's awards).

Awards are worn on a variety of State, evening or other occasions and the rules governing the wearing of orders according to dress are quite detailed. The subject is covered fully in Medals Will Be Worn *by Lieutenant Colonel Ashley R. Tinson (Token Publishing Ltd., 1999) and in* Spink's Guide to the Wearing of Orders, Decorations and Medals *(Spink, 1990). The wearing of awards in civilian clothes is also fully detailed in* Wearing Your Medals in Civilian Clothes *by Lieutenant Colonel Ashley R. Tinson (Token Publishing Ltd., 2003).*

The order of Wear

The order in which decorations and medals should be worn in the United Kingdom and the Commonwealth, is set out below, as announced by the Central Chancery of the Orders of Knighthood.

Victoria Cross
George Cross
Most Noble Order of the Garter
Most Ancient and Most Noble Order of the Thistle
Most Illustrious Order of St. Patrick
Knights Grand Cross, The Most Honourable Order of the Bath (GCB)
Order of Merit
Knight Grand Commander, The Most Exalted Order of the Star of India (GCSI)
Knights Grand Cross, The Most Distinguished Order of St. Michael and St. George (GCMG)
Knight Grand Commander, The Most Eminent Order of the Indian Empire (GCIE)
The Order of the Crown of India
Knights Grand Cross, The Royal Victorian Order (GCVO)
Knights Grand Cross, The Most Excellent Order of the British Empire (GBE)
Order of the Companions of Honour (CH)
Knight Commander, The Most Honourable Order of the Bath (KCB)
Knight Commander, The Most Exalted Order of the Star of India (KCSI)
Knight Commander, The Most Distinguished Order of St. Michael and St. George (KCMG)
Knight Commander, The Most Eminent Order of the Indian Empire (KCIE)
Knight Commander, The Royal Victorian Order (KCVO)
Knight Commander, The Most Excellent Order of the British Empire (KBE)
Baronet's Badge
Knight Bachelor's Badge
Companion, The Most Honourable Order of the Bath (CB)
Companion, The Most Exalted Order of the Star of India (CSI)
Companion, The Most Distinguished Order of St. Michael and St. George (CMG)
Companion, The Most Eminent Order of the Indian Empire (CIE)
Commander, The Royal Victorian Order (CVO)
Commander, The Most Excellent Order of the British Empire (CBE)
Distinguished Service Order (DSO)
Lieutenant, The Royal Victorian Order (LVO)

Officer, The Most Excellent Order of the British Empire (OBE)
Imperial Service Order (ISO)
Member, The Royal Victorian Order (MVO)
Member, The Most Excellent Order of the British Empire (MBE)
Indian Order of Merit—Military

DECORATIONS
Conspicuous Gallantry Cross
Royal Red Cross, Class 1
Distinguished Service Cross
Military Cross
Distinguished Flying Cross
Air Force Cross
Royal Red Cross, Class II
Order of British India
Kaisar-I-Hind Medal
Order of St John

GALLANTRY AND DISTINGUISHED CONDUCT MEDALS
Union of South Africa Queen's Medal for Bravery in gold
Distinguished Conduct Medal
Conspicuous Gallantry Medal
Conspicuous Gallantry Medal (Flying)
George Medal
Queen's Police Medal for Gallantry
Queen's Fire Service Medal for Gallantry
Royal West African Frontier Force Distinguished Conduct Medal
King's African Rifles Distinguished Conduct Medal
Indian Distinguished Service Medal
Union of South Africa Queen's Medal for Bravery in silver
Distinguished Service Medal
Military Medal
Distinguished Flying Medal
Air Force Medal
Constabulary Medal (Ireland)
Medal for Saving Life at Sea
Indian Order of Merit (Civil)
Indian Police Medal for Gallantry
Ceylon Police Medal for Gallantry
Sierra Leone Police Medal for Gallantry
Sierra Leone Fire Brigades Medal for Gallantry

Colonial Police Medal for Gallantry
Queen's Gallantry Medal
Royal Victorian Medal (gold, silver and bronze)
British Empire Medal
Canada Medal
Queen's Police Medal for Distinguished Service
Queen's Fire Service Medal for Distinguished Service
Queen's Volunteer Reserves Medal
Queen's Medal for Chiefs
War Medals, including the UN, EU, EC & NATO
    Medals in order of date of campaign for which
    awarded and the OSM, MFO and HPM
Polar Medals—in order of date of award
Imperial Service Medal

POLICE MEDALS FOR VALUABLE SERVICE

Indian Police Medal for Meritorious Service
Ceylon Police Medal for Merit
Sierra Leone Police Medal for Meritorious Service
Sierra Leone Fire Brigades Medal for Meritorious
    Service
Colonial Police Medal for Meritorious Service
Badge of Honour

JUBILEE, CORONATION, DURBAR MEDALS

Queen Victoria's Jubilee Medal 1887 (gold, silver and
    bronze)
Queen Victoria's Police Jubilee Medal 1887
Queen Victoria's Jubilee Medal 1897 (gold, silver and
    bronze)
Queen Victoria's Police Jubilee Medal 1897
Queen Victoria's Commemoration Medal 1900
    (Ireland)
King Edward VII's Coronation 1902
King Edward VII's Police Coronation 1902
King Edward VII's Durbar 1903 (gold, silver and
    bronze)
King Edward VII's Police Medal 1903 (Scotland)
King's Visit Commemoration Medal 1903 (Ireland)
King George V's Coronation Medal 1911
King George V's Police Coronation Medal 1911
King George V's Visit Police Commemoration Medal
    1911 (Ireland)
King George V's Durbar Medal 1911 (gold, silver and
    bronze)
King George V's Silver Jubilee Medal 1935
King George VI's Coronation Medal 1937
Queen Elizabeth II's Coronation Medal 1953
Queen Elizabeth II's Silver Jubilee Medal 1977
Queen Elizabeth II's Golden Jubilee Medal 2002
King George V's Long and Faithful Service Medal
King George VI's Long and Faithful Service Medal
Queen Elizabeth II's Long and Faithful Service
    Medal

EFFICIENCY AND LONG SERVICE
DECORATIONS AND MEDALS

Medal for Meritorious Service
Accumulated Campaign Service Medal
 Medal for Long Service and Good Conduct, Army
Naval Long Service and Good Conduct Medal
Medal for Meritorious Service (Royal Navy 1918–28)
Indian Long Service and Good Conduct Medal (for
    Europeans of Indian Army)
Indian Meritorious Service Medal (for Europeans of
    Indian Army)

Royal Marines Meritorious Service Medal (1849–1947
Royal Air Force Meritorious Service Medal 1918–28
Royal Air Force Long Service and Good Conduct
    Medal
Ulster Defence Regiment Long Service and Good
    Conduct Medal
Indian Long Service and Good Conduct Medal
    (Indian Army)
Royal West African Frontier Force Long Service and
    Good Conduct Medal
Royal Sierra Leone Military Forces Long Service and
    Good Conduct Medal
King's African Rifles Long Service and Good Conduct
    Medal
Indian Meritorious Service Medal (for Indian Army)
Police Long Service and Good Conduct Medal
Fire Brigade Long Service and Good Conduct Medal
African Police Medal for Meritorious Service
Royal Canadian Mounted Police Long Service Medal
Ceylon Police Long Service Medal
Ceylon Fire Services Long Service Medal
Sierra Leone Police Long Service Medal
Colonial Police Long Service Medal
Sierra Leone Fire Brigade Long Service Medal
Mauritius Police Long Service and Good Conduct
    Medal
Mauritius Fire Service Long Service and Good
    Conduct Medal
Mauritius Prisons Service Long Service and Good
    Conduct Medal
Colonial Fire Brigades Long Service Medal
Colonial Prison Service Medal
Army Emergency Reserve Decoration
Volunteer Officers' Decoration
Volunteer Long Service Medal
Volunteer Officers' Decoration (for India and the
    Colonies)
Volunteer Long Service Medal (for India and the
    Colonies)
Colonial Auxiliary Forces Officers' Decoration
Colonial Auxiliary Forces Long Service Medal
Medal for Good Shooting (Naval)
Militia Long Service Medal
Imperial Yeomanry Long Service Medal
Territorial Decoration
Ceylon Armed Service Long Service Medal
Efficiency Decoration
Territorial Efficiency Medal
Efficiency Medal
Special Reserve Long Service and Good Conduct Medal
Decoration for Officers of the Royal Naval Reserve
Decoration for Officers of the Royal Naval Volunteer
    Reserve
Royal Naval Reserve Long Service and Good Conduct
    Medal
Royal Naval Volunteer Reserve Long Service and
    Good Conduct Medal
Royal Naval Auxiliary Sick Berth Reserve Long
    Service and Good Conduct Medal
Royal Fleet Reserve Long Service and Good Conduct
    Medal
Royal Naval Wireless Auxiliary Reserve Long Service
    and Good Conduct Medal
Royal Naval Auxiliary Service Medal
Air Efficiency Award
Volunteer Reserves Service Medal
Ulster Defence Regiment Medal

Queen's Medal (for Champion Shots of the Royal Navy and Royal Marines)
Queen's Medal (for Champion Shots of the New Zealand Naval Forces)
Queen's Medal (for Champion Shots in the Military Forces)
Queen's Medal (for Champion Shots of the Air Force)
Cadet Forces Medal
Coast Guard Auxiliary Service Long Service Medal
Special Constabulary Long Service Medal
Canadian Forces Decoration
Royal Observer Corps Medal
Civil Defence Long Service Medal
Ambulance Service LS & GCM
Royal Fleet Auxiliary Service Medal
Rhodesia Medal
Royal Ulster Constabulary Service Medal
Union of South Africa Commemoration Medal
Indian Independence Medal
Pakistan Medal
Ceylon Armed Services Inauguration Medal
Ceylon Police Independence Medal (1948)

Sierra Leone Independence Medal
Jamaica Independence Medal
Uganda Independence Medal
Malawi Independence Medal
Fiji Independence Medal
Papua New Guinea Independence Medal
Solomon Islands Independence Medal
Service Medal of the Order of St. John
Badge of the Order of the League of Mercy
Voluntary medical Service Medal
Women's Voluntary Service Medal
South African Medal for War Services
Colonial Special Constabulary Medal
Honorary Membership of Commonwealth Orders (instituted by the Sovereign, in order of date of award)
Other Commonwealth Members, orders, Decorations and Medals (instituted since 1949 otherwise than by the Sovereign, and awards by States of Malaysia and Brunei in order of date of award)
Foreign Orders in order of date of award
Foreign Decorations in order of date of award
Foreign Medals in order of date of award

THE ORDER IN WHICH CAMPAIGN STARS AND MEDALS AWARDED FOR SERVICE DURING WORLD WAR I AND II ARE WORN

1914 Star with dated "Mons" clasp "15th AUGUST–22nd NOVEMBER 1914"
1914 Star
1914/15 Star
British War Medal
Mercantile Marine Medal
Victory Medal
Territorial Force War Medal

1939/45 Star
Atlantic Star
Air Crew Europe Star
Africa Star

Pacific Star
Burma Star
Italy Star
France and Germany Star
Defence Medal
Canadian/Newfoundland Volunteer Service Medal
1939/45 War Medal
1939/45 Africa Service Medal of the Union of South Africa
India Service Medal
New Zealand War Service Medal
Southern Rhodesia Service Medal
Australian Service Medal

POST-NOMINAL LETTERS

Recipients of some awards are entitled to use post-nominal letters including the following:

VC	Victoria Cross
GC	George Cross
KG	Knight, Most Noble Order of the Garter
KT	Knight, Most Ancient and Most Noble Order of the Thistle
KP	Knight, Most Illustrious Order of St Patrick
GCB	Knight Grand Cross, The Most Honourable Order of the Bath
OM	Order of Member
GCSI	Knight Grand Commander, The Most Exalted Order of the Star of India
GCMG	Knight Grand Cross—The Most Distinguished Order of St Michael and St George
GCIE	Knight Grand Commander. The Most Eminent Order of the Indian Empire
CI	The Order of the Crown of India (women only)
GCVO	Knight Grand Cross, The Royal Victorian Order
GBE	Knight Grand Cross, The Most Excellent Order of the British Empire
CH	Order of the Companion of Honour
KCB	Knight Commander, The Most Honourable Order of the Bath
DCB	Dame Commander, The Most Honourable Order of the Bath
KCSI	Knight Commander, The Most Exalted Order of the Star of India
KCMG	Knight Commander, The Most Distinguished Order of St Michael and St George
DCMG	Dame Commander, The Most Distinguished Order of St Michael and St George
KCIE	Knight Commander, The Most Eminent Order of the Indian Empire
KCVO	Knight Commander, The Royal Victorian Order
DCVO	Dame Commander, The Royal Victorian Order
KBE	Knight Commander, The Most Excellent Order of the British Empire
DBE	Dame Commander, The Most Excellent Order of the British Empire
Bt	Baronet

KB	Knight Bachelor
CB	Companion, The Most Honourable Order of the Bath
CSI	Companion, The Most Exalted Order of the Star of India
CMG	Companion, The Most Distinguished Order of St Michael and St George
CIE	Companion, The Most Eminent Order of the Indian Empire
CVO	Commander, The Royal Victorian Order
CBE	Commander, The Most Excellent Order of the British Empire
DSO	Distinguished Service Order
LVO	Lieutenant, The Royal Victorian Order
OBE	Officer, The Most Excellent Order of the British Empire
QSO	Queen's Service Order (NZ)
ISO	Imperial Service Order
MVO	Member, The Royal Victorian Order
MBE	Member, The Most Excellent Order of the British Empire
IOM	Indian Order of Merit (military)
OB	Order of Burma (gallantry)
CGC	Conspicuous Gallantry Cross
RRC	Royal Red Cross First Class
DSC	Distinguished Service Cross
MC	Military Cross
DFC	Distinguished Flying Cross
AFC	Air Force Cross
ARRC	Royal Red Cross, Second Class
OBI	Order of British India
OB	Order of Burma (distinguished service)
AM	Albert Medal
CGM (F)	Conspicuous Gallantry Medal (Flying)
DCM	Distinguished Conduct Medal
CGM	Conspicuous Gallantry Medal
GM	George Medal
KPM	King's Police Medal (gallantry)
QPM	Queen's Police Medal (gallantry)
KFSM	King's Fire Service Medal (gallantry)
QVRM	Queen's Volunter Reserves Medal
QFSM	Queen's Fire Service Medal (gallantry)
EM	Edward Medal
DCM	Distinguished Conduct Medal (West Africa Frontier Force)
DCM	Distinguished Conduct Medal (King's African Rifles)
IDSM	Indian Distinguished Service Medal
BGM	Burma Gallantry Medal
DSM	Distinguished Service Medal
MM	Military Medal
DFM	Distinguished Flying Medal
AFM	Air Force Medal
SGM	Sea Gallantry Medal
IOM	Indian Order of Merit (civil)
CPM	Colonial Police Medal
QGM	Queen's Gallantry Medal
QSM	Queen's Service Medal (NZ)
RVM	Royal Victorian Medal
BEM	British Empire Medal
EGM	Empire Gallantry Medal
CM/M DU C	Canada Medal
QPM	Queen's Police Medal (distinguished service)
QFSM	Queen's Fire Service Medal (distinguished service)
MSM	Meritorious Service Medal (Navy, awards up to 20.7.28)
ERD	Army Emergency Reserve Decoration
VD	Volunteer Officers' Decoration
TD	Territorial Decoration
ED	Efficiency Decoration
RD	Royal Naval Reserve Decoration
VRD	Royal Naval Volunteer Reserve Decoration
AE	Air Efficiency Award (officers)
UD	Ulster Defence Regiment Medal (officers)
CD	Canadian (Forces) Decoration

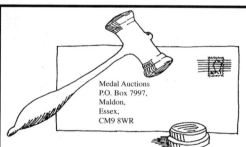

Collecting medal ribbons

There is nothing new or old about collecting medal ribbons, in fact the founders of the present Orders and Medals Research Society originally set out as medal ribbon collectors. The ribbon has, ever since the early 18th century, been an important complement to the medal or badge of an order and its importance has grown over the years. Since those early orders of chivalry when it was deemed necessary to identify the various religious or secular orders one belonged to by the colour of its ribbon, the emphasis has been on the ribbon to identify the order or medal. This practice has continued down through the centuries, even to today when the avid enthusiast can recognise a warriors medals simply by identifying his ribbons.

However, times are changing. The practice of wearing medals is on the decline, reserved only for ceremonial occasions, whilst the wearing of ribbon bars and the awarding of a single campaign or service medal with different ribbons to denote specific operations is on the increase. Our very own Operational Service Medal (OSM), the NATO medal and of course the plethora of United Nations medals are all classic examples of today's expansion of the medal ribbon. There is of course the growing cost of collecting medals and decorations compared to that of medal ribbons. There is also the down side to all of this, as the opportunity to acquire medal ribbons has become a challenge to many, as sources such as tailor's shops, small ribbon manufacturers or numerous regimental or quartermasters stores have all gone into decline, if not altogether vanished.

Before one can collect ribbons properly one must first be able to identify them. It is therefore important to have a reasonable reference library— nothing elaborate or expansive is needed. It is probably wise to start collecting ribbons of the United Kingdom before branching out into those of other countries. There are several good books on the subject and ribbons can be obtained quite easily.

The more one handles ribbons the quicker one starts to get a feel for the subject and gets to know which colours are used by certain countries or organisations, whether they always use silk or fine cottons, prefer moiré (watered) or corded ribbons whether they use wide or narrow ribbons, all are skills one picks up along the way, though sadly this art is slowly dying as the quality of many modern manufactured ribbons is really quite poor compared to the silk watered ribbons of bygone days.

Once over the initial teething problems of deciding how to store ribbons and ultimately mount or display them, the desire to expand and even specialise creeps in. Do you collect ribbons from just one country, state or organisation such as the Red Cross or the United Nations? Campaign medals and their numerous emblems? Famous chests? Regimental battle streamers? Religious or chivalric orders past and present? British or foreign orders and their various rosettes? The choice can be endless. Whatever the path you choose, you will almost certainly have to do a little research to obtain the reason for the award and the colours adopted for the ribbon. In reality, a true ribbon collector will know just as much about the medal or decoration as they will about the ribbon. Depending on the amount of time you have, research can lead you to museums, reading rooms or even portrait galleries, as well as societies such as the Ribbon Branch of the Orders and Medals Research Society. But whatever path is chosen you will be in awe of the sacrifices made by mankind down the centuries.

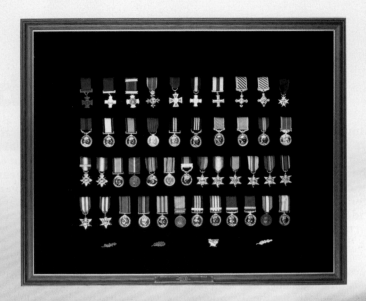

Miniature medals & decorations

The collecting of miniature medals has gained in popularity over the past few years and as a result groups and single miniatures that were once sold with their full-size counterparts, as an added extra, are now being traded in their own right. The market prices for these attractive and often superbly-produced little pieces are included in the catalogue section. Collectors wishing to learn more about miniature medals are invited to contact the Miniature Medals Branch of the Orders & Medals Research Society whose address can be found opposite.

Miniatures are small versions of orders, decorations and medals designed for formal evening wear. The custom appears to have developed in Continental Europe in the early years of the 18th century, but is now more or less universal, although the actual practice varies from country to country. In the United Kingdom, for example, miniatures are confined to mess kit and evening dress (white tie and tails), whereas in the United States it is quite common to see miniatures worn with dinner jackets. In Europe, miniatures are often worn without ribbons, suspended from a tiny chain, but in Britain and elsewhere miniatures are worn with exact replicas of the appropriate ribbons correspondingly reduced in size.

The scale of miniatures likewise varies from country to country. In Britain miniatures are usually half the size of the full-sized medals, but the Scandinavian countries use a 17mm size, while France and the Low Countries prefer a 14mm size, calculated from the diameter of medals or the badges of orders.

In the 18th and early 19th centuries the breast stars of orders were also worn in miniature, but nowadays only the badges of the orders are miniaturised. In Europe the higher classes of orders are designated by placing wings in silver, gold and silver, or gold, according to the class, below the rosette on the riband of the Officer Class. In Britain, however, miniatures are exact replicas of the badges they represent, and no additional rosettes or emblems are added to the ribands to denote a particular class.

Miniatures differ in one major respect from the full-scale; whereas the latter were produced by specific contractors, the former have been manufactured by many jewellers and goldsmiths.

Consequently, the quality may vary considerably, from a very faithful replica (doubtless produced by the same firm that made the originals and using scaled-down dies for the purpose), to quite crude imitations that differ in many details from the full sized version. In many instances, miniature medal groups may be found with the original case as supplied by the jeweller, so that identification is not a problem. Many other groups, however, have long since parted company from their presentation cases, and identification is then only possible from other factors, either stylistic or from marks. Some miniatures are hallmarked (i.e. they bear the punches of an assay office and the mark of the manufacturer), and in such cases the miniature can not only be identified, but even the date of manufacture adduced from the year letter. Not all miniatures by any means are hallmarked, especially if they fall below the statutory minimum weight, so that this aid to identification is not always present.

The value placed on miniatures is governed by condition, of course, but other factors that must be taken into consideration are the provenance and authenticity of the medal or group. Miniatures which are contemporary with the original award are rated more highly than replacements procured many years later. And miniature groups which can definitely be assigned to a particular recipient are worth a premium over those whose original owner cannot be determined. Unlike the full-scale originals, miniatures very seldom bear the name of the recipient. Nevertheless, this is a fascinating aspect of medal collecting, much less expensive than the full-size medals but often as rewarding for the human interest which miniatures represent.

Orders of Knighthood

The most colourful and romantic of all awards are those connected with the orders of chivalry. Many of them have their origins in the Middle Ages, when knights in armour formed the elite fighting force in every European country. This was the period when knights jousted in tournaments as a pastime, between going off to the Holy Land on the wars of Christendom known as the Crusades. This was the era of such popular heroes as Richard the Lionheart, William the Lion, Robert the Bruce, the Black Prince, Pepin of Herstal and John the Blind King of Bohemia. Their exploits have passed into the folklore of Europe, together with the legends of Roland and his Paladins or King Arthur and the Knights of the Round Table.

From the idea of a select band of knights, pledged to the support of a king or an ideal (usually religious), sprang the orders of chivalry. Many of these existed in the Middle Ages but most of them died out as feudalism went into decline. In some cases they survived; in others they disappeared for centuries, only to be resurrected at a later date. Still others were devised and instituted in relatively modern times, and indeed, continue to evolve. For example, Canada instituted the Order of Canada in 1967 and both Australia and New Zealand introduced their own orders in 1975.

In their original form membership of the orders of chivalry were just as highly coveted as they are today, but the insignia was usually simple or even non-existent. The complicated system of insignia which now surrounds these orders is fairly modern, dating from the 16th century or later. Nowadays most orders also exist in several classes, with the insignia becoming increasingly elaborate with each higher class.

Britain's senior order is the Garter, and although it consists of one class only it provides a good example of the pomp and ceremony which often surrounds these awards. It was founded by King Edward III and is said to derive its name from the fact that the King was attending a dance one day, when a lady's garter slipped from her leg and fell to the floor. To save her the embarrassment of retrieving her garter—and thus letting everyone know it was hers—the King himself picked it up and tied it round his own leg. Lest anyone should doubt that it was his garter he said, in court French, "Let evil be to him who evil thinks". From this curious incident came the idea of a very exclusive order of knighthood, consisting of the sovereign and 26 knights.

The insignia of this order consists of a Garter, a mantle of blue velvet lined with taffeta with the star of the Order embroidered on the left breast, a hood of crimson velvet, a surcoat of crimson velvet lined with white taffeta, a hat of black velvet lined with white taffeta, with a plume of white ostrich and black heron feathers fastened by a band of diamonds, a collar of gold composed of buckled garters and lovers' knots with red roses, the George (an enamelled figure of St George slaying the dragon) suspended from the collar, the Lesser George or badge, worn from a broad blue sash passing over the left shoulder to the right hip, and the star, a silver eight-pointed decoration bearing the red cross of St George surrounded by the garter and motto.

The insignia is exceptionally elaborate, the other orders of chivalry varying considerably in their complexity according to the class of the order. The full insignia is only worn on special occasions. In the case of the Garter usually the Lesser George and the breast star are worn on their own.

On the death of a Knight of the Garter the insignia must be returned to the Central Chancery of Orders of Knighthood, and therefore few examples of the Garter ever come on to the market. Those that do are usually examples from the 17th and 18th centuries when regulations regarding the return of insignia were not so strict. In the case of the lesser orders, insignia is returnable on promotion to a higher class. All collar chains are returnable, although that of the Order of St Michael and St George could be retained prior to 1948.

British orders are manufactured by firms holding contracts from the Central Chancery of Orders of Knighthood, and the values quoted in this Yearbook are for the official issues. It should be noted, however, that holders of orders frequently have replicas of breast stars made for use on different uniforms and it is sometimes difficult to tell these replicas from the originals as in many cases the replicas were made by the court jewellers responsible for making the originals. In addition, many jewellers in such European capitals as Vienna, Berlin and Paris have a long tradition of manufacturing the insignia of orders for sale to collectors.

The badges and breast stars of orders of chivalry are very seldom named to the recipient and therefore lack the personal interest of campaign medals and many gallantry awards. For this reason they do not command the same interest or respect of collectors. Nevertheless, in cases where the insignia of orders can be definitely proved to have belonged to some famous person, the interest and value are enhanced. In any case, these orders are invariably very attractive examples of the jeweller's art, and they often possess titles and stories as colourful and romantic as their appearance.

1. THE MOST NOBLE ORDER OF THE GARTER

KG Star
(a Victorian example)

Lesser George
(this early example has the
garter enamelled in blue)

Instituted: 1348.

Ribbon: 100mm plain dark blue. Not worn in undress uniform.

Garter: Dark blue velvet. Two versions may be encountered, with embroidered lettering and other details, or with gold lettering, buckle and tab. Worn on the left leg by gentlemen and on the left forearm by ladies.

Collar Chain: Gold composed of alternate buckled garters, each encircling a red enamelled rose, and lovers' knots in gold although sometimes enamelled white.

Collar badge: An enamelled figure of St George fighting the dragon.

Star: Originally always embroidered in metal thread, a style which continues in the mantle to this day. Prior to 1858 knights often purchased metal stars in addition and since that date metal stars have been officially issued. These consist of a silver eight-pointed radiate star bearing in its centre and red cross of St George on a white ground, surrounded by the garter and motto HONI SOIT QUI MAL Y PENSE (evil be who evil thinks).

Sash Badge: The Lesser George, similar to the collar badge but encircled by an oval garter bearing the motto.

Comments: *Membership of the Order of the Garter is confined to the reigning sovereign, the Prince of Wales and 25 other Knights, and is the personal gift of the monarch. In addition to the 25 Knights there have, from time to time, been extra Knights, occasionally non-Christians such as the Sultans of Turkey or the Emperor of Japan. The Emperor Hirohito, incidentally had the dubious distinction of being the only person awarded the Garter twice: in 1922 and again in 1971, having forfieted the original award as a result of the Japanese entry into the Second World War in 1941. Sir Winston Churchill was invested with the insignia originally presented in 1702 to his illustrious ancestor, the Duke of Marlborough. All official insignia is returnable to the Central Chancery of Knighthood on the death of the holder. Ladies (other than royalty) are now eligible for the Order.*

VALUE:

Collar chain	Rare
Collar badge (the George)	£50,000–100,000*
Star (in metal)	£3000–7000
Star (embroidered)	£850–2000
Mantle star	£850–1000
Sash badge (Lesser George)	£5000–40,000
Garter (embroidered)	£800–1000
Garter (gold lettering and buckle)	£3000–5000

Miniature

Star (metal)	£200–250

*Prices are for privately made examples many of which are jewelled and enamelled.

2. THE MOST ANCIENT AND MOST NOBLE ORDER OF THE THISTLE

KT Star

Instituted: 1687.

Ribbon: 100mm plain dark green. Not worn in undress uniform.

Collar Chain: Gold of alternate thistles and sprigs of rue enamelled in proper colours.

Collar Badge: The jewel is a gold and enamelled figure of St Andrew in a green gown and purple surcoat, bearing before him a white saltire cross, the whole surrounded by rays of gold.

Star: Silver, consisting of a St Andrew's cross, with other rays issuing between the points of the cross and, in the centre, on a gold background, a thistle enamelled in proper colours surrounded by a green circle bearing the Latin motto NEMO ME IMPUNE LACESSIT (no one assails me with impunity).

Sash Badge: The medal of the Order is a gold figure of St Andrew bearing before him a saltire cross, surrounded by an oval collar bearing the motto, surmounted by a gold cord fitted with a ring for suspension. Examples are found in plain gold, or with enamelling and/or set with jewels.

Comments: *This order is said to have been founded in AD 787, alluding to barefoot enemy soldiers who cried out when they trod on thistles and thus alerted the Scots of an imminent attack. The order had long been defunct when it was revived by King James VII and II and re-established in December 1703 by Queen Anne. It now consists of the sovereign and 16 Knights, making it the most exclusive of the orders of chivalry. At death, the official insignia is returned to the Central Chancery. Ladies (other than royalty) are now eligible for the Order.*

VALUE:

Collar chain	Rare
Collar badge	Rare
Star (metal)	£1500–4000
Star (embroidered)	£800–1000
Mantle star	£750–1400
Sash badge	£3000–8000
Miniature	
Star (metal)	£250–300

Examples of Sash Badges

3. THE MOST ILLUSTRIOUS ORDER OF ST PATRICK

KP Star

Sash badge

Instituted: February 5, 1783.

Ribbon: 100 mm sky-blue. Not worn in undress uniform.

Collar Chain: Gold, composed of five roses and six harps alternating, each tied together with a gold knot. The roses are enamelled alternately white petals within red and red within white.

Collar Badge: An imperial crown enamelled in proper colours from which is suspended by two rings a gold harp and from this a circular badge with a white enamelled centre embellished with the red saltire cross on which is surmounted a green three-petalled shamrock its leaves decorated with gold crowns, the whole surrounded by a gold collar bearing the Latin motto QUIS SEPARABIT (who shall separate us?) with the date of foundation in roman numerals round the foot MDCCLXXXIII.

Star: A silver eight-pointed star, having in its centre, on a white field, the saltire cross of St Patrick in red enamel charged with a green trefoil bearing a gold crown on each leaf.

Sash Badge: The saltire cross in red enamel surmounted by a green shamrock with gold crowns as above, surrounded by an oval collar of pale blue with the Latin motto round the top and the date of foundation round the foot, the whole enclosed by a gold and white enamel surround charged with 32 shamrocks.

Comments: *Founded by King George III to reward the loyalty of Irish peers during the American War of Independence, it originally comprised the monarch and 15 Knights. In 1833 it was extended to include the Lord-Lieutenant of Ireland and 22 Knights, with certain extra and honorary knights. Appointments of non-royal Knights to the Order ceased with the partition of Ireland in 1922, although three of the sons of King George V were appointed after that date—the Prince of Wales (1927), the Duke of York (1936) and the Duke of Gloucester (1934). It became obsolete in 1974 with the death of the last holder. All items of official insignia were returned at death. Unlike the other two great orders, the sash for this Order is worn in the manner of the lesser orders, over the right shoulder.*

VALUE:

Collar chain	Rare
Collar badge	£8000–12,000
Star (metal)	£2500–4500
Star (embroidered)	£800–1000
Mantle star	£800–1200
Sash badge	£4000–6000
Miniature	
Star (metal)	£200–250

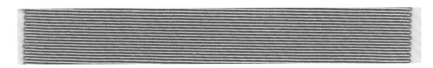

4. THE MOST HONOURABLE ORDER OF THE BATH

GCB Star (Military)

Instituted: 1725.

Ribbon: 38mm deep red.

Collar Chain: Gold composed of nine crowns and eight devices, each consisting of a rose, a thistle and a shamrock issuing from a sceptre all enamelled in their proper colours. The crowns and devices are joined by gold, white-enamelled knots.

Collar Badge: A skeletal gold badge with an oval collar inscribed TRIA JUNCTA IN UNO (three joined in one) in white enamelled letters, enclosing a thistle, rose and shamrock issuing from a sceptre, with a crown above the sceptre and two crowns below, at the sides.

Star: A silver flaming star surmounted by a circular gold band enamelled red bearing the motto round the top and having a laurel spray round the foot, enclosing three gold crowns enamelled in red.

Sash Badge: As the Collar Badge but smaller and without white enamelling.

Comments: *Established by King George I, this was a single-class Order comprising the monarch, a prince of the blood royal, a Great Master and 35 Knights of Companions (KB). It was re-organised at the conclusion of the Napoleonic Wars (see below). Ladies (other than royalty) are now eligible for the Order.*

VALUE:

Collar chain	£18,000–25,000
Collar badge	£3000–4000
Star (metal)	£2000–3500
Star (embroidered)	£400–800
Sash badge	£2000–3000

KNIGHT GRAND CROSS (GCB)

The Order was re-organised in 1815 in two divisions, Military and Civil. The Military Division had three classes: Knight Grand Cross (GCB), Knight Commander (KCB) and Companion (CB), while the Civil Division continued with the single class of Knight Grand Cross. In 1847 the Civil Division came into line with the Military, and divided into three classes.

Metal: Gold (1815–87), silver-gilt (1887–1901), silver gilt with gold centre (1902 on).

Collar Badge: The Military Badge is a gold Maltese cross of eight points, each point tipped with a small gold ball, and in each angle between the arms of the cross is a gold lion. In the centre of the cross is a device comprising a rose, thistle and shamrock issuing from a sceptre, and three imperial crowns . This device is surrounded by a red enamelled circle on which appears the Latin motto TRIA JUNCTA IN UNO (three joined in one) in gold lettering. The circle is surrounded by two branches of laurel, enamelled green, and below is a blue enamelled scroll with the German motto ICH DIEN (I serve) in gold.

The Civil Badge is of gold filigree work, and oval in shape. It consists of a bandlet bearing the motto, and in the centre is the usual device of the rose, thistle and shamrock issuing from a sceptre, together with the three crowns.

Star: A gold Maltese cross of the same pattern as the Military Badge, mounted on a silver flaming star (Military); or a silver eight-pointed star with a central device of three crowns on a silver ground, encircled by the motto on a red enamelled ribbon (Civil).

Sash Badges: Similar to the Collar Badges, they were originally made in gold but since 1887 silver-gilt has been substituted.

VALUE:	Military	Civil
Collar chain (gold)	£18,000–25,000	£18,000–25,000
Collar chain (silver gilt)	£8000–10,000	£8000–10,000
Collar badge (gold)	£2000–3500	£1000–1500
Star (metal)	£500–1000	£400–450
Star (embroidered)	£300–500	£200–300
Mantle star	£500–700	£400–600
Sash badge (gold)	£1800–3000	£1000–1200
Sash badge (gilt)	£800–1000	£400–600

4. THE MOST HONOURABLE ORDER OF THE BATH *continued*

KCB Star (Civil)

GCB Sash badge (Civil)

KCB Neck badge (Mili-

KNIGHTS COMMANDERS (KCB) AND COMPANIONS (CB)

Holders of the KCB wear a neck badge suspended by a ribbon as well as a breast star. Prior to 1917 Companions wore a breast badge, the same way as a medal: but in that year it was converted into a neck badge.

Star: (KCB): (Military) a star with the gold Maltese cross omitted, and in the shape of a cross pattée, the three crowns and motto in the centre surrounded by a green enamelled laurel wreath. (Civil) similar but omitting the laurel wreath.

Breast Badge (CB): Similar to the Star but smaller.

Neck Badge (KCB): Similar to the Collar badges of the GCB but smaller, in Military and Civil versions as above.

Neck Badge (CB): Similar to the above, but smaller.

VALUE:

	Military	*Miniature*	Civil	*Miniature*
Knight Commander				
Star (metal)	£650–850		£300–500	
Star (embroidered)	£250–400		£200–350	
Neck badge (gold)	£1200–1800		£600–800	
Neck badge (gilt)	£550–750		£300–400	
Companion				
Breast badge (gold)	£900–2000	£100–150	£400–500	£80–100
Breast badge (gilt)	£600–800	£30–50	£200–250	£30–50
Neck badge (gilt)	£400–500		£200–250	

5. THE ROYAL GUELPHIC ORDER

Instituted: 1815.
Ribbon: 44mm light blue watered silk.

KNIGHTS GRAND CROSS (GCH)

KCH Star (Military)

Collar Chain: Gold, with lions and crowns alternating, linked by scrolled royal cyphers.
Collar Badge: An eight-pointed Maltese cross with balls on each point and a lion passant gardant in each angle. (Obverse) in the centre, on a ground of red enamel, is a white horse of Hanover surrounded by a circle of light blue enamel with the motto in gold lettering NEC ASPERA TERRENT (difficulties do not terrify). Surrounding this circle is a green enamelled laurel wreath. (Reverse) the monogram GR in gold letters on a red ground, surmounted by the British crown and surrounded by a gold circle with the date of the institution MDCCCXV. In the Military version two crossed swords are mounted above the cross and below a Hanoverian crown. In the Civil version the swords are omited, and the wreath is of oak-leaves instead of laurel.
Star: A radiate star with rays grouped into eight points, the centre being similar to the Collar Badge. Behind the laurel wreathed centre are two crossed swords (Military); in the Civil version the swords are omitted and the wreath is of oak leaves.
Sash Badge: Similar to the Collar Badge but smaller.

Comments: *Founded by HRH the Prince Regent (later King George IV), it took its name from the family surname of the British sovereigns from George I onwards and was awarded by the crown of Hanover to both British and Hanverian subjects for distinguished services to Hanover. Under Salic Law, a woman could not succeed to the Hanoverian throne, so on the death of King William IV in 1837 Hanover passed to Prince Augustus, Duke of Cumberland, and thereafter the Guelphic Order became a purely Hanoverian award.*

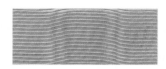

VALUE:

	Military	Civil
Collar chain (gold)	£10,000–12,000	£8000–10,000
Collar chain (silver gilt)	£6000–8000	£4000–5000
Collar Chain (copper gilt)	£4000–6000	£3000–4000
Collar badge	£5000–6000	£2500–3500
Star	£2000–2500	£1500–2000
Sash badge	£6000–8000	£3000–4000

KNIGHTS COMMANDERS (KCH) AND KNIGHTS (KH)

Knights Commanders wore a neck badge suspended by a ribbon, and a breast star, while Knights wore a breast badge only.
Star: As above, but smaller.
Neck Badge: Similar to the Collar Badge but smaller.
Breast Badge: Two versions, in gold and enamel or silver and enamel.

VALUE:

	Military	Miniature	Civil	Miniature
Star	£1500–2000		£1000–1200	
Neck badge	£2500–3500		£1500–2000	
Breast badge (gold)	£2000–2500	£250–300	£1000–1200	£200–250
Breast badge (silver)	£600–800			

KH Breast Badge (Military)

6. THE MOST DISTINGUISHED ORDER OF ST MICHAEL AND ST GEORGE

Instituted: 1818.
Ribbon: 38mm three equal bands of Saxon blue, scarlet and Saxon blue.

KNIGHTS GRAND CROSS (GCMG)

Knights Grand Cross wear a mantle of Saxon blue lined with scarlet silk tied with cords of blue and scarlet silk and gold, and having on the left side the star of the Order. The chapeau or hat is of blue satin, lined with scarlet and surmounted by black and white ostrich feathers. The collar, mantle and chapeau are only worn on special occasions or when commanded by the sovereign, but in ordinary full dress the badge is worn on the left hip from a broad ribbon passing over the right shoulder and the star on the left breast.

Collar Chain: Silver gilt formed alternately on lions of England, Maltese crosses enamelled in white, and the cyphers SM and SG with, in the centre, two winged lions of St Mark each holding a book and seven arrows.

Star: A silver star of seven groups of rays, with a gold ray between each group, surmounted overall by the cross of St George in red enamel. In the centre is a representation of St Michael encountering Satan within a blue circular riband bearing the motto AUSPICIUM MELIORIS AEVI (A token of a better age).

Sash Badge: A gold seven-pointed star with V-shaped extremities, enamelled white and edged with gold, surmounted by an imperial crown. In the centre on one side is a representation in enamel of St Michael encountering Satan and on the other St George on horseback fighting the dragon. This device is surrounded by a circle of blue enamel bearing the Latin motto in gold lettering. Silver-gilt was substituted for gold in 1887.

Comments: *Founded by HRH the Prince Regent and awarded originally to citizens of Malta and the Ionian Islands in the Adriatic Sea, both of which had been ceded to Britain during the Napoleonic Wars. The Ionian Islands were transferred to Greece in 1859. Towards the end of the 19th century, however, the Order was awarded to those who had performed distinguished service in the colonies and protectorates of the British Empire and in more recent times it has been widely used as an award to ambassadors and senior diplomats as well as colonial governors. Ladies are now eligible for this Order.*

VALUE:

Collar chain	£2500–3000
Star	£900–1200
Sash badge (gold)	£3000–4000
Sash badge (gilt)	£1200–1500

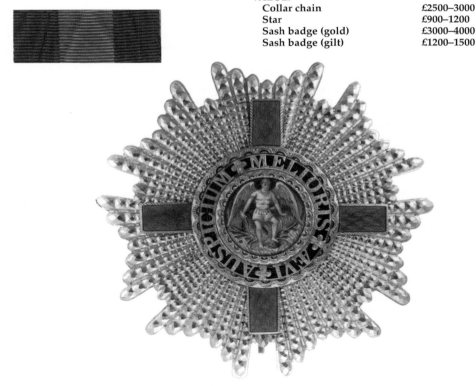

GCMG Star

6. THE MOST DISTINGUISHED ORDER OF ST MICHAEL AND ST GEORGE *continued*

KCMG Star

KNIGHTS COMMANDERS (KCMG) AND COMPANIONS (CMG)

Knights Commanders wear the badge suspended round the neck from a narrower ribbon of the same colours, and a breast star; Companions wear a neck badge. In undress uniform Knights Grand Cross and Knights Commanders wear the ribbon of Companions of the Order. Prior to 1917 Companions wore a breast badge, worn the same way as a medal, but this was then changed to a neck badge.

Star: A silver eight-pointed star charged with the red St George's cross and having the same central device as the GCMG Star. This was introduced in 1859.

Neck Badge: Similar to the sash badge of the GCMG but smaller. Those worn by Knight Commanders were of gold and enamel until 1887 but silver-gilt and enamel thereafter. The CMG neck badges are invariably of enamel and silver-gilt.

Breast Badge: Similar to the star of the KCMG but smaller and made of gold and enamel till 1887, and silver gilt and enamel from then till 1917.

VALUE:		*Miniature*
Knight Commander		
Star	£600–800	
Neck badge (gold)	£1000–1200	
Neck badge (gilt)	£400–500	
Companion		
Breast badge (gold)	£700–900	£80–100
Breast badge (gilt)	£500–600	£30–50
Neck badge (gilt)	£350–450	

7. THE MOST EXALTED ORDER OF THE STAR OF INDIA

Instituted: 1861.
Ribbon: Broad light blue with white edges (GCSI); 50mm plain white (KCSI); 38mm plain white (CSI).

KNIGHTS GRAND COMMANDERS (GCSI)

KCSI Neck badge

The insignia consisted of a gold collar and badge, a mantle of light blue satin with a representation of the star on the left side and tied with a white silk cord with blue and silver tassels. The collar and mantle were only worn on special occasions and in ordinary full dress uniform a GCSI wore the star on the left breast and the badge on the left hip from a broad sash of light blue edged in white.

Collar Chain: Gold formed of lotus flowers, palm branches and united red and white roses. Later chains are silver-gilt.

Badge: An onyx cameo bearing the left-facing bust of Queen Victoria wearing an imperial crown, set in a gold ornamental oval containing the motto of the Order HEAVEN'S LIGHT OUR GUIDE in diamonds, on a pale blue ground surmounted by a five-pointed star in chased silver.

Star: A five-pointed star in diamonds resting on a circular riband of light blue enamel bearing the motto in diamonds, the whole set on a circular star of golden rays.

Comments: *Founded by Queen Victoria a few years after the British Crown took over the administration of India from the Honourable East India Company, it was intended primarily as an award to loyal Indian princes. The highest class was designated Knight Grand Commander, rather than Cross, because the majority of recipient were not Christians (either Hindus or Muslims). The Order at first consisted of the sovereign, a Grand Master (the Viceroy of India), 36 Knights Grand Commanders (18 British and 18 Indian), 85 Knights Commanders and 170 Companions. The GCSI was the most lavish of all British orders. It lapsed in 1947 when the sub-continent attained independence. Until then all insignia of this Order was returnable on the death of recipients. After 1947, however, recipients or their heirs were allowed in certain cases to purchase the star and badges of any of the three applicable classes, but not the collar chain of the Knight Grand Commander.*

VALUE:

Collar chain	Rare
Star and badge	£30,000–40,000

KNIGHTS COMMANDERS (KCSI) AND COMPANIONS (CSI)

Knights Commanders wore a badge round the neck and a star on the left breast, while Companions originally had a breast badge which was transmuted into a neck badge from 1917 onwards.

Star: Similar to that of the GCSI but in silver.
Neck Badge: Similar to the collar badge of the GCSI but smaller and less ornate.
Breast Badge: Similar to the above but smaller and less ornate and fitted with a straight bar suspender. Subtle differences in the ornament at the foot of the blue border and the external ornament at the sides and foot of the oval.
Comments: *The second and third classes of the Order were awarded to Indian and British subjectsof the armed forces and Indian Civil Service for distinguished service of not less than 30 years' duration.*

VALUE: *Miniature*

Star and Neck badge (KCSI)	£4000–6000	
Breast badge (CSI)	£3500–4000	£200–300 (gold), £120–150 (gilt)
Neck badge (CSI)	£2500–2700	

8. THE MOST EMINENT ORDER OF THE INDIAN EMPIRE

Instituted: 1878.
Ribbon: Broad of imperial purple (GCIE); 50mm imperial purple (KCIE); 38mm imperial purple (CIE).

KNIGHTS GRAND COMMANDERS (GCIE)

KCIE Neck badge

The insignia consisted of a collar, badge and mantle of imperial purple or dark blue satin lined with white silk and fastened with a white silk cord with gold tassels, and having on the left side a representation of the Star of the Order. On ordinary full-dress occasions, however, Knights Grand Commanders wore the badge on the left hip from a broad sash, and a star on the left breast.

Collar Chain: Silver-gilt, composed of elephants, lotus flowers, peacocks in their pride and Indian roses with, in the centre, the imperial crown, the whole linked together by chains.

Badge: A gold five-petalled rose, enamelled crimson and with a green barb between each petal. In the centre is an effigy of Queen Victoria on a gold ground, surrounded by a purple riband originally inscribed VICTORIA IMPERATRIX but from 1901 onwards inscribed IMPERATRICIS AUSPICIIS (under the auspices of the Empress). The letters I N D I A are inscribed on the petals in the first version, but omitted in the second.

Star: Composed of fine silver rays with smaller gold rays between them, the whole alternately plain and scaled. In the centre, within a purple circle bearing the motto and surmounted by the imperial crown in gold, is the effigy of Queen Victoria on a gold ground.

Comments: *Founded by Queen Victoria after assuming the title of Empress of India, it was originally confined to Companions only, together with the Sovereign and Grand Master. Members of the Council of the Governor-General were admitted ex officio as Companions. It was intended for award in respect of meritorious services in India but from the outset it was regarded as a junior alternative to the Star of India. In 1886 the Order was expanded to two classes by the addition of Knights Commanders up to a maximum of 50 in number. In 1887, however, it was again re-organised into three classes: up to 25 Knights Grand Commanders (GCIE), up to 50 Knights Commanders (KCIE) and an unlimited number of Companions (CIE). The Order has been in abeyance since 1947.*

VALUE:

Collar chain	£12,000–15,000
Star and badge	£4500–5500

KNIGHTS COMMANDERS (KCIE) AND COMPANIONS (CIE)

The insignia of Knights Commanders consisted of a neck badge and a breast star, while that of Companions was originally a breast badge, converted to a neck badge in 1917.

Star: Similar to that of the GCIE but fashioned entirely in silver.

Neck badge: Similar to the collar or sash badge of the GCIE but in correspondingly smaller sizes and differing in minor details.

Breast badge: Similar to the sash badge of the GCIE but differing in minor details, notably the spacing ornament at the foot of the blue circle. Two versions exist, with or without INDIA on the petals of the lotus flower.

VALUE:		*Miniature*
Knights Commanders		
Star and Neck badge	£3000–3500	
Companions		
Breast badge (INDIA)	£1200–1400	£250–300 (gold)
Breast badge (smaller, without INDIA)	£450–550	£150–200 (gold)
Neck badge	£400–450	£100–200 (gilt)

9. THE ROYAL FAMILY ORDER

Instituted: 1820.

Ribbon: 50mm sky blue moire (1820); 38mm dark blue bordered by narrow stripes of yellow and broader stripes of crimson with narrow black edges (1902); 50mm pale blue moire (1911); 50mm pink moire (1937); 50mm pale yellow silk moire (1953). These ribbons are tied in a bow and worn on the left shoulder.

Descriptions: An upright oval heavily bordered by diamonds and surmounted by a crown, also embellished in diamonds. The oval contains a miniature portrait of the sovereign in enamels.

Comments: *Awarded to the Queen and female relatives of the reigning monarch. It was instituted by King George IV who conferred such orders on his sister, Princess Charlotte Augusta, wife of Frederick William, King of Wurttemberg, and his niece Princess Augusta Caroline, who married the Grand Duke of Mecklenburg-Strelitz. Queen Victoria instituted a separate Order (see next entry), but this Order was revived by King Edward VII in 1902 and continued by successive sovereigns ever since. Special badges are given to ladies-in-waiting. The insignia of these Family Orders very seldom appear on the market and on account of their immense rarity they are unpriced here.*

VALUE:	
George IV	Rare
Edward VIII	Rare
George V	Rare
George VI	Rare
Elizabeth II	Rare
Ladies-in-waiting badges	From £1000

10. THE ROYAL ORDER OF VICTORIA AND ALBERT

Instituted: 1862.

Ribbon: 38mm white moiré, in the form of a bow worn on the left shoulder.

Description: An upright oval onyx cameo bearing conjoined profiles of HRH Prince Albert, the Prince Consort and Queen Victoria. The badges of the First and Second Classes are set in diamonds and surmounted by an imperial crown similarly embellished, the badge of the Second Class being rather smaller. The badge of the Third Class is set in pearls, while that of the Fourth Class takes the form of a monogram "V & A" set with pearls and surmounted by an imperial crown.

VALUE:	
First Class	£24,000–26,000
Second Class	£16,000–18,000
Third Class	£10,000–12,000
Fourth Class	£4000–5000

11. THE IMPERIAL ORDER OF THE CROWN OF INDIA

Instituted: January 1, 1878.

Ribbon: 38mm light blue watered silk with narrow white stripes towards the edges, formed in a bow worn on the left shoulder.

Description: A badge consisting of the royal and imperial monogram VRI in diamonds, turquoises and pearls, surrounded by an oval frame and surmounted by a jewelled imperial crown.

Comments: *Awarded by Queen Victoria to the princesses of the royal and imperial house, the wives or other female relatives of Indian princes and other Indian ladies, and of the wives or other female relatives of any of the persons who had held or were holding the offices of Viceroy and Governor-General of India, Governors of Madras or Bombay, or of Principal Secretary of State for India, as the sovereign might think fit to appoint. This order, conferred on females only, became obsolete in 1947.*

VALUE:	
Breast badge	£8000–12,000

12. THE ROYAL VICTORIAN ORDER

Instituted: April 1896.
Ribbon: Dark blue with borders of narrow red, white and red stripes on either side.

KNIGHTS GRAND CROSS AND DAMES GRAND CROSS (GCVO)

The insignia consists of a mantle of dark blue silk, edged with red satin, lined with white silk, and fastened by a cordon of dark blue silk and gold; a gold collar and a badge, worn only on special occasions. Knights wear the badge on the left hip from a broad ribbon worn over the right shoulder, with a star on the left breast, while Dames wear a somewhat narrower ribbon over the right shoulder with the badge, and a star similar to that of the Knights. Dames' insignia are smaller than those of the Knights.

Collar: Silver gilt composed of octagonal pieces and oblong perforated and ornamental frames alternately linked together with gold. The pieces are edged and ornamented with gold, and each contains on a blue-enamelled ground a gold rose jewelled with a carbuncle. The frames are gold and each contains a portion of inscription VICTORIA BRITT. DEF. FID. IND. IMP. in letters of white enamel. In the centre of the collar, within a perforated and ornamental frame of gold, is an octagonal piece enamelled blue, edged with red, and charged with a white saltire, superimposed by a gold medallion of Queen Victoria's effigy from which is suspended the badge.

Badge: A white-enamelled Maltese cross of eight points, in the centre of which is an oval of crimson enamel bearing the cypher VRI in gold letters. Encircling this is a blue enamel riband with the name VICTORIA in gold letters, and above this is the imperial crown enamelled in proper colours.

Star: Of chipped silver of eight points on which is mounted a white-enamelled Maltese cross with VRI in an oval at the centre.

Comments: *Awarded for extraordinary, important or personal services to the sovereign of the Royal Family. Ladies became eligible for the Order in 1936. Most of the badges of the Royal Victorian Order are numbered on the reverse and are returnable on promotion. Honourary awards are unnumbered.*

VALUE:	Knights	Dames
Collar		
gold	£10,000–12,000	£12,000–15,000
silver gilt	£5000–6000	£7000–9000
Star and Badge (GCVO)	£1400–1600	£1200–1500

GCVO star

KNIGHTS COMMANDERS (KCVO), DAMES COMMANDERS (DCVO), COMMANDERS (CVO), LIEUTENANTS (LVO) AND MEMBERS (MVO)

The insignia of the Second, Third, Fourth and Fifth Classes follows the usual pattern. Knights wear a neck badge and a breast star, Dames a breast star and a badge on the left shoulder from a ribbon tied in a bow, Commanders the same neck badge (men) or shoulder badge (women), Lieutenants a somewhat smaller breast badge worn in line with other medals and decorations (men) or a shoulder badge (women) and Members breast or shoulder badges in frosted silver instead of white enamel. The two lowest classes of the Order were originally designated member Fourth Class or member Fifth Class (MVO), but in 1984 the Fourth Class was renamed Lieutenant (LVO) and the Fifth Class simply Member (MVO).

VALUE:	Gentlemen	*Miniature*	Ladies
Neck badge and breast star (KCVO)	£800–900		£700–900
Neck badge (CVO)	£350–400	£30–50	£450–500
Breast or shoulder badge (LVO)	£300–350	£30–50	£350–370
Breast or shoulder badge (MVO)	£230–250	£15–25	£300–350

13. ROYAL VICTORIAN MEDAL

Instituted: April 1896.
Ribbon: As for the Royal Victorian Order (above); foreign Associates, however, wear a ribbon with a central white stripe added.
Metal: Silver-gilt, silver or bronze.
Size: 30mm.
Description: (Obverse) the effigy of the reigning sovereign; (reverse) the royal cypher on an ornamental shield within a laurel wreath.
Comments: *Awarded to those below the rank of officers who perform personal services to the sovereign or to members of the Royal Family. Originally awarded in silver or bronze, a higher class, in silver-gilt, was instituted by King George V. Only two medals (both silver) were issued in the brief reign of King Edward VIII (1936) and only four bronze medals were issued in the reign of King George VI. Any person in possession of the bronze medal to whom a silver medal is awarded, can wear both, and the silver-gilt medal in addition if such be conferred upon him or her. Clasps are awarded for further services to each class of the medal, while the medals may be worn in addition to the insignia of the Order if the latter is subsequently conferred.*
To distinguish between British and foreign recipients, King George VI decreed in 1951 that the ribbon worn by the latter should have an additional stripe, these recipients to be designated Associates. In 1983 the order for wearing this medal was altered and it was no longer to be worn after campaign medals but took precedence over them.

	Silver-gilt	*Miniature*	Silver	*Miniature*	Bronze	*Miniature*
Victoria	—	£60–75	£160–180	£60–75	£140–150	£50–60
Edward VII	£250–300		£160–180	£50–60	£120–140	£40–50
George V	£250–300		£125–150	£25–30	£250–300	£20–25
Edward VIII	—		Rare		—	
George VI	£250–300		£140–150	£10–15	Rare	£10–15
Elizabeth II	£250–300		£160–180	£10–15	£250–300	£10–15

14. THE ROYAL VICTORIAN CHAIN

Instituted: 1902.
Ribbon: None.
Metal: Silver gilt
Description: A chain consisting of three Tudor roses, two thistles, two shamrocks and two lotus flowers (the heraldic flowers of England, Scotland, Ireland and India respectively), connected by a slender double trace of gold chain. At the bottom of the front loop is a centre piece consisting of the royal cypher in enamel surrounded by a wreath and surmounted by a crown. From this centrepiece hangs a replica of the badge of a Knight Grand Cross of the Royal Victorian Order. Ladies were the insignia in the form of a shoulder badge suspended from a miniature chain with links leading to a rose, thistle, shamrock and lotus. An even more elaborate collar, with diamonds encrusting the crown and cypher, was adopted in 1921 and there is a ladies' version of this as well.
Comments: *Sometimes regarded as the highest grade of the Royal Victorian Order, it is actually a quite separate Order and was introduced by King Edward VII for conferment as a special mark of the sovereign's favour, and then only very rarely, upon Royalty, or other especially distinguished personages, both foreign and British.*

VALUE

	Gentlemen	Ladies
Chain (1902–21)	Rare	Rare
Chain with diamonds	Rare	Rare

15. ORDER OF MERIT

Order of Merit obverse

Order of Merit reverse

Instituted: 1902.

Ribbon: 50mm half blue, half crimson.

Metal: Gold.

Size: Height 50mm; max. width 35mm.

Description: A pattée convexed cross, enamelled red, edged blue. (Obverse) FOR MERIT in the centre surrounded by a white band and a laurel wreath enamelled in proper colours. (Reverse) the royal cypher in gold on a blue ground with a white surround and a laurel wreath as above. The cross is surmounted by a Tudor crown to which is attached a ring for suspension. Naval and military recipients have crossed swords in the angles of the cross.

Comments: *This highly prestigious Order consists of the sovereign and a maximum of 24 members in one class only. There is, however, no limit on the number of foreign honorary members, although only ten have so far been admitted to the Order. It was intended for award to those whose achievements in the fields of art, music and literature were outstanding, but it was later extended to naval and military leaders in wartime. To date, fewer than 160 awards have been made, including only eight ladies, from Florence Nightingale (1907) to Baroness Thatcher. The insignia of those appointed since 1991 have to be returned on the death of the recipient. The insignia of members appointed prior to that date is retained, but understandably few items have come on to the market.*

VALUE:

	Military	Civil
Edward VII	£6000–8000	£5000–7000
George V	£6000–8000	£5000–7000
George VI	Rare	£5000–7000
Elizabeth II	Rare	£4500–6500
Miniature (modern example)		£100–150

16. THE MOST EXCELLENT ORDER OF THE BRITISH EMPIRE

GBE Star (2nd type)

CBE Badge (2nd type)

Instituted: June 1917.

Ribbon: 38mm originally purple, with a narrow central scarlet stripe for the Military Division; rose-pink edged with pearl grey, with a narrow central stripe of pearl-grey for the Military Division (since 1936). A silver crossed oakleaf emblem for gallantry was instituted in 1957.

Comments: *Founded by King George V during the First World War for services to the Empire at home, in India and in the overseas dominions and colonies, other than those rendered by the Navy and Army, although it could be conferred upon officers of the armed forces for services of a non-combatant character. A Military Division was created in December 1918 and awards made to commissioned officers and warrant officers in respect of distinguished service in action. The insignia of the Civil and Military Divisions is identical, distinguished only by the respective ribbons.*

KNIGHTS AND DAMES GRAND CROSS (GBE)

The insignia includes a mantle of rose-pink satin lined with pearl-grey silk, tied by a cord of pearl-grey silk, with two rose-pink and silver tassels attached. On the left side of the mantle is a representation of the star of the First Class of the Order. The mantle, collar and collar badge are only worn on special occasions. In dress uniform, however, the badge is worn over the left hip from a broad (96mm) riband passing over the right shoulder, while Dames wear the badge from a narrower (57mm) ribbon in a bow on the left shoulder; both with the breast star of the Order.

Collar: Silver-gilt with medallions of the royal arms and of the royal and imperial cypher of King George V alternately linked together with cables. In the centre is the imperial crown between two sea lions. The collar for Dames is somewhat narrower than that for Knights.

Badge: A cross patonce in silver-gilt the arms enamelled pearl-grey. In the centre, within a circle enamelled crimson, the figure of Britannia, replaced since 1936 by the conjoined left-facing crowned busts of King George V and Queen Mary, surrounded by a circle inscribed FOR GOD AND THE EMPIRE.

Star: An eight-pointed star of silver chips on which is superimposed the enamelled medallion as for the badge (Britannia or George V and Queen Mary). The star worn by Dames is smaller.

VALUE:	1st type Britannia	2nd type King and Queen
Knights Grand Cross		
Collar	£5000–6000	£5000–6000
Badge and star	£1500–1700	£1500–1700
Dames Grand Cross		
Collar	£6000–7000	£6000–7000
Badge and star	£1200–1400	£1200–1400

16. THE MOST EXCELLENT ORDER OF THE BRITISH EMPIRE *continued*
KNIGHTS COMMANDERS (KBE), DAMES COMMANDERS (DBE), COMMANDERS (CBE) AND MEMBERS (MBE)

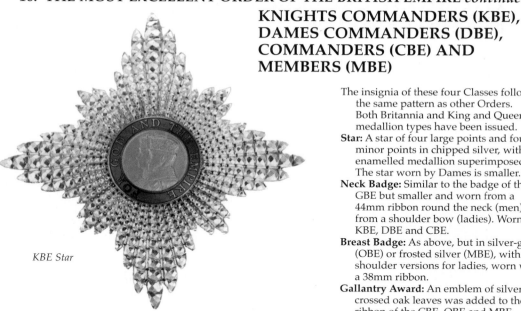

KBE Star

The insignia of these four Classes follows the same pattern as other Orders. Both Britannia and King and Queen medallion types have been issued.

Star: A star of four large points and four minor points in chipped silver, with the enamelled medallion superimposed. The star worn by Dames is smaller.

Neck Badge: Similar to the badge of the GBE but smaller and worn from a 44mm ribbon round the neck (men) or from a shoulder bow (ladies). Worn by KBE, DBE and CBE.

Breast Badge: As above, but in silver-gilt (OBE) or frosted silver (MBE), with shoulder versions for ladies, worn with a 38mm ribbon.

Gallantry Award: An emblem of silver crossed oak leaves was added to the ribbon of the CBE, OBE and MBE (1957–74).

Oak leaf emblem for gallantry.

VALUE:	1st type	*Miniature*	2nd type	*Miniature*
	Britannia		King&Queen	
Badge and Star (KBE,)	£650–850		£650–850	
Badge and Star (DBE)	£650–850		£650–850	
Neck badge (CBE)	£240–260	£20–25	£240–260	£20–25
Shoulder badge (CBE)	£240–250		£240–260	
Breast badge (OBE)	£85–95	£10–15	£85–95	£10–15
Shoulder badge (OBE)	£85–95		£85–95	
Breast badge (MBE)	£85–95	£10–12	£85–95	£10–12
Shoulder badge (MBE)	£85–95		£80–95	

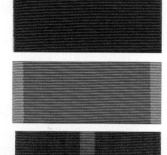

OBE badge (silver-gilt) and reverse of the MBE badge (frosted silver).

Ribbons: (top to bottom) OBE (Civil) 1st type, OBE (Civil) 2nd type, OBE (Military) 1st type and OBE (Military) 2nd type.

17. MEDAL OF THE ORDER OF THE BRITISH EMPIRE

Civil ribbon

Instituted: June 1917.
Ribbon: 32mm plain purple (Civil), with a narrow scarlet central stripe (Military).
Medal: Silver.
Size: 30mm.
Description: (Obverse) a seated figure of Britannia facing right, her left arm extended and her right holding a trident, with the inscription FOR GOD AND THE EMPIRE round the upper part of the circumference; (reverse) the royal and imperial cypher GRI surmounted by a Tudor crown, the whole enclosed in a cable circle. Fitted with a plain ring for suspension.
Comments: *Instituted as a lower award connected with the Order, it consisted originally of a Civil Division, but a Military Division, distinguishable solely by the ribbon, was added in December 1918. This medal was issued unnamed but many were subsequently engraved or impressed on the rim privately. Fewer than 2000 medals were awarded before they were discontinued in 1922.*

VALUE:

		Miniature
Medal unnamed as issued	£120–140	£30–40

18. EMPIRE GALLANTRY MEDAL

1st type rev.

Instituted: December 29, 1922.
Ribbon: Originally plain purple (Civil), with a thin scarlet central stripe (Military; from July 1937 rose-pink with pearl-grey edges (Civil) and a central pearl-grey stripe (Military). A silver laurel branch was added to the ribbon (1933), with a smaller version for wear on the ribbon alone.
Metal: Silver.
Size: 36mm.
Description: (Obverse) the seated figure of Britannia, her left hand resting on a shield and her right holding a trident, with a blazing sun upper right. The words FOR GOD AND THE EMPIRE inscribed round the upper part of the circumference, with FOR in the wave lower left above the exergue which bears the word GALLANTRY. (Reverse) 1st type has six lions passant gardant, with the Royal cypher in the centre surmounted by an imperial crown. The George VI issue has four lions, two either side and round the foot, in two concentric arcs, the words INSTITUTED BY KING GEORGE V. It is suspended from a straight bar ornamented with laurel leaves. Named in seriffed capitals engraved round the rim.
Comments: *This medal, officially known as the Medal of the Order of the British Empire for Gallantry, replaced the Medal of the Order of the British Empire and was awarded for specific acts of gallantry. It was abolished on the institution of the George Cross in September 1940, while it was announced in the London Gazette of April 22, 1941 that a recipient still living on September 24, 1940 should return it to the Central Chancery of the Orders of Knighthood and become a holder of the George Cross instead. Not all EGMs, however, were exchanged or returned. Only 130 medals were issued, 64 being civil, 62 military and 4 honorary.*

VALUE:

		Miniature
George V	£3000–3500	£70–100
George VI	£3000–3500	£50–80

19. BRITISH EMPIRE MEDAL

BEM (MIlitary) 2nd type

Instituted: December 1922.
Ribbon: As above, but without the silver laurel branch.
Metal: Silver.
Size: 36mm.
Description: As above, but with the words MERITORIOUS SERVICE in the exergue. Suspended from a straight bar ornamented with oak leaves. A silver bar decorated with oak leaves was introduced in March 1941 for further acts, and is denoted by a silver rosette on the ribbon worn on its own. An emblem of crossed silver oak leaves was introduced in December 1957 to denote a gallantry award, a smaller version being worn on the ribbon alone. Named in engraved capitals round the rim.
Comments: *Formally entitled the Medal of the Order of the British Empire for Meritorious Service, it is generally known simply as the British Empire Medal. It is awarded for meritorious service by both civil and military personnel although for some years it was issued as a third grade bravery award, particularly for air raid deeds not considered to be of the level of the GC or GM. The medal may be worn even if the recipient is promoted to a higher grade of the Order. The gallantry awards, instituted in December 1957, ceased in 1974 on the introduction of the Queen's Gallantry Medal. No British awards have been made for the BEM since 1995 but Commonwealth awards are still being made.*

VALUE:

	Military	Civil	Miniature	
George V	£200–250	£150–200	£15–20	
George VI GRI cypher	£180–200	£100–120	£10–15	
George VI GVIR cypher	£180–200	£100–120	£10–15	
Elizabeth II	£180–200	£100–120	£10–15	
Elizabeth II with gallantry emblem	£500–800	£500–800		

19A. QUEEN'S VOLUNTEER RESERVES MEDAL

Instituted: 1999.
Ribbon: Dark green with three narrow gold stripes.
Metal: Silver.
Size: 36mm.
Description: (Obverse) effigy of Queen Elizabeth II; (reverse) five ribbons containing the words THE QUEEN'S VOLUNTEER RESERVES MEDAL. The medal is fitted with a large ring for suspension.
Comments: *Awarded to men and women of any rank in the volunteer reserves of all three services in recognition of outstanding service which formerly would have merited an award within the Order of the British Empire. Holders are entitled to the post-nominal letters QVRM.*

VALUE: £300–500   *Miniature* £10–15

20. THE ORDER OF THE COMPANIONS OF HONOUR

Instituted: June 1917.

Ribbon: 38mm carmine with borders of gold thread.

Metal: Silver gilt.

Size: Height 48mm; max. width 29mm.

Description: An oval badge consisting of a medallion with an oak tree, a shield bearing the royal arms hanging from one branch, and on the left a knight armed and in armour, mounted on a horse. The badge has a blue border with the motto IN ACTION FAITHFUL AND IN HONOUR CLEAR in gold letters. The oval is surmounted by an imperial crown. Gentlemen wear the badge round their necks, while ladies wear it from a bow at the left shoulder.

Comments: *Instituted at the same time as the Order of the British Empire, it carries no title or precedence although the post-nominal letters CH are used. The Order consists of the sovereign and one class of members. Not more than 50 men or women who have rendered conspicuous service of national importance were admitted, but in 1943 this was increased to 65. The Order is awarded in Britain and the Commonwealth on a quota basis: UK (45), Australia (7), New Zealand (2), other countries (11). It is awarded for outstanding achievements in the arts, literature, music, science, politics, industry and religion.*

VALUE

Gentlemen	£2500–3000
Ladies	£2500–3000

Modern uniface miniature **£150–200**

21. THE BARONET'S BADGE

Baronet's badge—United Kingdom

Instituted: 1629.

Ribbon: 30mm orange watered silk (Nova Scotia); 44mm orange bordered with narrow blue edges (other Baronets).

Metal: Gold or silver-gilt.

Size: Height 55mm; max. width 41mm(Nova Scotia) or 44mm (later badges).

Description: An upright oval badge with a plain ring suspension. The badge of the Baronets of Nova Scotia was originally skeletal, with a shield bearing the lion rempant of Scotland, decorated with pearls and enamels, surmounted by a Scottish crown and surrounded by a blue border inscribed in gold FAX MENTIS HONESTAE GLORIA. The remaining badges (authorised in 1929) have a solid ground and a central shield with the red hand of Ulster surmounted by a crown and a border of gold and blue enamel decorated with roses (England), shamrocks (Ireland), roses and thistles combined (Great Britain) or roses, thistles and shamrocks combined (United Kingdom). Engraved on the reverse with the recipient's title and date of creation.

Comments: *By Letter Patent of 1611 James I created Baronets whose knighthood became hereditary. In 1624, to raise money independently of Parliament, James I sold grants of land in Nova Scotia (New Scotland) to Scotsmen. In 1625 Charles I conferred on the holders of this land the title and dignity of Baronets of Nova Scotia with the title of Sir, and decreed that they should wear round their necks "an orange tawny ribbon whereon shall be pendent an escutcheon". After the Union with England (1707) English and Scottish baronetcies ceased to be created, being replaced by baronetcies of Great Britain. Irish baronetcies continued to be created until 1801 after which all new creations were of the United Kingdom.*

VALUE:	Gold	Silver-gilt
Nova Scotia, 18th–early 19th centuries	£2000–3000	£800–1000
Nova Scotia, late 19th and 20th centuries	£1500–1800	£600–1000
England (rose surround)	£800–1200	£800–1000
Ireland (shamrock surround)	£800–1200	£800–1000
Great Britain (roses and thistles)	£800–1200	£800–1000
United Kingdom (roses, thistles and shamrocks)	£800–1200	£800–1000

22. THE KNIGHT BACHELOR'S BADGE

Instituted: April 21, 1926.
Ribbon: 38mm scarlet with broad yellow borders.
Metal: Silver-gilt and enamels. Some pre-war breast badges in base metal.
Size: Height 81mm; max. width 60mm. Reduced in 1933 and 1973.
Description: An upright oval medallion enclosed by a scroll, bearing a cross-hilted sword, belted and sheathed, pommel upwards, between two spurs, rowels upwards, the whole set about with the sword-belt.
Comments: *The title Knight Bachelor (KB) was introduced by King Henry III to signify a battelier (one who fought in battle). The badge was authorised by King George V in response to a request from the Imperial Society of Knights Bachelors who wished to have a distinctive badge denoting their rank. The original badge was of the dimensions given above and affixed to the breast by means of a pin on the reverse. This badge was reduced in size in 1933 and again in 1973 when it was fitted with a ring for suspension by a ribbon round the neck.*

VALUE:

		Miniature
First type (1929)	£300–350	£30–40
Smaller type (1933)	£300–350	(Skeletal type
Neck badge (1974)	£350–400	£20–35)

Knight Bachelor's badge

23. THE ORDER OF ST JOHN

Breast star

Shoulder badge

Instituted: May 14, 1888.
Ribbon: Plain black watered silk. Sash ribbons for Bailiffs, 100mm; Dames Grand Cross, 65mm. Ribbons for Chaplains and Knights, 57mm; Ribbons for Dames were formerly in a 32mm bow and ribbons for Commanders, officers and Serving Brothers 38mm and 32mm for ladies, but under new regulations (October 2001) all ribbons below Grand Cross are now standardised at 38mm.
Metal: Gold, silver-gilt and silver, or base metal.
Sash badge: An eight-pointed gold Maltese cross in white enamel with two lions and two unicorns in the angles. Confined to Bailiffs and Dames Grand Cross.
Neck badge: Hitherto in the grades Knight/Dame, Commander and Officer badges worn by women were smaller than those worn by men, but in 2001 this distinction was abolished. The badges worn by Knights of Justice and Chaplains are in gold, while those worn by Knights of Grace and Commanders are in silver.
Star: The eight-pointed Maltese cross in white enamel without the lions and unicorns (Grand Cross and Justice) or with lions and unicorns (Grace and Sub-Prelate). A sub-Prelate is an Order Chaplain (so his badge is

included above) who held high rank in the Church as distinct from the Order. The order ceased appointing Sub-Prelates in 1999, and as a result the Sub-Prelate's badge (gilt with animals) is now obsolescent.

Shoulder badge: Worn by Dames of Justice in gold and Dames of Grace, Commanders and Officers (Sisters) in silver. It is now mounted on a ribbon with "tails" as in other British orders. The shoulder badge illustrated here is now obsolescent.

Breast badges: Officers (Brothers) is the Order badge with animals, in silver (1926–36) and in silver and enamel subsequently. Those worn by Serving Brothers, and as shoulder badges by Serving Sisters, have undergone six main phases:

1892–1939: a circular badge with crosses and animals raised above the surface of the medal.

1939–1949: circular skeletal badge with ring suspension and the eight-point cross set in a silver rim.

1949–1974: the first badge resumed.

1974–1984: a badge of the same design but with the cross and animals flush with their background.

1984–1991: the cross and animals in white metal, slightly smaller than the Officer (Brother) cross and the whole convex on the obverse.

Since 1991: Cross and animals thicker, with each arm raised and shaped on both sides of a central channel, the whole in rhodium. Since 1999 a woman Officer or Serving Sister who was in uniform is invested with her breast badge on a straight ribbon.

Donats' badges: Gold, silver or bronze, consisting of the badge of the Order with the upper arm of the cross replaced by an ornamental piece of metal for suspension.

Comments: *The Most Venerable Order of the Hospital of St John of Jerusalem was incorporated by Royal Charter of Queen Victoria and granted the epithet Venerable in 1926 and Most in 1955; despite its title, it has no connection with the Knights Hospitallers of Jerusalem, who were subsequently based at Rhodes and Malta and are now located at Rome. In 1926 the Order was reorganised into five Classes like certain other Orders. A sixth class was added later. Both men and women are eligible for membership. Her Majesty the Queen is the Sovereign Head of the Order. Next in authority is the Grand Prior, followed by Bailiffs and Dames Grand Cross, Chaplains, Knights and Dames of Justice, Knights and Dames of Grace, Commanders, Officers, Serving Brothers and Sisters and Esquires. Associates were people who were not citizens of the United Kingdom, the British Commonwealth or the Republic of Ireland, or are non-Christians, who have rendered conspicuous service to the Order and may be attached to any grade of the Order. They wear the insignia of that grade, at one time distinguished only by a central narrow white stripe on the ribbon, but now all ribbons are identical. Donats are people who have made generous contributions to the funds of the Order. They are not enrolled as members of the Order but receive badges in gold, silver or bronze.*

VALUE:

	Gold	Silver/Gilt	Bronze	Miniature
Bailiff badge and star	£1500–2250	£800–1000	—	
Dame Grand Cross	£1500–2000	£600–700	—	
Knight of Justice neck badge and star	£800–900	£500–600	£150–250	
Dame of Justice shoulder badge and star	£800–900	£500–600	£200–300	
Knight of Grace neck badge and star	—	£350–400	£150–250	
Dame of Grace shoulder badge and star	—	£350–400	£150–250	£15–20
Commander (Brother) neck badge	—	£150–200	£60–80	
Commander (Sister) shoulder badge	—	£50–75	£30–50	
Officer breast badge, plain silver	—	£50–70	—	£10–15
Office breast badge, enamelled	—	£65–75	£30–50	£15–20
Officer (Sister) enamelled badge	—	£65–75	£30–50	
Serving Brother/Sister 1926–39	—	£50–75	£30–50	£10–12
Serving Brother/Sister 1939–49	—	£45–65	£40–60	£10–12
Serving Brother/Sister 1949–	—	—	£30–50	
Donat's badge	£120–150	£45–55	£30–40	£25–30

Honour the Air Forces

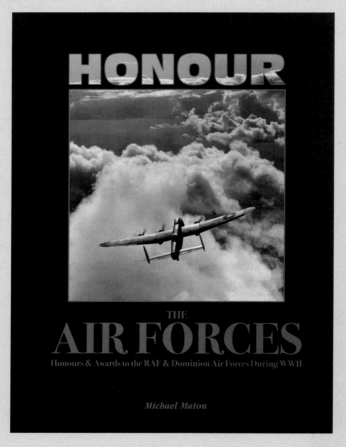

Honour the Air Forces, an important new work by Australian author Michael Maton, lists, for the first time, the names of over 40,000 recipients of gallantry and distinguished service awards made during WWII to members of the RAF and Dominion Air Forces, together with their service number, rank, honours awarded, *London Gazette* reference and the squadron or unit in which they served.

The book also lists the conventions used in establishing which awards and which individuals have been included together with other relevant material on the awards, each of which is described in a separate chapter with a number of citations shown in order to give the reader an idea of the events which led to such awards being bestowed.. There are a number of important tables showing the distribution of awards between the various air forces, by each year of the war, by rank and by squadron. There is also a table showing the number of multiple award combinations. Much of this statistical information has never been published before.

Priced at just £65 plus £5 p&p UK (overseas orders please add £10 standard airmail, at your own risk and £20 for "signed for" service), this hard-cased, A4 publication is a fascinating book and is essential for anyone interested in WWII or the Air Forces. It is a must have reference work for any collector specialising in Air Force medals.

TOKEN PUBLISHING LTD., ORCHARD HOUSE, DUCHY ROAD, HEATHPARK, HONITON EX14 1YD
TEL: 01404 44166 · FAX: 01404 44788 · sales@tokenpublishing.com · www.tokenpublishing.com

Decorations

The award of decorations for distinguished military service is an ancient institution. In his *Antiquities of the Jews*, the historian Josephus relates that, in the second century BC, King Alexander was so pleased with Jonathan the High Priest that he sent him a gold button as a mark of favour for his skill in leading the Jews in battle. Subsequently Jonathan was presented with a second gold button for his gallant conduct in the field, making these incidents among the earliest recorded for which specific military awards were granted. The award of jewels, gold buttons and badges for valour was carried on in most European countries on a sporadic basis but the present system of decorations is essentially a modern one dating back no farther than the middle of the seventeenth century. Earlier medals were quasi-commemorative and include the famous Armada Medal of 1588. A few medals in silver or gold were awarded to officers for distinguished service during the English Civil War, although the first "official" rewards in Britain were probably those issued by Parliament to naval officers following their victories over the Dutch fleet in 1653.

Decorations may be divided into those awarded for individual acts of heroism and those conferred in recognition of distinguished military, political or social service. In general terms collectors prefer a decoration awarded for bravery in the field rather than a political honour given automatically to a civil servant, just because he happens to have been in a particular grade for a certain number of years. The debasement of civil awards, such as the OBE and MBE, is reflected in the relative lack of interest shown by collectors.

It is generally true to say that military decorations are more desirable, but it is important to note that one decoration may be more highly prized than another, while the same decoration may well be more valuable to collectors when issued in one period rather than in another. At one extreme is the greatly coveted Victoria Cross, only 1354 of which (including three bars) have been awarded since its inception. VCs won during the Crimean War (111 awarded) are usuallyless highly regarded than Crosses awarded during the First World War, where, although numerically greater (633) they were far more dearly won. Second World War Crosses are correspondingly more expensive as only 182 were awarded and even now comparatively few of them have ever come on to the market. Today, while pre-1914 Crosses would rate at least £75,000 and those from the First World War slightly more, Second World War Crosses start around £120,000 but have been known to fetch several times as much, depending on the precise circumstances and the branch of the services.

At the other extreme is the Military Medal, of which no fewer than 115,589 were awarded during the First World War alone. For this reason a MM from this period can still be picked up for under £600, whereas one from the Second World War would usually fetch about four times as much, and awards made during the minor campaigns of the 1930s or the Korean War often rate at least ten times as much.

The value of a decoration, where its provenance can be unquestionably established, depends largely on the decoration itself, whether awarded to an officer or an enlisted man, the individual circumstances of the award, the campaign or action concerned, the regiment, unit or ship involved, and the often very personal details of the act or acts of bravery. These factors are extraordinarily difficult to quantify, hence the frequent large discrepancies in the prices fetched by decorations at auction.

The addition of even relatively common decorations, such as the Military Cross or the Military Medal to the average First World War campaign medal group, invariably enhances its value very considerably while the addition of bars for subsequent awards likewise rates a good premium. Decorations awarded to officers tend to fetch more than those awarded to other ranks, mainly because they are proportionately rarer but also because it is usually easier to trace the career details of an officer.

Sometimes the rank of the recipient may have a bearing on the demand for a particular decoration: e.g. Military Crosses awarded to warrant officers are scarcer than those awarded to subalterns and captains. The branch of the armed services may also have some bearing. Thus a Military Medal awarded to a member of the RAF rates far higher than one awarded to a soldier, while a medal awarded to a seaman in one of the naval battalions which fought on the Western Front is also equally desirable.

Initially the Distinguished Service Order could be won by commissioned officers of any rank but after 1914, when the Military Cross was instituted, it was usually restricted to officers of field rank. DSOs awarded to lieutenants and captains in the Army in both World Wars are therefore comparatively rare and invariably expensive, usually as they were awarded for acts of heroism which in earlier campaigns might have merited the VC. As part of the 1993 review of awards, the Conspicuous Gallantry Coss (CGC) replaced the DSO, CGM and DSM to remove the distiction between officers and other ranks.

The opportunity for individual acts of bravery varied from service to service, and in different conflicts. Thus sailors in the Second World War generally had less scope than air crew. Consequently specifically naval awards, such as the Conspicuous Gallantry Medal and the Distinguished Service Cross, are much more scarce than the corresponding RAF awards for Conspicuous Gallantry and the Distinguished Flying Cross.

The addition of bars to gallantry decorations greatly enhances the scarcity and value of such medals. The VC, for example, has been won by only three men on two occasions; none of these VC and bar combinations has ever come on the market, but should one come up for sale, it is certain that the price would be spectacular. The average First World War MM is today worth around £500, but with a bar for second award its value immediately jumps to about three times as much, while MMs with two or more bars are very much more expensive.

It is important to note that in some cases (the DSO for example) decorations were issued unnamed; for this reason the citation or any other supporting documents relevant to the award should be kept with the decoration wherever possible to confirm its attribution.

Engraving of Gallantry Decorations

After the special investiture for the South Atlantic campaign held on February 8, 1983, the question as to why certain awards were engraved with the date only was raised within the Ministry of Defence. A joint service working party considered the matter and recommended that procedures for all decorations and medals for gallantry in the face of the enemy and for the Air Force Cross when awarded for a specific act of gallantry should be brought into line. A submission was accordingly made to the Queen by the Committee on the Grant of Honours, Decorations and Medals and in April 1984 Her Majesty approved the following:

(i)   That the Distinguished Service Cross, Military Cross, Distinguished Flying Cross and Air Force Cross when awarded for gallantry should be engraved with the personal details of the recipient with effect from January 1, 1984.
(ii) That there should be no retrospection;
(iii) That the badge of a Companion of the Distinguished Service Order should not be engraved (in common with the badges of other orders); and
(iv) That the Royal Red Cross (RRC and ARRC) and the Air Force Cross when awarded for meritorious service should not be engraved.

Condition

The same terms are applied to describe the condition of medals and decorations as apply to coins, although the wear to which they are put is caused by other factors. In modern times, when the number of occasions on which medals are worn are relatively few and far between, the condition of most items will be found to be Very Fine (VF) to Extremely Fine (EF). Indeed, in many cases, the medals may never have been worn at all. A good proportion of Second World War medals and decorations are found in almost mint condition as they were not issued till long after the war, by which time their recipients had been demobilised. In some cases they even turn up still in the original cardboard box in which they were posted to the recipients or their next-of-kin.

Before the First World War, however, the wearing of medals was customary on all but the most informal occasions and when actually serving on active duty. Thus medals could be, and often were, subject to a great deal of wear. Medals worn by cavalrymen are often found in poor condition, with scratches and edge knocks occasioned by the constant jangling of one medal against another while on horseback. Often the medals in a group have an abrasive effect on each other. For this reason the Queen's Medal for Egypt (1882) is comparatively rare in excellent condition, as it was usually worn in juxtaposition to the bronze Khedive's Star whose points were capable of doing considerable damage to its silver companion. Apart from these factors it should also be remembered that part of the ritual of "spit and polish" involved cleaning one's medals and they were therefore submitted to vigorous cleaning with metal polish over long periods of service.

For these reasons medals are often sold by dealers "as worn"—a euphemism which conceals a lifetime of hardy service on the chest of some grizzled veteran. Because of the strong personal element involved in medal-collecting, however, genuine wear does not affect the value of a medal to the same degree that it would in other branches of numismatics. There is a school of thought which considers that such signs enhance the interest and value of a medal or group.

This line of thinking also explains the controversy over medal ribbons. Some military outfitters still carry extensive stocks of medal ribbons covering every campaign from Waterloo onwards, so that it is a very easy matter to obtain a fresh length of ribbon for any medal requiring it, and there is no doubt that the appearance of a piece is greatly improved by a clean, bright new ribbon. On the other hand, that ribbon was not the one actually worn by Corporal Bloggs on parade and, to the purist, it would spoil the total effect of the medal. Some collectors therefore retain the original ribbon, even though it may be faded and frayed. As ribbons are things which one cannot authenticate, however, there seems to be little material benefit to be gained from clinging rigidly to a tattered strip of silk when an identical piece can be obtained relatively cheaply. In reality, most collectors compromise by obtaining new ribbons while preserving the old lengths out of sentiment.

The prices quoted in this publication are average figures for medals and decorations as individual items. Combinations with other decorations and campaign medals will produce a value usually well in excess of the aggregate of the individual items. Value will depend to a large extent on the personal factors and circumstances of the award, but where general factors are involved (e.g. the design of the medal, the period of issue or the campaign concerned, or in some cases the branch of the services) these are itemised separately. "—" indicates that either no examples have come onto the market or no examples have been issued. The figure in brackets (where available) is the approximate number awarded. In the lists which follow, it should be assumed that decorations were instituted by Royal Warrant, unless otherwise stated.

MORTON & EDEN LTD

in association with **Sotheby's**

45 Maddox Street   London   W1S 2PE

Sold at auction, 18th April 2002

Sold at auction, 13th November 2002

Sold at auction, 3rd October 2003

Sold at auction, 13th December 2003

phone +44 (0)20 7493 5344   fax +44 (0)20 7495 6325   info@mortonandeden.com

24. THE VICTORIA CROSS

Instituted: January 1856.
Ribbon: Crimson. Originally naval crosses used a blue ribbon, but since 1918 the crimson (Army) ribbon has been used for all awards. A miniature cross emblem is worn on the ribbon alone in undress uniform.
Metal: Bronze, originally from Russian guns captured in the Crimea. Modern research, however, reveals that guns captured in other conflicts, e.g. China, have also been used at various periods.
Size: Height 41mm; max. width 36mm.
Description: A cross pattée. (Obverse) a lion statant gardant on the royal crown, with the words FOR VALOUR on a semi-circular scroll. (Reverse) a circular panel on which is engraved the date of the act for which the decoration was awarded. The Cross is suspended by a ring from a seriffed "V" attached to a suspension bar decorated with laurel leaves. The reverse of the suspension bar is engraved with the name, rank and ship, regiment or squadron of the recipient.
Comments: *Introduced as the premier award for gallantry, available for all ranks, to cover all actions since the outbreak of the Crimean War in 1854, it was allegedly created on the suggestion of Prince Albert, the Prince Consort. Of the 1354 awards since 1856, 832 have gone to the Army, 107 to the Navy, 31 to the RAF, ten to the Royal Marines and four to civilians. Second award bars have been awarded three times. The facility for posthumous awards, made retrospective to 1856, began in 1902 and was confirmed in 1907, while the early practice of forfeitures (eight between 1863 and 1908) was discontinued after the First World War.*

VALUE:

	Royal Navy/Army	RFC/RAF	Miniature
1856–1914 (522)	£80,000–100,000	—	£50–80
1914–18 (633)	£80,000–120,000	£100,000–150,000	£20–30
1920–45 (187)	£90,000–120,000	£100,000–150,000	£20–30
post-1945 (12)	From £100,000	—	£10–20

NB These prices can only be construed as a general guide. Quite a few awards would exceed these price ranges, particularly Commonwealth examples or those appertaining to well known actions.

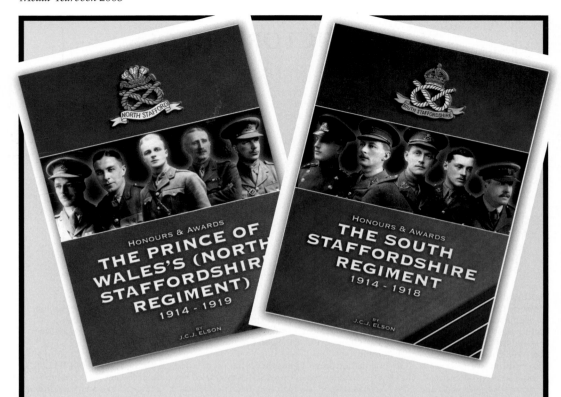

The Prince of Wales's North Staffordshire Regiment & The South Staffordshire Regiment

These major new works look at all the Honours and Awards earned by these two leading regiments during World War I. They are a must for any collector to the North Staffs or South Staffs

Hardbound and profusely illustrated – £24.95 each (+£3.00 p&p UK, £8 ROW) available from Token Publishing, Orchard House, Duchy Road, Heathpark, Honiton EX14 1YD. Tel: 01404 44166

Order on line
www.tokenpublishing.com

25. NEW ZEALAND CROSS

Instituted: 10 March 1869 (by an Order in Council, Wellington).
Ribbon: 38mm crimson.
Metal: Silver with gold appliqué.
Size: Height 52mm; max. width 38mm.
Description: A silver cross pattée with a six-pointed gold star on
   each limb. In the centre are the words NEW ZEALAND within
   a gold laurel wreath. The cross is surmounted by a gold Tudor
   crown which is attached by a ring and a seriffed "V" to a silver
   bar ornamented with gold laurel leaves, through which the ribbon
   passes. The recipient's name and details are engraved on the reverse.
Comments: *The rarest of all gallantry awards, it was conferred for bravery*
   during the second series of Maori Wars (1860-72). Only 23 Crosses
   were awarded, the last being authorised in 1910. This medal was called
   into being solely because local volunteer forces were not eligible for the
   VC. Replicas of the Cross have been authorised by the New Zealand
   government. Today the Cross, with slight amendments to the design, is
   New Zealand's premier civilian award for bravery (see NZ2).

VALUE: £30,000–40,000   *Miniature £250–750*
          Official copy £650–750

26. GEORGE CROSS

Instituted: 24 September 1940.
Ribbon: 38mm dark blue (originally 32mm). A silver miniature cross
   emblem is worn on the ribbon alone.
Metal: Silver.
Size: Height 48mm; max. width 45mm.
Description: A plain bordered cross with a circular medallion in
   the centre depicting the effigy of St George and the Dragon after
   Benedetto Pistrucci, surrounded by the words FOR GALLANTRY.
   In the angle of each limb is the Royal cypher GVI. The plain reverse
   bears in the centre the name of the recipient and date of the award.
   In the case of exchange awards, the date of the deed is given. The
   Cross hangs by a ring from a bar adorned with laurel leaves.
Comments: *The highest gallantry award for civilians, as well as for members*
   of the armed forces in actions for which purely military honours would not
   normally be granted. It superseded the Empire Gallantry Medal whose
   holders were then required to return it and receive the GC in exchange. By
   Warrant of December 1971 suviving recipients of the Albert and Edward
   Medals were also invited to exchange their awards for the GC—a move
   which created a controversy which is still continuing, particularly among
   those who received the Albert Medal. Perhaps the most famous Cross
   was that conferred on the island of Malta in recognition of its gallantry
   during the Second World War. Apart from exchange awards, between
   1940 and 1947 the GC was awarded to 102 men and three women; since
   1947 a further 40 awards have been made. To date no second award bars
   have been awarded. Since its inception in 1940 the George Cross has
   been awarded 155 times, including four women. In addition, 112 Empire
   Gallantry medallists, 65 Albert medallists and 68 Edward medallists who
   were eligible to exchange their awards for the GC have increased the total
   to 400. Most awards were made during World War II but it should be
   noted that since 1947 the GC has been awarded only 43 times (including
   one woman and the collective award to the Royal Ulster Constabulary,
   conferred by Her Majesty the Queen at Hillsborough Castle on 12 April
   2000, the most recent award).

VALUE:

Service awards 1940 to date	£8000–12,000
Civilian awards 1940 to date	£6000–10,000
Service exchange pre-1940	£5000–8000
Civilian exchange pre-1940	£4000–6000
Miniature	£10–15
	(in silver add £10)

27. DISTINGUISHED SERVICE ORDER

Instituted: 1886.
Ribbon: 29mm crimson with dark blue edges.
Metal: Originally gold; silver-gilt (since 1889).
Size: Height 44mm; max. width 41.5mm.
Description: A cross with curved ends, overlaid with white enamel. (Obverse) a green enamel laurel wreath enclosing an imperial crown; (reverse) the royal monogram within a similar wreath. It is suspended from its ribbon by a swivel ring and a straight laureated bar. Additional awards are denoted by bars ornamented by a crown. Silver rosettes on the ribbon alone are worn in undress uniform. Since its inception, the DSO has been issued unnamed, but since 1938 the year of award has been engraved on the reverse of the lower suspension bar as well as the reverse of the bars for second or subsequent awards.
Comments: *Intended to reward commissioned officers below field rank for distinguished service in time of war, and for which the VC would not be appropriate. Previously the CB had sometimes been awarded to junior officers, although intended mainly for those of field rank. It was also available to officers in both the other armed services. In September 1942 the regulations were relaxed to permit award of the DSO to officers of the Merchant Navy who performed acts of gallantry in the presence of the enemy. As a result of the 1993 Review of gallantry awards and resultant changes to the operational gallantry award system, the DSO is now awarded for "Leadership" only—theoretically to all ranks (it is not awarded posthumously). It has been replaced by the Conspicuous Gallantry Cross as the reward for gallantry.*

VALUE:	Unnamed single	Attributable group	Miniature
Victoria, gold (153)	£2000–2500	£4500–6000	£100–120
Victoria, silver-gilt (1170)	£1000–1200	£2500–6000	£60–80
Edward VII (78)	£1500–1800	£4500–5500	£80–100 (gold)
George V (9900)	£750–850	£1500–2500	£25 (gilt), £50 (gold)
George VI 1st type 1938–48 (4880)	£850–1000	£2000–3000	£40 (gilt)
George VI 2nd type 1948–52 (63)	£1500–1800	£3500–4500	£40 (gilt)
Elizabeth II	£3000–3500	£4000–5000	£30

28. IMPERIAL SERVICE ORDER

Instituted: August 1902.
Ribbon: 38mm three equal sections of crimson, blue and crimson.
Metal: Silver with gold overlay.
Size: Height 61mm; max. width 55mm.
Description: The badge consists of a circular gold plaque bearing the royal cypher and surrounded by the words FOR FAITHFUL SERVICE. This plaque is then superimposed on a seven-pointed silver star surmounted by a crown and ring for suspension. The badge of the ISO awarded to women is similar but has a laurel wreath instead of the star-shaped base.
Comments: *Instituted by King Edward VII as a means of rewarding long and faithful service in the Administrative and Clerical grades of the Civil Service at home and overseas. Women were admitted to the order in 1908. The order was awarded after at least 25 years service at home, 20 years and 6 months (India) and 16 years in the tropics, but in exceptional cases awards were made for "eminently meritorious service" irrespective of qualifying period. No UK awards have been made since 1995 but some Commonwealth awards continue to this day.*

VALUE:			Miniature
Edward VII	Gentleman (489)	£180–220	£25–30
	Lady (3)	£800–1000	£150–200
George V	Gentleman (909)	£180–220	£20–25
	Lady (2)	£800–1000	£150–200
George VI	Gentleman (608)	£180–200	£15–20
	Lady (8)	£800–1000	£150–200
Elizabeth II	Gentleman (2,153)*	£180–200	£10–15
	Lady (114)*	£600–800	£150–200
*1953–94			

29. IMPERIAL SERVICE MEDAL

Instituted: August 1902.
Ribbon: Same as above.
Metal: Silver and bronze.
Description: Originally similar to the ISO but with a silver plaque and bronze star or wreath. In 1920 the ISM was transformed into a circular medal of silver with the sovereign's effigy on the obverse and a reverse depicting a naked man resting from his labours, with FOR FAITHFUL SERVICE in the exergue.
Comments: *Instituted at the same time as the ISO but intended for junior grades of the Civil Service.*

VALUE:

			Miniature
Edward VII, 1903–10 (c. 4,500) Star (Gentleman)		£65–75	£15–20
Wreath (Lady)		£250–350	£150–200
George V, 1911-20 (c. 6,000) Star (Gentleman)		£60–70	£12–15
Wreath (Lady)		£300–350	£150–200
George V Circular type			
Coinage profile, 1920–31 (c. 20,000)		£18–25	£10–12
Crowned bust, 1931–37 (c. 16,000)		£18–25	£10–12
George VI			
Crowned bust INDIAE:IMP, 1938–48 (c. 36,000)		£18–25	£8–10
Crowned bust FID:DEF, 1949–52 (c. 16,000)		£18–25	£8–10
Elizabeth II			
Tudor crown BRITT:OMN, 1953–54 (c. 9,000)		£18–25	£8–10
Tudor crown DEI:GRATIA, 1955– (c. 150,000)		£18–25	£8–10

30. INDIAN ORDER OF MERIT

Instituted: 1837 (by the Honourable East India Company).
Ribbon: Dark blue with crimson edges (military) or crimson with dark blue edges (civil).
Metal: Silver and gold.
Size: Height 41mm; max. width 40mm.
Description: An eight-pointed star with a circular centre surrounded by a laurel wreath and containing crossed sabres and the relevant inscription. The star is suspended by a curvilinear suspension bar. The different classes were denoted by the composition of the star, noted below.
Comments: *The oldest gallantry award of the British Empire, it was founded in 1837 by the Honourable East India Company. Twenty years later it became an official British award when the administration of India passed to the Crown after the Sepoy Mutiny. Originally known simply as the Order of Merit, it was renamed in 1902 following the introduction of the prestigious British order of that name. There were three classes of the order, promotion from one class to the next being the reward for further acts of bravery. A civil division (also in three classes) was introduced in 1902. Ten years later the military division was reduced to two classes, when troops of the Indian Army became eligible for the VC. The civil division became a single class in 1939 and the military in 1945. Both divisions came to an end with the British Raj in 1947.*

VALUE:
Military Division
1837-1912 Reward of Valour

1st class in gold (42)	£4500–6000
2nd class in silver and gold (130)	£2000–3000
3rd class in silver (2740)	£1000–1500

1912-39 Reward of Valour

1st class in silver and gold (26)	£4500–6000
2nd class in silver (1215)	£350–450

continued

30. INDIAN ORDER OF MERIT continued

1939-44 Reward for Gallantry		
1st class in silver and gold (2)		Rare
2nd class in silver (332)		£750–900
1945-47 Reward for Gallantry (44mm diameter)		£1800–2500
Civil Division		
1902-39 For Bravery (35mm diameter)		
1st class in gold (0)		—
2nd class in silver and gold (0)		—
3rd class in silver (39)		£1500–1800
1939-47 For Bravery (26mm diameter)		
Single class (10)		£2500–3500
Miniature		£150–250

NB These prices represent unattributable pieces. Values can climb rapidly when in company with related campaign medals, particularly for the Victorian era.

30A. CONSPICUOUS GALLANTRY CROSS

Instituted: October 1993.
Ribbon: White with blue edges and a red central stripe.
Metal: Silver.
Size: Max. width 36mm
Description: A cross pattée imposed on a wreath of laurel, with the royal crown in a circular panel in the centre. Suspended by a ring from a plain suspension bar.
Comments: *As part of the decision to remove distinctions of rank in awards for bravery this decoration replaced the DSO for gallantry as well as the Conspicuous Gallantry Medal and the Distinguished Conduct Medal. It was first awarded in 1995 to Corporal Wayne Mills of the Duke of Wellington's Regiment and in 1996 to Colour Sergeant Peter Humphreys of the Royal Welch Fusiliers, both for gallantry in action during service with the UN Peacekeeping Forces in Bosnia. Two awards were made in respect of gallantry by members of the SAS and SBS in Sierra Leone in May–June 2000. A further two awards were made to members of the SAS and two awards to members of the SBS in Afghanistan in October 2001– March 2002, while awards to Justin Thomas, RM, and Lance Corporal Michael Flynn, Blues and Royals, both for gallantry in Iraq, were gazetted i October 2003, making a total of 10 in the first decade.*

VALUE: —   *Miniature* £15–18

31. ROYAL RED CROSS

First Class obverse

2nd Class reverse

Instituted: 27 April 1883.

Ribbon: 25mm dark blue edged with crimson, in a bow.

Metal: Gold (later silver-gilt) and silver.

Size: Height 41mm; max. width 35mm.

Description: (Obverse) The *1st class* badge was originally a gold cross pattée, enamelled red with gold edges, but from 1889 silver-gilt was substituted for gold. At the centre was a crowned and veiled portrait, with the words FAITH, HOPE and CHARITY inscribed on three arms, and the date 1883 on the lower arm. Subsequently the effigy of the reigning monarch was substituted for the allegorical profile; (reverse) crowned royal cypher. *2nd Class:* in silver, design as the 1st class but the inscriptions on the arms appear on the reverse. Awards from 1938 have the year of issue engraved on the reverse of the lower arm.

Comments: *This decoration had the distinction of being confined to females until 1976. It is conferred on members of the nursing services regardless of rank. A second class award was introduced in November 1915. Bars for the first class were introduced in 1917. Holders of the second class are promoted to the first class on second awards. Holders of the first class decoration are known as Members (RRC) while recipients of the second class are Associates (ARRC).*

VALUE:	First class (RRC)	Miniature	Second class (ARRC)	Miniature
Victoria, gold	£1000–1200	—	—	£90–100
Victoria, silver-gilt	£400–500	—	—	£60–70
Edward VII, gold	£800–1000	—	—	£90–100
George V	£250–300	£20–30	£120–150	£10–25
George V, with bar	£450–550	—	—	
George VI GRI	£300–350	£20–30	£180–220	£10–25
George VI GVIR	£350–400	£20–30	£200–250	£10–25
Elizabeth II	£300–350	£20–30	£200–250	£10–25

32. DISTINGUISHED SERVICE CROSS

Instituted: June 1901.

Ribbon: 36mm three equal parts of dark blue, white and dark blue.

Metal: Silver.

Size: Height 43mm; max. width 43mm.

Description: A plain cross with rounded ends. (Obverse) crowned royal cypher in the centre, suspended by a ring; (reverse) plain apart from the hallmark. From 1940 onwards the year of issue was engraved on the reverse of the lower limb.

Comments: *Known as the Conspicuous Service Cross when instituted, it was awarded to warrant and subordinate officers of the Royal Navy who were ineligible for the DSO. In October 1914 it was renamed the Distinguished Service Cross and thrown open to all naval officers below the rank of lieutenant-commander. Bars for second awards were authorised in 1916 and in 1931 eligibility for the award was enlarged to include officers of the Merchant Navy. In 1940 Army and RAF officers serving aboard naval vessels also became eligible for the award. Since 1945 fewer than 100 DSCs have been awarded. As a result of the 1993 Review of gallantry awards and resultant changes to the operational gallantry award system, this award is now available to both officers and other ranks, the DSM having been discontinued.*

VALUE:	Unnamed single	Attributable group	Miniature
Edward VII	Rare	£5000–7000	£200–250
George V	£400–600	£1000–1500	£20–30
George VI GRI	£450–600	£1000–1500	£15–20
George VI GVIR	Rare	£2500–3000	£25–30
Elizabeth II	Rare	£3500–5000	£12–15

33. MILITARY CROSS

Instituted: 31 December 1914.
Ribbon: 38mm three equal stripes of white, deep purple and white.
Metal: Silver.
Size: Height 46mm; max. width 44mm.
Description: An ornamental cross with straight arms terminating in broad finials decorated with imperial crowns. The royal cypher appears at the centre and the cross is suspended from a plain silver suspension bar.
Comments: *There was no gallantry award, lesser than the VC and DSO, for junior Army officers and warrant officers until shortly after the outbreak of the First World War when the MC was instituted. Originally awarded to captains, lieutenants and warrant officers of the Army (including RFC), it was subsequently extended to include equivalent ranks of the RAF when performing acts of bravery on the ground and there was even provision for the Royal Naval Division and the Royal Marines during the First World War. Awards were extended to majors by an amending warrant of 1931. Bars for second and subsequent awards have a crown at the centre. The MC is always issued unnamed, although since about 1938 the reverse of the cross or bar is officially dated with the year of issue. As a result of the 1993 Review of gallantry awards and resultant changes to the operational gallantry award system, this award is now available to both officers and other ranks, the Military Medal having been discontinued.*

VALUE:	Unnamed single	Attributable group	*Miniature*
George V 1914-20 (37,000)	£400–500	£900–1500	£15–20
George V 1914-20 one bar (3000)	£600–800	£1400–2000	
George V 1914-20 two bars (170)	£800–950	£3500–4500	
George V 1914-20 three bars (4)	Rare	Rare	
George V 1921-36 (350)	Rare	£1800–2500	
George V 1921-36 one bar (31)	Rare	£3000–5000	
George VI GRI 1939-46 (11,000)	£500–550	£1200–1800	£10–15
George VI GRI one bar (500)	£550–700	£3000–4000	
George VI GVIR (158)	Rare	£2500–3500	£10–15
Elizabeth II	£600–700	£3000–3500	£10–15
Elizabeth II one bar	Rare	Rare	

34. DISTINGUISHED FLYING CROSS

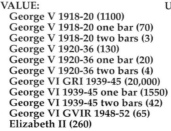

Instituted: June 1918.
Ribbon: 30mm originally horizontal but since June 1919 diagonal alternate stripes of white and deep purple.
Metal: Silver.
Size: Height 60mm; max. width 54mm.
Description: (Obverse) a cross flory terminating with a rose, surmounted by another cross made of propeller blades charged in the centre with a roundel within a laurel wreath. The horizontal arms bear wings and the crowned RAF monogram at the centre; (reverse) the royal cypher above the date 1918. The cross is suspended from a bar decorated with a sprig of laurel.
Comments: *Established for officers and warrant officers of the RAF in respect of acts of valour while flying in active operations against the enemy. The DFC is issued unnamed, but Second World War crosses usually have the year of issue engraved on the reverse of the lower limb. As a result of the 1993 Review of gallantry awards and resultant changes to the operational gallantry award system, this award is now available to both officers and other ranks, the Distinguished Flying Medal having been discontinued.*

VALUE:	Unnamed single	Attributable group	*Miniature*
George V 1918-20 (1100)	£750–850	£1800–2500	£20–25
George V 1918-20 one bar (70)	£900–1000	£4500–5500	
George V 1918-20 two bars (3)	Rare	Rare	
George V 1920-36 (130)	Rare	Rare	
George V 1920-36 one bar (20)	Rare	Rare	
George V 1920-36 two bars (4)	Rare	Rare	
George VI GRI 1939-45 (20,000)	£850–950	£1500–2500	£15–20
George VI 1939-45 one bar (1550)	£850–950	£2500–4000	
George VI 1939-45 two bars (42)	Rare	Rare	
George VI GVIR 1948-52 (65)	Rare	Rare	£15–20
Elizabeth II (260)	£1000–1200	£3000–4000	£12–15

(in silver add £5)

35. AIR FORCE CROSS

Instituted: June 1918.

Ribbon: 30mm originally horizontal but since June 1919 diagonal alternate stripes of white and crimson.

Metal: Silver.

Size: Height 60mm; max. width 54mm.

Description: (Obverse) the cross consists of a thunderbolt, the arms conjoined by wings, base bar terminating in a bomb, surmounted by another cross of aeroplane propellers, the finials inscribed with the royal cypher. A central roundel depicts Hermes mounted on a hawk bestowing a wreath; (reverse) the royal cypher and the date 1918.

Comments: *This decoration, awarded to officers and warrant officers of the RAF, was instituted in June 1918 for gallantry on non-operational missions and for meritorious service on flying duties. Since the 1993 Review of gallantry awards it is now available to all ranks (the Air Force Medal having been discontinued) for non-operational gallantry in the air only (no longer for meritorious service also).*

VALUE:	Unnamed single	Attributable group	*Miniature*
George V 1918-20 (680)	£700–800	£1200–1500	£20–25
George V 1918-20 one bar (12)	Rare	Rare	
George V 1918-20 two bars (3)	Rare	Rare	
George V 1920-36 (160)	£900–1000	£1800–2500	
George VI GRI (2000)	£650–750	£1200–1800	£15–20
George VI one bar (26)	£850–950	£2500–3000	
George VI two bars (1)	Rare	Rare	
George VI GVIR (980)	£650–750	£1200–1800	£15–20
Elizabeth II	£850–1000	£1500–2000	£10–12

(in silver add £5)

36. ORDER OF BRITISH INDIA

Instituted: 1837 by the Honourable East India Company.

Ribbon: Worn around the neck, the base colour of the ribbon was originally sky blue but this was altered to crimson in 1838, allegedly because the hair oil favoured by Indians of all classes would soon have soiled a light ribbon. From 1939 onwards the first class ribbon had two thin vertical lines of light blue at the centre, while the second class ribbon had a single vertical line. Originally these distinctive ribbons were only worn in undress uniform (without the insignia itself), but from 1945 they replaced the plain crimson ribbons when worn with the decoration.

Metal: Gold.

Size: Height 42mm; max. width 38mm.

Description: The first class badge consists of a gold star with a crown between the upper two points and a blue enamelled centre bearing a lion surrounded by the words ORDER OF BRITISH INDIA enclosed in a laurel wreath. The second class badge is smaller, with dark blue enamel in the centre and with no crown.

Comments: *Intended for long and faithful service by native officers of the Indian Army, it was thrown open in 1939 to officers of the armed forces, frontier guards, military police and officers of the Indian native states. There were two classes, promotion to the first being made from the second. Recipients of both classes were entitled to the letters OBI after their names, but holders of the first class had the rank of Sardar Bahadur, while those of the second were merely Bahadur. A few awards were made by Pakistan to British officers seconded to the Pakistani forces at the time of independence.*

VALUE:		*Miniature*
1st class, light blue centre and dark blue surround	£550–600	£150–200
1st class, sky blue centre and surround (1939)	£550–600	£150–200
2nd class	£550–600	£150–200

NB The prices quoted are for unattributable awards.

37. ORDER OF BURMA

Instituted 1940.
Ribbon: 38mm dark green with light blue edges.
Metal: Gold.
Size: Height 52mm; max. width 38mm.
Description: The badge consists of a gold-rayed circle with a central roundel charged with a peacock in his pride azure, surmounted by an imperial crown.
Comments: *Instituted by King George VI, three years after Burma became independent of British India. Only 24 awards were made, to Governor's Commissioned Officers for long, faithful and honourable service in the army, frontier force and military police of Burma. By an amendment of 1945 the order could also be awarded for individual acts of heroism or particularly meritorious service. It was abolished in 1947.*

VALUE: £4000–5000

38. KAISAR-I-HIND MEDAL

Victoria obv.

Instituted: May 1900.
Ribbon: 37mm bluish green.
Metal: Gold, silver or bronze.
Size: Height 61mm; max. width 34mm.
Description: An oval badge surmounted by the imperial crown. (Obverse) the royal cypher set within a wreath; (reverse) FOR PUBLIC SERVICE IN INDIA round the edge and KAISAR-I-HIND (Emperor of India) on a scroll across the centre against a floral background.
Comments: *Queen Victoria founded this medal for award to those, regardless of colour, creed or sex, who had performed public service in India. Originally in two classes George V introduced a 3rd Class in bronze. The medals were originally large and hollow but were changed to smaller in diameter and solid during the reign of George V.*

VALUE: (gold)	1st class	Miniature (silver)	2nd class	Miniature (bronze)	3rd class
Victoria	£700–800	£120–150	£250–300	£80–100	—
Edward VII	£700–750	£120–150	£220–260	£80–100	—
George V 1st	£600–700	£50–100	£200–250	£25–50	—
George V 2nd	£550–600	£50–100	£130–150	£25–50	£100–120
George VI	£600–700	£120–150	£140–180	£50–80	£100–120

Victoria rev.

George VI   *obv.*

rev.

39. ALBERT MEDAL

Instituted: 7 March 1866.

Ribbons: Originally 16mm blue with two white stripes (gold 1st class), changed on introduction of the 2nd class to 35mm blue with four white stripes. The 2nd class remained 16mm blue with two white stripes until 1904 when it was changed to 35mm blue with two white stripes. For the gold 1st class medal the ribbon was 35mm crimson with four white stripes, that for the 2nd class originally 16mm crimson with two white stripes, changing in 1904 to a 35mm ribbon.

Metal: Gold (early issues gold and bronze); bronze.

Size: Height 57mm; max. width 30mm.

Description: The badge consists of an oval enclosing the entwined initials V and A. The sea medals have, in addition, an anchor. The oval is enclosed by a bronze garter with the words FOR GALLANTRY IN SAVING LIFE, with AT SEA or ON LAND as appropriate, and enamelled in blue or crimson respectively. The whole is surmounted by a crown pierced by a ring for suspension. The first class medal was originally worked in gold and bronze and later in bronze alone, the second class in gold alone.

Comments: *Named in memory of the Prince Consort who died in 1861, this series of medals was instituted for gallantry in saving life at sea. An amendment of 1867 created two classes of medal and ten years later awards were extended to gallantry in saving life on land. In 1917 the title of the awards was altered, the first class becoming the Albert Medal in Gold and the second class merely the Albert Medal. It was last awarded in gold to a living recipient in April 1943, the last posthumous award being in May 1945. The last bronze medal awarded to a living recipient was in January 1949, and posthumous in August 1970. In 1949 the Medal in Gold was abolished and replaced by the George Cross and henceforward the Albert Medal (second class) was only awarded posthumously. In 1971 the award of the medal ceased and holders were invited to exchange their medals for the George Cross. Of the 65 eligible to exchange, 49 did so.*

VALUE:

	Civilian	Service	Miniature
Gold Sea (25)	£6000–8000	£8000–10,000	£70–90*
Bronze Sea (211)	£3500–4500	£4000–6000	£50–70
Gold Land (45)	£6000–8000	£800–10,000	£70–90*
Bronze Land (290)	£3500–4500	£4000–6000	£50–70
		*assumed gilt	

40. UNION OF SOUTH AFRICA KING'S/ QUEEN'S MEDAL FOR BRAVERY (WOLTEMADE MEDAL)

Instituted: 1939 by the Government of the Union of South Africa.

Ribbon: Royal blue with narrow orange edges.

Metal: Gold or silver.

Size: 37mm.

Description: (Obverse) an effigy of the reigning sovereign; (reverse) a celebrated act of heroism by Wolraad Woltemade who rescued sailors from the wreck of the East Indiaman *De Jong Thomas* which ran aground in Table Bay on 17 June 1773. Seven times Woltemade rode into the raging surf to save fourteen seamen from drowning, but on the eighth attempt both rider and horse perished.

Comments: *This medal was awarded to citizens of the Union of South Africa and dependent territories who endangered their lives in saving the lives of others. It was awarded very sparingly, in gold or silver.*

VALUE:

		Miniature
George VI Gold (1)	Rare	£500–600
George VI Silver (34)	Rare	£450–500
Elizabeth II Silver (1)	Rare	£450–500

41. DISTINGUISHED CONDUCT MEDAL

Instituted: 1854.

Ribbon: 32mm crimson with a dark blue central stripe.

Metal: Silver.

Size: 36mm.

Description: (Obverse) originally a trophy of arms but, since 1902, the effigy of the reigning sovereign; (reverse) a four-line inscription across the field FOR DISTINGUISHED CONDUCT IN THE FIELD.

Comments: *The need for a gallantry medal for other ranks was first recognised during the Crimean War, although previously the Meritorious Service Medal (qv) had very occasionally been awarded for gallantry in the field. The medals have always been issued named, and carry the number, rank and name of the recipient on the rim, together with the date of the act of gallantry from 1881 until about 1901. Bars are given for subsequent awards and these too were dated from the first issued in 1881 until 1916 when the more usual laurelled bars were adopted. Since 1916 it has ranked as a superior decoration to the Military Medal. As a result of the 1993 Review of gallantry awards and resultant changes to the operational gallantry award system, the decoration has been replaced by the Conspicuous Gallantry Cross.*

1st type obv.

VALUE:

Crimea (800)	£2500–5000
Indian Mutiny (17)	£700–10,000
India general service 1854-95	£3000–5000
Abyssinia 1867-8 (7)	£3500–4500
Ashantee 1873-4 (33)	£3500–5000
Zulu War 1877-9 (16)	£6000–10,000
Afghanistan 1878-80 (61)	£4000–6000
First Boer War 1880-1 (20)	£6500–10,000
Egypt & Sudan 1882-9 (134)	£5000–8000
India 1895-1901	£5000–6500
Sudan 1896-7	£4500–6500
Second Boer War 1899-1902 (2090)	£1500–3500
Boxer Rebellion 1900	£4500–8000
Edward VII	Many rarities
George V 1st type (25,000)	£750–1500
George V 2nd type 1930-7 (14)	£6000–8000
George VI, IND IMP 1937-47	£2500–4000
George VI, 2nd type 1948-52 (25)	£6000–8000
Elizabeth II, BR: OMN:	£5000–8000
Elizabeth II, DEI GRATIA	£6000–8000
Miniature (in silver add £5)	
Victoria	£40–50
Edward VII	£25–30
George V	Type I £20–25, II £70–100
George VI	Type I £15–20, II £25–40
Elizabeth II	£15–20

42. DISTINGUISHED CONDUCT MEDAL (DOMINION & COLONIAL)

Instituted: 31 May 1895.

Ribbon: 32mm crimson with a dark blue central stripe.

Metal: Silver.

Size: 36mm.

Description: As above, but the reverse bears the name of the issuing country or colony round the top.

Comments: *A separate DCM for warrant officers, NCOs and men of the colonial forces. Medals were struck for the Cape of Good Hope, Natal, New Zealand, New South Wales, Queensland, Tasmania, Natal and Canada, but only the last two actually issued them and the others are known only as specimens.*

VALUE:

Victoria Canada (1)	Rare
Victoria Natal (1)	Rare
Edward VII Natal (9)	Rare

43. DISTINGUISHED CONDUCT MEDAL (KAR & WAFF)

Instituted: early 1900s.

Ribbon: Dark blue with a central green stripe flanked by crimson stripes.

Metal: Silver.

Size: 3mm

Description: As no. 42, with either King's African Rifles or West Africa Frontier Force around the top of the reverse.

Comments: *Separate awards for gallantry were instituted in respect of the King's African Rifles (East Africa) and the West Africa Frontier Force (Nigeria, Sierra Leone, Gambia and the Gold Coast). These were issued until 1942 when they were superseded by the British DCM.*

VALUE:	Attributable groups
Edward VII KAR (2)	Rare
Edward VII WAFF (55)	£2500–3500
George V KAR (190)	£1500–2000
George V WAFF (165)	£1500–2000

44. CONSPICUOUS GALLANTRY MEDAL

Instituted: 1855.

Ribbon: 31mm white (RN) or sky blue (RAF) with dark blue edges.

Metal: Silver.

Size: 36mm.

Description: (Obverse) the effigy of the reigning monarch; (reverse) the words FOR CONSPICUOUS GALLANTRY in three lines within a crowned laurel wreath.

Comments: *Conceived as the naval counterpart to the DCM, it was instituted for award to petty officers and seamen of the Royal Navy and to NCOs and other ranks of the Royal Marines. Originally awarded only for gallantry during the Crimean War, it was revived in 1874 to recognise heroism during the Ashantee War and has since been awarded, albeit sparingly, for other wars and campaigns. The Crimean issue utilised the dies of the Meritorious Service Medal which had the date 1848 below the truncation of the Queen's neck on the obverse. The raised relief inscription MERITORIOUS SERVICE on the reverse was erased and the words CONSPICUOUS GALLANTRY engraved in their place. When the decoration was revived in 1874 a new obverse was designed without a date while a new die, with the entire inscription in raised relief, was employed for the reverse. In 1943 the CGM was extended to NCOs and other ranks of the RAF. Both naval and RAF medals are identical, but the naval medal has a white ribbon with dark blue edges, whereas the RAF award has a pale blue ribbon with dark blue edges. It ranks as one of the rarest decorations: the only three medals issued in the present reign were awarded to an airman in the RAAF for gallantry in Vietnam (1968), to Staff-Sergeant James Prescott, RE, during the South Atlantic War (1982) (posthumous) and to CPO Diver Philip Hammond, RN, during the Gulf War (1991). As a result of the 1993 Review and resultant changes to the operational gallantry award system, the decoration has been replaced by the Conspicuous Gallantry Cross.*

VALUE:	Attributable groups
Victoria 1st type (11)	£6000–10,000
Victoria 2nd type (50)	£6500–8500
Edward VII (2)	£8000–12,000
George V (110)	£5000–8000
George VI Navy/RM (72)	£6500–10,000
George VI RAF (103)	£6500–8500
Elizabeth II (3)	Rare
Miniature	
Victoria	£50–80
Edward VII	£50–80
George V	£20–30
George VI	£15–20
Elizabeth II	£15–20

45. GEORGE MEDAL

Instituted: 1940.

Ribbon: 32mm crimson with five narrow blue stripes.

Metal: Silver.

Size: 36mm.

Description: (Obverse) the effigy of the reigning monarch; (reverse) St George and the Dragon, modelled by George Kruger Gray, after the bookplate by Stephen Gooden for the Royal Library, Windsor.

Comments: *Awarded for acts of bravery where the services were not so outstanding as to merit the George Cross. Though primarily a civilian award, it has also been given to service personnel for heroism not in the face of the enemy. Of the approximately 2000 medals awarded, 1030 have been to civilians.*

VALUE:

	Civilian	Service
George VI 1st type 1940-47	£1500–2200	£1500–2500
George VI 2nd type 1948-52	£1500–2200	£1500–2500
Elizabeth II 1st type 1953	£1500–2200	£1500–2500
Elizabeth II 2nd type	£1500–2200	£1500–2500

Miniature	
George VI, Type I	£10–15 (Silver £20–25)
Type II	£20–25 (Silver £30–40)
Elizabeth II	£10–15 (Silver £20–25)

46. KING'S POLICE MEDAL

Instituted: 7 July 1909.

Ribbons: 36mm Originally deep blue with silver edges, but in 1916 a central silver stripe was added. Gallantry awards have thin crimson stripes superimposed on the silver stripes.

Metal: Silver.

Size: 36mm.

Description: (Obverse) the monarch's effigy; (reverse) a standing figure with sword and shield inscribed TO GUARD MY PEOPLE. The first issue had a laurel spray in the exergue, but in 1933 two separate reverses were introduced and the words FOR GALLANTRY or FOR DISTINGUISHED SERVICE were placed in the exergue.

Comments: *Instituted to reward "courage and devotion to duty" in the police and fire services of the UK and overseas dominions. Recognising the bravery of the firemen during the Blitz, the medal was retitled the King's Police and Fire Services Medal in 1940, but no change was made in the design of the medal itself. From 1950, the gallantry medals were only awarded posthumously and all medals were discontinued in 1954 when seperate awards were established for the two services (see numbers 47 and 48).*

VALUE:

		Miniature
Edward VII (100)	£800–1000	£25–30
George V 1st type coinage head (1900)	£350–450	£20–25
George V 2nd type crowned head	£350–450	£40–50
George V for Gallantry (350)	£650–800	£15–20
George V for Distinguished Service	£300–400	£15–20
George VI 1st type for Gallantry (440)	£650–800	£10–15
George VI 2nd type for Gallantry (50)	£1200–1500	£10–15
George VI 1st type for Distinguished Service	£300–400	£10–15
George VI 2nd type for Distinguished Service	£300–400	£10–15

47. QUEEN'S POLICE MEDAL

Instituted: 19 May 1954.
Ribbon: Three silver stripes and two broad dark blue stripes. Gallantry awards have thin crimson stripes superimposed on the silver stripes.
Metal: Silver.
Size: 36mm.
Description: (Obverse) effigy of the reigning sovereign; (reverse) a standing figure (as on the KPM) but the laurel spray has been restored to the exergue and the words FOR GALLANTRY or FOR DISTINGUISHED POLICE SERVICE are inscribed round the circumference.
Comments: *The QPM for Gallantry has been effectively redundant since November 1977 when it was made possible to award the George Medal posthumously. Prior to this the QPM was the posthumous equivalent of the GM for police officers. Issued in New Zealand under Regulations dated November 18, 1959 by the Minister in Charge of Police.*

VALUE:		*Miniature*
Elizabeth II for Gallantry (23)	£1500–2000	£70–80
Elizabeth II for Distinguished Service (1100)	£350–450	£50–60

48. QUEEN'S FIRE SERVICE MEDAL

Instituted: 19 May 1954.
Ribbon: Red with three yellow stripes (distinguished service) or similar, with thin dark blue stripes bisecting the yellow stripes (gallantry).
Metal: Silver.
Size: 36mm
Description: (Obverse) effigy of the reigning monarch; (reverse) standing figure with sword and shield (as on KPM), laurel spray in the exergue, and inscription round the circumference FOR GALLANTRY or FOR DISTINGUISHED FIRE SERVICE.
Comments: *Included in New Zealand under Regulations dated March 1, 1955 by the Minister of Internal Affairs.*

VALUE:		*Miniature*
Elizabeth II for Gallantry	Rare	£80–90
Elizabeth II for Distinguished Service	£550–650	£70–80

49. KING'S POLICE MEDAL (SOUTH AFRICA)

Instituted: 24 September 1937.
Ribbon: Silver with two broad dark blue stripes. Red stripes are added for gallantry awards.
Metal: Silver.
Size: 36mm.
Description: (Obverse) effigy of George VI and title including the words ET IMPERATOR (1937-49), George VI minus IMPERATOR (1950-52) and Queen Elizabeth II (1953-60). (Reverse) as UK (no. 47 above) but inscribed in English and Afrikaans. Inscribed FOR BRAVERY VIR DAPPERHEID or FOR DISTINGUISHED SERVICE VIR VOORTREFLIKE DIENS.
Comments: *Awarded to members of the South Africa Police for courage and devotion to duty. In 1938 it was extended to cover the constabulary of South West Africa.*

VALUE:		*Miniature*
George VI 1st type 1937-49		£300–350
for Gallantry (10)	Rare	
for Distinguished Service (13)	Rare	
George VI 2nd type 1950-52		
for Distinguished Service (13)	Rare	
Elizabeth II 1953-60		
for Gallantry (20)	Rare	
Elizabeth II 1953-69		
for Distinguished Service (3)	Rare	

50. EDWARD MEDAL (MINES)

Instituted: July 1907.

Ribbon: Dark blue edged with yellow.

Metal: Silver or bronze.

Size: 33mm.

Description: (Obverse) the monarch's effigy; (reverse) a miner rescuing a stricken comrade, with the caption FOR COURAGE across the top (designed by W. Reynolds-Stephens).

Comments: *Awarded for life-saving in mines and quarries, in two grades: first class (silver) and second class (bronze). Interestingly, the cost of these medals was borne not by the State but from a fund created by a group of philanthropic individuals led by A. Hewlett, a leading mine-owner. Medals were engraved with the names of the recipient from the outset, but since the 1930s the date and sometimes the place of the action have also been inscribed. Since 1949 the medal was only granted posthumously and in 1971 living recipients were invited to exchange their medals for the GC, under Royal Warrant of 1971. Two silver and seven bronze medallists elected not to do so. This is one of the rarest gallantry awards, only 77 silver and 318 bronze medals having been granted since its inception.*

VALUE:	Silver	Bronze
Edward VII	£850–1000	£750–850
George V 1st type	£850–1000	£750–850
George V 2nd type	£1200–1500	£850–1000
George VI 1st type	£1500–1800	£1200–1400
George VI 2nd type	—	Rare
Elizabeth II	Not issued	From £1800
Miniature		
Edward VII	£60–80	
George V	£50–60	
George VI	£70–80	

51. EDWARD MEDAL (INDUSTRY)

1st type rev.

2nd type rev.

Instituted: December 1909.

Ribbon: As above.

Metal: Silver or bronze.

Size: 33mm.

Description: (Obverse) effigy of the reigning monarch; (reverse) originally a worker helping an injured workmate with a factory in the background and the words FOR COURAGE inscribed diagonally across the top. A second reverse, depicting a standing female figure with a laurel branch and a factory skyline in the background, was introduced in 1912.

Comments: *Awarded for acts of bravery in factory accidents and disasters. Like the Mines medal it was also available in two classes, but no first class medals were awarded since 1948. Since 1949 the medal was only granted posthumously and in 1971 living recipients were invited to exchange their medals for the GC, under Royal Warrant of 1971. A total of 25 silver and 163 bronze awards have been issued. Two awards were made to women, the rarest gallantry award to a lady.*

VALUE:	Silver	Bronze
Edward VII	Rare	Rare
George V 1st Obv, 1st Rev	—	£1500–1800
George V 1st Obv, 2nd Rev	£1400–1500	£800–1000
George V 2nd Obv, 2nd Rev	Rare	£1200–1400
George VI 1st type	—	£1000–1200
George VI 2nd type	Not issued	Rare
Elizabeth II 1st type	Not issued	Rare
Elizabeth II 2nd type	Not issued	Rare
Miniature		
George V	£60–80	
George VI (modern)	£15–20	

52. INDIAN DISTINGUISHED SERVICE MEDAL

Instituted: 25 June 1907.
Ribbon: Crimson with broad dark blue edges.
Metal: Silver.
Size: 36mm.
Description: (Obverse) the sovereign's effigy; (reverse) the words FOR DISTINGUISHED SERVICE in a laurel wreath.
Comments: *Awarded for distinguished service in the field by Indian commissioned and non-commissioned officers and men of the Indian Army, the reserve forces, border militia and levies, military police and troops employed by the Indian Government. An amendment of 1917 extended the award to Indian non-combatants engaged on field service, bars for subsequent awards being authorised at the same time. It was formally extended to the Royal Indian Marine in 1929 and members of the Indian Air Force in 1940. Finally it was extended in 1944 to include non-European personnel of the Hong Kong and Singapore Royal Artillery although it became obsolete in 1947.*

VALUE:

		Miniature
Edward VII (140)	£800–1000	£50–70
George V KAISAR-I-HIND (3800)	£300–450	£30–40
George V 2nd type (140)	£800–1000	£30–40
George VI (1190)	£650–1000	£20–30

53. BURMA GALLANTRY MEDAL

Instituted: 10 May 1940.
Ribbon: Jungle green with a broad crimson stripe in the centre.
Metal: Silver.
Size: 36mm.
Description: (Obverse) the effigy of King George VI; (reverse) the words BURMA at the top and FOR GALLANTRY in a laurel wreath.
Comments: *As Burma ceased to be part of the Indian Empire in April 1937 a separate gallantry award was required for its armed services. The Burma Gallantry Medal was awarded by the Governor to officers and men of the Burma Army, frontier forces, military police, Burma RNVR and Burma AAF, although by an amendment of 1945 subsequent awards were restricted to NCOs and men. The medal became obsolete in 1947 when Burma became an independent republic and left the Commonwealth. Just over 200 medals and three bars were awarded, mainly for heroism in operations behind the Japanese lines.*

VALUE:
£3000–4000

Miniature
£15–20 for late example, contemporary example unknown

54. DISTINGUISHED SERVICE MEDAL

Instituted: 14 October 1914.

Ribbon: Dark blue with two white stripes towards the centre.

Metal: Silver.

Size: 36mm.

Description: (Obverse) the sovereign's effigy; (reverse) a crowned wreath inscribed FOR DISTINGUISHED SERVICE.

Comments: *Awarded to petty officers and ratings of the Royal Navy, NCOs and other ranks of the Royal Marines and all other persons holding corresponding ranks or positions in the naval forces, for acts of bravery in face of the enemy not sufficiently meritorious to make them eligible for the CGM. It was later extended to cover the Merchant Navy and Army, the WRNS and RAF personnel serving aboard ships in the Second World War. Of particular interest and desirability are medals awarded for outstanding actions, e.g. Jutland, Q-Ships, the Murmansk convoys, the Yangtze incident and the Falklands War. First World War bars for subsequent awards are dated on the reverse, but Second World War bars are undated. As a result of the 1993 Review of gallantry awards and resultant changes to the operational gallantry award system, this award has been replaced by the DSC which is now available both to officers and other ranks.*

VALUE:

		Miniature
George V uncrowned head 1914-30 (4100)	£650–1200	£20–25
George VI IND IMP 1938-49 (7100)	£900–1200	£15–20
George VI 2nd type 1949-53	£3000–4000	£30–40
Elizabeth II BR OMN 1953-7	£4000–5000	£8–10
Elizabeth II 2nd type	£3000–4000	£8–10

(in silver add £5)

55. MILITARY MEDAL

Instituted: 25 March 1916.

Ribbon: Broad dark blue edges flanking a central section of three narrow white and two narrow crimson stripes.

Metal: Silver.

Size: 36mm.

Description: (Obverse) the sovereign's effigy—six types; (reverse) the crowned royal cypher above the inscription FOR BRAVERY IN THE FIELD, enclosed in a wreath.

Comments: *Awarded to NCOs and men of the Army (including RFC and RND) for individual or associated acts of bravery not of sufficient heroism as to merit the DCM. In June 1916 it was extended to women, two of the earliest awards being to civilian ladies for their conduct during the Easter Rising in Dublin that year. Some 115,600 medals were awarded during the First World War alone, together with 5796 first bars, 180 second bars and 1 third bar. Over 15,000 medals were conferred during the Second World War, with 177 first bars and 1 second bar. About 300 medals and 4 first bars were awarded for bravery in minor campaigns between the two world wars, while some 932 medals and 8 first bars have been conferred since 1947. As a result of the 1993 Review of gallantry awards and resultant changes to the operational gallantry award system, this award has been replaced by the MC which is now available both to officers and other ranks.*

VALUE:

		Miniature
George V uncrowned head 1916-30		
Corps/RA—single	£220–250*	£15–20
in group	£350–450	
Regiment—single	£325–375	
in group	£600–900	
named to a woman	£2000–3000	
George V crowned head 1930-38	£3000–4000	£70–100
George VI IND IMP 1938-48		
Corps	£900–1200	£10–15
Regiment	£1200–1800	
George VI 2nd type 1948-53	£2500–3500	£25–40
Elizabeth II BR: OMN 1953-8	£3000–4000	£10–15
Elizabeth II 2nd type	£4000–6000	£10–15

(in silver add £5)

*Groups to RFC and RND will be considerably higher and obviously, medals with second (or more) award bars are also worth much more.

56. DISTINGUISHED FLYING MEDAL

Instituted: 1918.
Ribbon: Originally purple and white horizontal stripes but since July 1919 thirteen narrow diagonal stripes alternationg white and purple.
Metal: Silver.
Size: 42mm tall; 34mm wide.
Description: An oval medal, (obverse) the sovereign's effigy; (reverse) Athena Nike seated on an aeroplane, with a hawk rising from her hand. Originally undated, but the date 1918 was added to the reverse with the advent of the George VI obverse. The medal is suspended by a pair of wings from a straight bar.
Comments: *Introduced at the same time as the DFC, it was awarded to NCOs and men of the RAF for courage or devotion to duty while flying on active operations against the enemy. During the Second World War it was extended to the equivalent ranks of the Army and Fleet Air Arm personnel engaged in similar operations. First World War medals have the names of recipients impressed in large seriffed lettering, whereas Second World War medals are rather coarsely engraved. Approximately 150 medals have been awarded since 1945. As a result of the 1993 Review of gallantry awards and resultant changes to the operational gallantry award system, this award has been replaced by the DFC which is now available both to officers and other ranks.*

Example of WWI impressed naming

WWII engraved naming

VALUE:		Miniature
George V uncrowned head 1918-30 (105)	£3000–5000	£18–20
George V crowned head 1930-38	£8000–12,000	£70–100
George VI IND IMP 1938-49 (6500)	£1400–2000	£10–12
George VI 2nd type 1949-53	£4000–5000	£25–40
Elizabeth II	£4000–5000	£10–12

(in silver add £5)

57. AIR FORCE MEDAL

Instituted: 1918.
Ribbon: Originally horizontal narrow stripes of white and crimson but since July 1919 diagonal narrow stripes of the same colours.
Metal: Silver.
Size: 42mm tall; 32mm wide.
Description: An oval medal with a laurel border. (Obverse) the sovereign's effigy; (reverse) Hermes mounted on a hawk bestowing a laurel wreath. The medal is suspended by a pair of wings from a straight bar, like the DFM.
Comments: *Instituted at the same time as the AFC, it was awarded to NCOs and men of the RAF for courage or devotion to duty while flying, but not on active operations against the enemy. About 100 medals and 2 first bars were awarded during the First World War, 106 medals and 3 bars between the wars and 259 medals during the Second World War. After the 1993 Review of gallantry awards the AFM was discontinued; the AFC is now available both to officers and other ranks.*

VALUE:

		Miniature
George V uncrowned head 1918-30	£1500–1800	£25–30
George V crowned head 1930-38	£3000–4000	£80–100
George VI IND IMP 1939-49	£1800–2500	£10–15
George VI 2nd type 1949-53	£1800–2500	£30–40
Elizabeth II	£1800–2500	£10–15

(in silver add £5)

58. CONSTABULARY MEDAL (IRELAND)

1st type obv.

2nd type obv.

Instituted: 1842.
Ribbon: Originally light blue, but changed to green in 1872.
Metal: Silver.
Size: 36mm.
Description: (Obverse) a crowned harp within a wreath of oak leaves and shamrocks, with REWARD OF MERIT round the top and IRISH CONSTABULARY round the foot. In the first version the front of the harp took the form of a female figure but later variants had a plain harp and the shape of the crown and details of the wreath were also altered. These changes theoretically came in 1867 when the Constabulary acquired the epithet Royal, which was then added to the inscription round the top, although some medals issued as late as 1921 had the pre-1867 title. (Reverse) a wreath of laurel and shamrock, within which are engraved the recipient's name, rank, number, date and sometimes the location of the action.
Comments: *Originally awarded for gallantry and meritorious service by members of the Irish Constabulary. From 1872, however, it was awarded only for gallantry. It was first conferred in 1848 and became obsolete in 1922 when the Irish Free State was established. Bars for second awards were authorised in 1920. About 315 medals and 7 bars were awarded (or, in some cases, second medals—the records are inconclusive), mostly for actions in connection with the Easter Rising of 1916 (23) or the subsequent Anglo-Irish War of 1920 (180) and 1921 (55).*

VALUE:		*Miniature*
First type	£2000–2500	—
Second type	£1500–2000	£200–250

59. INDIAN POLICE MEDAL

1st type

Instituted: 23 February 1932.
Ribbon: Crimson flanked by stripes of dark blue and silver grey. From 1942 onwards an additional silver stripe appeared in the centre of the ribbon intended for the gallantry medal.
Metal: Bronze.
Size: 36mm.
Description: (Obverse) the King Emperor; (reverse) a crowned wreath inscribed INDIAN POLICE, with the words FOR DISTINGUISHED CONDUCT across the centre. In December 1944 the reverse was re-designed in two types, with the words FOR GALLANTRY or FOR MERITORIOUS SERVICE in place of the previous legend.
Comments: *Intended for members of the Indian police forces and fire brigades as a reward for gallantry or meritorious service. The medal became obsolete in 1950 when India became a republic.*

VALUE:

		Miniature
George V	£300–400	£20–25
George VI Distinguished Conduct	£300–400	£20–25
George VI for Gallantry	£450–550	£20–25
George VI for Meritorious Service	£300–400	£20–25

2nd type (after 1944)

60. BURMA POLICE MEDAL

Instituted: 14 December 1937.
Ribbon: A wide central blue stripe flanked by broad black stripes and white edges.
Metal: Bronze.
Size: 36mm.
Description: (Obverse) the effigy of George VI; (reverse) similar to the Indian medal (first type)and inscribed FOR DISTINGUISHED CONDUCT, irrespective of whether awarded for gallantry or distinguished service.
Comments: *Introduced following the separation of Burma from India, it was abolished in 1948. All ranks of the police, frontier force and fire brigades, both European and Burmese, were eligible.*

VALUE:

		Miniature
For Gallantry (53)	£1500–2000	£25–40
For Meritorious Service (80)	£800–1100	£25–40

61. COLONIAL POLICE MEDAL

Instituted: 10 May 1938.
Ribbon: Blue with green edges and a thin silver stripe separating the colours, but the gallantry award had an additional thin red line through the centre of each green edge stripe.
Metal: Silver.
Size: 36mm.
Description: (Obverse) the sovereign's effigy; (reverse) a policeman's truncheon superimposed on a laurel wreath. The left side of the circumference is inscribed COLONIAL POLICE FORCES and the right either FOR GALLANTRY or FOR MERITORIOUS SERVICE.
Comments: *Intended to reward all ranks of the police throughout the Empire for acts of conspicuous bravery or for meritorious service. The number to be issued was limited to 150 in any one year. Only 450 were awarded for gallantry (with nine second award bars), whilst almost 3000 were issued for meritorious service.*

VALUE:

		Miniature
George VI GRI for Gallantry	£800–1200	£40–50
George VI GRI for Meritorious Service	£350–450	£30–40
George VI GVIR for Gallantry	£800–1200	£40–50
George VI GVIR for Meritorious Service	£350–450	£30–40
Elizabeth II 1st type for Gallantry	£800–1200	£40–50
Elizabeth II 1st type for Meritorious Service	£350–450	£30–40
Elizabeth II 2nd type for Gallantry	£800–1200	£40–50
Elizabeth II 2nd type for Meritorious Service	£350–450	£30–40

62. COLONIAL FIRE BRIGADE MEDAL

Instituted: 10 May 1938.
Ribbon: As above.
Metal: Silver.
Size: 36mm.
Description: (Obverse) the effigy of the reigning sovereign; (reverse) a fireman's helmet and axe, with the inscription COLONIAL FIRE BRIGADES FOR GALLANTRY or FOR MERITORIOUS SERVICE.
Comments: *As No. 59 this medal was intended to reward all ranks of the Colonial fire brigades but very few were awarded for gallantry.*

VALUE:

		Miniature
George VI GRI for Gallantry	Rare	£40–50
George VI GRI for Meritorious Service	Rare	£30–40
George VI GVIR for Gallantry	Rare	£40–50
George VI GVIR for Meritorious Service	£300–500	£30–40
Elizabeth II 1st type for Gallantry	From £750	£40–50
Elizabeth II 1st type for Meritorious Service	£300–500	£30–40
Elizabeth II 2nd type for Gallantry	£600–800	£40–50
Elizabeth II 2nd type for Meritorious Service	£300–450	£30–40

63. QUEEN'S GALLANTRY MEDAL

Instituted: 20 June 1974.
Ribbon: Blue with a central pearl-grey stripe bisected by a narrow rose-pink stripe.
Metal: Silver.
Size: 36mm.
Description: (Obverse) the Queen's effigy; (reverse) an imperial crown above THE QUEEN'S GALLANTRY MEDAL flanked by laurel sprigs.
Comments: *Awarded for exemplary acts of bravery. Although intended primarily for civilians, it is also awarded to members of the armed forces for actions which would not be deemed suitable for a military decoration. With the introduction of the QGM the gallantry awards in the Order of the British Empire came to an end. To date, about 1,000 QGMs have been awarded, including 18 bars. A bar is added for a second award. A post-1990 SAS QGM and bar group sold at a recent auction for £26,000.*

VALUE:		Miniature
Service award	From £2000	£10–12
Civilian award	From £1500	

64. ALLIED SUBJECTS' MEDAL

Instituted: November 1920.
Ribbon: Bright red with a light blue centre, flanked by narrow stripes of yellow, black and white (thus incorporating the Belgian and French national colours).
Metal: Silver or bronze.
Size: 36mm.
Description: (Obverse) the effigy of King George V; (reverse) designed by C. L. J. Doman, the female allegory of Humanity offering a cup to a British soldier resting on the ground, with ruined buildings in the background.
Comment: *Shortly after the cessation of the First World War it was proposed that services rendered to the Allied cause, specifically by those who had helped British prisoners of war to escape, should be rewarded by a medal. The decision to go ahead was delayed on account of disagreement between the War Office and the Foreign Office, but eventually the first awards were announced in November 1920, with supplementary lists in 1921 and 1922. Medals were issued unnamed and almost half of the total issue, namely 56 silver and 247 bronze medals, were issued to women.*

VALUE:		Miniature
Silver (134)	£500–750	£40–50
Bronze (574)	£300–400	£45–55

NB These prices are for unattributable awards.

65. KING'S MEDAL FOR COURAGE IN THE CAUSE OF FREEDOM

Instituted: 23 August 1945
Ribbon: White with two narrow dark blue stripes in the centre and broad red stripes at the edges.
Metal: Silver.
Size: 36mm.
Description: (Obverse) the crowned profile of King George VI; (reverse) inscribed, within a chain link, THE KING'S MEDAL FOR COURAGE IN THE CAUSE OF FREEDOM.
Comments: *Introduced to acknowledge acts of courage by foreign civilians or members of the armed services "in the furtherance of the British Commonwealth in the Allied cause" during the Second World War. Like its First World War counterpart, it was intended mainly to reward those who had assisted British escapees in enemy-occupied territories. About 3200 medals were issued, commencing in 1947.*

VALUE: £250–300 (unattributable)   *Miniature* £30–40

66. KING'S MEDAL FOR SERVICE IN THE CAUSE OF FREEDOM

Instituted: 23 August 1945.
Ribbon: White with a central red stripe flanked by dark blue stripes.
Metal: Silver.
Size: 36mm.
Description: (Obverse) effigy of King George VI; (reverse) a medieval warrior in armour carrying a broken lance, receiving nourishment from a female.
Comments: *Introduced at the same time as the foregoing, it was intended for foreign civilians who had helped the Allied cause in other less dangerous ways, such as fund-raising and organising ambulance services. 2490 medals were issued.*

VALUE: £200–250 (unattributable)   *Miniature* £15–20

67. SEA GALLANTRY MEDAL

Instituted: 1855, under the Merchant Shipping Acts of 1854 and 1894.
Ribbon: Bright red with narrow white stripes towards the edges.
Metal: Silver or bronze.
Size: 58mm or 33mm.
Description: (Obverse) Profile of Queen Victoria; (reverse) a family on a storm-tossed shore reviving a drowning sailor. Both obverse and reverse were sculpted by Bernard Wyon.
Comments: *Exceptionally, this group of medals was authorised not by Royal Warrant but by Parliamentary legislation, under the terms of the Merchant Shipping Acts of 1854 and 1894. The 1854 Act made provision for monetary rewards for life saving at sea, but in 1855 this was transmuted into medals, in gold, silver or bronze, in two categories, for gallantry (where the rescuer placed his own life at risk) and for humanity (where the risks were minimal). The gold medal, if ever awarded, must have been of the greatest rarity. These medals, issued by the Board of Trade, were 58mm in diameter and not intended for wearing. The only difference between the medals lay in the wording of the inscription round the circumference of the obverse. In 1903 Edward VII ordered that the medal be reduced to 1.27 inches (33mm) in diameter and fitted with a suspension bar and ribbon for wearing. Both large and small medals were always issued with a minimum of the recipient's name and date of rescue round the rim. The last medal was awarded in 1980. Only one second award clasp has ever been issued—that to Ch.Off James Whiteley in 1921.*

VALUE:

	Silver	Bronze	*Miniature*
Victoria Gallantry	£450–550	£350–450	£100–150
Victoria Humanity (to 1893)	Rare	Rare	
Edward VII Gallantry (large)	£1400–1800	£1200–1400	
Edward VII Gallantry (small)	£450–600	£400–450	£100–150
Edward VII (2nd small type)	£450–600	£400–450	
George V	£350–450	£300–400	£50–75
George VI 1st type	Rare	Rare	
George VI 2nd type	—	Rare	
Elizabeth II	Rare	Rare	

68. SEA GALLANTRY MEDAL (FOREIGN SERVICES)

Type 4 rev.

Instituted: 1841.

Ribbon: Plain crimson till 1922; thereafter the same ribbon as the SGM above.

Metal: Gold, silver or bronze.

Size: 36mm or 33mm.

Description: The large medal had Victoria's effigy (young head) on the obverse, but there were five reverse types showing a crowned wreath with PRESENTED BY (or FROM) THE BRITISH GOVERNMENT inside the wreath. Outside the wreath were the following variants:
1. Individually struck inscriptions (1841-49 but sometimes later).
2. FOR SAVING THE LIFE OF A BRITISH SUBJECT (1849-54)
3. FOR ASSISTING A BRITISH VESSEL IN DISTRESS (1849-54)
4. FOR SAVING THE LIVES OF BRITISH SUBJECTS (1850-54)
There are also unissued specimens or patterns with a Latin inscription within the wreath VICTORIA REGINA CUDI JUSSIT MDCCCXLI.
The small medal, intended for wear, has five obverse types combined with four reverse types: as 2 above (1854-1906), as 3 above (1854-1896), as 4 above (1854-1926), or FOR GALLANTRY AND HUMANITY (1858 to the present day).

Comments: *Although intended to reward foreigners who rendered assistance to British subjects in distress some early awards were actually made for rescues on dry land. Originally a special reverse was struck for each incident, but this was found to be unnecessarily expensive, so a standard reverse was devised in 1849. Medals before 1854 had a diameter of 45mm and were not fitted with suspension. After 1854 the diameter was reduced to 33mm and scrolled suspension bars were fitted. Of the large medals about 100 gold, 120 silver and 14 bronze were issued, while some 10 gold and 24 bronze specimens have been recorded.*

VALUE:

	Gold	Silver	Bronze
Victoria large	Rare	£450–700	£400–500
Victoria small	£1000–1300	£250–350	—
Edward VII	£1000–1750	£400–500	—
George V	£1000–1300	£300–400	—
George VI	—	Rare	—
Elizabeth II	Rare	Rare	—
Miniature			£175–225

69. BRITISH NORTH BORNEO COMPANY'S BRAVERY CROSS

Instituted: 1890.

Ribbon: Gold (later yellow) watered silk 34mm.

Metal: Silver or bronze.

Size: 36mm.

Description: The cross pattée has a central medallion bearing a lion passant with the Company motto PERGO ET PERAGO (I carry on and accomplish) within a garter. The arms of the cross are inscribed BRITISH NORTH BORNEO with FOR BRAVERY in the lower limb. Three crosses have been recorded with the lower inscription for bravery omitted.

Comments: *Manufactured by Joseph Moore of Birmingham. The silver version bears the Birmingham hallmark for 1890. The reverse of the bronze medal is smooth. The cross was awarded for bravery in some 17 actions between 1883 and 1915, to the Company's Armed Constabulary Several of these actions involved fewer than 40 combatants, but at the other extreme 144 men took*

69. BRITISH NORTH BORNEO COMPANY'S BRAVERY CROSS *continued*

part in the major battle at Tambunan in 1900. Only five silver and four bronze crosses are known to have been awarded. Jemadar Natha Singh was the only officer to win both bronze (1892) and silver (1897). Examples with the word STERLING on the reverse are modern copies.

VALUE:

Silver	£750–1000
Bronze	£400–500 (but much more in either case if attributable)
Specimens/Copies	£100

70. KING'S MEDAL FOR NATIVE CHIEFS

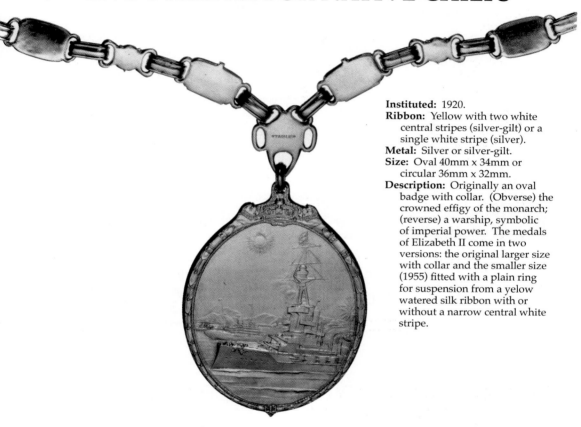

Instituted: 1920.
Ribbon: Yellow with two white central stripes (silver-gilt) or a single white stripe (silver).
Metal: Silver or silver-gilt.
Size: Oval 40mm x 34mm or circular 36mm x 32mm.
Description: Originally an oval badge with collar. (Obverse) the crowned effigy of the monarch; (reverse) a warship, symbolic of imperial power. The medals of Elizabeth II come in two versions: the original larger size with collar and the smaller size (1955) fitted with a plain ring for suspension from a yelow watered silk ribbon with or without a narrow central white stripe.

Comments: *Various large silver medals were struck for award to native chiefs in various parts of the world, from the eighteenth century onwards, and of these the awards to American Indian chiefs are probably the best known. In 1920, however, a standard King's Medal for Chiefs was instituted. It was awarded exceptionally in silver-gilt (first class), and usually in silver (second class). The oval medal was worn round the neck from a silver collar. The more modern issues, however, are smaller and intended for wear with a ribbon from the breast. The medal is normally returned on the death of the recipient.*

VALUE:

	Silver-gilt	Silver
George V		
First (couped) type	£1000–1200	£700–800
Second (larger bust) type	£1000–1200	£650–750
George VI	£1000–1200	£600–700
Elizabeth II		
First type	£1000–1200	£600–700
Second (small) type	£350–400	£300–400

Mentions and Commendations

A description of the various emblems denoting Mentions in Despatches and King's (or later Queen's) Commendations was published as a Supplement to the *London Gazette,* July 27, 1951. A special clasp to signify a Mention in Despatches was instituted during the First World War and continued to be awarded for active service up to August 10, 1920. It was worn on the ribbon of the Victory Medal (no. 170) and consisted of a bronze spray of oak leaves.

For Mentions in Despatches after August 10, 1920, or a King's Commendation for brave conduct or valuable service in the air, a bronze emblem consisting of a single oak leaf was worn on the appropriate medal ribbon, either a General Service Medal or the War Medal, 1939–45. King's or Queen's Commendations for brave conduct or valuable service in the air, in cases where no campaign or war medal was awarded, were worn on the breast in the position where an appropriate medal ribbon would have been worn, generally on the uniform tunic after any medal ribbons.

King's or Queen's Commendations in respect of bravery, granted to civilians for acts during or since the Second World War, are denoted by a silver emblem in the form of a spray of laurel leaves (this was originally a plastic oval badge). For service during the Second World War this emblem was worn on the ribbon of the Defence Medal (no. 185). Where no medal was awarded, it was sewn directly on to the coat, after any medal ribbons.

For civilians the King's or Queen's Commendation for Valuable Service in the Air, during the Second World War and subsequently, consisted of an oval silver badge, worn on the coat below any medals or medal ribbons, or in civil airline uniform, on the panel of the left breast pocket.

The emblems denoting Mentions and Commendations were revised on August 12, 1994, as shown in the table below.

Mention in Despatches emblem 1914–20

Mention in Despatches emblem 1920–94

FOR GALLANTRY			FOR VALUABLE SERVICE
IN ACTION WITH THE ENEMY (ALL ENVIRONMENTS)	NOT IN ACTION WITH THE ENEMY or OUT OF THEATRE (EXCEPT FLYING)	NOT IN ACTION WITH THE ENEMY or OUT OF THEATRE (FLYING)	IN-THEATRE BUT NOT IN ACTION WITH THE ENEMY
MENTION IN DESPATCHES	QUEEN'S COMMENDATION FOR BRAVERY	QUEEN'S COMMENDATION FOR BRAVERY IN THE AIR	QUEEN'S COMMENDATION FOR VALUABLE SERVICE
A single oak leaf in SILVER	A spray of laurel leaves in SILVER	A new emblem in SILVER	A spray of oak leaves in SILVER

Campaign
medals

The evolution of medals struck to commemorate, and later to reward participants in, a battle or campaign was a very gradual process. The forerunner of the modern campaign medal was the Armada Medal, cast in gold or silver, which appears to have been awarded to naval officers and distinguished persons after the abortive Spanish invasion of 1588. The obverse bears a flattering portrait of Queen Elizabeth (thought to have been designed by Nicholas Hilliard, the celebrated miniaturist) with a Latin inscription signifying "enclosing the most precious treasure in the world" (i.e. the Queen herself). On the reverse, the safety of the kingdom is represented by a bay tree growing on a little island, immune from the flashes of lightning which seem to strike it. This medal, and a similar type depicting the Ark floating calmly on a stormy sea, bore loops at the top so that a chain or cord could be passed through it for suspension from the neck of the recipient.

The Civil War produced a number of gallantry medals, mentioned in the previous section; but in 1650 Parliament authorised a medal which was struck in silver, bronze or lead to celebrate Cromwell's miraculous victory over the Scots at Dunbar. This was the first medal granted to all the participants on the Parliamentary side, and not restricted to high-ranking officers, or given for individual acts of heroism.

The Dunbar Medal thus established several useful precedents, which were eventually to form the criteria of the campaign medal as we know it today. After this promising start, however, the pattern of medals and their issue were much more restrictive. Naval medals were struck in gold for award to admirals and captains during the First Dutch War (1650–53), while the battle of Culloden (1746) was marked by a medal portraying the "Butcher" Duke of Cumberland, and granted to officers who took part in the defeat of the Jacobites.

In the second half of the eighteenth century there were a number of medals, but these were of a private or semi-official nature. The Honourable East India Company took the lead in awarding medals to its troops. These medals were often struck in two sizes and in gold as well as silver, for award to different ranks. The siege of Gibraltar (1779–83) was marked by an issue of medals to the defenders, but this was made on the initiative (and at the expense) of the garrison commanders, Generals Eliott and Picton, themselves.

During the French Revolutionary and Napoleonic Wars several medals were produced by private individuals for issue to combatants. Alexander Davison and Matthew Boulton were responsible for the medals granted to the officers and men who fought the battles of the Nile (1798) and Trafalgar (1805). Davison also produced a Trafalgar medal in pewter surrounded by a copper rim; it is recorded that the seamen who received it were so disgusted at the base metal that they threw it into the sea! At the same time, however, Government recognition was given to senior officers who had distinguished themselves in certain battles

and engagements and a number of gold medals were awarded. The events thus marked included the capture of Ceylon (1795–96) and the battles of Maida, Bagur and Palamos.

Towards the end of the Napoleonic Wars an Army Gold Medal was instituted in two sizes—large (generals) and small (field officers). Clasps for second and third battles and campaigns were added to the medal, but when an officer became eligible for a third clasp the medal was exchanged for a Gold Cross with the names of the four battles engraved on its arms. Clasps for subsequent campaigns were then added to the cross (the Duke of Wellington receiving the Gold Cross with nine clasps). A total of 163 crosses, 85 large and 599 small medals was awarded, so that, apart from their intrinsic value, these decorations command very high prices when they appear in the saleroom.

The first medal awarded to all ranks of the Army was the Waterloo Medal, issued in 1816 shortly after the battle which brought the Napoleonic Wars to an end. No action was taken to grant medals for the other campaigns in the Napoleonic Wars until 1847 when Military and Naval General Service Medals were awarded retrospectively to veterans who were then still alive. As applications were made, in some cases, in respect of campaigns more than fifty years earlier, it is hardly surprising that the number of medals awarded was comparatively small, while the number of clasps awarded for certain engagements was quite minute. The Military General Service Medal was restricted to land campaigns during the Peninsular War (1808–13), the American War (1812–14) and isolated actions in the West Indies, Egypt and Java, whereas the Naval GSM covered a far longer period, ranging from the capture of the French frigate La Cleopatra by HMS Nymphe in June 1793, to the naval blockade of the Syrian coast in 1840, during the British operations against Mehemet Ali. Thus Naval Medals with the clasp for Syria are relatively plentiful (7057 awarded) while in several cases clasps were awarded to one man alone, and in seven cases there were no claimants for clasps at all. It is worth bearing in mind that applications for the medals and clasps resulted mainly from the publicity given by printed advertisements and notices posted up all over the country. With the poor general standard of literacy prevalent at the time, many people who were entitled to the medals would have been quite unaware of their existence.

The Naming of Medals

The Military and Naval GSMs, with their multitudinous combinations of clasps, have long been popular with collectors, but the other campaign medals of the past century and a half have a strong following as well. With the exception of the stars and medals awarded during the Second World War, all British campaign medals have usually borne the name of the recipient and usually his (or her) number, rank and regiment, unit or ship as well. This brings a personal element into the study of medals which is lacking in most other branches of numismatics. The name on a medal is very important for two reasons. It is a means of testing the genuineness, not only of the medal itself, but its bar combination, and secondly it enables the collector to link the medal not only with the man who earned it, but with his unit or formation, and thus plays a vital part in the development of naval or military history, if only a small part in most cases.

Much of the potential value of a medal depends on the man who won it, or the unit to which he belonged. To form a coherent collection as opposed to a random accumulation of medals, the collector would be well advised to specialise in some aspect of the subject, restricting his interests perhaps to one medal (the Naval GSM) or a single group (British campaigns in India), or to medals awarded to the men of a particular regiment. The information given on the rim or back of a medal is therefore important in helping to identify it and assign it to its correct place. Even this has to be qualified to some extent. Some regiments are more popular than others with collectors and much depends on the part, active or passive, played by a unit in a particular battle or campaign for which the medal was awarded. Then again, the combination of event with the corps or regiment of the recipient must also be considered.

At one extreme we find the Royal Regiment of Artillery living up to its motto *Ubique* (everywhere) by being represented in virtually every land action (and not a few naval actions, as witness the Atlantic Star worn by former Maritime Gunners), so that a comprehensive collection of medals awarded to the RA would be a formidable feat.

At the other extreme one finds odd detachments, sometimes consisting of one or two men only, seconded from a regiment for service with another unit. The Indian GSM, with bar for Hazara (1891), is usually found named to personnel of the 11th Bengal Lancers and various battalions of the Bengal Infantry, but according to the medal rolls it was also given to six men of the 2nd Manchester Regiment, two men of the Queen's Regiment and one each to troopers of the 2nd and 7th Dragoon Guards. Whereas a specimen of the IGS medal with this bar is not hard to find named to a soldier in one of the Bengal units, it constitutes a major rarity when awarded to one of the "odd men" and its value is correspondingly high.

As the personal details given on a medal regarding the recipient are so important, it is necessary for the collector to verify two facts—that the person whose name is on the medal was actually present at the action for which either the medal or its bars were awarded, and secondly, that the naming of the bar and the attachment of the bars is correct and not tampered with in any way. As regards the first, the Public Record Office at Kew, London is a goldmine of information for all naval and military campaigns. Apart from despatches, reports and muster rolls covering the actions, there are the medal rolls compiled from the applications for medals and bars. Transcriptions of the medal rolls are held by regimental museums and also by such bodies as the Military Historical Association and the Orders and Medals Research Society. Details of these and other clubs and societies devoted to medal collecting can be found in the later chapters.

The presence of a name on the roll does not mean that a medal or clasp was inevitably awarded; conversely authenticated medals are known to exist named to persons not listed on the medal roll. There are often divergences between the muster and medal rolls. Moreover, discrepancies in the spelling of recipients' names are not uncommon and bars are sometimes found listed for regiments which were not even in existence when the battle was fought! This is explained, however, by the fact that a man may have been serving with one unit which took part in the campaign and subsequently transferred to another regiment. When claiming his medal he probably gave his *present* unit, rather than the one in which he was serving at the time of the action.

Unfortunately cases of medals having been tampered with are by no means rare, so it is necessary to be able to recognise evidence of fakery. A favourite device of the faker is to alter the name and personal details of the recipient and to substitute another name in order to enhance the medal's value. This is done simply by filing the inscription off the rim and adding a new one. In order to check for such alterations a similar medal of proven genuineness should be compared with a pair of fine callipers. Take the measurements at several points round the rim so that any unevenness should soon be apparent.

We cannot stress too much the importance of being closely familiar with the various styles of naming medals. Over the past 150 years an incredible variety of lettering—roman, italic, script, sans-serif, seriffed in all shapes and sizes—has been used at one time or another. In some cases the inscription was applied by impressing in raised relief; in others the inscription was punched in or engraved by hand. If a medal is normally impressed and you come across an engraved example you should immediately be on your guard. This is not an infallible test, however, as medals have been known with more than one style of naming, particularly if duplicates were issued at a much later date to replace medals lost or destroyed.

A rather more subtle approach was adopted by some fakers in respect of the Naval GSM. The three commonest clasps—*Algiers* (1362), *Navarino* (1137) and *Syria* (7057)—were awarded to many recipients possessing common names such as Jones or Smith which can be matched with recipients of some very rare clasps. In the case of the Naval GSM the ship on which the recipient served is not given, thus aiding the fraudulent substitution of clasps. It is necessary, therefore, to check the condition of clasps, even if the naming appears to be correct. Points to watch for are file or solder marks on the rivets which secure the clasps to each other and to the suspender of the medal. This test is not infallible as clasps *do* occasionally work loose if subject to constant wear (particularly if the recipient was a cavalryman, for obvious reasons). But clasps whose rivets appear to have been hammered should automatically be suspect, until a check of the medal rolls pass them as authentic. Examples of the earlier medals, particularly those awarded to officers, may be found with unorthodox coupling. Major L. L. Gordon, in his definitive work *British Battles and Medals*, mentions a Naval GSM awarded to one of his ancestors, with clasps for *Guadaloupe* and *Anse la Barque* in a large rectangular style which must have been unofficial. The medal is quite authentic, so it must be presumed that officers were allowed a certain degree of latitude in the manner in which they altered their medals.

Medals with clasps awarded for participation in subsequent engagements are invariably worth much more than the basic medal. In general, the greater number of clasps, the more valuable the medal, although, conversely, there are a few instances in which single-clasp medals are scarcer than twin-clasp medals. There is no short answer to this and individual rare clasps can enhance the value of an otherwise common medal out of all proportion. Thus the Naval GSM with clasp for *Syria* currently rates £350–400, but one of the two medals known to have been issued with the *Acheron* clasp of 1805 would easily rate twelve times as much. Again, relative value can only be determined by reference to all the circumstances of the award.

The person to whom a medal was issued has considerable bearing on its value. If the recipient belonged to a regiment which played a spectacular part in a battle, this generally rates a premium. The rank of the recipient also has some bearing; in general the higher the rank, the more valuable the medal. Medals to commissioned officers rate more than those awarded to NCOs and other ranks, and the medals of British servicemen rate more as a rule than those awarded to native troops. Medals granted to women usually command a relatively good premium. Another grim aspect is that medals issued to personnel who were wounded or killed in the campaign also rate more highly than those issued to servicemen who came through unscathed.

With the collector of British campaign medals the person to whom the medal was awarded tends to become almost as important as the medal itself. It is often not sufficient to collect the medal and leave it at that. The collector feels that he must investigate it and delve into the archives to find out all that he can about the recipient. The National Archives (Public Record Office) and regimental museums have already been mentioned, but do not overlook the usefulness of such reference tools as the monumental Mormon International Genealogical Index (now on microfiche and available in good public libraries and county record offices). All of these should help you to flesh out the bare bones of the details given in the muster and medal rolls.

Medal Groups

Apart from the combination of clasps on a medal and the significance of the recipient, there is a third factor to be considered in assessing the value of medals, namely the relationship of one medal to another in a group awarded to one person. Just as the number of clasps on a medal is not in itself a significant factor, so also the number of medals in a group is not necessarily important *per se*. Groups of five or more medals, whose recipient can be identified, are by no means uncommon. For example, a fairly common five medal group would consist of 1914–15 Medal, War Medal and Victory Medal (for the First World War) and the Defence Medal and War Medal (for the Second World War). Thousands of men served throughout the first war to do duty, in a less active role, during a part at least of the second, long enough to qualify for the latter pair of medals.

It should be noted that none of the medals awarded for service in the Second World War was named to the recipient, so that groups comprising such medals alone cannot be readily identified and are thus lacking in the interest possessed by those containing named medals. Six-medal groups for service in the Second World War are not uncommon, particularly the combination of 1939–45 Star, Africa Star, Italy Star, France and Germany Star, Defence Medal and War Medal awarded to Army personnel who served from any time up to late 1942 and took part in the campaigns of North Africa and Europe.

Conversely it would be possible for troops to have served over a longer period and seen more action, and only been awarded the 1939–45 Star, Burma Star (with Pacific bar) and the War Medal. Naval groups consisting of the 1939–45 Star, Atlantic Star (with bar for France and Germany), Italy Star and War Medal are less common and therefore more desirable (with, of course, the rider that it must be possible to identify the recipient), while the most desirable of all is the three-medal group of 1939–45 Star (with Battle of Britain bar), Air Crew Europe Star (with bar for France and Germany) and the War Medal. Such a group, together with a Distinguished Flying Cross awarded to one of The Few, is a highly coveted set indeed, providing, as always, that one can prove its authenticity. In any event, the addition of a named medal to a Second World War group (e.g. a long service award, a gallantry medal, or some other category of medal named to the recipient), together with supporting collateral material (citations, log-books, pay-books, service records, newspaper cuttings, etc), should help to establish the provenance of the group.

The prices quoted in this publication are average figures for medals and decorations as individual items. Combinations with other decorations and campaign medals will produce a value usually well in excess of the aggregate of the individual items. Value will depend to a large extent on the personal factors and circumstances of the award, but where general factors are involved (e.g. the design of the medal, the period of issue or the campaign concerned, or in some cases the branch of the services) these are itemised separately. "—" indicates that either no examples have come onto the market or no examples have been issued. The figure in brackets (where available) is the approximate number awarded.

71. LOUISBURG MEDAL

Date: 1758.

Campaign: Canada (Seven Years War).

Branch of Service: British Army and Navy.

Ribbon: 32mm half yellow, half blue, although not originally intended for wear and therefore not fitted with suspension or ribbon.

Metals: Gold, silver or bronze.

Size: 42mm.

Description: (Obverse) the globe surrounded by allegorical figures of victory and flanked by servicemen; (reverse) burning ships in the harbour.

Comments: *More in the nature of a decoration, this medal was only given to certain recipients for acts of bravery or distinguished service in the capture in July 1758 of Louisburg in Canada during the Seven Years War. James Wolfe and Jeffrey Amherst commanded the land forces and Edward Boscawen the fleet.*

VALUE:

Gold	Rare
Silver	£3000–4000
Bronze	£1500–2000

72. CARIB WAR MEDAL

Date: 1773.

Campaign: Carib rebellion, St Vincent.

Branch of Service: Local militia or volunteers.

Ribbon: None.

Metal: Silver.

Size: 52mm.

Description: (Obverse) bust of George III in armour; (reverse) Britannia offering an olive branch to a defeated Carib, the date MDCCLXXIII in the exergue.

Comments: *The Legislative Assembly of St Vincent in the West Indies instituted this award to members of the militia and volunteers who served in the campaign of 1773 which put down a native rebellion that had been fomented by the French.*

VALUE:

Silver	£1000–1200

73. DECCAN MEDAL

Date: 1784.

Campaign: Western India and Gujerat 1778-84.

Branch of Service: HEIC forces.

Ribbon: Yellow cord.

Metals: Gold or silver.

Size: 40.5mm or 32mm.

Description: (Obverse) a rather languid Britannia with a trophy of arms, thrusting a laurel wreath towards a distant fort. (Reverse) an inscription in Farsi signifying "As coins are current in the world, so shall be the bravery and exploits of these heroes by whom the name of the victorious English nation was carried from Bengal to the Deccan. Presented in AH 1199 [1784] by the East India Company's Calcutta Government".

Comments: *The first medals struck by order of the Honourable East India Company were conferred on Indian troops for service in western India and Gujerat under the command of Warren Hastings. They were struck at Calcutta in two sizes; both gold and silver exist in the larger size but only silver medals in the smaller diameter.*

VALUE:

40.5mm gold	£4000–6000
40.5mm silver	£1500–1800
32mm silver	£850–1000

74. DEFENCE OF GIBRALTAR

Date: 1783.

Eliott's medal   Picton's medal

Campaign: Siege of Gibraltar 1779-83.
Branch of Service: British and Hanoverian forces.
Ribbon: None.
Metal: Silver.
Size: 59mm (Picton) and 49mm (Eliott).
Description: Eliott's medal was confined to the Hanoverian troops, hence the reverse inscribed
BRUDERSCHAFT (German for "brotherhood") above a wreath containing the names of the three
Hanoverian commanders and General Eliott. The obverse, by Lewis Pingo, shows a view of the Rock and
the naval attack of 13 September 1782 which was the climax of the siege. Picton's medal, awarded to the
British forces, has a larger than usual diameter, with a map of the Rock on the obverse and a 22-line text—the
most verbose British medal—above a recumbent lion clutching a shield bearing the castle and key emblem of
Gibraltar on the reverse.
Comments: *Several medals of a private nature were struck to commemorate the defence of Gibraltar during the Franco-*
Spanish siege of 1779–83, but those most commonly encountered are the silver medals which were provided by George
Augustus Eliott and Sir Thomas Picton, the military commanders.

VALUE:

Picton medal	£1000–1200
Eliott medal	£700–1000

75. MYSORE MEDAL

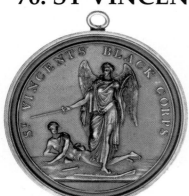

Date: 1792.
Campaign: Mysore 1790-92.
Branch of Service: HEIC forces.
Ribbon: Yellow cord.
Metal: Gold or silver.
Size: 43mm or 38mm.
Description: (Obverse) a sepoy of the HEIC Army holding British and Company flags over a trophy of arms with the fortress of Seringapatam in the background; (reverse) a bilingual inscription (in English and Farsi). The medal has a ring for suspension round the neck by a cord.
Comments: *Indian officers and men who served under Marquis Cornwallis and Generals Abercromby and Meadows received this medal for service in the campaign which brought about the downfall of Tippoo Sultan of Mysore.*

VALUE:

43mm gold (subadars)	£6000–8000
43mm silver (jemadars)	£1800–2200
38mm silver (other ranks)	£1000–1200

76. ST VINCENTS BLACK CORPS MEDAL

Date: 1795.
Campaign: Carib rebellion 1795.
Branch of Service: Local militia volunteers.
Ribbon: None.
Metal: Bronze.
Size: 48.5mm.
Description: (Obverse) the winged figure of Victory brandishing a sword over a fallen foe who has abandoned his musket; (reverse) native holding musket and bayonet, BOLD LOYAL OBEDIENT around and H.G.FEC. in exergue.
Comments: *Awarded to the officers and NCOs of the Corps of Natives raised by Major Seton from among the island's slaves for service against the rebellious Caribs and French forces.*

VALUE:

Bronze	Rare

77. CAPTURE OF CEYLON MEDAL

Date: 1796.
Campaign: Ceylon 1795.
Branch of Service: HEIC forces.
Ribbon: Yellow cord.
Metal: Gold or silver.
Size: 50mm.
Description: The plain design has an English inscription on the obverse, and the Farsi equivalent on the reverse.
Comments: *Awarded for service in the capture of Ceylon (Sri Lanka) from the Dutch during the French Revolutionary Wars. It is generally believed that the gold medals were awarded to Captains Barton and Clarke while the silver medals went to the native gunners of the Bengal Artillery.*

VALUE:

Gold (2)	—	
Silver (121)	£1200–1500 (original striking)	£400–500 (later striking)

78. DAVISON'S NILE MEDAL

Date: 1798.   **Campaign:** Battle of the Nile 1798.
Branch of Service: Royal Navy.
Ribbon: None, but unofficially 32mm, deep navy blue.
Metal: Gold, silver, gilt-bronze and bronze.   **Size:** 47mm.
Description: (Obverse) Peace caressing a shield decorated with the portrait of Horatio Nelson; (reverse) the
  British fleet at Aboukir Bay. The edge bears the lettering "From Alexr Davison, Esqr St James' Square=A
  Tribute of Regard".
Comments: *Nelson's victory at the mouth of the Nile on 1 August 1798 was celebrated in a novel manner by his prize
  agent, Alexander Davison, whose name and London address appear in the edge inscription of the medal designed by
  Kuchler. Originally issued without a suspender, many recipients added a ring to enable the medal to be worn. Admiral
  Nelson's medal was stolen in 1900 and is believed to have been melted down. Prices quoted below are for unnamed
  specimens, contemporary engraved medals are usually worth about twice as much.*

VALUE:	Gold (Nelson and his captains)	£6000–8000	Gilt-bronze (petty officers)	£500–800
	Silver (junior officers)	£1500–2000	Bronze (ratings)	£250–350

79. SERINGAPATAM MEDAL

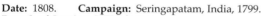

Date: 1808.   **Campaign:** Seringapatam, India, 1799.
Branch of Service: HEIC forces.
Ribbon: 38mm gold.
Metal: Gold, silver-gilt, silver, bronze and pewter.   **Size:** 48mm or 45mm.
Description: (Obverse) the British lion defeating Tiger of Mysore (Tippoo Sultan) with the date of the capture of
  the fortress IV MAY MDCCXCIX (1799) in the exergue; (reverse) the assault on Seringapatam.
Comments: *The British and native troops who took part in the renewed campaign against Tippoo Sultan were awarded
  this medal in 1808 in various metals without suspension (a number of different types of suspenders and rings were
  subsequently fitted by individual recipients). The medal was designed by Kuchler and struck in England and Calcutta,
  the latter version being slightly smaller. There are several different strikings of these medals.*

VALUE:

Gold 48mm (113)	£4000–6000	Gold 45mm		£3000–4000
Silver-gilt 48mm (185)	£1000–1200	Silver 45mm		£450–550
Silver 48mm (3636)	£600–800	Bronze 48mm (5000)		£200–280
		Pewter 48mm (45,000)		£200–220
		Miniature	Silver	£200–250

80. EARL ST. VINCENT'S MEDAL

Date: 1800.   **Campaign:** Mediterranean.
Branch of Service: Royal Navy.
Ribbon: None.
Metal: Gold or silver.   **Size:** 48mm
Description: (Obverse) left-facing bust of the Earl in Admiral's uniform; (reverse) a sailor and marine.
Comments: *A private medal presented by Earl St Vincent, when he struck his flag and came ashore in 1800, to the petty officers and men of his flagship* Ville de Paris *as a token of appreciation to his old shipmates. Contemporary engraved and named pieces with researched provenance are worth at least twice as much as unnamed specimens.*

VALUE:
Gold	£4500–6000
Silver	£450–650

81. EGYPT MEDAL 1801

Date: 1801.   **Campaign:** Egypt 1801.
Branch of Service: HEIC forces.
Ribbon: Yellow cord.
Metal: Gold or silver.   **Size:** 48mm.
Description: (Obverse) a sepoy holding a Union Jack, with an encampment in the background. A four-line Farsi text occupies the exergue; (reverse) a warship and the Pyramids.
Comments: *Issued by the Honourable East India Company to British and Indian troops in the Company's service who took part in the conquest of Egypt under Generals Baird and Abercromby.*

VALUE:
Gold (16)	Rare	
Silver (2200)	£1000–1200 (original striking)	£400–500 (later striking)

82. SULTAN'S MEDAL FOR EGYPT

Date: 1801.
Campaign: Egypt 1801.
Branch of Service: British forces.
Ribbon: The gold medals were originally suspended by gold hook and chain as shown. The silver medals were hung from a sand-coloured ribbon.
Metals: Gold or silver.
Size: Various (see below).
Description: The very thin discs have an elaborate arabesque border enclosing the *toughra* or sign manual of the Sultan.
Comments: *This medal was conferred by Sultan Selim III of Turkey on the British officers and NCOs who took part in the campaign against the French. It was produced in five gold versions for award to different ranks of commissioned officers, as well as one in silver for award to sergeants and corporals.*

VALUE:

Gold 54mm studded with jewels	Rare
Gold 54mm plain (less than 100 issued)	£3000–3500
Gold 48mm	£2000–2500
Gold 43mm	£1500–2000
Gold 36mm	£1000–1500
Silver 36mm	£1200–1500

Miniature
Gold	£150–200
Silver	£100–150

83. HIGHLAND SOCIETY'S MEDAL FOR EGYPT 1801

Date: 1801.
Campaign: Egypt 1801.
Branch of Service: British forces.
Ribbon: None.
Metals: Gold, silver and bronze.
Size: 49mm.
Description: The medal was designed by Pidgeon. (Obverse) the right-facing bust of General Sir Ralph Abercromby, with a Latin inscription alluding to his death in Egypt; (reverse) a Highlander in combat with the Gaelic inscription NA FIR A CHOISIN BUAIDH SAN EPHAIT(These are the heroes who achieved victory in Egypt) and the date 21 MAR 1801. On the edge is the inscription "On choumun Chaeleach D'on Fhreiceadan Dubh Na XLII RT" (From the London Highland Society to the Black Watch or 42nd Regt.).
Comments: *The Highland and Agricultural Society (now Royal) was founded in 1784 to promote the development of agriculture in Scotland generally and the Highlands in particular. General Abercromby (born at Tullibody, 1734) commanded the British expedition to Egypt, and the landing at Aboukir Bay on 2 March 1801 in the face of strenuous French opposition, is justly regarded as one of the most brilliant and daring exploits of all time. The French made a surprise attack on the British camp on the night of 21 March and Abercromby was struck by a ricochet; he died aboard the flagship seven days later. Medals in gold were presented to the Prince Regent and Abercromby's sons, but silver and bronze medals were later struck and awarded to senior officers of the expedition as well as soldiers who had distinguished themselves in the campaign.*

VALUE:
Gold	—
Silver	£600–800
Bronze	£250–300

84. BOULTON'S TRAFALGAR MEDAL

Date: 1805.
Campaign: Battle of Trafalgar 1805.
Branch of Service: Royal Navy.
Ribbon: None, but unofficially 32mm navy blue (originally issued without suspension).
Metals: Gold, silver, white metal, gilt-bronze or bronze.
Size: 48mm.
Description: (Obverse) bust of Nelson; (reverse) a battle scene.
Comments: *Matthew Boulton of the Soho Mint, Birmingham, struck this medal on his own initiative for presentation to the survivors of the battle of Trafalgar. It was awarded in white metal, but bronze and gilt-bronze specimens also exist. It was subsequently restruck on at least two occasions, the first and second strikings have the inscription impressed in large capitals around the rim TO THE HEROES OF TRAFALGAR FROM M:BOULTON, the last having the inscription omitted. As the original dies were used for each striking, they had to be polished before reuse, so the fine detail on Nelson's uniform and in the battle scene is less pronounced in the second and subsequent strikings. Examples of the original striking can sometimes be found engraved in various styles, but great care should be taken over checking the authenticity of such pieces. All gold specimens are restrikes. Silver medals were not awarded but were later ordered from Boulton or his descendants by officers who wished to have a medal to form a group with the 1848 NGS.*

VALUE:

Gold (c. 1905)	£2500–3500	Gilt-bronze	£500–700
Silver (1820–50)	£1500–1800	Bronze	£200–300
White metal	£300–400		

NB These prices are based on medals ssued from the original striking and are dependent on attribution.

85. DAVISON'S TRAFALGAR MEDAL

Date: 1805.
Campaign: Battle of Trafalgar 1805.
Branch of Service: Royal Navy.
Ribbon: None, but unofficially 32mm navy blue.
Metal: Pewter with a copper rim.
Size: 52mm.
Description: (Obverse) bust of Nelson; (reverse) a man-of-war with an appropriate biblical quotation from Exodus "The Lord is a Man-of-War".
Comments: *Alexander Davison, Nelson's prize agent, had this medal struck for award to the ratings of HMS* Victory *who took part in the battle.*

VALUE: £1200–1500

86. CAPTURE OF RODRIGUEZ, ISLE OF BOURBON AND ISLE OF FRANCE

Date: 1810.

Campaign: Indian Ocean 1809-10.

Branch of Service: HEIC forces.

Ribbon: Yellow cord.

Metal: Gold or silver.

Size: 49mm.

Description: (Obverse) a sepoy in front of a cannon with the Union Jack; (reverse) a wreath with inscriptions in English and Farsi.

Comments: *The East India Company awarded this medal to native troops of the Bengal and Bombay Armies for the capture of three French islands in the Indian Ocean (the latter two being better known today as Mauritius and Reunion) between July 1809 and December 1810.*

VALUE:	Original striking	Later striking
Gold (50)	£4000–6000	—
Silver (2200)	£1000–1500	£450–550

87. BAGUR AND PALAMOS MEDAL

Date: 1811.

Campaign: Peninsular War 1810.

Branch of Service: Royal Navy.

Ribbon: Red with yellow edges.

Metal: Gold or silver.

Size: 45mm.

Description: (Obverse) the conjoined crowned shields of Britain and Spain in a wreath with ALIANZA ETERNA (eternal alliance) round the foot; (reverse) inscription in Spanish GRATITUDE OF SPAIN TO THE BRAVE BRITISH AT BAGUR 10 SEPT. 1810, PALAMOS 14 SEPT. 1810.

Comments: *Awarded by the Spanish government to the crews of the British warships* Ajax, Cambrian *and* Kent *who landed at Bagur and Palamos to seize French ships. The British force was, in fact, driven back with very heavy losses.*

VALUE:	
Gold (8)	£4000–6000
Silver (600)	£800–1000

88. JAVA MEDAL

Date: 1811.

Campaign: Java 1811.

Branch of Service: HEIC forces.

Ribbon: Yellow cord.

Metals: Gold or silver.

Size: 49mm.

Description: (Obverse) the assault on Fort Cornelis; (reverse) inscriptions in English and Farsi.

Comments: *Awarded by the HEIC for the seizure of Java from the Dutch. The 750 British officers and men who took part in the operation were not only awarded this medal but were eligible for the Military GSM with Java clasp, issued 38 years later. Senior officers of the Company were given the gold medal, while junior officers, NCOs and sepoys received the silver version.*

VALUE:	Original striking	Later striking
Gold (133)	£6000–8000	£3000–3500
Silver (6519)	£900–1200	£300–400

89. NEPAUL MEDAL

Date: 1816.
Campaign: Nepal 1814-16.
Branch of Service: HEIC native troops.
Ribbon: Yellow cord.
Metal: Silver.
Size: 51mm.
Description: (Obverse) a fortified mountain-top with a cannon in the foreground; (reverse) Farsi inscription.
Comments: *This medal marked the campaign to pacify Nepal led by Generals Marley, Ochterlony and Gillespie (the last named being killed in action). At the conclusion of the war Ochterlony began recruiting Gurkha mercenaries, a policy which has continued in the British Army to this day. The clasp "Nepaul" was granted with the Army of India Medal to British forces in 1851.*

VALUE: Original striking £1400–1500   Later striking £350–450

90. CEYLON MEDAL

Date: 1818.
Campaign: Ceylon (Sri Lanka) 1818.
Branch of Service: British and HEIC forces.
Ribbon: 38mm deep navy blue.
Metal: Gold or silver.
Size: 35mm.
Description: The very plain design has "Ceylon 1818" within a wreath (obverse) and REWARD OF MERIT at top and bottom of the reverse, the personal details being engraved in the centre.
Comments: *Awarded by the Ceylon government for gallant conduct during the Kandian rebellion. Only selected officers and men of the 19th, 73rd and 83rd Foot, the 1st and 2nd Ceylon Regiments and 7th, 15th and 18th Madras Native Infantry received this medal.*

VALUE:

Gold (2)	—
Silver (45)	£2000–3000

91. BURMA MEDAL

Date: 1826.
Campaign: Burma 1824-26.
Branch of Service: HEIC native forces.
Ribbon: 38mm crimson edged with navy blue.
Metals: Gold or silver.
Size: 39mm.
Description: (Obverse) the Burmese elephant kneeling in submission before the British lion; (reverse) the epic assault on Rangoon by the Irrawaddy Flotilla.
Comments: *Granted to native officers and men who participated in the campaign for the subjugation of Burma. This was the first of the HEIC campaign medals in what was to become a standard 1.5 inch (38mm) diameter. The medal was fitted with a large steel ring for suspension and issued unnamed. British troops in this campaign were belatedly (1851) given the clasp "Ava" to the Army of India Medal.*

VALUE:		*Miniature*
Gold (750)	£3500–4500	—
Silver-gilt	£1000–1200	—
Silver (24,000)	£700–900	£250–300

92. COORG MEDAL

Date: 1837.
Campaign: Coorg rebellion 1837.
Branch of Service: HEIC loyal Coorg forces.
Ribbon: Yellow cord.
Metals: Gold, silver or bronze.
Size: 50mm.
Description: (Obverse) a Coorg holding a musket, with kukri upraised; (reverse) weapons in a wreath with the inscription FOR DISTINGUISHED CONDUCT AND LOYALTY TO THE BRITISH GOVERNMENT COORG APRIL 1837, the equivalent in Canarese appearing on the obverse.
Comments: *Native troops who remained loyal during the Canara rebellion of April-May 1837 were awarded this medal by the HEIC the following August. Bronze specimens were also struck but not officially issued and may have been restrikes or later copies. Bronzed and silvered electrotype copies are also known.*

VALUE:	Original striking	Later striking
Gold (44)	£5000–8000	—
Silver (300)	£1500–1800	£400–500
Bronze	£300–400	—

93. NAVAL GOLD MEDAL

Date: 1795.
Campaign: Naval actions 1795-1815.
Branch of Service: Royal Navy.
Ribbon: 44mm white with broad dark blue edges.
Metal: Gold.
Size: 51mm and 38mm.
Description: The medals were glazed on both sides and individually engraved on the reverse with the name of the recipient and details of the engagement in a wreath of laurel and oak leaves. (Obverse) the winged figure of Victory bestowing a laurel wreath on the head of Britannia standing in the prow of a galley with a Union Jack shield behind her, her right foot on a helmet, her left hand holding a spear.
Comments: *Instituted in 1795, a year after Lord Howe's naval victory on "the glorious First of June", this medal was awarded continually till 1815 when the Order of the Bath was expanded into three classes. Large medals were awarded to admirals and small medals went to captains. As medals were awarded for separate actions it was possible for officers to wear more than one; Lord Nelson himself had three. Two miniatures are recorded and would probably fetch at least £1000 if they came onto the market.*

VALUE:

Large medal (22)	From £80,000
Small medal (117)	From £40,000

94. NAVAL GENERAL SERVICE MEDAL

Date: 1847.

Campaign: Naval battles and boat actions 1793-1840.

Branch of Service: Royal Navy.

Ribbon: 32mm white with dark blue edges.

Metal: Silver.

Size: 36mm.

Description: (Obverse) the Young Head profile of Queen Victoria by William Wyon; (reverse) Britannia with her trident seated on a sea horse.

Clasps: No fewer than 230 different clasps for major battles, minor engagements, cutting-out operations and boat service were authorised. These either have the name or date of the action, the name of a ship capturing or defeating an enemy vessel, or the words BOAT SERVICE followed by a date. No fewer than 20,933 medals were awarded but most of them had a single clasp. Multi-clasp medals are worth very considerably more. The greatest number of clasps to a single medal was seven (two awards made); four medals had six clasps and fourteen medals had five clasps. For reasons of space only those clasps which are met with fairly often in the salerooms are listed below. At the other end of the scale it should be noted that only one recipient claimed the clasps for *Hussar* (17 May 1795), *Dido* (24 June 1795), *Spider* (25 August 1795), *Espoir* (7 August 1798), *Viper* (26 December 1799), *Loire* (5 February 1800), *Louisa* (28 October 1807), *Carrier* (4 November 1807), *Superieure* (10 February 1809), *Growler* (22 May 1812) and the boat actions of 15 March 1793, 4 November 1803, 4 November 1810 and 3-6 September 1814. In several cases no claimants came forward at all. The numbers of clasps awarded are not an accurate guide to value, as some actions are rated more highly than others, and clasps associated with actions in the War of 1812 have a very strong following in the USA as well as Britain. Clasps for famous battles, such as Trafalgar, likewise command a high premium out of all proportion to the number of clasps awarded. A medal to HMS *Victory* would be worth in excess of £5000.

Comments: *Instituted in 1847 and issued to **surviving** claimants in 1848, this medal was originally intended to cover naval engagements of the French Revolutionary and Napoleonic Wars (1793-1815) but was almost immediately extended to cover all naval actions of a more recent date, down to the expedition to Syria in 1840. It was fitted with a straight suspender.*

VALUE (for the most commonly encountered clasps):

v.	1 June 1794 (583)	£2000–2500	cxxviii.	Guadaloupe (484)		£900–1500
ix.	14 March 1795 (114)	£2500–3000	cxli.	Lissa (124)		£2500–3000
xv.	23 June 1795 (200)	£2000–2500	cxlvi.	Java (695)		£800–1200
xxxi.	St Vincent (364)	£1500–2000	clxi.	Shannon wh Chesapeake (42)	£5000–6000
xxxiv.	Camperdown (336)	£2000–2500	clxiii.	St Sebastian (288)		£1200–1500
xxxvi.	Mars 21 April 1798 (26)	£4000–6000	clxv.	Gluckstadt 5 Jany 1814 (44)	£3000–4000
xxxviii.	Lion 15 July 1798 (23)	£4000–6000	clxxvi.	Gaieta 24 July 1815 (88)	£2500–3000
xxxix.	Nile (351)	£3000–3500	clxxvii.	Algiers (1,362)		£900–1200
xli.	12 Octr 1798 (79)	£3000–3500	clxxviii.	Navarino (1,137)		£900–1200
xlv.	Acre 30 May 1799 (50)	£3500–4000	clxxix.	Syria (7,057)		£450–550
lxii.	Egypt (511)	£1000–1200				
lxiii.	Copenhagen (545)	£2500–3000	**Boat Service**			
lxv.	Gut of Gibraltar (144)	£2000–2500	cxcii.	16 July 1806 (51)		£2500–3500
lxxv.	Trafalgar (1,710)	£4500–6500	ccvi.	1 Novr 1809 (110)		£2000–3000
lxxvi.	4 Novr 1805 (297)	£2000–2500	ccx.	28 June 1810 (25)		£3000–4000
lxxvii.	St Domingo (406)	£1400–1600	ccxxiii.	29 Sepr 1812 (25)		£3000–4000
lxxix.	London 13 March 1806 (27)	£4000–6000	ccxxvii.	8 Ap and May 1813 (57)	£3000–4000
lxxxv.	Curacao 1 Jany 1807 (67)	£2500–3500	ccxxviii.	2 May 1813 (48)		£3000–4000
xcvii.	Stately 22 March 1808 (31)	£4000–5000	ccxxix.	8 April 1814 (24)		£4000–5000
cxiii.	Martinique (506)	£1000–1200	ccxxx.	24 May 1814 (12)		£5000–6000
cxvii.	Basque Roads (551)	£1200–1500	ccxxxiii.	14 Decr 1814 (205)		£2000–2500

Miniature

Without clasp £100–150, for each clasp add £75+ depending on the action.

Below are listed all of the clasps authorised for wear on the Naval General Service Medal. As they were not issued until some years after the events, in some cases very few were ever claimed and in some instances there were no claimants at all. The numbers issued are indicated in brackets.

i.	Nymphe 18 June 1793 (4)	lxiv.	Speedy 6 May 1801 (7)
ii.	Crescent 20 Octr 1793 (12)	lxv.	Gut of Gibraltar 12 July 1801 (144)
iii.	Zebra 17 March1794 (2)	lxvi.	Sylph 28 Septr 1801 (2)
iv.	Carysfort 29 May 1794 (0)	lxvii.	Pasley 28 Octr 1801 (4)
v.	1 June 1794 (583)	lxviii.	Scorpion 31 March 1804 (4)
vi.	Romney 17 June 1794 (2)	lxix.	Beaver 31 March 1804 (0)
vii.	Blanche 4 Jany 1795 (5)	lxx.	Centurion 18 Septr 1804 (12)
viii.	Lively 13 March 1795 (6)	lxxi.	Arrow 3 Feby 1805 (8)
ix.	14 March 1795 (114)	lxxii.	Acheron 3 Feby 1805 (2)
x.	Astraea 10 April 1795 (2)	lxxiii.	San Fiorenzo 14 Feby 1805 (13)
xi.	Thetis 17 May 1795 (2)	lxxiv.	Phoenix 10 Aug 1805 (29)
xii.	Hussar 17 May 1795 (1)	lxxv.	Trafalgar (1,710)
xiii.	Mosquito 9 June 1795 (0)	lxxvi.	4 Novr 1805 (297)
xiv.	17 June 1795 (42)	lxxvii.	St. Domingo (406)
xv.	23 June 1795 (200)	lxxviii.	Amazon 13 March 1806 (30)
xvi.	Dido 24 June 1795 (1)	lxxix.	London 13 March 1806 (27)
xvii.	Lowestoffe 24 June 1795 (6)	lxxx.	Pique 26 March 1806 (8)
xviii.	Spider 25 August 1795 (1)	lxxxi.	Sirius 17 April 1806 (20)
xix.	Port Spergui (4)	lxxxii.	Blanche 19 July 1806 (22)
xx.	Indefatigable 20 April 1796 (8)	lxxxiii.	Arethusa 23 Aug 1806 (17)
xxi.	Unicorn 8 June 1796 (4)	lxxxiv.	Anson 23 Aug 1806 (11)
xxii.	Santa Margarita 8 June 1796 (3)	lxxxv.	Curacoa 1 Jany 1807 (67)
xxiii.	Southampton 9 June 1796 (8)	lxxxvi.	Pickle 3 Jany 1807 (2)
xxiv.	Dryad 13 June 1796 (6)	lxxxvii.	Hydra 6 Aug 1807 (12)
xxv.	Terpsichore 13 Oct 1796 (3)	lxxxviii.	Comus 15 Aug 1807 (9)
xxvi.	Lapwing 3 Decr 1796 (2)	lxxxix.	Louisa 28 Octr 1807 (1)
xxvii.	Minerve 19 Decr 1796 (4)	xc.	Carrier 4 Novr 1807 (1)
xxviii.	Blanche 19 Decr 1796 (4)	xci.	Ann 24 Novr 1807 (0)
xxix.	Indefatigable 13 Jany 1797 (8)	xcii.	Sappho 2 March 1808 (4)
xxx.	Amazon 13 Jany 1797 (6)	xciii.	San Fiorenzo 8 March 1808 (17)
xxxi.	St Vincent (364)	xciv.	Emerald 13 March 1808 (10)
xxxii.	San Fiorenzo 8 March 1797 (8)	xcv.	Childers 14 March 1808 (4)
xxxiii.	Nymphe 8 March 1797 (5)	xcvi.	Nassau 22 March 1808 (31)
xxxiv.	Camperdown (336)	xcvii.	Stately 22 March 1808 (31)
xxxv.	Phoebe 21 Decr 1797 (5)	xcviii.	Off Rota 4 April 1808 (19)
xxxvi.	Mars 21 April 1798 (26)	xcix.	Grasshopper 24 April 1808 (7)
xxxvii.	Isle St. Marcou (3)	c.	Rapid 24 April 1808 (1)
xxxviii.	Lion 15 July 1798 (23)	ci.	Redwing 7 May 1808 (7)
xxxix.	Nile (351)	cii.	Virginie 19 May 1808 (21)
xl.	Espoir 7 Aug 1798 (1)	ciii.	Redwing 31 May 1808 (7)
xli.	12 Octr 1798 (79)	civ.	Seahorse wh Badere Zaffer (32)
xlii.	Fisgard 20 Octr 1798 (9)	cv.	Comet 11 Aug 1808 (4)
xliii.	Sybille 28 Feby 1799 (12)	cvi.	Centaur 26 Aug 1808 (42)
xliv.	Telegraph 18 March 1799 (0)	cvii.	Implacable 26 Aug 1808 (44)
xlv.	Acre 30 May 1799 (50)	cviii.	Cruizer 1 Novr 1808 (4)
xlvi.	Schiermonnikoog 12 Aug 1799 (9)	cix.	Amethyst wh Thetis (31)
xlvii.	Arrow 13 Sept 1799 (2)	cx.	Off the Pearl Rock 13 Decr 1808 (16)
xlviii.	Wolverine 13 Sept 1799 (0)	cxi.	Onyx 1 Jany 1809 (5)
xlix.	Surprise wh Hermione (7)	cxii.	Confiance 14 Jany 1809 (8)
l.	Speedy 6 Novr 1799 (3)	cxiii.	Martinique (506)
li.	Courier 22 Novr 1799 (3)	cxiv.	Horatio 10 Feby 1809 (13)
lii.	Viper 26 Decr 1799 (2)	cxv.	Supérieure 10 Feby 1809 (1)
liv.	Harpy 5 Feby 1800 (4)	cxvi.	Amethyst 5 April 1809 (27)
lv.	Fairy 5 Feby 1800 (4)	cxvii.	Basque Roads 1809 (551)
lvi.	Peterel 21 March 1800 (2)	cxviii.	Recruit 17 June 1809 (7)
lvii.	Penelope 30 March 1800 (11)	cxix.	Pompee 17 June 1809 (47)
lviii.	Vinciego 30 March 1800 (2)	cxx.	Castor 17 June 1809 (13)
lix.	Capture of the Désirée (24)	cxxi.	Cyane 25 and 27 June 1809 (5)
lx.	Seine 20 August 1800 (7)	cxxii.	L'Espoir 25 and 27 June 1809 (5)
lxi.	Phoebe 19 Feby 1801 (6)	cxxiii.	Bonne Citoyenne wh Furieuse (12)
lxii.	Egypt (511)	cxxiv.	Diana 11 Septr 1809 (8)
lxiii.	Copenhagen 1801 (545)	cxxv.	Anse la Barque 18 Decr 1809 (51)

cxxvi.	Cherokee 10 Jany 1810 (4)	cliii.	Griffon 27 March 1812 (3)
cxxvii.	Scorpion 12 Jany 1810 (8)	cliv.	Northumberland 22 May 1812 (63)
cxxviii.	Guadaloupe (484)	clv.	Growler 22 May 1812 (1)
cxxix.	Thistle 10 Feby 1810 (0)	clvi.	Malaga 29 May 1812 (18) (the date should have been 29 April 1812)
cxxx.	Surly 24 April 1810 (1)		
cxxxi.	Firm 24 April 1810 (1)	clvii.	Off Mardoe 6 July 1812 (47)
cxxxii.	Sylvia 26 April 1810 (1)	clviii.	Sealark 21 July 1812 (4)
cxxxiii.	Spartan 3 May 1810 (30)	clix.	Royalist 29 Decr 1812 (4)
cxxxiv.	Royalist May and June 1810 (3)	clx.	Weasel 22 April 1813 (8)
cxxxv.	Amanthea 25 July 1810 (23)	clxi.	Shannon wh Chesapeake (42)
cxxxvi.	Banda Neira (68)	clxii.	Pelican 14 Aug 1813 (4)
cxxxvii.	Staunch 18 Septr 1810 (2)	clxiii.	St. Sebastian (288)
cxxxviii.	Otter 18 Septr 1810 (8)	clxiv.	Thunder 9 Octr 1813 (9)
cxxxix.	Boadicea 18 Septr 1810 (15)	clxv.	Gluckstadt 5 Jany 1814 (45)
cxl.	Briseis 14 Octr 1810 (2)	clxvi.	Venerable 16 Jany 1814 (42)
cxli.	Lissa (124)	clxix.	Cyane 16 Jany 1814 (7)
cxlii.	Anholt 27 March 1811 (40)	clxx.	Eurotas 25 Feby 1814 (32)
cxliii.	Arrow 6 April 1811 (0)	clxxi.	Hebrus wh L'Etoile (40)
cxliv.	Off Tamatave 20 May 1811 (87)	clxxii.	Phoebe 28 March 1814 (36)
cxlv.	Hawke 18 Aug 1811 (6)	clxxiii.	Cherub 28 March 1814 (7)
cxlvi.	Java (695)	clxxiv.	The Potamac 17 Aug 1814 (108)
cxlvii.	Skylark 11 Novr 1811 (4)	clxxv.	Endymion wh President (58)
cxlviii.	Locust 11 Novr 1811 (2)	clxxvi.	Gaieta 24 July 1815 (89)
cxlix.	Pelagosa 29 Novr 1811 (74)	clxxvii.	Algiers (1,362)
cl.	Victorious wh Rivoli (67)	clxxviii.	Navarino (1,137)
cli.	Weasel 22 Feby 1812 (6)	clxxix.	Syria (7,057)
clii.	Rosario 27 March 1812 (7)		

BOAT SERVICE

These clasps have the words BOAT SERVICE separating the month and the years of the dates. They were only awarded for actions which culminated in an officer or the senior member present being promoted.

clxxx.	15 March 1793 (1)	ccvii.	13 Decr 1809 (9)
clxxxi.	17 March 1794 (29)	ccviii.	13 Feby 1810 (20)
clxxxii.	29 May 1797 (3)	ccix.	1 May 1810 (15)
clxxxiii.	9 June 1799 (4)	ccx.	28 June 1810 (27)
clxxxiv.	20 Decr 1799 (3)	ccxi.	27 Sept 1810 (36)
clxxxv.	29 July 1800 (4)	ccxii.	4 Novr 1810 (1)
clxxxvi.	29 Aug 1800 (25)	ccxiii.	23 Novr 1810 (42)
clxxxvii.	27 Octr 1800 (5)	ccxiv.	24 Decr 1810 (6)
clxxxvii.	21 July 1801 (7)	ccxv.	4 May 1811 (10)
clxxxviii.	27 June 1803 (5)	ccxvi.	30 July 1811 (4)
clxxxix.	4 Novr 1803 (2)	ccxvii.	2 Aug 1811 (9)
cxc.	4 Feby 1804 (11)	ccxviii.	20 Sept 1811 (6)
cxci.	4 June 1805 (10)	ccxix.	4 Decr 1811 (19)
cxcii.	16 July 1806 (52)	ccxx.	4 April 1812 (4)
cxciii.	2 Jan 1807 (3)	ccxxi.	1st Sept 1812 (21)
cxciv.	21 Jan 1807 (8)	ccxxii.	17 Sept 1812 (11) (Bars are known dated 17 Decr 1812 in error)
cxcv.	19 April 1807 (0)		
cxcvi.	13 Feby 1808 (2)	ccxxiii.	29 Sept 1812 (25)
cxcvii.	10 July 1808 (8)	ccxxiv.	6 Jany 1813 (25)
cxcviii.	11 Aug 1808 (17)	ccxxv.	21 March 1813 (3)
cxcix.	28 Novr 1808 (2)	ccxxvi.	29 April 1813 (2)
cc.	7 July 1809 (35)	ccxxvii.	Ap and May 1813 (56)
cci.	14 July 1809 (7)	ccxxviii.	2 May 1813 (48)
ccii.	25 July 1809 (36)	ccxxix.	8 April 1814 (24)
cciii.	27 July 1809 (10)	ccxxx.	24 May 1814 (14)
cciv.	29 July 1809 (11)	ccxxxi.	Aug and Septr 1814 (1)
ccv.	28 Aug 1809 (15)	ccxxxii.	3 and 6 Septr 1814 (1)
ccvi.	1 Novr 1809 (100)	ccxxxiii.	14 Decr 1814 (205)

95. ARMY GOLD CROSS

Date: 1813.

Campaigns: Peninsular War and War of 1812.

Branch of Service: British Army.

Ribbon: 38mm crimson edged with dark blue.

Metal: Gold.   **Size:** 38mm.

Description: A cross pattée with a laurel border having a rose at the centre on each of the four flat ends. At the centre of the cross appears a British lion statant. The scrolled top of the cross is fitted with an elaborate ring decorated with laurel leaves looped through a plain swivel ring fitted to the suspender. The arms of the cross on both obverse and reverse bear the names of four battles in relief.

Clasps: Large borders of laurel leaves enclosing the name of a battle in raised relief within an elliptical frame, awarded for fifth and subsequent battles.

Comments: *Arguably the most prestigious award in the campaign series, the Army Gold Cross was approved by the Prince Regent in 1813. It was granted to generals and officers of field rank for service in four or more battles of the Peninsular War. Three crosses had six clasps, two had seven, while the Duke of Wellington himself had the unique cross with nine clasps, representing participation in thirteen battles.*

VALUE:

Gold cross without clasp (61)	From £25,000
Miniature	£450–550

Battle of Vimiera.

96. MAIDA GOLD MEDAL

Date: 1806.

Campaign: Peninsular War, Battle of Maida 1806.

Branch of Service: British Army.

Ribbon: 38mm crimson edged with navy blue.

Metal: Gold.

Size: 39mm.

Description: (Obverse) laureated profile of George III; (reverse) winged figure of Victory hovering with a laurel wreath over the head of Britannia, shield upraised, in the act of throwing a spear. The name and date of the battle appears on Britannia's left, with the *trinacria* or three-legged emblem on the right.

Clasps: None.

Comments: *This small gold medal was authorised in 1806 and awarded to the thirteen senior officers involved in the battle of Maida in Calabria when a small British force under General Sir John Stuart defeated a much larger French army with heavy loss. A small unknown number of gold and silver specimens are known to exist.*

VALUE: from £35,000

97. ARMY GOLD MEDAL

Date: 1810.

Campaigns: Peninsular War 1806-14 and War of 1812.

Branch of Service: British Army.

Ribbon: 38mm crimson edged with navy blue.

Metal: Gold.

Size: 54mm and 33mm.

Description: (Obverse) Britannia seated on a globe, holding a laurel wreath over the British lion and holding a palm branch in her left hand while resting on a shield embellished with the Union Jack. The name of the first action is generally engraved on the reverse.

Clasps: For second and third actions.

Comments: *The Maida medal (no. 96) established a precedent for the series of medals instituted in 1810. The name of the battle was inscribed on the reverse, usually engraved, though that for Barossa was die-struck. These medals were struck in two sizes, the larger being conferred on generals and the smaller on officers of field rank. Second or third battles were denoted by a clasp appropriately inscribed, while those who qualified for a fourth award exchanged their medal and bars for a gold cross. The award of these gold medals and crosses ceased in 1814 when the Companion of the Bath was instituted.*

VALUE*:

Large medal	From £20,000
Small medal	From £9000

*Medals to British officers in the Portuguese Service generally sell for 20% less. Only one miniature is known to exist.

98. MILITARY GENERAL SERVICE MEDAL

Date: 1847.

Campaigns: French Revolutionary and Napoleonic Wars 1793-1814.

Branch of Service: British Army.

Ribbon: 31mm crimson edged with dark blue.

Metal: Silver.

Size: 36mm.

Description: (Obverse) the Wyon profile of Queen Victoria; (reverse) a standing figure of the Queen bestowing victor's laurels on a kneeling Duke of Wellington. The simple inscription TO THE BRITISH ARMY appears round the circumference, while the dates 1793-1814 are placed in the exergue. Despite this, the earliest action for which a clasp was issued took place in 1801 (Abercromby's Egyptian campaign).

Clasps: Only 29 battle or campaign clasps were issued but multiple awards are much more common than in the naval medal, the maximum being fifteen. While it is generally true to say that multi-clasp medals are worth more than single-clasp medals, there are many in the latter category (noted below) which command higher prices. The figures quoted below are based on the commonest regiments. Clasps awarded to specialists and small detached forces rate more highly than medals to the principal regiment in a battle or campaign. In particular, it should be noted that one naval officer, Lieut. Carroll, received the Military GSM and clasp for Maida, while a few other officers of the Royal Navy and Royal Marines received the medal with the clasps for Guadaloupe, Martinique or Java, and these, naturally, are now very much sought after. Paradoxically, the clasps for Sahagun and Benevente alone are very much scarcer than the clasp inscribed Sahagun and Benevente, awarded to surviving veterans who had participated in both battles. The clasps are listed below in chronological order. Medals to officers rate a premium.

Comments: *Like the Naval GSM, this medal was not sanctioned till 1847 and awarded the following year. Unlike the Naval medal, however, the Military GSM was confined to land actions up to the defeat of Napoleon in 1814 and the conclusion of the war with the United States. The regiment is now having a bearing on price, with medals to the 52nd, 88th or 95th Foot worth a good premium.*

VALUE:

i.	Egypt	£850–1000	xxi.	Chateauguay	£3000–3500
ii.	Maida	£1200–1400	xxii.	Chrystler's Farm	£3000–3500
iii.	Roleia	£900–1000	xxiii.	Vittoria	£650–800
iv.	Vimiera	£800–900	xxiv.	Pyrenees	£750–850
v.	Sahagun	£1500–1800	xxv.	St Sebastian	£800–900
vi.	Benevente	£4500–5500	xxvi.	Nivelle	£650–800
vii.	Sahagun and Benevente	£1500–1800	xxvii.	Nive	£650–800
viii.	Corunna	£700–800	xxviii.	Orthes	£650–800
ix.	Martinique	£700–850	xxix.	Toulouse	£650–800
x.	Talavera	£700–850	2 clasps		£800–1000
xi.	Guadaloupe	£750–900	3 clasps		£1000–1200
xii.	Busaco	£750–900	4 clasps		£1200–1500
xiii.	Barrosa	£750–900	5 clasps		£1400–1800
xiv.	Fuentes D'Onor	£750–900	6 clasps		£1500–2000
xv.	Albuhera	£900–1100	7 clasps		£2000–2300
xvi.	Java	£750–900	8 clasps		£2200–2600
xvii.	Ciudad Rodrigo	£900–1100	9 clasps		£2800–3400
xviii.	Badajoz	£900–1100	10 clasps		£3000–4000
xix.	Salamanca	£800–1000	11 clasps		£3500–4500
xx.	Fort Detroit	£3000–3500	12 or more clasps		From £4800

Miniature **without clasp** £100–150, **for each clasp add £75+ depending on the action.**

99. WATERLOO MEDAL

Date: 1815.
Campaign: Waterloo 1815.
Branch of Service: British Army.
Ribbon: 38mm, crimson edged in dark blue.
Metal: Silver.
Size: 37mm.
Description: (Obverse) the profile of the Prince Regent; (reverse) the seated figure of Victory above a tablet simply inscribed WATERLOO with the date of the battle in the exergue.
Comments: *This was the first medal awarded and officially named to all ranks who took part in a particular campaign. It was also issued, however, to those who had taken part in one or more of the other battles of the campaign, at Ligny and Quatre Bras two days earlier. The ribbon was intended to be worn with an iron clip and split suspension ring but many recipients subsequently replaced these with a more practical silver mount which would not rust and spoil the uniform. Some 39,000 medals were issued. The value of a Waterloo medal depends to a large extent on the regiment of the recipient. Medals awarded to those formations which saw the heaviest action and bore the brunt of the losses are in the greatest demand, whereas medals named to soldiers in General Colville's reserve division which did not take part in the fighting, are the least highly rated.*

VALUE:
Heavy Cavalry	£2200–3000
Scots Greys	£3500–4000
Light Cavalry	£2000–2500
Royal Artillery	£1000–1200
Royal Horse Artillery	£1200–1500
Foot Guards	£1500–2500
1st, 27th, 28th, 30th, 42nd, 44th, 52nd, 73rd, 79th, 92nd, 95th Foot	£2500–3500
Other Foot regiments	£1500–2000
Colville's division (35th, 54th, 59th, 91st Foot)	£1200–1500
King's German Legion	£1000–1200
Miniature	
Original	£50–200
Modern copy	£15–30

100. BRUNSWICK MEDAL FOR WATERLOO

Date: 1815.
Campaign: Battle of Waterloo 1815.
Branch of Service: Brunswick troops.
Ribbon: Cream with light blue stripes towards the edges.
Metal: Bronze.
Description: (Obverse) Duke Friedrich Wilhelm of Brunswick who was killed in the battle; (reverse) a wreath of laurel and oak leaves enclosing the German text "Braunschweig Seinen Kriegern" (Brunswick to its warriors) and the names of Quatre Bras and Waterloo.
Comments: *The Prince Regent authorised this medal for issue to the contingent from the Duchy of Brunswick.*

VALUE: £300–350

101. HANOVERIAN MEDAL FOR WATERLOO

Date: 1815.
Campaign: Battle of Waterloo 1815.
Branch of Service: Hanoverian troops.
Ribbon: Crimson edged with light blue.
Metal: Silver.
Description: (Obverse) the Prince Regent, his name and title being rendered in German. (Reverse) a trophy of arms below the legend HANNOVERSCHER TAPFERKEIT (Hanoverian bravery), with the name and date of the battle wreathed in the centre.
Comments: *The Prince Regent authorised this medal on behalf of his father George III in his capacity as Elector of Hanover and this was conferred on survivors of the battle. Suspension was by iron clip and ring similar to the British Waterloo Medal.*

VALUE: £350–450   *Miniature*   £100–150

102. NASSAU MEDAL FOR WATERLOO

Date: 1815.
Campaign: Battle of Waterloo 1815.
Branch of Service: Nassau forces.
Ribbon: Dark blue edged in yellow.
Metal: Silver.
Size: 25mm.
Description: (Obverse) Duke Friedrich of Nassau; (reverse) the winged figure of Victory crowning a soldier with laurels, the date of the action being in the exergue.
Comments: *Friedrich Duke of Nassau distributed this medal on 23 December 1815 to all of his own troops who had been present at the battle.*

VALUE: £250–300

103. SAXE-GOTHA-ALTENBURG MEDAL

Date: 1815.
Campaign: Germany and Waterloo 1814-15.
Branch of Service: Saxe-Gotha-Altenburg Foreign Legion.
Ribbon: Green with black edges and gold stripes.
Metal: Gilt bronze or bronze.
Size: 42mm.
Description: (Obverse) a crown with the legend IM KAMPFE FUER DAS RECHT (in the struggle for the right); (reverse) an ornate rose motif with the name of the duchy and the dates of the campaign in roman numerals.
Comments: *Gilded medals were issued to officers, but other ranks received a bronze version.*

VALUE:
          Gilt-bronze   £300–350
          Bronze   £250–300

104. ARMY OF INDIA MEDAL

Date: 1851.

Campaigns: India 1803–26.

Branch of Service: British and HEIC troops.

Ribbon: 32mm pale blue.

Metal: Silver.

Size: 35mm.

Description: (Obverse) the Wyon profile of Queen Victoria; (reverse) the seated figure of Victory beside a palm tree, with a wreath in one hand and a laurel crown in the other. The medal is fitted with an ornamental scroll suspender.

Clasps: The medal was not awarded without a campaign clasp and, unusually, in multi-clasp medals, the last clasp awarded was mounted closest to the medal itself, so that the battle roll has to be read downwards. There were two dies of the reverse, leading to the long- or short-hyphen varieties, both of comparable value. In all, some 4500 medals were awarded, but there is a very wide divergence between the commonest and rarest bars. Multi-clasp medals are rare, and medals awarded to Europeans are much scarcer than those to Indian troops.

Comments: *The last of the medals authorised in connection with the Napoleonic Wars, it was instituted and paid for by the Honourable East India Company in March 1851 for award to surviving veterans of the battles and campaigns in India and Burma between 1803 and 1826. Despite the dates 1799–1826 in the exergue, the medal was in fact awarded for service in one or other of four wars: the Second Mahratta War (1803–4), the Nepal War (1814–16), the Pindaree or Third Mahratta War (1817–18) and the Burmese War (1824–26), together with the siege of Bhurtpoor (1825–26). The medal is scarce, and examples with the clasps for the Second Mahratta War are much sought after, partly because few veterans were still alive 48 years after the event to claim their medals, and partly because of the war's association with Arthur Wellesley, the Duke of Wellington, who died in the very year in which the medal was awarded. Medals to the Royal Navy with the Ava clasp are very rare.*

Rev. die a, short hyphen

Rev. die b, long hyphen

VALUE:

Prices for medals bearing the following clasps are for European recipients. Medals to Indians are generally less expensive.

i.	Allighur (66)	£3000–3500
ii.	Battle of Delhi (40)	£3500–4500
iii.	Assye (87)	£3000–3500
iv.	Asseerghur (48)	£3500–4500
v.	Laswarree (100)	£3000–3500
vi.	Argaum (126)	£2500–3000
vii.	Gawilghur (110)	£3000–3500
viii.	Defence of Delhi (5)	Rare
ix.	Battle of Deig (47)	£3500–4500
x.	Capture of Deig (103)	£3000–3500
xi.	Nepaul (505)	£1500–1800
xii.	Kirkee (5)	Rare
xiii.	Poona (75)	£3000–3500
xiv.	Kirkee and Poona (88)	£3000–3500
xv.	Seetabuldee (2)	Rare
xvi.	Nagpore (155)	£2500–3000
xvii.	Seetabuldee and Nagpore (21)	£6000–8000
xviii.	Maheidpoor (75)	£3000–3500
xix.	Corygaum (4)	£6000–10,000
xx.	Ava (2325)	£1000–1200
xxi.	Bhurtpoor (1059)	£1200–1500
	2 clasps (300)	£2500–3500
	3 clasps (150)	£6000–8000
	4 clasps (23)	£8000–10,000
	5 or more clasps (10 x 5, 2 x 6, 1 x 7)	Rare
	Glazed gilt specimen	£400

*Miniature**

One clasp Ava	£200–250
Further clasps	£100–150 each

Note there are many silver reproductions and clasps on the market, value £10–20.

105. GHUZNEE MEDAL

Date: 1839.
Campaign: Ghuznee 1839.
Branch of Service: British and HEIC forces.
Ribbon: 35mm half crimson, half dark green (originally green and yellow)
Metal: Silver.
Size: 37mm.
Description: (Obverse) the impressive gateway of the fortress of Ghuznee; (reverse) a mural crown enclosed in a laurel wreath with the date of capture.
Comments: *This was the second medal awarded for a particular campaign (after Waterloo) and was granted to both British and Indian troops who took part in the assault on Ghuznee in July 1839 which brought the first Afghan War to a close, overthrew the pro-Russian Dost Mohamed and restored Shah Soojah who instituted the Order of the Dooranie Empire (awarded to British generals and field officers) in appreciation. The Ghuznee medal was issued unnamed by the Honourable East India Company, but many recipients subsequently had their names impressed or engraved in various styles. No clasps were issued officially, but unauthorised clasps are occasionally encountered.*

VALUE:

British recipient	**£500–600**
Indian recipient	**£300–400**
Unnamed as issued	**£420–500**
Miniature	*£150–300*

106. ST. JEAN D'ACRE MEDAL

Date: 1840.
Campaign: Syria 1840.
Branch of Service: Royal Navy, Royal Marines and British Army.
Ribbon: Red with white edges.
Metal: Gold, silver or copper (bronzed).
Size: 30mm.
Description: (Obverse) a fortress flying the Ottoman flag, with six five-pointed stars round the top. A commemorative inscription and date in Arabic appear at the foot; (reverse) the Toughra of the Sultan in a laurel wreath.
Comments: *Awarded by the Sultan of Turkey to British, Austrian and Turkish forces under Sir Charles Napier, taking part in the liberation of this important city on the Syrian coast after eight years of Egyptian occupation. The medal has a plain ring suspension. The clasp "Syria" to the Naval GSM was awarded in 1848 in respect to this operation, and this medal generally accompanies the St Jean d'Acre medal.*

VALUE:		*Miniature*
Gold (captains and field officers)	£500–700	—
Silver (junior officers)	£200–250	£150–200
Copper (petty officers, NCOs and other ranks)	£80–120	—

107. CANDAHAR, GHUZNEE, CABUL MEDAL

Date: 1842.

Campaign: Afghanistan 1841–42.

Branch of Service: British and HEIC troops.

Ribbon: 40mm watered silk of red, white, yellow, white and blue.

Metal: Silver.

Size: 35mm.

Description: Although the medals have a uniform obverse, a profile of the Queen captioned VICTORIA VINDEX, reverses are inscribed with the names of individual battles, or combinations thereof, within wreaths surmounted by a crown.

Comments: *The Honourable East India Company instituted this series of medals in 1842 for award to both HEIC and British troops who took part in the First Afghan War. The issue of this medal to units of the British Army, to Europeans serving in the Company's forces, and to Indian troops is further complicated by the fact that unnamed medals are generally common. In addition, the medal for Cabul is known in two versions, with the inscription CABUL or CABVL, the latter being a major rarity as only fifteen were issued. Beware of modern copies of the Candahar and Cabul medals.*

VALUE:	Imperial Regiments	Indian Units	Unnamed
i. Candahar	£600–650	£400–500	£300–350
ii. Cabul	£400–500	£250–350	£300–350
iii. Cabvl (15)	Rare	Rare	Rare
iv. Ghuznee/Cabul	£600–650	£350–450	£350–400
v. Candahar/Ghuznee/ Cabul	£650–700	£350–400	£350–400
Miniature	from £250 (depending on reverse)		

108. JELLALABAD MEDALS

Type 2 rev.

Type 1 obv.

Date: 1842.

Campaign: Afghanistan 1841-42.

Branch of Service: British and HEIC forces.

Ribbon: 44mm watered silk red, white, yellow, white and blue.

Metal: Silver.

Size: 39mm and 35mm.

Description: There are two different types of this medal, awarded by the HEIC to surviving defenders of the fortress of Jellalabad between 12 November 1841 and 7 April 1842. The first, struck in Calcutta, has a mural crown and JELLALABAD on the obverse, with the date of the relief of the garrison on the reverse; the second type shows the Wyon profile of Victoria (obverse) and the winged Victory with mountain scenery in the background and JELLALABAD VII APRIL round the top and the year in roman numerals in the exergue (reverse).

Comment: *The first type, struck in Calcutta, was considered to be unsuitable and holders were invited to exchange their medals for the second, more attractive, issue which was produced in London, although very few recipients took up the offer. The latter type was also awarded to the next of kin of soldiers killed in action.*

VALUE:	Imperial Regiments	Indian Units	Unnamed	*Miniature*
i. First type (Crown)	£750–850	£450–550	£400–500	£350–400
ii. Second type (Victory)	£1200–1500	—	£450–550	£250–350

109. MEDAL FOR THE DEFENCE OF KELAT-I-GHILZIE

Date: 1842.
Campaign: Afghanistan 1842.
Branch of Service: European and native troops, HEIC.
Ribbon: 40mm watered silk red, white, yellow, white and blue.
Metal: Silver.
Size: 36mm.
Description: (Obverse) a shield bearing the name of the fort, surmounted by a mural crown and encircled by laurels; (reverse) a trophy of arms above a tablet inscribed INVICTA (unbeaten) and the date in roman numerals.
Comments: *Awarded to those who took part in the defence of the fort at Kelat-i-Ghilzie in May 1842, it is the rarest medal of the First Afghan War. No British imperial regiments took part, but 55 Europeans in the Company's service received the medal. It was also awarded to 877 native troops (including a contingent supplied by Shah Soojah) but few of their medals appear to have survived.*

VALUE:

European recipients	£4500–5500
Indian recipients	£1800–2500
Unnamed	£800–1200
Miniature	£300–400

110. CHINA WAR MEDAL

Issued reverse

Date: 1842.
Campaign: China 1841-42.
Branch of Service: British and HEIC forces.
Ribbon: 39mm crimson with yellow edges.
Metal: Silver.
Size: 36mm.
Description: The medal has the usual Wyon obverse, but the reverse was to have shown a British lion with its forepaws on a dragon. This was deemed to be offensive to the Chinese and was replaced by an oval shield bearing the royal arms and a palm tree flanked by a capstan, anchor and naval cannon representing the Royal Navy (left) and a field gun, drum and regimental flag representing the Army (right), with the Latin motto ARMIS EXPOSCERE PACEM (to pray for peace by force of arms) round the top and CHINA 1842 in the exergue.
Comments: *Originally intended for issue to all ranks of the Honourable East India Company, it was subsequently awarded by the British government in 1843 to all who had taken part in the campaign in China popularly known as the First Opium War which ended with the seizure of Nanking.*

VALUE:

Royal Navy	£400–500
Indian and Bengal marine units	£400–500
British imperial regiments	£400–500
Indian Army	£350–450
Specimens of the original reverse	From £600–800
Miniature	£150–250

111. SCINDE MEDAL

Date: 1843.
Campaign: Scinde 1843.
Branch of Service: HEIC forces and 22nd Foot.
Ribbon: 44mm watered silk red, white, yellow, white and blue.
Metal: Silver.
Size: 36mm.
Description: The usual Wyon profile obverse was married to three different reverse types showing a crowned laurel wreath inscribed with the name of one or two campaigns and the date.
Comments: *Authorised in September 1843, this silver medal marked Sir Charles Napier's conquest of Scinde. The two major battles in the campaign, at Meeanee and Hyderabad, accomplished the complete rout of the forces of the Amirs of Scinde. The medals were originally issued with steel suspenders but the commanding officer of the 22nd Foot had the medals awarded to his men fitted with silver suspenders, at his own expense. Medals to the Indus Flotilla are particularly sought after by collectors.*

VALUE:

	22nd Foot	Indian units	HEIC ships
i. Meeanee	£750–950	£350–400	£1100–1500 (38)
ii. Hyderabad	£750–850	£350–400	£1100–1500 (52)
iii. Meeanee/Hyderabad	£650–850	£350–400	
Miniature	£150–250		

112. GWALIOR STAR

Date: 1843.
Campaign: Gwalior 1843.
Branch of Service: British and HEIC forces.
Ribbon: 44mm watered silk red, white, yellow, white and blue.
Metals: Bronze, with a silver centre.
Size: Max. width 45mm; max. height 52mm.
Description: Six-pointed bronze star with a silver centre star. The silver stars in the centre bear the name of one or other of the battles and the date 29 December 1843 on which both battles were fought. The plain reverse bears the name and regiment of the recipient.
Comments: *Bronze from guns captured at the battles of Maharajpoor and Punniar during the Gwalior campaign was used in the manufacture of these stars, thus anticipating the production of the Victoria Cross in the same manner. They were presented by the Indian government to all ranks who took part in these actions. When first issued, these stars were fitted with hooks to be worn like a breast decoration, but later ornate bar or ring suspensions were fitted to individual fancy and worn with the standard Indian ribbon of the period.*

VALUE:

			Miniature
i. Maharajpoor	£450–500		£200–250
ii. Punniar	£450–550		£250–350

Awards to Indian recipients are usually somewhat less.

113. SUTLEJ MEDAL

Date: 1846.

Campaign: Sutlej 1845-46.

Branch of Service: British and HEIC forces.

Ribbon: Dark blue with crimson edges.

Metal: Silver.

Size: 36mm.

Description: (Obverse) Wyon profile of Queen Victoria; (reverse) standing figure of Victory holding aloft a laurel crown, with a pile of captured weapons at her feet. The legend ARMY OF THE SUTLEJ appears round the top. The medal was fitted with an ornamental scroll suspender.

Clasps: Mounted above the suspender with roses between: Ferozeshuhur, Aliwal or Sobraon.

Comments: *The practice of issuing medals inscribed with different battles now gave way to the style of medals with specific battle or campaign clasps which set the precedent for the Naval and Military GSMs and later awards. As a compromise, however, the exergue of the reverse bears the name and date of the action for which the medal was first granted, and thus several different types are known.*

VALUE:	British regiments	Europeans in HEIC units	Indian units
i. Moodkee	£350–400	£300–450	£300–350
Moodkee 1 clasp	£450–500	£400–500	£350–400
Moodkee 2 clasps	£650–750	£600–700	£450–550
Moodkee 3 clasps	£850–950	£800–900	£700–900
ii. Ferozeshuhur	£350–400	£300–350	£300–350
Ferozeshuhur 1 clasp	£450–500	£400–450	£350–400
Ferozeshuhur 2 clasps	£650–750	£600–700	£450–550
iii. Aliwal	£300–350	£300–350	£300–350
Aliwal 1 clasp	£450–500	£400–500	£350–450
iv. Sobraon	£350–450	£350–400	£350–450
Glazed gilt specimen	£300–400		
Miniature	£100–150, for each clasp add £50		

114. PUNJAB MEDAL

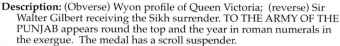

Date: 1849.

Campaign: Punjab 1848-49.

Branch of Service: British and HEIC forces.

Ribbon: Dark blue with yellow stripes towards the edges.

Metal: Silver.

Size: 36mm.

Description: (Obverse) Wyon profile of Queen Victoria; (reverse) Sir Walter Gilbert receiving the Sikh surrender. TO THE ARMY OF THE PUNJAB appears round the top and the year in roman numerals in the exergue. The medal has a scroll suspender.

Clasps: Mooltan, Chilianwala, Goojerat. Unusually the clasps read downwards from top to bottom

Comments: *This medal was granted to troops taking part in the campaigns which ended in the annexation of the Punjab. Unlike the Sutlej medal, however, this silver medal had a standard design. Large numbers of this medal were awarded to native troops, however many were melted down and therefore surprisingly few remain on the market in comparison with medals to European recipients.*

VALUE:	British units	Europeans in HEIC units	Indian units
No clasp	£250–300	£250–300	£200–250
i. Mooltan	£350–400	£300–350	£300–350
ii. Chilianwala	£350–400	£300–350	£300–350
iii. Goojerat	£350–400	£300–350	£300–350
iv. Mooltan/Goojerat	£500–650	£500–600	£400–500
v. Chilianwala/Goojerat	£450–650	£500–600	£400–500
24th Foot casualty at Chilianwala	£1000–1400	—	—
Glazed gilt specimen	£250–350		
Miniature	£75–100, for each clasp add £25		

115. SOUTH AFRICA MEDAL

Date: 1854.

Campaigns: Southern Africa 1834–53.

Branch of Service: Royal Navy and Army.

Ribbon: Gold with broad and narrow deep blue stripes towards each end.

Metal: Silver.

Size: 36mm.

Description: (Obverse) Wyon profile of Queen Victoria; (reverse) an African lion crouching in submission beside a protea shrub, the date 1853 being in the exergue.

Clasps: None.

Comments: *Authorised in November 1854, this medal was awarded in respect of three campaigns in southern Africa: 1834–35, 1846–47 and 1850–53, but as the medal was issued with a standard reverse and no campaign clasps it is impossible to tell when and where the recipient served without reference to the medal rolls. The majority of recipients were British troops but several hundred sailors of the Royal Navy also received the medal and a much smaller number of local forces. Of particular interest are medals awarded to men who survived the sinking of the troopship* Birkenhead *on its way to the Eastern Cape from Simons Town.*

VALUE:

British Army	£400–450
Royal Navy	£350–450
HMS *Birkenhead*	From £800
Local forces	£350–450
Miniature	£50–65

116. SIR HARRY SMITH'S MEDAL FOR GALLANTRY

Date: 1851.

Campaign: Eighth Frontier War 1850-51.

Branch of Service: Cape Mounted Rifles.

Ribbon: Dark blue with crimson edges.

Metal: Silver.

Size: 34mm.

Description: (Obverse) British lion passant gardant with a laurel wreath over its head; date 1851 in the exergue. (Reverse) PRESENTED BY round top and FOR GALLANTRY IN THE FIELD round the foot. HIS EXCELLENCY SIR H. G. SMITH and the name of the recipient appear across the centre.

Comments: *Sir Harry Smith (1787–1860) served with distinction in the Frontier War of 1834–35, gained his KCB in the Gwalior campaign and a baronetcy for his decisive victory at Aliwal in the Sikh War. In 1847 he returned to South Africa as governor of Cape Colony. Although short of troops he conducted the eighth Frontier War (1850–53) with great resourcefulness but was recalled to England in 1852 before the Xhosas had been subdued. Harrismith in the Orange Free State was named in his honour, while Ladysmith in Natal was named after his beautiful and spirited Spanish wife Juanita, the forces' sweetheart of her day. Sir Harry had this medal struck at his own expense and awarded to troopers of the Cape Mounted Rifles who took part in the epic ride through the enemy lines from Fort Cox to Kingwilliamstown in 1851. Only 31 medals were presented, of which 22 are believed to be still extant.*

VALUE:

Unnamed/named	£1500–1800
Named	£3000–4500
Miniature	One example known

117. INDIA GENERAL SERVICE MEDAL

Date: 1854.
Campaigns: Indian 1854-95.
Branch of Service: British and Indian forces.
Ribbon: Three crimson and two dark blue stripes of equal width.
Metal: Silver or bronze.
Size: 36mm.
Description: (Obverse) Wyon profile of Queen Victoria; (reverse) Victory crowning a semi-nude seated warrior.
Clasps: 24 (see below).
Comments: *This medal was the first of five general service medals issued to cover minor campaigns in India. It was instituted in 1854 and continued for forty-one years, retaining the original Wyon profile of Queen Victoria throughout the entire period. Although the medal itself is quite common, some of its clasps are very rare, notably* Kachin Hills 1892–93 *awarded to the Yorkshire Regiment and* Chin Hills 1892–93 *awarded to the Norfolk Regiment. The maximum number of clasps to one medal recorded is seven. At first the medal was awarded in silver to all ranks regardless of race or branch of the services, but from 1885 onwards it was issued in bronze to native support personnel such as bearers, sweepers and drivers.*

VALUE:

		RN/RM	British Army	Indian Army	Bronze
i.	Pegu	£200–250	£200–250	—	—
ii.	Persia	—	£300–350	£200–250	—
iii.	North West Frontier	—	£200–250	£150–200	—
iv.	Umbeyla	—	£200–250	£150–200	—
v.	Bhootan	—	£200–250	£150–200	—
vi.	Looshai	—	—	£300–400	—
vii.	Perak	£200–250	£200–250	£150–200	—
viii.	Jowaki 1877–78	—	£200–250	£150–200	—
ix.	Naga 1879–80	—	—	£180–250	—
x.	Burma 1885–87	£140–180	£150–180	£100–120	£100–120
xi.	Sikkim 1888	—	£250–300	£120–150	£120–150
xii.	Hazara 1888	—	£200–250	£120–150	£120–150
xiii.	Burma 1887–89	—	£200–250	£100–120	£100–120
xiv.	Burma 1887–9	—	£150–200	—	—
xv.	Chin Lushai 1889–90	—	£220–275	£150–180	£150–180
xvi.	Lushai 1889-92	—	£400–450	£180–250	£400–500
xvii.	Samana 1891	—	£200–250	£120–150	£120–150
xviii.	Hazara 1891	—	£200–250	£120–150	£120–150
xix.	NE Frontier 1891	—	£200–250	£120–150	£120–150
xx.	Hunza 1891	—	—	£200–350	£800–1000
xxi.	Burma 1889–92	—	£180–220	£120–150	£120–150
xxii.	Chin Hills 1892-93	—	£600–800	£180–250	£800–1000
xxiii.	Kachin Hills 1892-93	—	£700–900	£300–400	Rare
xxiv.	Waziristan 1894-95	—	£200–250	£120–150	£120–150

Miniature   £20–30, for each clasp add £10–15 (*Hunza, Chin Hills* and *Kachin Hills* clasps are rare)

118. BALTIC MEDAL

Date: 1856.

Campaign: Baltic Sea 1854–55.

Branch of Service: Royal Navy, Royal Marines and Royal Sappers and Miners.

Ribbon: Yellow with light blue edges.

Metal: Silver.

Size: 36mm.

Description: (Obverse) Wyon profile of Queen Victoria; (reverse) Britannia seated on a plinth decorated by a cannon, with a coastal scene in the background and BALTIC round the top.

Comments: *Authorised in 1856, this medal was granted to officers and men of the Royal Navy and Royal Marines for operations against Russia in the Baltic at the same time as the war in the Crimea. It was also awarded to about 100 members of the Royal Sappers and Miners engaged in the demolition of Russian fortifications of Bomarsund and Sveaborg. Medals were generally issued unnamed but often privately named afterwards, the exception being medals to the Sappers and Miners which were officially impressed.*

VALUE:

Unnamed	£140–150
Privately named	£140–150
Officially impressed to Sappers and Miners	£800–1000
Miniature	£40–50

119. CRIMEA MEDAL

Date: 1854.

Campaign: Crimea 1854–56.

Branch of Service: British Army, Navy and Marines.

Ribbon: Pale blue with yellow edges.

Metal: Silver.

Size: 36mm.

Description: (Obverse) Wyon profile of Queen Victoria; (reverse) a Roman soldier, armed with circular shield and short sword, being crowned by a flying Victory.

Clasps: Unusually ornate, being shaped like oak leaves with acorn finials: Alma, Inkerman, Azoff, Balaklava, Sebastopol, but the maximum found on any medal is four. Recipients of the Balaklava clasp were invariably entitled to other clasps. Unofficial clasps for Traktir, Mamelon Vert, Malakoff, Mer d'Azoff and Kinburn are sometimes found on medals awarded to French troops.

Comments: *Medals may be found unnamed, unofficially or regimentally named, or officially impressed. Medals awarded to participants in the most famous actions of the war—the Thin Red Line (93rd Foot) and the Charge of the Light and Heavy Brigades—rate a very high premium. The prices quoted are for medals named to the Army. Clasps awarded to the Royal Navy and Royal Marines (Azoff, Balaklava, Inkerman, Sebastopol) rate a good premium, especially those named to personnel on board HM Ships London, Niger, Rodney and Wasp.* No fewer than 19 VCs were awarded for gallantry at Inkerman alone, the largest number for a single action.*

VALUE :	Unnamed	Engraved	Regimentally impressed	Officially impressed Army
No clasp	£100–120	£100–110	£120–140	£140–160
i. Alma	£140–160	£140–180	£160–180	£180–220
ii. Inkerman	£140–160	£140–180	£140–160	£180–220
iii. Azoff	£180–220	£230–280	—	£450–500
iv. Balaklava	£160–180	£150–180	£180–220	£250–300
93rd Foot*	—	£400–500	£700–800	£1000–1200
Heavy Brigade*	—	£600–800	£900–1200	£1500–2000
Light Brigade (Charger)*	—	£1500–1800	£2500–3500	£8000–10,000
v. Sebastopol	£130–140	£140–160	£180–200	£220–280
2 clasps	£180–200	£180–220	£180–250	£250–350
3 clasps	£250–280	£250–300	£280–350	£400–500
4 clasps	£350–400	£300–400	£350–450	£600–800
Miniature	£20–30, for each clasp add £15			

**It is always difficult to price scarce or rare medals such as those marked as we have seen many engraved or Depot-style impressing that were probably named in the past 30 to 40 years. Also an engraved Crimea, together with a Mutiny and/or LS&GC would be worth considerably more than the prices indicated. Buyer beware!*

120. TURKISH CRIMEA MEDAL

Date: 1855.
Campaign: Crimea 1855-56.
Branch of Service: British, French and Sardinian forces.
Ribbon: Crimson with green edges.
Metal: Silver.
Size: 36mm (originally 18mm wide).
Description: (Obverse) a cannon, weapons and the four Allied flags with the name and date in the exergue; (reverse) the Toughra and Arabic date according to the Moslem calendar.
Clasps: None.
Comments: *Instituted by the Sultan of Turkey, this silver medal was conferred on troops of the three Allies who fought in the Crimea. The obverse types differed in the arrangement of the flags, corrsponding with the inscription in English, French or Italian in the exergue. Although the medals were intended to be issued to British, French and Sardinian troops respectively, they were issued haphazardly due to most of the British version being lost at sea. They were unnamed, but many were privately engraved or impressed later. Dangerous copies, emanating from the West Country of the UK, are known to be circulating.*

VALUE:		*Miniature*
i. **CRIMEA (British Issue)**	£85–100	£35–40
ii. **LA CRIMEE (French Issue)**	£150–185	Rare
iii. **LA CRIMEA (Sardinia Issue)**	£80–90	£25–30

121. INDIAN MUTINY MEDAL

Date: 1858.
Campaign: Sepoy mutiny, India 1857-58.
Branch of Service: British Army, Navy and Indian forces. It was also awarded to many civilians who took part in suppressing the Mutiny.
Ribbon: White with two red stripes.
Metal: Silver.
Size: 36mm.
Description: (Obverse) Wyon profile of Queen Victoria; (reverse) the standing figure of Britannia bestowing victor's laurels, with the British lion alongside. INDIA appears round the top with the dates 1857-1858 in the exergue.
Clasps: Delhi, Defence of Lucknow, Relief of Lucknow, Lucknow, Central India. The maximum recorded for a single medal is four (Bengal Artillery) or three (imperial troops, 9th Lancers).
Comments: *This medal was awarded to troops who took part in operations to quell the Sepoy mutiny which had been the immediate cause of the uprising, although it also served to focus attention on the Honourable East India Company's conduct of affairs and led directly to the transfer of the administration of India to the Crown. Medals with the clasp for the defence of Lucknow awarded to the original defenders rate a considerable premium, as do medals awarded to members of the Naval Brigade which witnessed most of the fighting in the mopping-up operations. Medals to Indian recipients although scarcer on the market, generally bring a little less than their British counterparts. Four-clasp medals to the Bengal Artillery bring from £800 if verified.*

VALUE:

		British Navy	**British Army**	*Miniature*
	No clasp	£600–800*	£220–250	£15–20
i.	Delhi	—	£300–350	£25–30
ii.	Defence of Lucknow			
	original defender	—	£1200–1500	£45–50
	first relief force	—	£550–650	
iii.	Relief of Lucknow	£700–800	§£300–350	£30–40
iv.	Lucknow	£700–800	£300–350	£25–30
v.	Central India	—	£300–350	£25–30, add
	2 clasps	£700–800	£450–550	£10 for each
	3 clasps (9th Lancers)	—	£900–1200	additional clasp
	4 clasps (Bengal Arty.)	—	£1800–2000	

66 medals to HMS Shannon *and 253 to HMS* Pearl.

122. SECOND CHINA WAR MEDAL

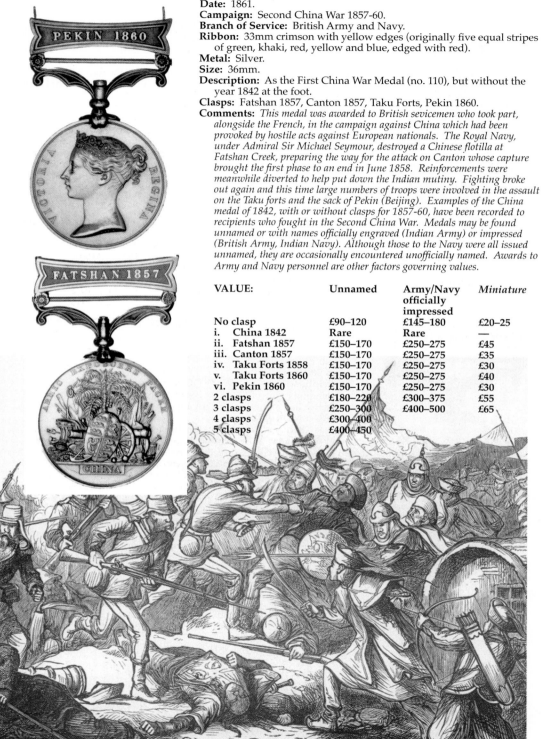

Date: 1861.
Campaign: Second China War 1857-60.
Branch of Service: British Army and Navy.
Ribbon: 33mm crimson with yellow edges (originally five equal stripes of green, khaki, red, yellow and blue, edged with red).
Metal: Silver.
Size: 36mm.
Description: As the First China War Medal (no. 110), but without the year 1842 at the foot.
Clasps: Fatshan 1857, Canton 1857, Taku Forts, Pekin 1860.
Comments: *This medal was awarded to British sevicemen who took part, alongside the French, in the campaign against China which had been provoked by hostile acts against European nationals. The Royal Navy, under Admiral Sir Michael Seymour, destroyed a Chinese flotilla at Fatshan Creek, preparing the way for the attack on Canton whose capture brought the first phase to an end in June 1858. Reinforcements were meanwhile diverted to help put down the Indian mutiny. Fighting broke out again and this time large numbers of troops were involved in the assault on the Taku forts and the sack of Pekin (Beijing). Examples of the China medal of 1842, with or without clasps for 1857-60, have been recorded to recipients who fought in the Second China War. Medals may be found unnamed or with names officially engraved (Indian Army) or impressed (British Army, Indian Navy). Although those to the Navy were all issued unnamed, they are occasionally encountered unofficially named. Awards to Army and Navy personnel are other factors governing values.*

VALUE:	Unnamed	Army/Navy officially impressed	Miniature
No clasp	£90–120	£145–180	£20–25
i. China 1842	Rare	Rare	—
ii. Fatshan 1857	£150–170	£250–275	£45
iii. Canton 1857	£150–170	£250–275	£35
iv. Taku Forts 1858	£150–170	£250–275	£30
v. Taku Forts 1860	£150–170	£250–275	£40
vi. Pekin 1860	£150–170	£250–275	£30
2 clasps	£180–220	£300–375	£55
3 clasps	£250–300	£400–500	£65
4 clasps	£300–400		
5 clasps	£400–450		

123. NEW ZEALAND MEDALS

Date: 1869.

Campaigns: First and Second Maori Wars 1845–47 and 1860–66.

Branch of Service: Army, Navy and local volunteers.

Ribbon: Blue with a central orange stripe.

Metal: Silver.

Size: 36mm.

Description: (Obverse) Veiled head of Queen Victoria. (Reverse) Date of service in a wreath, with NEW ZEALAND round the top and VIRTUTIS HONOR (honour of valour) round the foot. Suspender ornamented with New Zealand fern fronds.

Comments: *These medals were unusual in having the recipient's dates of service die-struck on the centre of the reverse, though medals were also issued without dates. As the medal was only awarded to surviving veterans, the numbers issued in respect of the earlier conflict are understandably small. Many of the dates are very scarce, especially those issued to naval personnel in the first war. Only naval personnel received dated medals in the first war.*

VALUE:		**Army**	**Navy/Royal Marines**
First war			
i.	Undated	£350–400	—
ii.	1845–46 (155)	—	£400–450
iii.	1845–47 (36)	—	£650–850
iv.	1846–47 (69)	—	£500–600
v.	1846 (10)	—	£800–1000
vi.	1847 (20)	£800–1000	£800–1000
Second war			
vii.	Undated	£300–350	—
viii.	1860	£700–800	Rare
ix.	1860-61	£450–500	£350–400
x.	1860-63	From £1550	—
xi.	1860-64	£350–450	—
xii.	1860-65	£350–450	—
xiii.	1860-66	£350–450	—
xiv.	1861	Rare	—
xv.	1861-63	Rare	—
xvi.	1861-64	£350–450	—
xvii.	1861-65	Rare	—
xviii.	1861-66	£350–450	—
xix.	1862-66	Rare	—
xx.	1863	£400–450	Rare
xxi.	1863-64	£400–450	£450–550
xxii.	1863-65	£350–450	Scarce
xxiii.	1863-66	£350–450	Rare
xxiv.	1864	£350–450	Rare
xxv.	1864-65	£350–450	—
xxvi.	1864-66	£350–450	—
xxvii.	1865	£350–450	£400–450
xxviii.	1865-66	£350–450	—
xxix.	1866	£350–450	—

Miniature		
Undated	£60–65	
Dated	£80+	

124. ABYSSINIAN WAR MEDAL

Date: 1869.
Campaign: Abyssinia (Ethiopia) 1867–68.
Branch of Service: Royal Navy, British and Indian Armies.
Ribbon: Red with broad white edges.
Metal: Silver.
Size: 33mm diameter.
Description: (Obverse) the veiled portrait of Victoria framed by a zigzag pattern with floral ornament alternating with the letters of the name ABYSSINIA. The recipient's name and unit were embossed in the centre of the reverse except most to Indian troops which were impressed. Suspension is by a ring via a large crown standing proud from the top of the medal.
Clasps: None.
Comments: *The imprisonment of British subjects by King Theodore of Abyssinia precipitated a punitive expedition under General Sir Robert Napier involving ships of the Royal Navy, a naval brigade and troops of the British and Indian armies. Because casualties were unusually light (only two killed and 27 wounded), medals from this campaign are not so highly rated as those from other nineteenth century wars.*

VALUE:

British troops	£350–400
Royal Navy	£350–400
RN Rocket Brigade	£550–650
Indian troops	£220–280
Miniature	£55–65

125. CANADA GENERAL SERVICE MEDAL

Date: 1899.
Campaign: Canada 1866–70.
Branch of Service: Royal Navy, British Army and Canadian units.
Ribbon: Three equal stripes of orange-red, white and orange-red.
Metal: Silver.
Size: 36mm.
Description: (Obverse) crowned and veiled Old Head bust of Queen Victoria by Sir Thomas Brock (reflecting the very late issue of the medal). (Reverse) Canadian flag surrounded by maple leaves.
Clasps: Fenian Raid 1866, Fenian Raid 1870, Red River 1870.
Comments: *This medal was not authorised until January 1899, thirty years after the event, and was issued by the Canadian government to British and Canadian local forces who took part in operations to put down the Fenian raids of 1866 and 1870 and the Red River rebellion of the latter year. Of the 16,100 medals awarded, 15,000 went to local forces. Naval medals command a premium.*

VALUE:

	Canadian forces	British Army	Royal Navy	*Miniature*
i. Fenian Raid 1866	£275–300	£350–400	£350–400	£60
ii. Fenian Raid 1870	£275–300	£350–400	£350–450	£65
iii. Red River 1870	£1000–1500	£1500–2000	£1000–1500	£85
2 clasps	£350–450	—	—	£80
3 clasps	Rare	—	—	—

126. ASHANTEE MEDAL

Date: 1874.

Campaign: Gold Coast 1873–74.

Branch of Service: Royal Navy, Army and native troops.

Ribbon: Orange with black stripes at the sides and two narrow black stripes towards the centre.

Metal: Silver.

Size: 36mm.

Description: The obverse and reverse are similar to the East and West Africa Medal of 1887–1900, differing solely in thickness and the method of naming. The veiled profile of Victoria graces the obverse while the reverse, designed by Sir Edwin Poynter, shows a skirmish in the jungle between British soldiers and Ashantee warriors.

Clasps: Coomassie.

Comments: *All ranks who took part in operations against King Kalkali of Ashantee, Gold Coast, were awarded this medal, approved in June 1874. The campaign lasted only four weeks but was fought with great ferocity and resulted in the award of four VCs. There was also a very high incidence of sickness and disease among the troops, notably the naval contingent. Unusually the medals are named in engraved capitals filled in with black.*

VALUE:

	Navy	Army	Natives	*Miniature*
No clasp	£240–280	£240–280	£180–220	£45–50
i. Coomassie	£400–450	£450–500	£280–350	£65–70

127. SOUTH AFRICA MEDAL

Date: 1879.

Campaign: South Africa 1877-79.

Branch of Service: Royal Navy, Army and colonial units.

Ribbon: As no. 115.

Metal: Silver.

Size: 36mm.

Description: The same design as no. 115, except that the date 1853 in the exergue is replaced by a Zulu shield and four crossed assegais.

Clasps: 1877, 1877–8, 1877–9, 1877–8–9, 1878, 1878–9, 1879.

Comments: *The campaign began in 1877 with an attack on the Fingoes by the Galeka and Gaika tribes and culminated in the showdown between the Zulus and the British when Lord Chelmsford's column was annihilated at Isandhlwana. When the 3000 Zulus advanced on Rorke's Drift, however, they were checked with heavy losses by a tiny garrison of 139 men. During the defence no fewer than eleven VCs were won—a very large number for a single action. The campaign concluded with the defeat of Dinizulu and his warriors at Ulundi.*

VALUE:

		Navy	Army	Colonial	*Miniature*
	No clasp	£280–300	£280–300	£220–250	£25
i.	1877	—	Rare	£1500–1800	—
ii.	1877–8	£500–600	£325–350	£300–350	£50
iii.	1877–9	—	Unique	£4500–6000	—
iv.	1877–8–9	£450–550	£380–450	£300–380	£35
v.	1878	—	£300–350	£250–300	£50–60
vi.	1878–9	—	£350–450	£350–380	£50–60
vii.	1879	£300–350	£375–450	£350–380	£40–50

Isandhlwana casualty	£4500–5500
Rorke's Drift participant	£15,000–18,000

128. AFGHANISTAN MEDAL

Date: 1881.
Campaign: Afghanistan 1878–80.
Branch of Service: British and Indian Armies.
Ribbon: Dark green with broad crimson edges.
Metal: Silver.
Size: 36mm.
Description: (Obverse) veiled profile of Queen Victoria. (Reverse) a column on the march, with an elephant carrying cannon. The dates 1878–79–80 appear in the exergue.
Clasps: Ali Musjid, Peiwar Kotal, Charasia, Kabul, Ahmed Kel, Kandahar. Maximum number of clasps per medal is four.
Comments: *This medal was awarded to all who took part in the campaigns against Afghanistan known as the Second Afghan War. In 1877 the Amir refused to accept a British resident and the following year raised an army which began harrassing the Indian frontier. A treaty with Russia, however, granting it protective rights in Afghanistan, precipitated an armed response from Britain. In 1880 General Roberts led a column from Kabul to Kandahar to relieve General Burrows and the resulting battle led to the defeat of the Afghans and the conclusion of the war. Medals awarded to the 66th Foot (Berkshire regiment) and E Battery of B Brigade, Royal Artillery rate a high premium as these units sustained the heaviest casualties at the battle of Maiwand in July 1880.*

VALUE:	British units	Indian units	*Miniature*
No clasp silver	£140–175	£90–125	£20
i. Ali Musjid	£250–280	£180–220	£30
ii. Peiwar Kotal	£250–280	£180–220	£30–40
iii. Charasia	£250–280	£180–220	£30–40
iv. Kabul	£250–280	£180–220	£25–30
v. Ahmed Khel	£250–280	£180–220	£30–40
vi. Kandahar	£250–280	£180–220	£25–30
2 clasps	£350–400	£250–300	£50–60
3 clasps	£450–500	£350–400	£65–75
4 clasps	£600–900	£450–500	£80–90
Maiwand casualties:			
66th Foot	£1800–2000	—	
E Bty, B Bde RHA	£1800–2000	—	

129. KABUL TO KANDAHAR STAR

Date: 1881.
Campaign: Afghanistan 1878–80.
Branch of Service: British and Indian Armies.
Ribbon: Watered silk red, white, yellow, white and blue.
Metal: Bronze from captured guns.
Size: Height 60mm, width 45mm.
Description: (Obverse) a rayed five-pointed star surmounted by a crown with a ring for suspension. The centre is inscribed KABUL TO KANDAHAR with 1880 at the foot and the VRI monogram of the Queen Empress in the centre. Stars were either issued unnamed, or had the recipient's name impressed (to British) or engraved (to Indian troops) on the reverse.
Clasps: None.
Comments: *This star, struck by Jenkins of Birmingham, was awarded to those who took part in the epic 300-mile march from the Afghan capital to Kandahar, led by General Roberts to relieve the beleaguered forces of General Burrows.*

VALUE:

Unnamed	£120–150
Impressed (British troops)	£250–300
Engraved (Indian troops)	£150–200

Miniature	Early pierced crown £50–65
	Later solid crown £40–50

Maiwand (see no. 128)

130. CAPE OF GOOD HOPE GENERAL SERVICE MEDAL

Date: 1900.
Campaign: Uprisings in Transkei, Basutoland and Bechuanaland 1880-97.
Branch of Service: Local forces and volunteers.
Ribbon: Dark blue with a central yellow stripe.
Metal: Silver.
Size: 36mm.
Description: (Obverse) Jubilee bust of Queen Victoria by Sir Joseph Boehm; (reverse) arms of Cape Colony.
Clasps: Transkei, Basutoland, Bechuanaland.
Comments: *Instituted by the Cape government, this medal acknowledged service in putting down the Transkei (1880-1) and Bechuana (1896-7) rebellions and dealing with the unrest that erupted sporadically in Basutoland for much of this period. The medal was awarded, with one or more campaign clasps, to local forces and volunteer regiments. Ten medals were, however, officially awarded without a clasp.*

VALUE:			*Miniature*
i.	**Transkei (1070)**	£300–350	£50–60
ii.	**Basutoland (2150)**	£180–220	£50–60
iii.	**Bechuanaland (2580)**	£160–200	£50–60
	2 clasps	£350–450	£65–80
	3 clasps (23)	Rare	—

131. EGYPT MEDAL 1882–89

Dated rev.

Undated rev.

Date: 1882.
Campaign: Egypt 1882–89.
Branch of Service: Royal Navy and Army.
Ribbon: Three blue and two white stripes.
Metal: Silver.
Size: 36mm.
Description: (Obverse) the veiled profile of Queen Victoria; (reverse) the Sphinx.
Clasps: 13, listed below. Maximum number for one medal is 7, but only one such award was made. Common two-clasp combinations are denoted below by / .
Comments: *British involvement in Egypt deepened after the opening of the Suez Canal in 1869, many British officers being seconded to the Khedive's Army. When the Army mutinied in 1882 and triggered off a general anti-European uprising, an Anglo-French expedition was mounted. Subsequently the French withdrew before a landing was effected. Trouble erupted in the Sudan (under Anglo-Egyptian administration) in 1884 where General Gordon was besieged at Khartoum. Further campaigns aimed at the overthrow of the Mahdi and the reconquest of the Sudan. These prolonged operations created immense logistical problems. Nile transportation in particular was a matter resolved only when Canadian voyageurs were recruited to handle the river-boats. In addition, a contingent of troops from New South Wales "answered the Empire's call" and medals awarded to them for the Suakin campaign of 1885 are much sought after. Except where noted, the prices quoted below are for medals awarded to British Army personnel. Medals awarded to Indian or Egyptian troops are generally worth about 25 per cent less than comparable awards to British Army units.*

VALUE:

			Miniature
i.	No clasp (dated)	£100–150	£15–20
ii.	No clasp (undated)	£100–150	£20–25
iii.	Alexandria 11th July	£240–280	£25–35
iv.	Tel-el-Kebir	£200–250	£20–25
v.	El-Teb	£275–325	£35–50
vi.	Tamaai	£275–325	£30–50
vii.	El-Teb/Tamaai	£240–300	£30–50
viii.	Suakin 1884	£200–245	£25–40
ix.	The Nile 1884-85	£240–280	£25–30
x.	The Nile 1884-85/Abu Klea	£650–950	£30–40
xi.	The Nile 1884-85/Kirbekan	£280–350	£30–40
xii.	Suakin 1885	£200–245	£25–30
xiii.	Suakin 1885/Tofrek	£280–350	£35–40
xiv.	Gemaizah 1888	£280–325	£40–50
xv.	Toski 1889	£340–380	£50–60
	2 clasps	£250–300	£40–50
	3 clasps	£300–350	£50–65
	4 clasps	£400–500	£70–80
	5 clasps	£800–900	—

Canadian boatmen	£1000–1200	
NSW units (Suakin 1885)	From £800	

132. KHEDIVE'S STAR

Date: 1882.
Campaign: Egypt 1882–91.
Branch of Service: Royal Navy and Army.
Ribbon: 37mm deep blue.
Metal: Bronze.
Size: Height 60mm; width 45mm.
Description: A five-pointed star with a circular centre showing the Sphinx and Pyramids surrounded by a band inscribed EGYPT followed by a year round the top, with 'Khedive of Egypt' and the year in the Moslem calendar in Arabic at the foot. (Reverse) the Khedive's monogram surmounted by a crown. The star is suspended by a ring from an ornamental clasp in the centre of which is a star and crescent.
Clasps: Tokar.
Comments: *This star, struck by Jenkins of Birmingham, was conferred by Khedive Tewfik of Egypt on those who qualified for the Egypt medal and it was invariably worn alongside, to the detriment of the silver medal which suffered abrasion from the points of the star. There was also an undated version found with or without a campaign clasp for Tokar, awarded in 1891. These stars were issued unnamed.*

VALUE:			*Miniature*
i.	1882	£50–60	£10–15
ii.	1884	£60–75	£12–16
iii.	1884-86	£55–65	£15–20
iv.	Undated	£70–80	£15–20
v.	Undated with Tokar bar	£145–165	£60-100

133. GENERAL GORDON'S STAR FOR THE SIEGE OF KHARTOUM

Date: 1884.
Campaign: Mahdist uprising, Sudan 1884.
Branch of Service: British and Sudanese forces.
Ribbon: Deep blue (?).
Metal: Silver or pewter.
Size: Height 80mm; maximum width 54mm.
Description: Star with three concentric circles and seven groups of rays on which are superimposed seven crescents and stars. Suspension by a ring from a Crescent and Star ornament.
Clasps: None.
Comments: *To boost the morale of the defenders Charles Gordon, commanding the garrison at Khartoum, had this star cast locally in a sand mould, using his own breast star of the Order of Mejidieh as the model. Exceptionally, recipients had to purchase their medals, the proceeds going to a fund to feed the poor.*

VALUE:	
Silver gilt	£900–1200
Silver	£600–800
Pewter	£500–600

134. NORTH WEST CANADA MEDAL

Date: 1885.

Campaign: Riel's rebellion 1885.

Branch of Service: Mainly local forces.

Ribbon: Blue-grey with red stripes towards the edges.

Metal: Silver.

Size: 36mm.

Description: (Obverse) bust of Queen Victoria; (reverse) the inscription NORTH WEST CANADA 1885 within a frame of maple leaves.

Clasps: Saskatchewan,

Comments: *Paradoxically, while the medal for the Fenian Raids of 1866–70 was not sanctioned till 1899, this medal for service in the North West was authorised immediately after the conclusion of operations against the Metis led by Louis Riel. It was issued unnamed, with or without the clasp for Saskatchewan where the bulk of the action took place. Of particular interest are medals to officers and men aboard the steamship* Northcote *involved in a boat action; exceptionally, their medals were impressed. Other medals may be encountered with unofficial naming. The medal was awarded to sixteen British staff officers but the majority of medals (5600 in all) went to local forces.*

VALUE:		Miniature
i. No clasp	£300–350	£50–60
ii. Saskatchewan	£550–650	£65–75
Northcote recipient	£1200–1400	

135. ROYAL NIGER COMPANY'S MEDAL

Date: 1899.

Campaign: Nigeria 1886–97.

Branch of Service: Officers and men of the Company's forces.

Ribbon: Three equal stripes of yellow, black and white.

Metal: Silver or bronze.

Size: 39.5mm.

Description: (Obverse) the Boehm bust of Queen Victoria; (reverse) the Company's arms in a laurel wreath.

Clasps: Nigeria 1886-97 (silver), Nigeria (bronze).

Comments: *This medal was issued in silver to Europeans and bronze to natives for service in the vast territories administered by the Royal Niger chartered company. Silver medals were impressed in capitals, but those in bronze were more usually stamped with the recipient's service (constabulary) number. Specimens of both versions were later struck from the original dies but these lack name or number.*

VALUE:		Miniature	
Silver named (85)	£3000–4000	no clasp	£150–200
Silver specimen	£80–100	—	
Bronze named (250)	£800–1000	Nigeria clasp	£200–250
Bronze specimen	£60–80	—	

136. IMPERIAL BRITISH EAST AFRICA COMPANY'S MEDAL

Date: 1890.
Campaign: East Africa (Kenya and Uganda) 1888–95.
Branch of Service: Company forces.
Ribbon: Plain blue.
Metal: Silver.
Size: 39mm.
Description: (Obverse) the Company badge, a crowned and radiant sun, with a Suaheli inscription in Arabic round the foot signifying "the reward of bravery"; (reverse) plain except for a wreath. Suspension is by a plain ring or an ornamental scroll.
Comments: *The rarest of the medals awarded by the chartered companies, this medal was originally intended solely as a gallantry award; but after the BEA Company was wound up in 1895 further issues were authorised by the Foreign Office for service in Witu (1890) and the Ugandan civil war (1890-91). Less than thirty medals are known.*

VALUE: From £900   *Miniature* £300–400

137. EAST AND WEST AFRICA MEDAL

Date: 1892.
Campaigns: East and West Africa 1887–1900.
Branch of Service: Royal Navy, Army and native forces.
Ribbon: As 126.
Metal: Silver or bronze.
Size: 36mm.
Description: As for the Ashantee Medal (q.v.), distinguished only by its clasps.
Clasps: 21 (see below). A 22nd operation (Mwele, 1895–96) was denoted by engraving on the rim of the medal.
Comments: *This medal was awarded for general service in a number of small campaigns and punitive expeditions. Though usually awarded in silver, it was sometimes struck in bronze for issue to native servants, bearers and drivers. British regiments as such were not involved in any of the actions, but individual officers and NCOs were seconded as staff officers and instructors and their medals bear the names of their regiments. Units of the Royal Navy were also involved in many of the coastal or river actions. Especially sought after are naval medals with the bar for Lake Nyassa 1893 in which the ships* Pioneer *and* Adventure *were hauled in sections overland through 200 miles of jungle.*

VALUE:		Royal Navy	Europeans	Natives	*Miniature*
i.	1887–8	£400–500	£180–220	£150–180	£40–45
ii.	Witu 1890	£180–220	£180–220	£150–180	£45–50
iii.	1891–2	£200–250	£180–220	£150–180	£45–50
iv.	1892	£1200–1500	£180–220	£150–180	£45–50
v.	Witu August 1893	£200–220	—	£150–180	£60–70
vi.	Liwondi 1893	£2000–2500	—	—	—
vii.	Juba River 1893	£2000–2500	—	—	—
viii.	Lake Nyassa 1893	£2500–3500	—	—	—
ix.	1893–94	£700–900	£180–220	£150–180	£50–60
x.	Gambia 1894	£200–250	—	£150–180	£50–60
xi.	Benin River 1894	£180–220	£180–220	£150–180	£40–50
xii.	Brass River 1895	£300–350	—	—	£45–50
xiii.	M'wele 1895–6 (Bronze)	£150–180	£180–220	£140–160 £800–1000	£100
xiv.	1896–98	—	£350–450	£220–300	£30–45
xv.	Niger 1897	—	£350–400	£220–300	£45–55
xvi.	Benin 1897	£180–220	£180–220	£220–300	£35–45
xvii.	Dawkita 1897	—	Rare	Rare	£100
xviii.	1897–98	—	£180–220	£150–180	£45–50
xix.	1898	£700–900	£180–220	£150–180	£45–50
xx.	Sierra Leone 1898–9	£200–250	£180–220	£150–180	£45–50
xxi.	1899	£900–1200	£250–300	£180–250	£45–50
xxii.	1900	—	£250–300	£180–250	£45–50
	2 clasps	£350–400	£250–350	£250–300	
	3 clasps	£500–600	—	£350–400	—
	4 clasps	—	—	£450–500	—

138. BRITISH SOUTH AFRICA COMPANY'S MEDAL

RHODESIA 1896

1st type rev.

Mashonaland (2nd) rev.

Date: 1896.
Campaign: South Africa 1890-97.
Branch of Service: British Army and colonial units.
Ribbon: Seven equal stripes, four yellow and three dark blue.
Metal: Silver.
Size: 36mm.
Description: (Obverse) the Old Head bust of Queen Victoria; (reverse) a charging lion impaled by a spear, with a mimosa bush in the background and a litter of assegais and a shield on the ground.
Clasps: Mashonaland 1890, Matabeleland 1893, Rhodesia 1896, Mashonaland 1897.
Comments: *Originally instituted in 1896 for award to troops taking part in the suppression of the Matabele rebellion, it was later extended to cover operations in Rhodesia (1896) and Mashonaland (1897). The medal, as originally issued, had the inscription MATABELELAND 1893 at the top of the reverse. The medal was re-issued with RHODESIA 1896 or MASHONALAND 1897 inscribed on the reverse, but holders of medals for their first campaign only added clasps for subsequent campaigns. Rather belatedly, it was decided in 1927 to issue medals retrospectively for the Mashonaland campaign of 1890; in this instance the name and date of the campaign were not inscribed on the reverse though the details appeared on the clasp. An unusually ornate suspender has roses, thistles, shamrocks and leeks entwined. Only two medals are known with all four clasps, while only fifteen medals had three clasps.*

VALUE:		*Miniature*
a. Undated reverse with Mashonaland 1890 clasp	£800–1000	£40–50
i. Matabeleland 1893	Rare	—
ii. Rhodesia 1896	Rare	—
iii. Mashonaland 1897	Rare	—
b. Matabeleland 1893 rev.	£300–350	£30–40
ii.Rhodesia 1896	£400–450	£30–40
iii. Mashonaland 1897	£400–450	£30–40
with 2 clasps	£600–800	£65–75
c. Rhodesia 1896 rev.	£300–350	£40–50
iii. Mashonaland 1897	£400–450	£50–60
d. Mashonaland 1897	£280–350	£45–60

139. HUNZA NAGAR BADGE

Date: 1891.
Campaign: Hunza and Nagar 1891.
Branch of Service: Jammu and Kashmir forces.
Ribbon: Large (46mm x 32mm) with a broad red diagonal band and white centre stripe and green upper left and lower right corners.
Metal: Bronze.
Size: 55mm x 27mm.
Description: A uniface rectangular plaque featuring three soldiers advancing on the crenellated hill fort of Nilt, with mountains in the background. The inscription HUNZA NAGAR 1891 appears lower right. It was intended to be worn as a brooch at the neck but subsequently many were fitted with a suspender for wear with a red and green ribbon.
Clasps: None.

Comments: *Gurney of London manufactured this badge which was awarded by the Maharajah of Jammu and Kashmir to his own troops who served in the operation against the border states of Hunza and Nagar and qualified for the Indian general service medal with clasp for Hunza 1891. The punitive expedition was led by Colonel A. Durand in response to the defiant attitude of the Hunza and Nagar chiefs towards the British agency at Gilgit.*

VALUE: £450–500

140. CENTRAL AFRICA MEDAL

Date: 1895.
Campaigns: Central Africa 1891–98.
Branch of Service: Mainly local forces.
Ribbon: Three equal stripes of black, white and terracotta representing the Africans, Europeans and Indians.
Metal: Silver or bronze.
Size: 36mm.
Description: Obverse and reverse as the East and West Africa (Ashantee) medal, distinguished only by its ribbon.
Clasps: Originally issued without a clasp but one for Central Africa 1894–98 was subsequently authorised.
Comment: *Though generally issued in silver, a bronze version was awarded to native servants. The first issue of this medal had a simple ring suspension and no clasp. For the second issue a clasp, Central Africa 1894–98 was authorised and the medal was issued with a straight bar suspender, which is very rare.*

VALUE: *Miniature*

Without clasp (ring suspension)		
To natives	£350–450	£80
To Europeans	£2000–3000	
With clasp (ring suspension)	£450–550	—
To natives	£800–900	
To Europeans	£1500–1800	
With clasp (bar suspension)	£800–900	£40
Bronze, unnamed	From £500	—

141. HONG KONG PLAGUE MEDAL

Date: 1894.
Campaign: Hong Kong, May-September 1894.
Branch of Service: Royal Navy, Royal Engineers, KSLI and local personnel.
Ribbon: Red with yellow edges and two narrow yellow stripes in the centre.
Metal: Silver.
Size: 36mm.
Description: (Obverse) a Chinese lying on a trestle table being supported by a man warding off the winged figure of Death while a woman tends to the sick man. The year 1894 appears on a scroll in the exergue, while the name of the colony in Chinese pictograms is inscribed on the left of the field. (Reverse) inscribed PRESENTED BY THE HONG KONG COMMUNITY round the circumference, and FOR SERVICES RENDERED DURING THE PLAGUE OF 1894 in seven lines across the centre. It was fitted with a plain ring for suspension.
Clasps: None.
Comments: *The colonial authorities in Hong Kong awarded this medal to nurses, civil servants, police, British Army and Royal Navy personnel who rendered assistance when the crown colony was stricken by a severe epidemic of bubonic plague in May 1894. Despite stringent measures, over 2500 people died in the ensuing three months. About 400 medals were issued in silver and awarded to 300 men of the King's Shropshire Light Infantry, 50 petty officers and ratings of the Royal Navy and NCOs and other ranks of the Royal Engineers, as well as about the same number of police and junior officials, while 45 were struck in gold for award to officers, nursing sisters and senior officials. However, the medal was not authorised for wear on uniform by British troops.*

VALUE:

		Miniature
Gold (45)	From £6000	£200–300
Silver (400)	£1800–2500	£150–200

142. INDIA MEDAL

Date: 1896.
Campaign: India 1895–1902.
Branch of Service: British and Indian forces.
Ribbon: Crimson with two dark green stripes.
Metal: Silver or bronze.
Size: 36mm.
Description: Issued with two different obverses, portraying Queen Victoria (1895–1901) and King Edward VII in field marshal's uniform (1901–02). (Reverse) British and Indian soldiers supporting a standard.
Clasps: Seven, mainly for actions on the North West Frontier (see below).
Comments: *This medal replaced the India GSM which had been awarded for various minor campaigns over a period of four decades from 1854. Combatant troops were given the medal in silver but native bearers and servants received a bronze version. Although the clasp Waziristan 1901–2 is rare to British recipients it was awarded to a number of regiments.*

VALUE:

	British regiments	Indian Army	Bronze	Miniature
i. Defence of Chitral 1895	—	£900–1200	Rare	£80–100
ii. Relief of Chitral 1895	£140–160	£120–150	£120–150	£20–25
iii. Punjab Frontier 1897-98	£120–150	£100–120	£100–120	£15–20
iv. Malakand 1897*	£500–700	£150–180	£150–200	£50–60
v. Samana 1897*	£150–180	£120–150	£100–120	£35–40
vi. Tirah 1897-98*	£150–180	£120–150	£100–120	£45–50
vii. Waziristan 1901-2	£300–350	£100–120	£100–120	£25–30
3 clasps	£200–250	£150–180	£150–180	£50–60
4 clasps	—	£200–250	—	£60–80

These clasps are always paired with clasp iii.

143. JUMMOO AND KASHMIR MEDAL

Date: 1895.
Campaign: Defence of Chitral 1895.
Branch of Service: Native levies.
Ribbon: White with red stripes at the edges and a broad central green stripe.
Metal: Bronze, silver.
Size: 35mm high; 38mm wide.
Description: This medal, by Gurney of London, has a unique kidney shape showing the arms of Jummoo (Jammu) and Kashmir on the obverse. (Reverse) a view of Chitral fort with troops in the foreground.
Clasps: Chitral 1895.
Comments: *Awarded by the Maharajah of Jummoo (Jammu) and Kashmir to the Indian troops who participated in the defence of Chitral (a dependency of Kashmir) during the siege of 4 March to 20 April by Chitralis and Afghans led by Umra Khan and Sher Afzul.*

VALUE:
Named	£400–500
Unnamed	£350–400
Silver	Rare

144. ASHANTI STAR

Date: 1896.
Campaign: Gold Coast 1896.
Branch of Service: British forces.
Ribbon: Yellow with two black stripes.
Metal: Bronze.
Size: 44mm.
Description: A saltire cross with a four-pointed star in the angles, surmounted by a circular belt inscribed ASHANTI 1896 around a British crown. The plain reverse is simply inscribed FROM THE QUEEN.
Clasps: None.
Comments: *Issued unnamed, but the colonel of the West Yorkshire Regiment had the medals of the second battalion engraved at his own expense. Some 2000 stars were awarded to officers and men serving in the expedition led by Major-General F.C. Scott against the tyrannical King Prempeh. It is believed that the star was designed by Princess Henry of Battenberg whose husband died of fever during the campaign.*

VALUE:

Unnamed	£140–160
Named to West Yorkshire Regiment	£280–325
Miniature	£35–40

INTERIOR OF CHITRAL FORT

(see nos. 142 & 143)

145. QUEEN'S SUDAN MEDAL

Date: 1899.
Campaign: Reconquest of the Sudan 1896–97.
Branch of Service: Royal Navy, Army and local forces.
Ribbon: Half-yellow and half-black representing the desert and the Sudanese nation, divided by a thin crimson stripe representing the British forces.
Metal: Silver or bronze.
Size: 36mm.
Description: (Obverse) the Jubilee bust of Queen Victoria. (Reverse) a seated figure of Victory holding palms and laurels with flags in the background, the word SUDAN appearing on a tablet at her feet.
Clasps: None.
Comments: *Unusually, no clasps were granted for individual actions which included the celebrated battle of Omdurman in which young Winston Churchill charged with the cavalry. Medals named to the 21st Lancers are especially desirable on that account.*

VALUE:

Bronze named	£250–300
Silver named to British Regt	£300–350
Indian Regt	£200–250
21st Lancers (confirmed charger)*	£1800–2400
RN/RM (46)	£1000–1500
War correspondent	£1000–1500

* Dependent on which Company the recipient served in.

Miniature	£30–35

146. KHEDIVE'S SUDAN MEDAL 1896–1908

(reverse)

Date: 1897.
Campaign: Sudan 1896-1908.
Branch of Service: Royal Navy and British and Egyptian Armies.
Ribbon: 38mm yellow with a broad central deep blue stripe, symbolising the desert and the River Nile.
Metal: Silver or bronze.
Size: 39mm.
Description: (Obverse) an elaborate Arabic inscription translating as 'Abbas Hilmi the Second' and the date 1314 (AD 1897); (reverse) an oval shield surrounded by flags and a trophy of arms. Bar suspender.
Clasps: Fifteen (see below) but medals with more than the two clasps 'The Atbara' and 'Khartoum' are unusual. Inscribed in English and Arabic.
Comments: *Instituted by the Khedive of Egypt in February 1897 and granted to those who served in the reconquest of Dongola province in the Sudan (1896-8) as well as in subsequent operations for the pacification of the southern provinces. It was awarded to officers and men of the British and Egyptian Armies and Royal Navy personnel who served on the Nile steamboats. In addition, the crews of the Royal Naval ships HMS Melita (139) and HMS Scout (149) were awarded silver medals with no clasps for Dongola 1896 (but were not awarded the Queen's Sudan Medal 1896–98). Medals to Royal Naval personnel with clasps are rare and command a high premium: Hafir (16), The Atbara (6), Sudan 1897 (12), Khartoum (33),*

VALUE:		*Miniature*				*Miniature*
No clasp silver	£100–120	£20–25	xi.	Jerok	£120–150	£50–60
No clasp silver (RN)	£200–250	—	xii.	Nyam-Nyam	£150–180	£50–60
No clasp bronze	£100–120	—	xiii.	Talodi	£150–180	£60–70
i. Firket	£120–150	£30–45	xiv.	Katfia	£150–180	£45–55
ii. Hafir	£120–150	£30–45	xv.	Nyima	£150–180	£35–40
iii. Abu Hamed	£120–150	£35–50				
iv. Sudan 1897	£120–150	£35–50	2 clasps		£150–200	Add £10–15
v. The Atbara	£130–150	£25–30	3 clasps		£180–220	per clasp
vi. Khartoum	£150–175	£25–30	4 clasps		£240–280	
vii. Gedaref	£120–150	£40–55	5 clasps		£300–350	
viii. Gedid	£120–150	£40–55	6 clasps		£350–380	
ix. Sudan 1899	£120–150	£25–35	7 clasps		£400–450	
x. Bahr-el-Ghazal 1900–2	£180–220	£60–75	8 clasps		£450–500	

147. EAST AND CENTRAL AFRICA MEDAL

Date: 1899.
Campaigns: East and Central Africa 1897–99.
Branch of Service: British, Indian and local forces.
Ribbon: Half yellow, half red.
Metal: Silver or bronze.
Size: 36mm.
Description: (Obverse) the Jubilee bust of Queen Victoria; (reverse) a standing figure of Britannia with the British lion alongside.
Clasps: Four (see below).
Comments: *Instituted for service in operations in Uganda and the southern Sudan, it was awarded in silver to combatants and in bronze to camp followers. Most of the medals were awarded to troops of the Uganda Rifles and various Indian regiments. The few British officers and NCOs were troop commanders and instructors seconded from their regiments and their medals are worth very much more than the prices quoted, which are for native awards.*

VALUE:

		Europeans	Natives	*Miniature*
No clasp				
silver		—	£220–240	£35–45
bronze		—	£300–400	—
i.	**Lubwa's (with clasp Uganda 1897-98)**	—	£350–450	£45–55
ii.	**Uganda 1897-98**	£600–800	£300–400	£45–55
iii.	**1898 (silver)**	—	£300–400	£45–55
iv.	**1898 (bronze)**	—	£500–600	—
v.	**Uganda 1899**	—	£300–400	£35–45

147A. UGANDA STAR

Instituted: 1897–98.
Campaign: Mutiny of Sudanese troops in Uganda.
Branch of Service: African civilians and soldiers.
Ribbon: None.
Metal: Silver.
Description: An eight-pointed uniface star surmounted by a crown, with the dates 1897 and 1898 on a circular rim enclosing the Old Head or Veiled Bust of Queen Victoria. Brooch-mounted. Manufactured by Carrington of London and issued in a blue plush-lined case.
Comments: *This award, approved by the Foreign Office and sanctioned by Queen Victoria, acknowledged the loyalty of African tribal leaders but, in a few cases, was also awarded to Sudanese troops (one, in fact, a Tunisian) who fought gallantly in quelling the serious mutiny of Sudanese troops of the Uganda Rifles. It was for this action that British, Indian and Local forces were awarded the East and Central Africa Medal with the bar for Lubwa's (see above). Only 39 stars were awarded.*

VALUE: From £2500

148. BRITISH NORTH BORNEO COMPANY'S MEDAL 1888–1916

Instituted: 1897.

Campaign: North Borneo (now Sabah, Malaysia), 1897-1916.

Ribbon: Initially gold (later yellow) watered silk 32mm, replaced in 1917 by a 32mm ribbon with maroon edges, two yellow stripes and a dark blue central stripe. The central stripe was originally 6mm wide but modern ribbons have a 10mm stripe.

Metal: Silver or bronze.

Size: 38mm, with a thickness of 5mm.

Description: (Obverse) the shield of the Company, supported by a warrior on either side. The Company motto at the foot is PERGO ET PERAGO (I carry on and accomplish); (reverse) the British lion facing left, standing in front of a bush adorned with the Company flag, with a small wreath in the exergue.

Clasps: Punitive Expedition (1897), Punitive Expeditions (1898-1915), Rundum (1915). The Punitive Expeditions clasp was awarded to those who took part in two or more actions, but it also replaced the earlier single Expedition clasp in due course.

Comments: *These medals were awarded for service in the 15 minor expeditions between 1883 and 1915, excluding the major action at Tambunan. The manufacturers, Spink, supplied 12 silver medals in 1898–9 for award to officers (only three being named). In 1906 a further 74 silver medals were issued, to be exchanged for the bronze medals initially awarded to other ranks. A further 11 silver medals were supplied later on, all unnamed. A total of 75 bronze medals were supplied, 25 of them stamped with a name and sometimes rank and number as well, and issued, both stamped and engraved, to other ranks.*

1st type rev.

VALUE:

	Type	Officially Named	Unnamed original	Spink copy	Stamped "Specimen"	Miniature
i. Punitive Expedition	Silver	£1400–1800	£300–500	£50–60	£60–80	£100–120
	Bronze	£1400–1800	£300–500	£50–60	£60–80	
ii. Punitive Expeditions	Silver	£1400–1800	£300–500	£50–60	£60–80	£50–70
	Bronze	£1400–1800	£300–500	£50–60	£60–80	
iii. Rundum	Silver	£1400–1800	£300–500	£50–60	£60–80	£60–75

148A. BRITISH NORTH BORNEO COMPANY'S MEDAL 1899–1900

2nd type obv.

Instituted: 1900.

Campaign: The final expedition in the Tambunan Valley against Mat Salleh.

Ribbon: 32mm yellow with a 10mm green stripe down the centre.

Metal: Silver or bronze.

Size: 38mm. Officially named medals are 5mm thick.

Description: (Obverse) the shield of the British North Borneo Company with BRITISH NORTH BORNEO round the top and the date 1900 below; (reverse) a wreath enclosing a device of one clothed and one naked arm supporting the Company's flag. The motto PERGO ET PERAGO is inscribed outside the wreath. The inscription SPINK & SON, LONDON appears in very tiny lettering at the foot.

Clasps: Tambunan.

Comments: *Instituted for award to those officers and men who took part in the expedition of January-February 1900 against Mat Salleh who had roused the Tegas against the Tiawan Dusuns in the Tambunan Valley. Salleh was killed on February 1, 1900 when Company forces stormed his stronghold and his followers were dispersed or killed. Eight silver medals were originally awarded to officers, but in 1906 some 106 were issued to be exchanged for the bronze medals initially issued to other ranks. A further 22 silver medals were later supplied, unnamed. A total of 125 bronze medals were supplied, 118 of them stamped with a name and sometimes also a rank and number, and issued, both stamped and engraved, to other ranks. Only 36 are recorded as replaced by silver medals, but it is known that some of these bronze medals were not returned to the authorities.*

VALUE:				
Type	Officially Named	Unnamed original	Spink copy	Stamped "Specimen"
Silver	£1800–2000	£300–500	£50–60	£60–80
Bronze	£1000–1500	£300–500	£50–60	£60–80
Miniature	£65–80			

2nd type rev.

149. SULTAN OF ZANZIBAR'S MEDAL

Date: 1896.

Campaign: East Africa 1896.

Branch of Service: Sultan's forces.

Ribbon: Plain bright scarlet.

Metal: Silver.

Size: 36mm.

Description: (Obverse) a facing bust of Sultan Hamid bin Thwain surrounded by a Suaheli inscription in Arabic; (reverse) same inscription set in four lines.

Clasps: Pumwani, Jongeni, Takaungu, Mwele (inscribed only in Arabic).

Comments: *Awarded to the Zanzibari contingent who served under Lieut. Lloyd-Matthews RN in East Africa alongside British and Imperial forces.*

VALUE:	£400–500	*Miniature*	£500–600

150. QUEEN'S SOUTH AFRICA MEDAL

Date: 1899.

Campaign: Anglo-Boer War 1899-1902.

Branch of Service: British and Imperial forces.

Ribbon: Red with two narrow blue stripes and a broad central orange stripe.

Metal: Silver or bronze.

Size: 36mm.

Description: (Obverse) the Jubilee bust of Queen Victoria; (reverse) Britannia holding the flag and a laurel crown towards a large group of soldiers, with warships offshore. The words SOUTH AFRICA are inscribed round the top.

Clasps: 26 authorised but the maximum recorded for a single medal is nine to the Army and eight to the Navy.

Comments: *Because of the large number of British and imperial forces which took part and the numerous campaign and battle clasps awarded, this is one of the most popular and closely studied of all medals, offering immense scope to the collector. A total of 178,000 medals were awarded. Numerous specialist units were involved for the first time, as well as locally raised units and contingents from India, Canada, Australia and New Zealand. Of particular interest are the medals awarded to war correspondents and nurses which set precedents for later wars. Although nurses received the medal they were not issued with clasps to which they were entitled. A small number of bronze medals without a clasp were issued to bearers and servants in Indian units. The original issue of the QSA depicts Britannia's outstretched hand pointing towards the R of AFRICA and bears the dates 1899–1900 on the reverse field. Less than 70 of these were issued to Lord Strathcona's Horse who had returned to Canada before the war ended, but as the war dragged on the date was removed before any other medals were issued, although some medals can be found with a "ghost" of this date still to be seen. On the third type reverse there is again no date but Britannia's hand points towards the F. The prices for clasps given opposite are for clasps issued in combination with others. Some clasps are much scarcer when issued singly than combined with other clasps and conversely some clasps are not recorded on their own. Verified ten-clasp medals to South African units are known.*

1st type rev.

2nd type rev. (occasionally ghost dates can be seen)

3rd type rev.

150. QUEEN'S SOUTH AFRICA MEDAL *continued*

VALUE:

	RN	British Army	SA/Indian	Aus/NZ	Canadian
No clasp bronze	—	—	£150–250	—	—
No clasp silver	£120–150	£60–80	£75–85	£100–150	£120–150
i. Cape Colony	£150–150	£60–70	£80–100	£100–150	£120–150
ii. Rhodesia	£1000–1200	£240–280	£160–200	£220–300	£300–350
iii. Relief of Mafeking	—	—	£280–350	£350–400	£400–450
iv. Defence of Kimberley	—	£250–280	£180–220	—	—
v. Talana	—	£200–250	£220–250	—	—
vi. Elandslaagte	—	£250–280	£240–280	—	—
vii. Defence of Ladysmith	£250–300	£120–150	£100–140	—	—
viii. Belmont	£250–300	£90–120	—	£200–250	—
ix. Modder River	£300–350	£90–120	—	£200–250	—
x. Tugela Heights	£300–350	£80–100	—	—	—
xi. Natal	£250–300	£100–150	£120–150	—	£220–250
xii. Relief of Kimberley	£750–900	£80–100	£80–100	£120–150	—
xiii. Paardeberg	£250–300	£80–100	£80–100	£120–150	£150–180
xiv. Orange Free State	£180–220	£70–80	£60–80	£120–150	£150–180
xv. Relief of Ladysmith	£250–300	£90–120	£80–100	—	—
xvi. Driefontein	£240–260	£80–100	—	£120–150	£200–250
xvii. Wepener	—	£600–800	£400–450	—	—
xviii. Defence of Mafeking	—	—	£950–1200	—	—
xix. Transvaal	£450–600	£70–80	£55–65	£90–100	£200–220
xx. Johannesburg	£250–300	£80–90	£80–90	£120–150	£120–150
xxi. Laing's Nek	£500–650	£80–90	—	—	—
xxii. Diamond Hill	£250–300	£80–90	£80–90	£120–150	£200–220
xxiii. Wittebergen	£1000–1200	£80–90	£80–90	£120–150	—
xxiv. Belfast	£250–300	£80–90	£80–90	£120–150	£120–150
xxv. South Africa 1901	£120–150	£60–80	£50–60	£80–100	£100–120
xxvi. South Africa 1902	£750–850	£60–80	£50–60	£80–100	£100–120
2 clasps	£180–220	£80–90	£80–90	£150–180	£150–180
3 clasps	£250–280	£90–100	£180–200	£180–200	£180–200
4 clasps	£300–350	£100–115	£100–120	£220–250	£200–220
5 clasps*	£380–450	£120–140	£120–140	£250–280	£220–250
6 clasps*	£550–650	£150–180	£180–200	£300–350	£300–350
7 clasps*	£800–900	£200–250	£350–400	£500–800	—
To Royal Marines	£1200–1300				
8 clasps*	£1200–1500	£600–800	£850–1000	—	—
9 clasps	—	—	£2000–2400	—	—
Relief dates on reverse	—	—	—	—	£2500–3500
Nurses	—	£200–250	—	—	—
War Correspondents	—	£1100–1200	—	—	—

* in addition to the South Africa 1901 clasp

Miniature
From £15 with no clasp to £45 with 6 fixed clasps—"slip-on" style clasps approx. 20% less.
With dated reverse £100–150

151. QUEEN'S MEDITERRANEAN MEDAL

Date: 1899.
Campaign: Mediterranean garrisons 1899-1902.
Branch of Service: British militia forces.
Ribbon: Red with two narrow dark blue stripes and a central broad orange stripe (as for Queen's South Africa Medal).
Metal: Silver.
Size: 36mm.
Description: Similar to the Queen's South Africa Medal but inscribed MEDITERRANEAN at the top of the reverse.
Clasps: None.
Comments: *Awarded to officers and men of the militia battalions which were sent to Malta and Gibraltar to take over garrison duty from the regular forces who were drafted to the Cape.*

VALUE:

Silver (5000)	£300–350	
		Miniature £55–65

152. KING'S SOUTH AFRICA MEDAL

Date: 1902.
Campaign: South Africa 1901–02.
Branch of Service: British and imperial forces.
Ribbon: Three equal stripes of green, white and orange.
Metal: Silver.
Size: 36mm.
Description: (Obverse) bust of King Edward VII in field marshal's uniform; (reverse) as for Queen's medal.
Clasps: Two: South Africa 1901, South Africa 1902.
Comments: *This medal was never issued without the Queen's medal and was awarded to all personnel engaged in operations in South Africa in 1901–02 when fighting was actually confined to numerous skirmishes with isolated guerrilla bands. Very few medals were awarded to RN personnel as the naval brigades had been disbanded in 1901. Apart from about 600 nurses and a few odd men who received the medal without a clasp, this medal was awarded with two clasps—most men were entitled to both clasps, single clasp medals being very rare. Only 137 were awarded to New Zealand troops.*

VALUE:

No clasp (nurses)	£200–250
i. South Africa 1901	
ii. South Africa 1902	
1901 / 1902 (RN) (33)	£750–1000
1901 / 1902 (Army)	£65–75
1901 / 1902 (Canada)	£80–100
1901 / 1902 (Aus)	£100–150
1901 / 1902 (NZ)	£300–350
1901 / 1902 (South African units)	£60–80
1902 alone	From £100
Miniature	£12–15 2-clasps £15–20

153. ST JOHN AMBULANCE BRIGADE MEDAL FOR SOUTH AFRICA

Date: 1902.
Campaign: South Africa 1899–1902.
Branch of Service: St John Ambulance Brigade.
Ribbon: Black with narrow white edges.
Metal: Bronze.
Size: 37mm.
Description: (Obverse) King Edward VII; (reverse) the arms of the Order with a legend in Latin, SOUTH AFRICA and the dates 1899 and 1902.
Clasps: None.
Comments: *Issued by the Order of St John of Jerusalem to the members of its ambulance brigade who served during the Boer War or who played an active part in the organisation, mobilisation and supply roles. Medals were engraved on the edge with the recipient's name and unit. It is most often associated with the two South Africa medals, but fourteen members who went on from South Africa to serve during the Boxer Rebellion were also awarded the China Medal.*

VALUE: Bronze (1,871)   £350–450   *Miniature* £80–90

153A. NATIONAL FIRE BRIGADE'S UNION MEDAL FOR SOUTH AFRICA

Date: 1902.
Campaign: South Africa 1899–1902.
Branch of Service: National Fire Brigade's Union.
Ribbon: Red with narrow orange edges and two orange stripes near the centre.
Metal: Bronze.
Size: 36mm.
Description: (Obverse) King Edward VII; (reverse) A bust of a helmeted fireman with a Geneva cross in the sky above. Around the circumference a spray of laurel leaves between the dates 1899 and 1902 and SOUTH AFRICA at top.
Comments: *Awarded to a small detachment of volunteers of the National Fire Brigades Union (Ambulance Department) who served in South Africa as stretcher bearers and ambulance personnel. Each volunteeer also received the St John's Ambulance Medal for South Africa and the Queen's South Africa Medal with the clasp Cape Colony. Only 42 were awarded.*

VALUE: £1200–1500   *Miniature* (silver) £175–225, (bronze) £200–250

154. KIMBERLEY STAR

Date: 1900.
Campaign: Defence of Kimberley 1899–1902.
Branch of Service: British and local forces.
Ribbon: Half yellow, half black, separated by narrow stripes of red, white and blue.
Metal: Silver.
Size: Height 43mm; max. width 41mm.
Description: A six-pointed star with ball finials and a circular centre inscribed KIMBERLEY 1899–1900 with the civic arms in the middle. (Reverse) plain, apart from the inscription MAYOR'S SIEGE MEDAL 1900. Suspended by a plain ring from a scrolled bar.
Clasps: None
Comments: *The Mayor and council of Kimberley awarded this and the following medal to the defenders of the mining town against the Boer forces. Two medals were struck in gold but about 5000 were produced in silver. Those with the "a" Birmingham hallmark for 1900 rate a premium over stars with later date letters.*

VALUE:

Hallmark "a"	£150–185	*Miniature*	£100–120
Later date letters	£150–170		

155. KIMBERLEY MEDAL

Date: 1900.
Campaign: Defence of Kimberley 1899–1900.
Branch of Service: Local forces.
Ribbon: As above.
Metal: Silver
Size: 38mm.
Description: (Obverse) the figure of Victory above the Kimberley Town Hall, with the dates 1899–1900 in the exergue. (Reverse) two shields inscribed INVESTED 15 OCT. 1899 and RELIEVED 15 FEB. 1900. The imperial crown appears above and the royal cypher underneath, with the legend TO THE GALLANT DEFENDERS OF KIMBERLEY round the circumference.
Comments: *Although awarded for the same purpose as MY154, this silver medal is a much scarcer award.*

VALUE: £800–1000

156. YORKSHIRE IMPERIAL YEOMANRY MEDAL

Date: 1900.
Campaign: South Africa 1900–02.
Branch of Service: Yorkshire Imperial Yeomanry.
Ribbon: Yellow.
Metal: Silver.
Size: 38mm.
Description: Three versions were produced. The first two had the numeral 3 below the Prince of Wales's feathers and may be found with the dates 1900–1901 or 1901–1902, while the third type has the figures 66, denoting the two battalions involved. The uniform reverse has the white rose of Yorkshire surmounted by an imperial crown and enclosed in a laurel wreath with the legend A TRIBUTE FROM YORKSHIRE.
Comments: *Many medals wre produced locally and awarded to officers and men of county regiments. The medals struck by Spink and Son for the Yorkshire Imperial Yeomanry, however, are generally more highly regarded as they were much more extensively issued, and therefore more commonly met with, than the others.*

VALUE:

		Miniature
3rd Battalion 1900–1901	£140–180	£120–140
3rd Battalion 1901–1902	£150–180	£100–120
66th Company 1900–1901	£180–220	£120–140

157. MEDAL FOR THE DEFENCE OF OOKIEP

Date: 1902.
Campaign: Defence of Ookiep 1902.
Branch of Service: British and colonial forces.
Ribbon: Dark brown with a central green stripe.
Metal: Silver or bronze.
Size: 36mm.
Description: (Obverse) a miner and copper-waggon, with the Company name and date of foundation (1888) round the circumference; (reverse) a thirteen-line text. Fitted with a scroll suspender.
Clasps: None.
Comments: *Commonly known as the Cape Copper Co. Medal, this medal was awarded by the Cape Copper Company to those who defended the mining town of Ookiep in Namaqualand when it was besieged from 4 April to 4 May 1902 by a Boer commando led by Jan Christian Smuts, later Field Marshal, Prime Minister of South Africa and a member of the Imperial War Cabinet. The defence was conducted by Lieut. Colonel Sheldon, DSO and Major Dean, the Company's manager. The garrison consisted of 206 European miners, 660 Cape Coloureds, 44 men of the 5th Warwickshire militia and twelve men of the Cape Garrison Artillery.*
VALUE:

Silver (officers)	£2000–2500
Bronze (other ranks)	£800–1000

158. CHINA WAR MEDAL 1900

Date: 1901.
Campaign: Boxer Rebellion 1900.
Branch of Service: British and imperial forces.
Ribbon: Crimson with yellow edges.
Metal: Silver or bronze.
Size: 36mm.
Description: (Obverse) bust of Queen Victoria; (reverse) trophy of arms, similar to the 1857-60 China Medal but inscribed CHINA 1900 at the foot.
Clasps: Taku Forts, Defence of Legations, Relief of Pekin.
Comments: *Instituted for service during the Boxer Rebellion and the subsequent punitive expeditions, this medal was similar to that of 1857-60 with the date in the exergue altered to 1900. There are three types of naming: in small, impressed capitals for European troops, in large impressed capitals for naval recipients, and in engraved cursive script for Indian forces. The medal was issued in silver to combatants and in bronze to native bearers, drivers and servants. The international community was besieged by the Boxers, members of a secret society, aided and abetted by the Dowager Empress. The relieving force, consisting of contingents from Britain, France, Italy, Russia, Germany and Japan, was under the command of the German field marshal, Count von Waldersee. The British Legation Guard, comprising 80 Royal Marines and a number of 'odd men', won the clasp for Defence of Legations, the most desirable of the campaign bars in this conflict.*

VALUE:

	Royal Navy	Army	Indian units	*Miniature*
Silver no clasp	£150–180	£150–180	£100–150	£15–20
Australian naval forces	£600–800			
Bronze no clasp	—	—	£100–150	—
i. Taku Forts	£400–450	—	—	£25–30
ii. Defence of Legations	£5000–6000	—	—	£50–60
iii. Relief of Pekin:				
Silver	£300–350	£350–400	£225–285	£25–30
Bronze	—	—	£225–285	—
2 clasps	£500–550	—	—	£40–50
No-clasp medal to a nurse	£1000–1500			
To a war correspondent (9)	£1000–1500			
ditto Relief of Pekin (1)	Rare			

159. TRANSPORT MEDAL

Date: 1903.
Campaigns: Boer War 1899-1902 and Boxer Rebellion 1900.
Branch of Service: Mercantile Marine.
Ribbon: Red with two blue stripes.
Metal: Silver.
Size: 36mm.
Description: (Obverse) bust of King Edward VII in the uniform of an Admiral of the Fleet; (reverse) HMS *Ophir* below a map of the world.
Clasps: S. Africa 1899-1902, China 1900.
Comments: *The last of the medals associated with the major conflicts at the turn of the century, it was instituted for award to the officers of the merchant vessels used to carry troops and supplies to the wars in South Africa and China.*

VALUE:

		Miniature
i. South Africa 1899–1902 (1219)	£650–750	£40–60
ii. China 1900 (322)	£900–100	£50–70
Both clasps (178)	£1200–1400	£80–100

160. ASHANTI MEDAL

Date: 1901.
Campaign: Gold Coast 1900.
Branch of Service: British and local forces.
Ribbon: Black with two broad green stripes.
Metal: Silver or bronze.
Size: 36mm.
Description: (Obverse) bust of King Edward VII in field marshal's uniform. (Reverse) a lion on the edge of an escarpment looking towards the sunrise, with a native shield and spears in the foreground. The name ASHANTI appeared on a scroll at the foot.
Clasps: Kumassi.
Comments: *A high-handed action by the colonial governor provoked a native uprising and the siege of the garrison at Kumassi. The medal was awarded to the defenders as well as personnel of the two relieving columns. Very few Europeans were involved as most were in South Africa fighting the Boers. The medal was awarded in silver to combatants and bronze to native transport personnel and servants.*

VALUE:

	Silver	Bronze	*Miniature*
No clasp	£225–250	£250–300	£25–35
i. Kumassi	£320–350	Rare	£45–55

161. AFRICA GENERAL SERVICE MEDAL

Date: 1902.
Campaigns: Minor campaigns in Africa 1902 to 1956.
Branch of Service: British and colonial forces.
Ribbon: Yellow with black edges and two thin central green stripes.
Metal: Silver or bronze.
Size: 36mm.
Description: (Obverse) effigies of Edward VII, George V and Elizabeth II; (reverse) similar to that of the East and Central Africa medal of 1897–99, with AFRICA in the exergue.
Clasps: 34 awarded in the reign of Edward VII, ten George V and only one Elizabeth II (see below).
Comments: *This medal replaced the East and West Africa Medal 1887–1900, to which 21 clasps had already been issued. In turn, it remained in use for 54 years, the longest-running British service medal. Medals to combatants were in silver, but a few bronze medals were issued during the 1903–04 operations in Northern Nigeria and the Somaliland campaigns of 1902 and 1908 to transport personnel and these are now much sought after, as are any medals with the effigy of George V on the obverse. With the exception of the 1902–04 Somali campaign and the campaign against the Mau Mau of Kenya (1952–56) European troops were not involved in any numbers, such personnel consisting mostly of detached officers and specialists.*

VALUE:

		RN	British units	African/Indian regiments
i.	N. Nigeria	—	—	£140–160
ii.	N. Nigeria 1902	—	—	£130–150
iii.	N. Nigeria 1903	—	—	£120–140
iv.	N. Nigeria 1903-04	—	—	£170–190
v.	N. Nigeria 1903-04 (bronze)	—	—	£180–200
vi.	N. Nigeria 1904	—	—	£150–170
vii.	N. Nigeria 1906	—	—	£150–170
viii.	S. Nigeria	—	—	£200–220
ix.	S. Nigeria 1902	—	—	£150–170
x.	S. Nigeria 1902-03	—	—	£150–170

continued opposite

161. AFRICA GENERAL SERVICE MEDAL *continued*

		RN	British units	African/Indian regiments
xi.	S. Nigeria 1903	—	—	£210–180
xii.	S. Nigeria 1903-04	—	—	£170–190
xiii.	S. Nigeria 1904	—	—	£140–160
xiv.	S. Nigeria 1904-05	—	—	£170–190
xv.	S. Nigeria 1905	—	—	£250–300
xvi.	S. Nigeria 1905-06	—	—	£160–180
xvii.	Nigeria 1918	—	—	£130–150
xviii.	East Africa 1902	—	—	£320–370
xix.	East Africa 1904	—	—	£180–220
xx.	East Africa 1905	—	—	£180–220
xxi.	East Africa 1906	—	—	£200–220
xxii.	East Africa 1913	—	—	£200–220
xxiii.	East Africa 1913-14	—	—	£200–220
xxiv.	East Africa 1914	—	—	£200–220
xxv.	East Africa 1915	—	—	£200–220
xxvi.	East Africa 1918	—	—	£200–220
xxvii.	West Africa 1906	—	—	£260–300
xxviii.	West Africa 1908	—	—	£200–240
xxix.	West Africa 1909-10	—	—	£200–220
xxx.	Somaliland 1901	—	—	£270–320
xxxi.	Somaliland 1901 (bronze)	—	—	£250–300
xxxii.	Somaliland 1902-04	£120–145	£125–150	£100–125
xxxiii.	Somaliland 1902-04 (bronze)	—	—	£250–300
xxxiv.	Somaliland 1908-10	£120–145	—	£100–125
xxxv.	Somaliland 1908-10 (bronze)	—	—	£200–250
xxxvi.	Somaliland 1920	£200–300	—	£120–150
	as above but RAF	—	£600–800	—
xxxvii.	Jidballi (with Somaliland 1902–04)	—	£200–250	£450–185
xxxviii.	Uganda 1900	—	—	£200–250
xxxix.	B.C.A. 1899-1900	—	—	£150–200
xl.	Jubaland	£220–250	—	£140–180
xli.	Jubaland (bronze)	—	—	£300–350
xlii.	Jubaland 1917-18	—	—	£180–200
xliii.	Jubaland 1917-18 (bronze)	—	—	£200–250
xliv.	Gambia	£600–800	—	£220–270
xlv.	Aro 1901-1902	£500–650	—	£150–170
xlvi.	Lango 1901	—	—	£250–300
xlvii.	Kissi 1905	—	—	£350–400
xlviii.	Nandi 1905-06	—	—	£120–150
xlix.	Shimber Berris 1914-15	—	—	£220–250
l.	Nyasaland 1915	—	—	£150–180
li.	Kenya	£350–500	£80–150	£50–70
lii.	Kenya (to RAF)	—	£100–125	—
2 clasps		£150–180	£200–250	£150–250
3 clasps		—	—	£200–400
4 clasps		—	—	£300–450
5 clasps		—	—	£400–600
6 clasps		—	—	£600–1000

Medal to war correspondent   £1200–1500

Miniature
Range from £30 to £75 depending upon clasp. "Slip-on" clasps are approx. 20% cheaper. Add £10 for each additional clasp.

162. TIBET MEDAL

Date: 1905.
Campaign: Tibet 1903–04.
Branch of Service: British and Indian regiments.
Ribbon: Green with two white stripes and a broad maroon central stripe.
Metal: Silver or bronze.
Size: 36mm.
Description: (Obverse) bust of King Edward VII; (reverse) the fortified hill city of Lhasa with TIBET 1903–04 at the foot.
Clasps: Gyantse.
Comments: *The trade mission led by Colonel Sir Francis Younghusband to Tibet was held up by hostile forces, against whom a punitive expedition was mounted in 1903. This medal was awarded mainly to Indian troops who took part in the expedition, camp followers being awarded the medal in bronze. A clasp was awarded to those who took part in the operations near Gyantse beteen 3 May and 6 July 1904.*

VALUE:

	British	Indian	Bronze	*Miniature*
Without clasp	£400–500	£250–300	£100–120	£30–40
i. Gyantse	£750–850	£350–400	£225–275	£50–60

163. NATAL REBELLION MEDAL

Date: 1907.
Campaign: Natal 1906.
Branch of Service: Local forces.
Ribbon: Crimson with black edges.
Metal: Silver.
Size: 36mm.
Description: (Obverse) right-facing profile of King Edward VII. (Reverse) an erect female figure representing Natal with the sword of justice in her right hand and a palm branch in the left. She treads on a heap of Zulu weapons and is supported by Britannia who holds the orb of empire in her hand. In the background, the sun emerges from behind storm clouds.
Clasp: 1906.
Comments: *The Natal government instituted this medal for services in the operations following the Zulu rebellion. Local volunteer units bore the brunt of the action and it is interesting to note that one of the recipients was Sergeant-Major M. K. Gandhi who later led India to independence.*

VALUE:

		Miniature
No clasp (2000)	£120–140	£15–20
i. 1906 (8000)	£150–160	£30–40
Natal Naval Corps		
without clasp (67)	£150–200	
clasp 1906 (136)	£250–300	

163A. MESSINA EARTHQUAKE COMMEMORATIVE MEDAL

Date: 1908.
Campaign: Messina earthquake relief.
Branch of Service: Royal Navy.
Ribbon: Green with white edges and central white stripe.
Metal: Silver.
Size: 31.5mm.
Description: (Obverse) left-facing profile of King Victor Emanuel III; (reverse) A wreath of oak leaves within which are the words MEDAGLIA COMMEMORATIVA / TERREMOTO CALABRO SICULO 28 DICEMBRE 1908.
Comments: *The King of Italy rewarded Royal Naval and other personnel who went to the aid of victims of the tragic earthquake that hit Messina in December 1908 with this silver medal. Officers and men serving on certain ships were eligible for the award as well as members of the Mercantile Marine and others who were engaged in relief operations. The Admiralty's published list of RN ships is as follows: HMS Duncan, HMS Euralyus, HMS Exmouth, HMS Lancaster, HMS Minerva and HMS Sutlej. However 52 medals were also awarded to personnel from HMS Boxer, which was omitted from the original list and a further 35 medals were awarded to the officers and men of HMS Philomel who had actually 'been engaged in work which was directly attributable to the rescue operations'. The medal was issued unnamed. In addition to the commemorative medal a special Messina Earthquake Merit Medal was awarded in two sizes (40mm and 30mm) bronze, silver and gold to organisations, vessels and various key individuals who played a part in the rescue operations.*

VALUE:

		Miniature
Unattributed single medal	£80–100	£60–80
Royal Navy (c. 3,500)	£120–160	
Royal Marines (481)	£140–180	
Mercantile Marine (c. 400)	£140–180	
Other	Rare	

Aftermath of the earthquake, Messina.

164. INDIA GENERAL SERVICE MEDAL

Date: 1909.
Campaigns: India 1908 to 1935.
Branch of Service: British and Indian forces.
Ribbon: Green with a broad blue central stripe.
Metal: Silver.
Size: 36mm.
Description: Three obverse types were used: Edward VII (1908–10), George V Kaisar-i-Hind (1910–30) and George V Indiae Imp (1930–35). (Reverse) the fortress at Jamrud in the Khyber Pass, with the name INDIA in a wreath at the foot.
Clasps: Fourteen, some in bronze (see below).
Comments: *This medal was awarded for a number of minor campaigns and operations in India before and after the First World War. The medals were struck at the Royal Mint in London and by the Indian government in Calcutta, the only difference being in the claw suspenders, the former being ornate and the latter plain. Medals with the bars North West Frontier 1908 and Abor 1911–12 were also issued in bronze to native bearers.*

VALUE:

		British Army	RAF	Indian regiments	*Miniature*
i.	North West Frontier 1908	£120–145	—	£60–80	£20–25
	bronze	—	—	£80–125	—
ii.	Abor 1911–12	—	—	£180–225	£20–25
	bronze	—	—	£250–300	—
iii.	Afghanistan NWF 1919	£60–90	£120–150	£35–55	£15–20
iv.	*Mahsud 1919–20 & Waziristan 1919–21	£120–150	£150–180	£60–85	£15–20
v.	Malabar 1921–22	£120–150	—	£55–85	£30–35
vi.	Waziristan 1921–24	£60–90	£120–150	£35–55	£15–20
vii.	Waziristan 1925	—	£800–1000	—	£20–25
viii.	NW Frontier 1930–31	£60–90	£120–150	£35–55	£15–20
ix.	Burma 1930–32	£70–95	Rare	£33–55	£15–20
x.	Mohmand 1933	£120–150	£250–300	£35–55	£15–20
xi.	NW Frontier 1935	£70–95	£120–150	£35–55	£20–25

*Usually found in combination with Waziristan 1919-21, but 10 medals were awarded either with this clasp alone or with the Afghanistan NWF clasp.

165. KHEDIVE'S SUDAN MEDAL 1910

Date: 1911.

Campaign: Sudan 1910 to 1922

Branch of Service: British and Egyptian forces.

Ribbon: Black with thin red and green stripes on either side.

Metal: Silver or bronze.

Size: 36mm.

Description: (Obverse) an Arabic inscription signifying the name of Khedive Abbas Hilmi and the date 1328 in the Moslem calendar (1910 AD). He was deposed in December 1914 when Egypt was declared a British protectorate, and succeeded by his nephew who was proclaimed Sultan. Sultan Hussein Kamil changed the Arabic inscription and date to AH 1335 (1916–17) on later issues of the medal. (Reverse) a lion poised on a plinth with the sunrise in the background.

Clasps: 16, inscribed in English and Arabic.

Comments: *Introduced in June 1911 as a replacement for the previous Khedive's Sudan medal of 1896–1908, it was awarded for minor operations in the southern Sudan between 1910 and 1922. The silver medal was issued with clasps to combatants, and without a clasp to non-combatants, while the bronze version was granted to camp followers. The medal is usually found unnamed although a few British recipient's medals are found named in small impressed capitals or arabic script. The prices below are for unnamed examples.*

VALUE:

Silver without clasp type I		£200–250
Silver without clasp type II		£180–200
Bronze without clasp type I		£400–450
Bronze without clasp type II		£250–300
i.	Atwot	£260–300
ii.	S. Kordofan 1910	£260–300
iii.	Sudan 1912	£280–310
iv.	Zeraf 1913-14	£300–325
v.	Mandal	£300–325
vi.	Miri	£300–325
vii.	Mongalla 1915-16	£300–325
viii.	Darfur 1916	£290–320
ix.	Fasher	£260–300
x.	Lau Nuer	£265–325
xi.	Nyima 1917-18	£250–300
xii.	Atwot 1918	£250–300
xiii.	Garjak Nuer	£250–300
xiv.	Aliab Dinka	£300–350
xv.	Nyala	£300–350
xvi.	Darfur 1921	£350–400
2 clasps		£350–450

Miniature
   Silver £50–75. Prices for clasps vary between £10 and £30.

The Camel Corps in the Sudan.

FIRST WORLD WAR MEDALS

Almost all World War I medals, like the earlier campaigns, continue to rise in price as more collectors come into the hobby and as more and more families endeavour to locate the medals of their forebears. Today radio and television documentaries continue to inspire collectors to buy medals that were once discarded as scrap. Many World War I medals were sold by the descendants of the original recipients at a time when no-one was interested in the past. Notoriously, the silver boom of the 1970s enticed many people to sell medals that were worth far more as scrap than as collectors' items and today we are reaping the consequences of the loss of the vast numbers of medals that went "into the pot". Fortunately today families are more aware of their history and do not wish to dispose of such heirlooms. Many of the auction houses are finding it increasingly difficult to source fresh items to sell but when medals do come on to the market for the first time, often the prices realised are out of proportion to their real value. The price for a gallantry group which has been bought and sold a number of times tends to settle down and is easy to value, but a similar group which has never been offered before can often astound the audience when two determined buyers battle it out on the auction floor.

Interestingly the popular "Medal Tracker" facility that appears each month in MEDAL NEWS and on the MEDAL NEWS website regularly features more World War I medals than any other campaign.

The main strong areas of collecting remain Gallipoli and The Somme, with the latter literally having monthly price increases. Other important areas include the Retreat from Mons, the Battle of Loos, Battle of Jutland and even actions around Delville Wod and Hill 60. Awards to casualties remain popular. Complete sets, i.e. the Trio, Plaque and Scroll remain hard to find and still command strong prices.

166. 1914 STAR

Date: 1917.
Campaign: France and Belgium 1914.
Branch of Service: British forces.
Ribbon: Watered silk red, white and blue.
Metal: Bronze.
Size: Height 50mm; max. width 45mm.
Description: A crowned four-pointed star with crossed swords and a wreath of oak leaves, having the royal cypher at the foot and a central scroll inscribed AUG NOV 1914. Uniface, the naming being inscribed incuse on the plain reverse.
Clasps: 5th Aug.–22nd Nov. 1914. The clasp was sewn on to the ribbon of the medal, the first of this type. A silver rosette is worn on the ribbon strip if the bar was awarded.
Comments: *Awarded to all those who had served in France and Belgium between 5 August and 22 November 1914. In 1919 King George V authorised a clasp bearing these dates for those who had actually been under fire during that period. The majority of the 400,000 recipients of the star were officers and men of the prewar British Army, the "Old Contemptibles" who landed in France soon after the outbreak of the First World War and who took part in the retreat from Mons, hence the popular nickname of Mons Star by which this medal is often known.*

VALUE:		Miniature
1914 Star	£65–85	£3–5
i. 5th Aug.–22nd Nov. 1914		
("Mons") clasp	£75–125	£5–7
To RN	£200–300	
RM	£65–100	
RND	£65–100	
1914 Star/BWM/Victory trio		
Corps	from £85	
Regiments	from £100	
Trio with plaque (no. 172)		
Corps	£200–250	
Regiments	£300–400	
RFC	£1200–1500	

167. 1914–15 STAR

Date: 1918.
Campaign: First World War 1914–15.
Branch of Service: British and imperial forces.
Ribbon: Watered silk red, white and blue (as above).
Metal: Bronze.
Size: Height 50mm; max. width 45mm.
Description: As above, but AUG and NOV omitted and scroll across
the centre inscribed 1914–15.
Clasps: None.
Comments: *Awarded to those who saw service in any theatre of war between
5 August 1914 and 31 December 1915, other than those who had already
qualified for the 1914 Star. No fewer than 2,350,000 were awarded, making
it the commonest British campaign medal up to that time.*

VALUE:

1914–15 Star	£20–45	*Miniature*	£3–4
1914–15 Star/BWM/Victory trio			
Corps	from £50		
Regiments	from £70		
Trio with plaque (no. 172)			
Corps	£200–250		
Regiments	£300–350		

168. BRITISH WAR MEDAL 1914–20

Date: 1919.
Campaign: First World War, 1914–20.
Branch of Service: British and imperial forces.
Ribbon: Orange watered centre with stripes of white and black at each
side and borders of royal blue.
Metal: Silver or bronze.
Size: 36mm.
Description: (Obverse) the uncrowned left-facing profile of King
George V by Sir Bertram Mackennal. (Reverse) St George on
horseback trampling underfoot the eagle shield of the Central
Powers and a skull and cross-bones, the emblems of death. Above,
the sun has risen in victory. The figure is mounted on horseback to
symbolise man's mind controlling a force of greater strength than
his own, and thus alludes to the scientific and mechanical appliances
which helped to win the war.
Clasps: None.
Comments: *This medal was instituted to record the successful conclusion of
the First World War, but it was later extended to cover the period 1919–20
and service in mine-clearing at sea as well as participation in operations
in North and South Russia, the eastern Baltic, Siberia, the Black Sea and
Caspian. Some 6,500,000 medals were awarded in silver, but about 110,000
in bronze were issued mainly to Chinese, Indian and Maltese personnel in
labour battalions. It was originally intended to award campaign clasps, but
79 were recommended by the Army and 68 by the Navy, so the scheme was
abandoned as impractical. The naval clasps were actually authorised (7
July 1920) and miniatures are known with them, though the actual clasps
were never issued.*

VALUE:		*Miniature*
Silver (6,500,000)	£15–20	£4–5
Bronze (110,000)	£85–100	£15–20
BWM/Victory pair		
Corps	from £25	
Regiments	from £35	
Pair with plaque (no. 172)	from £180	

169. MERCANTILE MARINE WAR MEDAL

Date: 1919.
Campaign: First World War 1914–18.
Branch of Service: Mercantile Marine.
Ribbon: Green and red with a central white stripe, symbolising port and starboard navigation lights.
Metal: Bronze.
Size: 36mm.
Description: (Obverse) Mackennal profile of King George V; (reverse) a steamship ploughing through an angry sea, with a sinking submarine and a sailing vessel in the background, the whole enclosed in a laurel wreath.
Clasps: None.
Comments: *Awarded by the Board of Trade to members of the Merchant Navy who had undertaken one or more voyages through a war or danger zone.*

VALUE:

Bronze (133,000)	£26–30
To women	£150–180
BWM/Mercantile Marine pair	from £60
Miniature	£20–25

170. VICTORY MEDAL

Date: 1919.
Campaign: First World War 1914–19.
Branch of Service: British forces.
Ribbon: 38mm double rainbow (indigo at edges and red in centre).
Metal: Yellow bronze.
Size: 36mm.
Description: (Obverse) the standing figure of Victory holding a palm branch in her right hand and stretching out her left hand. (Reverse) a laurel wreath containing a four-line inscription THE GREAT WAR FOR CIVILISATION 1914–1919.
Clasps: None.
Comments: *Issued to all who had already got the 1914 or 1914–15 Stars and most of those who had the British War Medal, some six million are believed to have been produced. It is often known as the Allied War Medal because the same basic design and double rainbow ribbon were adopted by thirteen other Allied nations (though the USA alone issued it with campaign clasps). The Union of South Africa produced a version with a reverse text in English and Dutch (not Afrikaans as is often stated).*

ALUE:

British pattern	£10–14
South African pattern	£25–35
Miniature	
Normal	£3–4
"CIVILIZATION" variety	£20–25
South African pattern	£70–80

171. TERRITORIAL FORCE WAR MEDAL

Date: 1919.
Campaign: First World War 1914–19.
Branch of Service: Territorial forces.
Ribbon: Watered gold silk with two dark green stripes towards the edges.
Metal: Bronze.
Size: 36mm.
Description: (Obverse) effigy of King George V; (reverse) a wreath enclosing the text FOR VOLUNTARY SERVICE OVERSEAS 1914–19.
Clasps: None.
Comments: *Granted to all members of the Territorial Force embodied before 30 September 1914, who had completed four years service by that date, and who had served outside the United Kingdom between 4 August 1914 and 11 November 1918. Those who had already qualified for the 1914 or 1914–15 Stars, however, were excluded. Only 34,000 medals were awarded, making it by far the scarcest of the First World War medals. The value of individual medals depends on the regiment or formation of the recipient.*

VALUE:

Infantry	£120–150
RA, RE or support units	£100–120
Yeomanry	£350–400
RFC or RAF	£600–800
Nursing sisters	£300–400
Miniature	£20–25

171A. BRITISH RED CROSS SOCIETY MEDAL FOR WAR SERVICE

Date: 1920.
Campaign: First World War.
Branch of Service: Members of the British Red Cross Society.
Ribbon: Plain white.
Metal: Bronze-gilt.
Size: 31mm.
Description: (Obverse) the Geneva Cross surrounded by a laurel wreath, with the legend BRITISH RED CROSS SOCIETY: FOR WAR SERVICE: 1914–1918 around; (reverse) a wreath enclosing the text INTER/ARMA/CARITAS ("Amidst the arms, love").
Clasps: None.
Comments: *Granted to all members of the BRCS including Voluntary Aid Detachments who had performed one year or 1,000 hours voluntary service during the war and who did not receive any British War Medal for services rendered in respect of Red Cross war work. The medal was unnamed for wear only on Red Cross or similar uniform.*

VALUE: £15–20 *Miniature* £20–25

172. MEMORIAL PLAQUE

Date: 1919.
Campaign: First World War.
Branch of Service: British forces.
Ribbon: None.
Metal: Bronze.
Size: 120mm.
Description: The plaque shows Britannia bestowing a laurel crown on a rectangular tablet bearing the full name of the dead in raised lettering. In front stands the British lion, with dolphins in the upper field, an oak branch lower right, and a lion cub clutching a fallen eagle in the exergue. The inscription round the circumference reads HE (or SHE) DIED FOR FREEDOM AND HONOVR. A parchment scroll was issued with each plaque giving the deceased's name and unit.
Comments: *Awarded to the next of kin of those who lost their lives on active service during the War. Plaques issued to the Army and the Navy can usually be differentiated by the size of the H in "HE". Those issued to the Navy have a narrower H when compared with the H of "HONOUR", whereas those to the Army are of equal size.*

VALUE: "He died" (1,355,000) From £45   "She died" (600) From £1500
Parchment scroll (male) from £25, (female) £800–1000
Miniature: Uniface and unnamed   £30–40

172A. SILVER WAR BADGE

Date: 12 September 1916.
Campaign: First World War.
Ribbon: None.
Metal: Silver.
Size: 33mm.
Description: A brooch-mounted circular badge with the crowned royal monogram in the centre and edge inscription FOR KING AND EMPIRE + SERVICES RENDERED +.
Comments: *Awarded to service personnel who sustained a wound or contracted sickness or disability in the course of the war as a result of which they were invalided out. It was worn on the lapel in civilian clothes. Each badge was numbered on the reverse. The purpose of the badge was to prevent men of military age but not in uniform from being harassed by women pursuing them with white feathers.*

VALUE: £14–20   *Miniature:*   £15–20

172B. CEYLON VOLUNTEER SERVICE MEDAL

Date: 1919.
Campaign: First World War.
Branch of Service: Ceylon volunteer forces.
Ribbon: None.
Metal: Bronze.
Size: 48mm x 44mm.
Description: An upright oval medal. (Obverse) a seated female figure bestowing a laurel crown on a kneeling soldier, with a radiant sun on the horizon; above, a six-line inscription: PRESENTED BY THE GOVERNMENT OF CEYLON TO THOSE WHO VOLUNTARILY GAVE THEIR SERVICES OVERSEAS IN THE GREAT WAR OF with the dates 1914 1919 in two lines on the right of the field; (reverse) the winged figure of Victory seated on a throne above a tablet inscribed with the name of the recipient.
Comments: *Awarded to volunteers from the Ceylon forces who served abroad during the war. Ceylon (now Sri Lanka) was the only British colony to issue such a medal for war service.*

VALUE: £100–150

173. NAVAL GENERAL SERVICE MEDAL 1915–62

Date: 1915.
Campaigns: Naval actions 1915 to 1962.
Branch of Service: Royal Navy.
Ribbon: White with broad crimson edges and two narrow crimson stripes towards the centre.
Metal: Silver.
Size: 36mm.
Description: (Obverse) effigy of the reigning monarch (see below).
   (Reverse) Britannia and two seahorses travelling through the sea.
Clasps: 16 (see below).
Comments: *Instituted for service in minor operations for which no separate medal might be issued, it remained in use for almost half a century. In that period five different obverses were employed: George V (1915-36), George VI Ind Imp (1936-49), George VI Fid Def (1949-52), Elizabeth II Br Omn (1952-53) and Elizabeth II Dei Gratia (1953-62). Medals issued with the first clasp include the name of the recipient's ship but this lapsed in later awards. The MALAYA clasp was issued with three types of medal: the George VI Fid Def and Elizabeth II Dei Gratia being the most common, the Elizabeth II Br Omn type being awarded mainly to SBS for special duties. The clasp BOMB & MINE CLEARANCE 1945–46 is very rare as it was apparently only awarded to the Royal Australian Navy. The clasp CANAL ZONE was instituted in October 2003 for service between October 1951 and October 1954.*

VALUE:

			Miniature
			(in silver add £5)
i.	Persian Gulf 1909-1914		
	RN (7,127)	£120–150	
	Army (37)	£500–800	£15–25
ii.	Iraq 1919-20 (116)	£1500–1800	£15–25
iii.	NW Persia 1919-20 (4)*	Rare	£25–50
iv.	Palestine 1936-39 (13,600)	£100–125	£15–25
v.	SE Asia 1945-46 (2,000)	£155–185	£15–25
vi.	Minesweeping 1945-51 (4,750)	£150–175	£15–25
vii.	Palestine 1945-48 (7,900)	£100–120	£15–25
viii.	Malaya (George VI, Elizabeth II 2nd type) (7,800)	£100–140	£15–25
	(Elizabeth II 1st type)	£125–155	£15–25
ix.	Yangtze 1949 (1,450)	£450–600	£15–25
	to HMS *Amethyst*	£1000–1500	
x.	Bomb and Mine Clearance 1945-53 (145)	£500–600	£40–60
xi.	Bomb and Mine Clearance 1945–46	Very rare	£40–60
xi.	Bomb and Mine Clearance Mediterranean (60)	£1800–2200	£40–60
xii.	Cyprus (4,300)	£130–150	£15–25
xiii.	Near East (17,800)	£95–120	£15–25
xiv.	Arabian Peninsula (1,200)	£200–240	£15–25
xv.	Brunei (900)	£200–250	£15–25
xvi.	Canal Zone	—	—

* The clasp NW Persia 1920 was withdrawn in favour of the clasp NW Persia 1919–20. Recipients were supposed to return their first clasp in exchange for the latter.

174. GENERAL SERVICE MEDAL 1918–62

Date: 1923.

Campaigns: Minor campaigns 1918 to 1962.

Branch of Service: Army and RAF.

Ribbon: Purple with a central green stripe.

Metal: Silver.

Size: 36mm

Description: (Obverse) six different effigies of the reigning monarch [George V coinage head (1918–30), George V crowned and robed bust (1931–36), George VI Ind Imp (1937–49), George VI Fid Def (1949–52), Elizabeth II Br Omn (1952–54) and Elizabeth II Dei Gratia (1955–62)]. (Reverse) a standing figure of Victory in a Greek helmet and carrying a trident, bestowing palms on a winged sword.

Clasps: 18 (see below).

Comments: *Awarded to military and RAF personnel for numerous campaigns and operations that fell short of full-scale war. It did not cover areas already catered for in the Africa and India general service medals. The George V crowned and robed bust was used only on the medal for Northern Kurdistan in 1931. The clasp CANAL ZONE was instituted in October 2003 for service between October 1951 and October 1954.*

VALUE:

		British units	RAF	Indian and local units	Miniature *(in silver add £5)*
i.	S. Persia (Brit. officers)	£150–200	Rare	£55–85	£15–25
ii.	Kurdistan	£80–100	£150–200	£55–85	£15–25
iii.	Iraq	£60–90	£200–250	£55–85	£15–25
iv.	N.W. Persia	£90–120	£250—300	£55–85	£15–25
v.	Southern Desert Iraq	—	£350–450	—	£20–30
vi.	Northern Kurdistan	£350–450	£750–850	—	£90–100
vii.	Palestine	£80–120	£60–80	£65–95	£15–25
viii.	S.E. Asia 1945-46	£80–100	£80–100	£35–45	£15–25
ix.	Bomb and Mine Clearance 1945-49	£300–350	£300–350	—	£40–60
x.	Bomb and Mine Clearance 1945-56	£450–500	£450–500	—	£40–60
xi.	Palestine 1945-48	£60–80	£50–60	£80–100	£15–25
xii.	Malaya (George VI)	£60–80	£45–55	£50–60	£15–25
xiii.	Malaya (Elizabeth II)	£60–80	£45–55	£50–60	£15–25
xiv.	Cyprus	£60–80	£50–60	£50–60	£15–25
xv.	Near East	£80–120	£80–120	—	£15–25
xvi.	Arabian Peninsular	£80–120	£60–80	£50–60	£15–25
xvii.	Brunei	£200–250	£180–220	£120–150	£15–25
xviii.	Canal Zone	—			

175. INDIA GENERAL SERVICE MEDAL 1936–39

Date: 1938.
Campaign: India 1936–39.
Branch of Service: British and Indian Armies and RAF.
Ribbon: Stone flanked by narrow red stripes, with broad green stripes at the edges.
Metal: Silver.
Size: 36mm
Description: (Obverse) crowned effigy of King George VI; (reverse) a tiger with the word INDIA across the top.
Clasps: North-West Frontier 1936–37, North-West Frontier 1937–39.
Comments: *The fifth and last of the IGS series, it was introduced when the change of effigy from George V to George VI became necessary, anticipating a similarly long life. It was not awarded after the outbreak of the Second World War, while the partition and independence of the Indian sub-continent afterwards rendered it obsolete. The medal was struck at the Royal Mint, London for award to British Army troops and RAF personnel, but the Calcutta Mint struck the medals awarded to the Indian Army.*

VALUE:	British Army	RAF	Indian Army	*Miniature*
North West Frontier				
i. 1936-37	£85–100	£80–125	£35–45	£12–15
ii. 1937-39	£85–100	£80–125	£35–45	£12–20
2 clasps	£100–150	£125–150	£50–60	£15–30

(slip-on clasps deduct 20%)

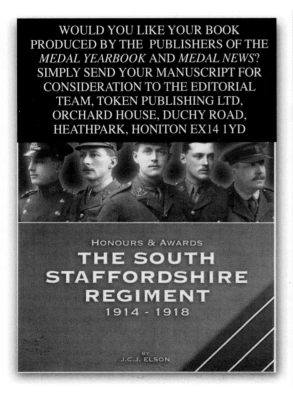

176. BRITISH NORTH BORNEO COMPANY'S GENERAL SERVICE MEDAL 1937–1941

Instituted: 1937.

Campaign: British North Borneo (now Sabah), 1937–41.

Branch of Service: British North Borneo Company staff, Constabulary and various civilians.

Ribbon: 35mm, half dark green, half yellow. Gallantry awards were denoted by a thin red central stripe.

Metal: Silver. Copies were made in bronze.

Size: 38mm diameter, with a thickness of 3mm.

Description: (Obverse) the shield of the Company flanked by warriors as supporters. Above the shield are two arms, one clothed and the other naked, supporting the Company's flag. Below the shield is the motto PERGO ET PERAGO (I carry on and accomplish); (reverse) the seated figure of Britannia facing right, holding a trident in her left hand, with her right hand resting on a shield which bears the Union flag. NORTH BORNEO GENERAL SERVICE MEDAL is inscribed round the top and in the exergue is a branch with 11 leaves.

Clasps: None.

Comments: *Only one gallantry award was ever made, to Leong Yew Pong, aged 15, gazetted August 3, 1939. For specially valuable or long and meritorious services 44 were issued, gazetted in 1937, 1938, 1939 and 1941, with one replacement in 1947. Recipients were government officials, armed constabulary, rubber planters, the Archdeacon of North Borneo, the Chairman of the Chamber of Commerce, railway managers, businessmen and local dignitaries.*

VALUE

Medal	Type	Officially named	Unnamed original	Spink copy	Specimen
For Gallantry	Silver	Unique	Rare	£250–300	£300–350
For Service	Silver	£1500–1750	Rare	£150–200	£150–200
Miniature	£180–200				

176A. SUDAN DEFENCE FORCE GENERAL SERVICE MEDAL

Instituted: November 1933.

Campaign: Minor campaigns in the Sudan after 1933.

Branch of Service: Sudan Defence Force (SDF) and Police.

Ribbon: Central stripe of royal blue, edged by two yellow stripes and two black stripes at the edges.

Metal: Silver.

Size: 36mm.

Description: (Obverse) the seal of the Governor-General of the Sudan; (reverse) a stationary group of Sudanese soldiers, with "The Sudan" in Arabic below.

Clasps: None.

Comments: *The medal was awarded on the recommendation of the Kaid el'Amm (SDF Commander) to native personnel of the SDF, Police and other approved Sudanese who served in the field on such operations as might be considered by the Governor-General as being of sufficient importance to warrant the grant of the medal. It was also awarded for action against Italian forces in the southern Sudan from June 1940 to November 1941. About 9,000 were issued.*

VALUE: £150–£200

SECOND WORLD WAR STARS

Eight different campaign stars were issued for the Second World War. Apart from some Commonwealth issues, these were issued unnamed. It was decided that the maximum number of stars that could be earned by any one person was five, while those who qualified for more received a clasp to be sewn on the ribbon of the appropriate star. Only one clasp per ribbon was permitted which was the first to be earned after qualifying for that star.

Thus the stars could bear the following clasps:

1 1939–45 Star	i. Battle of Britain
2 Atlantic Star	ii. Air Crew Europe *or* iii. France and Germany
3 Air Crew Europe Star	iv. Atlantic *or* iii. France and Germany
4 Africa Star	v. North Africa 1942-43, vi. 8th Army *or* vii. 1st Army
5 Pacific Star	viii. Burma
6 Burma Star	ix. Pacific
7 Italy Star	None
8 France and Germany Star	x. Atlantic

The ribbons are believed to have been designed by King George VI personally and have symbolic significance in each case.

When ribbons alone are worn, the clasp is usually denoted by a silver rosette. However, the Battle of Britain clasp is represented by a gilt rosette and the 8th Army and 1st Army clasps by small silver numerals. As the clasps were sewn on to the ribbon and the stars issued unnamed, it is difficult to put valuations on examples with campaign clasps, however, the prices quoted are for medals with the *original* clasps. When purchasing expensive groups it is advisable that the medals be supported by documentary provenance or form part of a group in which at least one of the medals is named to the recipient.

Many of the medals and stars of the Second World War are still being officially produced, therefore there are a number of different die varieties available. There are also a number of dangerous forgeries in existence so care should be taken when purchasing expensive items.

177. 1939–1945 STAR

Date: 1945.

Campaign: Second World War 1939–45.

Branch of Service: British and Commonwealth forces.

Ribbon: Equal stripes of dark blue, red and light blue symbolising the Royal Navy, Army and RAF respectively.

Metal: Bronze.

Size: Height 44mm; max. width 38mm.

Description: The six-pointed star has a circular centre with the GRI/VI monogram, surmounted by a crown and inscribed THE 1939-1945 STAR round the foot.

Clasps: Battle of Britain, sewn directly on to the ribbon.

Comments: *The first in a series of eight bronze stars issued for service in the Second World War, it was awarded to personnel who had completed six months' service in specified operational commands overseas, between 3 September 1939 and 2 September 1945, though in certain cases the minimum period was shortened. Any service curtailed by death, injury or capture also qualified, as did the award of a decoration or a mention in despatches. The clasp awarded to RAF aircrew for action during the Battle of Britain was denoted by a gilt rosette when the ribbon was worn alone. It is ironic that RAF ground crews who kept the Battle of Britain fighters in the air did not qualify for the 1939–45 Star and only received the Defence and War Medals, although those who assisted with the evacuation of troops from the beaches of Dunkirk did qualify.*

VALUE:		*Miniature*
1939-45 Star	£10–12	£3–5
With Battle of Britain clasp	£400–450	£6

178. ATLANTIC STAR

Campaign: Atlantic 1939-45.
Branch of Service: Mainly Royal and Commonwealth Navies.
Ribbon: Watered silk blue, white and green representing the ocean.
Metal: Bronze.
Size: Height 44mm; max. width 38mm.
Description: As above, but inscribed THE ATLANTIC STAR.
Clasps: Air Crew Europe, France and Germany.
Comments: *This star was awarded in the Royal Navy for six months' service afloat between 3 September 1939 and 8 May 1945 in the Atlantic or home waters, and to personnel employed in the convoys to North Russia and the South Atlantic. Personnel must have already qualified for the 1939–45 Star with the qualifying period for this not counting towards the Atlantic Star. Merchant Navy personnel also qualified, as did RAF and Army (maritime gunners and air crews—the latter only requiring 2 months service) who served afloat. In the last six months of operational service up to 8 May 1945, the Atlantic Star was awarded but not the 1939–45 Star. Entitlement to the France and Germany or Air Crew Europe stars was denoted by clasps to that effect, if the Atlantic Star was previously awarded. Only one clasp could be worn. Only two awards were made to WRNS: to an officer and a rating.*

VALUE:

		Miniature
Atlantic Star	£30–35	£3
Air Crew Europe clasp	Add £25	£6
France and Germany clasp	Add £15	£6

179. AIR CREW EUROPE STAR

Campaign: Air operations over Europe 1939-44.
Branch of Service: RAF and Commonwealth aircrew.
Ribbon: Pale blue (the sky) with black edges (night flying) and a narrow yellow stripe on either side (enemy searchlights).
Metal: Bronze.
Size: Height 44mm; max. width 38mm.
Description: As above, but inscribed THE AIR CREW EUROPE STAR.
Clasps: Atlantic or France and Germany.
Comments: *Awarded for operational flying from UK bases over Europe, for a period of two months between 3 September 1939 and 4 June 1944. Entitlement to either the Atlantic Star or France and Germany Star was denoted by the appropriate bar. This star is by far the most coveted of all the Second World War stars. Officially named stars to South Africans are the rarest of all the Second World War medals.*

VALUE:

		Miniature
Air Crew Europe Star	£160–180	£3
Atlantic Clasp	Add £60	£6
France and Germany Clasp	Add £15	£6

180. AFRICA STAR

Campaign: Africa 1940-43.
Branch of Service: British and Commonwealth forces.
Ribbon: Pale buff symbolising the sand of the desert, with a broad red central stripe, a dark blue stripe on the left and a light blue stripe on the right symbolising the three services.
Metal: Bronze.
Size: Height 44mm; max. width 38mm.
Description: As above, but inscribed THE AFRICA STAR.
Clasps: North Africa 1942-43, 8th Army, 1st Army.
Comments: *Awarded for entry into an operational area in North Africa between 10 June 1940 (the date of Italy's declaration of war) and 12 May 1943 (the end of operations in North Africa), but service in Abyssinia (Ethiopia), Somaliland, Eritrea and Malta also qualified for the award. A silver numeral 1 or 8 worn on the ribbon denoted service with the First or Eighth Army between 23 October 1942 and 23 May 1943. A clasp inscribed North Africa 1942-43 was awarded to personnel of the Royal Navy Inshore Squadrons and Merchant Navy vessels which worked inshore between these dates. RAF personnel also qualified for this clasp, denoted by a silver rosette on the ribbon alone.*

VALUE:

		Miniature
Africa Star	£12–15	£3
8th Army clasp	Add £15	£8
1st Army clasp	Add £15	£8
North Africa 1942–43 clasp	Add £15	£10

181. PACIFIC STAR

Campaign: Pacific area 1941-45.
Branch of Service: British and Commonwealth forces.
Ribbon: Dark green (the jungle) with a central yellow stripe (the beaches), narrow stripes of dark and light blue (Royal Navy and RAF) and wider stripes of red (Army) at the edges.
Metal: Bronze.
Size: Height 44mm; max. width 38mm.
Description: As above, but inscribed THE PACIFIC STAR.
Clasps: Burma.
Comments: *Awarded for operational service in the Pacific theatre of war from 8 December 1941 to 15 August 1945. Service with the Royal and Merchant navies in the Pacific Ocean, Indian Ocean and South China Sea and land service in these areas also qualified. Personnel qualifying for both Pacific and Burma Stars got the first star and a clasp in respect of the second.*

VALUE:		*Miniature*
Pacific Star	£30–35	£3
Burma clasp	Add £20	£6

182. BURMA STAR

Campaign: Burma 1941-45.
Branch of Service: British and Commonwealth forces.
Ribbon: Three equal bands of dark blue (British forces), red (Commonwealth forces) and dark blue. The dark blue bands each have at their centres a stripe of bright orange (the sun).
Metal: Bronze.
Size: Height 44mm; max. width 38mm.
Description: As above, but inscribed THE BURMA STAR.
Clasps: Pacific
Comments: *Qualifying service in the Burma campaign counted from 11 December 1941 and included service in Bengal or Assam from 1 May 1942 to 31 December 1943, and from 1 January 1944 onwards in these parts of Bengal or Assam east of the Brahmaputra. Naval service in the eastern Bay of Bengal, off the coasts of Sumatra, Sunda and Malacca also counted.*

VALUE:		*Miniature*
Burma Star	£15–20	£3
Pacific Clasp	Add £20	£6

183. ITALY STAR

Campaign: Italy 1943-45.
Branch of Service: British and Commonwealth forces.
Ribbon: Five equal stripes of red, white, green, white and red (the Italian national colours).
Metal: Bronze.
Size: Height 44mm; max. width 38mm.
Description: As above, but inscribed THE ITALY STAR.
Clasps: None.
Comments: *Awarded for operational service on land in Italy, Sicily, Greece, Yugoslavia, the Aegean area and Dodecanese islands, Corsica, Sardinia and Elba at any time between 11 June 1943 and 8 May 1945.*

VALUE:		*Miniature*
Italy Star	£12–15	£3

184. FRANCE AND GERMANY STAR

Date: 1945.
Campaign: France and Germany 1944-45.
Branch of Service: British and Commonwealth forces.
Ribbon: Five equal stripes of blue, white, red, white and blue
 (the national colours of the United Kingdom, France and the
 Netherlands).
Metal: Bronze.
Size: Height 44mm; max. width 38mm.
Description: As above, but inscribed THE FRANCE AND GERMANY
 STAR.
Clasps: Atlantic.
Comments: *Awarded for operational service in France, Belgium, the
 Netherlands or Germany from 6 June 1944 to 8 May 1945. Service in
 the North Sea, English Channel and Bay of Biscay in connection with
 the campaign in northern Europe also qualified. Prior eligibility for the
 Atlantic or Air Crew Europe Stars entitled personnel only to a bar for
 France and Germany. Conversely a first award of the France and Germany
 Star could earn an Atlantic bar.*

VALUE:		Miniature
France and Germany Star	£18–20	£3
Atlantic Clasp	Add £60	£6

185. DEFENCE MEDAL

Date: 1945.
Campaign: Second World War 1939-45.
Branch of Service: British and Commonwealth forces.
Ribbon: Two broad stripes of green (this green and pleasant land)
 superimposed by narrow stripes of black (the black-out), with a
 wide stripe of orange (fire-bombing) in the centre.
Metal: Cupro-nickel or silver.
Size: 36mm.
Description: (Obverse) the uncrowned effigy of King George VI;
 (reverse) two lions flanking an oak sapling crowned with the dates
 at the sides and wavy lines representing the sea below. The words
 THE DEFENCE MEDAL appear in the exergue.
Clasps: None.
Comments: *Awarded to service personnel for three years' service at home, one
 year's service in a non-operational area (e.g. India) or six months' service
 overseas in territories subjected to air attack or otherwise closely threatened.
 Personnel of Anti-Aircraft Command, RAF ground crews, Dominion forces
 stationed in the UK, the Home Guard, Civil Defence, National Fire Service
 and many other civilian units* qualified for the medal. The medal was
 generally issued unnamed in cupro-nickel, but the Canadian version was
 struck in silver.*

VALUE:		Miniature
Cupro-nickel	£16–18	£8
Silver (Canadian)	£16–18	£12

**The definitive list of eligible recipients was published by the Ministry of
 Defence in 1992 — Form DM1/DM2 and Annexe. This lists 50 different
 organisations and 90 sub-divisions of eligible personnel.*

186. WAR MEDAL 1939–45

Date: 1945.
Campaign: Second World War 1939-45.
Branch of Service: British and Commonwealth forces.
Ribbon: Narrow red stripe in the centre, with a narrow white stripe on
 either side, broad red stripes at either edge and two intervening stripes
 of blue.
Metal: Cupro-nickel or silver.
Size: 36mm.
Description: (Obverse) effigy of King George VI; (reverse) a triumphant
 lion trampling on a dragon symbolising the Axis powers.
Clasps: None.
Comments: *All fulltime personnel of the armed forces wherever they were
 serving, so long as they had served for at least 28 days between 3 September
 1939 and 2 September 1945 were eligible for this medal. It was granted in
 addition to the campaign stars and the Defence Medal. A few categories
 of civilians, such as war correspondents and ferry pilots who had flown in
 operational theatres, also qualified. No clasps were issued with this medal but
 a bronze oak leaf denoted a mention in despatches. The medal was struck in
 cupro-nickel and issued unnamed, but those issued to Australian and South
 African personnel were officially named. The Canadian version of the medal
 was struck in silver.*

VALUE:

		Miniature
Cupro-nickel	£10–12	£8
Silver (Canadian)	£12–15	£12

186A. KING'S BADGE FOR WAR SERVICE

Date: 1945.
Campaign: Second World War.
Ribbon: None.
Metal: Silver.
Size: 26mm.
Description: A circular buttonhole badge with the crowned monogram GRI
 in script capitals in the centre, inscribed FOR LOYAL SERVICE.
Comments: *Awarded to personnel who did not qualify for one or other of the service
 medals or campaign stars, and who had been invalided out of the services. The
 badges are not numbered or named.*

VALUE: £15–20   *Miniature*   £15–20

187. INDIA SERVICE MEDAL

Date: 1945.
Campaign: India 1939-45.
Branch of Service: Indian forces.
Ribbon: Dark blue with two wide and one central thin pale blue stripes.
Metal: Cupro-nickel.
Size: 36mm.
Description: (Obverse) the effigy of the King Emperor; (reverse) a map of
 the Indian sub-continent with INDIA at the top and 1939-45 at foot.
Clasps: None.
Comments: *Awarded to officers and men of the Indian forces for three years'
 non-operational service in India. In effect, it took the place of the Defence
 Medal in respect of Indian forces.*

VALUE: £12–15   *Miniature*   £10–12

188. CANADIAN VOLUNTEER SERVICE MEDAL

Date: 22 October 1943.

Campaign: Second World War 1939-45.

Branch of Service: Canadian forces.

Ribbon: Narrow stripes of green and red flanking a broad central stripe of dark blue.

Metal: Silver.

Size: 36mm.

Description: (Obverse) seven men and women in the uniforms of the various services, marching in step; (reverse) the Canadian national arms.

Clasps: Maple leaf clasp to denote overseas service. A clasp inscribed DIEPPE and surmounted by the Combined Operations emblem, was instituted on 28 April 1994 for award to all servicemen who took part in the Dieppe raid of 19 August 1942. A clasp inscribed Hong Kong, the 2 words being seperated by the letters HK entwined within a circle, was instituted on 28 April 1994 for award to those involved in the Battle of Hong Kong from 8–25 December 1941.

Comments: *Awarded for eighteen months' voluntary service in the Canadian forces from 3 September 1939 to 1 March 1947. The seven marching personnel are based on real people taken from National Defence photographs, representing the land, sea and air forces plus a nurse. The individuals are: first row: centre, 3780 Leading Seaman P. G. Colbeck, RCN; left, C52819 Pte D. E. Dolan, 1 Can. Para Bn; right, R95505 F/Sgt K. M. Morgan, RCAF. Second row: centre, W4901 Wren P. Mathie, WRCNS; left, 12885 L/Cpl J. M. Dann, CWAC; right, W315563 LAW O. M. Salmon, RCAF; back row: Lt N/S E. M. Lowe, RCAMC. 650,000 have been awarded including 525,500 with the overseas bar.*

VALUE:		Miniature
Silver medal	£18–£20	£8
i. Maple Leaf clasp	£20–£25	£12
ii. Dieppe clasp	£35–45	£15
iii. Hong Kong clasp	£35–45	

188A. CANADIAN MEMORIAL CROSS

Instituted: 1 December 1919.

Branch of Service: Relative of Canadian forces.

Ribbon: Violet 11mm with ring suspension only.

Metal: Dull silver.

Size: 32mm.

Description: A Greek cross with the royal cypher at the centre, superimposed on another with arms slightly flared at the ends. Maple leaves adorn three of the arms while the top arm has a crown surmounted by a suspension ring. (Reverse) The service number, rank, initials and name of the person being commemorated are engraved. There is also a sterling mark on the lower arm. Four versions of the cross exist: the original, with GRI cypher (1914–19), with GVIR cypher and ring suspension (1940–45), GVIR cypher with suspension bar (1945–52) and an EIIR version for Korea and later conflicts.

Comments: *Issued to wives and mothers of servicemen who had died during World War I. A second version was introduced in August 1940 for award to widows and mothers of World War II servicemen, but this was extended to include those of merchant seamen and civilian firefighters. Newfoundland service personnel became eligible after April 1, 1949.*

VALUE:

GVR, ring suspension (58,500)	From £80
GVIR, ring suspension ⎫ (32,500)	From £80
GVIR, bar suspension ⎭	From £80
EIIR, bar suspension (500)	From £120
Miniature £70–90	

189. AFRICA SERVICE MEDAL

Date: 1943.
Campaign: Second World War 1939-45.
Branch of Service: South African forces.
Ribbon: A central orange stripe, with green and gold stripes on either side.
Metal: Silver.
Size: 36mm.
Description: (Obverse) depicts a map of the African Continent; (reverse) bears a leaping Springbok. Inscribed AFRICA SERVICE MEDAL on the left and AFRIKADIENS-MEDALJE on the right.
Clasps: None, but a Protea emblem is worn on the ribbon by recipients of the King's Commendation.
Comments: *Awarded to Union service personnel who served at home and abroad during the War for at least thirty days. Medals were fully named and gave the service serial number of the recipient, prefixed by various letters, for example N (Native Military Corps), C (Cape Corps), M (Indian and Malay Corps), etc., no prefix indicated a white volunteer.*

VALUE:
Silver medal (190,000)	£12–15	*Miniature*	£10–12

190. AUSTRALIA SERVICE MEDAL

Date: 1949.
Campaign: Second World War 1939-45.
Branch of Service: Australian forces.
Ribbon: A broad central band of khaki bordered in red, with a dark blue and a light blue bar at either edge.
Metal: Cupro-nickel.
Size: 36mm.
Description: (Obverse) the effigy of King George VI; (reverse) the Australian arms supported by a kangaroo and an emu.
Clasps: None.
Comments: *Awarded to all Australian personnel who had seen eighteen months' overseas or three years' home service. The medals were named to the recipients. In the case of Army personnel, their service numbers were prefixed by the initial of their state: N (New South Wales), Q (Queensland), S (South Australia), T (Tasmania), V (Victoria) and W (Western Australia). In 1999 the time served for eligibility was reduced.*

VALUE:
Cupro-nickel medal (600,000)	£30–35	*Miniature*	£12–15

191. NEW ZEALAND WAR SERVICE MEDAL

Date: 1946.
Campaign: Second World War 1939-45.
Branch of Service: New Zealand forces.
Ribbon: Black with white edges.
Metal: Cupro-nickel.
Size: 36mm.
Description: (Obverse) effigy of King George VI; (reverse) the text FOR SERVICE TO NEW ZEALAND 1939-45 with a fern leaf below. Suspension was by a pair of fern leaves attached to a straight bar.
Clasps: None.
Comments: *Issued unnamed, to all members of the New Zealand forces who completed one month full-time or six months part-time service between September 1939 and September 1945, provided the applicant carried out the prescribed training or duties. This included Home Guard service and Naval Auxiliary Patrol service.*

VALUE:
Cupro-nickel medal (240,000)	£20–25	*Miniature*	£7–10

191A. NEW ZEALAND MEMORIAL CROSS

Instituted: 1960.
Campaign: Second World War, 1939–45.
Branch of Service: Relatives of New Zealand forces personnel.
Ribbon: 12mm royal purple
Metal: Dull Silver.
Size: 32 mm.
Description: A cross surmounted by a St Edward Crown, with fern leaves on each arm, in the centre, within a wreath, the Royal Cypher; (reverse) details of the person in respect of whose death the cross is granted.
Comments: *First announced in the New Zealand Gazette dated at Wellington, September 12, 1947 and approved by the King but not instituted until August 16, 1960. Originally granted to the next-of-kin of persons who had lost their lives on active service with the New Zealand forces during the Second World War, or who had subsequently died of wounds or illness contracted during that conflict. Provision was made for the grant of crosses to the parent(s) as well as the wife or eldest surviving daughter or son. It was subsequently awarded in respect of postwar campaigns: Korea (47), Malaya, South Vietnam (37), and East Timor (3).*
VALUE:

Silver (World War II)	From £90	Miniature £180–200
(Later campaigns)	Rare	

192. SOUTH AFRICAN MEDAL FOR WAR SERVICE

Date: 1946.
Campaign: Second World War 1939-46.
Branch of Service: South African forces.
Ribbon: Three equal stripes of orange, white and blue, the South African national colours.
Metal: Silver.
Size: 36mm.
Description: (Obverse) South African arms; (reverse) a wreath of protea flowers enclosing the dates 1939 and 1945. Inscribed in English and Afrikaans: SOUTH AFRICA FOR WAR SERVICES on the left and SUID AFRIKA VIR OORLOGDIENSTE on the right.
Clasps: None.
Comments: *Men and women who served for at least two years in any official voluntary organisation in South Africa or overseas qualified for this medal so long as the service was both voluntary and unpaid. Those who already had the Africa Service Medal were ineligible, but exceptions exist.*
VALUE:
  Silver (17,500) £35–40   *Miniature* £14–16

193. SOUTHERN RHODESIA WAR SERVICE MEDAL

Date: 1946.
Campaign: Second World War 1939-45.
Branch of Service: Southern Rhodesian forces.
Ribbon: Dark green with black and red stripes at each edge.
Metal: Cupro-nickel.
Size: 36mm.
Description: (Obverse) King George VI; (reverse) the Southern Rhodesian national arms. FOR SERVICE IN SOUTHERN RHODESIA round the top and the dates 1939-1945 at the foot.
Clasps: None.
Comments: *This very scarce medal was awarded only to those who served in Southern Rhodesia during the period of the War but who were ineligible for one of the campaign stars or war medals.*
VALUE:
  Cupro-nickel (1700) £240–260   *Miniature* £20–25

194. NEWFOUNDLAND VOLUNTEER WAR SERVICE MEDAL

Date: 1981.
Campaign: Second World War 1939-45.
Branch of Service: Newfoundland forces.
Ribbon: Deep claret with edges of red, white and blue.
Metal: Bronze.
Size: 37mm.
Description: (Obverse) the royal cypher of George VI surmounted by a crown topped by a caribou, the Newfoundland national emblem; (reverse) Britannia on a scallop shell background guarded by two lions.
Clasps:
Comments: *While the Second World War was being fought, Newfoundland was still a separate British colony which did not enter the Canadian Confederation till 1949. Consequently Newfoundland servicemen did not qualify for the Canadian Volunteer Service medal, and this deficiency was not remedied until July 1981 when the Newfoundland provincial government instituted this medal. Those who had served with the Canadian forces, on the other hand, and already held the Canadian medal, were not eligible for this award. The medal could be claimed by next-of-kin of those who died in or since the war.*

VALUE: Bronze (7,500)   £450–550   *Miniature*   £60–70

195. KOREA MEDAL

Date: July 1951.
Campaign: Korean War 1950-53.
Branch of Service: British and Commonwealth forces.
Ribbon: Yellow, with two blue stripes .
Metal: Cupro-nickel or silver.
Size: 36mm.
Description: (Obverse) Right-facing bust of Queen Elizabeth II by Mary Gillick; there are two obverse types, with or without BR: OMN; (reverse) Hercules wrestling with the Hydra, KOREA in the exergue.
Clasps: None.
Comments: *Awarded to all British and Commonwealth forces who took part in the Korean War between July 1950 and July 27, 1953. British and New Zealand medals were issued in cupro-nickel impressed in small capitals, medals to Australian forces were impressed in large capitals and the Canadian version was struck in silver and has CANADA below the Queen's bust. Particularly prized are medals issued to the "Glorious Gloucesters" who played a gallant part in the battle of the Imjin River.*

VALUE:		*Miniature*
British, first obverse		
Regiments	£120–150	£10–12
Corps/RN/RAF	£180–220	
British, second obverse	£120–150	£10–12
To Gloucester Regiment	£350–450	
Australian or New Zealand naming	£120–150	
Canadian, silver (over 20,000)	£90–120	£12–14

196. SOUTH AFRICAN MEDAL FOR KOREA

Date: 1953.
Campaign: Korea 1950-53.
Branch of Service: South African forces.
Ribbon: Sky blue central stripe flanked by dark blue stripes and edges of orange.
Metal: Silver.
Size: 38mm.
Description: (Obverse) maps of South Africa and Korea with an arrow linking them and the words VRYWILLIGERS and VOLUNTEERS in the field. (Reverse) the then South African arms surmounted by the crowned EIIR.
Clasps: None.
Comments: *Awarded to the 800 personnel in the contingent sent to Korea by the Union of South Africa. Suspension is by a ring and claw.*

VALUE:

Silver (800)	£400–500	*Miniature* £35–45
Pilot's issue	£1200–1500	

197. UNITED NATIONS KOREA MEDAL

Date: December 1950.
Campaign: Korea 1950-53.
Branch of Service: All UN forces.
Ribbon: Seventeen narrow stripes alternating pale blue and white.
Metal: Bronze.
Size: 35mm.
Description: (Obverse) the wreathed globe emblem of the UN; (reverse) inscribed FOR SERVICE IN DEFENCE OF THE PRINCIPLES OF THE CHARTER OF THE UNITED NATIONS.
Clasps: Korea.
Comments: *National variants were produced, but the British type was granted to all personnel of the British and Commonwealth forces who had served at least one full day in Korea or in support units in Japan. Moreover, as those who served in Korea after the armistice in July 1953 were also entitled to the UN medal it is sometimes found in groups without the corresponding British medal. The award was extended to cover the period up to July 27, 1954, the first anniversary of the Panmunjom Truce. Issues to South African personnel were named on the rim.*

VALUE: £20–25   *Miniature* £6–8

198. GENERAL SERVICE MEDAL 1962

Date: 1964.
Campaign: Minor campaigns and operations since 1962.
Branch of Service: British forces.
Ribbon: Deep purple edged with green.
Metal: Silver.
Size: 36mm.
Description: (Obverse) a crowned bust of Queen Elizabeth II; (reverse) an oak wreath enclosing a crown and the words FOR CAMPAIGN SERVICE. It has a beaded and curved suspension above which are mounted campaign clasps.
Clasps: 13 to date (see below); the maximum clasps awarded so far seems to be six.
Comments: *This medal was instituted for award to personnel of all services, and thus did away with the need for separate Army and Navy general service medals. Awards range from a mere 70 for South Vietnam to over 130,000 for service in Northern Ireland.*

VALUE:

			Miniature
i.	Borneo	£70–90	£8–10
ii.	Radfan	£90–120	£8–10
iii.	South Arabia	£60–100	£8–10
iv.	Malay Peninsula	£65–90	£8–10
v.	South Vietnam	Rare	£8–10
vi.	Northern Ireland	£50–65	£8–10
vii.	Dhofar	£150–200	£8–10
viii.	Lebanon	£700–800	£8–10
ix.	Mine Clearance	£800–1000	£8–10
x.	Gulf	£240–280	£8–10
xi.	Kuwait	£400–450	£8–10
xii.	N. Iraq & S. Turkey	£350–450	£8–10
xiii.	Air Operations Iraq	£350–450	£10–12
	2 clasps	£80–100	£12–16
	3 clasps	£150–180	£14–18
	4 clasps	£220–280	£16–20

198A. OPERATIONAL SERVICE MEDAL

Date: 1999.
Campaign: Operations after May 5, 2000.
Branch of Service: All branches of the armed forces.
Ribbon: Broad central red stripe, flanked by black and blue with green stripes (Sierra Leone) or buff edge stripes (Afghanistan).
Metal: Silver.
Size: 36mm.
Description: (Obverse) crowned profile of Queen Elizabeth; (reverse) a four-pointed star with different crowns impaled on each point, the centre having the Union Jack in a circle surrounded by the inscription FOR OPERATIONAL SERVICE. The medal has a scrolled suspender with ornamental finials.
Clasps: Afghanistan, Sierra Leone.
Comments: *Intended for minor campaigns for which a separate medal is not awarded, and operations for which the award of a UN or NATO medal is not merited. It replaces the General Service Medal 1962, except for Northern Ireland and Air Operations Iraq. It has so far been awarded for 30 days continuous service in Sierra Leone or 45 days outside the operational area (Operations Basilica or Silkman), or 14 days continuous in, or 21 days outside Sierra Leone (Operation Palliser), or one day or one sortie (Operations Maidenly or Barras). In the case of the last two, awards are denoted by rosettes on the ribbon, as for the South Atlantic Medal. The clasp AFGHANISTAN was instituted in October 2003 for service there since 11 September 2001.*

VALUE: £400–500

199. UNITED NATIONS EMERGENCY FORCE MEDAL

Date: 1957.
Campaign: Israel and Egypt 1956–57.
Branch of Service: All UN forces.
Ribbon: Sand-coloured with a central light blue stripe and narrow dark blue and green stripes towards each edge.
Metal: Bronze.
Size: 35mm.
Description: (Obverse) the UN wreathed globe emblem with UNEF at the top; (reverse) inscribed IN THE SERVICE OF PEACE. Ring suspension.
Clasps: None.
Comments: *Awarded to all personnel who served with the UN peace-keeping forces on the border between Israel and Egypt following the Sinai Campaign of 1956. These medals were awarded to troops from Brazil, Canada, Colombia, Denmark, Finland, Indonesia, Norway, Sweden and Yugoslavia.*

VALUE:

Bronze original issue	£35–45	*Miniature*	*£6–8*

200. VIETNAM MEDAL

Date: July 1968.
Campaign: Vietnam 1964-73.
Branch of Service: Australian and New Zealand forces.
Ribbon: A broad central stripe of bright yellow surmounted by three thin red stripes (the Vietnamese national colours) and bordered by broader red stripes, with dark and light blue stripes at the edges, representing the three services.
Metal: Silver.
Size: 36mm.
Description: (Obverse) the crowned bust of Queen Elizabeth II; (reverse) a nude male figure pushing apart two spheres representing different ideologies.
Clasps: None.
Comments: *Awarded to personnel who served in Vietnam a minimum of one day on land or 28 days at sea after 28 May 1964. The medal was impressed in large capitals (Australian) or small capitals (New Zealand).*

VALUE:

Australian recipient (18,000)	£220–250
New Zealand recipient (3,312)	£245–285
Miniature	£10–12

200A. VIETNAM LOGISTIC AND SUPPORT MEDAL

Instituted: 1993.
Campaign: Vietnam 1964–68.
Branch of Service: Australian forces.
Ribbon: A broad central stripe of yellow with three narrow red stripes superimposed. On the left are stripes of red and dark blue and on the right stripes of dark brown and light blue.
Metal: Nickel-silver.
Size: 36mm.
Description: (Obverse) crowned effigy of Queen Elizabeth and titles; (reverse) as MY200 above but with a cartouche containing a ram's head (Royal Australian Mint's mark) near the man's right foot. The suspension bar also differs from MY200 with graduated straight sides.
Clasps: None.
Comments: *Awarded to personnel who served in the Vietnam War but who did not qualify for the Vietnam Medal. It is estimated that about 20,000 individuals are eligible for this award. Recipients include Qantas air crew who took troop flights to Saigon, and civilian entertainers.*
VALUE:
    Australian recipient (5,121)   £150–250

201. SOUTH VIETNAM CAMPAIGN MEDAL

Date: May 12, 1964.
Campaign: Vietnam 1964–72.
Branch of Service: Allied forces in Vietnam.
Ribbon: White with two broad green stripes towards the centre and narrow green edges.
Metal: Bronze.
Size: Height 42mm; max. width 36mm.
Description: A six-pointed star, with gold rays in the angles. The gilt enamelled centre shows a map of Vietnam engulfed in flames; (reverse) a Vietnamese inscription in the centre.
Clasps: 1960- (bronze, cupro-nickel or silver gilt), 1965 (silver gilt).
Comments: *Awarded by the government of South Vietnam to Australian and New Zealand forces who served at least six months in Vietnam from March 1, 1961. The original issue, of Vietnamese manufacture, was relatively crude and issued unnamed. Subsequently medals were produced in Australia and these are not only of a better quality but bear the name of the recipient. A third version, made in the USA, has the suspension ring a fixed part of the medal.*
VALUE:
Unnamed	£15–20
Named	£20–30
Miniature	enamels £6–10, painted £5–8

202. RHODESIA MEDAL

Date: 1980.
Campaign: Rhodesia 1979–80.
Branch of Service: British and Rhodesian forces.
Ribbon: Sky blue, with a narrow stripe of red, white and dark blue in the centre.
Metal: Rhodium-plated cupro-nickel.
Size: 36mm.
Description: (Obverse) the crowned bust of Queen Elizabeth II; (reverse) a sable antelope with the name of the medal and the year of issue.
Clasps: None.
Comments: *This medal was awarded to personnel serving in Rhodesia for fourteen days between 1 December 1979 and 20 March 1980, pending the elections and the emergence of the independent republic of Zimbabwe. Medals were issued unnamed or named in impressed capitals. It was officially named to the armed forces and RAF personnel but unnamed to participating British Police. Examples with the word COPY in raised capitals immediately below the suspension fitment are believed to have been issued as replacements for lost medals, although examples with "R" for replacement are also known to exist.*
VALUE:
    Cupro-nickel (2500)   £350–450   *Miniature*   £30–50

203. SOUTH ATLANTIC MEDAL

Date: 1982.
Campaign: Falkland Islands and South Georgia 1982.
Branch of Service: British forces.
Ribbon: Watered silk blue, white, green, white and blue.
Metal: Cupro-nickel.
Size: 36mm.
Description: (Obverse) crowned profile of Queen Elizabeth II; (reverse) laurel wreath below the arms of the Falkland Islands with SOUTH ATLANTIC MEDAL inscribed round the top.
Clasps: None, but a rosette denoting service in the combat zone.
Comments: *Awarded to all personnel who took part in operations in the South Atlantic for the liberation of South Georgia and the Falkland Islands following the Argentinian invasion. To qualify, the recipient had to have at least one full day's service in the Falklands or South Georgia, or 30 days in the operational zone including Ascension Island. Those who qualified under the first condition were additionally awarded a large rosette for wear on the ribbon.*

VALUE:	Wth rosette	Without
Army (7000)	£400–500	£230–280
Parachute Regiment	£800–1200	—
Royal Navy (13,000)	£350–400	£230–280
Royal Marines (3700)	£600–900	£280–350
Royal Fleet Auxiliary (2000)	£350–450	£200–250
RAF (2000)	£350–400	£200–250
Merchant Navy and civilians (2000)	£350–400	£200–250
Miniature	£10–12	

203A. SOVIET 40th ANNIVERSARY MEDAL

Date: 1985.
Campaign: Second World War.
Branch of Service: British and Canadian forces who served mainly in RN or MN ships on Arctic convoys.
Ribbon: One half red, the other orange with three black stripes, edged with pale blue. Worn in the Russian style.
Metal: Bronze.
Size: 32mm.
Description: (Obverse) Group of servicemen and women in front of a five-pointed star flanked by oak leaves and the dates 1945–1985 above; (reverse) 40th anniversary of the Victory in the Great Patriotic War 1941–1945, in Russian.
Clasps: None.
Comments: *In 1994 Her Majesty the Queen approved the wearing of this medal awarded by the Soviet Government to selected ex-Servicemen, bearing in mind the changed circumstances in Russia since the award was first issued. Similar medals have also been issued for the 50th and 55th anniversaries.*

VALUE:		
	British striking	£15–20
	Russian striking	£15–20
	Miniature	£9–10

204. GULF MEDAL

Date: 1992.

Campaign: Kuwait and Saudi Arabia 1990-91.

Branch of Service: British forces.

Ribbon: Sand-coloured broad central stripe flanked by narrow stripes of dark blue, red and light blue (left) or light blue, red and dark blue (right) representing the sands of the desert and the three armed services.

Metal: Cupro-nickel.

Size: 36mm.

Description: (Obverse) crowned profile of Queen Elizabeth II; (reverse) an eagle and automatic rifle superimposed on an anchor, symbolising the three armed services. The dates of the Gulf War appear at the foot.

Clasps: 2 Aug 1990, 16 Jan–28 Feb 1991.

Comments: *Awarded to personnel who had thirty days continuous service in the Middle East (including Cyprus) between 2 August 1990 and 7 March 1991, or seven days between 16 January 1991 and 28 February 1991, or service with the Kuwait Liaison Team on 2 August 1990, the date of the Iraqi invasion. Two clasps were sanctioned and awarded to personnel who qualified for active service with the Liaison Team or in the operations to liberate Kuwait. A rosette is worn on the ribbon alone to denote the campaign clasps. Naming is in impressed capitals. More than 45,000 medals were awarded. See also the Kuwait and Iraq-Turkey clasps awarded to the General Service Medal 1962. About 1,500 civilians, including members of British Aerospace working at Dahran, also received the medal with the clasp 16 Jan to 28 Feb 1991.*

VALUE:

No clasp	£150–180
i. 2 Aug 1990	£2000–3000
ii. 16 Jan to 28 Feb 1991	
Regiments/RN/RAF	£250–350
Corps and Artillery	£200–250
Civilians	£200–250
Miniature	£10–12

205. SAUDI ARABIAN MEDAL FOR THE LIBERATION OF KUWAIT

Date: 1991.

Campaign: Gulf War 1991.

Branch of Service: British and Allied forces.

Ribbon: Green with edges of red, black and white (the Saudi national colours).

Metal: White metal.

Size: approx. 45mm across

Description: The white metal medal has a star of fifteen long and fifteen short round-tipped rays, surmounted by a bronze circle bearing a crowned and enwreathed globe on which appears a map of Arabia. Above the circle is a palm tree with crossed scimitars, the state emblem of Saudi Arabia. A scroll inscribed in Arabic and English LIBERATION OF KUWAIT appears round the foot of the circle.

Clasps: None.

Comments: *Awarded by the government of Saudi Arabia to all Allied personnel who took part in the campaign for the liberation of Kuwait, although only a few of the 45,000 British servicemen were subsequently given permission by the Foreign and Commonwealth Office to wear it. The contract for production was shared between Spink and a Swiss company, but subsequently a flatter version, more practicable for wear with other medals, was manufactured in the United States.*

VALUE: £20   *Miniature*   £12–14

205A. MULTINATIONAL FORCE AND OBSERVERS MEDAL

Date: March 1982.

Campaign: Sinai Peninsula.

Ribbon: 36mm with 10mm central white stripe, flanked by 3mm dark green stripes and 10mm orange stripes on the outside.

Metal: Bronze.

Size: 30mm.

Description: (Obverse) a dove clutching an olive branch surrounded by the inscription MULTINATIONAL FORCE & OBSERVERS; (reverse) UNITED IN SERVICE FOR PEACE in five lines.

Comments: *Awarded to personnel of the Multinational Force and Observers (MFO) created in 1979 to monitor the peace agreement between Egypt and Israel. Eligibility for the medal was originally 90 days continuous service in the force, but this was raised to 170 days in March 1985. Subsequent awards for each completed six-month tour is indicated by a silver numeral affixed to the ribbon. It was originally awarded personally by the MFO's first commander, the Norwegian General Fredrik Bull-Hansen. The Force has 3,000 personnel drawn from the armed services of Australia, Canada, Colombia, Fiji, France, Italy, the Netherlands, New Zealand, UK, USA and Uruguay.*

VALUE: £25–30   *Miniature* £7–10

206. KUWAITI LIBERATION MEDALS

4th grade

Date: 1991.

Campaign: Liberation of Kuwait 1991.

Branch of Service: Allied forces.

Ribbon: Equal stripes of green, white and red (the Kuwaiti national colours) with a black quadrilateral at the upper edge.

Metal: Various.

Size: Various.

Description: The circular medals have different decorative treatments of the Kuwaiti state emblem on the obverse, enshrined in a five-petalled flower (Second Grade), a five-pointed star with radiate background (Third Grade) and a plain medallic treatment (Fourth Grade). All grades, however, have a straight bar suspender of different designs.

Clasps: None.

Comments: *This medal was issued in five grades and awarded according to the rank of the recipient. The Excellent Grade was only conferred on the most senior Allied commanders, the First Grade went to brigadiers and major-generals, the Second Grade to officers of field rank (colonels and majors), the Third Grade to junior officers (captains, lieutenants and equivalent ranks in the other services), and the Fourth Grade to all other ranks. HM Government has decreed that British personnel may accept their medals as a keepsake but permission to wear them in uniform has so far been refused. The Canadian Government has followed the same policy, but the personnel of other Allied nations are permitted to wear their medals.*

VALUE: *Miniature*

2nd grade		£40–50	
3rd grade —		£20–30	
4th grade £10–15		£20–30	£12–14 (silver)

206A. NATO SERVICE MEDALS

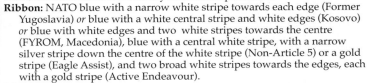

Instituted: December 20, 1994.

Campaigns: Any theatre or area of operations in the service of the North Atlantic Treaty Organization.

Branch of Service: NATO military and service personnel.

Ribbon: NATO blue with a narrow white stripe towards each edge (Former Yugoslavia) *or* blue with a white central stripe and white edges (Kosovo) *or* blue with white edges and two white stripes towards the centre (FYROM, Macedonia), blue with a central white stripe, with a narrow silver stripe down the centre of the white stripe (Non-Article 5) or a gold stripe (Eagle Assist), and two broad white stripes towards the edges, each with a gold stripe (Active Endeavour).

Metal: Bronze.

Size: 36mm.

Description: (Obverse) the NATO star emblem set in a wreath of olive leaves; (reverse) the title NORTH ATLANTIC TREATY ORGANIZATION and the words IN SERVICE OF PEACE AND FREEDOM in English and French. Two versions of this medal have been recorded: (a) light bronze, broad leaves in wreath, (b) dark bronze, narrow leaves.

Clasps: Former Yugoslavia, Kosovo, Non-Article 5, Macedonia, Eagle Assist, Endeavour. Additionally a special clasp inscribed MERITORIOUS was instituted in 2003 for meritorious service.

Comments: *The NATO medal was first instituted to reward personnel who took part in the Alliance operations in the former Yugoslavia. Any person serving under NATO command or operational control is eligible for the award. UK Service personnel cannot qualify for the NATO Medal and the UNPROFOR Medal (no. 207) in respect of the same period of service. The qualifying period for the medal is to be designated by the Secretary-General, however, for the operations in the former Yugoslavia the period has been set as 30 days continuous or accumulated service within the theatre of operations inside the former Yugoslavia and the Adriatic, or 90 days within the area of operations but outside the territory of the former Yugoslavia. The medal takes precedence equal to the General Service Medal in order of date of award. Numerals are worn on the ribbon to denote multiple tours. The Non-Article 5 medal (ribbon) replaces the three other NATO medals (ribbons) for services anywhere in the Balkans, commencing December 3, 2002. Article 5 of the NATO Charter states that an attack on one member state is an attack on the whole Alliance. Non-Article 5 operations are therefore those outside NATO territory.*

VALUE: £12–£15   *Miniature* £8–10

206B. EUROPEAN COMMUNITY MONITORING MISSION MEDAL

Date: 1995.

Campaigns: Former Yugoslavia.

Branch of Service: EC Community Peacekeeping.

Ribbon: Navy with stripes of white and red and thin yellow.

Metal: Silver.

Size: 36mm.

Description: (Obverse) Outline map of Yugoslavia surmounted by the words EC MONITOR MISSION surrounded by a ring of stars; (reverse) a dove of peace.

Comments: *Awarded or 21 days service between July 27, 1991 and June 30, 1993, in and around the former Yugoslavia.*

VALUE: £15–£20   *Miniature*   £30–40

206C. WESTERN EUROPEAN UNION MISSION SERVICE MEDAL

Date: 1997.

Campaigns: Operations in the Former Yugoslavia.

Branch of Service: Personnel serving with the Western European Union forces.

Ribbon: Bright blue with central broad yellow stripe.

Metal: Silver.

Size: 36mm.

Description: (Obverse) capital letters WEU arranged horizontally with U and O above and below the E to signify "Western European Union" and its French equivalent "Union de l'Europe Occidentale". Ten five-pointed stars are ranged around the lower half of the circumference; (reverse) PRO PACE UNUM ("One for peace") in three lines. A clasp signifying the area of service is worn on the ribbon.

Comments: *This medal was instituted to award service with missions under the auspices of the Western European Union. It was awarded to personnel who had served at least 30 days in the former Yugoslavia or 90 days in the Adriatic, Hungary or Rumania. The first British recipients (March 6, 1977) were 27 police officers who had served with the WEU Police Force in Bosnia-Herzegovina. A total of 15,982 medals had been awarded by September 2000. This medal is also known as the European Union Police Mission Medal.*

VALUE: £20–£25   *Miniature*   £40–45

207. UNITED NATIONS MEDAL

Style of lettering for clasps.

Date: 1951.
Campaigns: Various supervisory or observation roles since 1948.
Branch of Service: UN forces.
Ribbons: Various (see below).
Metal: Bronze.
Size: 35mm.
Description: (Obverse) the wreathed globe emblem surmounted by the letters UN; (reverse) inscribed "IN THE SERVICE OF PEACE".
Clasps: CONGO, UNGOMAP, OSGAP, UNSMIH, MINUGUA, UNCRO, ONUMOZ, UNSOM.
Comments: *Apart from the UN Korea and UNEF medals, there have been numerous awards to personnel who served in one or other of the UN peace-keeping actions around the world since the end of the Second World War. The all-purpose medal has been awarded with various distinctive ribbons for service in many of the world's trouble spots. Two versions of the medal exist: globe flat (European) and globe raised (US version). Issues to South African Personnel are named. Eligibility is generally 90 days, but some missions were 180 days. Subsequent awards for each six month tour completed with the same mission are indicated by a silver numeral affixed to the ribbon. The missions are listed below in chronological order.*

UNTSO   United Nations Truce Supervision Organization (Israel, Egypt, Syria since 1948).
Blue ribbon with two narrow white stripes towards the edges.
UNOGIL   United Nations Observation Group in Lebanon (1958).
Same ribbon as UNTSO.
ONUC   Organisation des Nations Unies au Congo (1960–64).
Originally the same ribbon as UNTSO with clasp CONGO, but a green ribbon, with white and blue edges was substituted in 1963.
UNTEA   United Nations Temporary Executive Authority (Netherlands New Guinea, 1962).
Blue ribbon with a white central stripe bordered green.
UNMOGIP   United Nations Military Observer Group in India and Pakistan since 1949.
Dark green ribbon shading to light green with white and blue edges.
UNIPOM   United Nations India Pakistan Observation Mission (1965–66).
Ribbon as UNMOGIP.
UNYOM   United Nations Yemen Observation Mission (1963–64).
Ribbon with brown centre, yellow stripes and light blue edges.
UNFICYP   United Nations Force in Cyprus (1964–   ).
Pale blue ribbon with central white stripe bordered in dark blue. Initially 30, then increased to 90 days.
UNEF 2   United Nations Emergency Force 2 patrolling Israeli-Egyptian cease-fire (1973–   ).
Pale blue ribbon with sand centre and two dark blue stripes.
UNDOF   United Nations Disengagement Observer Force, Golan Heights (1974–   ).
Ribbon of red, white, black and pale blue.
UNIFIL   United Nations Interim Force in Lebanon (1978–   ).
Pale blue ribbon with green centre bordered white and red.

UNGOMAP   United Nations Good Offices in Afghanistan and Pakistan.
   A bronze bar inscribed UNGOMAP was issued but as the mission was made up from observers from three other missions it can only be found on these ribbons: UNTSO, UNIFIL, UNDOF.
UNIIMOG   United Nations Iran-Iraq Monitoring Observation Group.
   Pale blue with red, white and green edges.
UNAVEM   United Nations Angola Verification Missions: I (1989–91), II (1991–95), III (1995–   ).
   Pale blue ribbon with yellow edges separated by narrow stripes of red, white and black (same for all three).
ONUCA   Observadores de las Naciones Unidas en Centro America (Nicaragua and Guatemala).
   Pale blue ribbon with dark blue edges and nine thin central green or white stripes.
UNTAG   United Nations Transitional Assistance Group (Namibia, 1989–90).
   Sand ribbon with pale blue edges and thin central stripes of blue, green, red, sand and deep blue.
ONUSAL   Observadores de las Naciones Unidas en El Salvador.
   Pale blue ribbon with a white central stripe bordered dark blue.

UNIKOM   United Nations Iraq Kuwait Observation Mission (1991–).
Sand ribbon with a narrow central stripe of pale blue.

MINURSO   Mission des Nations Unies pour la Referendum dans le Sahara Occidental (UN Mission for the Referendum in Western Sahara) (1991–).
Ribbon has a broad sandy centre flanked by stripes of UN blue.

UNAMIC   United Nations Advanced Mission in Cambodia (Oct. 1991–March 1992).
Pale blue ribbon with central white stripe bordered with dark blue, yellow and red stripes.

UNTAC   United Nations Transitional Authority in Cambodia (March 1992–Sept. 1993).
Green ribbon with central white stripe edged with red, pale blue and dark blue.

UNOSOM   United Nations Operations in Somalia (I: 1992–93 and II: 1993–95).
Pale yellow ribbon with central blue stripe edged with green.

UNMIH   United Nations Mission in Haiti
Pale blue ribbon with dark blue and red central stripes edged with white.

UNIMOZ   United Nations Operations in Mozambique (1992–).
Pale blue ribbon edged with white and green stripes.

UNPROFOR   United Nations Protection Force (1992–95) operating in the former Yugoslavia, especially Bosnia. *Blue ribbon with central red stripe edged in white and green or brown edges. See also UNCRO below.*

UNOMIL   United Nations Observer Mission in Liberia (1993–).
Pale blue ribbon flanked with white stripes with dark blue or red edges.

UNOMUR   United Nations Observer Mission in Uganda/Rwanda (1993–).
Pale blue central stripe edged by white and flanked by equal stripes of black, orange and red.

UNOMIG   United Nations Observer Mission in Georgia (1993–). For 180 days service.
Pale blue central stripe flanked by equal stripes of white, green and dark blue.

UNAMIR   United Nations Assistance Mission in Rwanda (1993–96).
Pale blue central stripe edged with white and flanked by equal stripes of black, green and red.

UNHQ   General service at UN headquarters, New York.
Plain ribbon of pale blue, the UN colour.

UNPREDEP   United Nations Preventative Deployment in Yugoslavia.
Blue ribbon with central red stripe bearing four yellow lines and flanked by white edging.

UNMOP   United Nations Mission of Observers in Pravlaka.
Dark blue ribbon with central yellow stripe edged with white, and two pale blue stripes.

UNTAES   United Nations Transitional Authority in Eastern Slavonia. (1995-96)
Pale blue ribbon with yellow, red edged with white, and green stripes.

UNMOT   United Nations Peacekeeping Force in Tadjikistan.
Blue ribbon with central green stripe flanked by white stripes.

UNMIBH   United Nations Mission in Bosnia Herzegovina (1995).
Blue ribbon with white central stripe, edged with one green and one red stripe.

UNMOGUA   United Nations Military Observers in Guatemala.
Purple with central blue stripe and two white stripes each with central green line.

UNSMIH   United Nations Support Mission in Haiti (July 1996–).
Same ribbon as UNMIH above, but with clasp UNSMIH.

UNCRO   United Nations Confidence Restoration Operation in Croatia (1995–96).
Same ribbon as UNPROFOR above, but with clasp UNCRO.

MINUGUA   Mision de las Naciones Unidas en Guatemala.
Same ribbon as UNMOGUA but clasp with initials in Spanish.

ONUMOZ   Operation des Nations Unies pour le referendum dans Mozambique.
Same ribbon as UNIMOZ above. Clasp with French initials.

UNSSM   United Nations Special Service Medal.
Awarded to personal serving at least 90 consecutive days under UN control in operations for which no other UN award is authorised. Blue ribbon with white edges. Clasps: UNOCHA, UNSCOM

OSGAP   Office of the Secretary General for Afghanistan and Pakistan.
Silver clasp worn by Canadian personnel on the ribbons of UNTSO, UNDOF or UNIFIL.

UNOMSIL   United Nations Observer Mission in Sierra Leone. (1998-)
Awarded for 90 days service. White ribbon with blue edges and the Sierra Leone colours (light blue flanked by green stripes) in the centre. This mission was redesignated UNAMSIL on October 1, 1999.

UNPSG   United Nations Police Support Group Medal.
A support group of 180 police monitors created in January 1998 initially to supervise the Croatian police in the return of displaced persons. 90 days qualifying service. White ribbon with a broad blue central stripe and narrow dark grey (left) and bright yellow (right) stripes towards the edges.

MINURCA   United Nations Verification Mission in the Central African Republic.
Mission instituted April 15, 1998 to monitor the restoration of peace following the Bangui agreement. 90 days qualifying service. Ribbon has a broad blue central stripe flanked by yellow, green, red, white and dark blue stripes on either side.

UNSCOM   United Nations Special Service Medal.
The UN Special Service Medal with UNSCOM clasp is awarded to personnel with a minimum of 90 days consecutive service or 180 days in all, with UNSCOM in Iraq. Ribbon is UN blue with a white stripe at each edge.

UNMIK   United Nations Mission in Kosovo (1999–).
Pale blue ribbon with wide central dark blue stripe edged with white. For 180 days service.

UNAMET   United Nations Mission in East Timor (1999–).
Pale blue ribbon with wide central white stripe edged with yellow and claret.
MONUC   United Nations Mission in the Congo (2000–).
Pale blue ribbon with wide central dark blue stripe edged with yellow.
UNMEE   United Nations Mission in Ethiopia / Eritrea.
Pale blue with central band of sand bisected by narrow dark green stripe.
MPONUH   United Nations Civil Police Mission in Haiti.
Central bands of dark blue and red, flanked by narrow silver stripes and broad blue bands
UNTMIH   United Nations Transitional Mission in Haiti.
Same ribbon as MPONUH but with a bar inscribed UNTMIH.
MICAH   International Civilian Support Mission in Haiti.
Same ribbon as MPONUH.
UNOSGI   The UN Office of the Secretary General in Iraq.
A clasp issued to a small police group assigned to Baghdad from February 1991 to December 1992.
UNHCR   United Nations High Commission for Refugees.
A clasp issued worldwide and still on-going.
UNAMSIL   United Nations Medal for Service in Sierra Leone.
Same ribbon as UNOMSIL.
UNMEE   United Nations Medal for Service in Ethiopia and Eritrea.
Pale blue ribbon with a central tan section divided by a narrow green stripe.

VALUE:

Any current issue medal regardless of ribbon	£15–20
Original striking for Cyprus	£25–30
Miniature	£6–8

207A. INTERNATIONAL CONFERENCE ON THE FORMER YUGOSLAVIA MEDAL

Date: 1995.
Campaigns: Former Yugoslavia.
Branch of Service: UN Observers.
Ribbon: Central broad orange stripe, flanked by narrow blue and white stripes and broad red edges, mounted in the Danish style.
Metal: Silver.
Size: 38mm.
Description: (Obverse) the wreathed globe emblem of the United Nations surrounded by 15 five-pointed stars representing the member nations of the conference, with the inscription round the edge: INTERNATIONAL CONFERENCE ON THE FORMER YUGOSLAVIA; (reverse) the Drina River and the mountains of Serbia and Montenegro surmounted by a peace dove in flight, with the words OBSERVER MISSION round the foot.
Comments: *This medal was awarded to about 100 observers who monitored the 17 land and two rail crossings between Serbia and Montenegro and Bosnia-Herzegovina during September 1994.*

VALUE: —   *Miniature*   £30–40

Long and Meritorious Service Medals

A large, varied but until recently relatively neglected category comprises the medals awarded for long service and good conduct or meritorious service. Their common denominator is that the grant of such awards is made in respect of a minimum number of years of unblemished service—"undetected crime" is how it is often described in the armed forces. As their title implies, long service and good conduct medals combine the elements of lengthy service with no transgressions of the rules and regulations. Meritorious service, on the other hand, implies rather more. Apart from a brief period (1916-28) when awards were made for single acts of gallantry, MSMs have generally been granted to warrant officers and senior NCOs as a rather superior form of long service medal.

Long service and good conduct medals do not appear to excite the same interest among collectors as campaign medals. Perhaps this may be accounted for by their image of stolid devotion to duty rather than the romantic connotations of a medal with an unusual clasp awarded for service in some remote and all but forgotten outpost of the Empire. Nevertheless their importance should not be overlooked. Especially in regard to groups consisting primarily of the Second World War medals, they serve a useful purpose in establishing the provenance of the group, on account of the fact that they are invariably named to the recipient.

Service medals include not only such well known types as the Army LSGC (known affectionately as "the mark of the beast" on account of its high incidence on the chests of sergeant-majors), but also awards to the Territorial and Reserve forces, the auxiliary forces, the nursing services, and organisations such as the Royal Observer Corps and the Cadet Force, the Police, the Red Cross and St John's Ambulance Brigade. The Special Constabulary and Fire Brigades also have their own medals bestowed according to length of service and distinguished conduct. These medals may lack the glamour of naval and military awards but in recent years they have become increasingly fashionable with collectors and will certainly repay further study in their own right.

As many of these medals have been in use for eighty years or more with a standard reverse, variation usually lies in the obverse, changed for each successive sovereign. In addition, considerable variety has been imparted by the use of crowned or uncrowned profiles and busts, and changes in titles.

The following is a summary of the principal obverse types which may be encountered, referred to in the text by their type letters in brackets:

Queen Victoria (A) Young head by William Wyon 1838–60
Queen Victoria (B) Veiled head by Leonard C. Wyon 1860–87
Queen Victoria (C) Jubilee head by Sir Joseph E. Boehm 1887–93
Queen Victoria (D) Old head by Sir Thomas Brock 1893–1901
Edward VII (A) Bareheaded bust in Field Marshal's uniform
Edward VII (B) Bareheaded bust in Admiral's uniform
Edward VII (C) Coinage profile by George W. de Saulles
George V (A) Bareheaded bust in Field Marshal's uniform
George V (B) Bareheaded bust in Admiral's uniform
George V (C) Crowned bust in Coronation robes
George V (D) Crowned bust in Delhi Durbar robes
George V (E) Coinage profile by Bertram Mackennal 1931–36
George VI (A) Crowned profile in Coronation robes
George VI (B) Crowned profile INDIAE: IMP 1937–48
George VI (C) Crowned profile FID: DEF 1949–52
George VI (D) Coinage profile IND: IMP 1937–48
George VI (E) Coinage profile FID: DEF 1949–52
Elizabeth II (A1) Tudor crown BR: OMN 1953–54
Elizabeth II (A) BR: OMN omitted 1954–80
Elizabeth II (B) St Edward crown 1980–
Elizabeth II (C) Coinage bust BRITT: OMN 1953–54
Elizabeth II (D) Coinage bust BRITT: OMN omitted 1955–

PRINCIPAL OBVERSE TYPES:

Queen Victoria (A) Young Head

Queen Victoria (B) Veiled Head

Queen Victoria (C) Jubilee Head

Queen Victoria (D) Old Head

Edward VII (A) Bareheaded bust in Field Marshal's uniform

Edward VII (B) Bareheaded bust in Admiral's uniform

George V (A) Bareheaded bust in Field Marshal's uniform

George V (B) Bareheaded bust in Admiral's uniform

George V (C) Crowned bust in Coronation robes

George V (E) Coinage profile by Bertram Mackennal

George VI (B) Crowned profile with INDIAE: IMP in legend 1937–48

George VI (C) Crowned profile with FID: DEF 1949–52

George VI (D) Coinage profile with IND: IMP 1937–48

George VI (E) Coinage profile with FID: DEF 1949–52

Elizabeth II (A) Tudor crown 1954–80 Elizabeth II (A1) as above but with BR.OMN. (1953–4)

Elizabeth II (B) Coinage bust with BRITT: OMN, 1953–54

Elizabeth II (C) Coinage bust without BR: OMN.

Elizabeth II (D) St Edward crown 1980–.

209

208. ROYAL NAVAL MERITORIOUS SERVICE MEDAL

Instituted: 14 January 1919, by Order in Council.
Branch of Service: Royal Navy.
Ribbon: Dark blue edged in white, with a central white stripe. Since 1977 the same ribbon as the Army MSM.
Metal: Silver
Size: 36mm.
Description: (Obverse) effigy of the reigning monarch; (reverse) imperial crown surmounting a wreath containing the words FOR MERITORIOUS SERVICE. The medal was named in large seriffed capitals round the rim.
Comments: *Awarded without annuity or pension to petty officers and ratings of the Royal Navy. Originally it was awarded either for specific acts of gallantry not in the presence of the enemy or for arduous and specially meritorious service afloat or ashore in action with the enemy. Bars were granted for second awards. It was superseded in 1928 by the British Empire Medal for Gallantry or Meritorious Service, but re-instated on 1 December 1977. In this guise it has been awarded to senior petty officers of the Royal Navy, warrant officers and senior NCOs of the Royal Marines, and equivalent ranks in the WRNS and QARNNS, who have at least 27 years service and are already holders of the LSGC medal and three good conduct badges. The medal is not awarded automatically when these criteria are satisfied, as no more than 59 medals may be awarded annually. The revived medal is identical to the Army MSM and can only be distinguished by the naming giving rank and name of ship.*

VALUE:		Miniature
George V (B)	Rare	—
George V (B) (1020)	£300–400	£20–30
Elizabeth II (D)	£350–450	£10–12

209. ROYAL MARINES MERITORIOUS SERVICE MEDAL

Instituted: 15 January 1849, by Order in Council (although medals dated 1848 are unknown).
Branch of Service: Royal Marines.
Ribbon: Plain dark blue, but later replaced by the RN MSM ribbon (above) and since 1977 the Army ribbon.
Metal: Silver.
Size: 36mm.
Description: (Obverse) effigy of the monarch; (reverse) a crowned laurel wreath enclosing the words FOR MERITORIOUS SERVICE.
Comments: *Annuities not exceeding £20 a year might be granted in addition to the medal for distinguished service. Sergeants with a minimum of 24 years service (the last fourteen as a sergeant), 'with an irreproachable and meritorious character' were considered eligible for the award which was extended to discharged sergeants in 1872 when the service qualification was reduced to 21 years. The award of the MSM for gallantry was discontinued in 1874 when the Conspicuous Gallantry Medal was reconstituted. Only six MSMs for gallantry were ever awarded. The medal was identical with the Army MSM, distinguished solely by its ribbon and the naming to the recipient. Under the royal warrants of 1916-19 Marine NCOs became eligible for immediate awards of the MSM for arduous or specially meritorious service. The medals in this case were worn with crimson ribbons with three white stripes and had the obverse showing the King in the uniform of an Admiral or a Field Marshal, depending on whether the award was for services afloat, or with the naval brigades on the Western Front. The use of this medal ceased in 1928 when the BEM for Gallantry was instituted. The Royal Marines MSM was revived in 1977 solely as a long service award and is the same as the naval MSM already noted, differing only in the details of the recipient.*

VALUE:	VR dated 1848		Miniature	
VR		£1200–1500		£45–60
VR		£700–1000		£70–80
EVIIIR		£600–800		£70–80
GVR		£400–600		£40–50
GVIR		£400–600		£25–30

210. ARMY MERITORIOUS SERVICE MEDAL

Instituted: 19 December 1845.

Branch of Service: Army.

Ribbon: Plain crimson (till 1916), white edges added (1916-17), three white stripes (since August 1917).

Metal: Silver.

Size: 36mm.

Description: (Obverse) effigy of the monarch; (reverse) a crowned laurel wreath inscribed FOR MERITORIOUS SERVICE.

Comments: *A sum of £2000 a year was set aside for distribution to recipients in the form of annuities not exceeding £20, paid for life to NCOs of the rank of sergeant and above for distinguished or meritorious service. The number of medals awarded was thus limited by the amount of money available in the annuity fund, so that medals and annuities were only granted on the death of previous recipients or when the fund was increased. Until November 1902 holders were not allowed to wear the LSGC as well as the MSM, but thereafter both medals could be worn, the LSGC taking precedence. In 1979, however, the order of precedence was reversed. Until 1951 the MSM could only be awarded when an annuity became available, but since then it has often been awarded without the annuity, the latter becoming payable as funds permit. From 1956 recipients needed at least 27 years service to become eligible, but this was reduced to 20 years in 2002. What was, in effect, a second type of MSM was introduced in October 1916 when immediate awards for exceptionally valuable and meritorious service were introduced. In January 1917 this was extended to include individual acts of gallantry not in the presence of the enemy. No annuities were paid with the immediate awards which terminated in 1928 with the institution of the Gallantry BEM. Bars for subsequent acts of gallantry or life-saving were introduced in 1916, seven being awarded up to 1928. The standard crown and wreath reverse was used but in addition to the wide range of obverse types swivelling suspension was used until 1926, and immediate and non-immediate awards may be distinguished by the presence or absence respectively of the recipient's regimental number. Recent awards of the Elizabethan second bust medals have reverted to swivelling suspension. By Royal Warrant of February 2002 the annual allocation was a maximum of 201 medals: Royal Navy (49), Royal Marines (3), Army (89) and RAF (60).*

VALUE:

		Miniature
Victoria (A) 1847 on edge (110)	£800–1000	—
Victoria (A) 1848 below bust (10)	£1500–2000	—
Victoria (A) (990)	£350–450	£30–50
Edward VII (725)	£230–350	£30–40
George V (A) swivel (1050)	£150–250	£18–25
George V (A) non-swivel (400)	£150–250	£10–18
George V (A) Immediate awards 1916–28 (26,211+7 bars):		
For Gallantry (366+1 bar)	£300–400	—
Meritorious services (25,845+6 bars)	£150–250	—
George V (E) (550)	£150–250	£18–20
George VI (D) (1090)	£100–180	£10–18
George VI (E) (5600)	£100–180	£10–18
George VI (B) (55)	£800–1000	£10–18
Elizabeth II (C) (125)	£400–650	£10–18
Elizabeth II (D) (2750)	£250–450	£10–18

211. ROYAL AIR FORCE MERITORIOUS SERVICE MEDAL

Instituted: June 1918
Branch of Service: Royal Air Force.
Ribbon: Half crimson, half light blue, with white stripes at the centre and edges. Since 1977 the same ribbon as the Army MSM.
Metal: Silver.
Size: 36mm.
Description: (Obverse) effigy of the monarch; (reverse) a crowned laurel wreath enclosing the words FOR MERITORIOUS SERVICE. Originally medals were named in large seriffed capitals and were issued in respect of the First World War and service in Russia (1918-20), but later medals were impressed in thin block capitals. The RAF version had a swivelling suspension, unlike its military counterpart.
Comments: *Awarded for valuable services in the field, as opposed to actual flying service. This medal was replaced by the BEM in 1928, but revived in December 1977 under the same conditions as the military MSM. No more than 70 medals are awarded annually. The current issue is similar to the naval and military MSMs, differing only in the naming which includes RAF after the service number.*

VALUE:		*Miniature*
George V (E) (854)	£350–450	£20–30
Elizabeth II (D)	£350–450	£10–15

212. COLONIAL MERITORIOUS SERVICE MEDALS

Instituted: 31 May 1895.
Branch of Service: Colonial forces.
Ribbon: According to issuing territory (see below).
Metal: Silver.
Size: 36mm.
Description: (Obverse) as British counterparts; (reverse) as British type, but with the name of the dominion or colony round the top.
Comments: *Awarded for service in the British dominions, colonies and protectorates.*

Canada: Ribbon as for British Army MSM. CANADA on reverse till 1936; imperial version used from then until 1958. No medals with the Victorian obverse were awarded, but specimens exist.
Cape of Good Hope: Crimson ribbon with central orange stripe. Only one or two Edward VII medals issued.
Natal: Crimson ribbon with a central yellow stripe. Exceptionally, it was awarded to volunteers in the Natal Militia. Fifteen Edward VII medals awarded.
Commonwealth of Australia: Crimson ribbon with two dark green central stripes. Issued between 1903 and 1975.
New South Wales: Crimson ribbon with a dark blue central stripe. Issued till 1903.
Queensland: Crimson ribbon with light blue central stripe. Issued till 1903.
South Australia: Plain crimson ribbon. Issued till 1903.
Tasmania: Crimson ribbon with a pink central stripe. Issued till 1903.
New Zealand: Crimson ribbon with a light green central stripe. Issued since 1898 (see also NZ21).

VALUE	Rare	*Miniature*	£100–200

213. INDIAN ARMY MERITORIOUS SERVICE MEDAL 1848

Instituted: 20 May 1848, by General Order of the Indian government.
Branch of Service: Forces of the Honourable East India Company and later the Indian armed services.
Ribbon: Plain crimson.
Metal: Silver.
Size: 36mm.
Description: (Obverse) the Wyon profile of Queen Victoria; (reverse) the arms and motto of the Honourable East India Company.
Comments: *Awarded with an annuity up to £20 to European sergeants, serving or discharged, for meritorious service. It was discontinued in 1873.*

VALUE: £500–600   *Miniature*   £200–250

214. INDIAN ARMY MERITORIOUS SERVICE MEDAL 1888

Instituted: 1888.
Branch of Service: Indian Army.
Ribbon: Plain crimson (till 1917); three white stripes added (1917).
Metal: Silver.
Size: 36mm.
Description: (Obverse) the sovereign's effigy; (reverse) a central wreath enclosing the word INDIA surrounded by the legend FOR MERITORIOUS SERVICE with a continuous border of lotus flowers and leaves round the circumference.
Comments: *For award to Indian warrant officers and senior NCOs (havildars, dafadars and equivalent band ranks). Eighteen years of exceptionally meritorious service was the minimum requirement, subject to the availability of funds in the annuity. At first only one medal was set aside for each regiment and thereafter awards were only made on the death, promotion or reduction of existing recipients. On promotion the medal was retained but the annuity ceased. It became obsolete in 1947.*

VALUE:		*Miniature*
Victoria (B)	£200–250	£80–100
Edward VII (A)	£150–200	£80–100
George V (D)	£70–100	£80–100
George V (C)	£70–100	£80–100
George VI (B)	£70–100	£80–100

215. AFRICAN POLICE MEDAL FOR MERITORIOUS SERVICE

Instituted: 14 July 1915.
Branch of Service Non-European NCOs and men of the colonial police forces in East and West Africa.
Ribbon: Sand-coloured with red edges.
Metal: Silver.
Size: 36mm
Description: (Obverse) effigy of the sovereign; (reverse) a crown surmounted by a lion passant gardant within a palm wreath and having the legend FOR MERITORIOUS SERVICE IN THE POLICE and AFRICA at the foot.
Comments: *Awarded for both individual acts of gallantry and distinguished, meritorious or long service. In respect of the lastnamed, a minimum of 15 years exemplary service was required. It was superseded by the Colonial Police Medal in 1938.*

VALUE:

George V (A) IND: IMP 1915-31	£350–450
George V (A) INDIAE IMP 1931-7	£350–450
George VI (B) 1938	Rare
Miniature	£70–90

216. UNION OF SOUTH AFRICA MERITORIOUS SERVICE MEDAL

Instituted: 24 October 1914, by Government gazette.
Branch of Service: Service personnel of South Africa, Southern Rhodesia and Swaziland.
Ribbon: Crimson with blue edges and a central white, blue and white band.
Metal: Silver.
Size: 36mm.
Description: As British military MSM.
Comments: *A total of 46 gallantry and 300 meritorious service awards were made up to 1952 when the medal was discontinued. Of these only two were awarded to South Africans in the RNVR.*

VALUE: Rare   *Miniature*   £200–250

216A. ACCUMULATED CAMPAIGN SERVICE MEDAL

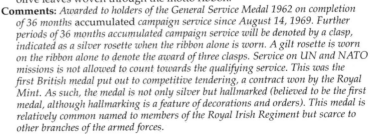

Instituted: January 1994.
Branch of Service: All branches of the armed services.
Ribbon: Purple and green with a gold stripe.
Metal: Silver.
Size: 36mm.
Description: (Obverse) crowned effigy of Queen Elizabeth; (reverse) the inscription FOR ACCUMULATED CAMPAIGN SERVICE set within a four-part ribbon surrounded by a branch of oak leaves with laurel and olive leaves woven through the motto ribbon.
Comments: *Awarded to holders of the General Service Medal 1962 on completion of 36 months accumulated campaign service since August 14, 1969. Further periods of 36 months accumulated campaign service will be denoted by a clasp, indicated as a silver rosette when the ribbon alone is worn. A gilt rosette is worn on the ribbon alone to denote the award of three clasps. Service on UN and NATO missions is not allowed to count towards the qualifying service. This was the first British medal put out to competitive tendering, a contract won by the Royal Mint. As such, the medal is not only silver but hallmarked (believed to be the first medal, although hallmarking is a feature of decorations and orders). This medal is relatively common named to members of the Royal Irish Regiment but scarce to other branches of the armed forces.*

VALUE: £200–300   *Miniature*   £8

217. ROYAL HOUSEHOLD FAITHFUL SERVICE MEDALS

1st type obv.

1st type rev.

Instituted: 1872 by Queen Victoria.

Branch of Service: Royal Household.

Ribbon: Originally Royal Stuart tartan; later, a different ribbon for each monarch: dark blue and red diagonal stripes descending from left to right (George V), the same but descending from right to left (George VI) or dark blue with three red stripes (Elizabeth II).

Metal: Silver.

Size: 27mm (Victoria); 29mm (later awards).

Description: (Obverse) the sovereign's effigy; (reverse) the personal details of the recipient engraved on it. The Victorian medal has a very elaborate suspension ornamented with the crowned royal monogram, with a laurel bar brooch fitting at the top. This medal was not originally intended to be worn with a ribbon, although it had a strip of Royal Stuart tartan behind it. The same medal, but struck in 22 carat gold, was presented to John Brown, the Queen's personal servant. The concept was revived by George V, a silver medal of more conventional appearance being struck with the text FOR LONG AND FAITHFUL SERVICE on the reverse. Thirty, forty and fifty year service bars were also awarded.

Comments: *Intended as a reward to servants of the Royal Household for long and faithful service of at least 25 years. A further 10 years merited a bar. Different ribbons were used for each monarch, corresponding to the crowned cypher joining the medal to the suspension bar on either side of which the recipient's years of service were inscribed. Only two medals have been recorded with the profile of Edward VIII (1936).*

VALUE:

		Miniature
Victoria	From £300	£250–300
Edward VIII	From £1500	—
George V (E)	From £300	£80–100
George VI (D)	From £300	£80–100
Elizabeth II (C)	From £350	£80–100

2nd type obv. (George V).

2nd type rev.

218. ROYAL NAVAL LONG SERVICE AND GOOD CONDUCT MEDAL

1st type obv.

1st type rev.

Instituted: 24 August 1831, by Order in Council.
Branch of Service: Royal Navy.
Ribbon: Plain dark blue (1831); dark blue with white edges (1848).
Metal: Silver.
Size: 34mm (1831); 36mm (1848).
Description: First type: (Obverse) an anchor surmounted by a crown and enclosed in an oak wreath; (reverse) the recipient's details. Plain ring for suspension.

   Second type, adopted in 1848: (Obverse) the sovereign's effigy; (reverse) a three-masted man-of-war surrounded by a rope tied at the foot with a reef knot and having the legend FOR LONG SERVICE AND GOOD CONDUCT round the circumference. This medal originally had a wide suspender bar 38mm, but a narrow suspender was substituted in 1874. Normally the obverse was undated, but about 100 medals were issued in 1849-50 with the obverse of the Naval GSM, with the date 1848 below the Queen's bust. Between 1875 and 1877 a number of medals had the years of service added to the recipient's details, either engraved or impressed on the edge—these medals (about 60 known) are now sought after by collectors. Engraved naming was used from 1875 to 1877, but from then until 1901 impressed naming was adopted. Later medals used the various obverse effigies noted below.

Comments: *Originally awarded for 21 years exemplary conduct, but the period was reduced to 10 years in 1874, then later increased to 15 years. Bars for additional periods of 15 years were instituted by George V. In March 1981 commissioned officers of the naval services became eligible after 15 years service, provided at least 12 years were served in the ranks.*

VALUE:

		Miniature
Anchor 1831-47 (644)	£600–800	—
Victoria (A) wide suspender (3572)	£350–400	—
1848 type (100)	£1000–1200	—
Victoria (A) narrow suspender (4400)	£120–150	£30–40
Year on edge variety (c. 40)	£250–350	
impressed naming (18,200)	£120–150	
Year on edge variety (c. 20)	£250–350	
Edward VII (B)	£65–70	—
George V (B) 1910-20 swivel	£50–75	£10–15
1920–30 non-swivelling bar	£50–75	£5–10
George V (E) 1931-36	£50–75	£10–12
George VI (D) 1937-48	£50–75	£10–12
George VI (E) 1949-52	£50–75	£10–12
Elizabeth II (C) 1953-54	£55–75	£10–12
Elizabeth II (D) 1954-	£55–75	£10–12

2nd type rev. wide suspender

2nd type rev. narrow suspender

2nd type obv. George V

219. ROYAL NAVAL RESERVE DECORATION

Instituted: 1908.
Branch of Service: Royal Naval Reserve.
Ribbon: Plain green ribbon, white edges being added from 1941 onwards.
Metal: Silver and silver-gilt.
Size: Height 54mm; max. width 33mm.
Description: A skeletal badge with the royal cypher in silver surrounded by an oval cable and reef knot in silver-gilt, surmounted by a crown and suspension ring.
Comments: *Granted for 15 years commissioned service (sub-lieutenant and above) in the Royal Naval Reserve, active service in wartime counting double. Bars are awarded for additional periods of 15 years. Recipients are entitled to the letters RD after their name. This decoration was replaced by the VRSM (No. 242A) in 2000.*

VALUE:		*Miniature*
Edward VII	£120–140	£25–30
George V	£120–140	£25–30
George VI (GRI)	£120–140	£25–30
George VI (GVIR)	£120–140	£25–30
Elizabeth II	£150–180	£25–30

220. ROYAL NAVAL RESERVE LONG SERVICE AND GOOD CONDUCT MEDAL

Instituted: 1908.
Branch of Service: Royal Naval Reserve.
Ribbon: Plain green, white edges and a central white stripe being added in 1941. On the amalgamation of the RNR and RNVR in 1958 the ribbon was changed to five equal stripes of blue, white, green, white and blue.
Metal: Silver.
Size: 36mm.
Description: (Obverse) effigy of the monarch; (reverse) a battleship with the motto DIUTERNE FIDELIS (faithful for ever) at the foot.
Comments: *Awarded to petty officers and ratings of the RNR for 15 years service, war service counting double, with bars for additional 15 year periods. This medal was replaced by the VRSM (No. 242A) in 2000.*

VALUE:		*Miniature*
Edward VII (B)	£40–50	£25–30
George V (B)	£30–40	£25–30
George V (E)	£30–40	£25–30
George VI (D)	£35–45	£25–30
George VI (E)	£35–45	£25–30
Elizabeth II (C)	£50–60	£25–30
Elizabeth II (D)	£50–60	£25–30

221. ROYAL NAVAL VOLUNTEER RESERVE DECORATION

Instituted: 1908.
Branch of Service: Royal Naval Volunteer Reserve.
Ribbon: 38mm originally plain dark green; dark blue with a central green stripe flanked by narrow red stripes (since 1919).
Metal: Silver and silver-gilt.
Size: Height 54mm; max. width 33mm.
Description: Similar to RNR decoration.
Comments: *Awarded to commissioned officers of the RNVR. The qualifying period was 20 years, service in the ranks counting half and war service counting double. In 1966 the decoration was replaced by the RD following the merger of the RNR and RNVR. Holders were entitled to the post-nominals letters VD, until 1947 when the letters VRD were substituted.*

VALUE:		*Miniature*
Edward VII	£140–150	£25–30
George V	£120–140	£25–30
George VI GRI	£120–140	£25–30
George VI GVIR	£120–140	£25–30
Elizabeth II	£150–180	£25–30

222. ROYAL NAVAL VOLUNTEER RESERVE LONG SERVICE AND GOOD CONDUCT MEDAL

Instituted: 1908.
Branch of Service: Royal Naval Volunteer Reserve.
Ribbon: Originally plain green, but subsequently a broad central green stripe edged in red with blue stripes at the ends was adopted.
Metal: Silver.
Size: 36mm.
Description: Identical to the RNR medal, but distinguished by the ribbon and the naming which includes the letters RNVR, RCNVR (Canada), RSANVR (South Africa), etc.
Comments: *Awarded to petty officers and ratings for 12 years service with the necessary training, character assessed as "very good" or better throughout the period. War service counted double. The award was extended to the Colonial Navies during the Second World War.*

VALUE:		*Miniature*
Edward VII (B)	Rare	£25–30
George V (B)	£45–60	£25–30
George V (E)	£50–70	£25–30
George VI (D)	£50–65	£25–30
George VI (E)	£50–65	£25–30
Elizabeth II (D)	£70–100	£25–30

223. ROYAL FLEET RESERVE LONG SERVICE AND GOOD CONDUCT MEDAL

Instituted: 1919.
Branch of Service: Royal Fleet Reserve.
Ribbon: Blue bordered with thin red stripes and white edges.
Metal: Silver.
Size: 36mm.
Description: Similar to the RNR LSGC but with ring suspension instead of a bar suspender.
Comments: *Awarded for 15 years service in the Fleet Reserve. This medal was discontinued in 2000.*

VALUE:		Miniature
George V (B)	£35–45	£25–30
George V (E)	£35–45	£25–30
George VI (D)	£35–45	£25–30
George VI (E)	£35–45	£25–30
Elizabeth II (C)	£50–60	£25–30
Elizabeth II (D)	£50–60	£25–30

224. ROYAL NAVAL AUXILIARY SICK BERTH RESERVE LONG SERVICE AND GOOD CONDUCT MEDAL

Instituted: 1919.
Branch of Service: Royal Naval Auxiliary Sick Berth Reserve.
Ribbon: Plain green but later green with a white central stripe and white edges.
Metal: Silver.
Size: 36mm.
Description: Identical to the RNR equivalent, but the letters RNASBR appear after the recipient's name.
Comments: *Arguably the longest title of any British medal, it continued until the RNASBR was disbanded in 1949. The Auxiliary Sick Berth Reserve was created in 1903, members being recruited from the St John Ambulance Brigade. About 780 medals were granted prior to the Second World War and a further 715 between 1939 and 1949.*

VALUE:		Miniature
George V (B)	£100–120	£25–30
George V (E)	£100–120	£25–30
George VI (D)	£100–120	£25–30

225. ROYAL NAVAL WIRELESS AUXILIARY RESERVE LONG SERVICE AND GOOD CONDUCT MEDAL

Instituted: 1939.
Branch of Service: Royal Naval Wireless Auxiliary Reserve.
Ribbon: Originally plain green, but subsequently a broad central green stripe edged in red with blue stripes at the ends was adopted.
Metal: Silver.
Size: 36mm.
Description: Identical to the RNR equivalent, but the letters RNWAR after the recipient's name. The last of the service medals with a battleship reverse.
Comments: *Issued till 1957 when the RNWAR was disbanded. It was awarded for 12 years service, only about 200 having been issued.*

VALUE:		Miniature
George VI (D)	£250–350	£25–30
Elizabeth II (C)	£250–350	£25–30

226. ROYAL NAVAL AUXILIARY SERVICE LONG SERVICE MEDAL

Instituted: July 1965.
Branch of Service: Royal Naval Auxiliary Service (RNXS), formerly the Royal Naval Minewatching Service.
Ribbon: Dark blue with a narrow green central stripe and broad white stripes at the edges bisected by thin dark green stripes.
Metal: Cupro-nickel.
Size: 36mm.
Description: (Obverse) the Queen's effigy; (reverse) a fouled anchor in an oak wreath surmounted by a naval crown.
Comments: *Awarded for 12 years service. Interestingly this medal was the last to be issued with a pure silk ribbon.*

VALUE: Elizabeth II (A)   £180–220   *Miniature*   £25–30

227. ROCKET APPARATUS VOLUNTEER LONG SERVICE MEDAL

First type obverse.

Instituted: 1911 by the Board of Trade.
Branch of Service: Rocket Life Saving Apparatus Volunteers,
Ribbon: Watered blue silk with broad scarlet edges.
Metal: Silver.
Size: 36mm.
Description: (Obverse) the effigy of the reigning monarch with the date 1911 below the truncation. (Reverse) exists in four types. The first refers to the Board of Trade but when that department handed over responsibility to the Ministry of Transport in 1942 the wording was amended to read ROCKET APPARATUS VOLUNTEER MEDAL round the circumference. In 1953 the inscription was changed to COAST LIFE SAVING CORPS and then in 1968 to COASTGUARD AUXILIARY SERVICE.
Comments: *Awarded for 20 years service with the Rocket Life Saving Apparatus Volunteers. The RLSAV became the Coast Life Saving Corps in 1953 and the Coastguard Auxiliary Service in 1968, these titles being reflected in the wording on the reverse.*

VALUE:		*Miniature*
George V (E)	£60–80	£50–100
George VI (D) BoT	£70–90	
George VI (D) Rocket Apparatus	£70–90	
Elizabeth II (D) Coast Life Saving	£120–145	
Elizabeth II (D) Coastguard Auxiliary	£120–150	

229. ARMY LONG SERVICE AND GOOD CONDUCT MEDAL

Instituted: 1830.
Branch of Service: Army.
Ribbon: Plain crimson was used till 1917 when white stripes were added to the edges. Dominion and colonial medals formerly had crimson ribbons with a narrow central stripe in dark green (Australia), light blue (NSW and Queensland), pink (Tasmania), orange (S. Africa), white (Canada), light green (NZ), broad white (Victoria), scarlet and light blue (Papua NG).
Metal: Silver.
Size: 36mm.
Description: Over the long period in which this medal has been in use it has undergone a number of changes. Until 1901 the obverse bore a trophy of arms with the royal arms in an oval shield in the centre while the reverse bore the inscription FOR LONG SERVICE AND GOOD CONDUCT. The first issue had the royal arms with the badge of Hanover on the obverse and small suspension ring with a plain crimson ribbon. A large ring was substituted in 1831. On the accession of Queen Victoria in 1837 the Hanoverian emblem was dropped from the arms. In 1855 a swivelling scroll suspension was substituted and in 1874 small lettering replaced the original large lettering on the reverse. From 1901, however, the effigy of the reigning sovereign

1st type obv. Trophy of Arms with badge of Hanover.

2nd type obv. with badge of Hanover omitted and swivel suspender.

was placed on the obverse although the reverse remained the same. In 1920 the swivelling scroll suspension gave way to a fixed suspender. In 1930 the title of the medal was changed to the Long Service and Good Conduct (Military) Medal; at the same time the design was modified. A fixed suspension bar was added, bearing the words REGULAR ARMY or the name of a dominion (India, Canada, Australia, New Zealand or South Africa). This replaced the Permanent Forces of the Empire LSGC Medal (see below).

Comments: *Originally awarded to soldiers of exemplary conduct for 21 years service in the infantry or 24 years in the cavalry, but in 1870 the qualifying period was reduced to 18 years. During the Second World War commissioned officers were permitted to acquire this medal so long as they had completed at least 12 of their 18 years service in the ranks. Canada discontinued the LSGC medal in 1950 when the Canadian Forces Decoration was instituted, while South Africa replaced it with the John Chard Medal later the same year. From 1930 onwards the lettering of the reverse inscription was in tall, thin letters. In 1940 bars for further periods of service were authorised. The LSGC is invariably named to the recipient. The William IV and early Victorian issues (to 1854) were impressed in the style of the Waterloo Medal and also bore the date of discharge and award. The 1855 issue was not dated, while lettering was impressed in the style of the Military General Service Medal. Later Victorian issues, however, were engraved in various styles, while medals from 1901 onwards are impressed in small capitals of various types. Medals to Europeans in the Indian Army are engraved in cursive script. Recent research by Irvin Mortensen, however, reveals that some medals after 1850 were issued unnamed, and this also accounts for various unofficial styles of naming found on later medals.*

VALUE:

		Miniature
William IV small ring 1830–31	£500–800	—
William IV large ring 1831–37	£500–800	—
Victoria without Hanoverian arms 1837–55	£200–300	—
Victoria swivelling scroll suspension 1855–74	£150–200	£30–40
Victoria small reverse lettering 1874–1901	£100–150	£25–30
Edward VII (A) 1902–10	£60–100	£25–30
George V (A) 1911–20	£50–80	£15–20
George V (A) fixed suspender 1920–30	£50–80	£15–20
George V (C) 1930–36	£50–80	£15–20
Commonwealth bar	From £75	£15–20
George VI (B) 1937–48	£50–80	£15–20
Commonwealth bar	From £75	£15–20
George VI (E) 1949–52	£50–80	£15–20
Elizabeth II (A/A1) 1953	Very rare	
Commonwealth bar	Very rare	
Elizabeth II (C) 1953–54	£55–80	£15–20
Elizabeth II (D) 1954–	£55–80	£15–20
Commonwealth bar	From £100	£15–20

1st type rev. large letters

2nd type rev. small letters with swivel suspension

3rd type obv. (George V).

229. ARMY LONG SERVICE & GOOD CONDUCT MEDAL *continued*

Modified design with fixed suspender obv. and rev.

George V obv. (type C) with "Commonwealth" bar

231. VOLUNTEER OFFICER'S DECORATION

Instituted: 25 July 1892.
Branch of Service: Volunteer Force.
Ribbon: Plain green.
Metal: Silver and silver-gilt.
Size: Height 42mm; max. width 35mm.
Description: An oval skeletal badge in silver and silver-gilt, with the royal cypher and crown in the centre, within a wreath of oak leaves. It is suspended by a plain ring with a laurel bar brooch fitted to the top of the ribbon. Although issued unnamed, many examples were subsequently engraved or impressed privately. Two versions of the Victorian decoration were produced, differing in the monogram—VR for United Kingdom recipients and VRI for recipients in the dominions and colonies.
Comments: *The basic qualification was 20 years commissioned service in the Volunteer Force, a precursor of the Territorial Army, non-commissioned service counting half. By Royal Warrant of 24 May 1894 the decoration was extended to comparable forces overseas, the qualifying period for service in India being reduced to 18 years. The colonial VD was superseded in 1899 by the Colonial Auxiliary Forces Officers Decoration and the Indian Volunteer Forces Officers Decoration. In the United Kingdom it was superseded by the Territorial Decoration, on the formation of the TF in 1908. A total of 4,710 decorations were awarded. Awards in Bermuda continued until 1930.*

VALUE:		*Miniature*
Victoria VR	£100–120	£30–40
Victoria VRI	£250–300	£50–60
Edward VII	£100–120	£25–35
George V	£100–120	£20–25

232. VOLUNTEER LONG SERVICE AND GOOD CONDUCT MEDAL

Instituted: 1894.

Branch of Service: Volunteer Force.

Ribbon: Plain green, but members of the Honourable Artillery Company were granted a distinctive ribbon in 1906, half scarlet, half dark blue with yellow edges—King Edward's racing colours.

Metal: Silver.

Size: 36mm.

Description: (Obverse) effigy of the reigning monarch; (reverse) a laurel wreath on which is superimposed ribbons inscribed FOR LONG SERVICE IN THE VOLUNTEER FORCE.

Comments: *This medal was awarded for 20 years service in the ranks. Officers could also receive the medal, being eligible on account of their non-commissioned service. Many officers then gained sufficient commissioned service to be awarded either the Volunteer Decoration or (from 1908) the Territorial Decoration. The medal was extended to Colonial Forces in June 1898, the titles of the monarch being appropriately expanded for this version. This medal was superseded by the Territorial Force Efficiency Medal in 1908, although it continued to be awarded until 1930 in Bermuda, India, Isle of Man (Isle of Man Vols.) and the 7th Volunteer Battalion of the King's (Liverpool) Regiment.*

VALUE:

		Miniature
Victoria Regina (C) (UK)	£65–85	
Unnamed	£35–45	£20–25
Victoria Regina et Imperatrix (C) (overseas)	£85–100	£20–25
Edwardus Rex (A)	£65–85	£15–25
Edwardus Rex et Imperator (A) (colonial)	£65–85	£15–25
Edwardus Kaisar-i-Hind (A) (India)	£80–100	£15–25
George V (A) (India)	£60–80	£15–20
George V (A) (Isle of Man)	£150–200	£15–20

233. TERRITORIAL DECORATION

Instituted: 29 September 1908.

Branch of Service: Territorial Force, later Territorial Army.

Ribbon: 38mm plain dark green with a central yellow stripe.

Metal: Silver and silver-gilt.

Size: Height 46mm; max. width 35mm.

Description: A skeletal badge with the crowned monogram of the sovereign surrounded by an oval oak wreath, fitted with a ring for suspension.

Comments: *Awarded for 20 years commissioned service, service in the ranks counting half and war service double. It was superseded by the Efficiency Decoration in 1930. A total of 4,783 decorations were awarded.*

VALUE:

		Miniature
Edward VII (585)	£120–140	£15–20
George V (4,198)	£100–120	£10–12

234. TERRITORIAL FORCE EFFICIENCY MEDAL

Instituted: 1908.
Branch of Service: Territorial Force.
Ribbon: 32mm plain dark green with a central yellow stripe.
Metal: Silver.
Size: Height 38mm; max. width 31mm.
Description: An oval medal fitted with claw and ring suspension. (Obverse) the sovereign's effigy; (reverse) inscribed with the name of the medal in four lines.
Comments: *Granted for a minimum of 12 years service in the Territorial Force. It was superseded in 1921 by the Territorial Efficiency Medal when the service was renamed. Bars were awarded for further periods of 12 years service.*

VALUE:		Miniature
Edward VII (A) (11,800)	£100–120*	£15–20
With bar (537)	£150–180	
With second bars (64)	£200–250	
George V (A) (37,726)	£55–85	£15–20
George V first clasps (362)	£100–150	

Medals to Yeomanry regiments command a higher premium.

234A. TERRITORIAL FORCE IMPERIAL SERVICE BADGE

Instituted: 1912.
Branch of Service: Members of the Territorial Force.
Ribbon: None.
Metal: Silver.
Size: 10mm x 43mm
Description: A horizontal bar surmounted by a royal crown, the bar inscribed in raised lettering IMPERIAL SERVICE.
Comments: *Awarded to members of the Territorial Force who were prepared to serve outside the United Kingdom in defence of the Empire, mainly during the First World War.*

VALUE: £12–15

235. TERRITORIAL EFFICIENCY MEDAL

Instituted: 1921.
Branch of Service: Territorial Army.
Ribbon: 32mm plain dark green with yellow edges.
Metal: Silver.
Size: Height 38mm; max. width 31mm.
Description: As above, but with the name amended and inscribed in three lines.
Comments: *Introduced following the elevation of the Territorial Force to become the Territorial Army. It was superseded by the Efficiency Medal in 1930.*

VALUE:			
George V (A)	£45–65	Miniature	£10–15

236. EFFICIENCY DECORATION

Instituted: 17 October 1930.
Branch of Service: Territorial Army (UK), the Indian Volunteer Forces and the Colonial Auxiliary Forces.
Ribbon: 38mm plain dark green with a central yellow stripe. In 1969, on the introduction of the T&AVR, the ribbon was altered to half blue, half green , with a central yellow stripe. Members of the Honourable Artillery Company wear half blue, half scarlet ribbon, with yellow edges.
Metal: Silver and silver-gilt.
Size: Height 54mm; max. width 37mm.
Description: An oval skeletal badge in silver and silver-gilt with the crowned monogram in an oak wreath, the ring for suspension being fitted to the top of the crown. It differs also from the previous decorations in having a suspender bar denoting the area of service: Territorial (UK), India, Canada, Fiji or other overseas country being inscribed as appropriate, but the previous ribbon was retained.
Comments: *Recipients in Britain were allowed to continue using the letters TD after their names, but in the Commonwealth the letters ED were used instead. The 20-year qualification was reduced to 12 years in 1949, bars for each additional 6 years being added. In 1969 the British bar was changed to T & AVR, on the establishment of the Territorial and Army Volunteer Reserve. In 1982 the title of Territorial Army was resumed, so the inscription on the bar reverted to TERRITORIAL but the blue, yellow and green ribbon was retained. This decoration was superseded by the VRSM (No. 242A) in 2000.*

VALUE:

	Territorial	T&AVR	Commonwealth
George V	£90–100	—	From £150
George VI (GRI)	£80–100	—	From £150
George VI (GVIR)	£80–100	—	—
Elizabeth II	£100–110	£100–120	From £150

Miniature £8–20

237. EFFICIENCY MEDAL

Instituted: 17 October 1930.
Branch of Service: Territorial Army (UK), Indian Volunteer Forces and Colonial Auxiliary Forces.
Ribbon: 32mm green with yellow edges. In 1969, on the introduction of the T&AVR, the ribbon was altered to half blue, half green, eith yellow edges. Members of the Honourable Artillery Regiment wear half blue, half scarlet ribbon, with yellow edges.

237. EFFICIENCY MEDAL *continued*

Metal: Silver.

Size: Height 39mm; max. width 32mm.

Description: An oval silver medal. (Obverse) the monarch's effigy; (reverse) inscribed FOR EFFICIENT SERVICE. In place of the simple ring suspension, however, there was now a fixed suspender bar decorated with a pair of palm leaves surmounted by a scroll inscribed TERRITORIAL or MILITIA (for UK volunteer forces), while overseas forces had the name of the country.

Comments: *This medal consolidated the awards to other ranks throughout the volunteer forces of Britain and the Commonwealth. The basic qualification was 12 years service, but war service and peacetime service in West Africa counted double. The Militia bar was granted to certain categories of the Supplementary Reserve until the formation of the Army Emergency Reserve in 1951. In 1969 the bar inscribed T & AVR was introduced. The bar TERRITORIAL was resumed in 1982 but the half blue, half green ribbon with yellow edges was retained. For the distinctive medal awarded in the Union of South Africa see number 254. Instead of the second obverse of Queen Elizabeth II, Canada adopted a type showing the Queen wearing the Imperial Crown. This medal was superseded by the VRSM (No. 242A) in 2000.*

VALUE:	Territorial	Militia	T&AVR	Commonwealth
George V (C)	£40–80	£80–120	—	From £80*
George VI (A)	£40–80	£65–85	—	From £80*
George VI (C)	£40–80	£65–85	—	From £80*
Elizabeth II (A)	£55–85	—	—	From £150*
Elizabeth II (B)	£55–85	—	£80–100	From £150*

Miniature from £15

*These prices are for the commoner Commonwealth types. However, some are extremely rare as can be seen in the table below where the issue numbers are indicated in brackets (where known).

George V (C)	George VI (A)	George VI (C)	Elizabeth II (A)	Elizabeth II (B)
—	—	—	Antigua (3)	—
Australia	Australia	Australia	Australia	Australia
Barbados	Barbados	Barbados	Barbados	Barbados
Bermuda	Bermuda	Bermuda	Bermuda	Bermuda
British Guiana (15)	British Guiana	British Guiana	British Guiana	—
British Honduras (1)	British Honduras (23)	British Honduras (3)	British Honduras (13) —	
—	Burma (111)	—	—	—
Canada	Canada	Canada	Canada (Rare)	Canada (Rare)
Ceylon	Ceylon	Ceylon	Ceylon (69)	—
—	Dominica (130)	—	—	—
Falkland Islands (29)	Falkland Islands (29)	—	Falkland Islands	Falkland Islands
Fiji (29)	Fiji (35)	Fiji (9)	Fiji (7)	Fiji (33)
—	—	Gibraltar (15)	Gibraltar	Gibraltar
—	Gold Coast (275)	Gold Coast (35)	—	—
—	Grenada (1)	—	—	—
—	Guernsey (3)	Guernsey (4)	Guernsey (3)	Guernsey (35)
Hong Kong (21)	Hong Kong (50)	Hong Kong (224)	Hong Kong (145)	Hong Kong (268)
India	India	—	—	—
Jamaica	Jamaica	Jamaica	Jamaica	—
—	Jersey (40)	Jersey (7)	—	Jersey (1)

237. EFFICIENCY MEDAL *continued*

George V (C)	*George VI (A)*	*George VI (C)*	*Elizabeth II (A)*	*Elizabeth II (B)*
—	Kenya (1)	Kenya (159)	Kenya (36)	—
—	Leeward Islands (49)	Leeward Islands (14)	Leeward Islands (2)	—
—	Malaya	Malaya	Malaya (54)	—
—	Malta (320)	Malta (84)	Malta (7)	Malta (36)
—	—	—	Mauritius (71)	—
—	—	—	—	Montserrat (6)
New Zealand (71)	New Zealand (34)	New Zealand	New Zealand	New Zealand
Nigeria (1)	—	Nigeria (7)	Nigeria (3)	—
—	—	—	Rhodesia/Nyasaland (7)	—
—	—	—	St Christopher Nevis (13)	—
—	St Lucia (2)	—	—	—
—	St Vincent (1)	—	—	—
S. Rhodesia (17)	S. Rhodesia (230)	S. Rhodesia (24)	S. Rhodesia (6)	—
—	Trinidad/Tobago (228)	Trinidad/Tobago (46)	Trinidad/Tobago (5)	—

238. ARMY EMERGENCY RESERVE DECORATION

Instituted: 17 November 1952.

Branch of Service Army Emergency Reserve.

Ribbon: 38mm dark blue with a central yellow stripe.

Metal: Silver and silver-gilt.

Size: Height 55mm; max. width 37mm.

Description: An oval skeletal badge, with the monarch's cypher surmounted by a crown in an oak wreath. Suspension is by a ring through the top of the crown and it is worn with a brooch bar inscribed ARMY EMERGENCY RESERVE.

Comments: *Awarded for 12 years commissioned service. Officers commissioned in the Army Supplementary Reserve or Army Emergency Reserve of Offices between 8 August 1942 and 15 May 1948 who transferred to the Regular Army Reserve of Officers after 10 years service were also eligible. War service counts double and previous service in the ranks counts half. The ERD was abolished in 1967 on the formation of the Territorial and Army Volunteer Reserve.*

VALUE:

Elizabeth II	£120–150	*Miniature*	£10–15

239. ARMY EMERGENCY RESERVE EFFICIENCY MEDAL

Instituted: 1 September 1953.

Branch of Service: Army Emergency Reserve.

Ribbon: 32mm dark blue with three central yellow stripes.

Metal: Silver.

Size: Height 39mm; max. width 31mm.

Description: This oval medal is similar to the Efficiency Medal previously noted but has a scroll bar inscribed ARMY EMERGENCY RESERVE.

Comments: *Awarded for 12 years service in the ranks or for service in the Supplementary Reserve between 1924 and 1948 prior to transferring to the Army Emergency Reserve. War service counted double. It was abolished in 1967 following the formation of the Territorial and Army Volunteer Reserve.*

VALUE:

Elizabeth II	£150–180	*Miniature*	£10–12

240. IMPERIAL YEOMANRY LONG SERVICE AND GOOD CONDUCT MEDAL

Instituted: December 1904, by Army Order number 211.
Branch of Service: Imperial Yeomanry.
Ribbon: 32mm plain yellow.
Metal: Silver.
Size: Height 38mm; max. width 31mm.
Description: Upright oval. (Obverse) the sovereign's effigy; (reverse) inscribed IMPERIAL YEOMANRY round the top and the usual long service and good conduct inscription in four lines across the middle.
Comments: *Awarded to NCOs and troopers of the Imperial Yeomanry for 10 years exemplary service. It became obsolete in 1908 when the Territorial Force was created. Nevertheless 48 medals were awarded in 1909, one in 1910, one in 1914 and one in 1917. All medals were issued with the bust of King Edward VII on the obverse.*

VALUE:

Edward VII (A) (1674)	£350–450	*Miniature*	£60–80

241. MILITIA LONG SERVICE AND GOOD CONDUCT MEDAL

Instituted: December 1904, by Army Order number 211.
Branch of Service: Militia.
Ribbon: 32mm plain light blue.
Metal: Silver.
Size: Height 38mm; max. width 31mm.
Description: An upright oval medal. (Obverse) the effigy of the monarch; (reverse) similar to the preceding but inscribed MILITIA at the top of the reverse.
Comments: *Qualifying service was 18 years and 15 annual camps. It was superseded by the Efficiency Medal with the Militia bar in 1930.*

VALUE:

		Miniature
Edward VII (A) (1446)	£350–450	£80–100
George V (C) (141)	£350–400	£70–80

242. SPECIAL RESERVE LONG SERVICE AND GOOD CONDUCT MEDAL

Instituted: June 1908, by Army Order.
Branch of Service: Special Reserve.
Ribbon: Dark blue with a central light blue stripe.
Metal: Silver.
Size: Height 38mm; max. width 31mm.
Description: As the foregoing but inscribed SPECIAL RESERVE round the top of the reverse.
Comments: *Awarded to NCOs and men of the Special Reserve who completed 15 years service and attended 15 camps. A total of 1,078 medals were awarded between 1908 and 1936 with solitary awards in 1947 and 1953.*

VALUE:

		Miniature
Edward VII (A)	£350–400	£90–100
George V (C)	£350–400	£70–80

242A. VOLUNTEER RESERVES SERVICE MEDAL

Instituted: 1999.
Branch of Service: Volunteer reserves of all three armed services.
Ribbon: Dark green with three narrow central stripes of dark blue, scarlet and light blue, separated from the green by two narrow stripes of gold.
Metal: Silver.
Size: Height 38mm; width 32mm.
Description: An oval medal. (Obverse) the sovereign's effigy; (reverse) inscribed FOR SERVICE IN THE VOLUNTEER RESERVES above a spray of oak.
Comments: *Awarded to all ranks of the volunteer reserves who complete ten years of continuous service. Bars for additional five-year periods of efficient service are also awarded. This medal replaces the Royal Naval Reserve Decoration, the Royal Naval Reserve Long Service and Good Conduct Medal, the Efficiency Decoration, the Efficiency Medal and the Air Efficiency Award. It carries no rights to the use of post-nominal letters.*

VALUE: £250–300   *Miniature*   £10–12

242B. ROYAL MILITARY ASYLUM GOOD CONDUCT MEDAL

Instituted: c.1850.
Branch of Service: Students in the Royal Military Asylum.
Ribbon: Plain red.
Metal: Silver.
Size: 36mm.
Description: (Obverse) the royal arms, garnished, crested and with supporters; (reverse) ROYAL MILITARY ASYLUM round the circumference enclosing a laurel wreath inscribed across the centre FOR GOOD CONDUCT. Fitted with a scrolled suspender and brooch. Engraved in upright capitals with the name of the recipient.
Comments: *The Royal Military Asylum was established for the education of the sons of soldiers who had been killed in action or who had died while in the service.*

VALUE: £100–150

243. INDIAN ARMY LONG SERVICE & GOOD CONDUCT MEDAL FOR EUROPEANS 1848

Instituted: 20 May 1848, by General Order of the Indian Government.
Branch of Service: Indian Army.
Ribbon: Plain crimson.
Metal: Silver.
Size: 36mm.
Description: (Obverse) a trophy of arms, not unlike its British counterpart, but a shield bearing the arms of the Honourable East India Company was placed in the centre. (Reverse) engraved with the recipient's name and service details. In 1859 some 100 medals were sent to India by mistake, with the Wyon profile of Queen Victoria on the obverse and a reverse inscribed FOR LONG SERVICE AND GOOD CONDUCT within an oak wreath with a crown at the top and a fouled anchor at the foot.
Comments: *Awarded to European NCOs and other ranks of the Indian Army on discharge after 21 years meritorious service. It was discontinued in 1873 after which the standard Army LSGC medal was granted.*

VALUE:

		Miniature
HEIC arms	£350–450	£100–150
Victoria (A) (100)	£400–550	£80–100

HEIC arms type.

Victoria type.

244. INDIAN ARMY LONG SERVICE AND GOOD CONDUCT MEDAL (INDIAN)

Instituted: 1888.
Branch of Service: Indian Army.
Ribbon: Originally plain crimson but white edges were added in 1917.
Metal: Silver.
Size: 36mm.
Description: (Obverse) the sovereign's effigy; (reverse) the word INDIA set within a palm wreath surrounded by a border of lotus flowers and leaves. The inscription FOR LONG SERVICE AND GOOD CONDUCT appears between the wreath and the lotus flowers.
Comments: *Awarded to native Indian NCOs and other ranks for 20 years meritorious service. The medal became obsolete in 1947 when India achieved independence.*

VALUE:

		Miniature
Victoria (B) Kaisar-i-Hind	£100–150	£90–100
Edward VII (A) Kaisar-i-Hind	£90–120	£90–100
George V (D) Kaisar-i-Hind	£50–80	£80–90
George V (C) Rex Et Indiae Imp	£50–80	£80–90
George VI (B)	£50–80	£80–90

245. INDIAN VOLUNTEER FORCES OFFICERS' DECORATION

Instituted: May 1899, but not issued until 1903.
Branch of Service: Indian Volunteer Forces.
Ribbon: Plain green.
Metal: Silver and silver-gilt.
Size: Height 65mm; max. width 35mm.
Description: An oval skeletal badge with the royal monogram within an oval band inscribed INDIAN VOLUNTEER FORCES surmounted by a crown fitted with a suspension bar and an elaborate silver brooch.
Comments: *Awarded for 18 years commissioned service, with any service in the ranks counting half. It was superseded by the Efficiency Decoration with India bar in 1930, although the first awards were not gazetted until 1933. A total of 1,163 decorations are known to have been awarded, the last in 1934. Although the decoration was issued unnamed, nearly all found so far are named. During the lifetime of the decoration seven different engravers for the naming have been identified.*

VALUE:		*Miniature*
Edward VII	£250–300	£40–50
George V	£250–300	£30–40

246. COLONIAL AUXILIARY FORCES OFFICERS' DECORATION

Instituted: 18 May 1899.
Branch of Service: Colonial Auxiliary Forces.
Ribbon: Plain green.
Metal: Silver and silver-gilt.
Size: Height 66mm; max. width 35mm.
Description: Similar to the previous decoration, with an oval band inscribed COLONIAL AUXILIARY FORCES.
Comments: *Awarded to officers of auxiliary forces everywhere except in India for 20 years commissioned service. Service in the ranks counting half and service in West Africa counting double. Although issued unnamed, it was usually impressed or engraved privately. Examples to officers in the smaller colonies command a considerable premium. It became obsolete in 1930.*

VALUE:		*Miniature*
Victoria	£250–300	£80–90
Edward VII	£200–250	£70–80
George V	£150–200	£50–60

247. COLONIAL AUXILIARY FORCES LONG SERVICE MEDAL

Instituted: 18 May 1899.
Branch of Service: Colonial Auxiliary Forces.
Ribbon: Plain green.
Metal: Silver.
Size: 36mm.
Description: (Obverse) the effigy of the reigning monarch; (reverse) an elaborate rococo frame surmounted by a crown and enclosing the five-line text FOR LONG SERVICE IN THE COLONIAL AUXILIARY FORCES.
Comments: *Awarded for 20 years service in the ranks, West African service counting double. It was superseded in 1930 by the Efficiency Medal with the appropriate colonial or dominion bar.*

VALUE:		Miniature
Victoria (D)	£100–120	£25–35
Edward VII (A)	£80–100	£20–25
George V (A)	£80–100	£12–15

248. COLONIAL LONG SERVICE AND GOOD CONDUCT MEDALS

Instituted: May 31, 1895.
Branch of Service: Indian and Colonial forces.
Ribbon: Crimson with a central stripe denoting the country of service (see no. 212).
Metal: Silver.
Size: 36mm.
Description: Similar to its British counterpart except that the name of the country appeared on the reverse.
Comments: *Awarded to warrant officers, NCOs and other ranks for distinguished conduct in the field, meritorious service and long service and good conduct. Medals of the individual Australian colonies were superseded in 1902 by those inscribed COMMONWEALTH OF AUSTRALIA. The Colonial LSGC medal was replaced in 1909 by the Permanent Forces of the Empire Beyond the Seas LSGC award.*

VALUE:	Rare	*Miniature*	£50–100

249. PERMANENT FORCES OF THE EMPIRE BEYOND THE SEAS LONG SERVICE AND GOOD CONDUCT MEDAL

Instituted: 1909.
Branch of Service: Colonial and Dominion forces.
Ribbon: Maroon bearing a broad white central stripe with a narrow black stripe at its centre.
Metal: Silver.
Size: 36mm.
Description: (Obverse) the effigy of the reigning sovereign; (reverse) the legend PERMANENT FORCES OF THE EMPIRE BEYOND THE SEAS round the circumference, with FOR LONG SERVICE AND GOOD CONDUCT in four lines across the centre.
Comments: *This award replaced the various colonial LSGC medals, being itself superseded in 1930 by the LSGC (Military) Medal with appropriate dominion or colonial bar. It was awarded for 18 years exemplary service.*

VALUE:		Miniature
Edward VII (A)	£300–400	£60–80
George V (A)	£100–150	£50–60

250. ROYAL WEST AFRICA FRONTIER FORCE LONG SERVICE & GOOD CONDUCT MEDAL

Instituted: September 1903.
Branch of Service: Royal West Africa Frontier Force.
Ribbon: Crimson with a relatively broad green central stripe.
Metal: Silver.
Size: 36mm.
Description: (Obverse) the effigy of the reigning monarch. Two reverse types were used, the word ROYAL being added to the regimental title in June 1928.
Comments: *Awarded to native NCOs and other ranks for 18 years exemplary service.*

VALUE: £300–350   *Miniature*   £25–30

251. KING'S AFRICAN RIFLES LONG SERVICE AND GOOD CONDUCT MEDAL

Instituted: March 1907.
Branch of Service: King's African Rifles.
Ribbon: Crimson with a broad green central stripe.
Metal: Silver.
Size: 36mm.
Description: Very similar to the foregoing, apart from the regimental name round the top of the reverse.
Comments: *Awarded to native NCOs and other ranks for 18 years exemplary service.*

VALUE:		*Miniature*
Edward VII	Rare	
George V	£250–300	£50–60
George VI (B)	£250–300	£40–50
Elizabeth II	£300–350	£25–35

252. TRANS-JORDAN FRONTIER FORCE LONG SERVICE AND GOOD CONDUCT MEDAL

Instituted: 20 May 1938.
Branch of Service: Trans-Jordan Frontier Force.
Ribbon: Crimson with a green central stripe.
Metal: Silver.
Size: 36mm.
Description: Similar to the previous medals, with the name of the Force round the circumference.
Comments: *This rare silver medal was awarded for 16 years service in the ranks of the Trans-Jordan Frontier Force. Service in the Palestine Gendarmerie or Arab Legion counted, so long as the recipient transferred to the Frontier Force without a break in service. Only 112 medals were awarded before it was abolished in 1948.*

VALUE: Rare

253. SOUTH AFRICA PERMANENT FORCE LONG SERVICE AND GOOD CONDUCT MEDAL

Instituted: 29 December 1939.
Branch of Service: South African forces.
Ribbon: Crimson with white stripes.
Metal: Silver.
Size: 36mm.
Description: (Obverse) Crowned effigy of King George VI; (reverse) FOR LONG SERVICE AND GOOD CONDUCT in four lines across the upper half and VIR LANGDURIGE DIENS EN GOEIE GEDRAG in four lines across the lower half. It also differs from its British counterpart in having a bilingual suspension bar.
Comments: *Awarded to NCOs and other ranks with a minimum of 18 years service.*

VALUE:		Miniature
George VI (B)	£120–140	£15–20
George VI (C)	£150–170	£15–20

254. EFFICIENCY MEDAL (SOUTH AFRICA)

Instituted: December 1939.
Branch of Service: Coast Garrison and Active Citizen Forces of South Africa.
Ribbon: 32mm plain dark green with yellow edges.
Metal: Silver.
Size: Height 38mm; max. width 30mm.
Description: An oval silver medal rather similar to the Efficiency Medal (number 237) but having a scroll bar inscribed UNION OF SOUTH AFRICA with its Afrikaans equivalent below. The reverse likewise bears a bilingual inscription.
Comments: *Awarded for 12 years non-commissioned service in the Coast Garrison and Active Citizen Forces. A bar, bearing in the centre a crown, was awarded for every six years of additional service. It was replaced in 1952 by the John Chard Medal.*

VALUE:	£65–75	Miniature	£30–40

254A. ROYAL HONG KONG REGIMENT DISBANDMENT MEDAL

Instituted: 1995.
Branch of Service: Royal Hong Kong Regiment (Volunteers).
Ribbon: Half red and half blue with a central yellow stripe.
Metal: Cupro-nickel.
Size: 38mm.
Description: (Obverse) Regimental badge with dates 1854 and 1995 either side and ROYAL HONG KONG REGIMENT THE VOLUNTEERS around. (Reverse) Coat of Arms of Hong Kong with DISBANDMENT MEDAL 3rd SEPTEMBER 1995 (date of disbandment) around.
Comment: *Available to those serving with the Regiment as the end of the Crown Colony became imminent. Recipients, however, had to purchase a full size and a miniature medal in a plush case.*

VALUE:	£75–100	Miniature	£50–60

255 (C30). CANADIAN FORCES DECORATION

Instituted: 15 December 1949.
Branch of Service: Canadian Forces.
Ribbon: 38mm orange-red divided into four equal parts by three thin white stripes.
Metal: Silver-gilt (George VI) or gilded tombac brass (Elizabeth II).
Size: Height 35mm; max. width 37mm.
Description: A decagonal (ten-sided) medal. The George VI issue has a suspension bar inscribed CANADA and the recipient's details engraved on the reverse, whereas the Elizabethan issue has no suspension bar, the recipient's details being impressed or engraved on the rim and the word "CANADA" appears at the base of the effigy. The reverse has a naval crown at the top, three maple leaves across the middle and an eagle in flight across the foot. In the George VI version the royal cypher is superimposed on the maple leaves.
Comments: *Awarded to both officers and men of the Canadian regular and reserve forces for 12 years exemplary service. A bar, gold in colour, bearing the shield from the arms of Canada surmounted by the crown is awarded for each additional 10 years of qualifying service. Approximately 6,000 medals and 4,500 clasps are awarded annually.*

VALUE:		Miniature
George VI (E)	£50–60	£10–20
Elizabeth II (D)	£40–50	£10–20

256. VICTORIA VOLUNTEER LONG AND EFFICIENT SERVICE MEDAL

1st type obv.

Instituted: 26 January 1881 but not given royal sanction until 21 April 1882.
Branch of Service: Volunteer Forces, Victoria.
Ribbon: White, with broad crimson stripes at the sides.
Metal: Silver.
Size: 39mm.
Description: (Obverse) the crowned badge of Victoria with LOCAL FORCES VICTORIA round the circumference; (reverse) inscribed FOR LONG AND EFFICIENT SERVICE. Two types of obverse exist, differing in the motto surrounding the colonial emblem. The first version has AUT PACE AUT BELLO (both in peace and war) while the second version is inscribed PRO DEO ET PATRIA (for God and country).
Comments: *Awarded to officers and men of the Volunteers in the colony of Victoria for 15 years service. Awards to officers ended in 1894 with the introduction of the Volunteer Officers Decoration. This medal was replaced by the Commonwealth of Australia LSGC medal in 1902.*

VALUE: Rare   *Miniature*   £80–130

2nd type obv.

257. NEW ZEALAND LONG AND EFFICIENT SERVICE MEDAL

Instituted: 1 January 1887.
Branch of Service: Volunteer and Permanent Militia Forces of New Zealand.
Ribbon: Originally plain crimson, but two white central stripes were added in 1917.
Metal: Silver.
Size: 36mm.
Description: (Obverse) an imperial crown on a cushion with crossed sword and sceptre and NZ below, within a wreath of oak-leaves (left) and wattle (right) and having four five-pointed stars, representing the constellation Southern Cross, spaced in the field; (reverse) inscribed FOR LONG AND EFFICIENT SERVICE. Plain ring suspension.
Comments: *Awarded for 16 years continuous or 20 years non-continuous service in the Volunteer and Permanent Militia Forces of New Zealand. It became obsolete in 1931 following the introduction of the LSGC (Military) medal with bar for New Zealand.*

VALUE: 1887-1931 £100–150   *Miniature* £25–30

258. NEW ZEALAND VOLUNTEER SERVICE MEDAL

Instituted: 1902.
Branch of Service: Volunteer Forces, New Zealand.
Ribbon: Plain drab khaki.
Metal: Silver.
Size: 36mm
Description: (Obverse) a right-facing profile of King Edward VII with NEW ZEALAND VOLUNTEER round the top and 12 YEARS SERVICE MEDAL round the foot; (reverse) a kiwi surrounded by a wreath. Plain ring suspension.
Comments: *This rare silver medal (obsolete by 1912) was awarded for 12 years service. Two reverse dies were used. In type I (1902–04) the kiwi's beak almost touches the ground, whereas in Type II (1905–12) there is a space between the tip of the beak and the ground. Only about 100 of Type I were produced, but 636 of Type II.*

VALUE: Type I   £250–350   *Miniature* £80–100
        Type II   £180–220

259. NEW ZEALAND TERRITORIAL SERVICE MEDAL

Instituted: 1912.
Branch of Service: Territorial Force, New Zealand.
Ribbon: Originally as above, but replaced in 1917 by a ribbon of dark khaki edged with crimson.
Metal: Silver.
Size: 36mm.
Description: (Obverse) left-facing bust of King George V in field marshal's uniform; (reverse) similar to the above.
Comments: *It replaced the foregoing on the formation of the Territorial Force on March 17, 1911, from which date the old Volunteer Force ceased to exist but became obsolete itself in 1931 when the Efficiency Medal with New Zealand bar was adopted.*

VALUE:
    George V   £80–100   *Miniature* £25–30

261. ULSTER DEFENCE REGIMENT MEDAL

Instituted: 1982.
Branch of Service: Ulster Defence Regiment.
Ribbon: Dark green with a yellow central stripe edged in red.
Metal: Silver.
Size: 36mm.
Description: (Obverse) crowned head of Elizabeth II (B); (reverse) crowned harp and inscription ULSTER DEFENCE REGIMENT with a suspender of laurel leaves surmounted by a scroll bar bearing the regiment's initials.
Comments: *Awarded to part-time officers and men of the Ulster Defence Regiment with 12 years continuous service since 1 April 1970. A bar for each additional six-year period is awarded. Officers are permitted to add the letters UD after their names. This medal is to be superseded by the Northern Ireland Home Service Medal.*

VALUE:

Elizabeth II (B)	£200–250	*Miniature*	£10–12

261A. ULSTER DEFENCE REGIMENT MEDALLION

Instituted: 1987.
Branch of Service: Relatives of the Ulster Defence Regiment.
Ribbon: Dark green with a central yellow stripe flanked by two narrow red stripes.
Metal: Silver.
Size: 36mm.
Description: Uniface medal showing a crowned Irish harp flanked by sprays of shamrocks. Ring suspension. Ribbons of awards to widows and other female relatives mounted as a bow with a brooch fitment.
Comments: *Designed by Colour Sergeant Win Clark and struck by Spink & Son, it was commissioned by the Regiment for presentation to the families of UDR personnel killed during the conflict in Northern Ireland as a token of appreciation.*

VALUE: —

262. CADET FORCES MEDAL

Instituted: February 1, 1950.
Branch of Service: Cadet Forces.
Ribbon: A broad green central band bordered by thin red stripes flanked by a dark blue stripe (left) and light blue stripe (right, with yellow edges.
Metal: Cupro-nickel.
Size: 36mm.
Description: (Obverse) the effigy of the reigning monarch; (reverse) a hand holding aloft the torch of learning. Medals are named to recipients on the rim, in impressed capitals (Army and Navy) or engraved lettering (RAF).
Comments: *Awarded to commissioned officers and adult NCOs for 12 years service in the Cadet Forces. A clasp is awarded for additional service; initially it was for each additional 8 years; but since April 1999 anyone who has completed 18 years' service will be entitled to the award of the clasp, i.e. 12 years for the medal and 6 years for the clasp. In 2002 the length of additional service for the clasp was reduced from 8 to 6 years. Issued to those qualifying in New Zealand under the terms of a Royal Warrant dated February 1, 1950 and the New Zealand Cadet Forces Medal Regulations dated January 13, 1954.*

VALUE:

		Miniature
George VI (C)	£70–90	£8–12
Elizabeth II (A1, BRITT: OMN)	£70–90	£8–12
Elizabeth II (A, DEI GRATIA)	£70–90	£8–12

263. ROYAL OBSERVER CORPS MEDAL

Instituted: 31 January 1950 but not awarded until 1953.
Branch of Service: Royal Observer Corps.
Ribbon: Pale blue with a broad central silver-grey stripe edged in dark blue.
Metal: Cupro-nickel.
Size: 36mm.
Description: (Obverse) effigy of the reigning monarch; (reverse) an artist's impression of a coast-watcher of Elizabethan times, holding a torch aloft alongside a signal fire, with other signal fires on hilltops in the background. The medal hangs from a suspender of two wings. An obverse die with the effigy of George VI was engraved, but no medals were struck from it.
Comments: *Awarded to part-time officers and observers who have completed 12 years satisfactory service and full-time members for 24 years service. A bar is awarded for each additional 12-year period. Home Office scientific officers and other non Royal Observer Corps members of the United Kingdom Warning and Monitoring Organisation were eligible for the Civil Defence Medal (no. 264) until being stood down on September 30, 1991. This entailed serving for 15 years alongside ROC members who received their own medal for 12 years' service.*

VALUE:		*Miniature*
Elizabeth II (C)	£90–120	**£8–12**
Elizabeth II (D)	£80–100	**£8–12**

264. CIVIL DEFENCE LONG SERVICE MEDAL

Instituted: March 1961.
Branch of Service: Civil Defence and other auxiliary forces.
Ribbon: Blue bearing three narrow stripes of yellow, red and green.
Metal: Cupro-nickel.
Size: Height 38mm; max. width 32mm.
Description: (Obverse) the effigy of the reigning monarch; (reverse) two types. Both featured three shields flanked by sprigs of acorns and oak leaves. The upper shield in both cases is inscribed CD but the initials on the lower shields differ, according to the organisations in Britain and Northern Ireland respectively—AFS and NHSR (British) or AFRS and HSR (Northern Ireland).
Comments: *Issued unnamed to those who had completed 15 years service in a wide range of Civil Defence organisations. It was extended to Civil Defence personnel in Gibraltar, Hong Kong and Malta in 1965. The medal became obsolescent in the UK after the Civil Defence Corps and Auxiliary Fire Service were disbanded in 1968, but members of the CD Corps in the Isle of Man and Channel Islands are still eligible.*

VALUE:		*Miniature*
British version	£25–30	**£30–40**
Northern Ireland version	£80–100	**£100–150**
Gibraltar	£100–125	
Hong Kong	£100–125	
Malta	£100–125	

British rev.

Northern Ireland rev.

264A. AMBULANCE SERVICE (EMERGENCY DUTIES) LONG SERVICE AND GOOD CONDUCT MEDAL

Instituted: 5 July 1996.

Branch of Service: Ambulance services in England and Wales, Scotland, Northern Ireland, the Isle of Man and the Channel Islands.

Ribbon: Green with, on either side, a white stripe on which is superimposed a narrow green stripe.

Metal: Cupro-nickel.

Size: 36mm.

Description: (Obverse) crowned effigy of the reigning monarch, ELIZABETH II DEI GRATIA REGINA F.D.; (reverse) FOR EXEMPLARY SERVICE round the top, with either the emblem of the Ambulance Services of Scotland or the remainder of the United Kingdom in the centre below. Fitted with a ring for suspension.

Comments: *Both full- and part-time members of Ambulance Services are eligible provided they are employed on emergency duties. Service prior to 1974 in ambulance services maintained by local authorities counts. For paramedics and technicians the qualifying service is 20 years. For ambulance officers and other management grades, at least seven of their 20 years' service must have been spent on emergency duties.*

VALUE:	UK version	£50–60	*Miniature*	£35–40
	Scottish version	£50–60		—

264B. ASSOCIATION OF CHIEF AMBULANCE OFFICERS SERVICE MEDAL

Instituted: —.

Branch of Service: Members of the Ambulance Service.

Ribbon: Dark green with twin central red stripe edged with yellow.

Metal: Bronze.

Size: 36mm.

Description: (Obverse) symbol of the Association (caduceus on a wheel) surrounded by ASSOCIATION OF CHIEF AMBULANCE OFFICERS; (reverse) FOR SERVICE surrounded by a laurel wreath.

Comments: *Issued by members of the Association to ambulancemen who have performed exemplary service.*

VALUE:	£40–60	*Miniature*	£50–60

264C. ROYAL FLEET AUXILIARY SERVICE MEDAL

Instituted: July 24, 2001 by Royal Warrant.

Branch of Service: Royal Fleet Auxiliary Service.

Ribbon: Central band of watered royal blue flanked by narrow stripes of cypress green, yellow-gold and purple.

Metal: Cupro-nickel.

Size: 38mm.

Description: (Obverse) the crowned effigy of the Queen; (reverse) the badge of the Royal Fleet Auxiliary Service with the inscription ROYAL FLEET AUXILIARY — FOR LONG SERVICE.

Comments: *The medal is awarded to all officers, petty officers and ratings of the RFA after 20 years' service. Clasps will be granted for a further 10 years service. The recipient's name and rank, together with date of qualification, are impressed on the rim. The first awards of this medal were made to three petty officers in 2003, a further 400 personnel being eligible.*

VALUE:	£200–250	*Miniature*	£40–50

265. WOMEN'S ROYAL VOLUNTARY SERVICE LONG SERVICE MEDAL

Instituted: 1961.
Branch of Service: Women's Royal Voluntary Service.
Ribbon: Dark green with twin white stripes towards the end and broad red edges.
Metal: Cupro-nickel.
Size: 36mm.
Description: (Obverse) the interlocking initials WRVS in an ivy wreath (the WVS acquired the Royal title in 1966, early issues of the medal use the initials WVS only); (reverse) three flowers, inscribed SERVICE BEYOND SELF round the circumference.
Comments: *Issued unnamed and awarded for 15 years service. Bars for additional 15 year periods are awarded. Although the majority of the 35,000 (approx.) medals have been awarded to women there has also been a substantial number of male recipients.*

Type 1 obv.

VALUE: £15–20   *Miniature*   £30–40

266. VOLUNTARY MEDICAL SERVICE MEDAL

Instituted: 1932.
Branch of Service: British Red Cross Society and the St Andrew's Ambulance Corps (Scotland).
Ribbon: Red with yellow and white stripes.
Metal: Originally struck in silver but since the 1960s it has been produced in cupro-nickel.
Size: 36mm.
Description: (Obverse) the veiled bust of a female holding an oil lamp, symbolic of Florence Nightingale; (reverse) the crosses of Geneva and St Andrew, with the inscription FOR LONG AND EFFICIENT SERVICE.
Comments: *Awarded for 15 years service, with a bar for each additional period of five years. The service bars are embellished with a Geneva cross or saltire (St Andrew) cross, whichever is the more appropriate.*

VALUE:
Silver	£20–25
Cupro-nickel	£15–20
Miniature	£20–30

267. SERVICE MEDAL OF THE ORDER OF ST JOHN

Instituted: 1898.

Branch of Service: The Most Venerable Order of the Hospital of St John of Jerusalem.

Ribbon: Three black and two white stripes of equal width.

Metal: Silver (1898-1947), silvered base metal (1947-60), silvered cupro-nickel (1960-66) and rhodium-plated cupro-nickel (since 1966).

Size: 38mm.

Description: (Obverse) an unusual veiled bust of Queen Victoria with her name and abbreviated Latin titles round the circumference. A new obverse was adopted in 1960 with a slightly reduced effigy of Queen Victoria and less ornate lettering. (Reverse) the royal arms within a garter surrounded by four circles containing the imperial crown, the Prince of Wales's feathers and the armorial bearings of the Order and of HRH the Duke of Clarence and Avondale, the first Sub-Prior of the Order. Between the circles are sprigs of St John's Wort. Round the circumference is the Latin inscription MAGNUS PRIORATUS ORDINIS HOSPITALIS SANCTI JOHANNIS JERUSALEM IN ANGLIA in Old English lettering.

Comments: *Originally awarded for 15 years service to the Order in the United Kingdom (12 in the Dominions and 10 in the Colonies) but the qualifying period has now been reduced to 12 years service, except that overseas service outside South Africa, New Zealand, Canada and Australia remains 10 years. A silver bar was introduced in 1911 for additional periods of five years. From then until 1924 the bar was inscribed 5 YEARS SERVICE but then a design showing a Maltese cross flanked by sprays of St John's Wort was substituted. Bars for 20 years service were subsequently instituted in silver-gilt. Suspension by a ring was changed in 1913 to a straight bar suspender. The medal is worn on the left breast. Although awarded for long service this medal should not be solely referred to as a long service award as it can also be awarded for conspicuous service—when so awarded it was distinguished by the addition of a silver palm leaf on the ribbon. The silver palm was discontinued in 1949, after only three years. It is believed to be the only medal still issued bearing the bust of Queen Victoria (the effigy was first sculptured by HRH Princess Louise, daughter of Queen Victoria).*

Ribbon embellishments:

5-year cross | Palm leaf for conspicuous service

Voluntary Aid Detachment | Military Hospital Reserve

Ribbon bars:

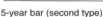

5-year bar (second type)

VAD (or MHR)

VALUE:

		Miniature
Silver, ring suspension	£20–25	£15–20
Silver, straight bar suspension	£20–25	£12–15
Base metal, first obverse	£15–20	£6–10
Base metal, second obverse	£15–20	£6–10

268. ROYAL AIR FORCE LONG SERVICE AND GOOD CONDUCT MEDAL

Instituted: 1 July 1919.

Branch of Service: Royal Air Force.

Ribbon: Dark blue and maroon with white edges.

Metal: Silver/silver-plated.

Size: 36mm.

Description: (Obverse) the effigy of the reigning monarch; (reverse) the RAF eagle and crown insignia.

Comments: *Awarded to NCOs and other ranks of the RAF for 18 years exemplary service, reduced in 1977 to 15 years. Provision for bars for further periods of service was made from 1944 onwards. Before 1945 conduct below the required standard was permitted to count if the airman had displayed higher exemplary conduct against the enemy, gallantry or some special service in times of emergency. From 1944 prior service in the Navy and Army up to a maximum of four years could be counted. In 1947 officers became eligible for the medal provided they had had at least 12 years service in the ranks. Recipients' details are inscribed on the rim. The later issues are of silver-plated base metal.*

VALUE:

		Miniature			Miniature
George V (E)	£80–100	£20–30	Elizabeth II (C)	£45–50	£20–30
George VI (D)	£50–60	£20–30	Elizabeth II (D)	£45–50	£20–30
George VI (E)	£50–60	£20–30			

269. ROYAL AIR FORCE LEVIES LONG SERVICE AND GOOD CONDUCT MEDAL

Instituted: 1948.

Branch of Service: RAF Levies, Iraq.

Ribbon: As the preceding.

Metal: Silver.

Size: 36mm.

Description: Similar to the previous type but was fitted with a clasp inscribed ROYAL AIR FORCE LEVIES IRAQ.

Comments: *Awarded to the locally commissioned officers and men of the RAF Levies in Iraq, for 18 years service (the last 12 to be of an exemplary nature). The Iraq Levies were raised in 1919 and became the responsibility of the RAF in 1922, maintaining law and order by means of light aircraft and armoured cars. The force was disbanded in 1955 when the RAF withdrew from Iraq. 309 medals were issued, 115 to officers and 194 to airmen.*

VALUE:

George VI (E)	£800–1000
Elizabeth II (C)	£900–1100
Elizabeth II (D)	£900–1100

270. AIR EFFICIENCY AWARD

Instituted: September 1942

Branch of Service: AAF, RAAF and RAFVR.

Ribbon: Green with two light blue stripes towards the centre.

Metal: Silver.

Size: Height 38mm; max. width 32mm.

Description: An oval medal with a suspender in the form of an eagle with wings outspread. (Obverse) the effigy of the reigning monarch; (reverse) inscribed AIR EFFICIENCY AWARD in three lines.

Comments: *Granted for 10 years efficient service in the Auxiliary and Volunteer Air Forces of the United Kingdom and Commonwealth. A bar was awarded for a further ten-year period. Officers are permitted to add the letters AE after their name. This award was replaced in 2000 by the VRSM (No. 242A).*

VALUE:

George VI (D)	£100–120
George VI (E)	£100–120
Elizabeth II (C)	£100–120
Elizabeth II (D)	£100–120
Miniature (all)	£20–30

271. POLICE LONG SERVICE AND GOOD CONDUCT MEDAL

Instituted: 14 June 1951.
Branch of Service: Police Forces.
Ribbon: Dark blue with twin white stripes towards each end.
Metal: Cupro-nickel
Size: 36mm.
Description: (Obverse) the effigy of the reigning monarch; (reverse) a standing female allegorical figure of Justice, with scales in one hand and a wreath in the other. Named on the rim.
Comments: *Awarded for 22 years full-time service in any UK constabulary. By a Royal Warrant of 1 May 1956 it was extended to police forces in Australia, Papua New Guinea and Nauru. The Australian award was replaced in 1976 by the National Medal.*

VALUE:		*Miniature*
George VI (C)	£35–45	£20–30
Elizabeth II (A)	£40–50	£20–30
Elizabeth II (D)	£40–50	£20–30

272. SPECIAL CONSTABULARY LONG SERVICE MEDAL

Instituted: 30 August 1919.
Branch of Service: Special Constabulary.
Ribbon: A broad red stripe in the centre flanked by black and white stripes.
Metal: Bronze.
Size: 36mm.
Description: (Obverse) the effigy of the reigning monarch; (reverse) a partial laurel wreath with a six-line text inscribed FOR FAITHFUL SERVICE IN THE SPECIAL CONSTABULARY. A second reverse was introduced in 1956 for 15 years service in the Ulster Special Constabulary, the text being modified to permit the inclusion of the word ULSTER. A third type was introduced in 1982 for 15 years service in the RUC Reserve and is thus inscribed.
Comments: *Awarded to all ranks in the Special Constabulary for 9 years unpaid service, with more than 50 duties per annum. War service with at least 50 duties counted triple. A clasp inscribed THE GREAT WAR 1914-18 was awarded to those who qualified for the medal during that conflict. Clasps inscribed LONG SERVICE, with the date, are awarded for additional ten-year periods.*

VALUE:		*Miniature*
George V (C)	£10–15	£5–8
With Great War 1914-18 clasp	£15–18	
George V (E)	£10–15	£5–8
George VI (D)	£10–15	£5–8
George VI (E)	£50–75	£8–10
Elizabeth II (C)	£35–40	£8–10
Elizabeth II (D)	£35–40	£8–10
Elizabeth II (D) Ulster	£120–150	£8–12
Elizabeth II (D) RUC Reserve	£120–150	£8–12
Elizabeth II (A1)	Very rare	

273. ROYAL ULSTER CONSTABULARY MEDAL

Instituted: 1982.

Branch of Service: RUC and its Reserve.

Ribbon: Green, with narrow central stripes of red, black and dark blue. Following the award of the George Cross to the RUC the ribbon of this medal was modified to reflect the award. The colour of the GC ribbon is now indicated by two vertical blue stripes at the outer edges.

Metal: Cupro-nickel.

Size: 36mm.

Description: (Obverse) the effigy of Queen Elizabeth II; (reverse) the crowned harp insignia of the RUC with the words FOR SERVICE round the foot.

Comments: *Awarded for 18 months continuous service since 1 January 1971, but the award was made immediate on the recipient also being awarded a gallantry decoration or a Queen's commendation.*

VALUE:

Elizabeth II (B)	£200–250	*Miniature*	£10–15

274. COLONIAL POLICE LONG SERVICE MEDAL

Instituted: 1934.

Branch of Service: Colonial police forces.

Ribbon: Green centre bordered with white and broad blue stripes towards the edges.

Metal: Silver.

Size: 36mm.

Description: (Obverse) the effigy of the reigning monarch; (reverse) a police truncheon superimposed on a laurel wreath.

Comments: *Originally awarded to junior officers who had completed 18 years exemplary service but latterly awarded to officers of all ranks who have the required service qualification. A bar is awarded on completing 25 years service and a second bar after 30 years. These are represented on the ribbon bar in working dress by silver rosettes. The number (where applicable), rank and name as well as (for George VI and later issues) the relevant force in which the recipient is serving at the time of the award is engraved on the rim, often locally and therefore in a variety of styles.*

VALUE:

		Miniature
George V (C)	£100–120	£20–30
George VI (B)	£70–85	£20–30
George VI (C)	£70–85	£20–30
Elizabeth II (A)	£70–85	£20–30
Elizabeth II (B)	£70–85	£20–30

275. COLONIAL SPECIAL CONSTABULARY LONG SERVICE MEDAL

Instituted: 1957.
Branch of Service: Colonial Special Constabulary.
Ribbon: Two thin white stripes on a broad green centre, with broad blue edges.
Metal: Silver.
Size: 36mm.
Description: (Obverse) the effigy of the reigning monarch; (reverse) the crowned royal cypher above the words FOR FAITHFUL SERVICE in a laurel wreath.
Comments: *Awarded for nine years unpaid or 15 years paid service in a colonial special constabulary. A bar is awarded for further ten-year periods.*

VALUE:

Elizabeth II (A)	£250–300	*Miniature*	£20–30

276. CEYLON POLICE LONG SERVICE AND GOOD CONDUCT MEDAL (I)

Instituted: 1925.
Branch of Service: Ceylon Police.
Ribbon: Very similar to that of the Special Constabulary Long Service Medal—a broad red stripe in the centre flanked by black and white stripes.
Metal: Silver.
Size: 36mm.
Description: (Obverse) coinage profile of King George V by Sir Bertram Mackennal; (reverse) an elephant surmounted by a crown. Ring suspension.
Comments: *Awarded for 15 years active service. It was superseded in 1934 by the Colonial Police Long Service Medal.*

VALUE:

George V (E)	£300–350	*Miniature*	£80–90

277. CEYLON POLICE LONG SERVICE AND GOOD CONDUCT MEDAL (II)

Instituted: 1950.
Branch of Service: Ceylon Police.
Ribbon: Dark blue edged with khaki, white and pale blue.
Metal: Cupro-nickel.
Size: 36mm.
Description: (Obverse) the effigy of the reigning monarch; (reverse) similar to the foregoing, but without the crown above the elephant, to permit the longer inscription CEYLON POLICE SERVICE. Straight bar suspender.
Comments: *Awarded for 18 years exemplary service. Bars for 25 and 30 years service were also awarded. It became obsolete when Ceylon (now Sri Lanka) became a republic in 1972.*

VALUE:

		Miniature
George VI (C)	£350–400	£30–40
Elizabeth II (A)	£350–400	£30–40

278. CEYLON POLICE MEDAL FOR MERIT

Instituted: 1950.
Branch of Service: Ceylon Police.
Ribbon: Broad central khaki stripe, flanked by narrow stripes of white, light blue and dark blue.
Metal: Silver.
Size: 36mm.
Description: (Obverse) the effigy of the reigning monarch; (reverse) an Indian elephant with the legend CEYLON POLICE SERVICE at the top and FOR MERIT at the foot.
Comments: *The medal became obsolete when Ceylon (now Sri Lanka) became a republic in 1972.*

VALUE		*Miniature*
George VI	Rare	—
Elizabeth II	£400–500	£30–40

278A. CEYLON POLICE MEDAL FOR GALLANTRY

Instituted: 1950.
Branch of Service: Ceylon Police.
Ribbon: As for the medal for Merit (above) but with the addition of a very narrow red stripe superimposed on the white stripes.
Metal: Silver.
Size: 36mm.
Description: Similar to the Medal of Merit (above) but reverse inscribed FOR GALLANTRY at the foot.
Comments: *It became obsolete when Ceylon (now Sri Lanka) became a republic in 1972.*

VALUE:		*Miniature*
George VI	—	£50–60
Elizabeth II	—	£50–60

279. CYPRUS MILITARY POLICE LONG SERVICE & GOOD CONDUCT MEDAL

Instituted: October 1929.
Branch of Service: Cyprus Military Police.
Ribbon: Yellow, dark green and yellow in equal bands.
Metal: Silver.
Size: 36mm.
Description: (Obverse) King George V; (reverse) the title of the police round the circumference and the words LONG AND GOOD SERVICE in four lines across the middle.
Comments: *Awarded to those who had three good conduct badges, plus six years exemplary service since the award of the third badge, no more than four entries in the defaulters' book and a minimum of 15 years service. Officers who had been promoted from the ranks were also eligible. No more than 7 officers and 54 other ranks were awarded this medal during its brief life before it was superseded in 1934 by the Colonial Police Long Service Medal.*

VALUE: Rare

279A. ROYAL FALKLAND ISLANDS POLICE JUBILEE MEDAL

Date: 1996
Branch of Service: Royal Falkland Islands Police
Ribbon: Blue with a central white stripe edged in black and a thin red central stripe.
Metal: Silver.
Size: 36mm.
Description: (Obverse) Elizabeth II (A); (reverse) arms of the colony; ROYAL FALKLAND ISLANDS POLICE round top and double dated 1846-1996 round foot. Fitted with ring suspension and a brooch clasp at the top of the ribbon.
Comments: *Awarded to all officers serving in the Royal Falkland Islands Police on 15 October 1996. Only 27 medals were awarded.*

VALUE: £1000–1500

280. HONG KONG POLICE MEDAL FOR MERIT

Instituted: May 3, 1862.
Branch of Service: Hong Kong Police.
Ribbon: Various, according to class (see below).
Metal: Gold, silver or bronze.
Size: 36mm.
Description: (Obverse) the effigy of the reigning monarch; (reverse) inscribed HONG KONG POLICE FORCE FOR MERIT within a laurel wreath and beaded circle. Examples have been recorded with the effigy of Queen Victoria as on the Abyssinian and New Zealand Medals (MY123–124), and King George V types C and E.
Comment: *Exceptionally awarded in five different classes according to the length and type of service. The 1st Class medal was struck in gold and worn with a maroon (VC) ribbon, the 2nd Class in silver with a plain yellow ribbon, the 3rd Class in bronze with a central black stripe on the yellow ribbon, the 4th Class in bronze with two central black stripes in the yellow ribbon, and the 5th Class (confined to the Police Reserve) in bronze had a green ribbon with two black central stripes. The 4th Class was engraved on the reverse above the wreath. These medals were superseded in April 1937 by the Hong Kong Police Silver Medal, only four of which was awarded before it was replaced by the Colonial Police Medal for Meritorious Service 1938.*

VALUE:	1st class	2nd class	3rd class	4th class
Victoria	—	£450–500	£400–450	£250–300
Edward VII	Rare	£450–500	£350–450	£250–300
George V (B)	Rare	£400–450	£300–350	£225–275
George V (C)	Rare	£$00–450	£300–350	£225–275

Miniature (all, silver or bronze)   £100–150

280A. HONG KONG DISTRICT WATCH FORCE MERIT MEDAL

Instituted: 1868.
Branch of Service: District Watch Force.
Ribbon: Very dark green with a central deep red stripe.
Metal: Silver or bronze.
Size: 31mm with a prominent rim.
Description: (Obverse) four Chinese characters "Great Britain Hong Kong" above a watchman's lamp, superimposed on a cutlass and police baton, with the Chinese characters for "District Watch Force" and "Medal" at the sides; (reverse) DISTRICT WATCHMEN'S FORCE FOR MERIT within a laurel wreath.
Comment: *While the Hong Kong Police was principally a mixed force of Europeans and Indians, operated in the business and higher class residential areas, and was paid for out of the colony's revenues, the District Watch Force was a purely Chinese organisation, raised by prominent citizens of the colony to patrol and police the Chinese parts of the city. Its members had statutory powers, were uniformed and were trained and functioned in the style of the old parish constables, rather than in the gendarmerie style of the Hong Kong Police which was colonial in nature and imposed on society rather than integrated with it. The District Watch Force ceased to function at the time of the Japanese invasion in 1941 and was not revived on liberation.*

VALUE: £500–550

280B. ROYAL HONG KONG POLICE COMMEMORATION MEDAL

Instituted: 1996.
Branch of Service: Royal Hong Kong Police.
Ribbon: Black, magenta and old gold (colours of the turban worn by the original Punjabi constables).
Metal: Silver.
Size: 38mm.
Description: (Obverse) the RHKP crest; (reverse) crossed tipstaves inside a laurel wreath with the dates 1844 and 1997.
Comment: *The medal, approved by Commissioner Eddie Hui Kion, is available on purchase (HK$1,000, about £80) to those who served in the Hong Kong Police (1844–1969) and the Royal Hong Kong Police (1969–97). Made by Spink & Son and cased. Apparently only about 2,000 of the 40,000 eligible have purchased the medal owing to the cost. Purchasers' details are engraved in bold upright capitals in a variety of formats. The medal, worn on the right breast, has the same status as the Royal Hong Kong Regiment Disbandment Medal (254A).*

VALUE: £100–120   *Miniature*   £90–100

280C. ROYAL HONG KONG AUXILIARY POLICE COMMEMORATION MEDAL

Instituted: 1996.
Branch of Service: Royal Hong Kong Auxiliary Police.
Ribbon: Black, magenta and old gold (colours of the turban worn by the original Punjabi constables).
Metal: Silver.
Size: 38mm.
Description: Similar to the above, but inscribed ROYAL HONG KONG AUXILIARY POLICE FORCE.
Comment: *Similar to the above this medal is available for purchase. Some 5,000 auxiliary policemen and women being eligible for the award.*

VALUE: £120–140   *Miniature*   £90–100

280D. HONG KONG MILITARY SERVICE CORPS MEDAL

Instituted: 1997.
Branch of Service: Hong Kong Military Service Corps.
Ribbon: Red, with a central yellow stripe.
Metal: Cupro-nickel.
Size: 36mm.
Description: (Obverse) a Chinese dragon on a scroll bearing the initials of the Corps. HONG KONG MILITARY SERVICE CORPS inscribed round the top and 1962-1997 at the foot; (reverse) the British royal arms with inscription round the top TO COMMEMORATE DISBANDMENT and the date 31 March 1997 at the foot.
Comments: *The Military Service Corps was a paramilitary unit formed in 1962 for defence of the Crown Colony and recruited locally. Members of the Corps were allowed to purchase this medal following its disbandment prior to the return of Hong Kong to China.*
VALUE: —

281. HONG KONG ROYAL NAVAL DOCKYARD POLICE LONG SERVICE MEDAL

Instituted: 1920.
Branch of Service: Hong Kong Royal Naval Dockyard Police.
Ribbon: Yellow with two royal blue stripes towards the centre.
Metal: Gilt bronze or silver.
Size: 31mm.
Description: (Obverse) the effigy of the reigning monarch; (reverse) the title of the Police within a laurel wreath. Ring suspension (two sizes).
Comments: *Awarded for 15 years service. Although the Dockyard closed in 1961 men who transferred to other police divisions continued to be awarded the medal up to 1973. About 280 medals in all were issued.*

VALUE:		Miniature
George V (E)	£350–450	£100–150
George VI (C)	£350–450	£100–150
George VI (D)	£350–450	£100–150
Elizabeth II (C)	£350–450	£100–150

281A. HONG KONG DISCIPLINED SERVICES MEDAL

Instituted: 1986.
Branch of Service: Hong Kong Customs & Excise and Immigration Service.
Ribbon: Green bordered by vertical stripes of dark blue with a strip of sky blue at each edge.
Metal: Silver.
Size: 36mm.
Description: (Obverse) crowned effigy of Queen Elizabeth II (B); (reverse) armorial bearings of Hong Kong, with the inscription "For Long Service and Good Conduct".
Clasps: Awarded after 25 and 30 years, denoted by silver rosettes on ribband in working dress.
Comments: *Awarded after 18 years continuous service. Engraved with name and rank on rim. Some 1,739 medals were awarded between 1987 and the return of Hong Kong to China on June 30, 1997. No other long service medal to Customs officers has been awarded in the British system.*

VALUE:	Customs	Immigration
Medal	£100–£150	£250–£300
1st clasp	£250–£300	£500–£700
2nd clasp	£400–£500	Unique

282. MALTA POLICE LONG SERVICE AND GOOD CONDUCT MEDAL

Instituted: 1921.
Branch of Service: Malta Police.
Ribbon: Dark blue with a narrow central silver stripe.
Metal: Silver.
Size: 36mm.
Description: (Obverse) the effigy of King George V; (reverse) an eight-
pointed Maltese cross in a laurel wreath with the title of the service and
FOR LONG SERVICE AND GOOD CONDUCT round the circumfer-
ence.
Comments: *Awarded to sergeants and constables with 18 years exemplary
service. Officers who had had 18 years in the ranks were also eligible for the
award. It was superseded by the Colonial Police Long Service Medal in 1934.
No more than 99 medals were awarded.*

VALUE:		*Miniature*
George V (E)	£350–450	£100–120
George V (C)	£350–450	£100–120

282A. MAURITIUS POLICE LONG SERVICE AND GOOD CONDUCT MEDAL: I

Instituted: —.
Branch of Service: Mauritius Police.
Ribbon: Three types: (a) 36mm half black, half white; (b) 33mm white with a
broad royal blue central stripe; (c) blue with two narrow white stripes towards
the edges.
Metal: Bronze.
Size: Oval, 40x33mm or 39x31mm.
Description: (Obverse) crown surmounting crossed tipstaves with the motto PAX
NOBISCUM (Peace be with us) and the legend POLICE DEPARTMENT round
the top and MAURITIUS at the foot; (reverse) palm fronds enclosing a theee-
line inscription FOR GOOD CONDUCT. Fitted with a ring for suspension.
Medals with 33mm ribbon fitted at top with a pin brooch by Hunt & Roskill.
Comment: *It is believed that the different ribbons indicated different periods of service,
but confirmation is sought. It is presumed that this medal was superseded by no.
282B.*

VALUE:	£200–250	*Miniature*	£75–100

282B. MAURITIUS POLICE LONG SERVICE AND GOOD CONDUCT MEDAL: II

Instituted: —.
Branch of Service: Mauritius Police
Ribbon: Green centre flanked by white stripes and broad blue stripes towards the edges.
Metal: Silver.
Size: 36mm.
Description: (Obverse) the effigy of Queen Elizabeth II; (reverse) police truncheon on a laurel wreath.
Comments: *This medal is identical to the Colonial Police Long Service Medal (no. 274) except that the inscription
substituted the name MAURITIUS for COLONIAL. It has been recorded in a medal group of 1976 and may have been
introduced in or about 1968 when Mauritius attained independence.*

VALUE: £100–150

283. NEW ZEALAND POLICE MEDAL

First type obverse.

Instituted: 1886.

Branch of Service: New Zealand Police.

Ribbon: Originally plain crimson but in 1917 it was changed to a pattern very similar to that of the Permanent Forces of the Empire Beyond the Seas LSGC medal.

Metal: Silver.

Size: 36mm.

Description: The original obverse was very similar to that of the NZ Long and Efficient Service Medal, with the crown, crossed sword and sceptre motif within a wreath of oak and fern leaves. Two types of suspension for this medal are known: the normal type has a bar suspender but a very rare variant has a ring suspender. By Royal Warrant of 8 September 1976 an obverse portraying Queen Elizabeth was introduced. The reverse was plain with the words FOR LONG SERVICE AND GOOD CONDUCT.

Comments: *Awarded for 14 years service. Bars for further eight-year periods were added in 1959, reduced to seven years in 1963, the total length of service being indicated on the bar. A new medal, introduced in 1994 but retaining the original name, will be found in the New Zealand section (no. NZ16).*

VALUE:

		Miniature
Regalia obverse, bar suspension	£100–120	£20–30
Elizabeth II obverse	£90–110	£20–30

283A. SEYCHELLES POLICE LONG SERVICE AND GOOD CONDUCT MEDAL

Instituted: —.

Branch of Service: Seychelles Police.

Ribbon: Crimson.

Metal: Bronze.

Size: Oval, 40x33mm.

Description: (Obverse) crown surmounting crossed tipstaves with legend POLICE DEPARTMENT round the top and SEYCHELLES at the foot; (reverse) palm fronds enclosing a three-line inscription FOR GOOD CONDUCT. Fitted with a ring for suspension.

Comments: *Thgis medal is similar to the Mauritius Police Medal (282A) and it is presumed that this medal also became obsolete on the introduction of the Colonial Police Long Service Medal in 1934. Details of qualifying terms of service and other regulations are sought.*

VALUE: £100–150

284. SOUTH AFRICA POLICE GOOD SERVICE MEDAL

Instituted: 1923.

Branch of Service: South Africa Police.

Ribbon: Broad black centre, flanked by white stripes and green borders.

Metal: Silver.

Size: 36mm.

Description: (Obverse) South African coat of arms; (reverse) bilingual inscriptions separated by a horizontal line. Three versions of the medal have been recorded. In the first version inscriptions were in English and Dutch, the latter reading POLITIE DIENST with VOOR TROUWE DIENST (for faithful service) on the reverse. In the second, introduced in 1932, Afrikaans replaced Dutch and read POLISIE DIENS and VIR GETROUE DIENS respectively. In the third version, current from 1951 to 1963, the Afrikaans was modified to read POLISIEDIENS and VIR TROUE DIENS.

Comments: *Awarded to other ranks for 18 years exemplary service or for service of a gallant or particularly distinguished character. In the latter instance a bar inscribed MERIT-VERDIENSTE was awarded. The medal was replaced by the South African Medal for Faithful Service.*

VALUE:	1st type	£30–35
	2nd type	£25–30
	3rd type	£20–25
	Miniature	£30–40

285. SOUTH AFRICAN RAILWAYS AND HARBOUR POLICE LONG SERVICE AND GOOD CONDUCT MEDAL

Instituted: 1934.
Branch of Service: South African Railways and Harbour Police.
Ribbon: Similar to the Police Good Service Medal but with the colours reversed—a green central stripe flanked by white stripes and blue edges.
Metal: Silver.
Size: 36mm.
Description: (Obverse) the Union arms with S.A.R. & H. POLICE at the top and S.A.S.- EN HAWE POLISIE round the foot, but this was changed in 1953 to S.A.S. POLISIE at the top and S.A.R. POLICE at the foot. (Reverse) six line bilingual inscription.
Comments: *Awarded for 18 years unblemished service. Immediate awards for gallant or especially meritorious service earned a bar inscribed MERIT - VERDIENSTE (later with the words transposed). The medal was superseded in 1960 by the Railways Police Good Service Medal.*

VALUE: 1st type £80–100   **2nd type** £75–100   *Miniature* £30–40

286. FIRE BRIGADE LONG SERVICE MEDAL

Instituted: 1 June 1954.
Branch of Service: Fire Services.
Ribbon: Red with narrow yellow stripes towards the end and yellow borders.
Metal: Cupro-nickel.
Size: 36mm.
Description: (Obverse) the Queen's effigy; (reverse) two firemen manning a hose. Ring suspension.
Comments: *Awarded to all ranks of local authority fire brigades, whether full- or part-time for 20 years exemplary service. Prior to the institution of this award most local authorities issued their own medals of individual design.*

VALUE:
   Elizabeth II £35–45   *Miniature* £10–12

286A. ASSOCIATION OF PROFESSIONAL FIRE BRIGADE OFFICERS LONG SERVICE MEDAL

Branch of Service: Association of Professional Fire Brigade Officers.
Ribbon: A red central stripe flanked by narrow white stripes and broad black edges (silver medal) or grey edges (bronze medal).
Metal: Silver or bronze.
Size: 38mm.
Description: (Obverse) allegorical female figure carrying a palm frond and bestowing a laurel crown on a kneeling fireman; an early fire appliance in the background; blank exergue; (reverse) an oak wreath enclosing a four-line inscription ASSOCIATION OF PROFESSIONAL FIRE BRIGADE OFFICERS FOR LONG SERVICE. Fitted with a swivelling bar suspension.
Comments: *The medal in silver was awarded to professional fire brigade officers for a minimum of 20 years full time service and in bronze for lesser periods. Engraved on the rim with the rank and name of the officer, together with the year of the award.*

VALUE: £40–50   *Miniature* £40–60

286B. BRITISH FIRE SERVICES ASSOCIATION MEDAL

Instituted: 1949.
Branch of Service: British Fire Services Association.
Ribbon: 33mm with a central silver-grey stripe flanked by black and white stripes and a broad red edge.
Metal: Silver or bronze.
Size: 38mm.
Description: (Obverse) identical to 286A; (reverse) badge of the Association: a wreathed flag within a circle inscribed FOR LONG SERVICE & EFFICIENCY, surmounted by a fireman's helmet and surrounded by ladders and hoses. THE BRITISH FIRE SERVICES ASSOCIATION round the circumference. The medal has an ornamental scrolled suspender with a bar inscribed BFSA. The recipient's name and service number are engraved on the rim.
Comments: *The British Fire Services Association was formed in 1949 by the amalgamation of the National Fire Brigades Association and the Professional Fire Brigades Association. This medal thus superseded 286A.*

VALUE:	Silver	£35–50	*Miniature*	£30–40
	Bronze	£20–30		

287. COLONIAL FIRE BRIGADE LONG SERVICE MEDAL

Instituted: 1934.
Branch of Service: Colonial Fire Services.
Ribbon: Blue with twin green central stripes separated and bordered by thin white stripes.
Metal: Silver.
Size: 36mm.
Description: (Obverse) the effigy of the reigning monarch; (reverse) a fireman's helmet and axe. Ring suspension.
Comments: *Awarded to junior officers for 18 years full-time exemplary service. Bars are awarded for further periods of service.*

VALUE:		*Miniature*
George V (E)	£300–350	£30–40
George VI (D)	£300–350	£30–40
George VI (E)	£300–350	£30–40
Elizabeth II (C)	£300–350	£30–40
Elizabeth II (D)	£300–350	£30–40

288. CEYLON FIRE BRIGADE LONG SERVICE & GOOD CONDUCT MEDAL

Instituted: 1950.
Branch of Service: Ceylon Fire Service.
Ribbon: Similar to the Police Medal, but with a thin central white stripe through the dark blue band.
Metal: Silver.
Size: 36mm.
Description: As the Police Medal, but with a reverse inscribed CEYLON FIRE SERVICES.

VALUE:	
George VI	£300–400
Elizabeth II	£300–400

288A. NORTHERN IRELAND PRISON SERVICE MEDAL

Instituted: 25 February 2002.

Branch of Service: Northern Ireland Prison Service.

Ribbon: Green with a broad navy blue band having at its centre a sky-blue stripe. Prison grade recipients have a ribbon with an addition thin red stripe bisecting the sky-blue stripe.

Metal: Cupro-nickel.

Size: 36mm.

Description: (Obverse) the crowned profile of the Queen with her name and titles: (reverse) a ring of flax flowers with three keys at the top, enclosing a four line inscription NORTHERN IRELAND PRISON SERVICE. The medal is fitted with a plain bar for suspension. The name of the recipient is stamped on the rim.

Comments: *The medal recognises "those who have rendered professional, committed and brave service as members of and by others in support of the Northern Ireland Prison Service".*

VALUE: £150–250

289. COLONIAL PRISON SERVICE LONG SERVICE MEDAL

Instituted: October 1955.

Branch of Service: Colonial Prison Services.

Ribbon: Green with dark blue edges and a thin silver stripe in the centre.

Metal: Silver.

Size: 36mm.

Description: (Obverse) Queen Elizabeth II; (reverse) a phoenix rising from the flames and striving towards the sun.

Comments: *Awarded to ranks of Assistant Superintendent and below for 18 years exemplary service. Bars are awarded for further periods of 25 or 30 years service.*

VALUE:
Elizabeth II	£200–250	*Miniature*	£30–40

290. SOUTH AFRICAN PRISON SERVICE FAITHFUL SERVICE MEDAL

Instituted: September 1922.

Branch of Service: South African Prison Service.

Ribbon: Broad green centre flanked by white stripes and blue edges.

Metal: Silver.

Size: 36mm.

Description: (Obverse) arms of the Union of South Africa, of identical design to no. 284 except with GEVANGENIS DIENST round the top and PRISONS SERVICE round the foot. (Reverse) inscribed FOR FAITHFUL SERVICE across the upper half and in Dutch VOOR TROUWE DIENST across the lower half.

Comments: *Awarded to prison officers with 18 years exemplary service. Immediate awards for gallantry or exceptionally meritorious service received the Merit bar. In 1959 this medal was superseded by a version inscribed in Afrikaans.*

VALUE: £40–50   *Miniature*   £30–40

291. SOUTH AFRICA PRISONS DEPARTMENT FAITHFUL SERVICE MEDAL

Instituted: 1959.
Branch of Service: South African Prisons Department.
Ribbon: Broad blue centre flanked by white stripes and green edges.
Metal: Silver.
Size: 36mm.
Description: (Obverse) arms of the Union of South Africa, of identical design to no. 284 except with DEPARTEMENT VAN GEVANGENISSE round the top and PRISONS DEPARTMENT round the foot. (Reverse) VIR TROUE DIENS across the upper half and FOR FAITHFUL SERVICE across the lower half.
Comments: *The conditions of the award were similar to the previous medal, the main difference being the change of title and the substitution of Afrikaans inscriptions for Dutch. This medal was superseded by the Prisons Department Faithful Service Medal of the Republic of South Africa, instituted in 1965.*

VALUE:	£30–40	*Miniature*	£30–40

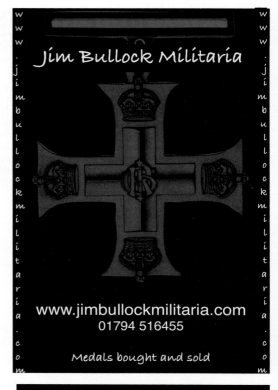

Coronation
and Jubilee
Medals

The first official royal medal was that cast by Henry Basse in 1547 for the accession of the young King Edward VI. It is known cast in gold or silver and is a curious example of bad design and poor workmanship for such an august occasion. No coronation medals were produced in honour of either Mary or Elizabeth I, but under James VI and I there was a small silver medal struck at the Royal Mint to mark the king's accession in 1603. These early medals celebrated the accession of the new sovereign, rather than the act of crowning itself.

To mark the coronation of James I, however, a small silver medalet was struck for distribution among the people who attended the ceremony, and this may be regarded as the forerunner of the modern series. This bore a Latin title signifying that James was Caesar Augustus of Britain and Heir to the Caesars. Thereafter medals in gold, silver or base metals were regularly struck in connection with the coronations of British monarchs. These were purely commemorative and not intended for wear, so they lack rings or bars for suspension.

By the early 19th century medals were being struck by many medallists for sale as souvenirs to the general public. At least fifteen different medals greeted the coronation of William IV in 1830 and more than twice that number appeared seven years later for the coronation of Queen Victoria. That paled into insignificance compared with the number produced for the coronation of Edward VII in 1902. On that occasion numerous civic authorities, organizations, industrial concerns and business firms issued medals in celebration—well over a hundred different medals and medalets were produced.

Sir George Frampton designed two silver medals, and one of these was mounted with a suspender and a blue ribbon with a thin white stripe and scarlet edges. This medal was distributed to notable personages attending the ceremony and established the precedent for subsequent coronation medals which came to be regarded as an award in recognition of services rendered in connection with the coronation, from the Earl Marshal of England to the private soldiers

taking part in the ceremonial parades. In more recent times the coronation medal has even been given to people who were not present at the ceremony but who performed notable public service in the coronation year.

Many other royal events have been commemorated by medals over the centuries. Royal weddings and the birth of the heir to the throne were regularly celebrated in this manner. Important anniversaries in long reigns have been the subject of numerous commemorative medals. The Golden Jubilee of George III in 1809-10, for example, resulted in over 30 different medals. Five times that number greeted the Golden Jubilee of Queen Victoria in 1887, but among them was an official medal intended for wear by those on whom it was conferred.

Even this, however, was not the first of the royal medals intended to be worn. This honour goes to a very large medal celebrating the proclamation of Victoria as Empress of India in 1877. Although fitted with a suspender bar and worn from a ribbon round the neck, it was not permitted for officers and men to wear this medal while in uniform. Later medals, however, were permitted to be worn when in uniform, but after other orders, decorations and campaign medals.

In the following listing (291A–291N) are the official Coronation Medals of James I, 1603, to Victoria, 1838. All were originally non-wearing, i.e. without suspension or ribbon, although some were later pierced or fitted with suspension for wearing. **Values are for silver medals only.**

291A. JAMES I CORONATION MEDAL

Date: 1603.
Metal: Silver.
Size: 28mm.
Description: (Obverse) Bust of King James I facing right. Legend: IAC: I: BRIT: CAE: AVG: HAE CAESArum cae D.D. (Reverse) Lion rampant facing left. Legend: ECCE PHA(R)OS POPVLIQ(VE) SALVS (Behold a lighthouse and safety of the people)

VALUE:
Silver:£350–450

291B. CHARLES I CORONATION MEDAL

Date: 1626.
Metal: Gold, silver.
Size: 28mm.
Designer: Nicholas Briot.
Description: Bust of Charles I facing right. Legend: CAROLVS. I. DG. MAG. BRITAN. FRAN. ET. HIB. REX. (Reverse) An arm issuing from a cloud and holding a sword. Legend: DONEC. PAX. REDDITA. TERRIS. (As long as Peace returns to the lands).

VALUE: Silver: £350–450

291C. CHARLES I CORONATION MEDAL

Date: 1633 (Scottish Coronation)
Metal: Gold, silver.
Size: 28mm.
Designer: Nicholas Briot.
Mintage: Gold (3), silver (Unknown)
Description: Bust of Charles I facing left. Legend: CAROLVS DG SCOTIAE. ANGLIAE. FR. ET. HIB. REX. (Reverse) A rose bush surmounted by a thistle. Legend: HINC. NOSTRAE. CREVERE. ROSAE (From this our roses abound). Exergue: CORON. 18 JVNII 1633

VALUE: Silver: £300–350

291D. CHARLES II CORONATION MEDAL

Date: 1651 (Scottish Coronation).
Metal: Gold, silver.
Size: 31mm.
Designer: Sir James Balfour.
Description: Bust of Charles II facing right. Legend: CAROLVS.2. D.G. SCO. ANG. FRA. ET. HI. REX. FI. DE. cor. i. ia. scon. 1651. (Reverse) Lion rampant facing left, holding a thistle. Legend: NEMO. ME. IMPVNE. LACESSET (No one touches me with impunity).

VALUE: Silver: £300–400

291E. CHARLES II CORONATION MEDAL

Date: 1661 (English Coronation).
Metal: Gold, silver.
Size: 30mm.
Designer: Thomas Simon.
Description: Bust of Charles II facing right. Legend:
CAROLVS .II.DG ANG. SCO. FR. ET. HI REX. (Reverse)
Charles II, wearing royal robe, seated on throne facing
left, holding sceptre. Angel hovering over him placing
crown on his head. Legend: EVERSO. MISSVS. SVC-
CVRRERE. SECLO. XXIII APR. 1661 (the times having
been turned upside down, he has been sent to succour
us)

VALUE: **Silver:** £150–250

291F. JAMES II CORONATION MEDAL

Date: 1685.
Metal: Gold, silver, copper (?)
Size: 34mm.
Designer: John Roettier.
Mintage: Gold (200), silver (800), copper (Un-
known).
Description: Bust of James II facing right, laure-
ate. Legend: JACOBVS. II. D.G. ANG. SCO. FR.
ET. HI. REX. (Reverse) Hand holding the crown
above a laurel branch resting on a pillow. Legend:
A. MILITARI. AD. REGIAM. (from soldiering to
the palace). Exergue: INAVGVRAT. 23. AP. 1685.

VALUE: **Silver:** £250–350

291G. WILLIAM AND MARY CORONATION MEDAL

Date: 1689.
Metal: Gold, silver, lead.
Size: 34mm.
Designer: John Roettier.
Mintage: Gold (515), silver (1,200), lead (Unknown).
Description: Conjoint busts of William and Mary
facing right. Legend: GVLIELMVS. ET. MARIA.
REX. ET. REGINA. (Reverse) Two-horse vehicle
lower left, Jove in cloud above right. Legend:
NE TOTVS ABSVMATVR. (let not the whole be
consumed). Exergue: INAVGVRAT. II. AP. 1689.

VALUE: **Silver:** £200–300

291H. ANNE CORONATION MEDAL

Date: 1702.
Metal: Gold, silver, base metal.
Size: 34mm.
Designer: John Croker.
Mintage: Gold (858), silver (1,200), base metal (Unknown).
Description: Bust of Queen Anne facing left. Legend: ANNA. D:G: MAG: BR. FR. ET. HIB: REGINA. (Reverse) Pallas Athene, left, with shield and lightning bolts, attacking recumbent monster, right. Legend: VICEM GERIT. ILLA. TONANTIS. Exergue: INAVGVRAT. XXIII. AP. MDCCII. (As, making sounds, she conducts herself).

VALUE: Silver: £150–200

291I. GEORGE I CORONATION MEDAL

Date: 1714.
Metal: Gold, silver, base metal.
Size: 34mm.
Designer: John Croker
Mintage: Gold (330), silver (1,200), base metal (Unknown).
Description: Bust of George I facing right. Legend: GEORGIVS. DG. MAG. BR. FR. ET. HIB. REX. (Reverse) Seated King, left, being crowned by Britannia standing right. Exergue: INAVGVRAT. XX. OCT. MDCCXIIII.

VALUE: Silver: £150–200

291J. GEORGE II CORONATION MEDAL

Date: 1727.
Metal: Gold, silver, base metal.
Size: 34mm.
Designer: John Croker
Mintage: Gold (238), silver (800), base metal (Unknown)
Description: Bust of George II facing left. Legend: GEORGIVS. II. D.G. MAG. BR. FR. ET. HIB. REX. (Reverse) King seated on throne, left being crowned by Britannia, standing right. Legend: VOLENTES. PER. POVLOS (through the will of the people) Exergue: CORON. XI. OCTOB. MDCCXXVII.

VALUE: Silver: £150–200

291K. GEORGE III CORONATION MEDAL

Date: 1761.
Metal: Gold, silver, bronze
Size: 34mm.
Designer: Lorenz Natter.
Mintage: Gold (858), silver (800), bronze (unknown)
Description: Bust of George III facing right. Legend: GEORGIVS. III. D.G. M. BRI. FRA. ET. HIB. REX. F.D. (Reverse) Britannia standing left, crowning King seated right. Legend: PATRIAE. OVANTI. (Crowned as the country rejoices). Exergue: CORONAT. XXII. SEPT. CI ƆIƆCCLXI

VALUE: Silver: £250–350

291L. GEORGE IV CORONATION MEDAL

Date: 1821.
Metal: Gold, silver, bronze
Size: 35mm.
Designer: Benedetto Pistrucci.
Mintage: Gold (1,060), silver (800), bronze (unknown, over 1,525)
Description: Bust of George IV, laureate, facing left. Legend: GEORGIVS IIII D.G. BRITANNIARUM REX F.D. (Reverse) Three standing ladies, left, facing seated King, right. Behind King stands angel holding crown above his head. Legend: PROPRIO JAM JURE ANIMO PATERNO (already by special right, inaugurated in the spirit of his father). Exergue: INAUGURATUS DIE JULII. XIX ANNO. MDCCXXI.
Comments: *A slightly smaller and thinner version of this medal was struck and pierced for suspension from a plain maroon ribbon. These medals are invariably named to members of the Buckinghamshire Yeomanry Cavalry Hussars who took part in lining the route of the procession. This is believed to be the first coronation medal designed to be worn.*

VALUE: Silver: £100–150

291M. WILLIAM IV CORONATION MEDAL

Date: 1831.
Metal: Gold, silver, bronze
Size: 34mm.
Designer: William Wyon
Mintage: Gold (1,000), silver (2,000), bronze (1,133)
Description: Head of William IV facing right. Legend: WILLIAM THE FOURTH CROWNED SEP: 8 1831 (Reverse) Head of Queen Adelaide facing right. Legend: ADELAIDE. QUEEN CONSORT. CROWNED SEP: 8 1831.

VALUE: Silver: £150–200

291N. VICTORIA CORONATION MEDAL

Date: 1838.
Metal: Gold, silver, bronze.
Size: 36mm.
Designer: Benedetto Pistrucci.
Mintage: Gold (1,369), silver (2,209), bronze (1,871)
Description: Head of Queen Victoria facing left. Legend: VICTORIA D.G. BRITANNIARUM REGINA F.D. (Reverse) Three ladies symbolic of England, Scotland and Ireland, standing left, presenting crown to Queen, seated on a dais, right. A lion lies behind her chair. Legend: ERIMUS TIBI NOBILE REGNUM (We shall be a noble Kingdom to you). Exergue: INAUGURATA DIE JUNII XXVIII MDCCCXXXVIII.

VALUE: Silver   £100–150

292. EMPRESS OF INDIA MEDAL

Date: 1877.
Ribbon: 42mm crimson edged in gold.
Metal: Gold or silver.
Size: 58mm.
Description: (Obverse) a left-facing bust of Queen Victoria wearing a veil and a coronet, her name and the date of her elevation being inscribed round the circumference. (Reverse) a broad zigzag border enclosing the words EMPRESS OF INDIA and its equivalent in Urdu and Hindi across the field.
Comments: *Issued to celebrate the proclamation of Victoria as Empress of India on 1 January 1877. It was awarded in gold to Indian princes and high-ranking British officials. Indian civilians and selected officers and men of the various British and Indian regiments serving in India at the time were awarded the silver medal. It was issued unnamed but many examples were subsequently engraved or impressed privately.*

VALUE:
    Gold   £2000–2500
    Silver   £375–450

Miniature
£250–350
£100–150

292A. VISIT OF THE PRINCE OF WALES TO INDIA MEDAL 1875

(reduced)

Date: 1875–76.
Ribbon: 38mm plain white (gold), pale blue with white edges (silver).
Metal: Gold, silver or white metal with a silver crown.
Size: Oval 48mmx77mm.
Description: (Obverse) left-facing effigy of the Prince of Wales (later King Edward VII) surrounded by a laurel wreath and surmounted by a crown fitted to a suspension ring; (reverse) Prince of Wales's emblem surrounded by the chain of the GCSI.
Comments: *A large oval medal was struck to commemorate the state visit of HRH the Prince of Wales to India. Some 48 medals were struck in gold, 165 in silver and an unknown number in white metal. The gold medals are impressed on the rim with a small numeral, and engraved with the recipient's name in block capitals. The medals were numbered and named in strict order of precedence. The silver medal has a frosted relief on a mirror table. 13 small silver badges were also presented. In addition a small silver medalet was issued with an obverse similar to the reverse of the large medal but with the initials A and E either side and a reverse inscribed HRH ALBERT EDWARD PRINCE OF WALES 1875–76.*

VALUE:

Gold (48)	£7000–8000
Silver (165)	£1000–1500
White metal	£200–250
Silver badge (13)	Rare
Silver medalet	£80–100

293. JUBILEE MEDAL 1887

Date: 1887.
Ribbon: Broad central blue band with wide white stripes at the edges.
Metal: Gold, silver or bronze.
Size: 30mm.
Description: (Obverse) the bust of Queen Victoria by Sir Joseph Edgar Boehm; (reverse) an elaborate wreath in which are entwined the heraldic flowers of the United Kingdom. This encloses an eight-line inscription surmounted by a crown: IN COMMEMORATION OF THE 50th YEAR OF THE REIGN OF QUEEN VICTORIA 21 JUNE 1887. The reverse was designed by Clemens Emptmayer.
Comments: *Struck to celebrate the 50th anniversary of Victoria's accession to the throne. The medal in gold was given to members of the Royal Family and their personal guests. The silver medal was given to members of the Royal Household, government ministers, senior officials, distinguished foreign visitors, naval and military officers involved in the Jubilee parade on 21 June 1887 and the captains of vessels taking part in the great Naval Review at Spithead. The bronze medal was given to selected NCOs and men who took part in the parade or the Spithead Review. All medals were issued unnamed with a ring for suspension. When the Diamond Jubilee was celebrated ten years later holders of the 1887 medal were given a clasp in the form of a cable entwined around the date 1897 and surmounted by an imperial crown. Twin loops at the ends enabled the clasp to be sewn on to the ribbon.*

VALUE:

	without clasp	with clasp	*Miniature*
Gold	£1300–1500	Rare	£100–150
Silver	£100–120	£175–200	£25–30 (add £30 for clasp)
Bronze	£100–120	£180–200	£25–30 (add £30 for clasp)

294. JUBILEE (POLICE) MEDAL 1887

Date: 1887.
Ribbon: Plain dark blue.
Metal: Bronze.
Size: 36mm.
Description: (Obverse) the veiled profile of Queen Victoria; (reverse) a wreath surmounted by a crown and enclosing the inscription: JUBILEE OF HER MAJESTY QUEEN VICTORIA. The year appears at the foot and the name of the force round the top.
Comments: *Issued to all ranks of the Metropolitan and City of London Police involved in the parades and celebrations on 21 June 1887. Medals are believed to have been issued with the inscription POLICE AMBULANCE round the top but confirmation of this is required. Clasps for 1897 were likewise issued ten years later.*

VALUE:

	without clasp	with clasp	*Miniature*
Metropolitan Police (1400)	£25–35	£35–45	£25–30
City of London Police (900)	£50–60	£70–90	£25–30 (add £10 for clasp)

295. JUBILEE MEDAL 1897

Date: 1897.
Ribbon: Dark blue with two broad white bands and dark blue edges (as for 293).
Metal: Gold, silver or bronze.
Size: 30mm.
Description: This medal is very similar to the 1887 issue, differing solely in the date and anniversary on the reverse. Around 980 medals were awarded to army officers.

VALUE:

		Miniature
Gold (73)	£1300–1500	£80–100
Silver (3040)	£100–120	£15–20
Bronze (890)	£100–120	£15–20

296. JUBILEE MEDAL (MAYORS AND PROVOSTS) 1897

Date: 1897.
Ribbon: White with two broad dark stripes bands and white edges.
Metal: Gold or silver.
Size: Height 48mm; max. width 40mm.
Description: A diamond-shaped medal with ring suspension, reminiscent of the *Klippe* coinage of central Europe. Both sides had circular centres with trefoil ornaments occupying the angles. (Obverse) the Wyon profile of the young Victoria at the time of her accession; (reverse) Sir Thomas Brock's Old Head veiled bust of the Queen.
Comments: *The gold version was presented to Lord Mayors and Lord Provosts while the silver medal was granted to Mayors and Provosts. Small silver medals of more conventional circular format were produced with these motifs and sold as souvenirs of the occasion.*

VALUE:

		Miniature
Gold (14)	Rare	£250–300
Silver (512)	£250–300	£80–120

297. JUBILEE (POLICE) MEDAL 1897

Date: 1897.
Ribbon: Plain dark blue.
Metal: Bronze.
Size: 36mm.
Description: Very similar to the 1887 issue with the dates suitably amended and the name of the service round the top of the reverse.
Comments: *Separate issues were made in respect of the Police Ambulance service, St John Ambulance Brigade and the Metropolitan Fire Brigade. Holders of the previous medal merely received the 1897 clasp.*

VALUE:		*Miniature*
Metropolitan Police (7500)	£30–35	£50–70
City of London Police (535)	£70–80	£50–70
Police Ambulance (210)	£200–250	£50–70
St John Ambulance Brigade (910)	£60–70	£50–70
Metropolitan Fire Brigade (950)	£60–70	£50–70

298. CEYLON DIAMOND JUBILEE MEDAL 1897

Date: 1897.
Ribbon: Plain red.
Metal: Gold or silver.
Size: 35mm.
Description: (Obverse) the Boehm bust of Queen Victoria with the dates 1837-1897 at the foot. (Reverse) an elephant and a stupa (dome-shaped Buddhist shrine), with two lines of concentric inscriptions: TO COMMEMORATE SIXTY YEARS OF HER MAJESTY'S REIGN and, unusually, THE RT. HON. SIR J. WEST RIDGEWAY K.C.B., K.C.M.G., GOVERNOR. A crown above the rim was fixed to a ring for suspension.
Comments: *Awarded to local dignitaries and leading officials in the Ceylon government.*

VALUE:		*Miniature*
Gold	Rare	£300–350
Silver	£200–250	£100–120

299. HONG KONG DIAMOND JUBILEE MEDAL

Date: 1897.
Ribbon: Three equal stripes of dark blue, maroon and dark blue (also known with gold ribbon with two white stripes).
Metal Silver, possibly also bronze.
Size: 36mm.
Description: (Obverse) the Boehm bust of Queen Victoria with the date 1897 at the foot; (reverse) a seascape with a British three-masted sailing ship and a Chinese junk in the background and two figures shaking hands in the foreground. The name of the colony appears at the top, while two concentric inscriptions read SIR WILLIAM ROBINSON G.C.M.G. GOVERNOR and TO COMMEMORATE SIXTY YEARS OF HER MAJESTY'S REIGN 1837-1897.
Comments: *Very little is known for certainty about this medal on account of the fact that the colonial records were destroyed during the Japanese occupation.*

VALUE:	
Silver	£300–400
Bronze	£180–200

299A. LAGOS DIAMOND JUBILEE MEDAL

Date: 1897.
Ribbon: Dark blue with two broad white stripes towards the edges.
Metal Silver.
Size: 34mm.
Description: (Obverse) the veiled crowned profile of Queen Victoria (similar to the Egypt Medal 1882, No. 131) inscribed VICTORIA QUEEN AND EMPRESS with a Tudor rose at the foot; (reverse) QUEEN'S DIAMOND JUBILEE LAGOS round the circumference, with JUNE 22ND 1897 in the centre.
Comments: *Issued to civil and military personnel associated with the Diamond Jubilee celebrations in the crown colony of Lagos (1886–1906 when it was incorporated in the colony and protectorate of Southern Nigeria).*

VALUE: Rare

299B. INDIA DIAMOND JUBILEE MEDAL

Date: 1897.
Ribbon: White.
Metal Silver.
Size: 34mm.
Description: (Obverse) the veiled crowned profile of Queen Victoria (similar to the Egypt Medal 1882, No. 131) inscribed VICTORIA QUEEN AND EMPRESS with a Star of India at the foot; (reverse) TO COMMEMORATE THE SIXTIETH YEAR OF THE REIGN OF H.M. QUEEN VICTORIA 1897 within a laurel wreath, with royal arms above and the Star of India below.
Comments: *Issued to civil and military personnel associated with the Diamond Jubilee celebrations in India.*

VALUE: Rare

300. VISIT TO IRELAND MEDAL 1900

Date: 1900.
Ribbon: Plain dark blue.
Metal: Bronze.
Size: 36mm.
Description: (Obverse) a half-length version of the Boehm bust of Queen Victoria; (reverse) the female allegorical figure of Hibernia looking out over Kingstown (Dun Laoghaire) harbour in which the Royal Yacht can be seen (far left). Unusually, the medal was mounted with a suspension bar decorated with shamrocks.
Comments: *The medal designed by G. W. de Saulles commemorated Queen Victoria's visit to Ireland in 1900. It was awarded to officers of the Royal Irish Constabulary and Dublin Metropolitan Police who were involved in security and policing the various events connected with the visit. The medal was worn with the same ribbon as the Jubilee Police medals.*

VALUE:
Bronze (2285)	£100–120	*Miniature*	£100–120

300A. VISIT TO THE COLONIES MEDAL 1901

Date: 1901.
Ribbon: Unknown.
Metal: Silver.
Size: Oval 20 x 24mm.
Description: (Obverse) a crowned anchor with the royal garter and
   rose emblem inset; (reverse) inscribed T.R.H. DUKE & DUCH-
   ESS OF CORNWALL & YORK—BRITISH COLONIES 1901 H.M.S.
   OPHIR.
Comments: *This small medalet was issued to commemorate the visit of the
   Duke and Duchess of Cornwall and York to the British Colonies aboard
   HMS Ophir in 1901.*

VALUE: Rare   *Miniature*   £100–120

301. CORONATION MEDAL 1902

Date: 1902.
Ribbon: Dark blue with a central red stripe and white edges.
Metal: Silver or bronze.
Size: Height 42mm; max. width 30mm.
Description: (Obverse) the left-facing conjoined busts of King Edward
   VII and Queen Alexandra, both crowned and wearing coronation
   robes. (Reverse) the crowned royal cypher above the date of the actual
   ceremony. The medal has an elaborate raised rim decorated with a
   wreath culminating in a crown through which the ring for suspension
   was looped.
Comments: *This medal, designed by Emil Fuchs and struck by Messrs. Elkington & Co., celebrated the coronation of King Edward VII on 9 August 1902.
   It was presented in silver to members of the Royal Family, foreign dignitiaries,
   high officials of the government, senior officials and service officers involved in
   the celebrations. Selected NCOs and other ranks of the Army and Navy taking
   part in the parades were awarded the medal in bronze. Both versions were
   issued unnamed.*

VALUE:		*Miniature*
Silver (3493)	£80–90	£10–15
Bronze (6054)	£60–70	£10–15

302. CORONATION MEDAL (MAYORS AND PROVOSTS) 1902

Date: 1902.
Ribbon: Dark blue with a narrow white central stripe and crimson bor-
   ders.
Metal: Silver.
Size: 32mm.
Description: (Obverse) conjoined right-facing busts of the King and
   Queen; (reverse) the crowned cypher and date. It differed from the
   ordinary medal by having flat, broad borders decorated with the heral-
   dic flowers of the United Kingdom culminating at the top in a simple
   suspension ring.
Comments: *The medal was designed by Emil Fuchs and struck by Messrs.
   Elkington & Co.*

VALUE:			
Silver	£140–150	*Miniature*	£100–120

303. CORONATION (POLICE) MEDAL 1902

Date: 1902.
Ribbon: Red, with a narrow dark blue central stripe.
Metal: Silver or bronze.
Size: 36mm.
Description: (Obverse) the left-facing bust of King Edward VII; (reverse) a crown above a nosegay of heraldic flowers with the words CORONATION OF HIS MAJESTY KING EDWARD VII 1902 in the upper field. The name or initials of the service appeared round the top, LCC MFB signifying London County Council Metropolitan Fire Brigade.
Comments: *Issued to all ranks of the police and associated services involved in the coronation celebrations, and awarded in silver or bronze to officers and other ranks respectively. The medal was designed by G. W. de Saulles.*

VALUE:	Silver	*Miniature*	Bronze	*Miniature*
Metropolitan Police	£400–500 (51)	£25–30	£25–30 (16,700)	£20–30
City of London Police	£600–800 (5)	£20–30	£60–70 (1060)	£20–35
LCC MFB	£500–600 (9)	£35–55	£50–60 (1000)	£50–60
St John Ambulance Brigade	—	£30–40	£50–60 (912)	£60–70
Police Ambulance Service	—	£40–50	£200–250 (204)	£90–100

304. CEYLON CORONATION MEDAL 1902

Date: 1902.
Ribbon: Plain blue.
Metal: Gold.
Size: 35mm.
Description: (Obverse) a crowned left-facing bust of King Edward VII; (reverse) the elephant and stupa motif previously used. The concentric inscription on the reverse now tactfully omitted any reference to the governor: IN COMMEMORATION OF THE CORONATION OF H.M. KING EDWARD VII 1902. The medal was fitted with a ring for suspension.
Comments: *Like its predecessor, this rare medal was struck for presentation to local dignitaries and government officials.*

VALUE:	Rare	*Miniature*	£250–300

305. HONG KONG CORONATION MEDAL 1902

Date: 1902.
Ribbon: None officially designated.
Metal: Bronze.
Size: 36mm.
Description: (Obverse) conjoined right-facing busts of King Edward VII and Queen Alexandra with their names round the circumference; (reverse) the maritime motif of the Diamond Jubilee medal with new inscriptions in two concentric curves: SIR HENRY A. BLAKE G.C.M.G. GOVERNOR (inner) and TO COMMEMORATE THE CORONATION OF THEIR MAJESTIES THE KING & QUEEN (outer). Fitted with a suspension ring.
Comments: *Issued to all British and Indian officers and other ranks serving in the colony as well as local police. Some 6,000 medals were produced by Edmonds & Son, London, and issued in cases.*

VALUE:	
Bronze	£65–85

305A. NATAL CORONATION MEDAL 1902

Date: 1902.
Ribbon: Dark blue with a central claret stripe.
Metal: Silver.
Size: 21mm, 29mm and 51mm.
Description: (Obverse) a right-facing crowned bust of King Edward VII with the inscription TO COMMEMORATE THE CORONATION OF KING EDWARD VII; (reverse) Royal coat of arms above two running wildebeests, inscribed (round top) EDWARDUS DEI GRATIA BRITANNIAR REX F:D and (round bottom) COLONY OF NATAL 26 JUNE 1902. Ring suspension.
Comments: *The small medal was distributed to schoolchildren whereas the large medal was restricted to native chiefs and is relatively scarce. It is believed that the middle-size medal was presented to local dignitaries.*

VALUE:		
	21mm	£20–30
	29mm	£85–100
	51mm	£350–450

306. DELHI DURBAR MEDAL 1903

Date: 1903.
Ribbon: Pale blue with three dark blue stripes.
Metal: Gold or silver.
Size: 38.5mm.
Description: (Obverse) a right-facing crowned bust of the King Emperor with DELHI DARBAR 1903 on the right side; (reverse) a three-line inscription in Farsi across the field, which translates as "By grace of the Lord of the Realm, Edward, King, Emperor of India, 1901", with an elaborate border of roses, thistles, shamrocks and Indian flowers. Ring suspension.
Comments: *Struck to celebrate the Durbar of the King Emperor at Delhi on 1 January 1903. It was awarded in gold to the rulers of the Indian princely states and in silver to lesser dignitaries, government officials, and officers and other ranks of the armed services actually involved in the celebrations.*

VALUE:		*Miniature*
Gold (140)	£1000–1200	—
Silver (2567)	£120–150	£15–20

307. VISIT TO SCOTLAND MEDAL 1903

Date: 1903.
Ribbon: Plain red.
Metal: Bronze.
Size: 36mm.
Description: Very similar to the Police Coronation medal but the year was changed to 1903 and the inscription SCOTTISH POLICE appeared round the top of the reverse. The medal was named to the recipient on the rim. An ornate clasp decorated with a thistle was worn above the suspension bar.
Comments: *This medal was designed by G. W. de Saulles and struck to commemorate Their Majesties' post-coronation tour of Scotland in May 1903. It was awarded to the police and troops involved in parades and escort duties, as well as the ancillary services such as the Fire Brigade and the St Andrew's Ambulance Association.*

VALUE:

Bronze (2957)	£70–90	*Miniature*	£40–50

308. VISIT TO IRELAND MEDAL 1903

Date: 1903.
Ribbon: Pale blue.
Metal: Bronze.
Size: 36mm.
Description: (Obverse) bust of King Edward VII; (reverse) as 1900 medal with the date altered at the foot. The suspension brooch is ornamented with shamrocks.
Comments: *This medal was designed by G. W. de Saulles and struck to mark the King's visit to Ireland in July 1903. It was awarded on the same terms as the Visit to Ireland Medal 1900.*

VALUE:
Bronze (7757)	£80–100	*Miniature*	£60–70

308A. VISIT OF THE PRINCE AND PRINCESS OF WALES TO INDIA

Instituted: 1905–06
Ribbon: Neck ribbon 55mm wide, maroon with wide blue stripes towards each edge.
Metal: Frosted silver.
Size: 46mm.
Description: (Obverse) conjoined busts of the Prince and Princess of Wales (later King George V and Queen Mary), facing right. ELKINGTON (manufacturers) inscribed below busts. (Reverse) badge of the Prince of Wales surrounded by the chain of the GCSI, with legend T.R.H. THE PRINCE & PRINCESS OF WALES VISIT TO INDIA 1905-6.
Comments: *Only 72 medals were struck, 70 of which were bestowed on British and Indian officials.*

VALUE: £300–400   *Miniature*   £50–60

308B. GEORGE PRINCE OF WALES MEDAL

Instituted: 1905-06.
Ribbon: 15mm, red, white and blue in equal parts.
Metal: Silver or gold.
Size: Oval 20 x 24mm.
Description: (Obverse) the Prince of Wales's plumes surrounded by the Garter and the chain and badge of the GCSI, flanked in the field by the letters G and M; (reverse) inscription T.R.H. GEORGE PRINCE OF WALES & VICTORIA MARY PRINCESS OF WALES with INDIA 1905-6 in the upper centre.
Comments: *The 26 gold medals were given by Their Royal Highnesses to their personal staff, while a total of 1,625 silver medals were presented to all hands aboard HMS* Renown *and* Terrible *and the Royal Yacht* Osborne.

VALUE:
Gold (26)	£800–1000
Silver (1625)	£80–120

309. CORONATION MEDAL 1911

Date: 1911.
Ribbon: Dark blue with two thin red stripes in the centre.
Metal: Silver.
Size: 32mm.
Description: (Obverse) conjoined left-facing busts of King George V
and Queen Mary in their coronation robes within a floral wreath;
(reverse) the crowned royal cypher above the date of the coronation
itself. Plain ring suspension.
Comments: *Designed by Sir Bertram McKennal, MVO, ARA, these*
medals were issued unnamed but may sometimes be found with unofficial
engraving. Those who were also entitled to the Delhi Darbar Medal received
a crowned clasp inscribed DELHI if they had previously been awarded
the coronation medal. This was the first occasion that the medal might be
awarded to those not actually present at the ceremony itself.

VALUE:

		Miniature
Silver (15,901)	£40–45	£5–10
Clasp Delhi (134)	£600–800	£50–60

310. CORONATION (POLICE) MEDAL 1911

Date: 1911.
Ribbon: Red with three narrow blue stripes.
Metal: Silver.
Size: 32mm.
Description: (Obverse) a crowned left-facing bust of King George V;
(reverse) an imperial crown with an ornate surround. The inscription
CORONATION 1911 appears at the foot and the name of the service at
the top. Ring suspension.
Comments: *By now the number of police and ancillary services had grown*
considerably, as witness the various reverse types which may be encountered in
this medal. The medal was designed by Sir Bertram McKennal, MVO, ARA,
VALUE:

		Miniature
Metropolitan Police (19,783)	£25–30	£15–20
City of London Police (1400)	£75–85	£20–25
County and Borough Police (2565)	£70–90	£20–25
Police Ambulance Service*	£300–350	£90–100
London Fire Brigade (1374)	£75–85	£90–100
Royal Irish Constabulary (585)	£100–120	£150–200
Scottish Police (2800)	£80–100	£50–60
St John Ambulance Brigade*	£50–60	£60–70
St Andrew's Ambulance Corps*	£120–150	£100–150
Royal Parks (109)	£300–350	£140–160

* A total of 2623 medals was awarded to these three services, the Police Ambulance medal being the scarcest
and St John Ambulance medal the commonest.

311. VISIT TO IRELAND MEDAL 1911

Date: 1911.
Ribbon: Dark green with thin red stripes towards either end.
Metal: Silver.
Size: 36mm.
Description: Very similar to the foregoing, distinguished only by the
reverse which is inscribed CORONATION 1911 round the top, with
the actual date of the visit round the foot.
Comments: *This medal was designed by Sir Bertram McKennal, MVO,*
ARA and was granted to prominent civic dignitaries and members of the
Irish police forces involved in the royal visit to Ireland which took place on
7-12 July 1911.

VALUE:
    Silver (2477)   £75–90   *Miniature*   £70–80

311A. EAST INDIAN RAILWAY COMPANY ROYAL VISIT TO INDIA MEDAL 1911

Date: 1911.
Ribbon: Dark blue with a central maroon stripe flanked by narrow gold stripes.
Metal: Gilded bronze.
Size: 32mm.
Description: (Obverse) the arms of the East Indian Railway Company surrounded by the inscription EAST INDIAN RAILWAY COMPANY with a winged wheel at the foot; (reverse) a ten-line inscription FOR SERVICES RENDERED DURING THE RAILWAY JOURNEYS OF THEIR MAJESTIES THE KING EMPEROR AND QUEEN EMPRESS IN INDIA 1911.
Comments: *Very little is known about this rare medal, but it is believed to have been awarded to members of the Honour Guard of the East Indian Railway Volunteer Rifle Corps and employees of the company present during the tour of India undertaken in 1911 by King George V and Queen Mary. It is believed that no more than 30 medals were issued.*

VALUE: £100–£120

312. DELHI DURBAR MEDAL 1911

Date: 1911.
Ribbon: Dark blue with two narrow red stripes in the middle.
Metal: Gold or silver.
Size: 38.5mm.
Description: (Obverse) the conjoined crowned busts of King George V and Queen Mary in a floral wreath; (reverse) an elaborate Farsi text which translates as "The Durbar of George V, Emperor of India, Master of the British Lands".
Comments: *This medal marked the Delhi Durbar held in the King Emperor's honour in December 1911. Most of the gold medals went to the Indian princely rulers and top government officials, 10,000 of the 30,000 silver medals were awarded to officers and other ranks of the British and Indian Armies for exemplary service, without their necessarily being present at the Durbar itself.*

VALUE:		Miniature
Gold (200)	£800–1000	—
Silver (30,000)	£45–50	£6–10

312A. VISIT OF KING GEORGE V AND QUEEN MARY TO INDIA 1911–12

Date: 1911–12.
Ribbon: None.
Metal: Silver.
Size: Oval 20 x 24mm.
Description: (Obverse): GRI entwined initials as a monogram above the dates 1911–12; (reverse) MRI monogram and dates, suspended from a bar by a simple ring and scroll suspender.

VALUE: £70–100

312B. VISIT OF THE PRINCE OF WALES TO INDIA 1921–22

Date: 1921–22.
Ribbon: Neck ribbon 55mm maroon with broad blue stripes towards each edge.
Metal: Frosted silver.
Size: 50mm.
Description: (Obverse) bust of Prince of Wales facing left with inscription EDWARD PRINCE OF WALES INDIA 1921–1922; (reverse) badge of the Prince of Wales surrounded by the chain of the GCSI. Fitted with a plain suspension ring.
Comments: *Only 84 medals were awarded in connection with the visit of HRH the Prince of Wales (later King Edward VIII and Duke of Windsor) to India in the course of his world tour aboard HMS Renown.*

VALUE: £500–650   *Miniature*   £80–100

312C. WELCOME HOME MEDAL FOR THE PRINCE OF WALES

Date: 1922.
Ribbon: Green with red central stripe.
Metal: Silver and bronze.
Size: Oval 43mm x 34mm.
Description: An oval medal with ornate edges. (Obverse) crowned and robed bust of the Prince of Wales with the inscription EDWARD PRINCE OF WALES KG; (reverse) The Prince of Wales's feathers with the inscription WELCOME HOME 1922. With integral ornate loop for suspension.
Comments: *Struck by F. Bowcher to mark the return of the Prince of Wales to England after his world tour.*

VALUE: Gold   £150–200
                   Silver   £70–100

312D. VISIT OF THE PRINCE OF WALES TO BOMBAY MEDAL 1921

Date: 1921.
Ribbon: Not known.
Metal: Bronze.
Size: Oval 38mm x 30mm.
Description: An oval medal. (Obverse) bust of the Prince of Wales facing right, with the inscription EDWARD PRINCE OF WALES and surmounted by the Prince of Wales's feathers and motto ICH DIEN; (reverse) VISIT OF HIS ROYAL HIGHNESS BOMBAY NOVEMBER 1921 in six lines.
Comment: *Presented to the leading military and civil dignitaries present during the visit of the Prince of Wales. The number issued is not known but is believed to be very small.*

VALUE: £60–£80

312E. VISIT OF THE PRINCE OF WALES TO PATNA 1921

Date: 1921.
Ribbon: Imperial Purple.
Metal: Bronze.
Size: 40mm.
Description: (Obverse) bust of the Prince of Wales facing with the inscription EDWARD PRINCE OF WALES, in an oval centre-piece, with an ornate floral decoration either side; (Reverse) centre blank, with the inscription VISIT OF HIS ROYAL HIGHNESS around the top half, and PATNA 22ND. DEC 1921 around the lower half of the reverse.
Comment: *Believed to have been presented to the leading military and civil dignitaries present during the visit of the Prince of Wales. The number issued is not known, but is believed to be very small.*

VALUE :   £80–£100

313. JUBILEE MEDAL 1935

Date: 1935.
Ribbon: Red with two dark blue and one white stripes at the edges.
Metal: Silver.
Size: 32mm.
Description: (Obverse) left-facing conjoined half-length busts of King George V and Queen Mary in crowns and robes of state; (reverse) a crowned GRI monogram flanked by the dates of the accession and the jubilee.
Comments: *This medal, designed by Sir William Goscombe John, RA, was issued to celebrate the Silver Jubilee of King George V and widely distributed to the great and good throughout the Empire.*

VALUE:
   Silver (85,234)   £20–25   *Miniature*   £6–10

313A. ISLE OF MAN SILVER JUBILEE MEDAL 1935

Date: 1935.
Ribbon: Three equal stripes of red, white and blue. However some medals had their ribbons substituted with black to mark the death of the King in 1936.
Metal: Silver.
Size: 32mm.
Description: (Obverse) conjoined busts of King George V and Queen Mary in an inner circle surrounded by the legend KING GEORGE V & QUEEN MARY REIGNED 25 YEARS; (reverse) Triskelion emblem with the legend IN COMMEMORATION OF THE SILVER JUBILEE 1935. Suspended from a brooch bar of seven overlapping panels. The centre panel has the royal cypher GvR while the outer panels have two leaves in each.
Comments: *This medal is an unofficial issue struck to celebrate the Silver Jubilee. It is included here as it was apparently presented to civic dignitaries and officials in the island.*

VALUE: £100–120

314. CORONATION MEDAL 1937

Date: 1937.
Ribbon: Blue edged with one red and two white stripes.
Metal: Silver.
Size: 32mm.
Description: (Obverse) conjoined busts of King George VI and Queen Elizabeth in their robes of state without any inscription. The stark simplicity of this motif was matched by a reverse showing the crowned GRI over the inscription CROWNED 12 MAY 1937, with the names of the King and Queen in block capitals round the circumference.
Comments: *Issued to celebrate the coronation of King George VI on 12 May 1937.*

VALUE:
    Silver (90,000)   £25–30   *Miniature*   £8–10

314A. GUILDHALL CORONATION MEDAL 1937

Date: 1937.
Ribbon: None
Metal: Silver.
Size: 34mm.
Description: A rectangular medal. (obverse) conjoined busts of King George VI and Queen Elizabeth in their robes of state on a shield wth palm and vine sprigs below and CORONATION in a tablet. The design struck on a rectangular base with two "steps" at each side in art deco style. Reverse blank, inscribed wih name of recipient. The medal is suspended from an ornate crowned coat of arms of the City of London with GUILDHALL above
Comments: *Issued to selected dignitaries by the City of London to celebrate the coronation of King George VI on 12 May 1937.*

VALUE: —

314B. ROYAL VISIT TO SOUTH AFRICA 1947

Obverse i.

Obverse ii.

Date: 1947.
Ribbon: Yellow.
Metal: Silver.
Size: Oval 25mm x 32mm or 65mm x 55mm.
Description: (Obverse) conjoined busts of King George VI and Queen Elizabeth in their robes of state without any inscription. (Reverse) (i) crowned GRE with the inscription ROYAL VISIT 1947; (ii) map of South Africa surmounted by crowned GRE cypher dividing the date 1947 with KONINKLIKE BESOEK above and ROYAL VISIT below.
Comments: *Issued to celebrate the coronation of King George VI on 12 May 1937. Two distinctly different obverses have been seen but little is known about these medals which were issued in two sizes. They appear to have been worn from a yellow neck ribbon.*

VALUE: —

315. CORONATION MEDAL 1953

Date: 1953.
Ribbon: Dark red with two narrow blue stripes in the centre and narrow white edges.
Metal: Silver.
Size: 32mm.
Description: (Obverse) a right-facing bust of Queen Elizabeth II in a Tudor crown and robes of state, the field being otherwise plain. (Reverse) a similar crown over the royal monogram EIIR with the legend QUEEN ELIZABETH II CROWNED 2ND JUNE 1953 round the circumference. Ring suspension.
Comments: *This medal celebrated the coronation of Queen Elizabeth II on 2 June 1953. News that Edmund Hillary and Sherpa Tenzing had successfully attained the summit of Everest reached London on the morning of the Coronation. Subsequently the members of the Hunt Expedition were invited to Buckingham Palace on 16 July 1953 where, on Her Majesty's own initiative, they were presented with coronation medals engraved MOUNT EVEREST EXPEDITION on the rim, following the precedent of the Mwele medals of 1895–96.*

VALUE:

		Miniature
Silver (129,000)	£30–35	£10–12
Mount Everest Expedition (37)	£800–1000	

315A. ROYAL VISIT TO NEW ZEALAND MEDAL 1953-54

Date: 1953.
Ribbon: Dark blue.
Metal: Copper-coloured alloy.
Size: 38mm.
Description: (Obverse) right-facing crowned bust of Queen Elizabeth II wearing Tudor crown; (reverse) the crowned New Zealand coat of arms surrounded by sprays of flowers and the inscription ELIZABETH II ROYAL VISIT 1953–54. The copper-coloured medal is hung by a ring from a scalloped suspender as illustrated.
Comment: *Issued to all New Zealand school-children in 1953, accompanied by a folder telling the story of the Royal Family, with pictures of the Coronation regalia, royal palaces and descriptions. The medals themselves are fairly common, but those with the accompanying folder are quite rare.*

VALUE: £2–3 (with accompanying folder £20–30)

316. JUBILEE MEDAL 1977

Date: 1977.
Ribbon: White with thin red stripes at the edges, a broad blue stripe in the centre and a thin red stripe down the middle of it.
Metal: Silver.
Size: 32mm.
Description: (Obverse) Right-facing profile of Queen Elizabeth II wearing the St Edward's crown—the first time this design was employed; (reverse) a crown and wreath enclosing the words THE 25TH YEAR OF THE REIGN OF QUEEN ELIZABETH II 6 FEBRUARY 1977. A distinctive reverse was used in Canada, showing the dates of the reign flanking the royal monogram round the foot, CANADA round the top and a large stylised maple leaf in the centre.
Comments: *The 25th anniversary of the Queen's accession was marked by the release of this unnamed medal.*

VALUE:

		Miniature
General issue (30,000)	£160–180	£6–10
Canadian issue (30,000)	£90–120	£6–10

317. QUEEN ALEXANDRA'S CHILDREN'S BANQUET MEDAL 1914

Date: 28 December 1914.
Ribbon: White, with red stripes at each edge.
Metal: Bronze.
Size: 38mm.
Description: (Obverse) bust of Queen Alexandra facing right with the
inscription A GIFT FROM QUEEN ALEXANDRA; (reverse) central
inscription FEAR GOD, HONOUR THE KING surrounded by the
legend GUILDHALL BANQUET TO OUR SOLDIERS' & SAILORS'
CHILDREN 28th DEC. 1914. The suspension is ornate and has the
arms of the City of London superimposed.
Comments: *This medal, designed and manufactured by Elkington, was issued
unnamed to 1,300 children and a small number of Chelsea pensioners who
attended a banquet at the Guildhall on 28 December 1914. The children,
between the ages of eight and thirteen, were the sons and daughters of men
in the Fleet or on the Western Front. One child was chosen from each family by Sir James Gildea of the Soldiers' and Sailors' Families' Association.
Relatively few medals appear to have survived.*

VALUE: £50–£70

318. GOLDEN JUBILEE MEDAL 2002

Date: February 2002.
Ribbon: Royal blue with thin red stripes at the edges, a broad white
stripe in the centre and a thin red stripe down the middle.
Metal: Gold-plated cupro-nickel.
Size: 32mm.
Description: (Obverse) a right facing profile of Queen Elizabeth II
wearing a crown; (reverse) the royal coat of arms flanked by the
dates 1952 and 2002.
Comments: *Issued to celebrate the 50th anniversary of the Queen's accession. It was granted to all personnel of the armed forces who had completed five or more years service on February 7, 2002. It was also issued
to members of the police, ambulance, coastguard, fire services, RNLI and
mountain rescue services. About 366,000 medals were issued.*

VALUE: £70–80   *Miniature*   £8–10

Miscellaneous Medals

Under this heading are grouped a very disparate range of medals whose only common denominator is that they do not fit conveniently into one or other of the preceding categories. They are not without considerable interest and many of them have a very keen following and a buoyant market.

319. KING'S AND QUEEN'S MESSENGER BADGE

Date: 1722.

Ribbon: Garter blue.

Metal: Silver gilt.

Size: Earliest issues variable according to monarch and jeweller; since George V—45mm x 34mm.

Description: (Issues since George V) an upright oval fitted with a plain suspension ring and having a greyhound suspended by a ring from the foot of the rim. (Obverse) the Garter inscribed HONI SOIT QUI MAL Y PENSE enclosing the royal cypher; (reverse) plain, engraved with an official number of issue and, on occasion, the name of the messenger.

Comments: *Messengers can be traced back to 1199, but prior to George I badges were not issued. Few of the earlier badges can be found due to a hand in and melt down order instituted by George III in 1762. During the reign of Victoria a number of different shapes and sizes were used for the badges due to a misunderstanding whereby individual messengers obtained their insignia from different jewellers instead of the Jewel Office. Since 1870 Garrards have been responsible for the design, submission and production of Messengers badges. From 1876 to 1951 the Foreign Office, as Controllers of the Corps of Messengers, purchased and held all badges for issue to those appointed as messengers. Since 1951 messengers, on satisfactorily completing a period of probation, are given a registered number and letter of permission to purchase their badges through the Crown Jewellers.*

VALUE:		
	George III	£1500–2000
	George IV	£1200–1500
	William IV	£1200–1500
	Victoria	£1000–1500
	Edward VII	£800–1000
	George V	£600–800
	George VI	£600–800
	Elizabeth II	£800–1000

320. ARCTIC MEDAL

Instituted: 30 January 1857.
Ribbon: 38mm watered white.
Metal: Silver.
Size: Height 46mm; max. width 32mm.
Description: An octagonal medal with a beaded rim, surmounted by a nine-pointed star (representing the Pole Star) through which the suspension ring is fitted. (Obverse) an unusual profile of Queen Victoria, her hair in a loose chignon secured with a ribbon. (Reverse) a three-masted sailing vessel amid icebergs with a sledge party in the foreground and the dates 1818-1855 in the exergue. The medal was issued unnamed, but is often found privately engraved.
Comments: *Awarded retrospectively to all officers and men engaged in expeditions to the polar regions from 1818 to 1855, including those involved in the on-going search for the ill-fated Franklin Expedition of 1845-8. Thus the medal was granted to civilians, scientists, personnel of the French and US Navies and employees of the Hudson's Bay Company who took part in a number of abortive search parties for Sir John Franklin and his crew. Some 1106 medals, out of 1486 in all, were awarded to officers and ratings of the Royal Navy.*

VALUE:
(unnamed) £550–750

Miniature £200–300

321. ARCTIC MEDAL

Instituted: 28 November 1876.
Ribbon: 32mm watered white.
Metal: Silver.
Size: 36mm
Description: A circular medal with a raised beaded rim and a straight bar suspender. (Obverse) a veiled bust of Queen Victoria wearing a small crown, dated 1876 at the foot; (reverse) a three-masted ship icebound.

Comments: *Granted to officers and men of HM ships* Alert *and* Discovery *who served in the Arctic Expedition between 17 July 1875 and 2 November 1876. The medal was later extended to include the crew of the private yacht* Pandora *commanded by Allen Young which cruised in polar waters between 25 June and 19 October 1875 and from 3 June to 2 November 1876. Medals were impressed with the name and rank of the recipient. Only 170 medals were awarded.*

VALUE:
(named) £2000–3000

Miniature £250–300

322. POLAR MEDAL

Instituted: 1904.

Ribbon: 32mm plain white.

Metal: Silver or bronze.

Size: 33mm octagonal.

Description: (Obverse) the effigy of the reigning sovereign; (reverse) a view of the Royal Research Ship *Discovery* with a man-handling sledge party in the foreground.

Comments: *Originally issued in silver to officers and in bronze to petty officers and ratings, but the bronze medals were discontinued in 1939 and since then only silver medals have been awarded. Bronze medals were also awarded to personnel on relief ships or those who did not land. On Scott's first expedition (1902–04) bronze medals were also awarded to officers, including Evans of the Broke. Apart from the 1904 issue of bronze medals, all Polar Medals have been fitted with a clasp giving details of the service for which they were awarded. However, those receiving the bronze medal for the first time (21) in 1917 also had no clasp, the date being on the rim. Those already having a bronze medal (3) received a 1917 dated clasp. The 1904 bronze issue included four dated 1902–03, 23 dated 1902–04 and 33 1903–04. Only three women have received the Polar Medal: Lady Virginia Fiennes, and one other the NZ scientist Mary Bradshaw. Medals are named to the recipient, engraved on the earlier and most recent issues and impressed in small capitals on the earlier Elizabethan issues. Clasps for subsequent expeditions are awarded. Altogether some 880 silver and 245 bronze medals for the Antarctic and 73 silver medals for the Arctic have been awarded to date. Of these almost 670 have been awarded in the present reign alone. 8 medals have been awarded for service in both the Arctic and Antarctic and 3 for Antarctic and Arctic (differentiating where first service took place). No bronze medals were issued for Arctic service. Only 18 persons received both the silver and bronze medals, including W. A. Horton who received a bronze clasp to his silver medal.*

VALUE:	Silver	Miniature	Bronze (no clasp)	Miniature (no clasp)
Edward VII	from £2500	£100–150	from £1500	£100–150
George V (B)	from £1500	£100–150	from £1500	£100–150
George V (C)	—	£100–150	from £1500	£100–150
George V (E)	from £1500	£100–150	—	£100–150
George VI	from £1500	£100–150	from £1500	£100–150
Elizabeth II	from £1500	£100–150	—	£100–150

323. KING EDWARD VII MEDAL FOR SCIENCE, ART AND MUSIC

Instituted: 1904

Ribbon: 35mm scarlet with a broad central stripe of dark blue and thin white stripes towards the edges.

Metal: Silver.

Size: 32mm.

Description: The raised rim consisted of a laurel wreath and has a ring for suspension. (Obverse) the conjoined busts of King Edward VII and Queen Alexandra; (reverse) the Three Graces engaged in various cultural pursuits.

Comments: *This short-lived medal was discontinued only two years later. It was awarded in recognition of distinguished services in the arts, sciences and music. The medal was struck by Burt & Co.*

VALUE:	£1200–1400

324. ORDER OF THE LEAGUE OF MERCY

Date: 1898.

Ribbon: 38mm watered white silk with a central broad stripe of dark blue.

Metal: Silver.

Size: Height 51mm; max. width 39mm.

Description: An enamelled red cross surmounted by the Prince of Wales's plumes enfiladed by a coronet, with a central medallion depicting a group of figures representing Charity, set within a laurel wreath. Reverse: a circular plaque inscribed LEAGUE OF MERCY 1898 in four lines.

Comments: *Appointments to the Order were sanctioned and approved by the sovereign on the recommendation of the Grand President of the League of Mercy as a reward for distinguished personal service to the League in assisting the support of hospitals. Ladies and gentlemen who rendered such aid for at least five years were eligible for the award. In 1917 King George V instituted a bar to be awarded to those who gave continuing service over a period of many years after receiving the Order itself. The Order was last awarded in 1946, the League itself ceased to exist in 1947. However, in March 1999, 100 years after its institution, the League was re-established and today it awards bronze medals for valuable service.*

VALUE:

Badge of the Order £50–60	*Miniature* £50–60
	with clasp £100–130

325. QUEEN ALEXANDRA'S IMPERIAL MILITARY NURSING SERVICE RESERVE MEDAL

Date: 1902

Branch of Sevice: Queen Alexandra's Imperial Military Nursing Service Reserve.

Ribbon: Black with two red stripes and two narrower white stripes towards the edges.

Metal: Silver.

Size: 38mm and 32mm.

Description: A uniface ring containing a prominent "R" surmounted by a Tudor crown fitted to a plain ring for suspension. The ring is inscribed in raised lettering QUEEN ALEXANDRA'S IMPERIAL MILITARY NURSING SERVICE RESERVE.

Comments: *This medal, usually referred to as a badge, was instituted in 1902. Its award merely signifies membership and was usually worn on the right hand side of the tippett or cape when on duty. A similar badge was issued for the Regular service with identical wording but omitting the RESERVE. After 1949, when the Service became Queen Alexandra's Royal Army Nursing Corps, the wording was changed to reflect the new name. The Reserve became obsolete in 1950. There also badges for Princess Christian's Army Nursing Service Reserve, Queen Alexandra's Military Families Nursing Service and the Indian Military Nursing Service.*

VALUE: £20–30   *Miniature* £30–40

326. TERRITORIAL FORCE NURSING SERVICE MEDAL

Date: 1908?

Branch of Sevice: Territorial Force Nursing Service.

Ribbon: Dark red with a narrow central white stripe.

Metal: Silver.

Size: Oval 50mm by 34mm

Description: A uniface oval ring surmounted by a Tudor crown attached to a plain ring for suspension. The ring has at the centre two ornamental letters "A" interlocking and set at an angle. The ring is inscribed in raised lettering: TERRITORIAL FORCE NURSING SERVICE. In 1920 when the TF became the TA the wording was changed to TERRITORIAL ARMY NURSING SERVICE and the motto "Fortitudo Meo Deus" (God give me strength) was placed in a scroll underneath.

Comments: *This medal (usually called a badge) was presumably instituted after the formation of the Territorial Force in 1908 and was worn as a badge of membership. When resigning, a nurse was expected to return the badge but they were often allowed to retain it after good service. Sometimes, for regulars, the right to retain is gazetted along with retirement.*

VALUE: £25–£30   *Miniature* £20–30

327. INDIAN TITLE BADGE

Instituted: 12 December 1911.

Ribbon: Light blue edged with dark blue (1st class); red edged with dark red (2nd class); or dark blue edged with light blue (3rd class).

Metal: Silver or silver-gilt.

Size: Height 58mm; max. width 45mm.

Description: A radiate star topped by an imperial crown with a curved laurel wreath below the crown and cutting across the top of a central medallion surrounded by a collar inscribed with the appropriate title. The medallion bears the crowned profile of King George V or King George VI. From the first issue of King George V's Title Badge on June 1, 1912 until 1933, his bust faced right. As from June 1, 1933 his bust faced left for the remainder of the reign. King George VI's Title Badges had his bust facing left. (Reverse) plain, but engraved with the name of the recipient.

Comments: *Introduced by King George V on the occasion of the Delhi Durbar of 1911 and awarded in three classes to civilians and Viceroy's commissioned officers of the Indian Army for faithful service or acts of public welfare. Recipients proceeded from the lowest grade to higher grades, each accompanied by a distinctive title. Each grade was issued in Hindu and Muslim versions, differing in title: Diwan Bahadur (Muslim) or Sardar Bahadur (Hindu), Khan Bahadur (Muslim) or Rai or Rao Bahadur (Hindu) and Khan Sahib (Muslim) or Rai or Rao Sahib (Hindu), in descending order of grade. These title badges took precedence after all British and Indian orders and decorations, and before campaign medals. The Title Badges with the bust of King George V facing left are much rarer than those with his bust facing right and worth approximately 30 per cent more.*

VALUE:

Diwan Bahadur	£70–90
Sardar Bahadur	£70–90
Khan Bahadur	£60–80
Rao Bahadur	£60–80
Khan Sahib	£60–80
Rao Sahib	£60–80
Miniature	£50–60

328. BADGES OF HONOUR (AFRICAN COUNTRIES)

Instituted: 1922.
Ribbon: Plain yellow, 38mm (neck) or 32mm (breast).
Metal: Bronze.
Size: 65mm x 48mm (neck); 45mm x 33mm (breast).
Description: Oval badges with a raised rim of laurel leaves terminating at the top in an imperial crown flanked by two lions. (Obverse) a crowned effigy of the reigning monarch; (reverse) the crowned cypher of the monarch or some emblem symbolic of the particular country with the country name in the exergue.
Comments: *The badge accompanied a certificate of honour awarded to chiefs and other persons of non-European descent who had rendered loyal and valuable service to the government of the territory. The original award was a neck badge suspended by a ribbon, but from 1954 onwards recipients were given the option of taking the award as a neck or breast badge. These awards were quite distinct from the decorations known as the Native Chiefs Medals (see number 70). They were first awarded to Ugandans but later extended to 14 other British territories in East and West Africa as well as the three High Commisson territories in Southern Africa. In particular the Badges issued for Nyasaland under Elizabeth II are rare, as Nyasaland became a Federation with Rhodesia in 1957. They are believed to have fallen into abeyance in the early 1980s.*

VALUE:

George V	£200–300
George VI	£150–200
Elizabeth II (neck)	£100–150
Elizabeth II (breast)	£100–150

329. BADGES OF HONOUR (NON-AFRICAN COUNTRIES)

Instituted: 1926.
Ribbon: 38mm watered silk mustard yellow.
Metal: Silver gilt.
Size: 41mm (George VI) or 32 mm (Elizabeth II).
Description: Circular with a raised rim of laurel leaves bearing a ring for suspension. (Obverse) crowned effigy of the reigning monarch; (reverse) the emblem of the country with the name round the foot.
Comments: *These medals accompanied certificates of honour awarded to indigenous persons who had rendered valuable service to the colony or protectorate. These awards appear to have been in abeyance since the early 1980s. Exceptionally, the New Hebrides badge was awarded to three British officers (Colonel (now General Lord) Guthrie (of Craigiebank), Lieutenant-Colonel C. H. C. Howgill, RM and HRH the Duke of Gloucester) in connection with the "Coconut War" in July 1980 instead of a campaign medal. The reverse types show the badges of 28 colonies or protectorate.*

VALUE:

George V	Rare
George VI	Rare
Elizabeth II	Rare

Miniature	£70–90 (only New Hebrides known)

330. NAVAL ENGINEER'S GOOD CONDUCT MEDAL

Instituted: 1842.
Ribbon: Originally plain dark blue but later broad blue with white edges.
Metal: Silver.
Size: 35mm.
Description: (Obverse) a two-masted paddle steamer with a trident in the exergue; (reverse) a circular cable cartouche enclosing a crowned fouled anchor and the legend FOR ABILITY AND GOOD CONDUCT. Between the cable and the rim the details of the recipient were engraved round the circumference. Considering the rarity of the award, it is even more remarkable that the medals have several unique features. Shaw's medal, for example, had oak leaves in the exergue, flanking the trident, but this feature was omitted from later medals. Medals have been recorded with a straight bar suspender, a steel clip and ring suspender or fixed ring suspension with one or two intermediate rings.
Comments: *This medal was abolished five years after it was instituted, only seven medals being awarded in that period: to William Shaw (1842), William Dunkin (1842), William Johnstone (1843), John Langley (1843), J.P. Rundle (1845), George Roberts (1845) and Samuel B. Meredith (1846). Restrikes were produced in 1875 and at a later date. The original medals have a grooved rim, the 1875 restrikes a diagonal grained rim and the later restrikes a plain, flat rim.*

VALUE:

Original	Rare
1875 restrike	£125–150
Later restrike	£80–100

331. INDIAN RECRUITING BADGE (GEORGE V)

Instituted: 1917.
Ribbon: Plain dark green.
Metal: Bronze.
Size: Height 45mm; max. width 48mm.
Description: A five-pointed star with ball finials, surmounted by a wreathed gilt medallion bearing a left-facing crowned bust of King George V, inscribed FOR RECRUITING WORK DURING THE WAR.
Comments: *Awarded to Indian officers and NCOs engaged in recruitment of troops. It could only be worn in uniform when attending durbars or state functions, but at any time in plain clothes.*

VALUE: George V   £80–100   *Miniature*   £50–60

332. INDIAN RECRUITING BADGE (GEORGE VI)

Instituted: 1940.
Ribbon: Emerald green divided into three sections interspersed by narrow stripes of red (left) and yellow (right).
Metal: Silver and bronze.
Size: Height 42mm; max. width 39mm.
Description: A multi-rayed silver breast badge surmounted by an imperial crown with a suspension ring fitted through the top of the crown. In the centre is superimposed a bronze medallion bearing the left-facing crowned profile of King George VI, within a collar inscribed FOR RECRUITING.
Comments: *Awarded to selected civilian and military pensioners, full-time members of the Indian Recruiting Organisation, fathers and mothers having at least three children in the armed services, and wives having a husband and at least two children serving in the defence forces.*

VALUE: George VI   £50–60   *Miniature*   £60–70

333. NAVAL GOOD SHOOTING MEDAL

Instituted: August 1902.
Ribbon: Dark blue with a red central stripe edged in white.
Metal: Silver.
Size: 36mm.
Description: (Obverse) the effigy of the reigning monarch; (reverse) a nude figure of Neptune holding five thunderbolts in each hand. In the background can be seen the bows of a trireme and the heads of three horses, with a trident in the field. The Latin motto VICTORIA CURAM AMAT (Victory loves care) appears round the circumference. Fitted with a straight suspension bar. The recipient's name, number, rank, ship and calibre of gun are impressed round the rim.
Comments: *Instituted to promote excellent gunnery performances in the annual Fleet Competitions, it was first awarded in 1903 but was discontinued in 1914. Subsequent success was marked by the issue of a clasp bearing the name of the ship and the date. A total of 974 medals and 62 bars were awarded. 53 men received one bar, three men got two bars and only one achieved three bars.*

VALUE:		Miniature
Edward VII	£250–300	£60–70 (in silver)
George V	£225–250	£60–70 "

334. ARMY BEST SHOT MEDAL

Instituted: 30 April 1869.
Ribbon: Watered crimson with black, white and black stripes at the edges.
Metal: Silver.
Size: 36mm.
Description: (Obverse) the veiled diademmed profile of Queen Victoria; (reverse) Victory bestowing a laurel crown on a naked warrior armed with a quiver of arrows and a bow and holding a target, impaled with arrows, in his other hand. Fitted with a straight suspension bar.
Comments: *This medal, sometimes referred to as the Queen's Medal, was awarded annually to the champion in the Army marksmanship contests held at Bisley. It was originally struck in bronze but was upgraded to silver in 1872. The award ceased in 1882 but was revived in 1923 and thereafter known as the King's Medal. The original reverse was retained, with the appropriate effigy of the reigning sovereign on the obverse. Since 1953 it has been known as the Queen's Medal again. In the post-1923 medals a bar bears the year of the award, with additional year clasps for subsequent awards. Until 1934 a single medal was awarded each year but in 1935 two medals were granted for the champion shots of the Regular and Territorial Armies respectively. Subsequently additional medals have been sanctioned for award to the military forces of India, Canada, Australia, New Zealand, Ceylon, Rhodesia, the British South Africa Police, the Union of South Africa, Pakistan, Jamaica and Ghana.*

VALUE:		Miniature
Victoria bronze	Rare	—
Victoria silver	Rare	—
George V	£800–1000	£30–40
George VI	£800–1000	£30–40
Elizabeth II	£800–1000	£10–15

335. QUEEN'S MEDAL FOR CHAMPION SHOTS OF THE ROYAL NAVY AND ROYAL MARINES

Instituted: 12 June 1953.
Ribbon: Dark blue edges with a broad red central stripe flanked by pale blue stripes.
Metal: Silver.
Size: 36mm.
Description: (Obverse) the effigy of Queen Elizabeth II; (reverse) Neptune (as on the Naval Good Shooting Medal).
Comments: *Instituted as the naval counterpart of the Army best shot medal with a bar which bears the year of the award.*

VALUE:

Elizabeth II	£800–1000	*Miniature*	£50–60

336. QUEEN'S MEDAL FOR CHAMPION SHOTS OF THE ROYAL AIR FORCE

Instituted: 12 June 1953.
Ribbon: Broad crimson centre flanked by dark blue stripes bisected by thin light blue stripes.
Metal: Silver.
Size: 36mm.
Description: (Obverse) the effigy of Queen Elizabeth II; (reverse) Hermes kneeling on a flying hawk and holding the caduceus in one hand and a javelin in the other. The recipient's details are engraved on the rim and the medal is fitted with a straight bar suspender.
Comments: *Competed for at the annual RAF Small Arms Meeting at Bisley. The medal was issued to the Champion Shot of the RNZAF uner the terms of the same Royal Warrant as the RAF.*

VALUE:

Elizabeth II	£800–1000	*Miniature*	£10–15

337. QUEEN'S MEDAL FOR CHAMPION SHOTS OF THE NEW ZEALAND NAVAL FORCES

Instituted: 9 July 1958.
Ribbon: Crimson centre bordered with white and broad dark blue stripes at the edges.
Metal: Silver.
Size: 36mm.
Description: (Obverse) the effigy of Queen Elizabeth II; (reverse) similar to that of the Naval Good Shooting Medal of 1903-14. Fitted with a clasp bearing the year of the award and a straight suspension bar.
Comments: *Awards were made retrospective to 1 January 1955. This medal is awarded for marksmanship in an annual contest of the New Zealand Naval Forces. Additional clasps are granted for further success. One contestant, Lt Cdr N. C. G. Peach, RNZN, has won this award ten times*

VALUE:

Elizabeth II	Rare	*Miniature*	—

338. UNION OF SOUTH AFRICA COMMEMORATION MEDAL

Instituted: 1910.
Ribbon: 38mm orange-yellow with a broad central dark blue stripe.
Metal: Silver.
Size: 36mm.
Description: (Obverse) the uncrowned effigy of King George V; (reverse) Mercury as God of Commerce and Prosperity, bending over an anvil, forging the links of a chain symbolic of the uniting of the four colonies (Cape Colony, Natal, Orange Free State and the Transvaal), with the date 1910 in the exergue and the legend TO COMMEMORATE THE UNION OF SOUTH AFRICA.
Comments: *This was the first medal struck in the reign of George V and resulted from the South Africa Act of 1909. This Act proclaimed the unification on 31 May 1910, of the self-governing four colonies into a legislative Union, becoming provinces of the Union of South Africa. This medal, the obverse of which was designed by Sir Bertram MacKennal, and the reverse by Mr Sydney Marsh, was struck to mark the opening of the first Parliament of the Union by HRH the Duke of Connaught. Awarded to those who took part in the inauguration of the Parliament. Additionally it was also awarded to certain officers and men of HMS Balmoral Castle, a Union Castle liner specially commissioned as a man-of-war to convey HRH the Duke of Connaught as the King's representative to South Africa for the celebrations. A total of 551 medals were struck by the Royal Mint, and were issued unnamed, although privately named medals are in existence.*

VALUE:	Named	£250–300
	Unnamed	£150–200
	Miniature	£20–30

339. DEKORATIE VOOR TROUWE DIENST

The other side is similar to no. 359 illustrated opposite

Instituted: 1920.
Ribbon: A broad dark blue central stripe flanked on one side by a gold stripe with a thin red stripe superimposed towards the edge, and on the other side by a yellow stripe with a thin white stripe towards the edge. Transvaal recipients wore the ribbon with the red to the centre of the chest; Orange Free State recipients wore the ribbon with the white stripe to the centre of the chest.
Metal: Silver.
Size: 36mm.
Description: (Obverse) the arms of the Transvaal; (reverse) the arms of the Orange Free State. Fitted with a fixed suspender. Recipients wore the medal with the appropriate state arms showing.
Comments: *This medal which is correctly named the Dekoratie Voor Trouwe Dienst was awarded by the Union of South Africa to officers of the two former Boer republics for distinguished service during the Second Boer War of 1899-1902.*

VALUE:

Silver (591)	£700–£800		*Miniature*	£60–70

340. ANGLO-BOERE OORLOG (WAR) MEDAL

Instituted: 1920.

Ribbon: Broad green and yellow stripes with three narrow stripes of red, white and dark blue in the centre. Transvaal recipients wore the ribbon with the green to the centre of the chest, while Orange Free State recipients wore it with the yellow towards the centre.

Metal: Silver.

Size: 36mm.

Description: Both sides inscribed ANGLO-BOERE OORLOG round the top, with the dates 1899-1902 round the foot. Medallions set in a border of a square and quatrefoil show the arms of the Orange Free State on one side and the Transvaal on the other. The medal was worn with the side showing the arms of the appropriate state uppermost. Fitted with a fixed suspender.

Comments: *Correctly named the Anglo-Boere Oorlog Medal, this was awarded by the Union government to officers and men of the former Boer republics for loyal service in the war against the British. To qualify for the medal proof had to be provided that they had fought against the British without surrendering or taking parole or the oath of allegiance prior to May 31, 1902.*

The other side is similar to no. 358 illustrated opposite.

VALUE: Silver   £140–160   *Miniature*   £60–70

Lint Voor Wonden (Wound Ribbon) Certificate value: £30; if with corresponding medal: value: £50.

341. COMMONWEALTH INDEPENDENCE MEDALS

Pakistan Independence Medal

Since the partition of the Indian sub-continent in 1947 and the emergence of the Dominions of India and Pakistan, it has been customary for medals to be issued to mark the attainment of independence. As these medals are invariably awarded to British service personnel taking part in the independence ceremonies, they are appended here, in chronological order of institution, the date of the actual award, where later, being given in parentheses. These medals invariably have symbolic motifs with the date of independence inscribed. The distinctive ribbons are noted alongside. All are 32mm wide unless otherwise stated.

India 1947 (1948) Three equal stripes of orange, white and green

Pakistan 1947 (1950) Dark green with a central thin white stripe

Ghana 1957 Nine alternating stripes of red, yellow and green

Nigeria 1960 (1964) Three equal stripes of green, white and green

Sierra Leone 1961 Three equal stripes of green, white and blue

Jamaica 1962 Black centre flanked by yellow stripes and green edges

Uganda 1962 (1963) Six stripes of black, yellow, red, black, yellow, red

Malawi 1964 Three equal stripes of black, red and green

Guyana 1966 Red centre flanked by yellow stripes and broad green edges. The green and yellow separated (left) by a thin black stripe and (right) by a thin pale blue stripe

Swaziland 1968 Three equal stripes of red, yellow and blue

Fiji 1970 Grey-blue with bars half red, half white, towards each end

Kenya 1973 Green with two equal red stripes towards the edges

Papua New Guinea 1975 Red bordered by thin stripes of yellow and white, with black edges

Solomon Islands 1978 Five equal stripes of blue, yellow, white, yellow and green

Gilbert Islands (Kiribati) 1980 Half red, half black, separated by a thin white stripe, and edged in yellow

Ellice Islands (Tuvalu) 1980 Equal stripes of red, white and red edged yellow. the white stripe bisected by a thin blue stripe

Zimbabwe 1980 Silver or bronze 38mm black centre flanked by red and yellow stripes with edges of green or blue

Vanuatu 1980 (1981) 30mm stripes of red and green with central thinner stripe of yellow edged by black

St Christopher, Nevis and Anguilla 1983 Bars of green (left) and red (right) with a black central bar having two thin white stripes, flanked by yellow stripes

VALUE: From £10   *Miniature* £10–100

342. MALTA GEORGE CROSS FIFTIETH ANNIVERSARY COMMEMORATIVE MEDAL

Instituted: 1992.
Ribbon: Dark blue with central stripes of white and red (the Maltese national colours).
Metal: Cupro-nickel.
Size: 36mm.
Description: (Obverse) the crowned arms of the island, which include the George Cross in the upper left corner, with the date 1992 at the foot. (Reverse) a replica of the George Cross with the eight-pointed Maltese Cross at the top and the date 1942 at the foot, with a legend BHALA SHIEDA TA'EROIZMU U DEDIKAZZJONI on one side and TO BEAR WITNESS TO HEROISM AND DEVOTION on the other. Suspension is by a fixed bar decorated with laurels, attached to a ring.
Comments: *Sanctioned by the government of Malta to celebrate the fiftieth anniversary of the award of the George Cross by King George VI to the island for its heroic resistance to prolonged Axis attack during the Second World War. The medal has been awarded to surviving veterans who served in Malta in the armed forces and auxiliary services between 10 June 1940 and 8 September 1943. Permission for British citizens to wear this medal was subsequently granted by the Queen. As a number of veterans applied for the medal after the cut-off date of 15 April 1994, the Maltese Government sanctioned a second striking—these medals carry the word COPY below the right arm of the George Cross.*

VALUE:
Cupro-nickel (original striking)   £80–100   *Miniature*   £8–10

343. SHANGHAI VOLUNTEER CORPS MEDAL

Date: 1854
Ribbon:
Metal: Silver.
Size: 38mm
Description:
Comment: *Awarded to the officers and men of the Shanghai Volunteers who took part in the battle of Soo Chow Creek (also known as the battle of Muddy Flats) which took place in April 28, 1854. Examples are of the greatest rarity and the last one to appear at auction was sold in 1991. Further details are sought.*

VALUE: £800–850

344. SHANGHAI JUBILEE MEDAL

Instituted: 1893.
Ribbon: Watered silk half bright red, half white or red with 4mm central white stripe.
Metal: Silver or bronze.
Size: 36mm.
Description: (Obverse) triple-shield arms of the municipality surrounded by a band with thistles, shamrocks and roses round the foot and NOVEMBER 17 1843 round the top. (Reverse) a scrolled shield with the words SHANGHAI JUBILEE and NOVEMBER 17 1843 and inscribed diagonally across the centre with the recipient's name in block capitals. The shield is flanked by Chinese dragons and above is a steamship and the sun setting on the horizon. The rim is engraved 'Presented by the Shanghai Municipality'. Issued with a small suspension ring, but often replaced by a straight bar. This medal has also been recorded with an ornamental silver brooch bearing the dates 1843–1893 on the second type of ribbon.
Comments: *The British settlement in Shanghai was founded in 1843 and formed the nucleus of the International Settlement established in 1854 under the control of an autonomous Municipal Council. In effect the International Settlement functioned as an autonomous City State administered by a Municipal Committee formed from those nations comprising the Settlement. This was abolished when Shanghai was overrun by Imperial Japanese troops in 1941.*

VALUE: Silver (625)   £250–300
                Bronze (100)   £250–300

345. SHANGHAI FIRE BRIGADE LONG SERVICE MEDAL

Instituted: Before 1904.
Ribbon: Black with broad crimson borders.
Metal: Silver.
Size: 31mm.
Description: (Obverse) an armorial device featuring a Chinese dragon standing on a symbolic high-rise building on which is displayed a flame on a pole crossed by a hook and ladder, with MIH-HO-LOONG SHANGHAI round the top and the motto "Say the word and down comes your house" round the foot; (reverse) engraved with recipient's details. It seems strange that no Chinese characters appear on the medal. Ring and double claw suspension, with a broad silver brooch bar at the top of the ribbon.
Comment: *Awarded for a minimum of twelve years regular service with the Municipal Fire Brigade. The award was presumably in abeyance following the Japanese invasion in 1937 and the wholesale destruction of the international commercial metropolis.*

VALUE: £300–350

346. SHANGHAI VOLUNTEER FIRE BRIGADE LONG SERVICE MEDAL

Instituted: 1904.
Ribbon: Red with white edges.
Metal: Gold, silver or bronze.
Size: 36mm.
Description: (Obverse) the arms and motto of the Municipality surrounded by a collar inscribed SHANGHAI VOLUNTEER FIRE BRIGADE ESTABLISHED 1866. (Reverse) originally simply engraved with name of unit, later a pair of crossed axes surmounted by a fireman's helmet under which is a horizontal tablet on which are engraved the recipient's dates of service. Round the circumference is inscribed FOR LONG SERVICE (top) and WE FIGHT THE FLAMES (foot) with quatrefoil ornaments separating the two inscriptions. Fitted with a swivelling scroll suspender.
Comments: *The medal in silver was awarded to members of the Volunteer Fire Brigade for five years service, for eight years service a clasp was added to the ribbon and for 12 years service the medal was awarded in gold. Bronze medals exist but are believed to have been specimens only.*

VALUE: £475–550

347. SHANGHAI VOLUNTEER CORPS LONG SERVICE MEDAL

Instituted: 1921.
Ribbon: Equal stripes of red, white and blue, the red bisected by a thin green stripe, the white by black and the blue by yellow.
Metal: Silver.
Size: 36mm.
Description: (Obverse) an eight-pointed radiate star bearing a scroll at the top inscribed 4th APRIL 1854. The arms of the Municipality superimposed on the star and surrounded by a collar inscribed SHANGHAI VOLUNTEER CORPS. Round the foot of the medal is a band inscribed FOR LONG SERVICE. (Reverse) plain, engraved with the name of the recipient and his period of service.
Comments: *The Volunteer Corps was raised in 1853 to protect the British and other foreign settlements. The date on the scroll alludes to the Corps' first engagement, the Battle of Muddy Flat. The Corps was cosmopolitan in structure, although the British element predominated. It was disbanded in September 1942, nine months after the Japanese overran the International Settlement. Awarded for 12 years good service, the last medal was awarded in 1941.*

VALUE: £275–325   *Miniature* £90–100

348. SHANGHAI MUNICIPAL POLICE DISTINGUISHED CONDUCT MEDAL

Instituted: 1924.
Ribbon: Red with a central blue stripe (1st class); red with a blue stripe at each edge (2nd class).
Metal: Silver or bronze.
Size: 36mm.
Description: (Obverse) arms of the Municipality and the inscription SHANGHAI MUNICIPAL POLICE; (reverse) the words FOR DISTINGUISHED CONDUCT. The recipient's name and rank were engraved around the rim.
Comments: *Awarded to officers and men of the Municipal Police in two classes, distinguished solely by their ribbons and the metal used (silver or bronze). A sliding clasp was fitted to the ribbon to denote a second award; this featured the Municipal crest and was engraved on the reverse with the details of the award. Only six awards were ever made, including two to Europeans.*

VALUE: Silver   £850–1000
        Bronze   £650–750

349. SHANGHAI MUNICIPAL POLICE LONG SERVICE MEDAL

Instituted: 1925.
Ribbon: Brown with a central yellow stripe edged in white.
Metal: Silver.
Size: 36mm.
Description: (Obverse) arms of the Municipality within a collar inscribed SHANGHAI MUNICIPAL POLICE; (reverse) plain apart from the inscription FOR LONG SERVICE in two lines across the centre. The recipient's name and rank were engraved round the rim in upper and lower case lettering. Awards to Indians were named in cursive script with the Hindi equivalent alongside. Fitted with a swivelling scroll suspender.
Comments: *Awarded for 12 years good service in the Shanghai Municipal Police, an international force composed largely of Sikhs, Chinese and White Russians as well as British ex-soldiers and policemen. Dated clasps for further five year periods of service were awarded. The medal was abolished in 1942.*

VALUE:		*Miniature*
Without clasp	£300–350	£45–50
With clasp	£400–500	£50–60

350. SHANGHAI MUNICIPAL POLICE (SPECIALS) LONG SERVICE MEDAL

Instituted: 1929.
Ribbon: Dark brown with three white bars, each bisected by a thin yellow stripe.
Metal: Silver.
Size: 36mm.
Description: (Obverse) the arms of the Municipality with the motto OMNIA JUNCTA IN UNO (all joined in one) round the circumference. (Reverse) inscribed SHANGHAI MUNICIPAL POLICE (SPECIALS) FOR LONG SERVICE in six lines. A unique award to A.L. Anderson (1930) was inscribed on the reverse FOR DISTINGUISHED AND VALUABLE SERVICES.
Comments: *Awarded for 12 years active and efficient service in the Special Constabulary. Some 52 medals and 8 clasps for additional service are recorded in the* Shanghai Gazette, *but the actual number awarded was probably greater. The medal was discontinued in 1942.*

VALUE :	
Without clasp	£450–500
With clasp	Very rare
Miniature	£200–250

355. FLORENCE NIGHTINGALE MEDAL

Date: 1912.
Ribbon: White with narrow red and broad stripes towards the edges.
Metal: Silver with enamels.
Size:
Description: An upright elliptical medal coming to a point at both ends, with a three-quarter length portrait of Florence Nightingale from the Crimean War period, inscribed MEMORIAM FLORENCE NIGHTINGALE 1820–1910 AD. The reverse bears the recipient's name.
Comments: *Instituted by the International Committee of the Red Cross for award to trained nurses, matrons, nursing organisers or voluntary aids for distinguished or exceptional service. Awards are made every other year on the anniversary of Miss Nightingale's birthday. This medal has been awarded very sparingly.*

VALUE: £500–700   *Miniature*   £400–500

356. ANZAC COMMEMORATIVE MEDAL

Date: 1967.
Ribbon: None.
Metal: Bronze.
Size: 76mm x 50mm.
Description: (Obverse) a medallion surmounted by a Royal Crown with a laurel wreath and the word ANZAC in a scroll below. In the field is the date 1915 above a picture of John Simpson and his donkey saving a wounded soldier at Gallipoli (based on a painting by 4/26A Spr Horace Moore-Jones, NZ Engineers. (Reverse) a map of Australia and New Zealand with the Southern Cross constellation. The reverse of the scroll has New Zealand fern leaves.
Comments: *This medal was instituted jointly by the governments of Australia and New Zealand and awarded to surviving veterans of the Australian and New Zealand Army Corps who served in the Gallipoli campaign. Designed by Australian artist Raymond Ewers. There is also a half-size lapel badge bearing the obverse design and is named on the reverse, as is the medal.*

VALUE: Medal   £60–80   Lapel badge   £30–40

357. NEW ZEALAND CADET DISTRICT MEDALS

Date: 1902.
Ribbon: Plain khaki or tan with a central pink flanked by dark green stripes.
Metal: Silver.
Size: 32mm.
Description: (Obverse) profile of Edward VII or George V with inscription FOR KING AND COUNTRY: PUBLIC SCHOOL CADETS, N.Z.; (reverse) DEFENCE NOT DEFIANCE round the top, with DISTRICT PRIZE (or CHALLENGE) MEDAL AWARDED TO in three lines, leaving space for the name of the recipient to be engraved below.
Comments: *These medals were instituted folllowing the establishment of the Public School Cadets in 1902 and were awarded in two classes in Challenge competitions or as prizes in the annual examinations.*

VALUE: District Challenge   £100
             District Prize   £90

358. DICKIN MEDAL

Date: 1943.
Ribbon: Three equal bands of green, dark brown and pale blue.
Metal: Bronze.
Size: 36mm.
Description: (Obverse) a laurel wreath enclosing the inscription "For Gallantry" in raised cursive script over the motto WE ALSO SERVE in block capitals; the initials PDSA in a tablet at the top of the wreath; (reverse) the date, name of recipient and details of the award. Fitted with a plain ring for suspension.
Comment: *Awarded by the People's Dispensary for Sick Animals to recognise acts of bravery by birds and animals in wartime, and consequently popularly known as the Animals' VC. It is very rarely awarded, only five medals having been granted since 1949. However, three medals were awarded following the terrorist attacks in the USA on September 11, 2001. Two were awarded to guide dogs who assisted their blind handlers to safety and the third was awarded to "Apollo", one of the search and rescue dogs who did such sterling work. "Apollo" was selected by ballot from out of the 300+ dogs involved. More recently in January 2003 another award was made, albeit posthumously, to "Sam" of the Royal Veterinary Corps for bravery in war-torn Bosnia in 1998. Originally, Mrs Dickin, founder of the PDSA also instituted a lesser award for acts of bravery by animals, known as the PDSA Silver Medal. This medal was last awarded in 1969 and has now been replaced by a Gold Medal—to date three animals have received this award.*

VALUE: £4000–£8000

359. NATIONAL CANINE DEFENCE LEAGUE MEDAL

Date: c. 1900.
Ribbon: Red.
Metal: Silver or bronze.
Size: 30mm.
Description: (Obverse) Victory standing with sword in hand over vanquished dragon, her right hand resting on a dog; NATIONAL CANINE DEFENCE LEAGUE inscribed round the top; (reverse) spray of oak leaves with a placard engraved with the name of the recipient and date of the award. Fitted with a plain ring for suspension
Comments: *Awarded for acts of bravery or exceptional humanity in the rescue of dogs from dangerous situations. Medals in bronze were intended for award to dogs for brave acts.*

VALUE:		
Silver (early issue)	£1000–£1500
Silver (late issue)	£200–300
Bronze	£150–200

360. THE PEOPLE'S DISPENSARY FOR SICK ANIMALS CROSS

Date: —
Ribbon: Broad red band with a narrow blue central stripe and broad white edges.
Metal: Silver.
Size: 32mm.
Description: A plain cross pattée with the initials PDSA on the arms. At the centre is a medallion bearing the figure of St Giles. The reverse is plain except for the name of the recipient and date of the award.
Comments: *Awarded to people who have performed acts of bravery involving animals. The PDSA also award medals to animals, the Dickin Medal (no. 358) being the most important.*

VALUE: £80–100

361. OUR DUMB FRIENDS LEAGUE MEDAL

Date:
Ribbon: Plain red.
Metal: Bronze.
Size: Heart-shaped, 45mm x 50mm.
Description: (Obverse) Figures of a horse, dog, cat and donkey within a heart-shaped ribbon inscribed OUR DUMB FRIENDS LEAGUE A SOCIETY FOR THE ENCOURAGEMENT OF KINDNESS TO ANIMALS; (reverse) engraved with the name of the recipient and date of the award.
Comments: *Awarded by the League for acts of bravery involving the rescue of animals.*

VALUE: £200–250

362. CORPS OF COMMISSIONAIRES MEDAL

Date:
Ribbon: Red, white and blue.
Metal: Silver.
Size: 40mm.
Description: A 16-point star bearing a central medallion with the Union Jack in the centre surrounded by the Latin mottoes: VIRTUTE ET INDUSTRIA (top) and LABOR VINCIT OMNIA (foot)—"by valour and industry" and "work conquers all" respectively. Fitted with a plain ring for suspension from the ribbon which bears an elaborate brooch consisting of crossed rifle and sabre on a fouled anchor with a cannon behind, representing the armed forces from which the Corps recruits its members.
Comments: *Awarded by the Corps of Commissionaires for long and exemplary service.*

VALUE: £30–45   *Miniature*   £200–250

363. NATIONAL EMERGENCY MEDAL

Date: 1926.
Ribbon: None.
Metal: Gold or bronze.
Size: 50mm.
Description: (Obverse) Britannia seated holding a laurel branch and resting on a shield. Above the inscription across the field FOR SERVICE IN NATIONAL EMERGENCY MAY 1926 appear the national emblems of England, Wales and Scotland; (reverse) three female figures with arms outstretched holding locomotives dividing the inscription LARGITAS MUNERIS SALUS REIPUBLICAE (the immensity of the task, the well-being of the country).
Comments: *These medals were designed by Edward Gillick and struck by the Royal Mint on behalf of the London, Midland and Scottish Railway for presentation to those volunteers who had served the company throughout the General Strike of May 1926. The medals were struck in bronze and issued in boxes unnamed to the recipients. According to Mint records, a few medals were also struck in gold, but none has so far been recorded.*

VALUE: £40–50

Medals for Saving Life

Until the establishment of the government's own gallantry awards for the saving of life (the Sea Gallantry Medal (Foreign Services), instituted in 1841 and the Sea Gallantry Medal of 1854 and the Albert Medal of 1866), it was left entirely to private individuals and organizations to reward those who risked their own lives to save the lives of others. Although the medals granted from the late eighteenth century onwards are unofficial, they are of considerable human interest and are now very much sought after, preferably with the citations, diplomas, printed testimonials and other collateral material. The most commonly found of these medals are listed in broadly chronological order of their institution. However, listed below is the very wide range of Institutions and other bodies who have issued or continue to give awards for life saving, as currently known to the Life Saving Awards Research Society. The Society would be very pleased to hear from readers of this Yearbook of any that are not on the list. Many of the following awards are as yet incompletely researched, and it is our intention to include many of these in this section when the research has been completed by the Life Saving Awards Research Society.

LIFE SAVING SOCIETIES / FUNDS

Royal Humane Society
Bath Humane Society
Bolton & District Humane Society
Bristol Humane Society
Carnegie Hero Fund Trust
Fleetwood Humane Society
Glasgow Humane Society
Grimsby Humane Society
The Hundred of Salford Humane Society
Jersey Humane Society
Lancashire Humane Society
Liverpool Shipwreck & Humane Society
Norfolk Humane Society
Northants Humane Society
Plym, Tamar, Lynher & Tavy Humane Society
Port of Plymouth Humane Society
The Royal National Lifeboat Institution
The (Royal) Society for the Protection of Life from Fire
The Royal Life Saving Society (Mountbatten Medal)
Sheffield Society for the Recognition of Bravery
Shipwrecked Fishermen & Mariners Royal Benevolent Society
Suffolk Humane Society
Tayleur Fund
Tynemouth Trust
Windsor & Eton Humane Society

NEWSPAPERS/MAGAZINES

Answers Medal
Associated Newspapers Medal
Daily Herald (Order of Industrial Heroism)
Daily Mirror
Daily Sketch Medal
Fleet (For Merit) Medal

Golden Penny Medal
Pluck Medal
Post Office Magazine (St. Martin's Medal)
The Quiver Medal
Ally Sloper's Medal
To-Day (Gallantry Fund) Medal

MUNICIPAL AND OTHER AUTHORITIES

Binney Memorial Award
Birmingham Fire Medal
Civil Aviation Authority
Dale Award
Dundee Corporation Medal for Bravery
Folkestone Bravery Medal
The Corporation of Glasgow Bravery Medal
Liverpool Corporation Medal for Bravery
Metropolitan/LCC/London Fire Brigade Bravery Medal
Plymouth City Police Bravery Medal
Southend-on-Sea Pier Department Life Saving Medal
The Strathclyde Bravery Medal

The Liverpool Corporation Medal for Bravery

YOUTH ORGANISATIONS

Boys Brigade
Church Lads Brigade
Girl Guards
Girl Guides Association
Scouts Association
Sea Cadets

ANIMAL SOCIETIES

Belfast Society for the Prevention of Cruelty to Animals
Dublin Society for the Prevention of Cruelty to Animals
National Canine Defence League
Our Dumb Friends League
Peoples Dispensary for Sick Animals
Royal Society for the Prevention of Cruelty to Animals

COMMERCIAL ORGANISATIONS

Automobile Association
Castle Mail Steam Packet Co.
Imperial Chemical Industries
Lever Brothers
Lloyds
Silk Cut
Surrey Commercial Dock Company

NON-COMMERCIAL ORGANISATIONS

Imperial Merchant Services Guild
Mercantile Marine Service Association
Royal Society for the Prevention of Accidents
St. Andrews Ambulance Association Bravery Medal
Order of St. John of Jerusalem Life Saving Medal
Shipping Federation

SPECIFIC RESCUES

Indian Chief Medal (Ramsgate Medal)
Carpathia and *Titanic* Medal
CQD Medal
SS *Drummond Castle*
Folkeatone, Hythe & Sandgate Medal
Gorleston *Christean* Medal
SS *Lusitania* (*Wanderer*)
Maharajah of Burdwan's Medal (HMS *Goliath*)
Osip Medal
HMS *Niger* Medal (Deal)
Henry Vernon Crew Fund Medal
Wreck of the *Chusan*
Wreck of the *Kent*
Wreck of the *Palme*

COLLIERY DISASTERS

Little Hulton 1866
Hamstead Colliery 1908
Hartley Colliery 1862
Hulton Coliery 1910
Sacriston Colliery 1903

OTHER DISASTERS

Glasgow Plague Medal 1900
Hong Kong Plague Medal
Maidstone Typhoid Medal 1897
Moray Floods Medal 1829

RAILWAYS

London, Midland & Scottish Railway
London & North Eastern Railway
London Passenger Transport Board
Midland Railway
Southern Railway

PRIVATE AWARDS

Too numerous to mention—but each a tale of heroism in its own right!

Maidstone Typhoid Medal 1897.

The Golden Penny Award.

Ally Sloper's Medal.

Illustrated are just some of the medals that are currently being researched by the Life Saving Awards Research Society and which it is hoped will feature in forthcoming issues of the MEDAL YEARBOOK.

L1. ROYAL HUMANE SOCIETY MEDALS

Date: 1774.

Ribbon: None (1774-1869); plain navy blue (1869); thin central yellow stripe and white edges added (silver medal, 1921).

Metal: Gold, silver or bronze.

Size: 51mm (1774-1869); 38mm (1869-).

Description: (Obverse) a cherub, nude but for a flowing cloak, blowing on a burnt-out torch explained by the Latin legend LATEAT SCINTILLVLA FORSAN (perhaps a tiny spark may be concealed). A three-line Latin text across the exergue reads SOC. LOND. IN RESUSCITAT INTERMORTUORUM INSTIT. with the date in roman numerals. (Reverse) an oak wreath containing the engraved details of the recipient and the date of the life-saving act. Round the circumference is a Latin motto HOC PRETIVM CIVE SERVATO TVLIT (He has obtained this reward for saving the life of a citizen). When the rescue attempt was unsuccessful, however, the medal was granted without this inscription. Later medals of similar design were struck also in bronze.

Comments: *The society was formed in 1774 for the specific purpose of diffusing knowledge about the techniques of resuscitation and saving life from drowning. From the society's inception large medals were struck in gold or silver. Monetary rewards, medals, clasps and testimonials were granted to those who saved life, or attempted to save life from drowning, but later the society's remit was broadened to include "all cases of exceptional bravery in rescuing or attempting to rescue persons from asphyxia in mines, wells, blasting furnaces or in sewers where foul air may endanger life".*

Although not intended for wear, the large medals were often pierced or fitted with a ring or bar for suspension from a ribbon. The details of the recipient and the act were engraved on the reverse.

In 1869 permission was given for the medals to be worn. As a result the diameter was reduced to 38mm and a scroll suspension was fitted for wear with a navy blue ribbon. At the same time the Latin text of the "unsuccessful" and "successful" medals was altered to read VIT. PERIC. EXPOS. D.D. SOC REG. HVM. (the Royal Humane Society presented this gift, his life having been exposed to danger) and VIT. OB. SERV. D.D. SOC, REG. HVM. (the Royal Humane Society presented this gift for saving life) respectively. Details of the recipient and the act were engraved on the rim. In 1921 the ribbon of the silver medal was changed to navy blue with a central yellow stripe and white edges, but the plain navy blue ribbon was retained for the bronze medal. Scrolled clasps with the initials R.H.S. were awarded for subsequent acts of lifesaving.

In 1873 the Stanhope Gold Medal, in memory of Captain C.S.S. Stanhope, RN, was instituted for award to the person performing the bravest act of life-saving during the year. The first Stanhope medals were similar to the society's small silver medal, differing only in the addition of a clasp inscribed STANHOPE MEDAL and the year, but since 1937 the Stanhope Medal has been identical to the other medals, differing solely in the metal. In 1921, however, the ribbon for the Stanhope Gold Medal was changed to one of navy blue with yellow and black edges.

VALUE:	Gold	Silver	Bronze
Large successful	—	£250–350	£150–180
Large unsuccessful	—	£250–350	£150–180
Small successful	—	£150–250	£90–120
Small unsuccessful	—	£180–280	£100–150
Stanhope Gold Medal	£2000–2500	—	—
Miniature Undated	£250–300	£40–45	£35–40
Dated	£300–400		

L2. GLASGOW HUMANE SOCIETY MEDALS

Instituted: 1780.
Ribbon: None.
Metal: Gold or silver.
Size: 42mm.
Description: (Obverse) a naturalistic treatment of the elements of the Glasgow civic arms: the tree that never grew, the bird that never flew, the fish that never swam and the bell than never rang, with edge inscription GLASGOW HUMANE SOCIETY INSTITUTED 1780; (reverse) PRESENTED BY THE GLASGOW HUMANE SOCIETY TO above a horizontal tablet engraved with the name of the recipient; below: FOR INTREPIDITY OF COURAGE AND SUCCESS IN SAVING THE LIFE OF A FELLOW CITIZEN.
Comments: *Awarded mainly for saving people from drowning in the Clyde and Kelvin rivers but also for rescues in the Firth of Clyde.*

VALUE:

Gold:	Rare
Silver:	£500–700

L3. HUNDRED OF SALFORD HUMANE SOCIETY MEDALS

Date: 1824.
Ribbon: Plain dark blue.
Metal: Gold, silver or bronze.
Size: 32mm (circular type); height 49mm; max. width 41mm (cruciform type).
Description: Circular silver or bronze medals were awarded from 1824 onwards, with the recipient's name and details engraved on the reverse, and featuring a cherub kindling a spark similar to the Royal Humane Society's medal, on the obverse. Around the time of the society's centenary in 1889, however, a more elaborate type of medal was devised, with the circular medal superimposed on a cross of distinctive shape, so that the society's name could be inscribed on the arms. The recipient's details are again found on the reverse. There is also a watch fob shield type in silver and enamel, named and dated on the reverse.
Comments: *This society was formed in 1789 to serve the needs of the Salford and Manchester area. After a few years it was dissolved, but was revived again in 1824. These awards ceased in 1922.*

VALUE:

	Gold	Silver	Bronze	*Miniature*
Circular medal	Rare	£150–180	£100–130	—
Cruciform medal	—	£90–120	—	—
Shield watch fob	—	£60–80	—	—

If you know of a British Life Saving medal that is not included in the MEDAL YEARBOOK we would be delighted to hear from you.

Or if you can supply us with a photograph of any of the medals not illustrated in this publication we would be pleased to include it next year.

If you can help, please contact the Managing Editor,
John Mussell, telephone 01404 46972 or at the address on page 1. Thank you!

L4. ROYAL NATIONAL LIFEBOAT INSTITUTION MEDALS

Date: 1825.

Ribbon: Plain blue.

Metal: Gold, silver or bronze.

Size: 36mm.

Description: The first medals bore the effigy of George IV on the obverse and it was not until 1862 that this was replaced by a garlanded profile of Victoria by Leonard C. Wyon. Medals portraying Edward VII and George V were introduced in 1902 and 1911 respectively, but when permission to portray George VI was refused in 1937 the RNLI adopted a profile of its founder, Sir William Hillary, instead. All but the Edwardian medals have a reverse showing a drowning seaman being rescued by three men in a boat with the motto LET NOT THE DEEP SWALLOW ME UP. The Edwardian medals have the seated figure of Hope adjusting the lifejacket on a lifeboatman. The twin-dolphin suspension (first fitted in the 1850s) has a plain blue ribbon, and clasps inscribed SECOND SERVICE, THIRD SERVICE and so on are awarded for subsequent acts of gallantry.

Comments: *The RNLI was founded, as the Royal National Institution for the Preservation of Life from Shipwreck, on 4 March 1824 and began awarding medals the following year to "persons whose humane and intrepid exertions in saving life from shipwreck on our coasts are deemed sufficiently conspicuous to merit honourable distinction". Its title changed to the Royal National Lifeboat Institution in 1854.*

VALUE:	Gold	Silver	*Miniature*	Bronze	*Miniature*
George IV	£1500–1800	£350–450	—	—	—
Victoria	£1500–1800	£300–400	£150–200	—	—
Edward VII	£2300–2500	£800–1000	£200–250	—	—
George V	£2000–2500	£400–500	£200–250	£300–400	£150–200
Hillary	£2000–2500	£600–750	£200–250	£300–400	£150–200

L5. MEDALS OF THE SOCIETY FOR THE PROTECTION OF LIFE FROM FIRE

Date: 1836.

Ribbon: Plain scarlet.

Metal: Silver or bronze.

Size: 52mm (I and II), 45mm (III), 42mm (IV &V) and 40mm (VI).

Description: The first medal (type I) had a radiate eye in garter on the obverse and a reverse giving the recipient's details in an oak-leaf wreath. They were fitted with a ring suspender. The Society was granted the Royal title in 1843 and a new medal (type II) was adopted the following year, with the word ROYAL added and the date at the foot of the obverse changed to 1844. In the early 1850s type III was introduced, with an obverse of a man carrying a woman away from a fire. This and type IV (1892) were struck in silver or bronze. As royal patronage ended with the death of Queen Victoria, a new medal (type V) was required in 1902 without the Royal title. Types IV and V show a man rescuing a woman and two children from a fire. The reverse of this medal has the words DUTY AND HONOR within a wreath, the recipient's details being placed on the rim. Type VI, awarded from 1984, is a bronze medal without suspension with the recipient's details engraved on the reverse.

VALUE:

		Silver	Bronze
I	Eye and garter (1836)	£650–750	—
II	Eye and garter (1844)	£650–750	—
III	Man and woman (1850s)	£300–350	Rare
IV	Man, woman and children (1892)	£450–500	Rare
V	As type IV but "Royal" removed (1902)	£200–250	£150–200
VI	As type IV but details on rev.	—	Rare
	Miniature (type IV)	£150–200	—

L6. LLOYD'S MEDALS FOR SAVING LIFE AT SEA

Date: 1836.
Ribbon: Blue, striped white, red and white in the centre.
Metal: Gold, silver or bronze.
Size: 73mm or 36mm.
Description: Both large and small medals had similar motifs. (Obverse) the rescue of Ulysses by Leucothoe; (reverse) an ornate wreath.
Comments: *The first medals, introduced in 1836, had a diameter of 73mm and were not intended for wear, but in 1896 the diameter was reduced to 36mm and a ring fitted for suspension with a ribbon.*

VALUE:

		Miniature
Large silver	£450–550	—
Large bronze	£350–400	—
Small silver	£250–350	£60–80
Small bronze	£200–250	£40–50

L7. LIVERPOOL SHIPWRECK AND HUMANE SOCIETY'S MARINE MEDALS

Date: 1839.
Ribbon: Plain dark blue.
Metal: Gold, silver or bronze.
Size: 54mm (type I), 45mm x 36mm (oval, type II) or 38mm (type III).
Description: (Obverse) a man on a spar of wreckage, taking an inert child from its drowning mother, with the stark legend LORD SAVE US, WE PERISH. This motif was retained for smaller, oval medals (type II) introduced around 1867 with the name of the Society round the edge, and a simple wreath reverse. The suspender was mounted with the Liver Bird emblem. A smaller circular version (type III) was adopted in 1874/75 and fitted with a scroll suspender. In this type the Liver Bird appeared in a wreath on the reverse. Bars engraved with the details were awarded for subsequent acts of life-saving. In addition to the general Marine medals there were distinctive awards in connection with specific marine rescues and funded separately. These had the type III obverse, but the reverse was inscribed CAMP & VILLAVERDE or BRAMLEY-MOORE. A glazed silver medal inscribed IN MEMORIAM was granted to the next of kin of those who lost their lives while attempting to save the lives of others.
Comments: *The Society was formed in 1839 to administer funds raised to help and reward those who distinguished themselves in saving life as a result of a hurricane which swept the Irish Sea in January of that year. The first medals were struck in 1844 and presented for rescues dating back to November 1839. They were large (54mm) in diameter, without suspension.*

VALUE:

	Gold	Silver	Bronze
Large (54mm) 1844	Rare	£250–350	—
Oval 1867	—	£400–450	—
Small (38mm) 1874/5	£1200–1500	£150–200	£100–120
Camp & Villaverde	—	£450–600	£400–450
Bramley-Moore	—	£450–600	£400–450
In Memoriam	—	£600–700	—
Miniature (type II)	£150–200	£100–150	£100–125
(type III)	£150–200	£100–150	£100–125

L8. SHIPWRECKED FISHERMEN AND MARINERS ROYAL BENEVOLENT SOCIETY MEDALS

Date: 1851.
Ribbon: Navy blue.
Metal: Gold or silver.
Size: 36mm.
Description: (Obverse) the Society's arms; (reverse) inscribed PRESENTED FOR HEROIC EXERTIONS IN SAVING LIFE FROM DROWNING with a quotation from Job 29: 13 at the foot. The circumference is inscribed ENGLAND EXPECTS EVERY MAN WILL DO HIS DUTY, a quotation from Lord Nelson's signal to the fleet at Trafalgar, 1805. The first medals had a straight suspender but by 1857 a double dolphin suspender had been adopted (five variations of this suspender can be identified). Details of the recipient's name and the date of the rescue are engraved on the edge.
Comments: *The Society was founded in 1839 to raise funds for shipwrecked fishermen and mariners and the families of those lost at sea.*

VALUE	Gold	Silver
Straight suspender	**Rare**	**£250–280**
Dolphin suspender	**Rare**	**£250–280**
Miniature	—	**£150–200**

L9. TAYLEUR FUND MEDALS

Date: 1854.
Ribbon: Dark blue.
Metal: Gold or silver.
Size: 45mm.
Description: (Obverse) a sinking ship with the legend TAYLEUR FUND FOR THE SUCCOUR OF SHIPWRECKED STRANGERS; (reverse) details of the award engraved.
Comments: *In January 1854 the emigrant ship* Tayleur *foundered in Bantry Bay, Ireland. A fund was started for the relief of the survivors and the surplus used to issue silver life-saving medals. The first awards were made in 1861. Medals are known to have been awarded for eight separate rescues, the last in 1875. In December 1913 the residue of the Tayleur Fund was transferred to the RNLI and the issue of medals terminated.*

VALUE:

Gold (2)	**Rare**
Silver (37)	**£350–550**

L10. HARTLEY COLLIERY MEDALS

Date: 1862.
Ribbon: None.
Metal: Gold or silver.
Size: 53mm
Description: (Obverse) an angel with mine rescuers and disaster victims. Details of the award were engraved on the reverse.
Comments: *Some 204 miners perished in the disaster which overtook the Hartley Colliery, Northumberland on 10 January 1862. This medal was awarded to those involved in the rescue operations.*

VALUE:

Gold (1)	**Rare**
Silver (37)	**£750–850**

L10A. JERSEY HUMANE SOCIETY MEDALS

Date: 1865.
Ribbon: Silver medal—purple 32mm wide;
          Bronze medal—royal blue 32mm wide.
Metal: Gold, silver or bronze.
Size: 38mm.
Description: The medal has a plain swivel type suspension, curved, 40mm wide. (Obverse) the escutcheon of Jersey—(Three lions passant guardant heraldic "leopards"). Above "HUMANE SOCIETY OF JERSEY" embossed in large capital letters. Below a naked mariner astride a ship's spar in heavy seas waving for assistance. Reverse: With a wreath "PRESENTED TO . . . . . FOR COURAGE AND HUMANITY" embossed in capital letters.
Comments: *The first society meeting to award medals took place in June 1865 when one gold (Philip Ahier Jnr.), and two silver medals (Alex. J. Bellis and Howard Morris) were awarded. Since then, the Society has remained active with only a break during the German Occupation 1940–45, when the Military Authorities ordered the Society to cease its function and hand over all documents and medals to the Germans. These were, however, hidden by the then Secretary until the Liberation.*

VALUE:

Gold (2)	Very rare
Silver (approx. 55)	£800–£1,000
Bronze (approx. 110)	£500–£600

L11. MERCANTILE MARINE SERVICE ASSOCIATION MEDALS

Date: 1872.
Ribbon: Blue.
Metal: Gold (2) and silver (74).
Size: 38mm.
Description: The obverse has a border with the legend "MERCANTILE MARINE SERVICE ASSOCIATION". In the centre are two seated figures of Neptune and Britannia. Neptune has a shield decorated with an anchor; Britannia a shield decorated with a sailing ship. Between the two figures are Cornucopias, Mercury's staff and a Liver bird. Beneath the two figures are the words "INCORPOR-ATED BY SPECIAL ACT OF PARLIAMENT", and the maker's name Elkington & Co. Liverpool. The reverse bears a wreath containing the engraved details of the incident and the recipient's name.
Comments: *The medal was instituted by the MMSA in 1875 but the first awards were made retrospectively for rescues in 1872. The award was generally given to the Master and senior officers of ships engaged in life saving actions, but towards the end of its issuance some of the recipients were not officers. The last known award was made in 1906.*

VALUE:

Gold	Silver
—	£350–450

L12. LIFE SAVING MEDALS OF THE ORDER OF ST JOHN

Date: 1874.

Ribbon: Black, embroidered with the eight-point cross in white (1874), black watered silk (1888), white inner and red outer stripes added, separated by a black line(1950) which was subsequently removed in 1954.

Metal: Gold, silver or bronze.

Size: 36mm.

Description: The first medals had a plain eight-pointed cross of the Order on the obverse with the legend AWARDED BY THE ORDER OF ST JOHN OF JERUSALEM IN ENGLAND. A second type of medal was adopted in 1888 and showed two tiny lions and two tiny unicorns in the interstices of the cross, the reverse shows sprigs of St John's wort and the legend FOR SERVICE IN THE CAUSE OF HUMANITY. Clasps for further awards were instituted in 1892.

Comments: *Instituted on 15 December 1874 and awarded for gallantry in saving life, these medals were originally granted in bronze or silver, but gold medals were also struck from 1907.*

VALUE:

	Gold	Silver	Bronze
1st type 1874	—	£1000–1200	£400–500
2nd type 1888	Rare	£800–1000	£400–500
Miniature	—	£200–250	£150–200

L12A. MAHARAJAH OF BURDWAN'S MEDAL FOR GALLANT CONDUCT—

BURNING OF HMS *GOLIATH* 1875

Date: 1875

Ribbon: Blue.

Metal: Silver. Bronze specimen's are known

Size: 36mm.

Description: The medal has a fixed ring suspender. (Obverse) Bust of Queen Victoria wearing a coronet and veil draped behind: she wears the Order of the Star of India: below "J. S. & A. B. Wyon": around "VICTORIA REGINA". (Reverse) Surrounding: "THE GIFT OF THE MAHARAJAH OF BURDWAN"; within "PRESENTED BY THE LORD MAYOR OF LONDON FOR GALLANT CONDUCT AT THE BURNING OF H.M.S. GOLIATH 22nd DECr 1875",

Comment: *HMS Goliath was a training ship lent by the Royal Navy to Forest Gate School Board in 1870. Moored off Grays, Essex, it held some 450 orphan boys, mostly from the East End of London and was used for training in Naval Service. On December 22, 1875 a fire accidentally broke out in the lamp-room and the ship was completely destroyed. One officer and 19 boys are believed to have died in the disaster. Such was the conduct of the boys that the Maharajah of Burdwan wrote to The Times expressing his desire to award a medal, through the Lord Mayor of London, to those boys who had particularly distinguished themselves. The medals were presented at the Mansion House in a private ceremony by the Lord Mayor.*

VALUE: £600–£800

L13. SHROPSHIRE SOCIETY LIFE SAVING MEDAL

Date: —

Ribbon: 30mm with two equal stripes of blue and yellow.

Metal: Silver.

Size: 50mm.

Description: (Obverse) a left-facing profile of Captain Matthew Webb whose name appears round the top, with the inscription BORN IN SHROPSHIRE 1848—SWAM THE CHANNEL 1875 round the foot. Fitted with a plain ring for suspension and a brooch bar at the top of the ribbon.

Comment: *Struck by John Pinches and presented by the Shropshire Society in London for outstanding acts of bravery in Shropshire. It is not known how many were awarded. An example of this medal, awarded in 1923, fetched £520 at Glendining's sale on March 28, 2001 against an estimate of £150–£200.*

VALUE: £500–700

L14. LIVERPOOL SHIPWRECK AND HUMANE SOCIETY'S FIRE MEDALS

Date: 1883.

Ribbon: Plain scarlet.

Metal: Gold, silver or bronze.

Size: 38mm.

Description: (Obverse) a fireman descending the stairs of a burning house carrying three children to their kneeling mother, her arms outstretched to receive them. (Reverse) the wreathed Liver Bird previously noted for the third type of Marine medal. The medal is fitted with a scroll suspender. Clasps engraved with the details are awarded for subsquent acts.

Comments: *The first recipient was William Oversly in November 1883, for rescuing a child from a burning house. The first woman recipient was Miss Julia Keogh (12 February 1895) who saved two children in a house fire.*

VALUE:

	Gold	Silver	Bronze
Fire medal	Rare	£300–350	£200–250
Miniature	£250–300	£200–250	£150–200

L15. LIVERPOOL SHIPWRECK AND HUMANE SOCIETY'S SWIMMING MEDALS

Date: 1885.

Ribbon: Five equal bars, three blue and two white.

Metal: Silver or bronze.

Size: Height 44mm; max. width 30mm.

Description: This extremely ornate medal has a twin dolphin suspender and a free form. (Obverse) a wreath surmounted by crossed oars and a trident, with a lifebelt at the centre enclosing the Liver Bird emblem on a shield; (reverse) plain, engraved with the recipient's name and details.

Comments: *Not granted for life-saving as such, but for proficiency in swimming and life-saving techniques.*

VALUE:

Silver	£60–80
Bronze	£50–65

L16. ANSWERS MEDAL FOR HEROISM

Date: 1892.
Ribbon: Equal stripes of blue, white, blue, white and blue.
Metal: Silver.
Size: 38mm.
Description: (Obverse) a wreath enclosing a lion crouching with a sunburst in the background; (reverse) HONORIS CAUSA within a wreath surrounded by the legend PRESENTED BY THE PROPRIE-TORS OF ANSWERS. Fitted with a scroll suspender.
Comments: *This medal is typical of the many awards made by newspapers and magazines in the late 19th century. The medals were accompanied by a first class diploma. Second class diplomas were projected but never issued. It was also intended to issue a gold medal but no trace of such awards has been found.*

VALUE: —

L17. LLOYD'S MEDALS FOR MERITORIOUS SERVICE

Second type.

Date: 1893.
Ribbon: Red with blue stripes towards the edges (1893); blue with broad white stripes towards the edges (since 1900).
Metal: Silver or bronze.
Size: 36mm x 38mm (star), 39mm x 29mm (oval), 36mm (circular).
Description: The original medal was a nine-pointed rayed star in bronze with the arms of Lloyd's on the obverse, suspended by a ring from a red ribbon with blue stripes towards the edge. A silver oval medal was introduced in 1900 with Lloyd's arms on the obverse and details of the recipient engraved on the reverse. This medal was fitted with a twin dolphin suspender and a blue ribbon with broad white stripes towards the edge. A third type, introduced in 1913, was a circular medal, struck in silver or bronze, with Lloyd's shield on the obverse. The fourth type, still current, was introduced in 1936 and has the full arms, with crest, motto and supporters, on the obverse. The ribbon is suspended by a ring.
Comments: *These medals have been awarded to officers and men for extraordinary services in the preservation of vessels and cargoes from peril.*

VALUE:

	Silver	Bronze
Star 1893	—	£120–150
Oval 1900	£400–450	—
Circular 1913	£320–350	£280–320
Circular 1936	—	—
Miniature (circular)	£200–250	—
(oval)	£250–300	—

L18. LIVERPOOL SHIPWRECK AND HUMANE SOCIETY'S GENERAL MEDALS

Date: 1894.
Ribbon: Five equal stripes, three red and two white.
Metal: Gold, silver or bronze.
Size: 38mm.
Description: (Obverse) a cross pattee with a wreathed crown at the centre and the legend FOR BRAVERY IN SAVING LIFE with the date 1894 at the foot; (reverse) the wreathed Liver Bird of the Marine medal, type III. Fitted with an ornate bar suspender. Bars for subsequent awards are granted.
Comments: *The first award was made on 9 June 1894 to Constables Twizell and Dean who were both injured whilst stopping runaway horses.*

VALUE:

	Gold	Silver	Bronze
General medal	Rare	£250–300	£200–250
Miniature	£250–300	£150–200	£100–150

L19. TODAY GALLANTRY FUND MEDALS

Date: 1894
Ribbon: Red with a central white stripe.
Metal: Silver and bronze.
Size: 38mm.
Description: (Obverse) standing figure of Britannia, lion and shield within a wreath; (reverse) the heraldic emblems of the United Kingdom with the legend ABSIT TIMOR (let fear depart) and AWARDED BY THE GALLANTRY FUND. The name of the recipient and date of the award are engraved within a wreath. The medal is fitted with an ornamental suspension bar.
Comments: *This medal was awarded by the magazine To—Day, published between 1893 and 1903. Its first editor was the novelist Jerome K. Jerome who enthusiastically promoted the idea of the Gallantry Fund, but when he gave up the editorship in 1897 the Fund soon fell into disuse. About 30 medals were issued.*

VALUE: —

L20. IMPERIAL MERCHANT SERVICE GUILD MEDALS

Date: c. 1895.
Ribbon: Blue
Metal: Silver with a silver—gilt rope and enamelled flag on a gold centre.
Size: 40mm and 63mm.
Description: A cross pattée in the centre of which, within a rope ring, is the Guild flag with the initials M.S.G. superimposed. (Reverse) plain but for the details of the recipient engraved with the formula "Presented by the Merchant Service Guild to . . . for heroism at sea (date)". The cross is suspended by a ring and hook, from a rod with a ball and point at each end. There is a brooch of similar design.
Comments: *Only three examples of this medal are known. The medal to C. Wood Robinson is 63mm and those to John H. Collin and W. Nutman are 40mm. No definite dates of issue for this award have been determined, but the rescues for which the known recipients got these awards were in 1895 and 1896.*

VALUE: —

L21. PLUCK AWARD FOR HEROISM

Date: 1895
Ribbon: Blue
Metal: Silver
Size: 32mm
Description: (Obverse) sprig of laurel and palm on left and right, with a cross pattée in the centre inscribed FOR HEROISM; (reverse) a sprig of laurel on the left of a scroll engraved with the recipient's name alongside the words PRESENTED BY PLUCK.
Comments: *Pluck was an adventure magazine for boys published from 1895 to 1916. Medals were issued from the inception of the periodical. In issue 8 it was announced that the award was to be known as the Answers—Pluck Award and until issue 24 the medal was similar to that given by Answers. From number 25 onwards the distinctive Pluck award was used. The last medals appear to have been issued in 1897.*

VALUE: —

L22. TYNEMOUTH MEDALS

Date: 1895.
Ribbon: Dark blue.
Metal: Gold or silver.
Size: Silver 51mm (gold smaller).
Description: Silver: (obverse) a scene viewed from the north of King Edward's Bay at Tynemouth, with Pen Bal Crag surmounted by a lighthouse. In the left foreground is a ship, sinking by the stern and a lifeboat putting off into stormy seas to the rescue. Around the top is the inscription PALAM QUI MERUIT and around the bottom TYNEMOUTH MEDAL; (reverse) recipient's engraved name surrounded by a laurel wreath. The medal is suspended by a scroll suspender with an ornate bar. **Gold:.** The obverse is similar to the silver medal but has no motto and there are numerous changes to the scene. The reverse carries the motto on a large lifebuoy within which are the details of the recipient.
Comments: *The Tynemouth Medal Trust was formed in response to a request from Mr E. B. Convers, a New York lawyer, who had witnessed a rescue in the Tynemouth area. He was so impressed that he had a medal designed and produced and sent 100 silver medals to the Trustees to be awarded for acts of heroism to Tynesiders worldwide, or for acts of heroism in the Tyne and the surrounding area. A variant to the silver medal exists in which the reverse of the medal is inverted in relation to the suspender—this is known as the Tynemouth Extension Medal.*

VALUE: Silver (approx. 100)   £350–500
            Gold   Rare

L23. DRUMMOND CASTLE MEDAL

Date: 1896.
Ribbon: Plain crimson.
Metal: Silver.
Size: 38mm.
Description: (Obverse) the veiled profile of Queen Victoria; (reverse) a wreath enclosing the name of the ship and the date of its sinking with the legend FROM QUEEN VICTORIA A TOKEN OF GRATITUDE. Fitted with a scrolled suspender.
Comments: *Presented on behalf of Queen Victoria by officials from the British Embassy in Paris to inhabitants of Brest, Ushant and Molene for their generosity and humanity in rescuing and succouring the survivors of the SS* Drummond Castle *which struck a reef off Ushant on 16 June 1896. Of the 143 passengers and 104 crew, all but three perished. 282 medals were struck and 271 of these were awarded to those who helped save the living and assisted in the recovery and burial of the victims.*

VALUE:

Silver (282)	£250–300	*Miniature* —

L24. NEWFOUNDLAND SILVER STAR FOR BRAVERY

Date: 1897.
Ribbon: Two equal stripes of dark blue and crimson.
Metal: Silver.
Size: 36mm max.
Description: A six-pointed radiate star with ball ornaments in the interstices, surmounted by a circular medallion showing a ship in distress and having the inscription FOR BRAVERY AT SEA in a collar. Fitted with a plain ring for suspension.
Comment: *Originally instigated by the Governor of Newfoundland, Sir Terence O'Brien, in 1893, as a bravery award. A total of 27 were made. In 1897 three were awarded to those who assisted in putting out a fire on the SS* Aurora *which, loaded with dynamite, was docked in St John's Harbour, Newfoundland. These three were altered to have the name of SS* Aurora *added to the legend.*

VALUE: £750–1000

L25. QUIVER MEDALS

Date: c.1897.
Ribbon: Dark blue, with a broad diagonal white stripe.
Metal: Silver (29) or bronze (29).
Size: 38mm.
Description: A thick medal weighing two ounces. (Obverse) a naked figure holding a rescued child, with the winged skeletal figure of Death hovering over a stormy sea in the background; (reverse) a laureated tablet bearing the name of the recipient and the date of the act. The circumference is inscribed round the top: FOR HEROIC CONDUCT IN THE SAVING OF LIFE and THE QUIVER MEDAL round the foot. The very elaborate suspension ring is in the form of a laurel wreath and is fitted to the suspender bar by means of a scroll inscribed THE QUIVER MEDAL. Brooch mounting at top of ribbon.
Comments: *The popular Victorian magazine* Quiver *took a keen interest in promoting safety at sea and organised a Lifeboat Fund which provided not only a number of lifeboats named* Quiver *but also this gallantry award. At least 58 silver and bronze medals were awarded of which four were presented to the survivors of the Margate surf boat disaster on December 2, 1897. A specially struck medal (of a different design) was awarded by* Quiver *to Captain Inch of "Volturne" fame.*

VALUE: Silver £500–800 Bronze £400–500

L26. HUMANE SOCIETY OF NEW ZEALAND MEDALS

Date: 1898.

Ribbon: Scarlet edged with broad beige stripes on which was embroidered gold fern leaves (1898–1914) or 32mm plain royal blue (from, 1915).

Metal: Gold, silver and bronze versions.

Size:

Description: Originally an eight-pointed cross with ball points, with a circular medallion at the centre showing two figures surrounded by an inscription ROYAL HUMANE SOCIETY at the top and NEW ZEALAND round the foot, the cross mounted on an oak wreath surmounted by a Royal Crown fitted with a plain ring for suspension. The reverse was engraved with the recipient's name, date and details of the award. The second type consists of a circular medal with (obverse) an allegorical life-saving scene, name of the Society round the top and FOR LIFE SAVING in two lines in the field; (reverse) a laurel wreath with the recipient's name and details engraved in the centre. Early versions of this medal had a scrolled swivel suspension bar but later versions had a plain bar suspension bar. The top of the ribbon is fitted with a plain brooch.

Comments: *Presented by the Governor General as Patron of the Royal Humane Society of New Zealand. Only one or two awards are made each year. The medal is worn on the right breast. Until 1913 the Society also awarded a special gold medal, known as the Stead Medal, for acts of outstanding bravery. It was similar to the gold medal but had a suspension bar inscribed STEAD MEDAL. It was revived in 1963 for award to unsuccessful nominees for the Stanhope Gold Medal.*

VALUE:	Gold	Silver	Bronze
Type I	£2000 (6)	£1000 (73)	£600 (89)
Type II	£1500 (10)	£600 (82)	£400 (449)
Stead Gold Medal	Rare		

L27. ROYAL NATIONAL LIFEBOAT INSTITUTION CROSS

Date: 7 May 1901.

Ribbon: Blue watered silk.

Metal: Gold or silver with enamels.

Size:

Description: A wavy cross in dark blue enamel, with the initials RNLI in the angles interlaced with a rope, surmounted by a Royal Crown fitted with a ring for suspension. First Class (gold) and Second Class (silver).

Comments: *The original decoration, designed by Charles Dibdin, the RNLI Secretary, was instituted as a reward for Branch Honorary Secretaries and Ladies Auxiliaries for long and devoted service. 36 awards were made initially, followed by 18 other awards in 1902–9. Thereafter a new decoration, awarded to men and women in two classes, was proposed. Designed by Mr Burke of the College of Heralds and manufactured by Garrards in 1912. Objections raised by King George V led to the cross being discontinued on May 14, 1914, by which time only ten gold awards had been made and no silver awards, the latter known only as a sample in the RNLI archives. No record of the design of the 1901–09 award has been preserved.*

VALUE: —

L28. BOYS' BRIGADE CROSS FOR HEROISM

Date: September 1902.

Ribbon: Originally royal blue with two equal white stripes, but changed to plain royal blue in 1941.

Metal: Bronze.

Description: A cross pattee formed of four V-shaped finials linked to a circular disc inscribed the BOYS' BRIGADE CROSS FOR HEROISM and enclosing the emblem of the Boys' Brigade. The cross has a suspension ring and a plain brooch bar at the top of ribbon. There are two types, with or without a Geneva cross behind the anchor in the emblem (added in 1926 when the Boys' Life Brigade amalgamated with the Boys' Brigade).

Comments: *First awarded in 1904, the cross was awarded only 194 times up to the end of 1985, including five posthumous awards. Simon Herriott, aged 8, became the youngest holder in 1980.*

VALUE:	First type (without central cross)	Rare
	Second type (with central cross)	£500

L29. BOYS' LIFE BRIGADE MEDAL

Date: 1905.

Ribbon: Red.

Metal: Bronze.

Size: 34mm.

Description: (Obverse) A Geneva cross within a crowned circle and a radiate background, the circle inscribed TO SAVE LIFE; a scroll round the foot inscribed THE BOYS LIFE BRIGADE; (reverse) personal details of the recipient. Fitted with a plain suspension ring. The brooch bar is the form of a scroll with a laurel wreath superimposed on the middle and a clasp bearing the date of the award.

Comments: *This medal was awarded for good attendance. The Boys' Life Brigade amalgamated with the Boys' Brigade in 1926 and the award of this medal was then abolished. The BLB Cross for Courage was also abolished at this time having been awarded only ten times in its history.*

VALUE: £20–30

L29A. GIRLS' LIFE BRIGADE MEDAL

Date: 1905.

Ribbon: Red.

Metal: Bronze.

Size: 34mm.

Description: Similar to the above, but inscribed THE GIRLS' LIFE BRIGADE.

Comments: *This medal was awarded to members of the Brigade in similar circumstances to those for the Boys' Life Brigade.*

VALUE: £30–40

L30. CARNEGIE HERO FUND MEDAL

Date: 1908.
Ribbon: None.
Metal: Bronze.
Size: 90mm.
Description: (Obverse) an angel and a nude male figure surrounded by an inscription "HE SERVES GOD
BEST WHO MOST NOBLY SERVES HUMANITY"; (reverse) two wreaths surrounding a central tablet
inscribed "FOR HEROIC ENDEAVOUR TO SAVE HUMAN LIFE 19…" surrounding a further inscription
"PRESENTED BY THE TRUSTEES OF THE CARNEGIE HERO FUND". Details of the recipient are engraved
on the rim.
Comments: *The Carnegie Hero Fund Trust was established in Scotland by Andrew Carnegie in 1908. The first medallion
was awarded posthumously on 26 November 1909 to Thomas Wright for a life saving act on 23 September 1908. To
date 173 medallions have been awarded.*

VALUE:
    Bronze   £550–750

L31. RSPCA LIFE-SAVING MEDALS

Date: 1909.
Ribbon: Blue with three white stripes in the centre, the central stripe
being narrower than the others (silver); blue with a central white
stripe flanked by narrow red and white stripes (bronze).
Metal: Silver or bronze.
Size: 36mm.
Description: (Obverse) a seated female figure surrounded by a cow,
sheep, cat, dog, goat and horse; (reverse) plain, with an inscription.
The recipient's name usually appears on the rim. Both medals have a
brooch bar inscribed FOR HUMANITY.
Comments: *Instituted in 1909 by the Royal Society for the Prevention of
Cruelty to Animals, this medal is awarded in silver or bronze for acts of
gallantry in saving the lives of animals.*

VALUE:			*Miniature*
Silver	£150–200		£150–200
Bronze	£100–150		£100–150

L32. SCOUT ASSOCIATION GALLANTRY MEDALS

Date: 1909.

Ribbon: Red (bronze), blue (silver) or half red, half blue (gilt).

Metal: Bronze, silver and gilt.

Size: 33mm.

Description: A cross pattée with the Scout fleur-de-lis emblem at the centre with the motto "BE PREPARED" and the words "FOR GALLANTRY" or "FOR SAVING LIFE". The name and details of the recipient are engraved on the plain reverse. Suspension is by a ring or straight bar. A plain bar is awarded for additional acts of gallantry.

Comments: *The Scout movement began informally in 1907 and the Boy Scouts Association was founded a year later. The Scout Association's highest award is the Cornwell Scout badge, named after the famous "Boy" Cornwell of Jutland fame. However, gallantry awards were instituted in 1908 and 1909. The bronze cross is the highest award of the Association for gallantry, granted for special heroism or action in the face of extraordinary risk. The silver cross is awarded for gallantry in circumstances of considerable risk. The gilt cross is awarded for gallantry in circumstances of moderate risk. A bar may be awarded to the holder of any gallantry award for further acts of gallantry in circumstances of similar risk.*

VALUE:		
	Bronze (146)	£800–1000
	Silver (1327)	£400–500
	Gilt	£250–300

L32A. CORNWELL SCOUT BADGE

Date: 1916.

Ribbon: None.

Metal: Bronze.

Size: 30 x 25mm.

Description: The fleur de lis of the Scout Association with a stylised capital C in the centre, suspended by a brooch pin with attached safety chain.

Comments: *This award was named after John Travers Cornwell who won a posthumous Victoria Cross at the Battle of Jutland. At the age of 16 Jack Cornwell was one of the youngest winners of the VC and had been a Scout before entering the Navy. It was originally awarded 'in respect of pre-eminently high character and devotion to duty, together with great courage and endurance' but is now reserved exclusively to members of a training section of the Scout Association under 25 years of age (until 2002, under 20 years of age) who have an outstanding record of service and efficiency. It is very rarely awarded, the last occasion being in 1998. To date a total of 634 badges have been awarded.*

VALUE:	Rare

L33. C.Q.D. MEDALS

Date: 1909.
Ribbon: Plain dark blue (silver) or dark red (bronze).
Metal: Silver or bronze.
Size: 45mm.
Description: (Obverse) the SS *Republic* with the initials C.Q.D. at the top; (reverse) the words FOR GALLANTRY across the middle, with a very verbose inscription round the circumference and continued in eight lines across the field. Ring suspension. Issued unnamed, but examples are known with the recipient's name and ship privately engraved.
Comments: *This medal takes its curious name from the CQD signal (All Stations Distress) sent out by the stricken White Star steamship* Republic *after it collided with the Italian stramer* Florida *on January 21, 1909. The liner* Baltic *responded to the call. The* Republic *was the more severely damaged vessel, but all of her passengers and crew were transferred, first to the* Florida *and then to the* Baltic, *before she sank. The saloon passengers of the* Baltic *and* Republic *subscribed to a fund to provide medals to the crews of all three ships in saving more than 1700 lives. The CQD radio signal was sent out by the Marconi operator Jack Binns aboard the* Republic. *Binns became a hero when the survivors reached New York and was given a welcome parade. This was the first time that radio was used to effect a rescue at sea and indirectly sealed the fate of the* Titanic *three years later, as the White Star Line wrongly assumed that any larger liner would take several hours to sink and radio would obtain help quickly within well-used whipping lanes and lifeboats would only be required to effect the transfer of passengers and crew. As a result the number of lifeboats on the* Titanic *was severely reduced. Incidentally, Jack Binns was offered the post of wireless officer on board the new* Titanic *but declined.*

VALUE:

Silver	£350–450
Bronze	£200–250

L34. CARPATHIA AND TITANIC MEDALS

Date: 1912.
Ribbon: Maroon.
Metal: Gold, silver or bronze.
Size: Height 40mm; max. width 35mm.
Description: The ornately shaped medal, in the best Art Nouveau style, has the suspension ring threaded through the head of Neptune whose long beard flows into two dolphins terminating in a fouled anchor and ship's spars. (Obverse) the Carpathia steaming between icebergs; (reverse) a twelve-line inscription, with the name of the manufacturer at the foot. It was worn from a straight bar suspender.
Comments: *This medal recalls one of the greatest tragedies at sea, when the White Star liner* Titanic *struck an iceberg on her maiden voyage and sank with the loss of 1490 lives. The 711 survivors were picked up by the* Carpathia *whose officers and men were subsequently awarded this medal in gold, silver or bronze according to the rank of the recipient.*

VALUE:

Gold (14)	£7000–10,000
Silver (110)	£3000–6000
Bronze (180)	£2500–3500

L35. LLOYD'S MEDALS FOR SERVICES TO LLOYDS

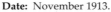

Date: November 1913.

Ribbon: Blue with broad white stripes towards the edge.

Metal: Silver.

Size: 36mm.

Description: (Obverse) Neptune in a chariot drawn by four horses; (reverse) an oak-leaf wreath enclosing a scroll inscribed FOR SERVICES TO LLOYD'S. Fitted with ring suspension.

Comments: *Instituted by Lloyd's Committee, this medal was intended to reward services of a general nature.*

VALUE:		*Miniature*
Gold (14)	£1500–2000	—
Silver (10)	£800–1000	£200–250

L36. ORDER OF INDUSTRIAL HEROISM

Date: 1923.

Ribbon: Bright watered red.

Metal: Bronze.

Size: 28mm.

Description: (Obverse) a modern interpretation of St Christopher carrying Christ (by Eric Gill); (reverse) inscription ORDER OF INDUSTRIAL HEROISM around the perimeter and in the upper half AWARDED BY THE DAILY HERALD above the recipient's name and date of award.

Comments: *Created by the* Daily Herald *and first issued in 1923. It was given as a reward to the "workers" who demonstrated bravery in the workplace and was initially only to be awarded to members of a Trade Union. However, there are numerous examples of the awards being given to non Union members and the definition of "workplace" was wide. The award was intimately associated with the* Daily Herald *throughout the lifetime of the newspaper and when it ceased publication in 1963 the award was discontinued. The medal was always awarded with a certificate and a monetary award. 440 were awarded.*

VALUE:	Bronze	£400–600

L37. CORPORATION OF GLASGOW BRAVERY MEDALS

Date: 1924

Ribbon: Green with red edges.

Metal: Gold, silver or bronze.

Size: 38mm (type I) or 33mm (type II).

Description: Type I: (obverse) Fame blowing a trumpet and holding a laurel wreath in front of a circular scrolled cartouche inscribed FOR BRAVERY; (reverse) plain, engraved with the name and details of the recipient. Type II: (obverse) wreath enclosing the words "FOR BRAVERY"; (reverse) Arms of the Corporation of Glasgow and details of the recipient. Fitted with a ring suspension and an ornate thistle brooch inscribed GALLANTRY in a scroll.

Comments: *Following the reorganisation of local government in Scotland in 1975, the award ceased and was replaced by the Strathclyde Regional Council Medal for Bravery.*

VALUE:	Type I	Type II
Gold	£300–350	£300–350
Silver	£250–300	£250–300
Bronze	£150–200	—

L37A. IMPERIAL CHEMICAL INDUSTRIES BRAVERY AWARD

Date: 1930.
Ribbon: Red with gold (9ct) brooch bar "Fortis".
Metal: Gold (9ct).
Size: 38mm x 26mm
Description: (Obverse) "Awarded for Bravery" with a lion rampant bearing the letters "I.C.I."; (reverse) inscription in raised letters (name, location and date of incident).
Comments: *A meeting of the ICI Central Council in 1929 proposed an award to be given for outstanding acts of bravery by ICI workers whilst at work. A bronze award was originally proposed, but extant examples all seem to have been 9ct gold. The first award was made to Harry Smithies in 1929 and the last to James Nicol in 1975. The award is still available for issue. 36 awards have been made to date.*

VALUE: £1000–1200

L38. RSPCA MARGARET WHEATLEY CROSS

Date: 1936.
Ribbon: 32mm blue with a white stripe towards each edge.
Metal: Bronze.
Size: 33mm square.
Description: Cross pattée with a central circular cross with rounded ends superimposed. R.S.P.C.A. across the top arm of the outer cross and INSTD. 1936 across the lower arm. THE MARGARET WHEATLEY CROSS inscribed in four lines across the centre. (Reverse) central circle inscribed FOR BRAVING DEATH ON BEHALF OF ANIMALS, above and below a raised horizontal panel engraved with the details of the award. Fixed ring for suspension.
Comments: *The RSPCA's highest award, it was named in memory of 16 year-old Margaret Wheatley who was killed by a train at Grange-over-Sands on June 4, 1936 while saving her dog who had got trapped on the railway line. She was posthumously awarded the RSPCA's Silver Medal and was also the first recipient of the cross named in her honour. To date, a total of 70 crosses have been awarded, at least 32 of them posthumously.*

VALUE: Rare

L39. LLOYD'S MEDAL FOR BRAVERY AT SEA

Date: 1940.
Ribbon: White with broad blue stripes at the sides.
Metal: Silver.
Size: 36mm.
Description: (Obverse) a seated nude male figure holding a laurel wreath, extending his hand towards a ship on the horizon; (reverse) a trident surmounted by a scroll inscribed BRAVERY, enclosed in a wreath of oak leaves. It has a ring suspender.
Comments: *Instituted by Lloyd's Committee, it was awarded to officers and men of the Merchant Navy and fishing fleets for exceptional bravery at sea in time of war. A total of 523 medals was awarded up to December 1947 when it was discontinued.*

VALUE:
Silver	£500–800	*Miniature*	£200–250

L40. LONDON, MIDLAND AND SCOTTISH RAILWAY MEDAL

Date: 1940.
Ribbon: Dark blue.
Metal: Silver.
Size: 38mm.
Description: (Obverse) Three different steam locomotive smoke stacks with a radiant sun in the right background with the inscription LONDON, MIDLAND AND SCOTTISH RAILWAY round the circumference; (reverse) a locomotive driving wheel on which is superimposed at the left a sprig of laurel, with the inscription FOR COURAGE or FOR MERIT round the top of the circumference. The date 1940 appears in the exergue. Fitted with a plain ring for suspension.
Comments: *Instituted by the Chairman of the LMS Company for acts of gallantry or meritorious service, hence the two different reverse types. The Chairman, Lord Stamp, was killed in an air raid in 1941 and it is believed that many of the records relating to this medal perished with him. Although the exact number of awards is not known, it is believed that about 20 awards were made.*

VALUE:

For courage	**Rare**
For merit	**Rare**

L41. SOUTHERN RAILWAY MERITORIOUS SERVICE MEDAL

Date: 1940.
Ribbon: Green with railway track and sleepers in gold.
Metal: Silver gilt.
Size: 32mm.
Description: (Obverse) a cross formy with SR in a circle at the centre, superimposed on a laurel wreath surrounded by a locomotive driving wheel; (reverse) FOR MERIT in seriffed capitals over a space for the recipient's name and SOUTHERN RAILWAY across the foot. The ornamental suspension bar is in the form of a vehicle spring. This medal was designed by Kruger Gray and struck at the Royal Mint.
Comments: *Instituted by the Directors of the Company for award to those employees who had been honoured by the King. 18 medals were awarded at a ceremony on August 16, 1940, and a further six medals were subsequently awarded.*

VALUE: Rare

L42. THE DALE AWARD

Instituted: November 1940.
Ribbon: White with broad blue and narrow black stripes towards the
    edges.
Metal: Silver.
Size: 33mm.
Description: (Obverse) a central medallion enamelled in white bearing
    the spires of Coventry Cathedral, surrounded by an inscription: THE
    DALE AWARD/COVENTRY.NOV.14.1940; (reverse) a laurel wreath
    enclosing a ten-line inscription across the middle: AWARDED BY
    THE COVENTRY HOSPITAL FUND FOR DEVOTION TO HOSPI-
    TAL & AMBULANCE DUTY DURING THE COVENTRY AIR RAID
    NOVEMBER 14th 1940. The rim bears the Birmingham assay marks
    and maker's mark of Thomas Fattorini. The medal was not named.
Comments: *This medal is known to have been awarded to a St John's Am-
    bulance driver but nothing further is known and details of the Dale Award
    and a list of recipients are sought.*

VALUE: —

L43. LONDON PASSENGER TRANSPORT
BOARD MEDAL FOR BRAVERY

Instituted: 1940.
Ribbon: Red with green central stripe and four narrow white stripes on
    either side.
Metal: Cupro-nickel.
Size: 38mm.
Description: (Obverse) a naked man kneeling and turning a large
    wheel; (reverse) the words LONDON TRANSPORT above a sprig of
    laurel, with a space for the recipient's name and a three-line inscrip-
    tion across the foot: FOR BRAVERY AND DEVOTION TO DUTY.
    Plain suspension bar and an ornamental brooch fitment at the top of
    the ribbon.
Comments: *This medal was instituted by Lord Ashfield, Chairman of the
    LPTB, to reward "special deeds of bravery" undertaken by LTPB staff
    during the Blitz. Only nine medals were awarded (all presented on Febru-
    ary 21, 1941) before the medal was discontinued, after some government
    pressure, to encourage nominations for the official civilian bravery awards
    of the George Cross and George Medal. A few unnamed specimens are
    known, possibly reaching the market from the stock of John Pinches when
    they ceased business.*

VALUE:
    Named   Rare
    Unnamed   £150

L44. LONDON AND NORTH EASTERN RAILWAY GALLANTRY MEDAL

Date: 1941.

Ribbon: Dark blue with a central white stripe flanked by narrow white stripes.

Metal: Silver with a matt finish.

Size: 38mm.

Description: (Obverse) a shield containing the arms of the company, superimposed on a laurel wreath surrounded by the inscription LONDON AND NORTH EASTERN RAILWAY on a raised band; (reverse) a scroll for the recipient's name superimposed on a laurel wreath with the rising sun in the background. The raised band is inscribed FOR COURAGE AND RESOURCE. Fitted with a plain suspension bar and an ornamental brooch bar at the top of the ribbon.

Comments: *Awarded "for outstanding acts of gallantry and resource which are not connected with enemy action, but which are of such a standard as would warrant recommendations for Government recognition had the acts been connected with enemy action". As some of the medals were awarded for actions resulting from enemy air raids the phrase "not connected with enemy action" was very liberally interpreted. A total of 22 medals were awarded, the last in 1947.*

VALUE: Rare

L45. BINNEY MEMORIAL MEDAL

Date: 1947.

Ribbon: None.

Metal: Bronze.

Size: 48mm.

Description: (Obverse) a bust of Captain R.D. Binney, CBE, RN; (reverse) inscription FOR COURAGE IN SUPPORT OF LAW AND ORDER and AWARDED TO above the recipient's name on a raised tablet.

Comments: *Instituted in memory of Captain Ralph Douglas Binney who was killed on 8 December 1944 in the City of London while attempting to apprehend two armed robbers single-handedly. It is awarded annually to the British citizen who displays the greatest courage in support of law and order within the areas under the jurisdiction of the Metropolitan Police and the City of London Police. The medal is not intended for wear. See MEDAL NEWS, August 1998 for a detailed article on the medal by Victor Knight.*

VALUE: £400–600

Awards of the British Commonwealth

In recent years many countries of the British Commonwealth have created their own individual systems of Honours and Awards. However, some British awards are still recognised within these systems. The medals and awards of these countries instituted prior to their own systems being introduced, are included in the main section of this book. In this section of the YEARBOOK we include the latest honours and awards of AUSTRALIA, CANADA, NEW ZEALAND and SOUTH AFRICA, together with their current Orders of Precedence encompassing their own and former British honours and awards. It is anticipated that the latest honours and awards for selected other countries of the former British Commonwealth, including those featured in earlier editions of the YEARBOOK, will be published in a separate volume at a future date.

There is a website for Australian Honours and Medals, maintained by the Awards and National Symbols branch in Canberra, ACT www.itsanhonour.gov.aus. The site is constantly being updated and, apart from listing the Australian honours and awards, has a search facility to enable researchers to trace medal details of Australians back to 1901, the year of Federation. It is also possible to search for awards by localities, defined by postcodes. This is an essential tool for military historians, medal collectors and family historians.

THE ORDER OF PRECEDENCE IN AUSTRALIA
(including British awards)

Victoria Cross
George Cross
Cross of Valour
Most Noble Order of the Garter
Most Ancient and Most Noble Order of the Thistle
Knight Grand Cross, the Most Honourable Order of the Bath
Order of Merit
Knight, the Order of Australia
Knight Grand Cross, the Most Distinguished Order of St Michael & St George
Knight Grand Cross, the Royal Victorian Order
Knight Grand Cross, the Order of the British Empire
Companion, the Order of Australia
Companion of Honour
Knight Commander, the Most Honourable Order of the Bath

Knight Commander, the Most Distinguished Order of St Michael & St George
Knight Commander, the Royal Victorian Order
Knight Commander, the Order of the British Empire
Knight Bachelor
Officer, the Order of Australia
Companion, the Most Honourable Order of the Bath
Companion, the Most Distinguished Order of St Michael & St George
Commander, the Royal Victorian Order
Commander, the Order of the British Empire
Star of Gallantry
Star of Courage
Distinguished Service Order
Distinguished Service Cross (Australian)

Member, the Order of Australia
Lieutenant, the Royal Victorian Order
Officer, the Order of the British Empire
Companion, the Imperial Service Order
Member, the Royal Victorian Order
Member, the Order of the British Empire
Conspicuous Service Cross
Nursing Service Cross
Royal Red Cross 1st Class
Distinguished Service Cross (British)
Military Cross
Distinguished Flying Cross
Air Force Cross
Royal Red Cross 2nd Class
Medal for Gallantry
Bravery Medal
Distinguished Service Medal (Australian)
Public Service Medal
Australian Police Medal
Australian Fire Service Medal
Member of the Order of Australia
Order of St John
Distinguished Conduct Medal
Conspicuous Gallantry Medal
George Medal
Conspicuous Service Medal
Antarctic Medal
Queen's Police Medal for Gallantry
Queen's Fire Service Medal for Gallantry

Distinguished Service Medal (British)
Military Medal
Distinguished Flying Medal
Air Force Medal
Queen's Gallantry Medal
Royal Victorian Medal
British Empire Medal
Queen's Police Medal for Distinguished Service
Queen's Fire Service Medal for Distinguished Service
Commendation for Gallantry
Commendation for Brave Conduct
Queen's Commendation for Brave Conduct
Commendation for Distinguished Service
War Medals in order of campaign
Australian Active Service Medal
Australian Service Medal
Australian Active Service Medal 1945–75
Australian Service Medal 1945–75
Police Overseas Service Medal
Civilian Service Medal
Polar Medal
Imperial Service Medal
Coronation/Jubilee Medals
Defence Force Service Medal
Reserve Force Decoration
Reserve Force Medal
National Medal
Champion Shots Medal
Long Service Medals

"The Australian and New Zealand troops have indeed proved themselves worthy sons of the Empire."

GEORGE R.I.

Australian medals

Since 1975 Australia has instituted a number of purely Australian awards. Medals and decorations pertaining to Australia, instituted prior to 1975 will be found in chronological sequence within the main text of this book.

The Australian system was inaugurated on February 14, 1975 when the Order of Australia, four bravery awards and the National Medal were established by Letters Patent. Since then a further 27 medals, decorations, commendations and citations have been introduced, which, including the various grades of the Order of Australia, brings the total to 37. A very detailed and comprehensive account of the Australian awards will be found in *The National Honours & Awards of Australia* by Michael Maton (1995). They are listed below in order of precedence. To date few of these new awards have come onto the market, thus we have not always been able to give an accurate valuation other than to indicate that the award is "Rare".

A1. VICTORIA CROSS FOR AUSTRALIA

Instituted: 1991.
Ribbon: Crimson 38mm wide.
Metal: Bronze.
Size: 35mm at each axis.
Description: A cross pattée with raised edges. (Obverse) a crowned lion standing on the royal crown, with the words FOR VALOUR on a semi-circular scroll below; (reverse) a circle containing the date of the action for which it was awarded. The Cross is suspended by a ring attached to the cross and a V-lug below a straight suspension bar ornamented with laurels.
Comments: *The Victoria Cross for Australia is identical to the British award and is awarded, with the approval of the Queen, by an instrument signed by the Governor-General on the recommendation of the Minister of Defence. Some 96 Australians have won the VC since 1856, the most recent being Warrant Officer Keith Payne for bravery in Vietnam (May 1969). No award of the Australian VC has yet been made.*

VALUE: As no. 24

A2. CROSS OF VALOUR

Instituted: 1975.
Ribbon: Magenta 38mm wide with a blood-red central band of 16mm.
Metal: Gold.
Size: 42mm.
Description: A straight-armed Greek cross with diminishing rays between the arms, ensigned by St Edward's crown and an integral suspension bar inscribed FOR VALOUR. The cross is surmounted by the heraldic shield of Australia topped by the Star of the Federation.
Comments: *Intended to replace the British civilian award of the George Cross. To date, only three CVs have been awarded.*

VALUE: Rare   *Miniature*   £100–150

A3. ORDER OF AUSTRALIA

Instituted: 1975.
Ribbon: Royal blue bearing scattered gold mimosa blossoms of various sizes (General Division); similar, but with gold edges (Military Division)

Neck/shoulder badge

Breast badge

KNIGHTS AND DAMES OF THE ORDER

The insignia consists of a neck badge and breast badge. In the case of a Dame there was the option of a neck badge or a shoulder badge, the latter being identical in every respect save the mounting. The neck badge is worn with a 16mm ribbon, while the shoulder badge of the Dame is worn with a 28mm ribbon. The breast badge is worn on the left side of a coat or outer garment.

Neck Badge: A gold disc 60mm in diameter, jewelled and having at its centre the arms of Australia enamelled in full colour on a blue ground decorated with two branches of mimosa. The whole is ensigned by the St Edward Crown in full colour with a suspension ring at the top.

Breast Badge: The emblem of the Order, 80mm in diameter, in gold, jewelled, and having the arms of Australia at the centre, surmounted by the St Edward Crown.

Comments: *There is also a miniature, 20mm in diameter, worn with the 16mm ribbon, a lapel badge, 10mm in diameter for ordinary civilian wear, and a ladies' badge mounted on a brooch bar. Knights and Dames are entitled to the prefix "Sir" or "Dame" and to use the postnominal letters AK or AD respectively. Between May 24, 1976, when the grade of Knights and Dames was introduced, and March 3, 1986 when these grades were abolished, a total of 11 Knights and two Dames were created, excluding the Queen (Sovereign of the Order) and the Prince of Wales.*

VALUE:		
Breast badge	Rare	
Neck/shoulder badge	Rare	
Miniature badge	—	

COMPANION OF THE ORDER

The insignia consists of a gold neck badge (men) or
shoulder badge (women) 60mm in diameter, similar
to the Knight's badge but having at its centre a
circlet of blue enamel edged in gold containing
two sprigs of mimosa and inscribed AUSTRALIA
at the foot. These badges are worn with a 16mm
neck ribbon or 38mm shoulder bow respectively.
Miniatures, lapel and brooch badges with jewelled
centres identical to those of the Knights or Dames,
are also worn. Companions have the postnominal
letters AC after their name.

Comments: *Up to 1994 214 Companions had been
appointed in the General Division and 17 in the Military
Division.*

VALUE: Neck badge   Rare
        Miniature badge   Rare

Companion's badge.

OFFICER OF THE ORDER

The insignia is a badge similar to that of the
Companion but only 55mm in diameter, and in
silver-gilt instead of gold. The miniature, lapel
badge and brooch badges have a blue enamel
centre. Officers have the postnominal letters AO
after their name.

Comments: *Up to 1994 1,164 Officers had been appointed,
990 in the General Division and 174 in the Military
Division.*

VALUE: Badge   £800–2000
        Miniature badge   £100-125

Officer's badge.

MEMBER OF THE ORDER

The insignia is a badge consisting of the emblem of the
Order, 45mm in diameter in silver-gilt but without
the enamelled centre, although the miniature, lapel
badge and brooch badges have a blue enamel centre.
Members have the postnominal letters AM.

*Comments: Up to 1994 3,727 Members had been appointed
to the Order, 3,064 in the General Division and 663 in the
Military Division.*

VALUE: Badge   £450–1000
        Miniature badge   £80–100

For the Medal of the Order of Australia (see no. A15)

Member's badge.

A4. STAR OF GALLANTRY

Instituted: 1991.

Ribbon: Deep orange with chevrons of light orange, points upwards.

Metal: Silver-gilt.

Size: 37mm.

Description: A seven-pointed Federation Star ensigned by a St Edward crown affixed to a suspension bar inscribed FOR GALLANTRY. (Obverse) a smaller Federation Star 22mm across, surrounded by stylised flames representing action under fire: (reverse) central horizontal panel on a stepped background.

Comments: *Second and subsequent awards are denoted by a silver-gilt 34mm bar with a replica of the Federation Star at the centre. Recipients are entitled to the postnominal letters SG. To date no award has been made.*

VALUE: — *Miniature* £60–80

A5. STAR OF COURAGE

Instituted: 1975.

Ribbon: Blood-red 32mm with a magenta central band 16mm wide.

Metal: Silver.

Size: 50mm.

Description: A seven-pointed, ribbed star surmounted by the heraldic shield of Australia and ensigned by a St Edward Crown affixed to a suspension bar inscribed FOR COURAGE.

Comments: *Subsequent awards are denoted by a silver bar bearing a replica of the star. Recipients are entitled to the postnominal letters SC. Since 1976 less than 60 Stars of Courage have been awarded. No awards were made in 1979 or 1982 and the most in any on year was 7 (1988 and 1991). One foreign award has been made, to Flight Lieutenant Holden, RNZAF, for his part in rescuing six trapped passengers from a helicopter crash in 1981.*

VALUE: £5000–12,000 *Miniature* £50–60

A6. DISTINGUISHED SERVICE CROSS

Instituted: 1991.

Ribbon: Ochre-red flanked by silver-blue bands.

Metal: Nickel-silver.

Size: 41mm.

Description: (Obverse) a modified Maltese cross with a seven-pointed Federation Star at the centre and flames in the interstices. It is ensigned with a St Edward Crown affixed to a plain suspension bar. (Reverse) plain but for a horizontal panel giving details of the award.

Comments: *Nickel-silver bars are granted for subsequent awards and have a Federation Star at the centre. Recipients are entitled to the postnominal letters DSC. So far only two awards have been made (November 1993) to senior Army officers commanding Australian forces assisting the UN peace-keeping operations in Somalia.*

VALUE: Rare

A7. CONSPICUOUS SERVICE CROSS

Instituted: 1989.
Ribbon: 32mm wide, with alternate diagonal stripes of bush green and sandy gold 6mm wide.
Metal: Nickel-silver.
Size: 38mm.
Description: A modified Maltese cross with fluted rays between the arms. (Obverse) the constellation of the Southern Cross within laurel leaves, ensigned with a St Edward's Crown affixed to a plain suspension bar. (Reverse) a horizontal panel for details of the award.
Comments: *Instituted to award all ranks of the armed services for outstanding service and devotion to duty in non-warlike situations. Since its inception only 129 crosses have been awarded (29 to the Navy, 39 to the RAAF and 61 to the Army). Recipients are entitled to the postnominal letters CSC.*

VALUE: £500–1000   *Miniature*   £50–60

A8. NURSING SERVICE CROSS

Instituted: 1991.
Branch of Service: Members of the Nursing Services of the Army, RAN and RAAF.
Ribbon: 32mm red flanked by broad white stripes.
Metal: Silver.
Size: 43mm.
Description: A stepped cross with straight arms, with a red enamelled plain cross at the centre and ensigned with the St Edward Crown affixed to a plain suspension bar. (Reverse) a horizontal panel superimposed on a pattern of fluted rays.
Comments: *Awarded for outstanding devotion and competency in the performance of nursing duties in support of the armed forces. Recipients are entitled to the postnominal letters NSC. To date, only four crosses have been awarded, two each to members of the RAAF and Army Nursing Services.*

VALUE: Rare   *Miniature*   £50–60

A9. MEDAL FOR GALLANTRY

Instituted: 1991.
Ribbon: 32mm light orange with chevrons of deep orange, points upwards.
Metal: Silver-gilt.
Size: 38mm.
Description: (Obverse) Federation Star surrounded by flames and surmounted by a St Edward Crown affixed to a suspension bar inscribed FOR GALLANTRY; (reverse) horizontal panel on a background of fluted rays.
Comments: *Awarded to all ranks of the armed services for acts of gallantry in action in hazardous circumstances. To date 13 medals have been awarded.*

VALUE: Rare   *Miniature*   £50–60

A10. BRAVERY MEDAL

Instituted: 1975.
Ribbon: 32mm with 15 alternating stripes of blood-red and magenta.
Metal: Bronze.
Size: 38mm.
Description: (Obverse) heraldic shield and Federation Star on a circular zigzag border; (reverse) zigzag pattern.
Comments: *Awarded to civilians and members of the armed services in non-warlike conditions for acts of bravery in hazardous circumstances. Recipients are entitled to the postnominal letters BN. Some 307 medals have been awarded since 1976.*

VALUE: £500–2000 *Miniature* £45–55

A11. DISTINGUISHED SERVICE MEDAL

Instituted: 1991.
Ribbon: 32mm silver-blue with three stripes of ochre-red.
Metal: Nickel-silver.
Size: 38mm.
Description: (Obverse) Federation Star with flames in the angles; (reverse) horizontal panel on a ground of fluted rays.
Comments: *Awarded to all ranks of the armed services for distinguished leadership in action. Recipients are entitled to the postnominal letters DSM. To date 21 awards of the DSM have been made, the first in November 1993 to Corporal Thomas Aitken as a section commander in Somalia during Operation Solace.*

VALUE: Rare

A12. PUBLIC SERVICE MEDAL

Instituted: 1989.
Ribbon: 32mm with 12 alternating stripes of green and gold of varying widths, the widest green on the left and widest gold on the right.
Metal: Nickel-silver.
Size: 38mm.
Description: (Obverse) an inner circle showing four planetary gears spaced equidistant from a central sun gear, surrounded by the inscription PUBLIC SERVICE. An outer circle shows 36 upright human figures representing a wide range of professions and activities. (Reverse) a wreath of mimosa surrounding the text FOR OUTSTANDING SERVICE.
Comments: *Awarded for outstanding public services at Commonwealth, State or Local Government levels. The number of medals allocated to each state is limited annually to 33 (commonwealth), 22 (New South Wales), 17 (Victoria), 11 (Queensland), 6 each (Western and Southern Australia), 3 (Tasmania) and 2 (Northern Territory). Awards may be made to Norfolk Island once every three years. Recipients are entitled to the postnominal letters PSM.*

VALUE: £100–200 *Miniature* £40–50

A13. AUSTRALIAN POLICE MEDAL

Instituted: 1986.
Ribbon: 32mm white with a central broad dark blue stripes.
Metal: Nickel-silver.
Size: 38mm.
Description: (Obverse) effigy of Queen Elizabeth within a Federation Star, with an outer pattern of fluted rays; (reverse) wreath of golden wattle enclosing the inscriptions AUSTRALIAN POLICE MEDAL and FOR DISTINGUISHED SERVICE.
Comments: *Awarded for distinguished service among members of the Australian Federal Police and the forces of the states and territories. Awards are limited annually to no more than one per thousand members (or proportionately) in each force, plus one additional medal for the whole of Australia. Recipients are entitled to the postnominal letters APM.*

VALUE: £250–400   *Miniature*   £40–50

A14. AUSTRALIAN FIRE SERVICE MEDAL

Instituted: 1988.
Ribbon: 32mm central gold band bearing an irregular pattern of red flames and flanked by green stripes.
Metal: Cupro-nickel.
Size: 38mm.
Description: (Obverse) effigy of Queen Elizabeth superimposed on a Federation Star composed of flames; (reverse) inscriptions AUSTRALIA FIRE SERVICE MEDAL and FOR DISTINGUISHED SERVICE on a background of flames.
Comments: *Awarded for distinguished service among members of the fire services on the basis of one annually for every 1,000 full-time and one for every 25,000 part-time or volunteer firemen. Recipients are entitled to the postnominal letters AFSM.*

VALUE: £250–400   *Miniature*   £40–50

A15. MEDAL OF THE ORDER OF AUSTRALIA

Instituted: 1976.
Ribbon: Royal blue 32mm, with gold mimosa decoration (General Division), or edged with gold (Military Division).
Metal: Silver-gilt.
Size: 40mm.
Description: (Obverse) emblem of the Order of Australia surmounted by St Edward crown affixed to a plain suspension bar.
Comments: *The medal of the Order is awarded for meritorious service. Holders of the medal are entitled to the postnominals OAM.*

VALUE: £250–350   *Miniature*   £20–25

A16. CONSPICUOUS SERVICE MEDAL

Instituted: 1989.
Ribbon: 32mm wide with alternating diagonal stripes of bush green and sandy gold 3mm wide.
Metal: Nickel-silver.
Size: 38mm.
Description: (Obverse) the Southern Cross encircled by laurel leaves; (reverse) a horizontal panel on a ground of fluted rays.
Comments: *Awarded to all ranks of the armed forces for meritorious achievement in non-warlike situations. Recipients are entitled to the postnominal CSM.*

VALUE: £200–350   *Miniature*   £40–50

A17. ANTARCTIC MEDAL

Instituted: 1987.
Ribbon: 32mm snow-white moire with 3mm edges in three shades of blue merging with the white.
Metal: Nickel-silver.
Size: 38mm.
Description: An octagonal medal surmounted by an ice crystal device affixed to a plain suspension bar. (Obverse) a global map of the Southern Hemisphere showing Australia and Antarctica, and the legend FOR OUTSTANDING SERVICE IN THE ANTARCTIC; (reverse) a polar explorer outside Sir Douglas Mawson's hut, leaning into a blizzard and wielding an ice-axe.
Comments: *Awarded to persons who have given outstanding service in connection with Australian Antarctic expeditions. Recipients must have a minimum of 12 months service in Antarctica. Clasps are inscribed with the year of service or with TO 1992 for persons who have served in Antarctica over several years. A total of 50 medals were awarded between 1987 and 1994, 1987 being the commonest date.*

VALUE: £350–500   *Miniature*   £45–55

A18. COMMENDATION FOR GALLANTRY

Instituted: 1991.
Ribbon: Plain orange 32mm wide and 90mm long.
Metal: Silver-gilt.
Size: 22mm.
Description: The insignia consists of a row of flames tapering towards the ends, with a seven-pointed Federation Star superimposed.
Comments: *Instituted for civilian acts of gallantry considered to be of lesser magnitude than those for which the star or medal would be awarded. To date three awards have been made.*

VALUE: Rare

A19. COMMENDATION FOR BRAVE CONDUCT

Instituted: 1975.
Ribbon: Blood-red 32mm wide and 90mm long.
Metal: Silver-gilt.
Size: 30mm.
Description: A sprig of mimosa, mounted diagonally near the foot of the ribbon.
Comments: *Intended to reward acts of bravery worthy of recognition but less than those for which the CV, SC or BM would be considered appropriate. Some 474 commendations were awarded between 1975 and 1994.*

VALUE: £150–500   *Miniature*   £25–30

A20. COMMENDATION FOR DISTINGUISHED SERVICE

Instituted: 1991.
Ribbon: Ochre-red 32mm wide and 90mm long.
Metal: Nickel-silver.
Size: 22mm.
Description: A central Federation Star mounted on a row of flames tapering towards the end.
Comments: *Awarded for distinguished performance of duties. To date 33 awards have been made, including six to the RAN (Gulf War) and six to the Army (Somalia).*

VALUE: Rare

A21. AUSTRALIAN ACTIVE SERVICE MEDAL

Instituted: 1991.
Ribbon: 32mm with a central red stripe, flanked by stripes of silver-green, light-green, gold, dark green and brown.
Metal: Nickel-silver.
Size: 38mm.
Description: (Obverse) a seven pointed Federation Star within a laurel wreath; (reverse) FOR ACTIVE SERVICE within a laurel wreath.
Clasps: Balkans, Cambodia, East Timor, Kuwait, Somalia, Vietnam 1975,
Comments: *Awarded for active service in various conflicts, denoted in each case by a campaign clasp. The Kuwait clasp recognised service in the Gulf theatre of operations between January 17, 1991 and February 28, 1991. Service before and after those dates was awarded by the Australian Service Medal with the appropriate clasp. The Somalia clasp was awarded for active service between January 10, 1993 and May 21, 1993 during Operation Solace. The Cambodia clasp was awarded for active service with UNTAC between October 1991 to October 1993. In August 1998 the Governor General altered the regulations and the Vietnam 1975 and Cambodia clasps are now awarded to the AASM. Holders of the Australian Service Medal (No. A22) will now receive the AASM.*

VALUE:

	RAN	RAAF	Army
Kuwait	£250–300 (937)	£300–450 (126)	£400–500 (41)
Somalia	£400–500 (20)	—	£250–350 (1016)

Miniature	£25–30

A22. AUSTRALIAN SERVICE MEDAL

Instituted: 1991.
Ribbon: 32mm with a central brown stripe flanked by stripes of dark
   green, light green, gold and silver-green.
Metal: Nickel-silver.
Size: 38mm.
Description: (Obverse) a modified heraldic shield on a background of
   the lines of longitude, surmounted by a St Edward crown affixed
   to a plain suspension bar; (reverse) clusters of mimosa blossom,
   surrounding a Federation Star inscribed FOR SERVICE.
Clasps: Balkans, Bougainville, Cambodia, East Timor, Ethiopia/Eritrea,
   Guatemala, Gulf, Iran-Iraq, Kashmir, Korea, Kuwait, Middle East,
   Mozambique, Namibia, Peshawar, Rwanda, SE Asia, Sierra Leone,
   Sinai, Solomon Is., Somalia, Special Ops, West Sahara, Uganda.
Comments: *For service with multinational peacekeeping forces. In many
   cases, the appropriate UN medal was also awarded. Some 2,363 medals
   and clasps have been issued to the RAN, 632 to the RAAF and 2,618 to the
   Army.*

VALUE: £200–500   *Miniature*   £20–25

A23. POLICE OVERSEAS SERVICE MEDAL

Instituted: 1992.
Ribbon: 32mm with a chequerboard pattern of black and white
   squares.
Metal: Nickel-silver.
Size: 38mm.
Description: (Obverse) globe surmounted by a branch of wattle, the
   whole enclosed in a chequerboard pattern and surmounted by a St
   Edward crown affixed to a plain suspension bar.
Clasp: Cyprus, Cambodia (20), Somalia (2), Mozambique (20), Haiti
   (30), Bouganville (22) and East Timor (300+) denoted by a globe
   emblem on the ribbon bar. Several officers have received two or
   three clasps and at least five officers have five clasps.
Comments: *Awarded to members of Australian police forces serving as
   members of peace-keeping missions under the auspices of the United
   Nations. Consequently recipients also receive the appropriate UN medals.*

VALUE: £200–500   *Miniature*   £25–30

A24. DEFENCE FORCE SERVICE MEDAL

Instituted: 1982.
Ribbon: 32mm azure blue with two gold stripes.
Metal: Cupro-nickel.
Size: 38mm.
Description: A circular chamfered medal bearing a Federation Star on
   which appears the insignia of the three defence forces. The medal
   is ensigned by the St Edward Crown affixed to a plain suspension
   bar. (Reverse) inscription FOR EFFICIENT SERVICE IN THE
   PERMANENT FORCES.
Clasp: Awarded for further periods of five years service.
Comments: *The medal is granted for 15 years service in the Defence Force, of
   which 12 years must have been as a member of the permanent Force.*

VALUE: £75–100   *Miniature*   £20–25

A25. RESERVE FORCE DECORATION

Instituted: 1982.
Ribbon: 32mm azure blue with a broad central band of gold.
Metal: Cupro-nickel.
Size: Oval 44mm high and 36mm wide.
Description: (Obverse) the joint services emblem on a radiate ground within a wreath of wattle; (reverse) inscribed FOR EFFICIENT SERVICE IN THE RESERVE FORCES.
Clasps: bar with the Royal Cypher flanked by sprigs of wattle.
Comments: *Awarded for a minimum of 15 years service as an officers in the Reserve Forces. Clasps for additional service of five years are granted.*

VALUE: £200–250   *Miniature*   £30–35

A26. RESERVE FORCE MEDAL

Instituted: 1982.
Ribbon: 32mm azure blue with narrow gold edges.
Metal: Cupro-nickel.
Size: Oval 44mm high and 36mm wide.
Description: (Obverse) insignia of the joint services on a rayed background; (reverse) inscription FOR EFFICIENT SERVICE IN THE RESERVE FORCES.
Comments: *Awarded to non-commissioned officers and other ranks of the reserve forces on completion of 15 years service. Clasps for further five-year periods of service have the Royal Cypher flanked by sprigs of wattle*

VALUE: £175–250   *Miniature*   £30–35

A26A. DEFENCE LONG SERVICE MEDAL

Instituted: 1998.
Ribbon: 32mm with central 10mm panel of seven narrow alternating stripes of azure blue and gold flanked by 7mm broad azure stripes and 4mm gold edges.
Metal: Nickel-silver.
Size: 38mm.
Description: A circular medal ensigned with the St Edward Crown attached to the suspension bar. (Obverse) the Australian Defence Force emblem surrounded by two sprays of wattle leaves and blossom; (reverse) a central horizontal panel surrounded by the inscription FOR SERVICE IN THE AUSTRALIAN DEFENCE FORCE.
Clasps: Bar with the Royal Cypher flanked by sprigs of wattle.
Comments: *This medal supersedes the Defence Force Service Medal, the Reserve Force Decoration and Reserve Force Medal. It is awarded on completion of 15 years service, clasps being awarded for further periods of service.*

VALUE: —

A27. NATIONAL MEDAL

Instituted: 1975.
Ribbon: 32mm with 15 alternating gold and blue stripes.
Metal: Bronze.
Size: 38mm.
Description: (Obverse) arms of the Commonwealth of Australia on a ground of mimosa blossom within a recessed circle. Incuse inscription round the edge: THE NATIONAL MEDAL FOR SERVICE. (Reverse) plain.
Comments: *Awarded to members of the various uniformed services for long service and good conduct, being a minimum of 15 years in one service or an aggregate of 15 years in two or more services. An amendment by Letters Patent in 1987 extended the award of this medal to the prison services. Bars for further periods of 10 years service are available.*

VALUE: £80–100   *Miniature*   £20–25

A28. CHAMPION SHOTS MEDAL

Instituted: 1988.
Ribbon: 32mm central dark blue stripe flanked by red and light blue stripes.
Metal: Antiqued brass.
Size: 38mm.
Description: (Obverse) a wreathed vertical panel with the Southern Cross and two crossed rifles; (reverse) plain.
Comments: *Only three medals are awarded annually, to the respective champion shots of the RAN, RAAF and Army. Of the seven RAAF awards, Sgt Philip MacPherson has won the medal three times (1991–3) and Sgt Brett Graeme Hartman has won it four times (1988–90 and 1994).*

VALUE: Rare   *Miniature*   £35–40

A29. CIVILIAN SERVICE MEDAL, 1939–1945

Instituted: 1994.
Ribbon: 32mm ochre-red central stripe flanked by narrow white stripes and broad stripes of opal green towards the edges.
Metal: Bronze.
Size: 38mm.
Description: (Obverse) the Southern Cross superimposed on a globe surrounded by mimosa blossoms; (reverse) horizontal panel for the recipient's name, with 1939 above and 1945 below.
Comments: *Awarded to civilians who had assisted Australia's war effort in a wide variety of organisations and who served under quasi-military conditions for at least 180 days. The medal may be awarded posthumously and presented to the next-of-kin. It is estimated that up to 70,000 people are eligible for this medal.*

VALUE: £100–150   *Miniature*   £8–10

A30. AUSTRALIAN ACTIVE SERVICE MEDAL, 1945–1975

Instituted: 1995.
Ribbon: 32mm central thin red stripe flanked by narrow yellow stripes and broad stripes of pale blue, dark green and purple towards the edge.
Metal: Nickel-silver.
Size: 38mm.
Description: (Obverse) the seven-pointed Federation star surrounded by the legend THE AUSTRALIAN ACTIVE SERVICE MEDAL 1945–1975; (reverse) a wreath of mimosa sourrounding a plaque for the recipient's details.
Clasp: Korea, Malaya, Malaysia, Thailand, Thai-Malay, Vietnam.
Comments: *This medal fills a gap between the Australian Service Medal (no. 190) and the current Australia Service Medal which was instituted in 1975. It is awarded to all ranks of the armed forces for warlike service in theatres of operation between the end of the Second World War and February 13, 1975. The medal is worn immediately after any Second World War awards and before any other campaign awards.*

VALUE: £100–150   *Miniature*   £10–12

A31. AUSTRALIAN SERVICE MEDAL, 1945–1975

Instituted: 1995.
Ribbon: 32mm central thin yellow stripe flanked by narrow green stripes flanked by khaki with wide navy blue stripe at left and pale blue at right.
Metal: Nickel-silver.
Size: 38mm.
Description: (Obverse) the arms of the Commonwealth of Australia surrounded by the legend THE AUSTRALIAN SERVICE MEDAL 1945–1975; (reverse) seven-pointed Federation star with space for recipient's details, surrounded by mimosa leaves.
Clasps: Berlin, FESR, Germany, Indonesia, Japan, Kashmir, Korea, Middle East, PNG, SE Asia, Special Ops, SW Pacific, Thailand, W New Guinea.
Comments: *This medal fills a gap between the Australia Service Medal (no. 190) and the current Australian Service Medal which was instituted in 1975. It is awarded to all ranks of the Australian Defence Force for non-warlike service in theatres of operation between the end of the Second World War and February 13, 1975. It is estimated that about 65,000 people are eligible for this medal. The medal is worn after campaign awards and before long service and foreign awards.*

VALUE: £100–150   *Miniature*   £12–15

A32. UNIT CITATION FOR GALLANTRY

Instituted: 1991.
Ribbon: Green encased in a silver-gilt rectangular frame with flame decoration. A seven-pointed Federation Star in silver-gilt in worn in the centre.
Comments: *This system was borrowed from the USA, many Australian formations and units receiving American unit citations during the Vietnam War. So far, however, no Unit Citations for Gallantry have been awarded. The citation is worn by all members of the unit receiving the citation for extraordinary gallantry in action, and appears on the right breast (Army and RAAF) or below the medal ribbons on the left breast (RAN). The first Unit Citation for Gallantry was awarded to a squadron of the SASR for gallantry in 13 major engagements in Iraq in 2003.*

VALUE: —

A33. MERITORIOUS UNIT CITATION

Instituted: 1991.

Ribbon: Gold encased in a rhodium-plated silver frame with flame decoration. A rhodium-plated silver Federation Star is mounted in the centre.

Comments: *Awarded to members of a unit for sustained outstanding service in warlike operations. So far only three Meritorious Unit Citations have been issued, all to units of the RAN for service in the Gulf War, 1990–91.*

VALUE: Rare

A34. AUSTRALIAN MERCHANT NAVY SERVICE CROSS

Instituted: 1998.

Branch of Service: Australian Merchant Navy.

Ribbon: Blue with narrow white central stripe and white edges.

Metal: Silver.

Size: 36mm.

Description: A cross fourchée on which is superimposed a small circular medallion bearing the insignia of the Australian Merchant Navy. Fitted with bar suspender.

Clasp: A gold laurel spray.

Comments: *This semi-officialmedal was created in 1998 to mark United Nations Year of the Ocean, September 24 being designated by the UN International Maritime Organisation as Day of the Merchant Mariner. The cross is awarded to officers for 15 years bona fide service on Articles of Agreement. Clasps are awarded for each additional 15 years service.*

VALUE: —

A35. AUSTRALIAN MERCHANT NAVY MERITORIOUS MEDAL

Instituted: 1998.

Branch of Service: Australian Merchant Navy.

Ribbon: Watered silk white with broad blue edges and central stripe.

Metal: Silver.

Size: 38mm.

Description: (Obverse) the crowned insignia of the Merchant Navy; (reverse) AUSTRALIAN MERCHANT NAVY MERITORIOUS MEDAL. Fitted with an ornamental bar suspender.

Comments: *This semi-official medal is awarded for an exceptional contribution to the Merchant Navy over a long period of time, but may also be awarded for an individual act of bravery by a seafarer.*

VALUE: —

A36. AUSTRALIAN MERCHANT NAVY COMMENDATION

Instituted: 1998.

Branch of Service: Australian Merchant Navy.

Ribbon: Watered silk with a dark blue centre, white stripes and light blue edges.

Metal: Silver.

Size: 36mm.

Description: A laurel wreath joined at the top by a merchant navy crown attached to a ring for suspension.

Comments: *This semi-official medal is awarded for an ongoing or individual contribution by a person in one of the many fields of maritime endeavour including education, research and development, maritime business, industrial relations and professional achievement.*

VALUE: —

A37. GALLIPOLI MEDAL

Instituted: 25 April 1990.
Branch of Service: ANZAC veterans of the Gallipoli campaign.
Ribbon: Central broad deep blue stripe, flanked by narrow crimson stripes and broad edges of yellow and light blue respectively.
Metal: Bronze.
Size: 36mm.
Description: A small circular medal superimposed on an eight-pointed star with ring suspension. (Obverse) a Tudor crown surrounded by the inscription GALLIPOLI 1914-15.
Comments: *This medal was originally approved by King George V but was never issued at the time. In April 1990 it was presented unofficially to the 200 surviving Gallipoli veterans to mark the 75th anniversary of the ill-fated landings on the Turkish coast, although we understand that it is still available via commercial sources.*

VALUE: £60–80

A38. ARMISTICE REMEMBRANCE MEDAL

Instituted: 2000.
Branch of Service: Surviving veterans of the First World War.
Ribbon: Red with a black central stripe and narrow black edges.
Metal: Silver.
Size: 36mm.
Description: (Obverse) a 'Digger' in the uniform of the First World War with the legend 80TH ANNIVERSARY ARMISTICE REMEMBRANCE MEDAL; (reverse) the words LEST WE FORGET in three lines within a wreath of ferns surmounted by a seven-pointed star. Fitted with a suspension bar with a Tudor crown on both sides.
Comments: *Awarded to all veterans of the First World War who were still alive on 11 November 1998, the 80th anniversary of the Armistice.*

VALUE: —

A39. NEW SOUTH WALES CORRECTIVE SERVICE BRAVERY MEDAL

Instituted: 1989.
Ribbon: Dark blue with a broad crimson central stripe.
Metal: Silver-gilt.
Description: A cross pattée with radiations in the angles and surmounted by a St. Edward's crown fitted to a ring for suspension. (Obverse) the arms of New South Wales within a circular band inscribed CORRECTIVE SERVICE N.S.W., with a scroll at the foot inscribed FOR BRAVERY; (reverse) plain.
Comments: *Awarded to prison officers for bravery.*

VALUE: —

A40. NEW SOUTH WALES CORRECTIVE SERVICE EXEMPLARY CONDUCT CROSS

Instituted: 1989.
Ribbon: Navy blue with a broad gold central stripe.
Metal: Silver.
Descrpiton: A seven-pointed star surmounted by a large St. Edward's crown fitted to a suspension ring. (Obverse) the arms of New South Wales within a circular band inscribed CORRECTIVE SERVICE N.S.W., with a scroll at the foot inscribed EXEMPLARY CONDUCT; (reverse) plain.
Comments: *Awarded to prison officers for exemplary conduct.*

VALUE: —

A41. NEW SOUTH WALES CORRECTIVE SERVICE MERITORIOUS SERVICE MEDAL

Instituted: 1989.
Ribbon: Red with a broad central gold stripe.
Metal: Bronze.
Size: 36mm.
Description: An elongated circle fitted with a suspension bar. (Obverse) the arms of New South Wales, with N.S.W. CORRECTIVE SERVICE at the top and LONG SERVICE at the foot; (reverse) FOR TWENTY YEARS SERVICE in four lines within a wreath.
Comments: *Awarded for 20 years service in the New South Wales prison service. Originally a bronze clasp for 30 years service was added after a further ten years, but this was replaced on 14 May 1999 by a bronze clasp for 25 years and silver clasps for 30, 35 and 40 years service.*

VALUE: —

A42. NEW SOUTH WALES CORRECTIVE SERVICE LONG SERVICE MEDAL

Instituted: 1989.
Ribbon: Navy blue with two silver stripes.
Metal: Bronze.
Size: 36mm.
Description: A circular medal fitted with a plain suspension bar. (Obverse) the crowned emblem of the Corrective Service with a wreath at the foot; (reverse) a laurel branch round the left side, with the words FOR FIFTEEN YEARS SERVICE in four lines on the right.
Comments: *Awarded for 15 years service in the New South Wales prison service.*

VALUE: —

A43. COMMISSIONER'S VALOUR AWARD

Instituted: 1987.
Ribbon: Light blue with narrow white stripes towards the edges and dark blue edges.
Metal: Silver.
Description: A cross pattée with a crowned and enamelled centrepiece bearing the insignia of the New South Wales Police Service within a wreath, inscribed FOR BRAVERY.
Comments: *Awarded to police officers where an act of conspicuous merit involving exceptional bravery is in evidence. It is very sparingly awarded, although eight awards were made in both 1993 and 1994.*

VALUE: —

A44. COMMISSIONER'S COMMENDATION FOR COURAGE

Instituted: 1970.
Ribbon: Light blue with a narrow central white stripe and narrow white edges.
Description: The insignia of the New South Wales Police Service affixed directly to the ribbon.
Comments: *Awarded to police officers where the risk to life has been less apparent, but where sufficient courage has been shown under hazardous circumstances to warrant the award. There is no restriction on the number of awards and about 90 are made annually.*

VALUE: —

A45. COMMISSIONER'S COMMENDATION FOR SERVICE

Instituted: 1970.
Ribbon: Light blue with narrow white edges.
Description: The insignia of the New South Wales Police Service affixed directly to the ribbon.
Comments: *Awarded to police officers for outstanding service. About ten commendations are awarded annually.*

VALUE: —

A46. COMMISSIONER'S UNIT CITATION

Instituted: 1994.
Description: A silver bar in the form of a wreath containing a light blue insert.
Comments: *Awaded to units, patrols, groups, squads and commands where outstanding service involving bravery or actions of obvious merit have been evident. The emblem is worn by each member of the unit, while the unit receives a framed citation for display. About five citations are awarded annually.*

VALUE: —

A47. QUEENSLAND PRISON SERVICE SUPERINDENDENT'S LONG SERVICE MEDAL

Instituted: Before 1988.
Ribbon: Dark blue with three narrow silver stripes.
Description: An eight-pointed Maltese cross superimposed on a wreath surmounted by a St. Edward's crown attached to a ring for suspension from a rectangular bar inscribed MERITORIOUS SERVICE. The top of the ribbon has a similar brooch bar with the recipient's details engraved on the reverse. The centre of the cross has the arms of Queensland.

VALUE: —

A48. QUEENSLAND PRISON SERVICE OFFICERS LONG SERVICE MEDAL

Instituted: Before 1988.
Ribbon: Silver with two narrow dark blue stripes.
Description: A circular medal fitted with a loop for suspension via a ring attached to an ornamental rectangular bar. The brooch bar at the top of the ribbon bears the recipient's personal details on the reverse. (Obverse) the crowned and wreathed insignia of the Queensland Prison Service with the inscription LONG AND MERITORIOUS SERVICE round the foot.

VALUE: —

A49. QUEENSLAND POLICE VALOUR AWARD

Instituted: 1993.
Ribbon: Maroon, light blue and dark blue in equal widths.
Metal: Silver.
Description: A Maltese cross superimposed on a wreath, with an enamelled centrepiece featuring the St. Edward's crown within a wreath and surrounded by the inscription QUEENSLAND POLICE VALOUR AWARD.
Comments: *This decoration is apparently similar to the Queensland Police Award which was discontinued in the 1930s.*

VALUE: —

A49A. HUMANITARIAN OVERSEAS SERVICE MEDAL

Instituted: 16 April 1999.
Ribbon: Green with a central gold stripe.
Metal: Nickel-silver.
Size: 38mm.
Description: A circular medal (obverse) a stylised eucalyptus tree surrounded by a ring of gum nuts; (reverse) a ring of gum nuts with the recipients details engraved in the centre.
Clasps: Somalia, Vietnam, Great Lakes, Cambodia, Balkans, East Timor, South Sudan.
Comments: *This medal is intended to be awarded to civilians who have provided outstanding humanitarian service overseas (although service personnel may be considered for the award in exceptional circumstances) and is believed to be the first medal of its kind. As most government employees will be eligible for the Australian Service medals, it is anticipated that this medal will be awarded to non-government employees or volunteers and as there is no time limit to the award it can be awarded retrospectively.*

VALUE: —

A49A. QUEENSLAND POLICE SERVICE MEDAL

Instituted: December 1998.
Ribbon: Blue with a broad central stripe of light blue and silver edges.
Metal: Silver.
Size: 36mm.
Description (Obverse) the state arms with the inscription DILIGENT AND ETHICAL SERVICE round the circumference; (reverse) QUEENSLAND POLICE SEVICE MEDAL round the circumference with the name of the recipient engraved in the centre.
Comments: Awarded to police officers after a minimum of 10 years service, but prospective candidates must demonstrate an unblemished record of diligence and ethical service. Clasps for further periods of service will be awarded.

VALUE: —

A50. AUSTRALIAN CADET FORCES SERVICE MEDAL

Instituted: December 1999.
Ribbon: Stripes of blue and gold with three outer stripes of navy, red and light blue.
Metal:
Description: (Obverse) the emblem of the Australian Cadet Force ensigned with St Edward's Crown; (reverse) the Commonwealth Star overlayed by a bar engraved with the recipient's name.
Comment: *Awarded to officers and instructors of cadets, for efficient long service of 15 years, with a additional clasp for each additional five years.*

VALUE: —

A51. EMERGENCY SERVICE MEDAL

Instituted: 1999.
Ribbon: Orange and white chequered pattern edged in blue.
Metal: Silver and bronze coloured metals.
Description: (Obverse) a triangular device containing a seven-pointed Commonwealth Star surrounded by 24 dots representing emergency services operating around the clock.
Comment: *Awarded for outstanding duty be members of the emergency services, including state organisations and voluntary emergency services, and to persons who render distinguished service relating to emergency management, training or education Only one award is made to any one person. Holders are entitled to the postnominal letters ESM.*

VALUE: —

A52. AMBULANCE SERVICE MEDAL

Instituted: 1999.
Ribbon: Chevrons of white, red and silver.
Metal: Silver and bronze.
Description: A circular medal featuring a Maltese cross, with the seven-pointed Commonwealth Star at the centre, surrounded by 24 dots symbolising a 24 hour service.
Comment: *Awarded for distinguished service by members of the civilian ambulance services. Only one award is made to any individual, entitled to the post-nominal letters ASM.*

VALUE: —

A53. AUSTRALIAN SPORTS MEDAL

Instituted: 2000.
Ribbon: Sand-coloured with four narrow black stripes towards the right side, of varying widths.
Metal: Silver.
Description: (Obverse) a stylised view of the Sydney Olympic Stadium with the Southern Cross constellation above; (reverse) the Olympic Stadium and inscription 'To commemorate Australian sporting achievement' and the date 2000.
Comments: *This medal was only awarded during the year of the Sydney Olympic Games and was intended to reward Australian sporting achievement. Both current and former sports men and women have been honoured, as well as coaches, sports scientists, officials, team managers and even those who maintain playing fields and sporting facilities.*

VALUE: —

A54. CENTENARY MEDAL

Instituted: January 2001.
Ribbon: Deep blue with a central yellow stripe bearing three thin red stripes.
Metal: Silver.
Size: 36mm.
Description: (Obverse) a seven-pointed star with a central band inscribed CENTENARY OF FEDERATION 1901 – 2001.
Comments: *Awarded to all Australian citizens who were born on or before December 31, 1901. About 3,000 centenarians received this medal. In the case of centenarians who died after January 1, 2001 posthumous awards were made to their next of kin. The medal was also conferred on 'a cross-section of the general community in recognition of their diverse contributions to Australia'.*

VALUE: —

A55. ANNIVERSARY OF NATIONAL SERVICE MEDAL

Instituted: April 2001.
Ribbon: White with a central gold stripe flanked by thin royal blue stripes, with bottle green, pale blue stripes and sand-coloured edges.
Metal: Gold-plated base metal.
Size: 36mm.
Description: (Obverse) the emblem of the armed forces surrounded by the text ANNIVERSARY OF NATIONAL SERVICE 1951-1972; (reverse) the sun radiating towards the Southern Cross constellation with a cogwheel surround. The medal is surmounted by a royal crown attached to a bar for suspension.
Comments: *All 325,800 National Servicemen, including the next-of-kin of the 187 who were killed on active service, are eligible for this medal.*

VALUE: —

A56. A.C.T. COMMUNITY POLICING MEDAL

Instituted:
Ribbon: White with a thin central strip and broad edges of dark blue, the central stripe flanked by two thin gold stripes.
Metal: Bronze.
Size: Upright oval 52 x 42mm.
Description: (Obverse) the arms of the Australian Capital Territory with the inscription A.C.T. COMMUNITY POLICING MEDAL round the top; (reverse) inscribed FOR DILIGENT SERVICE above a horizontal plaque for the name of the recipient. Fitted with a straight suspension bar.
Comments: *Awarded for service in the A.C.T. Police (Canberra).*

VALUE: —

A57. GROUP CITATION FOR BRAVERY

Instituted:
Ribbon: Pale blue encased in a rhodium-plated silver frame with a bronze waratah blossom in the centre.
Comments: *Awarded to members of a military formation for collective bravery in action.*

VALUE: —

Canadian
medals

Apart from such British campaign awards as the Louisburg Medal of 1758 (71), the Canada General Service Medal (125) awarded to those who helped to put down the Fenian Raids of 1866 and 1870 and the Red River rebellion of the latter year and the North West Canada Medal (134), distinctive medals relating to military service in Canada date from 1902 when Canadian versions of the Meritorious Service Medal (212) and Colonial Long Service and Good Conduct Medal (248) were instituted. Subsequently there were also Canadian versions of the Permanent Forces of the Empire Beyond the Seas Long Service and Good Conduct Medal (249) and the military Long Service and Good Conduct Medal (229). Similarly, both the Efficiency Decoration (236) and the Efficiency Medal (237) were issued with suspension bars denoting service in Canada. Distinctive versions of certain British medals, such as the Defence Medal (185), War Medal (186) and the Korea Medal (195), struck in silver instead of base metal, will also be found in the appropriate sections of this volume.

Several awards which were purely Canadian in character will also be found in earlier sections of this book, as they were authorised or instituted by the imperial government. Thus the Canadian Volunteer Service Medal (188), instituted to recognise volunteer service during World War II, comes under this category, as the various types of Canadian Memorial Cross (188A) awarded to the relatives of service personnel who gave their lives in both world wars and since the Korean War. Also included are awards by Newfoundland which did not enter the Confederation of Canada until 1949. For this reason Newfoundland servicemen were not eligible for the Canadian Volunteer Service Medal, and it was not until 1981 that this deficiency was remedied by the institution of a separate Newfoundland Volunteer War Service Medal (194).

The move towards purely Canadian medals, however, began to develop in the inter-war period, but the earliest awards were confined to the Royal Canadian Mounted Police and include a number of medals which were authorised by the various provinces. In 1967 Canada celebrated the centenary of confederation and the opportunity was then taken to institute the Order of Canada, with its associated Medal of Service and Medal of Courage, as well as the Centennial Medal. Five years later, Canada inaugurated a full range of honours and awards and over the intervening years this has been extended considerably.

THE ORDER OF PRECEDENCE IN CANADA

Victoria Cross (VC)
Cross of Valour (CV)
Companion of the Order of Canada (CC)
Officer of the Order of Canada (OC)
Member of the Order of Canada (CM)
Commander of the Order of Military Merit (CMM)
Commander of the Order of Merit of the Police Forces (COM)
Commander of the Royal Victorian Order (CVO)
Officer of the Order of Military Merit (OMM)
Officer of the Order of Merit of the Police Forces (OOM)
Lieutenant of the Royal Victorian Order (LVO)
Member of the Order of Military Merit (MMM)
Member of the Order of Merit of the Police Forces (MOM)
Member of the Royal Victorian Order (MVO)
The Most Venerable Order of the Hospital of St John of Jerusalem *(all grades)*
Order of Quebec (Ordre National du Québec) (GOQ, OQ, CQ) (in French only)
Saskatchewan Order of Merit (SOM)
Order of Ontario (OOnt)
Order of British Columbia (OBC)
Alberta Order of Excellence (AOE)
Order of Prince Edward Island (OPEI)
Order of Manitoba (OM)
Order of New Brunswick (ONB)
Order of Nova Scotia (ONS)
Star of Military Valour (SMV)
Star of Courage (SC)
Meritorious Service Cross (MSC)
Medal of Military Valour (MMV)
Medal of Bravery (MB)
Meritorious Service Medal (Civil or Military) (MSM)
Royal Victorian Medal (Gold, Silver & Bronze) (RVM)
Korea Medal
Canadian Volunteer Service Medal for Korea
Gulf and Kuwait Medal

Somalia Medal
South-West Asia Service Medal
General Campaign Star with Bars
General Service Medal with Bars
Special Service Medal with Bars
Canadian Peacekeeping Service Medal
United Nations' Medals
NATO Medals
International Commission and Organisation Medals
Canadian Centennial Medal, 1967
Queen Elizabeth II's Silver Jubilee Medal, 1977
125th Anniversary of the Confederation of Canada Medal, 1992
Queen Elizabeth II's Golden Jubilee Medal, 2002
Royal Canadian Mounted Police Long Service Medal
Canadian Forces Decoration (CD)
Police Exemplary Service Medal
Corrections Exemplary Service medal
Fire Services Exemplary Service Medal
Canadian Coast Guard Exemplary Service Medal
Emergency Medical Services Exemplary Service Medal
Queen's Medal for Champion Shot
Ontario Medal for Good Citizenship (OMC)
Ontario Medal for Police Bravery
Ontario Medal for Firefighters Bravery
Saskatchewan Volunteer Medal (SVM)
Ontario Provincial Police Long Service and Good Conduct Medal
Service Medal of the Most Venerable Order of the Hospital of St John of Jerusalem
Commissionaire Long Service Medal
Newfoundland and Labrador Bravery Award
Newfoundland and Labrador Volunteer Service Medal
British Columbia Fire Services Long Service and Bravery Medal
Commonwealth Orders, Decorations and Medals
Foreign Orders, Decorations and Medals

347

C1. VICTORIA CROSS (CANADA)

Date: 1 January 1993.
Ribbon: Crimson.
Metal: Bronze.
Size: 38mm.
Description: (Obverse) a cross pattée with raised edges having in the centre a lion standing on the royal crown partially circumscribed by a banner bearing the words PRO VALORE; (reverse) a circle containing the date of the action for which it was awarded. A straight suspender bar with a design of laurel leaves is used attached to the upper arm of the cross by a ring and "V" shaped lug.
Comments: *Available with effect from 1 January 1993 to members of the Canadian Forces or a member of an allied force serving with them for an act of supreme courage, self-sacrifice or devotion to duty in the face of an enemy. It is identical to the awards of the UK, Australia and New Zealand with the important exception of the inscription within the banner on the obverse. The two official languages of Canada (English and French) mitigated against the use of the English inscription FOR VALOUR as on the three other awards and the Latin translation PRO VALORE was chosen for the Canadian award. Recipients are entitled to use the post-nominals VC. None have been awarded yet.*

VALUE: —

C2. CROSS OF VALOUR

Date: 1 May 1972.
Ribbon: Light crimson—worn around the neck (men) or on a bow (women).
Metal: Gold and red enamel.
Size: 38mm.
Description: (Obverse) a cross with straight arms in red enamel edged in gold with a central medallion of a gold maple leaf on a red enamel ground encircled by a gold wreath of laurel; (reverse) the royal cypher (EIIR) surmounted by a crown on the upper arm with the words VALOUR VAILLANCE across the centre above the engraved name of the recipient and date of the incident.
Comments: *Awarded for acts of conspicuous courage in circumstances of extreme peril to Canadian citizens and foreign nationals for an act in Canada or elsewhere if the act is considered to be in the interest of Canada and merits recognition by the country. A second award is signified by a gold maple leaf worn on the larger of the two suspension rings. The first award was made on 20 May 1972. 19 have been awarded to this date. Recipients are entitled to use the post-nominals CV.*

VALUE: Rare   *Miniature*   £50–60

C3. ORDER OF CANADA
COMPANION (CC), OFFICER (OC), MEMBER (CM)

Date: 1 July 1967.

Ribbon: Red with a broad central stripe in white—a neck ribbon for the two higher levels (companion and officer) and a breast ribbon for members. In undress uniform a small maple leaf is worn on the ribbon in red (CC) gold (OC) or silver (CM).

Metal: Gold or silver with enamels.

Size: 57mm (companion), 47.5mm (officer) and 38mm (member).

Description: (Obverse) A white enamelled stylised snowflake of six points (hexagonal in shape) edged in gold or silver with a central medallion comprising a maple leaf in red enamel (CC), gold (OC) or silver (CM) on a white enamel field all surrounded by a red enamel outer band bearing the words DESIDERANTES MELIOREM PATRIAM (they desire a better country) in gold or silver. A St Edward crown in gold (CC and OC) or silver (CM) with red enamel is placed at the top of the central medallion on the upper point of the snowflake; (reverse) a small box in which is inscribed a serial number with the word CANADA above. The CC and OC are worn with neck ribbons, a ring suspender is used for the CM.

Comments: *Established to reward Canadian citizens who exemplify the highest qualities of citizenship which enrich the lives of their fellow citizens. Honorary membership is available to foreigners. There are three levels—Companion, Officer and Member—with the qualifying criteria differing for each. Appointments are made in July and December each year with a maximum of 15 (CC) companions, 64 (OC) officers and 136 (CM) members appointed each year. The maximum number of living companions at any one time will not exceed 165 although there is no limit to the number of officers and members. The Order initially had a single class—Companion—with the officer and member levels being introduced on 1 July 1972. Prior to this a Medal of Service was a part of the Order but it was discontinued in 1972 and all holders made officers of the Order of Canada. A Medal of Courage was also attached to the Order but was never awarded and discontinued on the introduction of the Bravery Decorations (CV, SC and MB).*

VALUE:				
	Companion (370)	£2,500–3,500		
	Officer (1592)	£1,500–2,000		
	Member (2815)	£1,000–1,500	*Miniature*	£50–60

C4. ORDER OF MILITARY MERIT
COMMANDER (CMM), OFFICER (OMM), MEMBER (MMM)

Date: 1 July 1972.

Ribbon: Blue with gold edges (4.8 mm) worn around the neck (commander) or on the breast (OMM and MMM).

Metal: Enamelled gold or silver.

Size: 38mm (OMM and MMM)

Description: (Obverse) a cross pattée with the arms in blue enamel edged with gold (CMM and OMM) or silver (MMM). A central medallion has a maple leaf at the centre in red (CMM), gold (OMM) or silver (MMM) on a gold or silver background surrounded by an outer band in red enamel inscribed with the words MERIT MÉRITE CANADA in the appropriate metal; (reverse) left plain apart from a serial number. A straight suspender bar with a laurel leaf design is used for officers (in gold) and members (in silver).

Comments: *Instituted to recognise conspicuous merit or exceptional service by all members of the Canadian armed forces. The total of all levels which can be awarded annually cannot exceed one-tenth of one per cent of the average number of personnel in the preceding year, currently it adds up to about 89 awards a year of which 6% are at the CMM level, 30% at the OMM level and 64% at the MMM level. There is no limit to the total number at any level. Commanders are most usually of the rank of brigadier-general/commodore and above, officers are majors to colonels and members all those of lower rank including NCOs and junior officers. Appointments are made in July and December each year. In undress uniform the level of the award is indicated by a blue cross worn on the ribbon with a maple leaf placed centrally in red, gold or silver. Prior to 1983 a maple leaf of the appropriate colour was worn alone.*

VALUE:				
	Commander (178)	£750–850		
	Officer (872)	£500–600		
	Member (2058)	£350–400	*Miniature*	£50–60

C5. ORDER OF MERIT OF THE POLICE FORCES

COMMANDER (COM), OFFICER (OOM), MEMBER (MOM)

Date: 2 October 2000.

Ribbon: Bands of blue, gold and blue, all of equal width. A neck ribbon is worn for the rank of commander and a breast ribbon for officers and members.

Metal: Gold, silver and enamels.

Size: 38mm (OOM and MOM).

Description: (Obverse) a cross pattée in dark blue enamel with a central medallion bearing a maple leaf and an outer band inscribed with the word MERIT (left) and MÉRITE (right) in the upper circumference and CANADA at the bottom. A St Edward's crown is on the upper arm of the cross. The maple leaf in the central medallion is red for commanders, gold for officers and silver for a member. The outer band is red with gold lettering for commanders and officers and red with silver lettering for members. A silver suspender bar with a laurel leaf pattern and three small sings is used for the MOM, the bar is gold for the OOM.

Comments: *The most recent addition to the awards available to police officers is a continuation of the series of Orders first established in 1967 with the introduction of the Order of Canada and continued in 1972 with the Order of Military Merit. The Order of Merit of the Police Forces ranks immediately after the Order of Military merit in the order of precedence. It was introduced to recognise the impact of the Police Service on society and honour those officers with careers of particular merit or who otherwise deserve formal recognition and is available in three classes—commander (COM), officer (OOM) and member (MOM). The first commander appointed to the Order was Commissioner Zaccardelli of the RCMP. In any one year there will be a maximum number of new appointees equivalent to one-tenth of one per cent of the number of police officers serving in Canada in the preceding year and is expected that they will number no more than 50. Officers from any police force in Canada are eligible although it is a living order and retired officers are not eligible, neither can it be awarded posthumously.*

VALUE:		
	Commander (10)	Rare
	Officer(34)	Rare
	Member (53)	Rare

C6. L'ORDRE NATIONAL DU QUÉBEC

GRAND OFFICIER (GOQ), OFFICIER (OQ), CHEVALIER (CQ)

Date: 20 June 1984.

Ribbon: Blue with a white central stripe, all of equal width. Worn around the neck (grand officier and officier) or on the breast (chevalier).

Metal: Gold (GOQ) or silver (OQ and CQ).

Size: —

Description: (Obverse) a Greek cross with very broad arms and the space between them so small that it is almost square. The upper left and lower right have an irregular highly polished area resulting in a very reflective quality with the space between the two in a matt finish giving the overall appearance of a river running between two land masses. In the bottom left corner, superimposed on the matt area is a fleur-de-lys. All the elements and ribbon colour are taken from the flag of Québec. The insignia for a chevalier has the cross mounted on a circular silver disc with a ring suspender.

Comments: *Membership of the Order is open to any citizen of Québec without distinction to recognise outstanding work in the Province for the benefit of all. Any person can nominate any other citizen for the award. Honorary membership is available to those not resident in Québec. An award ceremony takes place once a year although special arrangements can be made if the recipient does not reside in the Province. Recipients are entitled to use the post-nominals GOQ, OQ or CQ.*

VALUE:	£100–150

C7. SASKATCHEWAN ORDER OF MERIT

Date: 1985.
Ribbon: Dark green with a gold central stripe, all of equal width.
Metal: Enamelled gold.
Size: —
Description: (Obverse) a six-point star in white enamel edged in gold and with gold lines along the centre of each point. There is a central medallion in the shape of the shield from the Saskatchewan coat of arms in enamels (a lion above three sheaves of wheat) surmounted by a crown in gold. The neck ribbon is attached to the upper point of the star by a small suspender ring.
Comments: *Awarded to recognise individual excellence and outstanding achievement to the social, cultural and economic well-being of the Province and its people. A maximum of ten appointments can be made in any one year. Any resident, past or present of Saskatchewan is eligible for membership although members of parliament, legislative assembly and judges are barred whilst in office. Recipients are entitled to use the post-nominals SOM.*

VALUE: £70–80   *Miniature*   £45–50

C8. ORDER OF ONTARIO

Date: 18 December 1986.
Ribbon: Red with a central stripe in dark green flanked by a white stripe bisected by a thin gold line.
Metal: Enamelled gold.
Size: —
Description: (Obverse) a stylised version of the provincial flower (trillium) with three petals in white enamel superimposed on three dark green enamel sepals, all edged in gold. In the centre is the shield taken from the Ontario coat of arms in enamels surmounted by a crown in gold. A small ring suspender is used.
Comments: *Awarded to residents of Ontario who have shown excellence and achievement of the highest standard and whose contributions have enriched the lives of others and helped make a better society in Ontario. Recipients have the right to use the post-nominals O Ont. Elected officials at federal, provincial or municipal level are barred from membership of the Order whilst in office.*

VALUE: £70–80

C9. ORDER OF BRITISH COLUMBIA

Date: 12 April 1989.
Ribbon: Dark green with two stripes of white either side of a central dark green stripe each bisected by a thin gold line.
Metal: Gold and enamel.
Size: —
Description: (Obverse) a stylised representation of the six-petal provincial flower of British Columbia (pacific dogwood) in white and green enamels edged by gold. At the centre is the shield of the provincial coat of arms in enamels topped by a crown. A small ring suspender is used.
Comments: *Awarded in recognition of distinction and excellence in any field of endeavour for the benefit of people in British Columbia and elsewhere. Recipients are entitled to use the post-nominals OBC.*

VALUE: £70–80

C10. ALBERTA ORDER OF EXCELLENCE

Date: 16 November 1979.

Ribbon: The same design as the previous order but with the dark green replaced by dark blue.

Metal: Silver gilt and enamel.

Size: —

Description: (Obverse) a cross pattée with the arms in dark blue enamel edged with gold superimposed on a circular disc visible between the arms of the cross and decorated with a design of roses and rose leaves to represent the provincial flower. A central medallion has the full achievement of arms of Alberta on a red background within an outer band of white enamel bearing the words THE ALBERTA ORDER OF EXCELLENCE in gold; (reverse) a maple leaf and sheaf of wheat.

Comments: *Awarded in October each year to Canadian citizens living in Alberta from all walks of life who have performed excellent and distinctive works at provincial, national or international level. It is the highest award that can be bestowed by the Province of Alberta. An important provision is that the work will stand the test of time. Recipients are entitled to use the post-nominals AOE.*

VALUE: £70–80   *Miniature*   £45–50

C11. ORDER OF PRINCE EDWARD ISLAND MEDAL OF MERIT

Date: 1996.

Ribbon: A broad stripe of brown (left) and one of green (right) separated by a narrow white stripe and with a white line at each edge.

Metal: Enamelled gold.

Size: —

Description: (Obverse) circular with the shield from the provincial coat of arms in gold with red and white enamel on a background of gold enamel all within an outer band of blue enamel bearing the words MERIT (upper) and PRINCE EDWARD ISLAND (lower) in gold. A second version with the inscriptions in French is also available— MÉRITE (upper) and ÎLE-DU-PRINCE-EDOUARD. The ribbon, which is worn around the neck attached to the disc by two rings—one small, one large. A miniature is awarded for wear on less formal occasions— the design is the same but the ribbon is green with a central brown band, all of equal width, separated by white lines and with white edges.

Comments: *The Order is the highest that can be bestowed by the Province and given to any resident (present or former long-term) who contributes to the social, economic and cultural life of Prince Edward Island. Not more than three people can be admitted to the Order in any one year. In common with other provincial orders elected officials are not eligible whilst they remain in office. Recipients are entitled to use the post-nominals OPEI.*

VALUE: £80–100

C12. ORDER OF MANITOBA

Date: 14 July 1999.

Ribbon: White with a central stripe in red and a pale blue stripe towards each edge.

Metal: Enamelled gold.

Size: —

Description: (Obverse) a stylised representation of the provincial flower (crocus) with six petals in pale blue enamel edged in gold bearing the shield from the provincial coat of arms at the centre in enamels topped by a crown in gold.

Comments: *Established to recognise current or former long-term residents of Manitoba who have demonstrated excellence and achievement in any field leading to the social, economic or cultural well-being of the Province. A maximum of eight awards can be made in any one year although the initial investiture saw 20 people honoured. Members are entitled to the use of the post-nominals OM. Certain elected officials are not eligible whilst in office.*

VALUE: £70–80

C12A. ORDER OF NEW BRUNSWICK

Instituted: December 2000

Ribbon: Red with a central blue stripe flanked by yellow stripes. Worn as a neck ribbon.

Metal: Gold and enamels.

Description: (Obverse) a stylised purple violet, the provincial floral emblem, in enamels bordered with gold. In the centre is the provincial arms surmounted by a crown, the shield depicting an ancient gallery topped by a lion (an alusion to the arms of the Duchy of Brunswick, a possession of King George III in 1784 when New Brunswick was established). The ribbon is attached to the top of the crown between the two uppermost petals of the flower.

Comments: *Awarded to Canadian citizens who are present or long—term residents of New Brunswick and who have distinguished themselves in various fields (as above). A maximum of ten awards will be made each year. Recipients are entitled to the post—nominal letters ONB.*

VALUE: £80–90

C12B. ORDER OF NOVA SCOTIA

Instituted: 2001

Ribbon: Blue with a narrow central stripe of red flanked by white, a black line and a gold line, the colours of the provincial flag. Worn as a neck ribbon.

Metal: Gold and enamels.

Description: (Obverse) in the shape of a stylised mayflower, the provincial floral emblem, in white enamel edged with gold and with green enamel between each petal. In the centre is the provincial coat of arms (a blue Saltire cross surmounted by the Scottish lion in red and gold), all surmounted by a crown on the uppermost petal to which is affixed a thin red ring for suspension.

Comments: *Awarded to Canadian citizens who are present or long-term residents of Nova Scotia and who have distinguished themselves by outstanding achievement in a number of fields bringing honour and prestige to the Province. Certain public officials are not eligible while holding office. The award is available posthumously if the person is nominated within a year of death. Five appointments will be made each year after the inaugural year when there were ten recipients. Recipients are entitled to the post-nominal letters ONS.*

VALUE: £80–90

C13. STAR OF MILITARY VALOUR

Date: 1 January 1993.
Ribbon: Crimson with a white stripe towards each edge.
Metal: Gold with silver.
Size: 44mm
Description: (Obverse) a four-point star with a maple leaf between the points. A central medallion has a maple leaf placed centrally on a red background all surrounded by a circular wreath of laurel in silver; (reverse) the royal cypher (EIIR) surmounted by a crown with the inscription PRO VALORE. The rank and name of the recipient is engraved below the inscription. A suspension ring is attached to the upper point of the star.
Comments: *The second highest military valour decoration in Canada. It is awarded to any member of the Canadian Forces or allies serving with the Canadians for distinguished and valiant service in the presence of an enemy on or after January 1, 1993. Any second or subsequent award is indicated by a gold bar bearing a maple leaf in the centre. It can be awarded posthumously. Recipients are entitled to use the post-nominals SMV or ÉVM in French. None have been awarded to date.*

VALUE: —

C14. STAR OF COURAGE

Date: 1 May 1972.
Ribbon: Red with a stripe of blue towards each edge.
Metal: Silver with gold.
Size: 44mm
Description: (Obverse) identical to the Star of Military Valour but in silver with a gold wreath of laurel around the central medallion bearing a gold maple leaf in its center; (reverse) the royal cypher (EIIR) surmounted by a crown on the upper arm of the cross with the inscription COURAGE below. The name of the recipient and date of the act are engraved below.
Comments: *The second highest honour for courage awarded for acts of conspicuous courage in circumstance of great peril. It is available to Canadian citizens and foreign nationals for the performance of an act in Canada or elsewhere if the act is in the interest of Canada. The first award was made on 20 July 1972. Second or subsequent awards are indicated by a gold bar with a maple leaf at its centre. In common with most Canadian national honours the award is named in English and French but the initials of the two are not the same. The post-nominals are therefore different—SC (English) or ÉC (French "Étoile du Courage"). 396 have been awarded to date.*

VALUE: £350–400   *Miniature*   £45–50

C15. MERITORIOUS SERVICE CROSS (MILITARY AND CIVIL DIVISIONS)

Date: 11 June 1984 (military) and 6 June 1991 (civil).
Ribbon: Bright blue with a white stripe (6 mm) towards each edge. The civil division is indicated by the addition of a central white stripe (1 mm).
Metal: Silver.
Size: 38mm.
Description: (Obverse) a Greek cross with splayed ends with a wreath of laurel between the arms. A crown is attached to the upper arm of the cross to which is joined the plain straight suspender bar. A central medallion bears a maple leaf at its centre; (reverse) two concentric circles with the royal cypher (EIIR) in the centre and the words MERITORIOUS SERVICE MÉRITOIRE (separated at the bottom by a maple leaf) around the second of the two circles.
Comments: *The Cross was initially introduced for award to the military only but extended in 1991 to civilians and made retrospective to 1984. The criteria are similar for both divisions—a deed or activity performed in a highly professional manner or of a high standard bringing benefit or great honour to the Canadian armed forces (military) or Canada (civil). Second or subsequent awards are indicated by a silver bar with a maple leaf in its centre. Both awards are available to Canadians and foreign nationals. The name of the recipient is engraved at the back of the suspension bar and the date on the reverse of the top arm of the cross. Recipients are entitled to use the post-nominals MSC or CSM in French. 109 MSC's have been awarded to date (80 military, 29 civilian).*

VALUE: £125–150

C16. MEDAL OF MILITARY VALOUR

Date: 1 January 1993.
Ribbon: Crimson with white stripes in the centre and at each edge.
Metal: Gold.
Size: 36mm.
Description: (Obverse) circular with a maple leaf surrounded by a wreath of laurel tied at its base by a bow; (reverse) the royal cypher (EIIR) surmounted by a crown with the inscription PRO VALORE. The suspender bar is in the shape of a fleur-de-lys attached to the disc by a claw fitting. The rank and name of the recipient are engraved on the rim.
Comments: *Awarded to members of the Canadian Forces and allies serving with or in conjunction with the Canadians for an act of valour or devotion to duty in the presence of an enemy. A gold bar with a maple leaf at its centre is available for any second or subsequent award. It can be awarded posthumously. Recipients are entitled to use the post-nominals MMV or MVM in French. None have been awarded to date.*

VALUE: —

C17. MEDAL OF BRAVERY

Date: 1 May 1972.
Ribbon: Crimson with dark blue stripes in the centre and at each edge.
Metal: Silver.
Size: 36mm.
Description: (Obverse) identical to the previous award; (reverse) the royal cypher (EIIR) surmounted by a crown with the words BRAVERY (right) and BRAVOURE (left) at the circumference.
Comments: *Awarded to all Canadian citizens (civilian and military) and foreign nationals as defined for previous awards for acts of bravery in hazardous circumstances. It can be awarded posthumously. The first award was made on 20 July 1972. Bars are of silver with a maple leaf placed centrally. The name of the recipient is engraved on the rim. Recipients are entitled to use the post-nominals MB. 2,121 have been awarded to date.*

VALUE: £300–350   *Miniature* £45–50

C18. MERITORIOUS SERVICE MEDAL (MILITARY AND CIVIL DIVISIONS)

Date: 6 June,1991.
Ribbon: Bright blue with two white stripes towards each edge. The civil division is indicated by the addition of a central white stripe (1mm).
Metal: Silver.
Size: 36mm.
Description: (Obverse) a Greek cross with splayed ends with a wreath of laurel between the arms and a maple leaf in the central medallion all superimposed on a disc. A crown is attached to the upper arm of the cross to which is joined the ring suspender; (reverse) two concentric circles with the royal cypher (EIIR) in the centre and the words MERITORIOUS SERVICE MÉRITOIRE (separated at the bottom by a maple leaf) around the second of the two circles.
Comments: *The criteria are similar for both divisions—a deed or activity performed in a highly professional manner or of a high standard bringing benefit or honour to the Canadian armed forces (military) or Canada (civil). Second or subsequent awards are indicated by a silver bar with a maple leaf in its centre. Both awards are available to Canadians and foreign nationals and can be awarded posthumously. The name of the recipient is engraved on the rim and the date on the top part of the reverse. 357 MSM's have been awarded to date (146 mil, 211 civ). Recipients are entitled to the use of the post-nominals MSM.*

VALUE: £100–150

C19. CANADIAN VOLUNTEER SERVICE MEDAL FOR KOREA

Date: 12 July,1991
Ribbon: Yellow with a broad stripe in UN blue (7mm) at each edge and a central stripe of red, white and red (all 2mm).
Metal: Silver coloured copper and zinc alloy.
Size: 36mm.
Description: (Obverse) the crowned profile of Queen Elizabeth II with the word CANADA below and ELIZABETH II DEI GRATIA REGINA around the circumference; (reverse) a wreath of laurel tied at the base by a bow with a maple leaf above it. In the central field is the inscription KOREA/VOLUNTEER/1950–1954/VOLONTAIRE/COREE. A plain straight suspender was used.
Comments: *Awarded to former members of the Canadian armed forces who were in the qualifying area of Korea and adjacent areas between June 27, 1950 and July 27, 1954 with four further provisos. The recipients were eligible if they were on the strength of a unit in Korea for one day, were on active service aboard a ship for at least 28 days, flew one sortie over Korea or Korean waters or had accumulated at least 28 days service in the qualifying area. The medal could be awarded posthumously and 18,289 awards were made. Issued unnamed.*

VALUE: £60–80   *Miniature*   £30–35

C20. GULF AND KUWAIT MEDAL

Date: 3 June,1991.
Ribbon: A sand coloured central stripe (8mm) flanked by stripes of dark blue (5mm), red (2mm) and light blue (5mm) to represent the three branches of the armed forces.
Metal: Silver coloured copper and zinc alloy.
Size: 36mm.
Description: (Obverse) the crowned profile of Queen Elizabeth II with the word CANADA below and ELIZABETH II DEI GRATIA REGINA around the circumference; (reverse) a wreath of laurel tied at the base by a bow with a maple leaf above it. In the central field is the inscription THE GULF/AND KUWAIT/1990–1992/LE GOLFE/ET KUWAIT in five lines. A plain straight suspender was used.
Comments: *Awarded to all members of the Canadian armed forces who served in the theatre of operations between August 2, 1990 and June 27, 1991 for a minimum of 30 days cumulative service or who served during actual hostilities for at least one day between January 16 and March 30, 1991. The bar was awarded to all those who served during the hostilities for at least one day. The bar has a silver maple leaf at its centre. 4,436 medals were awarded, including 3,184 with bar. Issued unnamed*

VALUE: £60–80   *Miniature*   £30–35

C21. SOMALIA MEDAL

Date: 8 April, 1997

Ribbon: White with United Nations blue stripes (5 mm) at each edge and a central stripe of three colours (dark blue, red and light blue to represent the three armed services) flanked by stripes of a sand colour—all 2.5 mm wide).

Metal: Gold-plated bronze.

Size: 36mm.

Description: (Obverse) three over-lapping Canadian maple leaves above two branches of laurel and with the word CANADA above; (reverse) the royal cypher (EIIR) surmounted by a crown with the words SOMALIA (left) SOMALIE (right) and the dates 1992–93 (lower) around the circumference. A ring suspender was used.

Comments: *Available to any member of the Canadian armed forces or anyone attached to or working with them for a minimum of 90 days cumulative service in Somalia between November 16, 1992 and June 30, 1993. Anyone with a minimum of 60 days service who died, was evacuated or redeployed was also eligible. It was awarded posthumously. 1,408 were awarded, it was issued unnamed.*

VALUE: £60–70   *Miniature*   £30–35

C22. SOUTH-WEST ASIA SERVICE MEDAL

Date: 31 July, 2002

Ribbon: 32mm in width with a white stripe in the middle (12mm), on either side of which are stripes of black (4mm), red (2mm) and sand (4mm).

Metal: Nickel-plated red brass

Size: 36mm

Description: (Obverse) the Queen's effigy, wearing the King George IV State Diadem, facing right, circumscribed with the legend: ELIZABETH II • DEI GRATIA REGINA and at the base of the effigy, the word CANADA flanked by two small maple leaves; (reverse) a representation of the mythical figure of Hydra transfixed by a Canadian sword and over the design is the Latin phrase, ADVERSE MALUM PUGNAMUS - "We are fighting evil". A claw at the top of the medal, is in the form of a cluster of olive leaves representing peace is attavhed to a straight suspension bar.

Comments: *Awarded to Canadian Forces members deployed with, or in direct support of the operations against terrorism in South-West Asia. The medal with the AFGHANISTAN bar is awarded for 30 days cumulative service after 11 September, 2001 in the theatre of operations of South-West Asia while it is awarded without the bar for a minimum of 90 days cumulative service in direct support of these operations such as service with the Headquarters, Canadian Joint Task Force South-West Asia in Tampa Bay, Florida; the Stragtegic Airlift Detachment in Ramstein, Germany and other similar tasks. The medal is issued unnamed. Over 7,497 medals and 7,200 bars have been issued to date.*

*V*ALUE: —   *Miniature*   £30–35

C23. GENERAL CAMPAIGN STAR

Date: March 24 ,2004

Ribbon: 32mm in width with a green central stripe of 12mm on either side of which are stripes of white (2mm) and red (8mm).

Metal: Gold-plated bronze.

Size: 44mm.

Description: a four pointed star bearing (Obverse) a wreath of maple leaves open at the top to include the Royal Crown, two crossed swords, the blades and hilts forming four additional points to the Star, an anchor and a flying eagle; (reverse) within a raised circle, the Royal Cypher ensigned by the Royal Crown, a plain space for engraving and three maple leaves on one stem. A ring is fitted to a small ball at the tip of the top point of the Star. Recipient's details are engraved on the reverse of the Star.

Comments: *Awarded to Canadian Forces members who deploy into a specific theatre of operations to take part in operations in the presence of an armed enemy. The Star is always awarded with bars to specify the operation being recognised, each bar having its own criteria. This award will be available for distribution for fall 2004.*

Bars: ALLIED FORCE: Created June 17, 2004 and awarded to fighter pilots and AWACS crew members who took part in at least five missions in the theatre of operations during the air campaign in Kosovo between March 24 and June 10, 1999.

ISAF + FIAS: Created June 17, 2004 and awarded for 30 days of service in Afghanistan as part of the Canadian contribution to the International Security and Assistance Force since April 24, 2003.

VALUE: —

C24. GENERAL SERVICE MEDAL

Date: March 24, 2004

Ribbon: 32mm in width with a red central stripe of 18mm on either side of which are stripes of white (2mm) and green (5mm).

Metal: Cupro-nickel.

Size: 36mm.

Description: (Obverse) a contemporary crowned effigy of The Queen circumscribed by the inscriptions "ELIZABETH II DEI GRATIA REGINA" and "CANADA" seperated by small crosses patée; (reverse) two crossed swords, an anchor and a flying eagle surmounted by the Royal Crown and surrounded by two branches of maple leaves. The straight suspension bar is ornamented with 3 overlapping maple leaves. Recipient's details are engraved on the rim.

Comments: *Awarded to Canadian Forces members and Canadian civilians who deploy outside Canada but not necessarily into a defined theatre of operations, to provide direct support, on a full-time basis, to operations conducted in the presence of an armed enemy. The Medal is always awarded with bars to specify the operation being recognised, each bar having its own criteria. This award will be available for distribution for fall 2004.*

Bars: ALLIED FORCE: Created June 17, 2004 and awarded to personnel who served at least 30 days in Aviano and/or Vicenza, Italy in direct support of the air campaign in Kosovo between March 24 and June 10, 1999.

ISAF + FIAS: Created June 17, 2004 and awarded for 90 days of service in locations outside Afghanistan such as Camp Mirage and Turkey, in direct support of the Canadian contribution to the International Security and Assistance Force since the spring of 2003 (start dates vary depending on location).

VALUE: —

C25. SPECIAL SERVICE MEDAL

Date: 16 June, 1984.

Ribbon: A dark green central stripe (12mm) flanked by stripes of white (5mm) and red (5mm) at the edges.

Metal: Nickel-plated copper

Size: 36mm.

Description: (Obverse) A wreath of laurel tied at the base by a bow with a maple leaf in the central field; (reverse) the Royal cypher (EIIR) surmounted by the Royal Crown with the words SPÉCIAL SERVICE SPÉCIAL around the circumference. A plain straight suspender bar is used. The Medal is issued unnamed.

Comments: *Awarded to members of the Canadian Forces for service performed under exceptional circumstances, in a clearly defined locality for a specific duration. The medal is always issued with a bar, each having its own criteria.*

Bars: PAKISTAN 1989-90: Created 6 June, 1991 for 90 days of service with the Mine Awareness and Clearance Training Program in Pakistan from 15 March, 1989 to 29 July, 1990. 50 were awarded on 27 January, 1992. Recipients can now exchange this award for the United Nations Special Service Medal.

PEACE - PAIX: Created 26 November, 1992 for 180 days of service in approved peacekeeping operations since November 1947. This bar was superseded by the Canadian Peacekeeping Service Medal on 21 June 2001. 2267 Peace Bars have been issued.

ALERT: Created 26 November, 1992 for 180 days of service at Canadian Forces Station Alert since 1 September 1958. 7113 issued.

NATO + OTAN: Created 26 November, 1992 for 180 days service with NATO since 1 January 1951 (some restrictions apply). 62,341 issued.

HUMANITAS: Created 9 March, 1993 for 30 days of service on approved humanitarian operations since 11 June, 1984. 674 issued.

JUGOSLAVIJA: Created 9 March, 1993 for 90 days of service with the European Community Monitor Mission in Yugoslavia (ECMMY) from 4 September, 1991. This bar was cancelled and replaced by the ECMMY Medal (206B).

RANGER: Created 1 October, 1999 for 4 years service with the Canadian Rangers including completion of 3 sovereignty patrols in remote and isolated regions of Canada since 1947. To date, more than 2,411 Ranger bars have been issued.

VALUE: £10–15   *Miniature*   £30–35

C26. CANADIAN PEACEKEEPING SERVICE MEDAL

Date: 25 April 1997.

Ribbon: A light blue central stripe flanked by equal stripes of white, red and green.

Metal: Antique Silvered Copper

Size: 36mm.

Description: (Obverse) a depiction of three Canadian peacekeepers taken from the National Peacekeeping Monument in Ottawa. One figure is an unarmed UN military observer holding a pair of binoculars, another a kneeling female figure shouldering a radio and the third a guard with a rifle. The words PEACEKEEPING (upper) and SERVICE DE LA PAIX (lower) lie at the circumference; (reverse) a maple leaf with the royal cypher (EIIR) topped by a crown in the centre with a branch of laurel on either side and the word CANADA below. The plain straight suspender bar is attached by a maple leaf.

Comments: *Inspired by the award in 1988 of the Nobel Peace Prize to all UN peacekeepers. Awarded to Canadian citizens for a minimum of 30 days service on a peacekeeping or observing mission since 14 November, 1947. Military personnel, police officers and civilians are eligible. Recipients are also entitled to wear any UN, NATO or other international medal issued. 70,218 have been awarded to date, it is issued unnamed.*

VALUE: £35–40   *Miniature*   £25–30

C27. CANADIAN CENTENNIAL MEDAL

Date: 1 July 1967.
Ribbon: White with four red stripes (1mm) equally spaced and red stripes (5mm) at the edges.
Metal: Silver.
Size: 36mm.
Description: (Obverse) the Canadian maple leaf superimposed by the royal cypher (EIIR) surmounted by a crown and the words CONFEDERATION (left) CANADA (upper) and CONFÉDÉRATION (right) around the circumference; (reverse) the full achievement of arms of Canada above the dates 1867–1967. A plain suspender in a wide, shallow triangular shape was used.
Comments: *Awarded in celebration of the centenary of Canadian confederation to those recommended by national and provincial governments and a variety of other bodies and associations. Approximately 29,500 medals were awarded, including 8,500 to the military.*

VALUE: £60–80   *Miniature*   £25–30

C28. QUEEN ELIZABETH II'S SILVER JUBILEE MEDAL (Canada)

Date: 6 February 1977.
Ribbon: White with thin red stripes at the edges, a broad blue stripe in the centre and a thin red stripe down the middle of it.
Metal: Silver
Size: 32mm
Description: (Obverse) Right-facing profile of Queen Elizabeth II wearing the St Edward's crown–the first time this design was employed; (reverse) a large stylised maple leaf with 'CANADA' around the top of the rim and, around the bottom of the rim, the Royal Cypher EIIR surmounted by the Crown and the dates 1952 and 1977 on each side in small lettering.
Comments: *Awarded to Canadians who have made a significant contribution to their fellow citizens, their community or to Canada on the occasion of the 25th anniversary of Her Majesty's Accession to the Throne as Queen of Canada. The recipients were selected by a number of partner organisations in every field of Canadian Life. Approximately 30,000 medals were awarded including 7,000 to the military.*

VALUE: £90–120   *Miniature*   £25–30

C29. 125th ANNIVERSARY OF THE CONFEDERATION OF CANADA MEDAL

Date: 7 May 1992.
Ribbon: White with five red stripes (1mm) equally spaced and blue stripes (4.5mm) at the edges.
Metal: Rhodium plated copper and zinc alloy.
Size: 36mm.
Description: (Obverse) the Canadian maple leaf superimposed by the royal cypher (EIIR) surmounted by a crown and the words CONFEDERATION (left) and CONFÉDÉRATION (right) and the dates 1867–1992 (lower) around the circumference; (reverse) the shield taken from the Canadian coat of arms within a belt bearing the words DESIDERANTES MELIOREM PATRIAM and surmounted by a lion. The legend A MARI USQUE AD MARE is inscribed around the lower circumference half. A plain straight suspender is used.
Comments: *Awarded to Canadian citizens who had made a significant contribution to Canada, their community or their fellow citizens in celebration of the 125th anniversary of federation. Approximately 44,000 were awarded, including 4,000 to the military.*

VALUE: £45–50   *Miniature*   £35–40

C30. CANADIAN FORCES DECORATION

Instituted: 15 December 1949.
Branch of Service: Canadian Forces.
Ribbon: 38mm orange-red divided into four equal parts by three thin white stripes.
Metal: Silver-gilt (George VI) or gilded tombac brass (Elizabeth II).
Size: Height 35mm; max. width 37mm.
Description: A decagonal (ten-sided) medal. The George VI issue has a suspension bar inscribed CANADA and the recipient's details engraved on the reverse, whereas the Elizabethan issue has no suspension bar, the recipient's details being impressed or engraved on the rim and the word "CANADA" appears at the base of the effigy. The reverse has a naval crown at the top, three maple leaves across the middle and an eagle in flight across the foot. In the George VI version the royal cypher is superimposed on the maple leaves.
Comments: *Awarded to both officers and men of the Canadian regular and reserve forces for 12 years exemplary service, with a bar. A bar, gold in colour, bearing the shield from the arms of Canada surmounted by the crown is awarded for each additional 10 years of qualifying service.*

VALUE:			*Miniature*
George VI (E)	£50–60		£10–20
Elizabeth II (D)	£30–40		£10–20

C31. QUEEN ELIZABETH II'S GOLDEN JUBILEE MEDAL (Canada)

Date: 23 February 2002.
Ribbon: 33mm in width with two outer stripes of 2mm of red, followed by 10mm stripes of royal blue, 3mm stripes of white and a central 2mm stripe of red.
Metal: Gold-plated bronze
Size: 32mm
Description: (Obverse) the current Canadian coinage effigy of the Queen circumscribed by the legend "QUEEN OF CANADA - REINE DU CANADA" ; (reverse) the Royal Crown above a stylized maple leaf bearing the Royal Cypher with *CANADA* at the bottom and the years 1952 and 2002 on the left and right. There is a small ring at the top of the medal, through which passes a larger ring to accommodate the ribbon which is the same as for the British Golden Jubilee Medal.
Comments: *Awarded to Canadians who have made a significant contribution to their fellow citizens, their community or to Canada on the occasion of the 50th anniversary of Her Majesty's Accession to the throne as Queen of Canada. The recipients were selected by a number of partner organisations in every field of Canada Life. Approximately 46,000 medals were awarded including approximately 9,000 to the military. The Canadian Forces awarded its 9,000 medals proportionally through its ranks according to an automatic formula based on the component, service, rank, trade and length of service of every member of the Canadian Forces.*

VALUE: £75–100   *Miniature* £45–50

C32. ROYAL CANADIAN MOUNTED POLICE LONG SERVICE MEDAL

Date: 6 March 1934.

Ribbon: Dark blue with two yellow stripes towards the edges.

Metal: Silver.

Size: 36mm.

Description: (Obverse) the effigy of the reigning monarch; (reverse) the insignia of the RCMP consisting of the head of a buffalo within a buckled belt inscribed with the words MAINTENEZ LE DROIT all topped by a crown. On either side of the belt are five maple leaves. The name of the Force is contained in a banner below the belt. The words FOR LONG SERVICE (above) and AND GOOD CONDUCT (below) are inscribed around the circumference. A plain straight suspender is attached by a claw fitting.

Comments: *RCMP: Awarded for 20 years of service in the RCMP. Different bars exist to denote subsequent periods of service (bronze with one star for 25 years, silver with 2 stars for 30 years, gold with 3 stars for 35 years and gold and silver with 4 stars for 40 years), only the last bar awarded is worn. When Queen Elizabeth came to the throne and the medal was redesigned to display her effigy on the obverse, changes were also made to the reverse to substitute the Queen's crown for the King's that had been used from the medal's introduction. The opportunity was also taken to reduce the size of the insignia of the RCMP and move the inscription to read continuously around the circumference. In 1989 a French language version of this new design was introduced with the inscription on the reverse reading POUR ANCIENNETÉ ET BONNE CONDUITE. The recipients have the right to choose which version they would prefer. The name of the recipient is engraved on the rim. Approximately 75 Medals and close to 1,000 various bars are issued evry year.*

VALUE:

George V (C)	£500–600	
George V (E)	£500–600	
George VI (B)	£450–500	
George VI (C)	£450–500	
Elizabeth II (A)	£250–300	
Elizabeth II (French)	£500–600	*Miniature* (all) £45–50

C33. POLICE EXEMPLARY SERVICE MEDAL

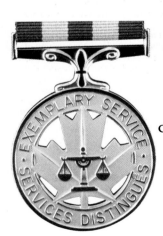

Date: 12 August 1982.

Ribbon: Five equal stripes of dark blue (three) and yellow (two).

Metal: Silver.

Size: 36mm.

Description: (Obverse) a circular medal with a maple leaf in the centre bearing a representation of the scales of justice and an outer band with the words EXEMPLARY SERVICE in the upper half and SERVICES DISTINGUÉS in the lower. It is of a skeletal design with the outer band attached to the leaves and stem of the maple leaf; (reverse) plain apart from the royal cypher (EIIR) topped by the Queen's crown in the centre of the maple leaf.

Comments: *Awarded on completion of 20 years' service to officers of any recognised Canadian police force who showed industry, efficiency and good conduct during their careers. Although members of the RCMP or Canadian Military Police are not eligible, any full-time service in either of those bodies can be counted towards the necessary number of years' service. Bars (bearing a stylised maple leaf) are available for additional periods of ten years. The medal is not a purely long service award and will be withheld if an officer with the required number of years' service does not meet the appropriate standards of behaviour necessary. It can be awarded posthumously. The name of the recipient is engraved on the rim. 32,835 have been issued to date.*

VALUE: £40–45   *Miniature* £40–45

C34. CORRECTIONS EXEMPLARY SERVICE MEDAL

Date: 11 June 1984.

Ribbon: Five equal stripes of green (three) and yellow (two).

Metal: Silver.

Size: 36mm.

Description: (Obverse) a circular medal with a maple leaf in the centre bearing a crossed key and torch and an outer band with the words EXEMPLARY SERVICE in the upper half and SERVICES DISTINGUÉS in the lower. It is of a skeletal design with the outer band attached to the leaves and stem of the maple leaf; (reverse) plain apart from the royal cypher (EIIR) topped by the Queen's crown in the centre of the maple leaf.

Comments: *Awarded on completion of 20 years' full-time paid service to officers of the Canadian Correctional Service (federal, provincial or territorial) who showed industry, efficiency and good conduct during their careers. The service need not have been continuous. Bars (bearing a stylised maple leaf) are available for additional periods of ten years. The medal is not a purely long service award and will be withheld if an officer with the required number of years' service does not meet the appropriate standards of behaviour necessary. It can be awarded posthumously. The name of the recipient is engraved on the rim. 7,602 have been issued to date.*

VALUE: £40–45

C35. FIRE SERVICES EXEMPLARY SERVICE MEDAL

Date: 25 August 1985.

Ribbon: Five equal stripes of red (three) and yellow (two).

Metal: Silver.

Size: 36mm.

Description: (Obverse) a circular medal with a maple leaf in the centre bearing a pair of crossed axes and fire hydrant within an outer band with the words EXEMPLARY SERVICE in the upper half and SERVICES DISTINGUÉS in the lower. It is of a skeletal design with the outer band attached to the leaves and stem of the maple leaf; (reverse) plain apart from the royal cypher (EIIR) topped by the Queen's crown in the centre of the maple leaf.

Comments: *Awarded on completion of 20 years' service with a recognised Canadian fire service (including fire marshal's offices, fire commissioner's offices and the Canadian Armed Forces Fire Service) to officers showed industry, efficiency and good conduct during their careers. The service need not have been continuous. Bars (bearing a stylised maple leaf) are available for additional periods of ten years. The medal is not a purely long service award and will be withheld if an officer with the required number of years' service does not meet the appropriate standards of behaviour necessary. It can be awarded posthumously. The name of the recipient is engraved on the rim.37,857 have been issued to date.*

VALUE: £40–45   *Miniature*   £40–45

C36. CANADIAN COAST GUARD EXEMPLARY SERVICE MEDAL

Date: 14 March 1991.

Ribbon: Dark blue with a narrow white stripe in the centre and a broader yellow stripe towards each edge.

Metal: Silver.

Size: 36mm.

Description: (Obverse) a solid circular medal with the crest of the Canadian Coast Guard in the centre and an outer band bearing the inscriptions EXEMPLARY SERVICE (left) and SERVICES DISTINGUÉS (right); (reverse) plain apart from the royal cypher (EIIR) topped by the Queen's crown in the centre of the maple leaf.

Comments: *Awarded on completion of 20 years' service with the Department of Transport which must include 10 years with the Canadian Coast Guard in duties with a potential risk. Officers must have shown industry, efficiency and good conduct during their careers. The service need not have been continuous. Bars (bearing a stylised maple leaf) are available for additional periods of ten years, five of which must have involved duties where there was a potential risk of danger. The medal is not a purely long service award and will be withheld if an officer with the required number of years' service does not meet the appropriate standards of behaviour necessary. It can be awarded posthumously. The name of the recipient is engraved on the rim. 278 have been issued to date.*

VALUE: £50–55

C37. EMERGENCY MEDICAL SERVICES EXEMPLARY SERVICE MEDAL

Date: 7 July 1994.

Ribbon: Gold with three stripes of black all equally spaced and with a stripe of orange (2.3mm) bisecting each of the three black stripes.

Metal: Silver.

Size: 36mm.

Description: (Obverse) a circular medal with a maple leaf in the centre bearing the star of life, staff and serpent within an outer band with the words EXEMPLARY SERVICE in the upper half and SERVICES DISTINGUÉS in the lower. It is of a skeletal design with the outer band attached to the leaves and stem of the maple leaf; (reverse) plain apart from the royal cypher (EIIR) topped by the Queen's crown in the centre of the maple leaf.

Comments: *Awarded on completion of 20 years' service in the field of pre-hospital emergency medical care. Ten of these years must have involved duties involving a potential risk. Recipients must have shown industry, efficiency and good conduct during their careers. The service need not have been continuous. Bars (bearing a stylised maple leaf) are available for additional periods of ten years. The medal is not a purely long service award and will be withheld if an officer with the required number of years' service does not meet the appropriate standards of behaviour necessary. It can be awarded posthumously. The name of the recipient is engraved on the rim. 746 have been issued to date.*

VALUE: £50–55

C38. QUEEN'S MEDAL FOR CHAMPION SHOT IN CANADA

Date: 28 August 1991.
Ribbon: Dark crimson with stripes of black, white and black (each 3mm) at the edges.
Metal: Silver.
Size: 38mm.
Description: (Obverse) the crowned head of Queen Elizabeth II with the inscription ELIZABETH II DEI GRATIA REGINA around the circumference and CANADA at the bottom; (reverse) the figure of Fame on the right rising from her throne and crowning a warrior with a laurel wreath. The warrior holds a bow and quiver of arrows in his right hand and has a target with three arrows in the centre resting on his left knee. Until 2002, a plain straight suspender was used attached by a claw fitting, since then it is a straight suspender ornemented with a fleur-de-lis. The date of the award is showed on a plain silver clasp. Any subsequent award of the medal is indicated by a clasp only.
Comments: *There are two medals awarded each year, one to the regular member of the Canadian armed forces and another to the officer of the Royal Canadian Mounted Police who obtains the highest aggregate score in the two stages of the Queen's Medal Competition. The name of the recipient is engraved on the rim.*

VALUE:

Victoria bronze	Rare
Victoria silver	Rare
George V	£700–800
George VI	£700–800
Elizabeth II	£700–800

C39. ONTARIO MEDAL FOR GOOD CITIZENSHIP

Date: 1973.
Ribbon: White with a central stripe in gold and a broad green stripe at the edges.
Metal: Silver.
Size: 36mm.
Description: (Obverse) circular with the full achievement of arms of Ontario in the lower two-thirds and the inscription FOR GOOD CITIZENSHIP at the upper circumference; (reverse) the provincial flower—a trillium. A scrolled suspender bar is used attached to the top of the disc.
Comments: *Awarded to any citizen of Ontario to recognise good citizenship displayed by their generous, kind or self-effacing manner in improving the quality of life in the Province. It is not awarded posthumously or for acts of courage. A maximum of twelve medals are presented each year. Recipients can use post-nominals OMC.*

VALUE: £25–30

C40. ONTARIO MEDAL FOR POLICE BRAVERY

Date: 1975.
Ribbon: Royal blue with two gold stripes towards the edges.
Metal: Gold plated sterling silver with blue and white enamel.
Size: 57mm wide by 68mm high (with crown).
Description: (Obverse) a cross in blue enamel on gold with the provincial flower (white trillium) in white in a small central medallion and a maple leaf between the arms of the cross. A Queen's crown tops the upper arm; (reverse) left plain.
Comments: *Awarded to officers from any police force in the province to reward any act of superlative courage and bravery performed in the line of duty and is also intended to encourage the virtue of bravery and focus attention and support of the public behind the efforts of the police forces. The medals are presented at a special ceremony held in early November each year.*

VALUE: £100–125

C41. ONTARIO MEDAL FOR FIREFIGHTERS BRAVERY

Date: 1976.
Ribbon: Red with two gold stripes towards the edges.
Metal: Gold plated sterling silver with red and white enamel.
Size: 57mm wide by 68mm high (with crown).
Description: (Obverse) a cross in gold with a pattern on each arm in red enamel to symbolise fire and a maple leaf between the arms. The provincial flower (white trillium) in white enamel lies in a small central medallion. A Queen's crown tops the upper arm; (reverse) left plain.
Comments: *Awarded to firefighters in the Province to reward any act of superlative courage and bravery performed in the line of duty and is also intended to encourage the virtue of bravery and focus attention and support of the public behind the efforts of the firefighters. The medals are presented at a special ceremony held on 9 November each year. The medal can be awarded posthumously.*

VALUE: £100–125

C42. SASKATCHEWAN VOLUNTEER MEDAL

Date: —
Ribbon: Green with a gold central stripe, all of equal width.
Metal: Silver and enamel.
Size: 36mm.
Description: (Obverse) a circular silver medal with the shield from the Saskatchewan coat of arms surmounted by a crown placed in the centre. The name of the Province lies along the lower circumference and the inscription NOS IPSOS DEDIMUS (we give of ourselves) at the upper edge. The plain straight suspender bar is attached by a stylised letter "V".
Comments: *Awarded each year to a maximum of ten current or former long-term residents of Saskatchewan who have served in a voluntary capacity above and beyond the call of duty to improved daily life in the Province. Elected officials and members of the judiciary are barred from receiving the award whilst they remain in office. Recipients can use post-nominals SVM.*

VALUE: £25–30

C43. ONTARIO PROVINCIAL POLICE LONG SERVICE AND GOOD CONDUCT MEDAL

Date: 15 December 1949.

Ribbon: Crimson with two green stripes each bordered by white lines on both sides.

Metal: Silver.

Size: 38mm.

Description: (Obverse) the Coat of Arms of the Province of Ontario with the word ONTARIO written below; (reverse) the inscription ONTARIO PROVINCIAL POLICE in three lines in the central field and FOR LONG SERVICE AND GOOD CONDUCT around the circumference and two crossed maple leaves in the exergue. An ornate, non-swivelling, suspender was attached to the top of the medal.

Comments: *Ontario is one of only two provincial police forces that remain in Canada. The medal was awarded to members of the Force who had served for not less than 20 years, the last ten of which must have been with good conduct and satisfactory service. Bars were awarded for each additional period of five years' qualifying service. For 25 and 30 years' service a plain silver bar decorated with one or two white trilliums (the provincial flower) was awarded and for 35 or 40 years qualifying service gold bars were issued also bearing one or two trillium motifs.*

VALUE: £30–35

C44. COMMISSIONAIRES LONG SERVICE MEDAL

Date: August 20, 1948.

Ribbon: 32mm in width with a broad centre stripe of crimson on each side of which are stripes of white and navy blue.

Metal: Nickel-plated copper

Size: 36mm.

Description: (Obverse) within a buckled belt inscribed with the words VIRTUTE ET INDUSTRIA are superimposed on a natural maple leaf a crossed sword and anchor and a flying eagle; (reverse) the inscription THE CANADIAN CORPS OF COMMISSIONAIRES - LE CORPS CANADIEN DES COMMISSIONNARES surrounding a plain field. The medal is attached to a suspension bar bearing the inscription LABOR OMNIA VINCIT by three small rings.

Comments: *Initially awarded in bronze for 10 years but now only awarded in silver for 12 years of service in the Canadian Corps of Commissionaires. Bars are awarded for subsequent periods of 5 years of service, a maximum of 3 bars may be awarded to an individual.*

VALUE: £20–30

THE ORDER OF PRECEDENCE IN NEW ZEALAND
(including British Awards)

Victoria Cross
George Cross
Order of the Garter
Knights Grand Cross, The Most Honourable Order of the Bath
Order of Merit
New Zealand Cross
Baronet's Badge
Knights Grand Cross, The Most Distinguished Order of St Michael and St George (GCMG)
Knights Grand Cross, The Royal Victorian Order
Knights Grand Cross, The Most Excellent Order of the British Empire
Order of Companions of Honour
Order of New Zealand
Knight Commander, The Most Honourable Order of the Bath
Knight Commander, The Most Distinguished Order of St Michael and St George
Knight Commander, The Royal Victorian Order
Knight Commander, The Most Excellent Order of the British Empire
Knight Bachelors badge
Companion, The Most Honourable Order of the Bath
Companion, The Most Distinguished Order of St Michael and St George
Commander, The Royal Victorian Order
Commander, The Most Excellent Order of the British Empire
Distinguished Service Order
Lieutenant, The Royal Victorian Order
Officer, The Most Excellent Order of the British Empire
Queen's Service Order
Imperial Service Order
Member, The Royal Victorian Order
Member, The Most Excellent Order of the British Empire
Royal Red Cross (Member)
Distinguished Service Cross
Military Cross
Distinguished Flying Cross
Air Force Cross
Royal Red Cross (Associate)
Order of St John (All classes)
Albert Medal
Distinguished Conduct Medal
Conspicuous Gallantry Medal
George Medal
Queen's Police Medal for Gallantry
Distinguished Service Medal
Military Medal
Distinguished Flying Medal

Air Force Medal
Empire Gallantry Medal
Queen's Gallantry Medal
Royal Victorian Medals
Queen's Service Medal
British Empire Medal
Queen's Police Medal for Distinguished Service
Queen's Fire Service Medal for Distinguished Service
War Medals in order of campaign
New Zealand Operational Service Medal
New Zealand General Service Medal
Polar Medal
Imperial Service Medal
Coronation and Jubilee Medals in date order
New Zealand 1990 Commemoration Medal
New Zealand Suffrage Centennial Medal 1993
New Zealand Meritorious Service Medal
New Zealand Armed Forces Award
New Zealand Army Long Service and Good Conduct Medal
Royal New Zealand Navy Long Service and Good Conduct Medal
Royal New Zealand Air Force Long Service and Good Conduct Medal
New Zealand Police Long Service and Good Conduct Medal
New Zealand Fire Brigades Long Service and Good Conduct Medal
New Zealand Prison Service Medal
New Zealand Traffic Service Medal
Colonial Auxiliary Forces Decoration
Colonial Auxiliary Forces Long Service Medal
New Zealand Efficiency Decoration
New Zealand Efficiency Medal
Royal New Zealand Naval Volunteer Reserve Decoration
Royal Naval Reserve Decoration
Royal New Zealand Naval Volunteer Reserve Long Service and Good Conduct Medal
Royal Naval Reserve Long Service and Good Conduct Medal
Air Efficiency Award
Queen's Medal for Champion Shots of the New Zealand Naval Forces
Queen's Medal for Champion Shots of the Military Forces
Queen's Medal for Champion Shots of the Air Forces
Cadet Forces Medal
Rhodesia Medal 1980
Service Medal of the Order of St John
Other Commonwealth Members' Orders, Decorations and Medals in date of award
Approved Foreign Orders, Decorations and Medals in order of date of award

New Zealand
medals

Between 1848 and 1996 New Zealanders were eligible for the various British or Imperial honours and awards. The first step towards an independent honours system was taken in 1975 when the Queen's Service Order and Queen's Service Medal were instituted.

Thereafter a range of distinctive New Zealand medals was gradually adopted for the defence forces, the police, fire and prison services, this culminated in the introduction of a totally separate New Zealand Royal Honours System in May 1996. With a few exceptions, all honours and awards are conferred by, or in the name of, the sovereign (Queen Elizabeth) on the advice of Her Majesty's New Zealand ministers. A distinctive feature of many New Zealand orders, decorations and medals is the influence of Maori art forms.

Medals and decorations which were specific to New Zealand but made under Royal Warrants prior to 1975 are listed in the main body of this book. A new range of New Zealand gallantry and bravery awards has recently been developed, and this includes the creation of a Victoria Cross for New Zealand as well as the highest non-combatant bravery award, the New Zealand Cross. The new medals and decorations are given below in order of precedence. To date very few of these awards have come onto the market. and information on their rarity and other details have not been available, so prices in this section, where given, can only be regarded as a rough guide.

NZ1. VICTORIA CROSS FOR NEW ZEALAND

Instituted: September 20, 1999.
Ribbon: Crimson 38mm wide.
Metal: Bronze.
Size: 35mm at each axis.
Description: A cross pattée with raised edges, identical to the British and Australian Victoria Crosses (MYB24 and A1).
Comments: *Although identical to the existing VC, awards will be made under a New Zealand, as opposed to a British, Royal Warrant. Recipients are entitled to the postnominal letters VC and their name will be engraved on each award. It may be awarded posthumously.*

VALUE: —

NZ2. NEW ZEALAND CROSS

Instituted: September 20, 1999.
Ribbon: Bright blue.
Metal: Silver with gold applique.
Size: Height 52mm, width 38mm.
Description: Similar to the original New Zealand Cross of 1869 (MYB25) but incorporating changes which were first proposed in 1885 and only now implemented, viz. fern fronds have replaced laurel leaves. (Reverse) inscribed FOR BRAVERY—MO TE MAIA.
Comments: *The premier civilian award for bravery, it now supersedes the George Cross so far as New Zealand citizens are concerned. Recipients are entitled to the postnominal letters NZC.*

VALUE: —

NZ3. ORDER OF NEW ZEALAND

Instituted: 1987.
Ribbon: Red ochre with a narrow white stripe towards either edge.
Metal: 9 carat gold.
Description: An oval medal decorated with coloured enamels bearing in the centre the heraldic shield of New Zealand within a Kowhaiwhai rafter pattern.
Comments: *Instituted as a first-level non-titular order, it is modelled on the British Order of Merit (1917) and the Order of the Companions of Honour (1917). The Order comprises the Queen as Sovereign and no more than 20 ordinary members who are entitled to the postnominal letters ONZ. Additional members may be appointed in commemoration of important royal, state or national occasions. Honorary membership includes citizens of Commonwealth nations of which the Queen is not Head of State, and of foreign countries. The badge must be returned on the death of the holder. No miniature exists, but a lapel badge was instituted in 1990.*

VALUE: —   *Miniature* £250–300

NZ4. NEW ZEALAND ORDER OF MERIT

Breast star

Instituted: May 30, 1996.
Ribbon: Plain red ochre (kokowai).
Comments: *An order of chivalry designed alongBritish lines and intended to replace the various British orders to which New Zealanders were formerly appointed. It consists of five classes whose insignia are noted separately below. In addition, there is a collar of the order, worn only by the Sovereign of the Order and the Chancellor (the Governor-General of New Zealand). The collar is composed of links of the central badge and gold koru (in the form of the letter S) with a pendant badge featuring the New Zealand arms. Distinctive lapel badges denoting membership of the Order are worn in civilian clothes. On the abolition of Knighthoods an amending warrant dated May 18, 2000, replaced Knights and Dames with Principal and Distinguished Companions.*

VALUE: —

NZ4. NEW ZEALAND ORDER OF MERIT (contd.)
PRINCIPLE COMPANIONS (PCNZM)
Badge: A cross in white enamel set in silver-gilt with, in the centre, a medallion comprising the New Zealand arms in coloured enamel surrounded by a circle of green enamel inscribed in gold FOR MERIT / TOHU HIRANGA and surmounted by a royal crown. The badge is worn from a sash over the right shoulder and resting on the left hip.

Star: A gold breast star of eight points, each arm bearing in relief a representation of a fern frond, superimposed in the centre of which is a smaller representation of the badge of the order.

DISTIGUISHED COMPANIONS (DCNZM)
A badge and breast star similar to that above, except that the badge is worn from either a neck ribbon or a bow on the left shoulder. The breast star is in silver, with the badge of the order in the centre.

COMPANIONS (CNZM)
A badge similar to that above, worn from a 38mm wide neck ribbon or a bow on the left shoulder.

OFFICERS (ONZM)
A smaller representation of the badge in silver-gilt, with the motto in green enamel. Worn from a ribbon on the left lapel or from a 38mm wide ribbon tied in a bow and worn on the left shoulder.

MEMBERS (MNZM)
Badge as for Officers but in silver.

NZ5. NEW ZEALAND GALLANTRY STAR

Instituted: September 20, 1999.
Branch of Service: New Zealand armed forces.
Ribbon: Crimson with a purple central stripe bordered by thin white stripes.
Metal: Silver and gilt.
Size: 45mm.
Description: (Obverse) faceted silver 8-pointed star of equal points surmounted by a gilt crown surrounded by a wreath of New Zealand fern. (Reverse) inscribed FOR GALLANTRY —MO TE TOANGA. With ring suspension.
Comments: *This decoration supersedes the British Distinguished Service Order, Distinguished Conduct Medal and Conspicuous Gallantry Medal. Recipients are entitled to the postnominal letters NZGS and their name will be inscribed on the reverse.*

VALUE: —

NZ6. QUEEN'S SERVICE ORDER

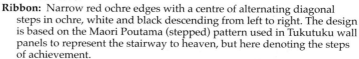

Instituted: 1975.
Ribbon: Narrow red ochre edges with a centre of alternating diagonal steps in ochre, white and black descending from left to right. The design is based on the Maori Poutama (stepped) pattern used in Tukutuku wall panels to represent the stairway to heaven, but here denoting the steps of achievement.
Metal: Frosted sterling silver.
Description: A badge based on the stylised representation of a manuka flower, consisting of five large and five small stylised petals. Superimposed in the centre is a silver-gilt medallion bearing the crowned effigy of the Queen within a circle of red enamel bearing the words FOR COMMUNITY SERVICE or FOR PUBLIC SERVICES as appropriate and surmounted by St Edward's Crown. The full name of the recipient is engraved on the reverse.
Comments: *The single non-titular order is divided into two divisions for Community Service and for Public Services respectively. Ordinary membership is limited to 30 appointments per annum. Members of the Royal Family may be appointed as Extra Companions and include so far the Duke of Edinburgh (1981), Prince Charles (1983) and the Princess Royal (1990). Recipients are entitled to the postnominal letters QSO, and appropriate lapel badges for everyday wear.*

VALUE: —   *Miniature*   £150–200

NZ7. NEW ZEALAND GALLANTRY DECORATION

Instituted: September 20, 1999.
Branch of Service: New Zealand armed forces.
Ribbon: 32mm wide. Crimson with central purple stripe and two equal white stripes.
Metal: Silver and gilt.
Size: 46mm.
Description: (Obverse) A simple faceted silver cross surmounted by the royal crown and fern frond wreath emblem; (reverse) inscribed FOR GALLANTRY —MO TE TOANGA. With ring suspension.
Comments: *This decoration supersedes the British DSC, MC, DFC, AFC, DSM, MM, DFM and AFM. Recipients are entitled to the postnominal letters NZGD.*

VALUE: —

NZ8. NEW ZEALAND BRAVERY STAR

Instituted: September 20, 1999.
Branch of Service: New Zealand police forces, fire brigades and civilians.
Ribbon: 32mm wide. Bright blue with two narrow red ochre stripes.
Metal: Silver and gilt.
Size: 46mm
Description: (Obverse) an 8-pointed faceted star with four long and four short points in the angles surmpounted by a gilt royal crown and fern frond wreath emblem; (reverse) inscribed FOR BRAVERY—MO TE MAIA. With ring suspension.
Comments: *This decoration superseded the British George Medal and is the second grade award for civilian acts of bravery. Recipients are entitled to the postnominal letters NZBS.*

VALUE: —

NZ9. NEW ZEALAND BRAVERY DECORATION

Instituted: September 20, 1999.
Branch of Service: Civilians and members of the armed forces in non-combat situations.
Ribbon: 32mm wide. Bright blue with three equal stripes of red ochre.
Metal: Silver and gilt.
Size: 45mm.
Description: (Obverse) a cross pattée surmounted by a small faceted four-pointed star with the royal crown and fern frond wreath emblem; (reverse) inscribed FOR BRAVERY—MO TE MAIA. With ring suspension.
Comments: *This decoration is awarded for acts of bravery in a non-combat situation. It supersedes the British QGM, QPM, QFSM, AFC and AFM. Recipients are entitled to the postnominal letters NZBD.*

VALUE: —

NZ10. NEW ZEALAND GALLANTRY MEDAL

Instituted: 1998.
Branch of Service: New Zealand armed forces.
Ribbon: 32mm wide. Crimson with two central purple stripes and two outer white stripes.
Metal: Bronze.
Size: 38mm.
Description: (Obverse) the Rank-Broadley effigy of Her Majesty Queen Elizabeth II with the legend ELIZABETH II QUEEN OF NEW ZEALAND; (reverse) FOR GALLANTRY / MO TE TOANGA surrounded by a fern frond wreath with the royal crown above.
Comments: *This decoration replaces the Mention in Despatches. Recipients are entitled to the postnominal letters NZGM. The name of the recipient will be engravd on each award.*

VALUE: —

NZ11. NEW ZEALAND BRAVERY MEDAL

Instituted: September 20 ,1999.
Branch of Service: Civilians or members of the New Zealand armed forces in a non-combat situation.
Ribbon: 32mm wide. Bright blue with four red ochre stripes.
Metal: Bronze.
Size: 38mm.
Description: (Obverse) the Rank-Broadley effigy of Her Majesty Queen Elizabeth II with the legend ELIZABETH II QUEEN OF NEW ZEALAND; (reverse) FOR BRAVERY / MO TE MAIA surrounded by a fern frond wreath with the royal crown above.
Comments: *This decoration replaces the Queen's Commendations for Brave Conduct and Valuable Service in the Air. Recipients are entitled to the postnominal letters NZBM.*

VALUE: —

NZ12. QUEEN'S SERVICE MEDAL

Instituted: March 13, 1975.
Ribbon: Same as the Queen's Service Order.
Metal: Silver.
Size: 38mm.
Description: (Obverse) effigy of Queen Elizabeth surrounded by the royal styles and titles; (reverse) New Zealand arms with THE QUEEN'S SERVICE MEDAL round the top. Two versions of the reverse exist, inscribed at the foot either FOR COMMUNITY SERVICE or FOR PUBLIC SERVICES. The medal is fitted with a suspension ring.
Comments: *Awards are made for valuable voluntary service to the community or meritorious and faithful services to the Crown or similar services within the public sector. Military service is ineligible. The name of the recipient is engraved on the rim. Recipients are entitled to the postnominal letters QSM.*

VALUE: — *Miniature* £60–70

NZ13. NEW ZEALAND OPERATIONAL SERVICE MEDAL

Instituted: July 2002.
Branch of Service: All New Zealand personnel previously awarded an operational medal for service since September 3, 1945.
Ribbon: 32mm wide. Black with six white stripes.
Metal: Silver plated base metal.
Size: 38mm.
Description: (Obverse) New Zealand arms; (reverse) a kiwi with NEW ZEALAND between two stars, with three wavy lines and the inscription FOR OPERATIONAL SERVICE below.
Comments: *Awarded to New Zealanders who have taken part in operational service on or after September 3, 1945. Personnel holding the NZGSM, East Timor, UN, Vietnam, Rhodesia or NATO medals qualified for this award. Seven days service towards an operational medal will also qualify for this medal. The medal is to be worn immediately after the New Zealand War Service Medal 1939–45 and before any other war medal.*

Value: £50–75   *Miniature* £25–30

NZ14. NEW ZEALAND GENERAL SERVICE MEDAL

Instituted: July 2002.
Branch of Service:
Ribbon: 32mm, the colours to vary according to the campaign for which the medal is first awarded. The first awards (2003) were for Afghanistan (bright green with a central red stripe bisected by a thin black stripe) and the Solomon Islands (dark green with a yellow central stripe flanked by narrow dark blue stripes).
Metal: Silver-plated base metal.
Size: 36mm.
Description: (Obverse) the effigy of Queen Elizabeth; (reverse) the inscription THE NEW ZEALAND GENERAL SERVICE MEDAL within a wreath of New Zealand flora surmounted by a Royal Crown.

VALUE: —   *Miniature* £25–30

NZ15. NEW ZEALAND SERVICE MEDAL 1946–1949

Instituted: November 3, 1995.
Branch of Service: New Zealand armed forces, merchant navy and civil airline crews.
Ribbon: 32mm white with a central red stripe and black stripes at the edges.
Metal: Rhodium plated steel.
Size: 38mm.
Description: (Obverse) New Zealand arms; (reverse) FOR SERVICE TO NEW ZEALAND 1946–1949 with a fern frond below.
Comments: *Awarded to about 7300 personnel despatched direct from New Zealand who had not had previous service in the Second World War, as well as about 5,000 troops stationed in Italy at the end of the war who were then sent to the Far East to take part in the police and peacekeeping operations in Japan between March 23, 1946 and March 31, 1949, a minimum of 28 days' service being required.*

Value: £40–50   *Miniature* £25–30

NZ16. NEW ZEALAND GENERAL SERVICE MEDAL (WARLIKE OPERATIONS)

Instituted: May 7, 1992.
Branch of Service: New Zealand armed forces.
Ribbon: 32mm dark blue with a central black stripe flanked by red stripes.
Metal: Silver.
Size: 38mm.
Description: (Obverse) crowned effigy of Queen Elizabeth; (reverse) THE NEW ZEALAND GENERAL SERVICE MEDAL within a wreath of pohutakawa blossom, fern fronds and kowhai blossom, ensigned by a royal crown affixed to a plain suspension bar.
Clasps: Malaya 1960–64, Kuwait, Vietnam, Near East.
Comments: *Awarded for service in warlike operations. The ribbon is based on the New Zealand War Medal ribbon (see MY123). In 2003 it was replaced by the General Service Medal (NZ14) without clasps but with a ribbon appropriate to the mission.*

VALUE: £85–120

NZ17. NEW ZEALAND GENERAL SERVICE MEDAL (PEACEKEEPING OPERATIONS)

Instituted: May 7, 1992.
Branch of Service: New Zealand armed forces.
Ribbon: 32mm dark blue with a white central stripe flanked by narrow red stripes.
Metal: Bronze.
Size: 38mm.
Description: As above.
Clasps: Mozambique, Cambodia, Peshawar, Somalia, Arabian Gulf, Iraq, Bouganville, Korea 1954-57, Indian Ocean, Ruwanda.
Comments: *Awarded for peacekeeping operations only if the relevant UN medals were not awarded. A person may qualify for both the NZGSM (Peacekeeping) and the NZGS (Warlike) if completing the required service in any theatre covered by each award. The ribbon is based on the New Zealand War Medal ribbon (see MY123). In 2003 it was replaced by the General Service Medal (NZ14) without clasps but with a ribbon appropriate to the mission.*

VALUE: £60–75

NZ18. EAST TIMOR MEDAL

Instituted: April 25, 2000.

Ribbon: Broad green central stripe flanked by narrow red, wider black and white stripes towards the edges.

Metal: Silvered alloy.

Size: 36mm.

Description: (Obverse) the effigy of the Queen by Ian Rank-Broadley with ELIZABETH II QUEEN OF NEW ZEALAND round the circumference; (reverse) the head of a kiwi facing right and overshadowing a map of East Timor with the words EAST TIMOR below and a sprig of olive leaves above. Fitted with a plain suspension bar.

Clasp: A silver clasp inscribed EAST TIMOR for additional service of 365 days or more, continuous or aggregate, in the operational area.

Comments: *Awarded to members of the New Zealand Defence Force, civilian personnel and police taking part in the International Force in East Timor from 19 June 1999 onwards. The medals was awarded for a day or more on the strength of a formation on land in the operational area, seven days' service afloat or after completing seven sorties as aircrew, or for 30 or more days, continuous or aggregated, on inspections or other service of a temporary nature. About 2,000 awards were made. The medal was designed by Philip O'Shea, LVO, New Zealand Herald of Arms, and struck by Thomas Fattorini of Birmingham. The first investiture of medals took place in the New Zealand Parliament, Wellington on 28 March 2001.*

Value: £100–120   *Miniature*   £30–35

NZ19. NEW ZEALAND SPECIAL SERVICE MEDAL

Instituted: July 2002.

Branch of Service: New Zealand service personnel and civilians.

Ribbon: An orange-yellow central stripe, flanked by narrow crimson stripes, then narrow red and white stripes and thin black edges.

Metal: Gold-plated.

Size: 36mm.

Description: (Obverse) the arms of New Zealand; (reverse) fern fronds and sprigs of pohutakawa, manuka, kowhai blossom and Mount Cook lilies.

Comments: *Awarded to New Zealanders sent by their government to observe atmospheric nuclear tests in the Pacific, from Operation Grapple (Christmas Island, 1957-8) to French testing at Muraroa Atoll in 1972.*

Value: £100–125

NZ20. NEW ZEALAND 1990 COMMEMORATION MEDAL

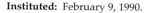

Instituted: February 9, 1990.

Ribbon: 32mm nine narrow stripes, black at the centre flanked by alternate white and red ochre.

Metal: Silver-gilt.

Size: 38mm.

Description: (Obverse) effigy of Queen Elizabeth with inscription ELIZABETH II . QUEEN OF NEW ZEALAND incuse on a raised rim; (reverse) stylised Kotuku or White Heron with inscription NEW ZEALAND 1990 COMMEMORATION.

Comments: *Awarded during the sesquicentennial year of British annexation to recognise achievements of New Zealanders in community service and the public services or their contribution to the country. The medal is accompanied by a certificate.*

Value: £40–50

NZ21. NEW ZEALAND MERITORIOUS SERVICE MEDAL

Instituted: May 6, 1985.

Branch of Service: NCOs of the rank of sergeant or petty officer or above in the armed forces.

Ribbon: 32mm crimson with a narrow green central stripe.

Metal: Silver.

Size: 38mm.

Description: (Obverse) bare-headed effigy of Queen Elizabeth; (reverse) FOR MERITORIOUS SERVICE within a laurel wreath surmounted by a royal crown and the legend NEW ZEALAND. Reverse similar to 212.

Comments: *Awarded for a minimum of 21 years full-time service in the armed forces, although this may be reduced to 18 years in the case of those invalided out of the services on grounds of disability. The recipient must be in possession of the Long Service & Good Conduct Medal. Service before the age of 17 does not count. At present the medal is limited to 10 serving members of RNZN, 20 Army and 15 RNZAF.*

Value: £180–250   *Miniature* £45–50

NZ22. NEW ZEALAND ARMED FORCES AWARD

Instituted: May 6, 1985.

Branch of Service: Officers of the armed forces.

Ribbon: 32mm dark blue, crimson and light blue with a central stripe of black.

Metal: Silver.

Size: 38mm.

Description: (Obverse) crowned effigy of Queen Elizabeth; (reverse) crossed swords, eagle and naval crown with two fronds below and inscription NEW ZEALAND ARMED FORCES AWARD.

Comments: *Awarded to Regular Force commissioned officers of the armed services for 15 years full-time service back-dated to 1977. Clasps for each additional 15 years may be awarded. Where an officer has been commissioned from the ranks at least 8 years must be commissioned service.*

Value: £85–120

NZ23. ROYAL NEW ZEALAND NAVY LONG SERVICE MEDAL

Instituted: May 6, 1985.
Branch of Service: Royal New Zealand Navy.
Ribbon: 32mm dark blue edged in white.
Metal: Silver.
Size: 38mm.
Description: (Obverse) uncrowned effigy of Queen Elizabeth; (reverse) HMS *Victory* surrounded by the inscription FOR LONG SERVICE AND GOOD CONDUCT.
Comments: *Awarded for naval ratings with 15 years service. Clasps may be awarded for each additional 15 years, denoted in undress uniform by a silver rosette on the ribbon bar. Indistinguishable from the Royal Navy LS&GC Medal, apart from the recipient's details.*

Value: £60–75   *Miniature*   £15–20

NZ24. NEW ZEALAND ARMY LONG SERVICE & GOOD CONDUCT MEDAL

Instituted: May 6, 1985.
Branch of Service: New Zealand Army, Regular Forces.
Ribbon: 32mm crimson edged in white.
Metal: Silver.
Size: 36mm.
Description: (Obverse) crowned effigy of Queen Elizabeth; (reverse) FOR LONG SERVICE AND GOOD CONDUCT attached to an ornamental title bar bearing the words NEW ZEALAND in raised lettering.
Comments: *Similar to the British Army LS&GC Medal (229) but with a distinctive New Zealand suspension bar. Only soldiers of the Regular Force serving from December 1, 1977 onwards, are eligible for this medal, a minimum of 15 years full-time irreproachable service being required. Clasps for additional periods of 15 years may be granted.*

Value: £40–50   *Miniature*   £15–20

NZ25. ROYAL NEW ZEALAND AIR FORCE LONG SERVICE MEDAL

Instituted: May 6, 1985.
Branch of Service: Royal New Zealand Air Force.
Ribbon: 32mm equal stripes of dark blue and crimson edged in white.
Metal: Silver.
Size: 36mm.
Description: (Obverse) uncrowned effigy of Queen Elizabeth; (reverse) an eagle with outstretched wings surmounted by a royal crown encircled by the inscription FOR LONG SERVICE AND GOOD CONDUCT.
Comments: *This medal replaces the award of the British RAF LS&GC Medal (MY 268). It is, in fact, indistinguishable from the British award except for the recipient's details engraved on the rim.*

Value: £60–75   *Miniature*   £15–20

NZ26. NEW ZEALAND POLICE LONG SERVICE & GOOD CONDUCT MEDAL

Instituted: September 8, 1976.

Ribbon: 32mm crimson with a central dark blue stripe flanked with white stripes.

Metal: Silver.

Size: 38mm.

Description: (Obverse) crowned effigy of Queen Elizabeth; (reverse) St Edward's Crown, sceptre and sword on a cushion within a wreath of oak leaves and fern fronds, surrounded by the inscription NEW ZEALAND POLICE—FOR LONG SERVICE AND GOOD CONDUCT.

Comments: *This medal is similar to the NZ Police LS&GC Medal (MY283) issued under Imperial Warrant, but differs in the ribbon and the inscription on the reverse. Awards made to police officers employed on or after January 1, 1976, with a qualifying period of service of 14 years. Clasps for additional periods of seven years are also awarded. The recipient's name is engraved on the rim.*

VALUE: £75–100   *Miniature*   £35–40

NZ27. NEW ZEALAND FIRE BRIGADES LONG SERVICE AND GOOD CONDUCT MEDAL

Instituted: September 8, 1976.

Ribbon: 32mm vermilion with a central black stripe flanked by narrow yellow stripes.

Metal: Silver.

Size: 38mm.

Description: (Obverse) crowned effigy of Queen Elizabeth (reverse) NEW ZEALAND FIRE BRIGADES—FOR LONG SERVICE AND GOOD CONDUCT above a fern frond.

Comments: *Originally awarded for 14 years full or part time services as a fireman, but amended by Royal Warrant (October 15, 1981) to include fire brigades maintained or operated by companies as well as the forces under the control of the NZ Fire Service Commission. Clasps are awarded every additional period of seven years service. The recipient's name is engraved on the rim.*

VALUE: £75–100   *Miniature*   £35–40

NZ28. NEW ZEALAND PRISON SERVICE MEDAL

Instituted: October 15, 1981.

Ribbon: 32mm crimson with a central dark blue stripe flanked by narrow green stripes.

Metal: Silver.

Size: 36mm.

Description: (Obverse) crowned effigy of Queen Elizabeth II; (reverse) St Edward's crown and inscription NEW ZEALAND PRISON SERVICE FOR LONG SERVICE AND GOOD CONDUCT.

Comments: *Awarded for 14 years service with bars further 7 year periods. This medal superseded the NZ Prison Service Long Service Medal originally instituted in 1901. The recipient's name is engraved on the rim.*

VALUE: £75–100   *Miniature*   £35–40

NZ29. NEW ZEALAND SUFFRAGE CENTENNIAL MEDAL

Instituted: July 1, 1993.
Ribbon: 32mm purple with narrow central stripes of white, yellow and white.
Metal: Antiqued bronze.
Size: 38mm.
Description: (Obverse) crowned effigy of Queen Elizabeth; (reverse) wreath of fern and camellia enclosing the inscription 1893 THE NEW ZEALAND SUFFRAGE CENTENNIAL 1993.
Comments: *Awarded to selected persons who by their virtues, talents and loyalty have made a recognised contribution to the rights of women in New Zealand or to women's issues in New Zealand. It was only awarded during the centennial year of the granting of votes to women—New Zealand being the first country in the world to do so.*

VALUE: £200–250

NZ30. NEW ZEALAND ENFORCEMENT LONG SERVICE MEDAL

Instituted: September 28, 1970.
Ribbon: Light blue with a central white stripe with black stripes each side.
Metal: Silver
Size: 38mm.
Description: A circular medal bearing the coat of arms of New Zealand, with a suspender of stylised fern leaves.
Comments: *This medal, rendered obsolete in 1987 on the introduction of the Traffic Service Medal (NZ29), was awarded to members of the Traffic and Road Safety forces of the Ministry of Transport upon 15 years continuous service.*

VALUE: £75–100   *Miniature*   £50–60

NZ33. NEW ZEALAND TRAFFIC SERVICE MEDAL

Instituted: May 30, 1994.
Ribbon: Bright blue with a narrow central white stripe flanked by black stripes.
Metal: Silver.
Size: 38mm.
Description: (Obverse) crowned effigy of Queen Elizabeth; (reverse) crowned wreath of fern fronds enclosing the word THE NEW ZEALAND TRAFFIC SERVICE MEDAL.
Comments: *Awarded to uniformed traffic officers in service after January 1, 1987 and before July 1, 1992 who had completed 14 years service. Clasps for each additional period of seven years are also awarded. The recipient's name is engraved on the rim.*

VALUE: £40–50   *Miniature*   £30–40

NZ34. ROYAL NEW ZEALAND NAVAL RESERVE DECORATION

Instituted: May 6, 1985.
Ribbon: 38mm green edged with white.
Metal: Silver and gold.
Size: 54mm high and 33mm wide.
Description: A skeletal badge consisting of an oval loop of rope in silver surrounding the Royal Cypher in gold.
Comments: *Awarded to commissioned officers of the Royal New Zealand Naval Reserve, with a minimum of 15 years service. Clasps for each additional period of 10 years are also awarded. The names of recipients are engraved on the reverse. Recipients are entitled to the postnominal letters RD. This medal replaced MY219.*

VALUE: £100–125   *Miniature*   £20–25

NZ35. ROYAL NEW ZEALAND NAVAL VOLUNTEER RESERVE DECORATION

Instituted: May 6, 1985.
Ribbon: 38mm dark blue with a central broad green stripe flanked by narrow crimson stripes.
Metal: Silver and gold.
Size: 54mm high and 33mm wide.
Description: A skeletal badge, similar in design to the above.
Comments: *Awarded to commissioned officers in the Royal New Zealand Naval Volunteer Reserve, with a minimum of 15 years service. Clasps for each additional period of 10 years are awarded. The names of recipients are engraved on the reverse. Recipients are entitled to the postnominal letters VRD. These decorations replaced the British RD and VRD, the latter being obsolete and the organisation of the Royal New Zealand Navy being such that the British Admiralty Board regulations were no longer applicable.*

VALUE: £100–125   *Miniature*   £20–25

NZ36. ROYAL NEW ZEALAND NAVAL VOLUNTEER RESERVE LONG SERVICE AND GOOD CONDUCT MEDAL

Instituted: 1985.
Ribbon: 32mm dark blue with a central broad stripe of green between narrow crimson stripes.
Metal: Silver.
Size: 36mm.
Description: (Obverse) uncrowned effigy of Queen Elizabeth; (reverse) a battleship with the motto DIUTURNE FIDELIS (faithful of long duration).
Comments: *Awarded to RNZVR ratings serving on or after December 1, 1977, with a minimum of 15 years service. Clasps for each additional period of 10 years are awarded. This medal replaced MY221.*

VALUE: £50–75   *Miniature*   £15–20

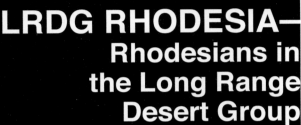
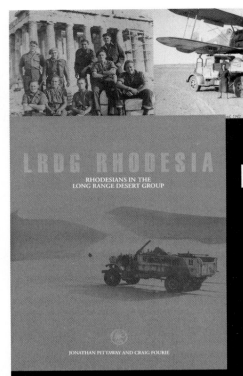

South African
medals

Apart from the various British campaign medals from 1834 onwards, distinctive medals relating to military service in South Africa date from 1896 when a version of the Meritorious Service Medal (MYB210) was provided with the name of the Cape of Good Hope on the reverse. This was accompanied by similar versions of the Distinguished Conduct Medal (MYB42) and the Long Service and Good Conduct Medal (MYB229). The following year similar awards were instituted for Natal. Moreover, there were also a number of military and naval medals issued under Dutch, and later Boer, administrations which are outside the scope of this Yearbook.

Cape and Natal colonists received British awards from the earliest days of the British occupation, and numerous instances have been recorded of awards to South Africans of both the orders of chivalry and gallantry decorations. This situation coninued after the formation of the Union of South Africa in 1910. As a rule, these were identical to the British versions in every respect but there were a few notable exceptions. The Victory Medal (MYB170) was struck with a bilingual (English and Dutch) reverse for award to South African forces. Distinctive medals for the police, railway and harbour police and prison services (MYB284–285 and 290–291) were awarded but as they were instituted by Royal Warrant they are included in the main body of this Yearbook.

Other South African awards which will be found in the main section are the King's Police Medal for gallantry or bravery (MYB49), the Africa Service Medal (MYB189), the South African Medal for War Service (MYB192) and the South African Medal for Korea (MYB196). There were also South African versions of the Efficiency Decoration (MYB236), Efficiency Medal (MYB254), the Permanent Force LS&GC (253) and Air Efficiency Award (MYB270). Finally, there are three miscellaneous medals: the Union of South Africa Commemoration Medal of 1910 (MYB357), the Dekoratie Voor Trouwe Dienst of 1920 (MYB358) and the Anglo-Boere Oorlog Medal instituted at the same time (MYB359).

In 1952 the Union of South Africa instituted its own system of awards for gallantry in action, bravery in a non-combat situation and for distinguished service. Nine of these awards had a standard reverse showing the arms of the Union of South Africa surmounted by the royal cypher. In 1961, when South Africa became a republic and left the Commonwealth, the royal cypher was removed. The tenth award was the Union Medal which was completely redesigned and renamed the Permanent Force Good Service Medal (SA11 below).

For the purposes of this insertion it has been necessary to limit full coverage to military awards because of the absolute plethora of orders, decorations and medals that have made their appearance in the last 50 years while South Africa was ruled by the National Party. Not only were separate and independent award structures set up with their own orders, decorations and medals for all branches of the public service: Military, Police, Railway Police, Prisons, as well as the National Intelligence Service, but the situation was further complicated when the Nationalist Party Government in terms of its apartheid policy set up Homeland Governments that were given independence from the Republic of South Africa, each with their own set of awards for Military, Police and Prison departments—Transkei, Ciskei, KwaZulu, Bophuthatswana, Venda, Lebowa, Gazankulu and Qwa-qwa, etc. After 1994 the situation has been compounded by the issue of medals awarded retrospectively to members of the forces of freedom fighters or terrorists—MK (Mkhonto Wesizwe) and APLA (Azanian People's Liberation Army).

The awards instituted and awarded in South West Africa by the South African Government until this SA administered territory gained its independence and became Namibia in 1990 through world pressure, must not be overlooked either. The South African award system also reveals great instability through the frequent abolition of awards, their supersession and further proliferation by the introduction of new awards! Although this insertion has a primary focus on military awards, some of the awards to the South African Police, Prisons and Railway Police that may occur in medal groups with some regularity, have been included.

For information purposes a full list of orders, decorations and medals instituted since 1952 to the Police, Railway Police and Prisons, appears overleaf. The date in brackets next to each award indicates the year of gazetting of that award. The awards are listed in order of precedence for that particular compartment of the public service. These lists are preceded by a listing of South African civilian orders and decorations that are not confined to any particular public service compartment of awards.

SOUTH AFRICAN CIVILIAN AWARDS

ORDERS
Order of the Southern Cross (1986/87)—Two Classes
Order of the Star of South Africa (Non Military) (1988)—Five Classes
Order for Meritorious Service (1986)—Two Classes
Order of Good Hope (1973/88)—Five Classes

DECORATIONS FOR BRAVERY
The Queen's Medal for Bravery (Gold and Silver) (1953)
The Woltemade Decoration for Bravery (1970/88) Gold
The Woltemade Decoration for Bravery (1970/88) Silver
Civil Defence Medal for Bravery (1976)

MERITORIOUS SERVICE
Civil Defence Medal for Meritorious Service (1976)
State President's Sports Merit Award (1971)

SOUTH AFRICAN POLICE

ORDERS
South African Police Star for Distinguished Leadership (1979)

DECORATIONS FOR BRAVERY
South African Police Cross for Bravery (1963)
South African Police Cross for Bravery (1989) (Gold/Silver/ungraded)
South African Police Silver Cross for Gallantry (1985)

AWARDS FOR DISTINGUISHED, LONG AND MERITORIOUS SERVICE
South African Police Star for Distinguished Service (1963)
South African Police Star for Distinguished Service (1979)
South African Police Star for Outstanding Service (1979)
South African Police Star for Merit (1963)
South African Police Medal for Faithful Service (1963)
South African Police Star for Faithful Service (1979)

SERVICE
South African Police Medal for Combating Terrorism (1974)

COMMEMORATIVE
South African Police Seventy-Fifty Anniversary Commemorative Medal (1988)

SOUTH AFRICAN RAILWAYS POLICE

ORDERS
South African Railways Police Star for Distinguished Leadership (1980)

DECORATIONS FOR BRAVERY
South African Railways Police Cross for Valour (1966)
South African Railways Police Cross for Valour (1980)

South African Railways Police *continued*

AWARDS FOR DISTINGUISHED, LONG AND MERITORIOUS SERVICE
South African Railways Police Star for Distinguished Service (1980) *
Decoration for Distinguished Service in the SA Railways Police Force (1966)
Decoration for Outstanding Service in the South African Railways Police Force (1980)
Star for Merit in the South African Railways Police Force (1966)
Star for Merit in the South African Railways Police Force (1980)
South African Railways Police Star for Faithful Service (1980)
Medal for Faithful Service in the South African Railways Police Force (1966)
Medal for Faithful Service in the South African Railways Police Force (1980)

SERVICE
South African Railways Police Medal for Combating Terrorism

SOUTH AFRICAN PRISONS
(later Department of Correctional Services)

ORDERS
Nil.

DECORATIONS FOR BRAVERY
Decoration for Valour in the South African Prisons Service (1968)
South African Prisons Service Cross for Valour (Diamond) (1980)
South African Prisons Service Cross for Valour (Ruby) (1980)

AWARDS FOR DISTINGUISHED, LONG AND MERITORIOUS SERVICE
South African Prisons Service Star for Excellence (1980)
South African Prisons Service Star for Distinction (1980)
South African Prisons Service Star for Merit (1980)
South African Prisons Service Cross for Merit (1980)
Medal for Merit in the South African Prisons Service (1968)
South African Prisons Service Medal for Merit (Commissioned Officers) (1980)
South African Prisons Service Medal for Merit (Non-Commissioned Officers) (1980)
Faithful Service Medal in the Prisons Department (1959)
Faithful Service Medal, Prisons Department (1965)
Medal for Faithful Service in the South African Prisons Service (1968)
South African Prisons Service Medal for Faithful Service (1980)—Gold Medal (30 years); Silver Medal (20 years); Bronze Medal (10 years)

* *name later changed to Star for Distinguished Devotion*

**SPECIAL NOTE ON THE PRICING OF POST 1952
SOUTH AFRICAN DECORATIONS AND MEDALS AWARDED TO MEMBERS OF
THE ARMY, NAVY AND AIR FORCE**

In 1952 the Union Defence Force made a decision to cease naming its medals. Instead each medal would be impressed with a serial number and the number, rank and name, etc. of the recipient entered against the serial number of the medal recorded down the left-hand margin of the register. The registers have since been misplaced. The register system was replaced by the computer and when a recipient received a medal, the medal number was recorded in many cases on this computerised record of service. However, these records are held by the Department of Defence and their system is not geared up to print out a full list of recipients of a particular medal with medal numbers.

    (i)   In certain cases, after the award of the medal, the recipient's number, rank, name and unit, along with the serial number of the medal awarded, was published in Part II Unit orders.

    (ii)   Since approximately 1988, the certificates of award have recorded the serial number of the medal awarded. Prior to that time, no medal serial number was printed on the certificate.

    In order to establish that the medal in the group or as a singleton was awarded to a particular recipient (i) or (ii) above, are a prerequisite = PRICE A (Medal certificate must be the original in (ii) to qualify).

    If a medal is numbered and has an un-numbered original certificate of award as supporting documentation = PRICE B.

    If a medal is numbered (or unnumbered) without any supporting documentation = PRICE C.

    It must be stressed that even if a recipient was awarded a medal, there is nothing to prove that that particular medal was actually awarded to the recipient, unless the serial number on the medal can be tied to that recipient through supporting documentation. Obviously gallantry awards must be accompanied by a copy of the citation for which the award was made.

    An A, B and C price will be given for each SA Military award. For medals awarded to the Police, two prices will be given: named medals and unnamed specimens, as the Police continued to name their medals (they actually impressed the day, month and year of award as well). As Prisons medals were engraved by a variety of jewellers after 1980, three prices are given for medals awarded from 1980. A: with certificate; B: named; C: unnamed.

    For verification of the Permanent Force LSGC Medal (18 years) (MYB SA29) and identification of the recipient, an unpublished roll has been compiled from Part II orders. This may be consulted by contacting Mr J. Louw at chevjlouw@hotmail.com. He will provide a copy of the roll entry at a fee. Such verification places verified medals in Category A.

SOUTH AFRICAN DEFENCE FORCE

ORDERS
SA1. STAR OF SOUTH AFRICA

Instituted: 1952.
Ribbon: 44.5mm orange with three 3mm green stripes in centre, 6mm apart.
Metal: Silver.
Description: A multi-facetted five-point star, fitted with a ring and oblong loop through which the ribbon is passed for suspension round the neck.
Comments: *Awarded for recognising exceptionally meritorious service, in time of peace or war, by officers of the SA Defence Force or of other armed forces attached to or serving with, or rendering service to the SA Defence Force. The award could recognize a particular instance or service over a period of time.*
Further awards were denoted by a silver bar embossed in the centre with a miniature replica of the Star. None were awarded but an example of the bar is on display at the SA Museum of Military History. The reverse of the order has the embellished coat of arms of the Union of SA in relief, surmounted by the Royal cypher. After 1961 the Royal cypher was erased from existing medal stock. Those officers who were still serving in 1975 could exchange their Star of South Africa for the Order of the Star of South Africa. Post nominal title: SSA.

VALUE

	A	B	C	Miniature
With Royal cypher	£500	£400	£250	£80
Royal cypher erased	£300	£150	£100	£20
Coat of arms reverse	£250	£150	£100	£20

SA2. ORDER OF THE STAR OF SOUTH AFRICA (MILITARY)

Instituted: 1975.

Ribbon: Blue, 37mm (neck ribbon), 80mm (sash), 44mm (breast ribbon) or 20mm (miniature). A narrow central white stripe denotes the second class (redesignated silver award in 1977).

Metal: Enamelled gold or silver depending on class.

Description: An eight-pointed Maltese cross with an eight-pointed star superimposed at the centre and having a circular Protea wreath behind. *First Class:* A Protea ornament at the top joins the star to a five-pointed badge in the form of a ground plan of the Castle of Good Hope, enclosing a circular device featuring the insignia of the Defence Force. This is linked by a chain to circular medallions embellished with eight-pointed stars forming the neck collar of the order. In addition to the neck badge and collar there is a gold breast star. An eight pointed multi-rayed star is surmounted by a circular protea wreath superimposed with a blue enamel Maltese Cross edged in gold, in turn surmounted by an eight pointed star with alternate long and short rays in gold. The centre of the neck badge is mounted with a diamond. The neck collar or chain was discontinued in 1978. *Second Class:* award is similar in every respect to the First Class except there is no diamond in the centre and the metal is silver and there is no neck collar.

Comments: *The Order of the Star of SA (Military) is divided into two classes:*

Class I Gold: Post nominal title: SSA. Awarded to generals and higher officers or officers of comparable rank who distinguished themselves by meritorious military service that promoted efficiency and contributed lastingly to the security of the nation.

Class II Silver: Post nominal title: SSAS. Awarded to brigadiers and higher officers or officers of comparable rank who distinguished themselves by exceptionally meritorious service of major military importance.

To all intents and purposes the award of this order was confined to members of the South African Permanent Force. If an officer was promoted to Class I of the order his Class II insignia would be returnable. The 1988 amendments to the warrant eliminated the inclusion of non-South African citizens of the appropriate rank for consideration. The amendments to regulations to cover the division that was not exclusively military but could include civilians, was introduced in 1978 but space does not permit lengthy explanation of the various classes: Grand Cross, Grand Officer, Commander, Officer and Knight.

VALUE:

	A	B	C	Miniature
Class I Neck collar and badge and breast badge	£1000	£700	£600	—
Class I ditto but in base metal gilt plated for presentation purposes or museums	—	—	£400	—
Class I Neck badge and breast badge.	£700	£500	£400	£40
Class I ditto in base metal	—	—	£200	—
Class II Neck and breast badge	£350	£250	£200	£20

DECORATIONS FOR BRAVERY

SA3. CASTLE OF GOOD HOPE DECORATION

Instituted: 1952.
Ribbon: 44.5mm green.
Metal: Gold.
Description: A five-pointed star representing in outline the Castle of Good Hope (the first major fortress in South Africa) the whole surrounded by a moat. The raised centre is in the form of a circle in which is depicted the arrival of Jan Van Riebeek, in his flag ship *Drommedaris* in Table Bay on 6 April 1652 against a background of Table Mountain, surrounded by a garland of Protea (the national flower) and the inscription: CASTEEL DE GOEDE HOOF DEKORASIE round the top and CASTLE OF GOOD HOPE DECORATION round the foot. (Reverse) Serial number and Royal cypher. Recently the loop for neck wear has been replaced by a ring for breast wear.
Comments: *Awarded for a signal act of valour or most conspicuous bravery or some daring or pre-eminent act of self-sacrifice or extreme devotion to duty in the presence of an enemy. The decoration could be awarded posthumously. This is South Africa's highest gallantry award but to date it has not been awarded. As no examples of the full size decoration have been awarded, no price is given—any specimens that come on to the market should be regarded with great suspicion. A gold miniature of the decoration is worn on the ribbon on the tunic.*

VALUE:

		Miniature (hallmarked gold)
Base metal-gilt plated specimen for museums or presentation sets of medals	£60	£150–200

SA4. LOUW WEPENER DECORATION

Instituted: 1952.
Ribbon: 35mm divided into equal stripes, six orange and five white.
Metal: Silver.
Description: Scene at the battle of Thaba Bosigo, Basutoland (now Lesotho) in 1865 in which Louw Wepener, shown in the foreground, was the hero. Inscribed LOUW WEPENER round the top and DECORATION DEKORASIE round the foot. Fitted with a scrolled suspension bar.
Comments: *It was awarded in recognition of acts of most conspicuous courage and self-sacrifice performed in the execution of or beyond the call of military duty in time of peace or war, by members of the SADF or attached troops, in saving or endeavouring to save the lives of others on land, sea or in the air or in the execution of duty for which other purely military honours are not normally granted. Post nominal title: LWD. The award was rendered obsolete by the Honoris Crux Decoration in 1975. Further awards were to have been denoted by a silver bar centred with a silver button inscribed with the initials LWD, but none were ever manufactured.*

VALUE:

	A	B	C	Miniature
Royal cypher reverse	£700	£300	£150	£35
Royal cypher erased	£700	£300	£100	£30
SA coat of arms	£600	£300	£70	£60

SA5. VAN RIEBEECK DECORATION

Instituted: 1952.
Ribbon: 32mm sky blue.
Metal: Silver-gilt.
Description: In shape of a five-pointed star representing the outline of the Castle of Good Hope. The suspension consists of a cluster of eight protea leaves. In the centre of the obverse is the full figure of Jan Van Riebeeck (first Governor of the Cape of Good Hope) in relief against a background of three rings representing his three ships—*Drommedaris, De Rijger* and *De Goede Hoop.*
Comments: *The decoration was awarded to officers of the SA Defence Force or auxiliary services or attached troops who distinguished themselves by outstanding resourcefulness, perseverance or personal courage or by their outstanding leadership or responsibility and personal example against an enemy in the field. Post nominal title: DVR. The award was rendered obsolete by the Honoris Crux Decoration in 1975. A specimen of the bar embossed with a miniature cannon in silver gilt to denote further awards, is on display at the SA Museum of Military History.*

VALUE:

	A	B	C	Miniature
Royal cypher reverse	£650	£450	£100	£30
Royal cypher erased	£650	£450	£70	£60
SA coat of arms reverse	£550	£400	£70	£30

SA6. VAN RIEBEECK MEDAL

Instituted: 1952.
Ribbon: 32mm sky blue with 6mm white central stripe.
Metal: Silver.
Description: Very similar to the Van Riebeeck Decoration (above) but differing in the ribbon. It, too, was discontinued in August 1975.
Comments: *In all respects identical to the Van Riebeeck Decoration except the medal was awarded to Warrant Officers, NCOs and Men. The medal was rendered obsolete by the Honoris Crux Decoration in 1975. Post nominal title: VRM. Additional award bar as for the decoration, except metal is silver. Specimen on display at the SA Museum of Military History.*

VALUE:

	A	B	C	Miniature
Royal cypher reverse	£475	£325	£100	£40
Royal cypher erased	£475	£325	£100	£65
SA coat of arms reverse	£375	£235	£100	£30

SA7. HONORIS CRUX

Instituted: 1952.
Ribbon: 32mm leaf-green with 3mm red outer and 2mm white inner edges.
Metal: Silver gilt and enamels.
Description: An eight-pointed Maltese Cross in silver gilt: in each angle formed by the cross is an eagle in silver gilt, facing to the right. Centre circle of the cross is enamelled in the three colours of the flag of Union of South Africa. The design was significantly influenced by the Order of the Golden Eagle that was proposed in 1894 but was rejected by the Transvaal Volksraad.
Comments: *There have been six recipients of this award. It was awarded to members of the South African Defence Force, auxiliary services, attached troops who regardless of their own safety and through personal courage and determination, perform a gallant act or deed against an enemy in the field. Subsequent deeds may entitle a recipient to a bar in silver-gilt embossed in the centre with a miniature eagle. A specimen bar is on display at the SA Museum of Military History. Post nominal title: HC.*

VALUE:

	A	B	C	Miniature
Royal cypher reverse	£1000	£650	£120	£25
Royal cypher erased	£1000	£650	£120	£25
SA coat of arms	£800	£550	£120	£25

SA8. LOUW WEPENER MEDAL

Instituted: 1967.
Ribbon: 35mm in width, orange divided into five broad stripes of equal width by four white stripes of 1.5mm
Metal: Bronze
Description: Identical to the Louw Wepener Decoration with the words "MEDALJE/MEDAL" substituted for"DECORATION/ DEKORASIE".
Comments: *Conditions of award as for Louw Wepener Decoration for deeds of a lesser nature to those for which the Louw Wepener Decoration was awarded. The award could be made posthumously. Subsequent awards were recognized by a bar with a centred circle containing the letters LWM. Post nominal title: LWM. The medal was rendered obsolete by the Honoris Crux Decoration in 1975.*

VALUE:

A	B	C	Miniature
£475	£350	£120	£40

SA9. HONORIS CRUX DECORATION

Instituted: 1975.
Ribbon: 32mm orange with additional white stripes according to class.
Metal: Enamelled gold or silver, according to class.
Description: An eight-pointed enamelled Maltese cross superimposed on a wreath with crossed swords in the angles, with a central roundel divided horizontally into orange, white and blue. Fitted with an ornamental suspension loop.
Comments: *This award replaced SA4, 5, 6, 7 and 8 above and was divided into four classes, distinguished by their ribbons and the embellishment of the obverse.*
Honoris Crux Diamond. Plain orange ribbon, 32mm, with a green circular border to centre roundel mounted with eight diamonds awarded to those who distinguished themselves. Awarded for performing deeds of outstanding valour, at extreme risk to their lives
Honoris Crux Gold. Orange ribbon with a 1mm central white stripe. Made of silver gilt with gold border to centre roundel. Awarded for performing outstanding deeds of bravery in extreme danger.
Honoris Crux Silver. Orange ribbon with a 1mm white stripe 13mm from each edge. Made of silver with silver border to centre roundel. Awarded for performing exceptional deeds of bravery whilst in great danger.
Honoris Crux. Orange with 2mm white edges and 1mm white stripe 5mm from each edge. Made of silver. The centre roundel has a silver border but the arms of the cross are white enamel instead of green as in the other three classes. Awarded for performing deeds of bravery in dangerous circumstances.
The post-nominal titles are: HCD, HCG, HCS and HC respectively. Further awards are denoted by a bar with miniature replica of the decoration—in gold for the first two classes and silver for the second two. Only 4 HCGs were awarded—one with a bar. In 1993 the HCD and HCG were discontinued. The crosses have a SA Mint hallmark. The first striking has voiding round the protea wreath whereas subsequent strikings have no voiding at all.

VALUE:

	A	B	C	Miniature
HC (Diamond)	—	—	—	—
HC (Gold)	£1800	£1500	£220	£100
HC (Silver)	£1500	£1200	£180	£80
HC	£1000	£750	£150	£75

SA10. PRO VIRTUTE DECORATION

Instituted: 1987.

Ribbon: 32mm in width, 20mm orange central stripe edged with a narrow pale blue stripe of 6mm each.

Metal: 9ct gold.

Description: A five linked white enamelled Maltese Cross edged with gold. The centre is of dark red enamel on which is superimposed the embellished coat of arms of the Republic of South Africa. The cross is connected with the suspender by an inverted V from which extends two proteas. The reverse bears the words "PRO VIRTUTE". Awarded to officers of the SA National Defence Force who have distinguished themselves by distinguished conduct and exceptional combat leadership during military operations.

Comments: *Post Nominal Title PVD. Subsequent awards are denoted by a silver gilt bar with a miniature Protea emblem embossed in the centre of the bar.*

VALUE:

A	B	C	Miniature
£1000	£650	£125	£30

SA11. PRO VIRTUTE MEDAL

Instituted: 1987.

Ribbon: 32mm in width, orange outer stripes of 10mm with two 4mm central light blue stripes divided by an orange 4mm central stripe.

Metal: Silver

Description: The obverse bears the outline of the cross of the Pro Virtute Decoration. The reverse bears the title PRO VIRTUTE Surmounted by the coat of arms of the Republic of South Africa and a wreath of proteas as a surround on three sides.

Comments: *Awarded to warrant officers and other ranks with a similar bar for further awards, except in silver. Conditions of award as for PVD. Post nominal title: PVM.*

VALUE:

A	B	C	Miniature
£650	£450	£45	£15

SA12. AD ASTRA DECORATION

Instituted: 1987.

Ribbon: 30mm diagonal alternating narrow light blue and white stripes of 3mm.

Metal: Gold plated silver with hallmark.

Description: In the centre of a five-pointed star is the outline of the Castle of Good Hope in relief on which is depicted the badge of the SA Air Force in gold on a light blue background edged with white. The reverse shows the embellished coat of arms of the Republic of South Africa above the words "AD ASTRA". The star is suspended from an eagle with outstretched wings attached to a ring at the top of the star.

Comments: *This award is made to air crew members for excellent flying skill or outstanding ingenuity or skill during emergencies or unusual situations on board aircraft. Post nominal title: AAD.*

VALUE:

A	B	C	Miniature
£650	£450	£200	£30

SA13.   THE S.A.D.F. CROSSES

Army Cross

Air Force Cross

Navy Cross

SA Medical Services Cross

Instituted: 1987.

Ribbons: A. Army Cross: 30mm wide. White with central 10mm guardsman red stripe; **B. Air Force Cross:** 30mm wide. White with central broad light blue stripes of 12mm divided by a narrow gold stripe of 2mm; **C. Navy Cross:** 30mm wide. White with central broad navy blue stripe of 10mm; **D. SA Medical Services Cross:** 30mm wide. White with central broad purple stripe of 10mm.

Metal: Silver

Description: A silver cross with fixed straight suspender decorated with laurel leaves. The suspender is attached to the top arm of the cross. The arms of the cross have a double border and rise to a higher point from the edge which is 2mm thick. There is a central roundel for each cross covered in shiny epoxy and bordered with three circles of laurel leaves.
A. Army Cross: orange roundel; with badge of the SA Army in gold; **B. Air Force Cross:** light blue roundel with the badge of the SA Air Force in gold; **C. Navy Cross:** navy blue roundel with the badge of the SA Navy in gold; **D. SA Medical Services Cross:** a purple roundel with the badge of the SA Medical Services in gold.

Comments: *The reverse bear the embellished coat of arms of the Republic of South Africa. A bar in silver denotes a subsequent award and bears a miniature protea. Post-nominal titles are as follows: **A. Army Cross:** CM (Crux Militere); **B. Air Force Cross:** CA (Crux Aeronautica); **C. Navy Cross:** CN (Crux Navalis); **D. SA Medical Services Cross:** CC (Crux Curationis).*
Recent events—the sinking of the Oceana *and the Mozambique floods—have seen a number of these crosses awarded, particularly to Air Force personnel. The crosses are awarded to all ranks of the SA Defence Force and auxiliary service for the SA Defence Force and other armed forces attached to or serving with or rendering service to the SA Defence Force, who have distinguished themselves by their exceptional ingenuity and skill in handling equipment, weapons, vehicles, aircraft and vessels concomitant with exemplary personal leadership, dedication and courage in peril of their lives (non-operational).*

VALUE:

A	B	C	*Miniature*
£500	£350	£150	£50

MEDALS AWARDED FOR DISTINGUISHED, LONG AND MERITORIOUS SERVICE

SA14. SOUTHERN CROSS MEDAL (1952)

Instituted: 1952.
Ribbon: 32mm dark blue with 3mm orange and white central stripes.
Metal: Hallmarked silver and enamel.
Description: A circular medal with raised 4mm rimmed border decorated with a single wreath of oak leaves with suspender also decorated with oakleaves. Within the wreath the field of dark blue enamel shows the Southern Cross constellation.
Comments: *This decoration was superseded in 1975 when it was split into two classes: the Southern Cross Decoration and the Southern Cross Medal (of different design). Recipients are entitled to the postnominal SM. The medal was awarded in times of peace or war to members of the SA Defence Force, or of an auxiliary service or other attached armed forces, irrespective of rank, who distinguished themselves by displaying outstanding devotion to duty, either in a particular instance or over a period of time.*

VALUE:

	A	B	C	Miniature
Royal cypher reverse	£120	£110	£100	£20
Royal cypher erased	£100	£80	£70	£15
SA coat of arms	£85	£80	£75	£25

SA15. SOUTHERN CROSS DECORATION (1975)

Instituted: 1975.
Ribbon: 32mm blue with 1mm white stripes 3mm from each edge.
Metal: Silver and enamels.
Description: An eight-pointed Maltese cross superimposed on a larger, broader cross in the same form, with a beaded enamelled medallion at the centre bearing the constellation of the Southern Cross. Fitted with a protea emblem for suspension from a straight bar.
Comments: *Awarded to commissoned officers of the South African Defence Force or of related forces who contributed to the security of the nation, in recognition of outstanding service of the highest order and the utmost devotion to duty displayed in time of peace or war. In 1993 a bar (silver gilt) was authorised with a protea emblem embossed in its centre, for subsequent awards. Recipients are entitled to the post-nominal SD.*

VALUE:

A	A with bar	B	C	Miniature
£100	£120	£85	£80	£75

SA16. SOUTHERN CROSS MEDAL (1975)

Instituted: 1975.
Ribbon: (1975)—32mm in width, dark blue with 2mm white edges and
1mm white stripes 13mm from each edge. (1986)—32mm in width,
divided as follows: white 4mm, dark blue 9mm, white 1mm, dark
blue 4mm and then repeated in reverse.
Metal: Enamelled silver.
Description: A five-pointed radiate star with circular radiate sectors
between the arms, having a beaded central medallion depicting
the constellation of the Southern Cross. Fitted with a plain ring for
suspension from a straight bar.
Comments: *Awarded to commissioned officers of the SA Defence Force or
other armed forces attached to or serving with or rendering service to the
SADF, in recognition of exceptionally meritorious service and particular
devotion to duty displayed in time of peace and war. This medal replaced the
Southern Cross 1952 (SA14). Bar for subsequent awards as for Southern
Cross Decoration (see SA15). Since 1993, recipients have been entitled to
the post-nominal SM.*

VALUE:

A	A with bar	B	C	Miniature
£70	£85	£65	£55	£65

SA17. PRO MERITO MEDAL (1967)

Instituted: 1967.
Ribbon: 32mm sky blue with a dark blue centre flanked by narrow
white and orange stripes.
Metal: Oxidised silver.
Description: An enamelled disa flower in relief encircled by a wreath of
leafed protea flowers on the obverse. The embellished coat of arms
of South Africa is on the reverse. With a foliate suspender.
Comments: *Awarded to Warrant Officers, NCOs and other ranks of the SA
Defence Force and related forces for outstanding devotion to duty. 374
medals were awarded in total. Recipients are entitled to the post-nominal
PMM. In 1975 this award was discontinued when it was split into two
classes: The Pro Merito Decoration and The Pro Merito Medal (of different
design).*

VALUE:

A	B	C	Miniature
£120	£100	£90	£25

SA18. PRO MERITO DECORATION (1975)

Instituted: 1975.
Ribbon: 32mm blue with a 4mm white central stripe.
Metal: Enamelled silver gilt.
Description: A white enamelled Maltese Cross bordered in gold with
centre roundel charged with a red disa flower. The reverse has the
embellished coat of arms of South Africa. At the top is a protea
flower emblem for suspension from a straight bar.
Comments: *It is awarded to Warrant Officers and NCOs and other ranks of
the SA Defence Force or of related forces contributing to the defence of the
Republic of South Africa, who have distinguished themselves by rendering
outstanding service of the highest order and displaying the utmost devotion
to duty. In 1993 a silver gilt bar with protea emblem on its centre was
introduced to denote a subsequent award. Recipients are entitled to the
post-nominal PMD.*

VALUE:

A	B	C	Miniature
£95	£85	£80	£35

SA19. PRO MERITO MEDAL (1975)

Instituted: 1975.

Ribbon: (1975)—32mm in width, blue with 2mm white edges and 4mm white central stripe. (1986)—32mm, sky blue edged by 5mm white stripes with one 4mm white central stripe.

Metal: Oxidised silver.

Description: A five pointed radiate star with radiate sectors between the arms, having a beaded central medallion of blue enamel with a red disa flower. The reverse bears the embellished coat of arms of South Africa. In 1993, a silver bar with a protea embossed in its centre was introduced to indicate a susbequent award. In 1993 the post-nominal title of PMM was introduced. Fitted with a plain ring for suspension from a straight bar.

Comments: *This medal replaced the original Pro Merito Medal of 1976 (SA 17) when that decoration was divided into two classes. The medal was awarded for exceptionally meritorious service and particular devotion to duty in peace or war to Warrant Officers, NCos and other ranks.*

VALUE:

A	B	C	Miniature
£85	£70	£60	£30

SA20. COMMANDANT GENERAL OF THE SOUTH AFRICAN DEFENCE FORCE COMMENDATION (1968)

Instituted: 1968.

Ribbon: None.

Metal: Bronze.

Description: A protea emblem sewn on to the tunic and not worn on medal ribbons.

Comments: *Awarded for mentions in despatches. It was superseded in 1974 by the Chief of the South African Defence Force Commendation Medal (SA21) for which it could be exchanged.*

VALUE:

A	B	C	Miniature
£15	£8	£5	£2

SA21. CHIEF OF THE SA DEFENCE FORCE COMMENDATION MEDAL (1974)

Instituted: 1974.

Ribbon: 32mm orange centre flanked by sky blue stripes and dark blue edges.

Metal: Bronze.

Description: A circular medal with concave curves between twelve points and a plain ring for suspension from a rectangular bar. In the centre, a beaded medallion of the South African Defence Force.

Comments: *Awarded o members of the SA Defence Force (an auxiliary service established to assist the SA Defence Force) who have distinguished themselves by rendering service of a high order which could not be suitably recognised in any other manner. In 1993 this medal was superseded by the Military Merit Medal.*

VALUE:

A	B	C	Miniature
£30	£27	£25	£12

Note: If awarded for downgraded gallantry award with citation: £50

SA22. MILITARY MERIT MEDAL

Instituted: 1993.

Ribbon: As for chief of SA Defence Force Commendation Medal (SA21).

Metal: Bronze plated brass.

Description: As for Chief of SA Defence Force Commendation Medal (SA21) but with fixed suspender.

Comments: *The medal replaced SA21 but with greatly enhanced status. The medal is now awarded to members of the SA Defence Force who have rendered outstanding service of vital importance/permanent significance of the highest order. Because of the anomaly of the previous title of the medal—only the State President and not the Chief of Defence Force could institute the medals, those who had been awarded the Chief of the SA Defence Force Commendation Medal were empowered to change the name of their medal to the new title and like the recipients of the new awards, could enjoy the post-nominal MMM. In 1993 a bar to denote a subsequent award was introduced. The bronze bar carries a centrally placed embossed protea emblem.*

VALUE:

A	B	C	Miniature
£25	£22	£20	£15

SA23. DANIE THERON MEDAL

Instituted: 1970

Ribbon: 32mm green with three narrow yellow stripes.

Metal: Silver.

Description: An eagle hovering over mountain peaks, with three stars on either side and DANIE THERON round the top and MEDALJE MEDAL at the foot. Scrolling spurs secure the medal to the plain suspension bar.

Comments: *This medal was named after the most famous Boer scout of the Anglo-Boer War 1899–1902. From 1970 to 1975, this medal was awarded to officers who were members of the commandos of the SA Defence Force, had completed not less than 10 years service in the SA Defence Force and had not yet received any other awards in recognition of outstanding devotion to duty or exceptionally diligent and outstanding service. In 1975, on the abolition of the Jack Hindon Medal, the Danie Theron Medal now covered the provisions of the Jack Hindon Medal. Recipients of the award are entitled to use the post-nominal DTM.*

VALUE:

A	B	C	Miniature
£100	£90	£80	£25

SA24. JACK HINDON MEDAL

Instituted: 1970

Ribbon: 32mm yellow with a narrow central green stripe and broad green stripes at the edges.

Metal: Bronze.

Description: An upright oval medal showing the sun rising over a mountain peak. In the foreground Jack Hindon and two companions unfurling the Vierkleur (Boer flag) during the battle of Spion Kop on January 24, 1900. Inscription JACK HINDON round the top, with MEDALJE MEDAL at the foot. Fitted with scrolled spurs to a plain suspension bar.

Comments: *This medal was named in honour of Captain Oliver John Hindon who fought for the South African Republic (Transvaal) against the British in the Boer war. (He was born in Stirling, Scotland on 20 April 1874 and he deserted from the British Army while serving in Natal in 1888, after severe treatment at the hands on an NCO of his unit. During the early part of the Anglo-Boer war, Hindon, now a citizen of the Transvaal Republic, was a member of Danie Theron's scout corps and was appointed to head a special corps whose function was to disrupt British lines of communication through the derailment of British trains and the cutting of telegraph lines. So successful was he that he became one of the Boer heroes of the war.)The conditions of this award are as the Danie Theron Medal (SA23) but the Jack Hindon medal was awarded to Warrant Officers, NCOs and other ranks. The medal was superseded by the Danie Theron Medal in 1975. Recipients are entitled to the post-nominal JHM.*

VALUE:

	A	B	C	Miniature
	£120	£100	£60	£25

SA25. COMMANDANT GENERAL'S MEDAL

Instituted: 1956.

Ribbon: 32mm in with, orange with 6.4mm sky blue edges and 6.4mm dark blue central stripe.

Metal: Oxidised silver.

Description: A laurel wreath enclosing a five-sided polygon divided into sectors. In the centre is a circle enclosing crossed rifles above a circular target and bushveld scenery. In the exergue is the inscription KOMMANDANT GENERAALS MEDALJE COMMANDANT GENERALS MEDAL. The top of the polygon has a fluted bar connecting it to the suspension bar decorated with laurel sprays.

Comments: *This medal was awarded for outstanding marksmanship. Subsequent awards of the medal are denoted by bars with a centrally placed silver button inscribed with the year of award. This medal was superseded in 1975 by the SADF Champion Shot Medal (SA26).*

VALUE:

	A	B	C	Miniature
	£120	£110	£50	£25

SA26. SADF CHAMPION SHOTS MEDAL

Instituted: 1975.

Ribbon: As SA25.

Metal: oxidised silver.

Description: Identical to SA25 except for the inscription in the exergue which now reads SAW KAMPIOENSKUTMEDALJE / SADF CHAMPION SHOT MEDAL.

Comments: *Awarded annually to the champion shot. Subsequent awards of the medal are denoted by bars with centrally placed silver button inscribed with the year of award. The award replaced the Commandant General's Medal (SA25).*

VALUE:

A	B	C	Miniature
£105	£100	£50	£25

SA27. CADET CORPS CHAMPION SHOT MEDAL

Instituted: 1987.

Ribbon: 32mm orange ribbon each side edged with a 6mm green stripe.

Metal: Silver.

Description: Obverse: A prancing springbok facing to the left enclosed on three sides by a wreath of laurels. Reverse: In semicircular format—top: GROOTKAMPIONSKUT, bottom: GRAND CHAMPION SHOT and centrally placed in two lines: KADETKORPS and CADET CORPS.

Comments: *The imaginative concept was that winners' achievements would not be lost on leaving school but they could mount this medal along with their SA Defence Force awards in after years. The medal is unique in that never before has a school cadet been authorised to wear a medal. In 1994 the School Cadet Corps were abolished by the President of South Africa, so the award became obsolete. By that date, 16 awards had been made and these were backdated to 1978.*

VALUE:

A	B	C	Miniature
£120	£100	£80	£25

SA28. UNION MEDAL

Instituted: 1952.

Branch of service: Union of South Africa Permanent Defence Force.

Ribbon: 32mm equal stripes of orange, white and navy blue repeated three times to make a total of 9 stripes.

Metal: Silver.

Description: A scalloped medal with an ornamental suspender of wattle leaves and mimosa flowers. Obverse: Coat of arms of South Africa and the inscription UNION MEDAL—UNIE MEDALJE. Reverse: the Royal Cypher EIIR with crown.

Bar for 12 years

Ribbon emblem

Comments: *This medal was awarded to members of the Union Defence Force Permanent Force, irrespective of rank, for a minimum of 18 years service of an impeccable character. It was superseded in 1961 by the Permanent Force Good Service Medal. This medal replaced no. 253 except its award was extended to include commissioned officers as well. Approximately 1,400 medals were awarded. Those completing an extra 12 years service were eligible for a silver bar with centrally embossed coat of arms of South Africa. When the ribbon alone was worn the bar to the awards was represented by a miniature silver coat of arms.*

VALUE:

A	B	C	Miniature
£45	£40	£35	£15

SA29. PERMANENT FORCE GOOD SERVICE MEDAL

Instituted: 1961.

Ribbon: As for Union Medal (SA28)

Metal: Silver.

Description: A scalloped medal. Obverse as for SA28 except "UNION MEDAL—UNIE MEDALJE" has been removed. Reverse: carries details over seven lines: VIR LANGDURIGE DIENS EN GOEIE GEDRAG / FOR LONG SERVICE AND GOOD CONDUCT.

Comments: *Awarded for a minimum of 18 years service. A silver bar in the form of the republican arms was added to the ribbon for further periods of 12 years service (as for SA28). About 2,700 of these medals were awarded.*

VALUE:

A	B	C	Miniature
£32	£28	£25	£15

SA30. SOUTH AFRICAN DEFENCE FORCE GOOD SERVICE MEDAL

1st striking

Instituted: 1975.

Ribbon: 32mm green with different stripes according to the class and branch of service. In 1986 the nine ribbons were reduced to three: gold medal—green with two 7mm yellow stripes 6mm from each edge; silver medal—green edged with 7mm white stripes with a central 6mm white stripe; bronze medal—green edged with two 10mm bronze brown stripes.

Metal: Silver gilt/gilt coated brass for 30 years; silver/silver coated brass for 20 years; bronze/bronze coated brass/bronze sprayed on brass for 10 years.

Description: A scalloped medal bearing (obverse): the coat of arms of the Republic. (Reverse) the inscription VIR TROUE DIENS/FOR GOOD SERVICE. Ornamental suspender of wattle leaves and mimosa flowers.

Comments: *This medal superseded the Permanent Force Good Service Medal of 1961 (see SA29) and was divided into three classes, each having distinctive ribbons as follows:*
> *Gold Medal:*
>> *Permanent Force. Three narrow white stripes towards each edge*
>> *Citizen Force. Three narrow blue stripes towards each edge*
>> *Commandos. Three narrow orange stripes towards each edge*
> *Silver Medal:*
>> *Permanent Force. Two narrow white stripes towards each edge*
>> *Citizen Force. Two narrow blue stripes towards each edge*
>> *Commandos. Two narrow orange stripes towards each edge*
> *Bronze Medal:*
>> *Permanent Force. One narrow white stripe 2mm from edge*
>> *Citizen Force. One narrow blue stripe 2mm from edge*
>> *Commandos. One narrow orange stripe 2mm from edge.*

> *Members of the Citizen Force or Commandos had the option of choosing this series instead of the John Chard series for Citizen Force or the De Wet series for the Commandos. A silver gilt bar identical to the bar mentioned in SA28 and SA29 was awarded for 40 years service and this was sewn on to the ribbon of the 30 year medal. The reverse of the medal bears the title: VIR TROUWE DIENS/ FOR GOOD SERVICE in relief. In the first two strikings of this medal the suspender was decorated with wattle leaves and mimosa flowers on the obverse while the reverse of the suspension was plain.*

There are three strikings to each medal:
1st striking: SA Mint marks.
2nd striking: No Mint marks, no rim to the reverse while the bronze medal is brass coated with bronze and the gauge of the medals is almost 50 per cent thinner.
3rd striking: No Mint marks, reverse rim restored and medal of proper thickness with double faced suspension bar. Brass coated in gold, silver and bronze sprayed-on paint.

VALUE:

	A	B	C	Miniature
First striking:				
Gold:	£45	£38	£35	£15
Silver:	£28	£25	£25	£12
Bronze:	£17	£15	£15	£5
Second striking:				
Gold:	£35	£32	£30	£15
Silver:	£25	£22	£20	£10
Bronze:	£15	£14	£12	£5
Third striking:				
Gold:	£35	£32	£30	£15
Silver:	£28	£22	£20	£10
Bronze:	£18	£15	£12	£5

SA31. SOUTH AFRICAN DEFENCE FORCE GOOD SERVICE MEDAL FOR 40 YEARS SERVICE

Instituted: 1986.

Ribbon: 32mm green with central portion 1mm white, 3mm black, 3mm white, 3mm orange and 1mm white. In 1994 the ribbon was changed however, reducing the central portion to 10mm, 5x2mm stripes of blue, yellow, black, white and red.

Metal: 9 carat gold.

Description: Obverse: The embellished coat of arms of South Africa. Reverse: The Roman numerals XL within a circular laurel wreath open at the top and the medal suspended from a double faced scrolled suspender.

Comments: *This medal is awarded to all members of the South African Permanent Force, Citizen Force or Commandos for 40 years of meritorious and irreproachable service.*

VALUE:

A	B	C	Miniature
£120	£110	£50	£30

SA32. JOHN CHARD DECORATION

Instituted: 1952.

Ribbon: 32mm dark red with 3mm dark blue (outer) and 2mm white (inner) edges.

Metal: Silver/chromed brass.

Description: An upright oval medal fitted with a ring for suspension. The centre shows a view of Rorke's Drift in 1879. At the top is the inscription JOHN CHARD and at the foot DECORATION: DEKORASIE. See descriptions below for details of the various reverses.

Comments: *This decoration replaced the Efficiency Decoration and was named in memory of Lieutenant John Chard, VC, who commanded the garrison at the defence of Rorke's Drift during the Zulu War, 1879. The medal ribbon is worn with a silver button embossed with the initials JCD. The measurement from the top to bottom of the upright oval was designed to exactly match the proportions of the Efficiency Decoration (No. 236). A silver bar with crown (as for the Efficiency Medal) was awarded to denote an extra 10 years, i.e. 30 years service up until 1961. In 1962 a bar of silver with centred circle enclosing the initials JCD was awarded for 30 years service. Silver emblems indicate the branch of service: a fouled anchor on the ribbon for the navy, crossed swords for the army and an eagle with outstretched wings for the air force. Holders are entitled to the post-nominals JCD.*

VALUE:

Type	Description	A	B	C	Miniature
I	Royal cypher EIIR above SA coat of arms	£75	£65	£60	£35
II	Royal cypher erased	£65	£60	£45	£30
III	Large coat of arms of SA —voided acorn	£55	£50	£35	£6
IV	Unvoided acorn suspender and no rim on reverse, with coat of arms	£50	£45	£35	£4
V	As for IV but metal chromed brass, with coat of arms	£45	£40	£30	—
VI	Reverse rim, voided acorn of poor detail and medal stamped silver, with coat of arms	£60	£50	£45	£6

SA33. JOHN CHARD MEDAL

Instituted: 1952.

Ribbon: As for John Chard decoration (SA32).

Metal: Bronze; bronze coated brass; brass sprayed with bronze paint.

Description: Identical to SA32 but with inscription MEDALJE: MEDAL round the foot.

Comments: *This medal replaced the Efficiency Medal and Air Efficiency Medal. Silver emblems indicate the branch of service as in SA32.*

VALUE:

Type	Description	A	B	C	Miniature
I	Royal cypher EIIR on	£55	£40	£35	£30
	SA coat of arms				
II	Royal cypher erased	£50	£45	£40	£25
III	Large coat of arms,	£30	£28	£25	£4
	solid bronze medal				
IV	Unvoided acorn and no rim	£30	£25	£20	£2
	on reverse, bronze coated brass, with coat of arms				
V	Poor detailed voided acorn,	£25	£22	£20	£4
	brass sprayed with bronze paint, with coat of arms				

SA34. DE WET DECORATION

Instituted: 1965.

Ribbon: 32mm orange with a broad central blue stripe and 3mm green edges separated from the orange by narrow white stripes.

Metal: Silver.

Description: Two sprays of protea blossom enclose a vignette of General Christiaan De Wet, leader of Boer Forces in 1901–02, on horseback with the inscription DEKORASIE—DE WET—DECORATION round the top of the field, enclosed in a wreath of protea blossom. Foliate spurs link the top of the rim to a plain suspension bar.

Comments: *Awarded to all ranks of Commandos for 20 years service. An additional 10 years service is denoted by a silver bar with centrally placed circle with embossed initials DWD. Holders are entitled to the post nominals DWD.*

VALUE:

A	B	C	Miniature
£85	£75	£60	£40

SA35. DE WET MEDAL

Instituted: 1987.

Ribbon: 32mm central panel (made up of 7mm stripes of navy blue, yellow and navy blue), flanked by 3mm green and 2mm white stripes on either side.

Metal: Brass with lacquered bronze paint.

Description: As for De Wet Decoration (SA34) except inscribed MEDALJE—DE WET—MEDAL on the obverse. Suspender of similar design but double width and uniface.

Comments: *Awarded for 10 years service in the Commandos.*

VALUE:

A	B	C	Miniature
£55	£50	£30	£35

SA36. CADET CORPS MEDAL

Instituted: 1966.

Ribbon: 32mm orange with 5mm blue edges separated from the orange by 1.5mm white stripes.

Metal: Oxidised silver.

Description: A prancing springbok enclosed in a laurel wreath with the inscription CADET CORPS MEDAL and KADETKORPS MEDALJE at the sides.

Comments: *Awarded for 20 years service as an officer in the Cadet Corps. Those who had completed 30 years service were eligible for a silver bar with a prancing springbok embossed in the centre of the bar. It was abolished in August 1976 when the Cadet Corps ceased to exist as a separate force, being absorbed into the Commandos or Citizen Force.*

VALUE:

A	B	C	Miniature
£55	£48	£42	£45

SERVICE MEDALS

SA37. PRO PATRIA MEDAL

Instituted: 1974.

Ribbon: 32mm orange with a broad band of dark blue divided by a thin central orange stripe, with narrow white stripes towards the edges.

Metal: Brass with gilt finish.

Clasp: Cunene clasp awarded for operations into Angola in 1976, sewn on to the ribbon of the Pro Patria Medal.

Description: An eight sided medal with rectangular motifs in each sector with a central dark blue medallion depicting a stylised aloe plant in gold. It has a plain ring attached to a straight suspension bar with a protean emblem flanked by laurel sprays—type I and II have a link suspender whereas type III has a fixed suspender.

Comments: *Awarded for service in the defence of the Republic of South Africa or for supression or prevention of terrorism with specified conditions of award. There are a number of variations in manufacture for type III.*

VALUE:

Type	Description	A	B	C	Miniature
I	*Link suspender. SA Mint striking—serial numbers 1.25mm high*	£50	£40	£30	
II	*Link suspender*	£35	£20	£15	£2
III	*Fixed suspender*	£15	£10	£5	£10
	With Cunene clasp	£15	£12	£10	£10

(This value should be added to types I, II and III if there is a Cunene clasp)

SA38. SOUTHERN AFRICA MEDAL

Instituted: 1989.

Ribbon: 32mm, central black stripe of 12mm centred with 2mm white stripe, flanked on either side with a 5mm red and 5mm yellow stripe.

Metal: Nickel silver.

Description: An eight sided medal with suspender ornamented with protea flower on each scrolled arm. Obverse: A leopard on the prowl beneath an acacia tree to indicate the strike power of the South African Defence Force. Reverse: A laurel wreath open at its uppermost point to embrace a small embellished coat of arms of South Africa, below are the words SUIDER-AFRICA / SOUTHERN AFRICA.

Comments: *The medal was awarded for participation in specified cross-border activites in defence of the Republic of South Africa. The award was to have originally been called the "Trans Jati Medal", the "Jati" being the cut line. The medals were to have been made from the metal of a captured Russian T34 tank but the metal was found to be unsuited for the purpose. Instead a small amount of melted metal from the tank was mixed with nickel silver. There were two strikings of the medal—the first with a uniface suspender struck as an integral part of the medal, the second with a double faced suspender attached to the medal.*

VALUE:	A	B	C	Miniature
Type I	£35	£25	£16	£10
Type II	£38	£28	£18	—

SA39. GENERAL SERVICE MEDAL

Instituted: 1989.

Ribbon: 32mm, 6mm navy blue stripe, 2mm white stripe, 7mm orange stripe, 2mm navy blue stripe, then the first three stripes repeated in reverse.

Metal: Nickel silver.

Description: Obverse: A laurel wreath open at its uppermost point and enclosing the badge of the South African Defence Force which combines the swords, wings and anchor of the Army, Air Force and Navy, on an outline of the Castle of Good Hope. Reverse: The embellished coat of arms of South Africa with GENERAL SERVICE / ALGEMENE DIENS to the right and left of the coat of arms. Suspenders / strikings as for SA38.

Comments: *The medal was awarded for service within the borders of the Republic of South Africa since 1 January 1983.*

VALUE:	A	B	C	Miniature
Type I	£10	£7	£5	£10
Type II	£12	£10	£8	—

COMMEMORATIVE—SA40. UNITAS MEDAL

Instituted: 1994.

Ribbon: 32mm, pale blue with central green stripe of 8mm edged each side by a white stripe of 4mm.

Metal: Lacquered brass.

Description: Obverse: A seven pointed star with central circle enclosing the Greek letter Alpha. Reverse: A small embellished coat of arms of South Africa with date 1994 below. The whole is enclosed by a circle made up of the word "Unity" in all eleven official languages of the new South Africa. Suspender is uniface and struck as one piece with the medal.

Comments: *Awarded to all those who rendered service through being members of a serving force (Permanent Force, Citizen Force, Commandos, members of the armed forces of the former self-governing territories, the armed wing of the ANC (the MK) and APLA) during the period of South Africa's first non-racial elections and inauguration of Mr Mandela as the first black State President in South Africa between 27 April and 10 May 1994. Those medals awarded to members of the British Military Advisory Team in South Africa at the time, for which Her Majesty Queen Elizabeth II granted permission for wear must be considered a rarity.*

VALUE:	A	B	C	Miniature
	£10	£8	£5	£10

MISCELLANEOUS

SA41. MENTION IN DESPATCHES

Instituted: 1967.
Metal: Gilt or bronze.
Description: A miniature replica of the embellished coat of arms of South Africa.
Comments: *Worn either on the ribbon of the Pro Patria Medal or General Service Medal. Prior to the institution of these medals, a bronze version was worn on uniform fabric of the tunic and not affixed to a medal.*

VALUE:

A with Citation	A	B	C	Miniature
£15 to £20	£10	£6	£2	£8

SOUTH AFRICAN NATIONAL DEFENCE FORCE INTERIM AWARDS: 1996 TO 2003

In 1994 South Africa entered a new era when the ANC came into power after the Nationalist Government ceased to hold the reigns of government. The armed forces underwent a period of transformation where former so called terrorists who had formed part of the armed wing of the African National Congress (MK, Mkhonto Wesizwe), and the Azanian People's Party (APLA, Azanian People's Liberation Army) had to be integrated into the armed forces of South Africa. In keeping with this, the South African Defence Force now became the South African National Defence Force.

Former MK and APLA members entered the SANDF with ribbonless chests. To remedy the situation 18 new medals were instituted for award to members of MK and APLA in 1996—two years after these forces had been disbanded. The awards recognised deeds of bravery or service before 27 April 1994. This decision had a South African president. In 1913 members of the armed forces of the old Boer republics of the Orange Free State and Transvaal had been absorbed into the newly formed Union Defence Force. Because of the outbreak of the First World War in 1914, an initiative to recognise the service and meritorious service of former members of the Boer Forces was postponed until 1920. That year the Dekoratie Voor Troue Dienst (see MY339) and the Anglo-Boere Oorlog Medalje (MY340) were instituted.

The new awards for former MK and APLA members consisted of three bravery awards in three classes for MK with a corresponding allocation for APLA. Similarly three merit and three long service awards were allocated to MK and APLA. A list of the 18 new awards with post nominal titles is as follows:

• Bravery. APLA Guild Star for Bravery (GSB) Bravery Star in Silver (BSS) Star for Conspicuous Leadership (SCL)	• Excellent Service, MK Gold Decoration for Merit in Gold (DMG) Merit Medal in Silver (MMS) Merit Medal in Bronze (MMB)
• Bravery. MK Star for Bravery in Gold (SBG) Star for Bravery in Silver (SBS) Conspicuous Leadership Star (CLS)	• Long Service, APLA Gold Service Medal (GSM) (30 yrs) Silver Service Medal (SSM) (20 yrs) Bronze Service Medal (BSM) (10 yrs)
• Excellent Service, APLA Gold Decoration for Merit (GDM) Silver Medal for Merit (SMM) Bronze Medal for Merit (BMM)	• Long Service, MK Service Medal in Gold (SMG) (30 yrs) Service Medal in Silver (SMS) (20 yrs) Service Medal in Bronze (SMB) (10 yrs)

COMMENTS
1. Orange and red were used as the basic ribbon colour for the bravery awards; blue for merit and green for long service.
2. The design of the medals and structure of the award system was modeled on that of the SADF instituted in 1975 (see MY SA9 for bravery; MY SA15+16+22 for merit and MY SA30 for long service.)
3. The bravery awards design was a new departure: the MK awards being a five pointed star and the APLA awards a ten pointed star. The centre of the bravery awards has a roundel with the South African Lion.

4. The official coat of arms of the Republic of South African was placed on the reverse of all the new awards
5. The obverse of the merit and long service awards carry the symbols of MK (African shield with wheel of industry plus vertical spear and angled AK47 assault rifle) and APLA (African shield with crossed spear and AK47 assault rifle.)
6. The metal used for the bravery awards and "gold" merit and "gold" long service awards is silver, plated in gold "Enamel" work is in fact not enamel but epoxy covered paint. The obverse of all the medals was poorly struck with a very shallow die so that the design is virtually flat, on a level with the surface of the medal. The medal series gives the over-all impression of hasty preparation which was exactly what had occurred.
7. The medals were issued with a serial number and certificate (see introduction to SA Decorations and Medals regarding the pricing of medals (page 375).
8. To date only a few unissued numbered specimen medals have appeared for sale without documentation.

SOUTH AFRICAN NATIONAL DEFENCE FORCE NEW AWARDS 2003

The new honours and awards system was instituted on April 27, 2003. All recommendations after that date are to be for the new honours. The new decorations and medals will be issued to all ranks of the SANDF, to any auxiliaries of the SANDF and in certain circumstances to foreign military personnel.

1. Three decorations for bravery are as follows with post nominal titles: Golden Leopard (NG); Silver Leopard (NS); Bronze Leopard (NB). Bars are awarded for subsequent awards of the same decoration.
2. Three decorations for leadership, meritorious conduct or devotion to duty are awarded. Golden Protea (PG); Silver Protea (PS); Bronze Protea (PB) As is the case with the bravery awards, further awards of the same decoration are indicated by bars.
3. A single bronze long service medal replaces the previous awards for 10, 20 and 30 years service, in bronze, silver and gold. The Medal for Loyal Service will be awarded for ten years service, characterised by good conduct. For each additional period of ten years qualifying service, to a maximum of 40 years, extra bars will be awarded to represent each ten year period. For Reserve Force members, a monogram of the letters RD will be attached to the ribbon. These letters stand for "Reserve Distinction" to accord special recognition to part time members of the Reserves.
4. A campaign medal, the General Service Medal, will reward recipients for periods of operational service, minor campaigns and other operations

It is disappointing to note that in the development of this new series, acknowledged medal experts were not consulted. The Military Medal Society of South Africa offered its services to make recommendations and give advice regarding the design of the new series. Such offers were ignored until the eleventh hour when assistance was required regarding the actual production of the medals.

The new series is a disappointment when it comes to design, as persons with little medallic knowledge or imagination developed these medals. In addition, the chance of breaking away from the flawed system of numbering medals and moving to the naming of medals with recipients number, rank, initials, surname and unit was not seized. A great opportunity to give South Africa a world class medal series has been missed.

NOTE: As it will be some years before any of the new awards come onto the market, it has been decided not to illustrate them.

POLICE AWARDS

Those listed here are the medals most commonly encountered by collectors. The information is taken from Gallantry Awards of the South African Police 1913–1994 by Terence King assisted by Audrey Portman by courtesy of Rhino Research. The book contains in-depth details of the gallantry medals listed.

SA42. SOUTH AFRICAN POLICE STAR FOR OUTSTANDING SERVICE (SOE)

Instituted: 1979

Ribbon: 36mm green divided by two stripes of yellow, blue and white. a

Metal: Gilded silver

Description: A star composed of the cross of St Cuthbert, each limb notched of four and in each angle, an engrailed ray. (Obverse): in the centre, a white roundel bearing an aloe with three racemes. (Reverse): the unembellished coat of arms of the Republic of South Africa within the legend *STELLA OFFICII ENGREGII* SA POLICE. A bar denoting subsequent awards depicts an aloe with three racemes. A miniature replica of this clasp is attached to the ribbon when the ribbon alone is worn by a recipient who has been awarded a bar. All decorations and bars were issued named to the recipient and stamped with the serial number, rank and name.

Comments: *Awarded to a member of the South African Police or reserve police who: (a) in the execution of his duties in protecting or saving, or endeavouring to protect or save, life or property, has displayed particular gallantry, exceptional ingenuity, skill or perseverance; (b) in the execution of his duties has rendered outstanding services to members of a dynasty or to Heads of State or of Governments; (c) has distinguished himself through outstanding resourcefulness, leadership, and sense of responsibility or by setting a personal example in any branch of the Force. In addition, it could be awarded to any other persons who distinguished themselves through outstanding services rendered to the South African Police. This decoration was also awarded to recognize acts of gallantry as well as acts of outstanding service. In 1989 all references to gallantry were removed where they occurred in the original warrant, and the award was to officers of the general staff. This was in consequence of the institution of the 1989 version of the South African Police Cross for Bravery. Recipients of this decoration are entitled to use the post nominal letters SOE (STELLA OFFICII EGREGII).*

VALUE: Named £100
Unnamed £50
Awards for gallantry £1,000

Miniature £40 (add £5 for bar)

SA43. SOUTH AFRICAN POLICE STAR FOR MERIT

Instituted: 1963.
Ribbon: 32mm, orange with white central stripe edged with blue.
Metal: Silver.
Description: (Obverse): two forearms with hands overlaying the letter V resting on the letter M and holding aloft a flame. (Reverse): the badge of the South African Police, with the words VERDIENSTE above and MERIT below. A silver bar with an embossed letter V resting on an M was authorised to denote a subsequent award or completion of 30 years service. When the ribbon alone is worn, the award of a bar is indicated by this circular emblem. All decorations and bars were issued named to the recipient and stamped with the serial number, rank and name.

Comments: *The award is granted to: (a) members of the South African Police or reserve police force who, in the discharge of their duties, have rendered services of a particularly meritorious or exemplary nature; (b) a member who has completed thirty years service (not necessarily continuous), and who has displayed an irreproachable character and exemplary conduct. The medal is also awarded to other persons (civilians) who have rendered services of a particularly meritorious nature to the South African Police. This medal is awarded for long service and good conduct as well as being a decoration for particularly exemplary or meritorious service (gallantry). The majority of awards to members of the police or reserve police were for acts of gallantry.*

VALUE: Named   £45
　　　　Gallantry award   £250–300　　　　*Miniature*   £20

SA44. SOUTH AFRICAN POLICE MEDAL FOR FAITHFUL SERVICE

Instituted: 1963.
Ribbon: 32mm, royal blue with 3mm old gold centre stripe.
Metal: Bronze.
Description: (Obverse): the coat of arms of the Republic of South Africa surrounded by a laurel. (Reverse): the official badge of the South African Police with the words TROUE DIENS and FAITHFUL SERVICE in embossed capital letters around.

Comments: *This medal replaced the Police Good Service Medal and was awarded to members of the South African Police who had displayed an irreproachable character and exemplary conduct and served for a qualifying period. A bronze bar embossed with the letters TDFS (Troue Diens/Faithful Service) in ornamental script was awarded for subsequent qualifying periods.*

VALUE　　Named   £15　　Unnamed   £10　　*Miniature*   £10

SA45. SOUTH AFRICAN POLICE STAR FOR FAITHFUL SERVICE

Instituted: 1979.
Ribbon: 36mm, divided into 11 parts: yellow 2mm, green 3mm, yellow 4mm, blue 2mm, yellow 4mm, green 6mm, repeated in reverse.
Metal: Silver.
Description: A circular medal with (obverse): an eight-pointed star, charged in the centre with a medallion, with four aloes in cross, each with three racemes, all in natural colours. (Reverse): the official badge of the South African Police with the words TROUE DIENS and FAITHFUL SERVICE around.

Comments: *This medal was an award to complement the two long service and good conduct awards already in existence.The qualifying period changed over the years and a gold bar bearing the letters TDFS in ornamental script was awarded for further periods of service. Medals were now awarded for 10 years service (Medal for Faithful Service), 20 years service (Star for Faithful Service), 30 years service (Star for Merit) and 40 years service (Bar to Star for Faithful Service).*

VALUE:　　Named   £15　　Unnamed   £10　　*Miniature*   £15

SA46. SOUTH AFRICAN POLICE MEDAL FOR COMBATING TERRORISM

Instituted: 1974.
Ribbon: 31.75mm red, with three wide and two narrow silver stripes.
Metal: Silver.
Description: (Obverse): A six-pointed star, with three long and three short points. Attached to the ribbon by means of a V-shaped silver clevis, which is in turn attached to the medal by means of a rimmed shield depicting a candlestick aloe with four leaves and three candles. (Reverse): The words BEKAMPING VAN TERRORISME—COMBATING TERRORISM around the official badge of the South African Police. A silver bar was authorised to denote a subsequent award. This plain bar bears, in the centre, a silver clasp corresponding to the design on the shield. A maximum of two bars only can be awarded, irrespective of any further qualification period. All medals were issued named to the recipient with the serial number, rank and name stamped on the reverse of the V shaped clevis.

Comments: *Awarded to a member of the South African Police or others who, in support of the police, on or at any time after 26 August 1966 (a) had been involved in combat with terrorists, or in the course of the performance of duties in connection with the prevention and combating of terrorism, sustained injuries arising from terrorist activities; or who, in the execution of such duties, displayed exceptional zeal, ingenuity, skills or leadership; (b) had performed counter insurgency duties for at least six months, which may be cumulative, in an area (operational area) fixed by the Minister; (c) had rendered exceptional and outstanding service to the South African Police in connection with the combating of terrorism. The original qualifying period of six months was later changed to sixty days. Any member of the South African Police who was stationed permanently for a continuous period of at least twelve months in an operational area and behaved in an exemplary manner also qualified for the award of the medal.*

VALUE: Named   £20   Unnamed   £10   *Miniature*   £12

SA47. SOUTH AFRICAN POLICE 75th ANNIVERSARY MEDAL

Instituted: 1988.
Ribbon: Royal blue 32mm edged with light blue and old gold stripes.
Metal: Bronze.
Description: (Obverse): The figures "75", surmounted with an aloe with three racemes and the police motto "SERVAMUS ET SERVIMUS" above and the dates "1913-1988" below. (Reverse): The badge of the South African Police.

Comments: *Instituted to commemorate the 75th anniversary of the founding the South African Police on 1 April 1988. Awarded to permanent and temporary members of the Police Force and Reserve Police Force on 1 April 1988, or people who had rendered service of a particularly meritorious nature to the South African Police. A bar, bearing the figures "75" surmounted by an aloe and three racemes, is to be awarded to those still serving in the Force on 1 April 2013. All awards were issued named and were engraved on the reverse with the serial number, rank and name of the recipient.*

VALUE: Named   £10   Unnamed   £5   *Miniature*   £15

SOUTH AFRICAN PRISONS AWARDS
(Later Department of Correctional Services)

SA48. MEDAL FOR MERIT IN THE SOUTH AFRICAN PRISONS SERVICE

Instituted: 1968.

Ribbon: 35mm in width divided into seven parts: blue 6mm; white 5mm; orange 6mm; white 1mm; then repeated in reverse.

Metal: Silver.

Description: Suspender in form of a lifebuoy. Obverse: DEPARTMENT VAN GEVANGENISSE / PRISONS DEPARTMENT at edge of medal with embellished South African coat of arms. Reverse: FOR MERIT (top) and VIR VERDIENSTELIKHEID (below).

Comments: *Awarded to members of the SAPS who had rendered particularly meritorious or exemplary service or distinguished himself by his ingenuity, proficiency or perseverance for a period of not less than 35 years, displaying irreproachable character and exemplary conduct. Impressed naming on reverse. A plain bar of silver with the coat of arms of SA embossed in the centre was awarded for subsequent acts of distinction. Replaced by SA51 (NCOs) in 1979.*

VALUE:

Named with bar	£75
Named	£40
Unnamed	£15
Miniature	£15

SA49. SOUTH AFRICAN PRISONS SERVICE STAR FOR MERIT

Instituted: 1980

Ribbon: 32mm Green with two vertical white stripes each 2mm wide and 12mm from the side.

Metal: Silver.

Description: A 10-point cross with protea flowers in the angles and a plain ring for suspension from a straight bar.

Comments: *Awarded to Commissioned officers for outstanding services rendered on the grounds of ability, efficiency, perseverance or devotion in the discharge of duties. Post nominal title: SPM (Stella Pro Merito). 496 were issued.*

VALUE:

Named with certificate	£70
Named	£40
Unnamed	£20
Miniature (silver)	£30

SA50. SOUTH AFRICAN PRISONS SERVICE CROSS FOR MERIT

Instituted: 1980.

Ribbon: 32mm green with three vertical white stripes each 2mm wide and 2mm from each other with the outer white stripes 11mm from each side.

Metal: Silver with gold plated border to cross.

Description: A cross pattée very similar to the German Iron Cross in appearance, but without any detail on the front. Fitted with a plain ring for suspension from a straight bar.

Comments: *No clasps granted for additional awards. Award conditions as for South Africa Prisons Service Star for Merit (SA49) but awarded to non-commissioned officers. Post nominal title: CPM (Crux Pro Merito). 2655 were issued.*

VALUE:

Named	£40
Unnamed	£20
Miniature	£30

SA51. SOUTH AFRICAN PRISONS SERVICE MEDAL FOR MERIT

Instituted: 1980.
Ribbon: For Commissioned Officers: 32mm divided into seven parts—
white 4mm; green 8mm; white 2mm; green 4mm and then repeated in
reverse. **For NCOs:** 32mm, divided into nine parts; white 4mm; green
8mm; white 2mm; green 4mm white 2mm and then repeated in reverse.
Metal: Silver.
Description: A radiate star with an open protea floriate centre and an
inverted V and ring for suspension from a straight bar.
Comments: *Same conditions of award as SA49 and SA50 except the word
"outstanding" is replaced by "special". For the Officer's Medal the eight single
rays are gold plated and the eight pairs of narrow rays are silver. The open
protea flower in the centre is gold plated. The NCOs Medal is plain silver.
1,248 issued to officers and 5,059 issued to NCO's.*

VALUE:

Named	£40
Unnamed	£20
Miniature	Officers £45
	NCOs £40

SA52. FAITHFUL SERVICE MEDAL, PRISONS DEPARTMENT

Instituted: 1965.
Ribbon: 31mm, divided into five parts: green 6mm; white 5mm; blue 9mm;
and then repeated in reverse.
Metal: Silver.
Description: Obverse: coat of arms of the Republic of South Africa
with the words DEPARTMENT VAN GEVANGENISSE—PRISONS
DEPARTMENT. Reverse: VOOR TROUE DIENS—FOR FAITHFUL
SERVICE.
Comments: *Awarded (1) for 18 years service (not necessarily continuous) that
displayed exemplary conduct and unimpeachable character or (2) had displayed
devotion to duty in a distinguished or gallant manner. This medal superseded
No. 291. A bar with the words: VERDIENSTELIK/MERITORIOUS was
granted for gallant or distinguished conduct.*

VALUE:

If awarded for (1)	£36
If awarded for (2)	£100
With bar	£75
Unnamed	£25
Miniature	£35

SA53. MEDAL FOR FAITHFUL SERVICE IN THE SOUTH AFRICAN PRISONS SERVICE

Instituted: 1968.
Ribbon: 35mm divided into five parts: blue 6mm; white 5mm; green 13mm
and then repeated in reverse.
Metal: Bronze.
Description: Obverse: In the form of the official badge of the Prisons
Department with the circumscription DEPARTMENT VAN
GEVANGINISSE (top) and PRISONS DEPARTMENT (bottom). Reverse:
FOR FAITHFUL SERVICE (above) and VIR TROUE DIENS (below). In
the central area the space received the engraved name, etc., and date of
the award of the recipient.
Comments: *Awarded For: (1) as for (1) in SA52. (2) If the recipient had
received SA52 for condition of 2 of SA52 then he would receive this medal
on completion of 18 years service, etc. (3) If the recipient was in possession of
SA52 after 18 years service he could receive this medal after a completion of
a further 12 years. A bar of bronze with the Prisons Department badge in the
centre denoted a further 15 years service following the award of the medal.*

VALUE:

Named	£15
Unnamed	£10
Miniature	£25

SA54. SOUTH AFRICA PRISONS SERVICE MEDAL FOR FAITHFUL SERVICE

Instituted: 1980.
Ribbon: 32mm yellow with two sets of three green stripes each 2mm wide and 2mm apart, the outer stripe set being 2mm from each edge (Gold); two sets of two green stripes each 2mm wide and 2mm apart, the outer stripe set being 2mm from each edge (Silver); or two green stripes each 2mm wide and 2mm from each edge (Bronze).
Metal: Silver-gilt, silver or bronze to denote 30, 20 or 10 years service.
Description: A circular medal with the arms of the Republic in the centre and a garland of protea blossom round the circumference.
Comments: *This replaced SA53. A silver-gilt bar for the gold medal was authorised, embossed with a central circle in the form of the obverse of the medal to indicate a further 10 years service.*

VALUE:

	Named	Unnamed	*Miniature*
With Bar to Gold	£50	£30	£35
Gold (1,130)	£40	£25	£40
Silver (5,594)	£30	£20	£45
Bronze (13,350)	£20	£10	£50

Unofficial
medals

Interest has been steadily growing in recent years in unofficial medals, a subject on the fringes of medal collecting. The term is deliberately vague and encompasses a very wide range of medals, medalets and medallions of a commercial, private or local nature. Such a generic term would, for example, include regimental medals awarded for marksmanship or good conduct, often associated with official medal groups of the 19th century. This is a very esoteric group, often consisting of medals which were specially engraved for the occasion and therefore exceedingly difficult to quantify.

On the other hand, many of the earlier medals, now highly regarded as forerunners of the general campaign series, were unofficial in origin, and relied upon the enterprise of public-spirited indviduals and prize agents such as Alexander Davison (nos. 78 and 85) or Matthew Boulton (no. 84), generals such as Elliot (no. 74), Earl St Vincent (no. 80) or Gordon of Khartoum (no. 133) or even private bodies such as the Highland Society (no. 83).

Then there is the large and fascinating group of civic or institutional medals which were presented to volunteers returning from the Boer War of 1899–1902. M.G. Hibbard, in his splendid monograph *Boer War Tribute Medals* (1982), recorded no fewer than 78 such medals, 40 from towns and cities in England, 25 from other parts of the United Kingdom and 13 from Commonwealth countries. Some of these were fitted with ribbons and were obviously intended for wear alongside the official medals of the war; others were 'danglers' intended to be fitted to watch-chains; and others still were not fitted with any form of suspension and were thus in the nature of commemorative medals intended purely as a memento of volunteer service.

So far as can be ascertained, such tribute medals were not produced in previous conflicts, which were predominantly fought by regular troops; and such was the scale of the involvement of volunteers and later conscripts in the First World War that the cost of providing civic medals of this nature would have been prohibitive. Instead, returning soldiers had to be content with some form of paper testimonial, at best. A notable exception was the gold medal presented by the Lord Mayor of London to the members of the anti-aircraft gun crews which shot down the first Zeppelin (listed below).

Apart from that, the Boer War group therefore constitutes a unique, but clearly defined group. They are, however, generally outside the scope of this YEARBOOK, although it should be noted that several medals in this category have long been accepted in the regular canon: the Kimberley Star (no. 154), the Kimberley Medals (no. 155), the Yorkshire Imperial Yeomanry Medal (no. 156)

and the Medal for the Defence of Ookiep (no. 157). The reason for their acceptance is quite arbitrary, and just why the Yorkshire Imperial Yeomanry medal should be so highly regarded while others are not seems to rest on the fact that this medal is more commonly met with than the others—which is hardly a valid criterion.

For the sake of completing the record we have endeavoured to introduce a number of unofficial medals, particularly as groups including certain of these medals are coming onto the market and inevitably some purchasers are curious to know their origins.

In addition there are a number of other unofficial medals available to veterans such as the "Battle for Britain" medal with its various clasps but **it is not the intention to make this a definitive guide**, so we have decided to limit this section to those medals that were initially commissioned or supported by the relevant veterans associations and mainly produced in recent years in order to fill the gap left in the official series.

Credit for reviving such medals must go to the Mayor of Dunkirk on whose initiative the medal awarded to survivors of the 1940 evacuation was instituted in 1965. Subsequently distribution of this medal was taken over by the Dunkirk Veterans' Association, applications being strictly limited to those who could prove that they had taken part in that historic event. This practice continued with the commissioning of the Bomber Command Medal by their Association (following a design competition in *Medal News*) in response to the long-standing grievance of veterans of the Second World War who felt that their contribution to the ultimate victory had been deliberately ignored for political reasons. The success of this medal encouraged the production of similar awards for other categories of servicemen, or for campaigns which many felt should have had a distinctive campaign medal.

It must be stressed that all of these medals are available for purchase only by bona-fide veterans or their proven next of kin with sales also benefitting related charities. The wearing of these medals has always been a contentious issue, with many veterans choosing to wear them below but never alongside their official decorations.

As many of the modern medals are still being struck, it has been decided not to give valuations for these.

U1. CHERRY MEDAL

Date: 1904.
Campaign: China, 1900–4
Branch of Service: Royal Navy.
Ribbon: Cherry red.
Metal: Silver.
Size: 38mm.
Description: (Obverse) a bare cherry tree with five naval officers in the foreground and a large number of other officers, all in frock coats, moving up in single file, with a scroll across the foot inscribed in Latin SUB HOC CERESO MANEMUS (under this cherry tree we remain); (reverse) a fouled anchor flanked by the Golden Fleece and a Chinese Dragon with the legend ARGONAUT CHINA 1900–1904 round the circumference. The medal is fitted with a plain suspension ring.
Comments: *The name of the medal and the colour of ribbon allude to Captain George Henry Cherry RN, commander of HMS* Argonaut *which served on the China Station in 1900-4. The five officers on one side of the tree represent the only ones remaining of the original number when the ship was paid off: Lieutenant Arthur Vernon Ross, Captain T. H. Hawkins RM, Chief Engineer A. W. Turner, Senior Engineer T. W. Cleave and Chaplain T. A. Dexter. The other line represents those officers who left the ship during the commission. The obverse motto contains a spelling error: CERESO instead of CERASO. This medal started off as a joke. Captain Cherry was a terrible martinet and his disgruntled officers felt that they deserved a medal for having to put up with him. It was designed by Miss Ross, sister of the senior watchkeeper, and struck by Gamage's of London. Only 100 medals were struck. Originally it was intended to be given only to the five officers who had stuck it out to the bitter end, but others complained and thus were awarded the medal with a bar indicating each year of service. Many years later, Admiral Cherry was offered one of the medals and graciously received it.*

VALUE: £150–200

U1A. EMIN RELIEF EXPEDITION STAR

Date: 1889.
Campaign: Sudan.
Ribbon:
Metal: Sterling silver.
Size: 50mm.
Description: A five-pointed star with a plain reverse and a central medallion bearing the monogram of the Royal Geographical Society, surrounded by an incuse inscription EMIN RELIEF EXPEDITION / 1887-9.
Comments: *This medal was awarded mainly to the Zanzibaris forming the bulk of the expedition organised in 1889 to discover the whereabouts of Emin Pasha, Governor of Equatoria, who had retreated south with Egyptian troops, officials and their families in the aftermath of the Mahdist revolt and the fall of Khartoum. The expedition, led by H. M. Stanley, located Emin and his followers in April 1888. Emin, in fact, refused to be relieved and the expedition not only failed in its primary objective but was a disaster, most Europeans and many Zanzibaris perishing before they returned empty-handed. The Royal Geographical Society commissioned the medals from Carrington. Some 200 were produced and of these 178 were issued to surviving members of the expedition. Of these, only nine were named to the recipients.*

VALUE: £400–500

U2. SECOND CRUISER SQUADRON MEDAL

Date: 1908.
Campaign: Goodwill tour of South America and South Africa.
Branch of Service: Royal Navy.
Ribbon: Pale blue.
Metal: Bronze.
Size: 36mm.
Description: (Obverse) a right-facing lady in Edwardian dress waving to distant ships, with the words SOUTH AFRICA and SOUTH AMERICA round the edge on either side of the suspender; (reverse) a seven-line inscription: 2ND CRUISER SQUADRON—GOOD HOPE, DEVONSHIRE, ANTRIM, CARNARVON—1908. The words CLOSER UNION appear at the sides.
Clasps: 14—Buenos Aires, Monte Video, Rio de Janerio, St Helena, Capetown, Simonstown, Port Elizabeth, East London, Ladysmith, Bloemfontein, Johannesburg, Pretoria, Pietermaritzburg, Durban.
Comments: *Privately issued and named to members of the goodwill cruise. It is uncertain how many medals were issued but they can be encountered with various combinations of clasps or none at all. It appears that there were two distinct strikings, the named examples being on a slightly thicker flan. The thinner, unnamed versions are believed to have been restrikes for specimen purposes. It is not known who funded or manufactured these medals.*

VALUE: £120–300 dependent on number of clasps

U2A. NATIONAL SERVICE LEAGUE MEDAL

Date: 1912.
Ribbon: White with a narrow central red stripe and narrow blue edges.
Metal: Bronze, silver or gold.
Size: 32mm (bronze) or 26mm (others).
Description: (Obverse) Standing figure of Britannia, helmeted and cloaked, her hands resting on the pommel of an unsheathed broadsword, with the inscription FOR KING AND COUNTRY round the upper part of the circumference. Fitted with a plain ring for suspension, with a brooch bar at the top of the ribbon inscribed NATIONAL SERVICE LEAGUE; (reverse) THE PATH OF DUTY IS THE PATH OF SAFETY and wreath.
Comments: *The National Service League was founded by Field Marshal Lord Roberts in the aftermath of the Boer war. The aim of the League was to warn Britain of the German menace and encourage young men to become proficient marksmen. Its wider aims were "to secure the legislative adoption of universal naval and military training for national defence". Ironically, Lord Roberts was proved right all too soon, and the League was dissolved in 1921.*

VALUE: £40–60

U2B. EMDEN MEDAL

Date: 1915.
Campaign: First World War.
Branch of Service: Royal Australian Navy.
Ribbon:
Metal: Silver.
Size: 60mm x 36mm.
Description: Mexican silver dollar surmounted by a crown and two concentric scrolls at the top inscribed NOV. 9. 1914 and HMAS SYDNEY / SMS EMDEN.
Comments: *Shortly after the outbreak of the War the Australian cruiser Sydney located the German light cruiser Emden in the Cocos Islands. After a brief engagement the Emden was boarded and captured. A quantity of Mexican silver dollars were found on board and these were subsequently mounted by the firm of W. Kerr of Sydney and presented to the crew of the Sydney as a memento of the action.*

VALUE: £400–450

U3. LORD MAYOR OF LONDON'S MEDAL FOR THE DESTRUCTION OF ZEPPELIN L15

Date: 1916.
Campaign: First World War.
Branch of Service: Royal Artillery.
Ribbon:
Metal: 9 carat gold.
Size: 29mm.
Description: (Obverse) the arms of Sir Charles Wakefield within a double ring inscribed PRESENTED BY THE LORD MAYOR round the top and COLONEL SIR CHARLES WAKEFIELD round the foot; (reverse) An anti-aircraft gun and two scrolls inscribed WELL HIT and MARCH 31st and number L15. It is engraved near the top with the rank and name of the recipient. It was issued unmounted but various ornamental suspensions loops were later fitted privately.
Comments: *The Lord Mayor of London offered a reward of £500 to the first gun crew to shoot down a Zeppelin. On 3 April 1916 Capt. J. Harris submitted a claim on behalf of the Purfleet gun crew that they were responsible for the bringing down of the airship L15, but it later transpired that gun crews from Abbey Wood, Dartford, Erith, North Woolwich, Plumstead and the Royal Arsenal, among others, were also involved. It was decided to use the prize money in procuring these medals, a total of 353 being awarded.*

VALUE: £800–1000

U4. DUNKIRK MEDAL

Date: 1960.
Campaign: Dunkirk evacuation, 1940
Branch of Service: All British and Allied forces.
Ribbon: Chrome yellow with one thin and one wide red stripe each side with two very thin black lines bisecting both sides.
Metal: Bronze.
Size: 36mm wide.
Description: (Obverse) a shield bearing the arms of Dunkirk (a lion passant above a heraldic dolphin) mounted on an anchor; (reverse) a circle bearing a burning lamp with DUNKERQUE 1940 beneath, surrounded by a laurel wreath and surmounted by crossed swords; the whole mounted on and surrounded by a laurel wreath.
Comments: *This medal was first made available to veterans of the Dunkirk evacuation and later administered by the now disbanded Dunkirk Veterans Association. It was created by the French National Association of Veterans of the Fortified Sector of Flanders and of Dunkirk and awarded in recognition of the sacrifice of 30,000 combatants between 29 May and 3 June 1940.*

VALUE: £50–60   *Miniature*   £10–15

U5. BOMBER COMMAND MEDAL

Date: 1985.
Campaign: Second World War.
Branch of Service: RAF Bomber Command.
Ribbon: Midnight blue with a central flame stripe and blue-grey edges.
Metal: Cupro-nickel.
Size: 36mm.
Description: (Obverse) A Tudor crown surmounting a laurel wreath containing the letters RAF, flanked by smaller wreaths containing the brevet letters of the aircrew signifying courage, team spirit and leadership; (reverse) a Lancaster bomber flanked by the dates 1939 and 1945 with inscription A TRIBUTE TO THE AIRCREW OF BOMBER COMMAND round the circumference.
Comments: *Produced at the behest of Air Vice Marshal Donald Bennett following a design competition in MEDAL NEWS. The competition was the brainchild of author Alan Cooper campaigning on behalf of Bomber Command veterans. The first medal was struck by Lady Harris (widow of the wartime commander of Bomber Command).*

U5A. ARMY CADET FORCE ANNIVERSARY MEDAL

Instituted: 1985.
Branch of Service: Army Cadet Force.
Ribbon: Red and blue separated by a thin yellow stripe.
Metal: Enamelled white metal.
Size: 55 x 85mm.
Description: (Obverse) the insignia of the ACF superimposed by figures of an officer and cadet shaking hands, the dates 1860 and 1985 flanking the motto at the foot. Fitted with a ring above the crown for suspension. (Reverse) plain, apart from the manufacturer's mark of Reu & Company of Heubach, Wurttemberg, Germany. A brooch bar in the form of a scroll 20mm deep is fitted to the top of the ribbon and bears a three-line inscription: ARMY CADET FORCE 125H ANNIVERSARY ONE DAY MARCH 26TH OCTOBER 1985.
Comments: *The medal was awarded to all members of the ACF who took part in the one-day march to celebrate the 125th anniversary of the Force.*

U6. NORMANDY CAMPAIGN MEDAL

Date: 1987.
Campaign: Service in the Normandy campaign between June 6 and August 20, 1944.
Branch of Service: All British and Allied forces.
Ribbon: Dark red with deep navy blue stripes towards the edges and light blue edges, symbolising the three services.
Metal: Cupro-nickel.
Size: 36mm.
Description: (Obverse) insignia of the combined services surrounded by 13 stars (representing the USA) and the inscription BLESSENT MON COEUR D'UNE LANGUEUR MONOTONE ("wounds my heart with monotonous languor"), a quotation from Verlaine broadcast by the BBC on June 5, 1944 to signal the start of the D-Day operations. (Reverse) a tank landing craft with its ramp on the beaches of France symbolised by fleurs-de lis; NORMANDY CAMPAIGN round the top and the date of the campaign inscribed on the ramp. The medal is fitted with a plain suspension bar while the ribbon bears a clasp inscribed NORMANDY between oak leaves.
Comments: *Commissioned by the Normandy Veterans Association whose Welfare and Benevolent Fund benefits from the proceeds of sales.*

U7. ARCTIC CAMPAIGN MEDAL

Date: 1991.
Campaign: Second World War.
Branch of Service: Personnel of the Russian convoys.
Ribbon: 32mm watered weave in equal stripes of blue and white representing ice and sea.
Metal: Cupro-nickel.
Size: 36mm.
Description: (Obverse) a liberty ship framed in the cross-hair of a U-boat periscope, with the inscription FOR SERVICE IN THE ARCTIC ZONE 1939-45 round the top; (reverse) four figures representing merchant seaman, Royal Naval, Army and RAF personnel, with the inscription THE ARCTIC CAMPAIGN round the top.
Comments: *This award was proposed by the Russian Convoy Club in conjunction with the North Russia Club who are the beneficiaries of the project.*

U8. MERCHANT NAVAL SERVICE MEDAL

Date: 1998.
Campaign: —
Branch of Service: Merchant Navy and DEMS Gunners.
Ribbon: Dark blue with a central narrow white stripe flanked by broader green and red stripes, representing the navigation lights of an approaching ship.
Metal: Cupro-nickel.
Size: 36mm.
Description: (Obverse) a stockless anchor encompassed by its heavy cable, surmounted by the initials MN; (reverse) a capstan surmounted by a naval crown and flanked by grotesque sea monsters, the whole encircled by a rope tied at the foot in a reef knot. The outer circumference is inscribed FOR MERCHANT NAVAL SERVICE. The medal is fitted to a plain suspension bar by an ornamental scroll.
Comments: *Veterans were eligible for this medal in respect of at least two years' service in the Merchant Navy. The award was inspired by the fact that although service in the mercantile marine was recognised after World War I it was ignored after World War II. King George's Fund for Sailors' benefits from the sale of this medal.*

U9. ALLIED EX-PRISONERS OF WAR MEDAL

Date: 1991.
Campaign: All wars of the 20th century.
Branch of Service: Prisoners of war.
Ribbon: Green with red edges. The centre has a broad black stripe edged in white, having a white strand of barbed wire running down the middle.
Metal: Cupro-nickel.
Size: 36mm.
Description: (Obverse) a young bird trapped by barbed wire, against a globe of the world, with the inscription INTERNATIONAL PRISONERS OF WAR; (reverse) a twisted barb of wire whose four strands divide the inscription INTREPID AGAINST ALL ADVERSITY. Fitted with a plain suspension bar.
Comments: *This award proposed by the National Ex Prisoners of War Association is applicable to any former PoWs whose countries were allies of Britain at the time of their capture irrespective of whether the United Kingdom was itself involved in the conflict.*

U10. RESTORATION OF PEACE MEDAL

Date: 1995.
Campaign: Second World War.
Branch of Service: Armed forces and civilians involved in the war effort.
Ribbon: Rich claret with a central broad gold stripe.
Metal: High-security HS1 gold-coloured alloy.
Size: 36mm.
Description: (Obverse) the letter V enclosing the date 1945, superimposed on a globe with the inscription A TIME FOR PEACE round the circumference; (reverse) a simple wreath enclosing the inscription FOR ALL WHO STRIVED FOR PEACE. The plain suspension bar is fitted to the medal by a peace dove on both sides.
Comments: *Produced at the behest of the British Red Cross Society to mark the 50th anniversary of the cessation of hostilities in the Second World War.*

U11. SUEZ CANAL ZONE MEDAL

Date: 1995.
Campaign: Suez Canal Zone, 1945-57.
Branch of Service: British and French forces.
Ribbon: Sand-coloured edged with narrow stripes of red, white and blue. A broad central crimson stripe has a light blue stripe down the middle.
Metal: High-security HS1 gold-coloured alloy.
Size: 36mm.
Description: (Obverse) the Sphinx and Pyramid flanked by the dates 1951-54 and 1956-57, representing the two most recent periods of conflict; (reverse) stylised papyrus grass with the words TO MARK SERVICE IN THE CANAL ZONE at left. Fitted with an ornamental suspension bar in the form of Pharaonic wings.
Comments: *The Ex-Services Mental Welfare Society (Combat Stress) is the beneficiary of this project.*

U12. NATIONAL SERVICE MEDAL

Date: 1991.
Campaign: Period of conscription, 1939-60.
Branch of Service: National Service, both military and civilian.
Ribbon: Dark blue with a narrow central gold stripe and narrow white and red stripes at the edges representing the involvement of the Royal British Legion.
Metal: Cupro-nickel.
Size: 36mm.
Description: (Obverse) the seated figure of Britannia supported by a lion, with the inscription NATIONAL SERVICE 1939-1960; (reverse) a wreath enclosing the inscription FOR CROWN AND COUNTRY. Fitted with scrolled suspension.
Comments: *Between January 1939 when the National Service Act was passed, and December 1960 when it was repealed, some 5,300,000 young people were conscripted into the armed services. The medal was proposed by the Royal British Legion and almost 100,000 have been issued to date.*

U13. JORDAN SERVICE MEDAL

Instituted: April 1997.
Branch of Service: British ex-service personnel who served in the Hashemite Kingdom of Jordan between 1948 and 1957 and again during the 1958 emergency, i.e. the 16th Independent Parachute Brigade and attached units.
Ribbon: Golden sand, edged on both sides with four thin stripes of the Jordanian national colours (black, white, green and red).
Metal: Gilt brass.
Size: 36mm.
Description: (Obverse) Effigy of King Hussein; (reverse) inscription in raised lettering: FOR SERVICE IN THE HASHEMITE KINGDOM OF JORDAN, with or without the date 1958 below.
Comments: *This medal was produced on the initiative of G. E. Harris of Haverfordwest with the approval of the late King Hussein. Sales of the medal benefit the SSAFA Forces Help charity. It was manufactured by the Bigbury Mint, Ermington, Devon. To date nearly 2,000 veterans have applied for the medal (either version), including two of the four female nurses who served in Jordan.*

U14. HONG KONG SERVICE MEDAL

Instituted: 1999.
Branch of Service: All former civil and military personnel who served for a minimum of six months in the Crown Colony of Hong Kong, or their next of kin.
Ribbon: Pale blue with a central yellow stripe.
Metal: Gilt metal.
Size: 36mm.
Description: (Obverse) Bird of Paradise surounded by the words HONG KONG SERVICE MEDAL 1841–1997; (reverse) HONG KONG in Cantonese characters surrounded by a circular wreath. The medal is suspended from a unique suspender depicting two mythical Chinese dragons.
Comments: *SSAFA Forces Help, the ex-servicemen's charity, benefits from the sales of this medal.*

U15. BRITISH FORCES GERMANY MEDAL

Instituted: 1999.
Branch of Service: All British service personnel in Germany, 1945–89.
Ribbon: 32mm NATO blue with central narrow stripes of black, red and gold (the German national colours).
Metal: Rhodium-plated cupro-nickel.
Size: 36mm.
Description: (Obverse) Standing figures of a soldier and airman holding the Union Jack, BRITISH FORCES GERMANY round the top with ARMY 1945–1989 RAF round the foot; (reverse) a laurel wreath incorporating the recipient's name, rank and service number over the years of service. Plain suspension bar. Royal Naval personnel who served in Germany are awarded a clasp to the medal.
Comments: *All men and women who served with the British Forces in Germany from the end of World War II until 1989 are eligible for this medal designed by Martin Duchemin and available from Royal British Legion Industries.*

U16. ROYAL NAVAL PATROL SERVICE MEDAL

Instituted: 1999.
Branch of Service: Royal Naval Patrol Service of World War II.
Ribbon: Watered dark and light green with a central orange stripe edged with black.
Metal: Cupro-nickel.
Size: 36mm.
Description: (Obverse) The badge of the RNPS with a shark swimming around it.
Comments: *Commissioned by the Royal Naval Patrol Service Association to commemorate service. Available only to veterans or their next of kin.*

U17. HORS DE COMBAT MEDAL

Instituted: 2001.
Branch of Service: All uniformed British service personnel.
Ribbon: Rich red bordered by narrow bands of blue with wider outer edges of white.
Metal: Cupro-nickel.
Size: 36mm.
Description: (Obverse) A gladiator kneeling before a female figure with the legend IN THE LINE OF DUTY; (reverse) a stylised rendering of the surgeon's knot with the same legend.
Comments: *For all those who sustained wounds or injury in the line of duty. Also available to next of kin. The Ex-Services Mental Welfare Society (Combat Stress) benefits from the sale of this medal.*

U18. INTERNATIONAL SUBMARINE SERVICE MEDAL

Instituted: 2002.
Branch of Service: Submariners of all nations.
Ribbon: Navy blue with a thin red stripe flanked by thin black and white stripes.
Metal: Cupro-nickel
Size: 36mm.
Description: (Obverse) a modern submarine viewed from the bow, with inscription INTERNATIONAL SUBMARINE SERVICE; (reverse) a depth gauge with the inscription BY SKILL AND STEALTH WE COME UNSEEN.
Comments: *Commissioned by London Submariners and the International Submarine Association in recognition of the men who have served, and continue to serve, beneath the world's oceans.*

U19. QUEEN'S GOLDEN JUBILEE COMMEMORATIVE MEDAL

Instituted: 2002.
Branch of Service: All service personnel, past or present, including police, coastguard, ambulance and other services.
Ribbon: Broad gold bands at the edges, with thin white, purple and white stripes in the centre.
Metal: Gilt brass.
Size: 36mm.
Description: (Obverse) left-facing robed bust of the Queen inscribed QUEEN ELIZABETH II GOLDEN JUBILEE 2002; (reverse) royal arms.
Comments: *This attractive medal was produced for the benefit of the SSAFA (Soldiers, Sailors and Air Forces Association) on the initiative of G. E. Harris who also instigated the Jordan Service Medal (no. U13) and is manufactured by the Bigbury Mint. It provides a need for those who were not entitled to the official medal.*

U20. NORTH AFRICA SERVICE MEDAL

Instituted: 1999.
Branch of Service: Veterans of the North African campaigns of World War II.
Ribbon: Yellow and sky-blue stripes at the edges, with navy blue, red and air force blue in the centre representing the armed services.
Metal: Bronze.
Size: 36mm.
Description: (Obverse) a camel standing beside a desert rat, with the inscription FOR SERVICE IN NORTH AFRICA, M.E.L.F.; (reverse) ornamental edge with centre blank for engraving with the name of the recipient.
Comments: *Designed and manufactured by the Bigbury Mint on the initiative of Ron Skeates of Aveton Gifford.*

U21. CAMERONIANS (SCOTTISH RIFLES) MEDAL

Instituted: 1999.
Branch of Service: Those who served in the regiment either as regulars or on National Service, including wives.
Ribbon: Three stripes of blue, black and dark green taken from the regimental tartan.
Metal: Silver-plated brass.
Size: 36mm.
Description: (Obverse) regimental badge of the Cameronians; (reverse) FOR SERVICE IN THE CAMERONIANS SCOTTISH RIFLES.
Comments: *The regiment was named in memory of the Covenanting leader Richard Cameron and was raised at Douglas, Lanarkshire in 1689. It later merged with the 90th (Perthshire) Regiment, at which point it adopted the Graham tartan.*

Abbreviations and initials

The medal collector is constantly coming across initials and abbreviations on medals and in documents—many of which are commonplace and easily decipherable. However, there are many more which can cause problems when trying to identify a medal recipient. The following list represents only a small selection of the inexhaustible number of abbreviations encountered, but hopefully it will be of some assistance to the collector. The *"Token Book of Militarisms"* contains literally hundreds more if you cannot find the abbreviation you are looking for here.

1 E Ang   1st East Anglian Regiment
1 R Dgns   1st Royal Dragoons
1 QDG   1st Queen's Dragoon Guards
11H   11th Royal Hussars
12L   12th Royal Lancers
13/18H   13th/18th Royal Hussars
14/20H   14th/20th Royal Hussars
15/19H   15th/19th Royal Hussars
3 E Ang   3rd East Anglian Regiment
4 QOH   4th Queen's Own Hussars
4H   4th Royal Hussars
5 DGds   5th Royal Inniskilling Dragoon Guards
7QOH   7th Queen's Own Hussars
7GR   7th Gurkha Rifles
A/   Acting
A Avn   Army Aviation
Abn Inf   Airborne Infantry
A/CWEM   Acting Chief Weapons Engineering Mechanic
A/LMEM   Acting Leading Marine Engineering Mechanic
A/LRO(G)   Acting Leading Radio Operator (General)
A/PO   Acting Petty Officer, Acting Pilot Officer
A&SH   The Argyll and Sutherland Highlanders
AAC   Army Air Corps
AAF, Aux F   Auxillery Air Force
AAU   Air Ambulance Unit
AB   Able Seaman; Airborne
ABDS   Army Bomb Disposal Squad
AC1   Aircraftman 1st Class
ACC   Army Catering Corps, Armoured Car Company
ACF   Army Cadet Force
ADALS   Assistant Director, Army Legal Service
ADC   Aide de Camp
AE   Army Education Officer, Air Efficiency Award
AER   Army Emergency Reserve
AFC   Air Force Cross
AFM   Air Force Medal
AGS   Africa General Service Medal
AIF   Australian Imperial Forces
AIY   Ayrshire Imperial Yeomanry
ALO   Air Liaison Officer
ALS   Army Legal Services
AM   Albert Medal
AM1   Air Mechanic 1st Class
AMA   Acting Master at Arms
AMS   Assistant Military Secretary; Army Medical Staff

AOC   Army Ordnance Corps
APC   Army Pay Corps
APL   Aden Protectorate Levies
APTC   Army Physical Training Corps
AQ   Assistant Quartermaster; Administrative Quartermaster
Armd   Armoured
ASC   Army Service Corps; Air Service Command
ATO   Ammunition Technical Officer
Aux AF   Auxiliary Air Force
B&H   The Bedfordshire & Hertfordshire Regiment
B&R   Blues & Royals
BAAT   British Army Advisory Team
BATT   British Army Training Team
BAO   British Army of Occupation
Bdr   Bombadier
BDU   Bomb Disposal Unit
BEM   British Empire Medal
BF   British Forces
BGS   Brigadier, General Staff
BIY   Bedford Imperial Yeomanry
BM   Brigade Major
BORD.R   Border Regiment
BR   British
Brig   Brigadier
Br Coy   Bearer Company
BSA Police   British South Africa Police
Buffs   The Buffs (Royal East Kent Regiment)
BW   Black Watch (Royal Highland Regiment)
BWM   British War Medal
C&TC   Commissariat and Transport Corps
C/Sgt   Colour Sergeant
C&S   Command & Staff
CAC   Canadian Armoured Corps
CADAC   Canadian Army Dental Corps
CAEA   Chief Air Engineering Artificer
CAHTC   Cape Auxiliary Horse Transport Corps
CAMN HIGH   Cameron Highlanders
Capt   Captain
CAR   Central African Rifles
CASC   Canadian Army Service Corps
CATO   Commander Ammunition Technical Officers
CB   Commander of the Order of the Bath
CBE   Commander of the Order of the British Empire
CBF   Commander British Forces
CC   Cadet Corps; Coastal Command; Combat Command
CCAEA   Charge Chief Air Engineering Artificer

CCCC   Cape Colony Cyclist Corps
CCF   Combined Cadet Force
CCMEA   Charge Chief Marine Engineering Artificer
CCS   Casualty Clearing Station
C de G   Croix de Guerre
Cdr   Commander
CE   Canadian Engineers
CEO   Chief Executive Officer; Chief Education Officer
CG   Coast Guard; Commanding General
CGC   Conspicuous Gallantry Cross
CGM   Conspicuous Gallantry Medal
Cheshire   The Cheshire Regiment
CI   Crown of India, Imperial Order; Counter-Intelligence
CIV   City Imperial Volunteers
CIE   Companion of the Order of the Indian Empre
CLY   County of London Yeomanry
CMEM   Chief Marine Engineering Mechanic
CMFR   Commonwealth Monitoring Force Rhodesia
CMG   Companion of the Order of St Michael and St George
CMM   Commander of the Order of Military Merit
CMO   Chief Medical Officer
CMMP   Corps of Military Mounted Police
CMP   Corps of Military Police
CMSC   Cape Medical Staff Corps
CMR   Cape Mounted Riflemen
CO   Commanding Officer
Col   Colonel
Coldm Gds   Coldstream Guards
Comd   Commander
COS   Chief of Staff
CP   Cape Police
Cpl   Corporal
CPO   Chief Petty Officer
CPOAEA   Chief Petty Officer Air Engineering Artificer
CPOWEA   Chief Petty Officer Weapons Engineering Artificer
CQMS   Company Quartermaster Sergeant
CSI   Companion of the Order of the Star of India
CSM   Company Sergeant Major; Campaign Service Medal
CT, C/T, Ch Tech   Chief Technician
CVO   Commander of the Royal Victorian Order
D   Diver
D Comd   Deputy Commander
D&D   The Devon and Dorset Regiment
DAD   Deputy Assistant Director
DADOS   Deputy Assistant Director of Ordnance Services
DADVRS   Deputy Assistant Director Veterinary & Remount Section
DAMA   Department of the Army Material Annex
DANS   Director of Army Nursing Services
DAPM   Deputy Assistant Provost Marshall
DAT   Director of Army Training
DBE   Dame Commander, Order of the British Empire
DCLI   The Duke of Cornwall's Light Infantry
DCM   Distinguished Conduct Medal
DCMG   Dame Commander of the Order of St Michael and St George
DCO   Duke of Cambridge's Own; Duke of Connaught's Own
DCOS   Deputy Chief of Staff
DCVO   Dame Commander of the Royal Victorian Order
DDSD   Deputy Director Staff Duties
DEO   Duke of Edinburgh's Own

DERR   The Duke of Edinburgh's Royal Regiment (Berkshire & Wiltshire)
Det   Detached; Detachment
Devon   The Devonshire Regiment
DFC   Distinguished Flying Cross
DFM   Distinguished Flying Medal
DG   Dragoon Guards
DI   Defence Intelligence
DLI   The Durham Light Infantry
DMT   District Mounted Troops
Dorset   The Dorset Regiment
DOS   Director of Ordnance Services
DS   Defence Secretary; Deputy Secretary; Defensive Section
DSC   Distinguished Service Cross
DSM   Distinguished Service Medal
DSO   Distinguished Service Order
DWR   The Duke of Wellington's Regiment
EAR   East African Rifles
ED   Efficiency Decoration
EF   Expeditionary Force
EGM   Empire Gallantry Medal
EM   Edward Medal; Efficiency Medal
EOD   Explosive Ordnance Disposal
ERA   Engine Room Artificier
ERD   Emergency Reserve Decoration
ERE   Extra Regimentally Employed
FA   Field Ambulance
FANYC   First Aid Nursing Yeomanry Corps
FBRA   Field Battery Royal Artillery
FC   Fighter Command
Fd   Field
FELF   Far East Land Forces
FF   Field Force
FFL   French Foreign Legion
FFR   Frontier Force Rifles
FL, F/L, Flt Lt   Flight Lieutenant
FM   Field Marshal
FMR   Frontier Mounted Rifles
FO, F/O, Fg Off   Flying Officer
FS   Fighter Squadron; Field Security
FS, F/S, Flt/Sgt   Flight Sergeant
Fus   Fusilier
G Howards   Green Howards (Alexandra, Princess of Wales's Own Yorkshire Regiment)
G Or   General Operational Requirements
GBE   Grand Cross, Order of the British Empire
GC   George Cross
GC, G/C, GpCapt   Group Captain
GCB   Knight Grand Cross Order of the Bath
GCH   Knight Grand Cross Hanoverian Order
GCIE   Knight Grand Commander Order of the Indian Empire
GCLH   Grand Cross Legion of Honour
GCM   Good Conduct Medal
GCMG   Knight Grand Cross Order of St Michael and St George
GCSI   Knight Grand Commander Order of the Star of India
GCVO   Knight Grand Cross Royal Victorian Order
Gdsmn   Guardsman
GLI   Guernsey Light Infantry
Glosters   The Gloucestershire Regiment (28th/61st Foot)
GM   George Medal
Gnr   Gunner
GOC   General Officer Commanding
Gordons   The Gordon Highlanders (75th/92nd Regiment)

423

GPR Glider Pilot Regiment
GR Gurkha Rifles
GS General Service
GSC General Service Corps
GSM General Service Medal
GSO General Staff Officer
HA Horse Artillery
HAC Honourable Artillery Company
HBM Her Britannic Majesty
HCR Household Cavalry Regiment
HG Home Guard; Horse Guards
HLI The Highland Light Infantry
HQ Headquarters
IAOC Indian Army Ordnance Corps
IASC Indian Army Service Corps
IC In Charge
IDSM Indian Distinguished Service Medal
IE Order of the Indian Empire
IG Irish Guards
Int Intelligence
Int Corps Intelligence Corps
Int & Sy Coy Intelligence and Security Company
IO Intelligence Officer
IOM Indian Order of Merit
IRC Infantry Reserve Corps
ISM Imperial Service Medal
ISO Imperial Service Order
IY Imperial Yeomanry
JSSC Joint Services Staff College
KAR King's African Rifles
KB Knight Bachelor
KBE Knight of the Order of the British Empire
KC Knight Commander
KCB Knight Commander Order of the Bath
KCH Knight Commander of the Royal Hanoverian Guelphic Order
KCIE Knight Commander Order of the Indian Empire
KCIO King's Commissioned Indian Officer
KCMG Knight Commander Order of St Michael and St George
KCSI Knight Commander Order of the Star of India
KCVO Knight Commander Royal Victorian Order
KDG King's Dragoon Guards
KG Knight of the Order of the Garter
KGCB Knight Grand Cross Order of the Bath
KGL King's German Legion
Kings The King's Regiment (Liverpool)
KLH Knight of the Legion of Honour
KM King's Medal
KOM Knight of the Order of Malta
KORB The King's Own Royal Border Regiment
KOSB The King's Own Scottish Borderers
KOYLI The King's Own Yorkshire Light Infantry
KPM King's Police Medal
KRRC The King's Royal Rifle Corps
KSG Knight of the Order of St George
KSLI The King's Shropshire Light Infantry
KT Knight of the Order of the Thistle
L/Cpl Lance Corporal
L/Sgt Lance Sergeant
LAC Leading Aircraftman
Lanc Fusiliers The Lancashire Fusiliers
Lanc R The Queen's Lancashire Regiment
LC Labour Corps
Leic The Royal Leicestershire Regiment
LG Life Guards; London Gazette
LI Light Infantry
Linc The Royal Lincolnshire Regiment
LM Legion of Merit

LMA Leading Medical Assistant
LS Leading Seaman
LS&GC Long Service and Good Conduct (medal)
Lt Lieutenant
Lt-Cdr Lieutenant Commander
Lt-Col Lieutenant-Colonel
LVO Lieutenant of the Royal Victorian Order
MA Military Attache
Maint Maintenance
Maj Major
Maj-Gen Major-General
Mal.LBC Maltese Labour Corps
MBE Member of the Order of the British Empire
MC Military Cross
MEM Marine Engineering Mechanic
MFA Mercantile Fleet Auxiliary
MFS Medical Field Service
MGC Machine Gun Corps
MGS Military General Service (medal)
MH Medal of Honour
MI Mounted Infantry
MID Mentioned in Despatches
MKW Military Knights of Windsor
MM Military Medal; Medal of Merit
MMGS Motor Machine Gun Service
MMWM Mercantile Marine War Medal
Mne Marine
MMR Mercantile Marine Reserve
MR Middlesex Regiment
MRCVS Member Royal College of Veterinary Surgeons
MSC Medical Staff Corps
MSM Meritorious Service Medal
MTO Motor Transport Office
MVO Member of the Royal Victorian Order
NACS Naval Air Commando Squadron
NAS Naval Air Squadron
NCO Non-Commissioned Officer
NFA Natal Field Artillery
NGS Naval General Service (Medal)
NZEF New Zealand Expeditionary Force
OBE Officer of the Order of the British Empire
OBLI Ox and Bucks Light Infantry
OC Officer Commanding
OCS Officer Cadet School
OEO Ordnance Executive Officer
OHBMS On Her Britannic Majesty's Service
OM Order of Merit
OR Operational Requirements; Other Ranks; Organised Reserve
Ord Ordnance
OS Ordinary Seaman; Ordnance Survey
PAOCVA Prince Albert's Own Cape Volunteer Rifles
PAVG Prince Albert's Volunteer Guard
Para The Parachute Regiment
PO Petty Officer
PO, P/O, Plt Off Pilot Officer
PO/AC Petty Officer Aircrewman
POMA Petty Officer Medical Assistant
POMEM Petty Officer Marine Engineering Mechanic
PR Public Relations
PSO Personal Staff Officer
Pte Private
PVCP Permanent Vehicle Check Point
PWO The Prince of Wales's Own Regiment of Yorkshire
Q Ops Quartermaster General Branch Operations

QARANC   Queen Alexandra's Royal Army Nursing Corps
QCBA   Queen's Commendation for Bravery in the Air
QCBC   Queen's Commendation for Brave Conduct
QCVS   Queen's Commendation for Valuable Service
QCVSA   Queen's Commendation for Valuable Service in the Air
QFSM   Queen's Fire Service Medal
QDG   The Queen's Dragoon Guards
QGM   Queen's Gallantry Medal
QLR   The Queen's Lancashire Regiment
QM   Quartermaster
QMAAC   Queen Mary's Auxiliary Ambulance Corps
QMS   Quartermaster Sergeant
QPM   Queen's Police Medal
QRIH   Queen's Royal Irish Hussars
QSA   Queen's South Africa (Medal)
Queens   The Queen's Regiment—Queen's Division
QVRM   Queen's Volunteer Reserves Medal
R Anglian   Royal Anglian Regiment
R Fus   Royal Fusiliers (City of London Regiment)
R Innis   Royal Inniskilling
R Signals   Royal Corps of Signals
RA   Royal Artillery
RAAF   Royal Australian Air Force
RAC   Royal Armoured Corps
RAChD   Royal Army Chaplains Department
RAEC   Royal Army Educational Corps
RAF   Royal Air Force
RAFVR   Royal Airforce Volunteer Reserve
RAMC   Royal Army Medical Corps
RAOC   Royal Army Ordnance Corps
RAPC   Royal Army Pay Corps
RARO   Regular Army Reserve of Officers
RASC   Royal Army Service Corps
RAVC   Royal Army Veterinary Corps
R Aux AF   Royal Auxillery Airforce
RB   The Rifle Brigade
RCAF   Royal Canadian Air Force
RCT   Royal Corps of Transport
RE   Corps of Royal Engineers
RECC   Reconnaissance Corps
REME   Corps of Royal Electrical and Mechanical Engineers
RF   Royal Fusiliers
RFA   Royal Field Artillery
RFC   Royal Flying Corps
Rfmn   Rifleman
RFR   Royal Fleet Reserve
RGJ   Royal Greenjackets
RHA   Royal Horse Artillery
RHF   The Royal Highland Fusiliers
RHG   Royal Horse Guards
RHIGHRS   Royal Highlanders
RI   Royal Irish Rangers (27th (Inniskilling), 83rd and 87th)
RI Regt   Royal Irish Regiment
RIC   Royal Irish Constabulary
RIF   The Royal Irish Fusiliers
RM   Royal Marines
RMA   Royal Military Academy
RMC   Royal Military College
RMLI   Royal Marine Light Infantry
RMP   Corps of Royal Military Police
RN   Royal Navy
RNAS   Royal Naval Air Services
RNASBR   Royal Naval Auxiliary Sick Berth Reserve
RNF   The Royal Northumberland Fusiliers

RNR   Royal Naval Reserve
RNVR   Royal Naval Volunteer Reserve
RNZAF   Royal New Zealand Air Force
RNWAR   Royal Naval Wireless Auxiliary Reserve
RO   Radio Operator
RPC   Royal Pioneer Corps
RRC   Royal Red Cross (Medal)
RRF   Royal Regiment of Fusiliers
RRW   Royal Regiment of Wales
RS   The Royal Scots (The Royal Regiment)
RSDG   Royal Scots Dragoon Guards
RSF   Royal Scots Fusiliers
R Sig   Royal Signals
RSM   Regimental Sergeant Major
RSO   Regimental Supply Officer
RTR   Royal Tank Regiment, Royal Armoured Corps
RUC   Royal Ulster Constabulary
RUR   The Royal Ulster Rifles
RVM   Royal Victorian Medal
RVO   Royal Victorian Order
RWF   The Royal Welsh Fusiliers
RWK   The Queen's Own Royal West Kent Regiment
RW Kent R   Royal West Kent Regiment
S/L, S/Ldr, Sqn Ldr   Squadron Leader
S/Sgt   Staff Sergeant
SAAF   South African Air Force
SAC   Senior Aircraftman
SAS   Special Air Service Regiment
SC   Staff College; Staff Captain; Second in Command; Signal Corps
SF   Special Forces
SG   Scots Guards
SGM   Sea Gallantry Medal
Sgmn   Signalman
Sgt   Sergeant
SI   Star of India (Order)
SJAB   St John Ambulance Brigade
SMIO   Special Military Intelligence Officer
SMIU   Special Military Intelligence Unit
Smn   Seaman
SO1   Staff Officer, Grade 1
Som LI   Somerset Light Infantry
SWB   The South Wales Borderers
TA   Territorial Army
T&AVR   Territorial and Army Volunteer Reserve
TD   Territorial Decoration
TEM   Territorial Efficiency Medal
TF   Territorial Force
TFEM   Territorial Force Efficiency Medal
TFWM   Territorial Force War Medal
TG   Town Guard
Trg Gp   Training Group
UKLF   United Kingdom Land Forces
UNM   United Nations Medal
UNSM   United Nations Service Medal
V&A   Victoria and Albert (Order)
VC   Victoria Cross
VM   Victory Medal
WAAF   Women's Auxiliary Air Force
WAFF   West Afican Frontier Force
W/C, W/Cdr, Wg Cdr   Wing Commander
W&S   Worcestershire & Sherwood Foresters
WEA   Weapons Engineering Artificer
WG   Welsh Guards
Wilts   Wiltshire Regiment
WO   Warrant Officer
WOI   Warrant Officer Class I
WOII   Warrant Officer Class II
WRAC   Women's Royal Army Corps
WRAF   Women's Royal Air Force

Current
regiments

As many British medals carry the names of regiments that no longer exist, we list here all of the regiments of the British Army as published in the current *Army List*, together with their predecessors, and the dates of amalgamations and redesignations The current regiment title is indicated in bold type with former names underneath in normal type. Old regimental numbers are included in brackets. The dates are of amalgamations and redesignations taken from the *Army List 2000*.

HOUSEHOLD CAVALRY
Life Guards (*June 1928*)
    1st Life Guards
    2nd Life Guards
Blues and Royals (Royal Horse Guards and 1st Dragoons) (*29 March 1969*)
    Royal Horse Guards (The Blues)
    Royal Dragoons (1st Dragoons)

ROYAL ARMOURED CORPS
1st The Queen's Dragoon Guards (1 January 1959)
    1st The King's Dragoon Guards
    Queen's Bays (2nd Dragoon Guards)
Royal Scots Dragoon Guards (Carabiniers and Greys) (*2 July 1971*)
    3rd Dragoon Guards (Prince of Wales's)
    Carabiniers (6th Dragoon Guards)
    3rd/6th Dragoon Guards
    3rd Carabiniers (Prince of Wales's Dragoon Guards)
    Royal Scots Greys (2nd Dragoons)
Royal Dragoon Guards (1 August 1992)
    4th Royal Irish Dragoon Guards
    7th Dragoon Guards (Princess Royal's)
    4th/7th Dragoon Guards
    4th/7th Royal Dragoon Guards
    5th Dragoon Guards (Princess Charlotte of Wales's)
    Inniskillings (6th Dragoon Guards)
    5th/6th Dragoons
    5th Inniskillling Dragoon Guards
    5th Royal Inniskilling Dragoon Guards
Queen's Royal Hussars (The Queen's Own & Royal Irish) (*1 September 1993*)
    3rd The King's Own Hussars
    7th The Queen's Own Hussars
    Queen's Own Hussars
    4th The Queen's Own Hussars
    8th The King's Royal Irish Hussars
    Queen's Royal Irish Hussars
9th/12th Royal Lancers (Prince of Wales's)
    (*11 September 1960*)
    9th Queen's Royal Lancers
    12th Royal Lancers (Prince of Wales's)

King's Royal Hussars (*4 December 1992*)
    10th Royal Hussars (Prince of Wales's Own)
    11th Hussars (Prince Albert's Own)
    Royal Hussars (Prince of Wales's Own)
    14th King's Hussars
    20th Hussars
    14th/20th Hussars
    14th/20th King's Hussars
Light Dragoons (*1 December 1992*)
    13th Hussars
    18th Royal Hussars (Queen Mary's Own)
    13th/18th Hussars
    13th/18th Royal Hussars (Queen Mary's Own)
    15th The King's Hussars
    19th Royal Hussars (Queen Alexandra's Own)
    15th/19th Hussars
    15th The King's Royal Hussars
    15th/19th The King's Royal Hussars
Queen's Royal Lancers (*25 June 1993*)
    16th The Queen's Lancers
    5th Royal Irish Lancers
    16th/5th Lancers
    16th/5th The Queen's Royal Lancers
    17th (Duke of Cambridge's Own Lancers)
    21st (Empress of India's) Lancers
    17th/21st Lancers
Royal Tank Regiment (*4 April 1939*)
    Heavy Branch Machine Gun Corps
    Tank Corps
    Royal Tank Corps

ARTILLERY
Royal Regiment of Artillery
    Royal Horse Artillery
    Royal Regiment of Artillery

ENGINEERS
Corps of Royal Engineers

SIGNALS
Royal Corps of Signals

GUARDS DIVISION
Grenadier Guards
Coldstream Guards
Scots Guards
Irish Guards
Welsh Guards

SCOTTISH DIVISION
Royal Scots (The Royal Regiment)(1)
Royal Highland Fusiliers (Princess Margaret's Own Glasgow and Ayrshire Regiment)(21, 71 & 74)
  (*20th January 1959*)
    Royal Scots Fusiliers (21)
    Highland Light Infantry (City of Glasgow Regiment) (71 & 74)
King's Own Scottish Borderers (25)
Black Watch (Royal Highland Regiment) (42 & 73)
Highlanders (Seaforth, Gordons and Camerons) (72, 75, 78, 79 & 92) (*17 September 1994*)
    Seaforth Highlanders (Ross-shire Buffs, Duke of Albany's) (72 & 78)
    Queen's Own Cameron Highlanders (79)
    Queen's Own Highlanders (Seaforth & Camerons) (72, 78 & 79)
    Gordon Highlanders
Argyll & Sutherland Highlanders (Princess Louise's) (91 & 93)

QUEEN'S DIVISION
Princess of Wales's Royal Regiment (Queen's & Royal Hampshire) (2, 3, 31, 35, 37, 50, 67, 70, 97 & 107) (*9 September 1992*)
    Queen's Royal Regiment (West Surrey) (2)
    East Surrey Regiment (31 & 70)
    Queen's Royal Surrey Regiment
    Buffs (Royal East Kent Regiment) (3)
    Queen's Own Royal West Kent Regiment (50 & 97)
    Queen's Own Buffs (The Royal Kent Regiment)
    Royal Sussex Regiment (35 & 107)
    Middlesex Regiment (Duke of Cambridge's Own) (57 & 77)
    Queen's Regiment
    Royal Hampshire Regiment (37 & 67)
Royal Regiment of Fusiliers (5, 6, 7 & 20) (*23 April 1968*)
    Royal Northumberland Fusiliers (5)
    Royal Warwickshire Regiment (6)
    Royal Fusiliers (City of London Regiment)(7)
    Lancashire Fusiliers (20)
Royal Anglian Regiment (9, 10, 12, 16, 17, 44, 48, 56 & 58) (*1 September 1964*)
    Bedfordshire & Hertfordshire Regiment (16)
    Essex Regiment (44 & 56)
    3rd East Anglian Regiment (16th/44th Foot)
    Royal Norfolk Regiment (9)
    Suffolk Regiment (12)
    1st East Anglian Regiment (Royal Norfolk & Suffolk)
    Royal Lincolnshire Regiment (10)
    Northamptonshire Regiment (48 & 58)
    2nd East Anglian Regiment (Duchess of Gloucester's Own Royal Lincolnshire & Northamptonshire)
    Royal Leicestershire Regiment (17)

KING'S DIVISION
King's Own Royal Border Regiment (4, 34 & 55) (*1 October 1959*)
    King's Own Royal Regiment (Lancaster) (4)
    Border Regiment (34 & 55)
King's Regiment (8, 63 & 96) (*13 December 1968*)
    King's Regiment (Liverpool) (8)
    Manchester Regiment (63 & 96)
    King's Regiment (Manchester & Liverpool) (8, 63 & 96)
Prince of Wales's Own Regiment of Yorkshire (14 & 15) (*24 April 1958*)
    West Yorkshire (Prince of Wales's Own)(14)
    East Yorkshire Regiment (Duke of York's Own)(15)
Green Howards (Alexandra, Princess of Wales's Own Yorkshire Regiment) (19)
Queen's Lancashire Regiment (30, 40, 47, 59 81 & 82) (*25 March 1970*)
    East Lancashire Regiment (30 & 59)
    South Lancashire Regiment (The Prince of Wales's Volunteers) (40 & 82)
    Lancashire Regiment (Prince of Wales's Volunteers)
    Loyal Regiment (North Lancashire) (47 & 48)
Duke of Wellington's Regiment (West Riding) (33 & 76) (*Later no date*)
    Duke of Wellington's Regiment (33)
    76th Regiment of Foot
    Halifax Regiment

PRINCE OF WALES'S DIVISION
Devon & Dorset Regiment (11, 39, & 54) (*17 May 1958*)
    Devon Regiment (11)
    Dorset Regiment (39 & 54)
Cheshire Regiment (22)
Royal Welch Fusiliers (23)
Royal Regiment of Wales (24th/41st Foot)
    South Wales Borderers (24)
    Welch Regiment (41 & 69)
Royal Gloucestershire, Wiltshire & Berkshire Regiment (28, 49, 61, 62, 66 & 99) (*27 April 1994*)
    Wiltshire Regiment (Duke of Edinburgh's) (62 & 99)
    Royal Berkshire Regiment (Princess Charlotte of Wales's) (49 & 66)
    Duke of Edinburgh's Royal Regiment (Berkshire and Wiltshire)
    Gloucestershire Regiment (28 & 61)
Worcestershire & Sherwood Foresters Regiment (29th/45th Foot) (*28 February 1970*)
    Worcestershire Regiment (29 & 36)
    Sherwood Foresters (Nottingham & Derbyshire Regiment) (45 & 95)
Staffordshire Regiment (The Prince of Wales's) (38, 64, 80 & 98) (*31 January 1959*)
    South Staffordshire Regiment (38 & 80)
    North Staffordshire Regiment (Prince of Wales's) (64 & 98)

LIGHT DIVISION
Light Infantry (13, 32, 46, 51, 53, 68, 85, 105 & 106) (*10 July 1968*)
    Duke of Cornwall's Light Infantry (32 & 46)
    Somerset Light Infantry (Prince Albert's) (13)

LIGHT DIVISION *continued*

> Somerset & Cornwall Light Infantry (13, 32 & 46)
> King's Own Yorkshire Light Infantry (51 & 105)
> King's Shropshire Light Infantry (53 & 85)
> Durham Light Infantry (68 & 106)

Royal Green Jackets (43rd & 52nd, King's Royal Rifle Corps, Rifle Brigade) (*1 January 1966*)

> Oxfordshire & Buckinghamshire Light Infantry (43 & 52)
> 1st Green Jackets (43 & 52)
> King's Royal Rifle Corps (60)
> 2nd Green Jackets (King's Royal Rifle Corps)
> Rifle Brigade (Prince Consort's Own)
> 3rd Green Jackets (The Rifle Brigade)

INFANTRY NOT INCLUDED IN THE DIVISIONS
Royal Irish Regiment (27th (Inniskilling), 83rd, 87th and Ulster Defence Regiment)

> Royal Inniskilling Fusiliers (27 & 108)
> Royal Ulster Rifles (83 & 86)
> Royal Irish Rifles (83 & 86)
> Royal Irish Fusiliers (Princess Victoria's) (87 & 89)
> Ulster Defence Regiment
> Royal Irish Rangers

Parachute Regiment

GURKHA BRIGADE
Royal Gurkha Rifles (*1 July 1994*)+

> 2nd King Edward VII's Own Gurkha Rifles (The Sirmoor Rifles)
> 6th Queen Elizabeth's Own Gurkha Rifles
> 7th Duke of Edinburgh's Own Gurkha Rifles
> 10th Princess Mary's Own Gurkha Rifles
> Queen's Gurkha Engineers
> Queen's Gurkha Signals
> Queen's Own Gurkha Transport Regiment

SPECIAL AIR SERVICE
Special Air Service Regiment

ARMY AIR CORPS
Army Air Corps

> Glider Pilot Regiment

OTHER CORPS
Royal Army Chaplains' Department
Royal Logistic Corps

> Royal Army Service Corps
> Royal Corps of Transport
> Royal Army Ordnance Corps
> Royal Pioneer Corps

Royal Army Medical Corps
Royal Electrical & Mechanical Engineers
Adjutant General's Corps
Adjutant General's Corps (Staff and Personnel Support Branch)

> Royal Army Pay Corps
> Women's Royal Army Corps (less those to Regiments)
> Royal Army Ordnance Corps Staff Clerks
> Regimental Clerks

Adjutant General's Corps (Provost Branch) (RMP) (MPS)

> Royal Military Police
> Military Provost Staff Corps
> Military Provost Guard Service

Adjutant General's Corps (Education & Training Service Branch)

> Royal Army Education Corps

Adjutant General's Corps (Army Legal Branch)

> Army Legal Corps

Royal Army Veterinary Corps
Small Arms School Corps
Royal Army Dental Corps
Intelligence Corps
Army Physical Training Corps
Queen Alexandra's Royal Army Nursing Corps

> Queen Alexandra's Imperial Military Nursing Service

Corps of Army Music

TERRITORIAL ARMY
Royal Monmouth Royal Engineers (Militia)
Honourable Artillery Company

YEOMANRY OF THE ROYAL ARMOURED CORPS
Royal Yeomanry

> Royal Wiltshire Yeomanry (Prince of Wales's Own)
> Sherwood Rangers Yeomanry
> Leicestershire and Derbyshire (Prince Albert's Own) Yeomanry
> Kent and City of London Yeomanry (Sharpshooters)
> Inns of Court and City Yeomanry
> Westminster Dragoons (2nd City of London Yeomanry)

Royal Wessex Yeomanry

> Royal Wiltshire Yeomanry (Prince of Wales's Own)
> Royal Gloucestershire Hussars.
> Royal Devon Yeomanry
> Dorset Yeomanry

Royal Mercian and Lancaster Yeomanry

> Queen's Own Warwickshire and Worcestershire Yeomanry
> Staffordshire Yeomanry (Queen's Own Royal Regiment)
> Shropshire Yeomanry
> Cheshire Yeomanry (Earl of Chester's)
> Duke of Lancaster's Own Yeomanry (Royal Tank Regiment)

Queen's Own Yeomanry

> Queen's Own Yorkshire Yeomanry
> Ayrshire Yeomanry (Earl of Carrick's Own)
> Northumberland Hussars
> Fife and Forfar Yeomanry (Scottish Horse)
> North Irish Horse

ARTILLERY
Royal Regiment of Artillery

ENGINEERS
Corps of Royal Engineers
Engineer and Logistic Staff Corps Royal Engineers (Volunteers)

SIGNALS
Royal Corps of Signals

SCOTTISH DIVISION
52nd Lowland Regiment
51st Highland Regiment

QUEEN'S DIVISION
3rd (Volunteer) Battalion The Princess of Wales's
    Royal Regiment (Queen's & Royal Hampshire
London Regiment
East of England Regiment

KING'S DIVISION
Lancaster and Cumbrian Volunteers
Tyne-Tees Regiment
East and West Riding Regiment

PRINCE OF WALES'S DIVISION
West Midlands Regiment
Kings and Cheshire Regiment
Royal Welsh Regiment

LIGHT DIVISION
Royal Rifle Volunteers
Rifle Volunteers
4th/5th Battalion The Royal Irish Rangers
    (Volunteers)
4th (Volunteer) Battalion The Parachute Regiment

ARMY AIR CORPS
7th Regiment Army Air Corps (Volunteers)

OTHER CORPS
Royal Army Chaplains' Department
Royal Logistic Corps
Royal Army Medical Corps
Royal Electrical & Mechanical Engineers

Adjutant General's Corps (Staff and Personnel
    Support Branch)
Adjutant General's Corps (Army Legal Branch)
Adjutant General's Corps (Education Service
    Branch)
Adjutant General's Corps (RMP)
Adjutant General's Corps (MPS)
Royal Army Veterinary Corps
Army Physical Training Corps
Small Arms School Corps
Royal Army Dental Corps
Intelligence Corps
Queen Alexandra's Royal Army Nursing Corps
Officer Training Corps
Royal Gibraltar Regiment

SOME DISBANDED REGIMENTS WITH NO KNOWN "PARENT"
22nd Dragoons
23rd Hussars
24th Lancers
25th Dragoons
26th Hussars
27th Lancers
Reconnaissance Regiment
Royal Irish Regiment (18)
Cameronians (Scottish Rifles) (26 &90)
York and Lancaster Regiment (65)
Connaught Rangers (88 & 94)
Prince of Wales's Leinster Regiment (Royal
    Canadians) (100 & 109)
Royal Munster Fusiliers (101 & 104)
Royal Dublin Fusiliers (102 & 103
Royal Guernsey Light Infantry
Army Cyclist Corps
Machine Gun Corps
Army Remount Service
Cyprus Regiment

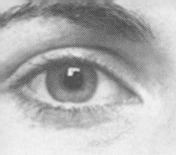

Researching your medals

The fact that many British medals are named enables the serious collector to engage in researching both the life and service history of the recipient as well as being able to learn about the history of the regiment/ship/unit or whatever with which he served. There is no easy or definitive guide to the range of research materials that are available, nor to the range of information likely to be found. The sort of information available varies greatly depending on whether the recipient was an officer or other rank, the service and unit with which he served, and the period during which he served. The experience and perseverance of the researcher can also affect the outcome. For those who are new to research, or who live a long way from the original sources, it may be wise to employ a professional researcher, at least initially. The PRO keeps a list of independent researchers who undertake this kind of work

When researching a medal and its recipient, experienced collectors regularly refer to a mixture of manuscript and printed sources:

Manuscript Sources

The National Archive, previously the Public Record Office (Ruskin Avenue, Kew, Surrey TW9 4DU) and the Oriental & India Office Collections (OIOC, British Library, 96 Euston Road, London NW1 2DB) are the two major depositories of official records of interest to the medal collector. Generally speaking the collector of medals to the British Armed Services will find the National Archive records essential to their enquiries, whilst anyone interest in the Indian Army and Navy (formerly the armed services of the Honourable East India Company), also the participation of British Forces in Indian campaigns, will find the OIOC to be an essential source of information. County Record Offices, Libraries and Museums, and also Regimental Museums can also have important holdings of manuscript records.

A first visit to the National Archive and the OIOC can be daunting. The range of records held by both Record Offices is also awe-inspiring once research has gone beyond consulting medal rolls and service papers.

Whilst there is no substitute for *experience* in learning successfully to branch out from the main stream of records, it is essential to be well prepared. It is important to have some idea of where to start looking and to realise the scope and limitations of the documents—it should be noted that the National Archive is subject to the standard 30 year closure rule for records, with many personal records being closed for longer periods. A great deal of time can be spent in simply locating the relevant references. To help you be more informed and to help eliminate time-wasting there are a number of important guides available that will aid in the location of the most relevant documents:

Cox, J. and Padfield, T., *Tracing your Ancestors in the Public Record Office* (1983).
Farrington, A., *Guide to the Records of the India Office Military Department* (1981).

Hamilton-Edwards, Gerald, *In Search of Army Ancestry* (1977).
Holding, N., *The Location of British Army Records: A National Directory of World War I Sources* (1984).
Holding, N., *World War I Army Ancestry* (1982).
Rodger, N.A.M., *Naval Records for Genealogists* (1988).

In addition it is worth noting that:

1.   The National Archive produces a range of leaflets which provide useful information about particular classes of records—records relating to military, naval and air services are particularly well-covered. The leaflets are free to visitors.
2.   The Mormons have published a wide range of guides to genealogical research which cover subjects of interest to medal/military researchers.
3.   The National Army Museum occasionally holds a study day on the subject of military research.
4.   New information is becoming available all the time and in new forms.
   Additionally, it is important to be aware that new documents are released periodically to public access. Probably the most important in recent years are those at the National Archive relating to World War I.

Medal Entitlement/Verification

Most collectors start their research by checking with the campaign medal roll (if available) that the recipient is indeed entitled to the medal and any clasps. It is a logical point at which to begin. This is often regarded as a simple, routine procedure, but for the unwary there are pitfalls and complications. The following points should always be borne in mind:

1.   Printed medal rolls will always contain errors in transcription, thus any discrepancies between a medal and the roll should, whenever possible, be checked back with the original manuscript roll. The more complex the original roll, the more transcription errors are likely to occur (for example, the claimants' lists for the Naval General Service Medal 1793-1840

and even the Military General Service Medal 1793-1814 are good examples of rolls where difficulties are likely to arise).

2. Some rolls have not survived—for example that for the Gwalior Campaign 1843. In such instances prize or bhatta rolls may exist at either the Public Record Office or the India Office. The inclusion of a recipient's name will at least indicate that he was most likely "entitled" to a medal and/or clasp (prize rolls indicate the share of money—realised from the loot captured in an action and then sold—allocated to each participant; bhatta is an extra allowance of pay made for field service).

3. Some medal rolls are incomplete, as with some of the regimental rolls for the Crimea Medal 1854–56.

4. With some campaign medal rolls, supplementary lists and late claimants' documentation have not survived.

5. Some medal rolls are difficult to search and therefore one has to take time in understanding the background to the documents one is looking at—the various lists of recipients for the Military General Service Medal 1794–1814 is a case in point.

It is important to note that the establishment of a recipient's entitlement is not the same thing as verifying a medal. Verification also requires the numismatic knowledge to know that the medal and clasps appear genuine. Where entitlement cannot be confirmed from the medal rolls, some collectors may be happy to rely on their numismatic knowledge to assure themselves that a medal is "genuine".

Published Sources

The published literature on medals is far-reaching and diverse, ranging from simply-produced booklets to detailed studies published in several volumes. A full bibliography of medallic and related works would in itself fill several volumes, particularly if fully cross-referenced.

The references which follow seek to provide a useful list of publications which either relate to orders, decorations and medals in general or to specific items in particular; the list includes medal rolls and casualty lists. No attempt has been made to include journal articles, as this would be an immense task; however a list of useful periodicals, some of which publish regular indexes, appears at the end.

Suggestions for other works that might be considered for inclusion in the next Yearbook *are welcomed.*

Most collectors seek to build up a solid library which reflects their main interests, but inevitably there are always books that have to be consulted elsewhere. Major libraries and national museums, such as the British Museum Library, the National Army Museum, the Imperial War Museum, the Hendon Royal Air Force Museum, the Greenwich Maritime Museum, and the Portsmouth Naval Musuem have extensive holdings of relevant material which can be consulted on the premises. City and County Reference Libraries are important for collectors who rarely visit London. Some Regimental Museums have libraries attached. Most libraries of any size will have a subject index to their collection of books (and sometimes manuscripts and photographs).

ORDERS, DECORATIONS AND MEDALS

GENERAL WORKS
(listed in alphabetical order by author)

Alexander, E. G. M., Barron, G. K. B. and Bateman, A. J., *South African Orders, Decorations and Medals* (1986).

Blatherwick, Surg. Cmdr. F. J., *Canadian Orders, Decorations and Medals* (4th edition, 1994).

Brine, F., *British Decorations from 1348 to the Present Time, Together with Those Given by Allies* (1880).

Buckman, Richard, *The Royal Sussex Regiment Honours and Awards* (2001).

Burke, J. B., *The Book of Orders of Knighthood and Decorations of Honour of All Nations* (1858).

Campion, Roger, *Police Medals of the World* (2002).

Central Office of Information, *Honours and Titles*. Part of the Aspects of Britain series.

Chapman, Roger, *Beyond Their Duty: Heroes of the Green Howards* (2001).

Downey, M., *The Standard Catalogue of Orders, Decorations and Medals Awarded to Australians* (1971).

Dymond, Steve, *Researching British Military Medals, a Practical Guide* (1999).

Eaton, Col.Hon.H.F. (later Lord Cheylesmore)., *Naval and Military Medals* (1897).

Elvin, C.N., *A Handbook of the Orders of Chivalry, War Medals and Crosses with Their Clasps and Ribbons and Other Decorations* (1892).

Floyd., J. B. (ed), *United States Decorations Awarded to the Armed Forces of the British Empire in World War II, Part I* (1997).

Gibson, J.H., *British War Medals and Other Decorations, Military and Naval* (1866).

Gibson, J.H., *British Military and Naval Medals and Decorations* (1880).

Gordon, Major L.L., *British Orders and Awards* (1959).

Hall, D.C. (in association with Wingate, C.), *British Orders, Decorations and Medals* (1973).

Hastings, Irwin D., *War Medals and Decorations* (1910).

Hieronymussen, Paul, *Orders, Medals and Decorations of Britain and Europe* (1967).

Hayward, J. B. & Son (pub.) *Honours and Awards of the Army, Navy and Air Force 1914-20* (1979).

Irwin, Ross W. , *War Medals and Decorations of Canada* (1969).

Jocelyn, A., *Awards of Honour* (1956).

Johnson, S. C., *Medals of our Fighting Men* (1916).

Johnson, S. C., *The Medal Collector* (1921).

Johnson, S. C., *Everybodys Medals: Including Medals, Decorations, Honours and Orders* (1914).

Joslin, E., C., *The Observers Book of British Awards and Medals* (1974).

Letcher, Owen., *Medals and Decorations of the British Commonwealth of Nations - Medaljes en Dekorasies van de Britse Gemenebes van Nasies* (1941).

Litherland, A. R. and Simpkin, B. T., *Spink's Standard Catalogue of British Orders, Decorations and Medals* (1990).

McClenaghan, Tony, *Indian Princely Medals: A Record of the Orders, Decorations and Medals of the Indian Princely States* (1997).

Maton, Michael, *The National Honours & Awards of Australia* (1995).

Mayo, J. H., *Medals and Decorations of the British Army and Navy* (1897).

Mericka, V., *Book of Orders and Decorations* (1975).

Monick, S., *South African Military Awards 1912-1987* (1988).

Monick, S., *Awards of the South African Uniformed Public Services 1922-1987* (1988).

Morrissey, Paul B. and Westlake, William R., *British Orders, Decorations and Medals Awarded to American Forces for the Korean War* (2003).

Narbeth, Colin, *Collecting Military Medals* (1971).

Nicolas, N.H., *History of the Orders of Knighthood of the British Empire; of the Order of the Guelphs of Hanover, and of the Medals, Clasps and Crosses, Conferred for Naval and Military Services* (1842).

Oldham, G. P. and Delahunt, B., *Orders, Decorations and Medals Awarded to New Zealanders.* (1991).

Pamm, Anthony N., *Honours and Rewards in the British Empire and Commonwealth*, 2 vols. (1995).

Payne, A.A., *A Handbook of British and Foreign Orders, War Medals and Decorations awarded to the Army and Navy* (1911).

Purves, A.A., *Collecting Medals and Decorations* (1968).

Purves, A.A., *The Medals, Decorations and Orders of the Great War 1914-18* (1975).

Purves, A.A., *The Medals, Decorations and Orders of World War II 1939-45* (1986).

Purves, Alec A., *Orders, Decorations and Medals, a Select Bibliography* (1958).

Steward, W.A., *War Medals and Their History* (1915).

Steward, W.A., *The ABC of War Medals and Decorations* (1918).

Tancred, G., *Historical Record of Medals and Honorary Distinctions* (1891).

Taprell-Dorling, Captain H. (ed. Alec A. Purves), *Ribbons and Medals* (1983).

Tinson, Lt-Col. Ashley R., *"Medals Will Be Worn", Wearing Medals Past and Present 1844–1999* (1999).

Williamson, Howard, *The Collector and Researchers Guide to the Great War* (2003).

ORDERS
(listed by the Order of Precedence)

GENERAL

CB Printers Group (Pubr)., *Orders of Chivalry and Gallantry Awards* (1963).

De la Bere, Sir I. *The Queen's Orders of Chivalry* (1961).

Harbord, R.E., *Supplement to the Royal Family Orders, Badges of Office, Royal Household Medals and Souvenirs* (1954)

Hunter, John., *A Concise Description of the Insignia of the Orders of British Knighthood*

James, G.P.L., *The Royal Family Orders, Badges of Office, Royal Household Medals and Souvenirs* (1951)

Neville, D.G. *A History of the Early Orders of Knighthood and Chivalry.*

Patterson, Stephen, *Royal Insignia* (1996).

Risk, J.C., *British Orders and Decorations* (1973).

ORDER OF THE GARTER

Anstis, J., *The Register of the Most Noble Order of the Garter* (1724).

Ashmole, E., *The Institution, Laws and Ceremonies of the Most Noble Order of the Garter* (1672).

Ashmole, E., *History of the Most Noble Order of the Garter* (1715).

Begent, P. J. and Chesshyre, H., *The Most Noble Order of the Garter: 650 Years* (1999).

Beltz, G. F., *Memorials of the Most Noble Order of the Garter* (1839).

Buswell, J., *An Historical Account of the Most Noble Order of the Garter* (1757).

Dawson, T., *Memoirs of St George The English Patron: And of the Most Noble Order of the Garter* (1714).

Fellowes, Rev. E.H., *The Knights of the Garter 1348-1939* (1939).

Harrison, A.P., *Order of the Garter: Armorial Registry of the Sovereign and the Knights of the Most Noble Order of the Garter—Their Names, Titles, Election, Installment and Demise* (1845).

Heylyn, P., *The History of that Most Famous Saint and Soldier of Christ Jesus: St George of Cappadocia...The Institution of the Most Noble Order of St George, named The Garter. A Catalogue of all the Knights Thereof Until this Present* (1631).

Holmes, Grace, *The Order of the Garter: Its Knights and Stall Plates, 1384–1984* (1984).

Hope, W.H. St J., *The Stall Plates of the Knights of the Order of the Garter 1348-1485* (1901).

Leake, S.M., *The Statutes of the Most Noble Order of The Garter* (1766).

ORDER OF THE THISTLE

Innes of Learney, Sir T., *The Foundation of the Most Ancient and Most Noble Order of the Thistle* (1959).

Lyon King of Arms, Lord, and Warrack, J., *The Knights of the Most Ancient and Most Noble Order of the Thistle* (1911).

ORDER OF ST PATRICK

Galloway, Peter, *The Order of St Patrick & Its Knights* (1999).

Galloway, Peter, *The Most Illustrious Order* (1996).

Grierson, G.A. & Grierson, J.F., *Statutes and Ordinan-ces of the Most Illustrious Order of St. Patrick* (1831).

ORDER OF THE BATH

Anstis, J., *Observations Introductory to an Historical Essay Upon the Knighthood of the Bath* (1725).

Perkins, Canon J., *The Most Honourable Order of the Bath* (1913).

Risk, J. C., *The History of the Order of the Bath and its Insignia* (1982).

ORDER OF ST MICHAEL AND ST GEORGE

Abela, A. E., *The Order of St Michael and St George in Malta* (1988).

Galloway, Peter, *The Order of St Michael and St George* (2000).

ROYAL VICTORIAN ORDER AND FAMILY ORDERS

Galloway, P., Martin, S., Pownall, H., Risk, J., Stanley, D. and Tamplin, J. *Royal Service, Volumes I–III* (1996, 2001/2).

Malloch, R. J., *The Royal Victorian Chain and Other Honors of the Sovereign*, (The Orders and Medals Society of America 1990).

Royal Victorian Order: Statutes and Lists of Members (1930).

ORDER OF THE BRITISH EMPIRE

Burke, *Handbook to the Order of the British Empire* (1921).

Galloway, Peter, *The Order of the British Empire* (1996).

Thorpe, A. Winton (ed.), *Burke's Handbook to the Most Excellent Order of the British Empire* (1921).

ORDER OF ST JOHN OF JERUSALEM

Bedford, W.K.R., and Holbeche, R., *The Order of the Hospital of St John of Jerusalem* (1902).

Fincham, H.W., *The Order of the Hospital of St John of Jerusalem and its Grand Priory of England* (1915).

The Grand Priory in the British Realm of the Venerable Order of the Hospital of St John of Jerusalem, *Roll of the Order 1931; Centenary Issue* (1936).

King, Col. E. J., *The Knights of St John in England* (1924).

King, Col. E. J., *The Knights of St John in the British Empire, Being the Official History of the British Order of the Hospital of St John of Jerusalem* (1934).

King, Sir Edwin, revised and continued by Sir Harry Luke, *The Knights of St John in the British Realm* (1967).

Luke, Sir H., *An Examination of Certain Claims to be an Order of St John* (1965).

Puddy, E., *A Short History of the Order of the Hospital of St John of Jerusalem in Norfolk* (1961).

Renwick, E.D., *A Short History of the Order of St John* (1959).

Tozer, C.W., *The Insignia and Medals of the Grand Priory of the Most Venerable Order of the Hospital of St John of Jerusalem* (1975).

DECORATIONS
(listed in alphabetical order by name of medal)

GENERAL
Abbott, P.E. and Tamplin, J.M.A., *British Gallantry Awards* (1981).

Abela, A.E., *Maltas George Cross and War Gallantry Awards*.

Bles, G (pub.) *Naval Honours and Awards 1939-1940* (1942).

Brown, G.A., *Commando Gallantry Awards of World War II*.

Campbell, G.L., *Royal Flying Corps (Military Wing) — Honours, Awards and Casualties 1914-17* (1917).

Campion, Roger, *The Call of Duty* (1997).

Chatterton-Dickson,W.W.F., *Seedie's List of Coastal Forces Awards for World War II*.

Chatterton-Dickson, W.W.F., *Seedies List of Fleet Air Arm Awards 1939-1969*.

Chatterton-Dickson,W.W.F., *Seedie's Roll of Naval Honours & Awards 1939-59* (1990).

Chatterton-Dickson, W.W.F., *Seedie's List of Submarine Awards for World War II*.

Chatterton-Dickson, W.W.F., *Seedie's List of Awards to the Merchant Navy for World War II* (1997).

Clarke, John D., *Gallantry Medals and Decorations of the World* (1993).

Elson, J., *Honours and Awards: the South Staffordshire Regiment 1914-18* (2004).

Elson, J., *Honours and Awards: the Prince of Wales's (North Staffordshire) Regiment 1914-19* (2004).

Escott, Beryl, *20th Century Women of Courage* (1999).

Eyre, Philip, *Those Who Dared — Gallantry Awards to the SAS and Attached SBS Units 1941-46* (2002).

Greenhill (pub.) *South African Honours and Awards 1899-1902*.

Hayward J. B. & Son (pub.) *Honours & Awards to the Indian Army 1914-21* (1992).

Hayward J. B. & Son (pub.) *Honours & Awards of the Old Contemptibles* (1992).

Housley, C., *British Gallantry Awards to Sherwood Foresters* (1999).

Hypher, P.P., *Deeds of Valour Performed by Indian Officers and Soldiers During the Period from 1860 to 1925* (1927).

Jacob, J.R., *Court Jewellers of the World* (1978).

King, Terence, *Gallantry Awards of the South African Police 1913-94 including a Complete Roll of Honour*, (2000).

King, Terence and Portman, Audrey, *South African Police Medal of Honour for Courage and Faithfulness 1963-2001* (2001).

McInness, I. and Webb, J.V., *Contemptible Little Flying Corps* (1991).

Midland (pub.) *Tank Corps Honours & Awards 1916-1919* (1982).

O'Shea, P., *An Unknown Few: The Story of Those Holders of the George Cross, the Empire Gallantry Medal, and the Albert Medals Associated with New Zealand*.

Pamm, Anthony N., *Honours and Rewards in the British Empire* (1995) (2 vols.).

Pitchfork, Graham, *Men Behind the Medals* (2004).

Royal Flying Corps: *Casualties and Honours During the War of 1914-17* (1987).

Stanistreet, A. *'Gainst All Disaster: Above and Beyond the Call of Duty* (1986).

Tucker, S/L N. G., *In Adversity — Exploits of Gallantry and Awards to the RAF Regiment and its Associated Forces 1921-1995* (1997).

Wilson, Sir A., and McEwen, Capt. J. H. F., *Gallantry* (1939).

ALBERT MEDAL
Henderson, D.V., *For Heroic Endeavour* (1988).

Stanistreet, Allan, *Heroes of the Albert Medal* (2002).

CHIEFS' MEDALS
Jamieson, A.M., *Indian Chief Medals and Medals to African and Other Chiefs* (1936).

CONSPICUOUS GALLANTRY MEDAL
Cooper, A.W., *In Action With The Enemy: The Holders of the Conspicuous Gallantry Medal (Flying)*.

Brown, G. and Penhall, R., *Conspicuous Gallantry Medal* (1977).

McDermott, P., *For Conspicuous Gallantry*.

DISTINGUISHED CONDUCT MEDAL
Abbott, P.E., *The Distinguished Conduct Medal 1855-1909* (1987).

Ashton, M., *The Canadian Medal Rolls — Distingushed Conduct and Military Medal (1939-45 & 1950-53)*.

Brown, George A., *For Distinguished Conduct in the Field: The Register of the DCM 1939-92* (1993).

Mackinlay, Gordon, *True Courage: The Distinguished Conduct Medal to Australians 1939-1972* (1993).

McDermott, P., *For Distinguished Conduct in the Field: The Register of the DCM 1920-92* (1994).

Polaschek, A.J., *The Complete New Zealand Distinguished Conduct Medal* (1978).

Walker, R.W., *The Distinguished Conduct Medal 1914-20(1981)*.

DISTINGUISHED CONDUCT MEDAL (AFRICAN)
Arnold J., *The African DCM to the King's African Rifles and the West African Frontier Force* (1998).

DISTINGUISHED FLYING CROSS
Carter, N. and C., *The Distinguished Flying Cross and How it was Won 1918–1995*, 2 vols. (1998).

Nelson, K. J., *The Royal Air Force Awards. 1918–1919* (2001).

DISTINGUISHED FLYING MEDAL
Ashton, M., *The Canadian Medal Rolls — Distinguished Flying Medal (1939-1945)*.

Tavender, Ian, *The Distinguished Flying Medal: A Record of Courage* (1990).

Tavender, Ian, *The DFM Registers for the Second World War* (1999).

DISTINGUISHED SERVICE CROSS
Fevyer, W. H., *Distinguished Service Cross 1901-1938* (1990).

Witte, R. C., *Fringes of the Fleet and the Distinguished Service Cross* (1997).

DISTINGUISHED SERVICE MEDAL
Chhina, Rana, *The Indian Distinguished Service Medal* (2001).

Fevyer, W.H., *The Distinguished Service Medal, 1914–1920* (1982).

Fevyer, W.H., *The Distinguished Service Medal, 1939–1946* (1981).

DISTINGUISHED SERVICE ORDER

Creagh, General Sir O'Moore and Humphris, H.M.,
The D.S.O.: A Complete Record of Recipients (1978).

EDWARD MEDAL

Henderson, D.V., *For Heroic Endeavour* (1988).

EMPIRE GALLANTRY MEDAL

Henderson, D.V., *For Heroic Endeavour* (1988).

GEORGE CROSS

Bisset, Lieut. Colonel Ian, *The George Cross* (1961).
Dowling, Dr C., *The Victoria Cross and George Cross* (1970).
Hare-Scott, K., *For Gallantry — The George Cross* (1951).
Smyth, Sir J., *The Story of the George Cross* (1968).
This England (pub.), *The Register of the George Cross* (1990).

GEORGE MEDAL

Fevyer, W.H., *The George Medal*.
Henderson, D.V., *Dragons Can Be Defeated* (1984).
Henderson, D.V., *Fashioned into a Bow* (1995).

INDIAN DISTINGUISHED SERVICE MEDAL

Chhina, Rana, *The Indian Distinguished Service Medal* (2001).

INDIAN ORDER OF MERIT

Hypher, P.P., *Deeds of Valour of the Indian Soldier Which Won the Indian Order of Merit During the Period From 1837 to 1859* (1925).
Peterson, C., *Unparalleled Danger Unsurpassed Courage: Recipients of the Indian Order of Merit in the Second World War* (1997).

KING'S POLICE MDAL

Farmery, J. P., *Police Gallantry: The King's Police Medal, The King's Police and Fire Service Medal and the Queen's Police Medal for Gallantry 1909–1979* (1995).

MILITARY MEDAL

Abbink, H. and C., *The Military Medal: Canadian Recipients 1916-1922*.
Ashton, M., *The Canadian Medal Rolls — Distingushed Conduct and Military Medal (1939-45 & 1950-53)*.
Bate, Chris and Smith, Martin, *For Bravery in the Field: Recipients of the Military Medal 1919-1939, 1939-1945* (1991).

VICTORIA CROSS

Biggs, M., *The Story of Gurkha VCs*.
Chapman., Roger, *Beyond Their Duty, Heores of the Green Howards* (2001).
Clayton, Ann, *Chavasse, Double VC* (1992).
Clayton Ann, *Martin-Leake, Double VC* (1995).
Cooksley, Peter, *The Air VCs* (1998).
Creagh, General Sir O'Moore and Humphris, H.M., *The Victoria Cross 1856-1920* (1993).
Crook, M.J., *The Evolution of the Victoria Cross* (1975).
Dowling, Dr C., *The Victoria Cross and George Cross* (1970).
Gerard, M., *The Victoria Cross* (1892).
Hare-Scott, K., *For Valour — The Victoria Cross* (1949).
Harvey, David, *Monuments to Courage* (1999).
Haydon, A.L., *The Book of the Victoria Cross* (1906).
Hunt, Derek, *Valour Beyond All Praise* (2003).
Laffin, John, *British VCs of World War 2: A Study in Heroism* (1997).
Lee, P.H., *The Victoria Cross* (1912).

Lennox, Lord W., *The Victoria Cross: The Rewarded and Their Services* (1857).
Leyland, R., *For Valour: The Story of the Victoria Cross*.
Little, M.G., *The Royal Marines Victoria Crosses*.
May, P. R. S., *Beyond Five Points, Masonic Winners of the VC and GC* (2001).
Muddock, J.E., *For Valor — the Victoria Cross 1856-1895* (1895).
Mundell, F., *Stories of the Victoria Cross* (1890).
Mulholland, J. and Jordan, A., *Victoria Cross Bibliography* (1999).
Napier, Gerald, *The Sapper VCs* (1998).
O'Byrne, R.W., *The Victoria Cross* (1865).
Pillinger, D. and Staunton, A., *Victoria Cross Locator* (1991).
Parry, D.H., *Britain's Roll of Glory, or the Victoria Cross, Its Heroes and Their Valour* (1895)
Parry, D.H., *The VC, Its Heroes and Their Valour* (1913).
Perrett, Bryan, *For Valour* (2004).
RAMC Historical Museum, *The Medical Victoria Crosses*.
Sarkar, D., *Guards VC: Blitzkrieg 1940* (1999).
Smyth, Brig. Sir John, *The Story of the Victoria Cross* (1964).
Snelling, Stephen, *VCs of World War I: Gallipoli* (1995).
Stewart, Lt.Col.Rupert., *The Victoria Cross: The Empire's Roll of Valour* (1916).
This England (pub.), *Register of the Victoria Cross* (1988).
Toomey, T.E., *The Victoria Cross and How Won 1854-1889* (1889).
Toomey, T.E., *Heroes of the Victoria Cross* (1895).
Turner, J.F., *VCs of the Air* (1961).
Turner, J.F., *VCs of the Army 1939-51* (1962).
Turner, J.F., *VCs of the Royal Navy* (1956).
Uys, Ian., *Victoria Crosses of the Anglo-Boer War* (2000).
Wilkins, P.A., *The History of the Victoria Cross* (1904).

CAMPAIGN MEDALS

(listed in chronological order by date of campaign medal)
GENERAL

Carter, T. and Long, W.H., *War Medals of the British Army 1650-1891* (1972).
Dickson, Bill Chatterton, *Seedie's List of Awards to the Merchant Navy for World War II* (1997).
Douglas-Morris, Captain K.J., *Naval Medals 1793-1856* (1987).
Douglas-Morris, Capt K.J. *Naval Medals Vol. II 1856-1880*.
Johnson, Derek E., *War Medals* (1971).
Joslin, E.C., Litherland, A.R. and Simpkin, B.T., *British Battles and Medals* (1988).
Kerr, Major W.J.W., *Notes on War Medals 1794-1840* (1948).
Laffin, J., *British Campaign Medals*.
Long, W.H., *Medals of the British Navy* (1895).
Poulsom, Major N.W.A., *Catalogue of Campaign and Independence Medals Issued During the Twentieth Century to the British Army* (1969).
Power, J.R., *Identification Data on British War Medals and Their Interpretation* (1962).
Power, J.R., *Addenda and Corrigenda to Identification Data on British War Medals and their Interpretation* (1963).
Purves, A.A., *Some Notes on War Medals for the Collector* (1958).
Steward, W., Augustus, *War Medals and their History* (1915).
Vernon S.B., *Collector's Guide to Orders, Medals and Decorations (With Valuations)* (1990).
Williams, R.D. *Medals to Australians: with Valuations*.

MILITARY GENERAL SERVICE MEDAL 1793-1814
Caldwell, G.J., Cooper, R.B.E., *Rifle Green in the Peninsula, Vol. 1* (1998).
Foster, Col. Kingsley O.N., *The Military General Service Medal Roll 1793-1814* (1947).
Mullen, A.L.T., *The Military General Service Medal 1793-1814.*
Newnham, A.J., *The Peninsula Medal Roll 1793-1814* (privately produced).
Vigors, Lieutenant Colonel D.D. and Macfarlane, Lieutenant Colonel A.M., *The Three Great Retrospective Medals 1793-1840 Awarded to Artillerymen* (1986).
Wilson, B., *Canadian Recipients of the MGS, Egypt (1882-9) and NW Canada Medals.*

NAVAL GENERAL SERVICE MEDAL 1793-1840
Douglas-Morris, Captain K.J., *The Naval General Service Medal Roll, 1793-1840* (1982).
Hailes, Colonel D.A., *Naval General Service Medal Roll 1793-1840* (privately produced).
MacKenzie, Col R.H., *The Trafalgar Roll: The Ships and the Officers* (1989).
Message, C.W., *Alphabetical Naval General Service Medal Roll 1793-1840* (1995).
Newnham A.J., *Naval General Service Medal Roll 1793-1840* (privately produced).
O'Byrne, William, *Naval Biographical Dictionary* (2 vols, 1849).
Roberts, *The Trafalgar Roll* (1995).
Vigors, Lieutenant Colonel D.D. and Macfarlane, Lieutenant Colonel A.M., *The Three Great Retrospective Medals 1793-1840 Awarded to Artillerymen* (1986).

ARMY OF INDIA MEDAL 1799-1826
Gould, R.W. and Douglas-Morris, Captain K.J., *The Army of India Medal Roll 1799-1826* (1974).
Vigors, Lieutenant Colonel D.D. and Macfarlane, Lieutenant Colonel A.M., *The Three Great Retrospective Medals 1793-1840 Awarded to Artillerymen* (1986).

WATERLOO MEDAL
Caldwell, G.J., Cooper, R.B.E., *Rifle Green at Waterloo* (1990).
Dalton, C., *The Waterloo Roll Call* (1904).
Haythornthwaite, P. J., *Waterloo Men* (2000).
Lagden, A. and Sly, J., *The 2/73rd at Waterloo: Including a Roll of All Ranks Present, with Biographical Notes* (1998).

INDIAN CAMPAIGN MEDALS
Biddulph, Major H., *Early Indian Campaigns and the Decorations Awarded for Them* (1913).
Cook, H. C. B., *The Sikh Wars 1845-6, 1848-9* (1975).
Stone, A.G., *The First Afghan War 1839-1842 and Its Medals* (1967).
Punjab Campaign 1848-9 Casualty Roll.
The Army of the Sutlej 1845-6 Casualty Roll

SOUTH AFRICA MEDAL 1835-53
Everson, Gordon R., *The South Africa 1853 Medal Roll* (1978).
Sole, T.E., *The Military Casualties of south Africa: Vol 1 1834-1878.*

NEW ZEALAND MEDAL 1845-66
Cowan, J., *The New Zealand Wars* (2 volumes) (1969).
Gudgeon, T.W., *Heroes of New Zealand and Maori History of the War* (1887).
Longley, H.G., *The New Zealand Wars 1845-1866* (1967).
Stowers, R., *The New Zealand Medal to Colonials: Detailed Medal Rolls for the New Zealand Wars 1845–72* (1999).

INDIA GENERAL SERVICE MEDAL 1854-95
Parritt, Colonel B.A.H., *Red With Two Blue Stripes* (1974).

CRIMEA MEDAL 1854-56
Caldwell, G.J., Cooper, R.B.E., *Rifle Green in the Crimea* (1996).
Cook, F. and Cook, A., *Casualty Roll for the Crimea 1854-55* (1976).
Duckers, P. and Mitchell, N., *The Azoff Campaign 1855* (1997).
Lummis, Canon W.M., *Honour the Light Brigade* (1973).
Mitchell, N. and Duckers, P., *Presented to the Queen: The Crimea Medal Award Ceremony, 18 May 1855* (1996).
Research Publications and Productions (pub.), *Returns Relating to Officers of the Army in the Crimea* (1989).
Savannah Publications (pubs.), *Casualty Roll for the Crimea 1854-55* (1999).

INDIA MUTINY MEDAL 1857-59
Asplin, K. J., *Indian Mutiny Medal Roll (British Forces)* (1999).
Tavender, I.T., *Casualty Roll for the India Mutiny 1857-59* (1983).

CANADA GENERAL SERVICE MEDAL 1866-70
Neale, G. N. and Irwin, R. W., *The Medal Roll of the Red River Campaign in 1870 in Canada* (1982).
Thyen, R., *Canada General Service Medal Roll 1866–70* (1999).

ABYSSINIAN WAR MEDAL 1867–68
Bates, Darrell, *The Abyssinian Difficulty* (1979).

SOUTH AFRICA MEDAL 1877-79
Forsyth, D.R., *South African War Medal 1877-8-9: The Medal Roll.*
Holme, N., *The Silver Wreath. The 24th Regiment at Isandhlwana and Rorke's Drift 1879* (1979).
Knight, Ian, *Brave Men's Blood* (1990).
Knight, Ian, *Zulu: Isandlwana and Rorke's Drift 22nd–23rd January 1879* (1997).
Mackinnon, J.P. and Shadbolt, S.H., *The South Africa Campaign of 1879* (1882).
Sole, T.E. *The Military Casualties of South Africa: Vol 1 1834-1878.*
Tavender, I.T., *Casualty Roll for the Zulu and Basuto Wars, South Africa 1877-79* (1985).
Whybra, J., *The Roll Call for Isandhlwana and Rorke's Drift* (1990).
Holme, N., *The Noble 24th, Biographical Records of the 24th Regiment in the Zulu War and the South African Campaigns 1877–1879* (2000).

AFGHANISTAN MEDAL 1878-80
Farrington, A., *The Second Afghan War 1878-80 Casualty Roll* (1986).
Robson, Brian, *The Road to Kabul: The Second Afghan War 1878–1881* (1986).
Shadbolt, S.H., *The Afghanistan Campaigns of 1878-80* (1882).

CAPE OF GOOD HOPE GS MEDAL 1880-97
Forsyth, D.R., *Cape of Good Hope General Service Medal: The Medal Roll.*

EGYPT MEDAL 1882-89
Maurice, Colonel J.F., *The Campaign of 1882 in Egypt.*
Webb, J.V., *Abu Klea Medal Roll.*

KHARTOUM STAR 1884
Fearon, D., *General Gordon's Khartoum Star* (1967).

NORTH WEST CANADA MEDAL 1885
Pacific Publishing Co (pub.), *North-West Canada Medal Roll (The Riel Rebellion 1885)* (1974).

BRITISH SOUTH AFRICA CO. MEDAL 1890-97
Forsyth, D.R., *British South Africa Co. Medal 1890-1897.*
Owen, C.R., *British South African Company Medal Roll 1890-1897.*
Roberts (pub.), *The British South Africa Company Medal Rolls 1890-1897* (1993).

HONG KONG PLAGUE MEDAL
Platt, J. J., Jones, M. E. and Platt, A. K., *The Whitewash Brigade: The Hong Kong Plague 1894* (1999).

INDIA MEDAL 1895–1902
Farrington, A., *India General Service Casualty Roll* (1987).
Barthorp, Michael, *The Frontier Ablaze: The North-West Frontier Rising 1897–98* (1996).

ASHANTI STAR 1896
McInnes, Ian and Fraser, Mark, *The Ashanti Campaign 1896.*

QUEEN'S & KING'S SOUTH AFRICA MEDAL 1899-1902
Biggins, David, *Elandslaagte: Account and Medal Roll* (2004).
British Naval Brigades in the South Africa War 1899-1902 (Reprint).
Dooner, M.G., *The Last Post: Roll of All Officers Who Gave Their Lives in the South African War 1899-1902* (1980).
Fevyer, W.H. and Wilson, J.W., *The Queen's South Africa Medal to the Royal Navy and Royal Marines* (1983).
Gray, S., *The South African War 1899-1902 - Service Records of British and Colonial Women.*
Hayward, J. B. & Son (pub.), *List of Casualties of the South Africa Frontier Force* (Reprint 1972).
Hayward, J. B. & Son (pub.), *South African War Casualty Roll: Natal Field Force* (1980).
Kaplan, Stan, *The Relief of Kimberley Bar for the QSA.*
Kaplan, Stan, *The Wepener Bar for the QSA.*
Lusted, C.A (pub.), *The Queens South Africa Medal 1898-1902* (1974).
Mitchell, Dr F.K., *Roll Of The Bar, Defence of Mafeking, on the Queen's Medal for South Africa, 1899-1902* (1963).
Palmer, A., *The Boer War Casualty List* (1999).
Stirling, J., *British Regiments in South Africa 1899-1902* (reprint) (1994).
Stirling, J., *The Colonials in South Africa* (1990).

CAPE COPPER COMPANY'S MEDAL 1902
Forsyth, D.R., *Medal Roll of the Cape Copper Company's Medal.*

CHINA MEDAL 1900
Fevyer, W.H. and Wilson, J.W., *The China War Medal 1900 to the Royal Navy and Royal Marines* (1985).
Narbeth, C., *Taku Forts* (1980).

OOKIEP DEFENCE MEDAL
Kieran, Brian L., *O'okiep* (1996).

AFRICA GENERAL SERVICE MEDAL 1902
Fevyer, W.H. and Wilson, J.W. *African General Service Medal to the RN and RM.*
Magor, R.B., *African General Service Medals.*

TIBET MEDAL 1903–04
Fleming, Peter, *Bayonets to Lhasa* (revised 1985).
Roberts (pub.), *The Tibet Campaign 1904 and the Royal Fusiliers.*

NATAL REBELLION MEDAL 1906
Forsyth, D.R., *Natal Native Rebellion 1906: The Medal Roll.*
Roberts Medals Publications Ltd (pub.), *The Natal Zulu Rebellion 1906.*

INDIA GENERAL SERVICE MEDAL 1908–35
Stiles, Richard G. M., *The Story of the India General Service Medal 1908–35* (1992).
Naval & Military Press (pub.), *India General Service Medal 1908–1935 to the Royal Air Force* (1994).

FIRST WORLD WAR MEDALS 1914-19
Adler, Revd. M (ed.), *British Jewry Book of Honour 1914-1918* (1922 and reprint 1997).
Bell, E.W., *Soldiers Killed on the First Day of the Somme* (1977).
Christie, N.M. *Officers of the Canadian Expeditionary Force who Died Overseas 1914-1919.*
Fevyer, W. H. and Wilson, J. W., *The 1914 Star to the Royal Navy and the Royal Marines* (1995).
Hayward, J. B. & Son (pub.), *Officers Died in the Great War* (1988).
Hayward, J. B. & Son (pub.), *Soldiers Died in the Great War* (80 parts).
Hobson, C., *Airmen Died in the Great War 1914-18: The Roll of Honour of the British and Commonwealth Air Services of the First World War* (1995)
Imperial War Museum (pub.), *Drake, Royal Naval Division Roll of Honour.*
Imperial War Museum (pub.), *Hawke, Royal Naval Division Roll of Honour.*
Imperial War Museum (pub.), *Hood, Royal Naval Division Roll of Honour.*
Imperial War Museum (pub.), *Howe, Royal Naval division Roll of Honour.*
Imperial War Museum (pub.), *Nelson, Royal Naval division Roll of Honour.*
Jarvis, S.D. and Jarvis, D.B., *The Cross of Sacrifice* (1990-1994) (several volumes).
Laslo, A.J., *The Interallied Victory Medals of WWI* (1986).
Merewhether, Lt-Col L. A., CIE and Smith Sir F., Bart., *The Indian Corps in France* (1919).
Mitchell, F.K., *Medals of the Great War Awarded to South Africans* (1983).
New Zealand Expeditionary Force Roll of Honour (Reprint).
Parks, Major Edwin, *The Royal Guernsey Militia* (1993).
Ruvigny, Marquis de., *The Roll of Honour 1916-1919.*
Walker, R., *To What End Did They Die? — Officers Died At Gallipoli.*
Williams, R.D., *Guide to Collecting and Researching Campaign Medals of the Great War* (1993).
Williamson, H.J., *The Roll of Honour, Royal Flying Corps and Royal Air Force for the Great War 1914-18* (1992).

SECOND WORLD WAR MEDALS
Devereux, J. and Sacker, G., *Roll of Honour, Land Forces World War 2 Volume I* (Cavalry, Yeomanry, RAC, Reconnaissance Corps, RTR and Brigade of Guards—other volumes to follow) (1999).
Hayward, J. B. & Son (pub.), *Prisoners of War (British, Empire and Commonwealth Forces)* (3 vols, reprint).
Purves, A. A., *The Medals, Decorations & Orders of World War II* (1986).
Savannah Publications (pubs.), *Roll of Honour Land Forces WWII* (2000).

NAVAL GENERAL SERVICE MEDAL 1915

Fevyer, W.H. and Wilson, J.W., *NGS Medal 1915-1962 to the Royal Navy and Royal Marines for the Bars Persian Gulf 1909-1914, Iraq 1919-1920, NW Persia 1920* (1995).

KOREA MEDALS 1950-53

Dyke, P., *Korea 1950-53: Mentions-in-Despatches* (1989).

Gaston, P., *Korea 1950-1953, Prisoners of War, The British Army.*

Harding, Colonel E.D., *The Imjin Roll* (1976).

Ingraham, Kevin R., *The Honors, Medals and Awards of the Korean War 1950-1953* (1993).

MERITORIOUS SERVICE MEDALS

Chamberlain, Howard, *Service Lives Remembered, The MSM in New Zealand and its Recipients 1895–1994* (1995) and *Supplement* (1997).

McInnes, Ian, *The Meritorious Service Medal to Aerial Forces* (1984).

McInnes, Ian, *The Meritorious Service Medal to Naval Forces* (1983).

McInnes, Ian, *Meritorious Service Medal. The Immediate Awards 1916-1928* (1992).

McInnes, Ian, *The Annuity Meritorious Service Medal* (1994).

Sainsbury, Major J.D., *For Gallantry in the Performance of Military Duty* (1980).

LONG SERVICE & GOOD CONDUCT MEDALS

Bolton, R., Howie, L. and Mandry, R., *Badges of the Brigade.* (2000).

Douglas-Morris, Captain K.J., *The Naval Long Service Medals* (1991).

Lees, J.R., *Recipients of the Long Service & Good Conduct Medal 1833-1916 to the Somerset Light Infantry (Prince Alberts).*

McInnes, I. and Gregson, J. B., *The Army Long Service & Good Conduct Medal 1830–1848* (1996).

Pallas, S.M., *Canadian Recipients of the Colonial Auxiliary Forces Officers Decoration and the Colonial Auxiliary Forces Long Service Medal.*

Tamplin, J.M.A., *The Army Emergency Reserve Decoration and the Efficiency Medal (Army Emergency Reserve)* (1989).

Tamplin, J.M.A., *The Colonial Auxiliary Forces Long Service Medal* (1984.)

Tamplin, J.M.A., *The Colonial Auxiliary Forces Officers' Decoration: the Indian Volunteer Forces Officers' Decoration* (1981).

Tamplin, J.M.A., *The Efficiency Decoration Instituted 1930* (1987).

Tamplin, J.M.A., *The Imperial Yeomanry Long Service and Good Conduct Medal* (1978).

Tamplin, J.M.A., *The Militia Long Service and Good Conduct Medal* (1979).

Tamplin, J.M.A., *The Special Reserve Long Service and Good Conduct Medal* (1979).

Tamplin, J.M.A., *The Territorial Decoration 1908-1930* (1983).

Tamplin, J.M.A., *The Territorial Force Efficiency Medal 1908-1921 and the Territorial Efficiency Medal 1922-1930* (1980).

Tamplin, J.M.A., *The Volunteer Long Service Medal* (1980).

Tamplin, J.M.A., *The Volunteer Officers' Decoration* (1980).

Williams, R.D., *The Victoria Volunteer Long and Efficient Service Medal & the Volunteer Officers' Decoration* (1976).

LIFE SAVING AWARDS

Barclay, C., *Royal Humane Society Medals* (1999).

Besley, Edward, *For Those in Peril* (2004).

Brown, G., *Lloyds War Medal for Bravery at Sea* (1992).

Cox, Barry, *Lifeboat Gallantry: The Complete Record of Royal National Lifeboat Institution Gallantry Medals and How They Were Won 1824–1996* (1998).

Cumming, Sir J., *Literature of the Life-Boat 1785-1947* (1947).

Dibdin, C., *History of the Institution's Gold and Silver Medals* (1909).

Fevyer, William H., *Acts of Gallantry, Vol. 2, 1871–1950* (1997).

Fevyer, William H. and Barclay, Craig, *Acts of Gallantry, Vol. 3, 1951-2000* (2003).

Gawler, J., *Lloyds Medals 1836-1989.*

Jeffery, S., *The Liverpool Shipwreck and Humane Society 1839-1939* (1939).

Lamb, Sir J.C., *The Life Boat and Its Work* (1911).

Mundell, F., *Stories of the Royal Humane Society* (1895).

Scarlett, R., *Under Hazardous Circumstances: Lloyds War Medal for Bravery at Sea.*

Young, L., *Acts of Gallantry: Being a Detailed Account of Each Deed of Bravery in Saving Life from Drowning in All Parts of the World for which the Gold and Silver Medals and Clasps of the Royal Humane Society Have Been Awarded from 1830-1871.*

ANIMAL AWARDS

Le Chene, Evelyn, *Silent Heroes: The Bravery and Devotion of Animals in War* (1994).

OTHER MEDALS

Balmer, Major J.L., *TD, British and Irish Regimental and Volunteer Medals 1745-1895.*

Blatherwick, F. J. *Canadian Orders Decorations and Medals* (1994).

Bolton, R., Howie, L., Mandry, B., *Badges of the Brigade* (2000). (Boy's Brigade Badges and Medals)

Borts, L.H., *UN Medals and Missions* (1998).

Buckman, richard, *The Royal Sussex Regiment Military Honours and Awards* (2002).

Cole, H. N., *Coronation and Royal Commemorative Medals 1887-1977* (1977).

Condon, Major J.P.B., MBE, *The Kings and Queens Medals for Shooting (Regular Army).*

Dalzell, M. and Riches, P., *Mentioned in Despatches 1948-1968* (1999).

Duckers, P., *The Delhi Durbar Medal 1911 to The British Army* (1995).

Fevyer, W. H., Wilson, J. W. and Cribb, J., *The Order of Industrial Heroism* (2000).

Harris, D., *A Guide to Military Temperance Medals* (2002).

Hibbard, M.G., *Boer War Tribute Medals* (1982).

James G.P.L., *The Royal Family Orders, Badges of Office, Royal Household Medals and Souvenirs* (1951).

Maloyd, Tony, *South African War 1899-1902 Mentioned in Despatches.*

Owen, D., *The King's and Queen's Medal for Shooting* (1999).

Poulsom, Major N.W., *The White Ribbon: a Medallic Record of British Polar Expeditions* (1968).

Poulsom, Major N.W., *Catalogue of Campaign and Independence Medals Issued During the Twentieth Century to the British Army* (1969).

Rouse, Malcolm, *By Grace of the Lord of the Realm — The Delhi Durbar 1903* (2002).

Scarlett, R. J., *The Naval Good Shooting Medal 1903-1914* (1990).

Wilson, J. W. and Perkins, R., *Angels in Blue Jackets: The Navy at Messina, 1908.*

Wright, Col. Tim B., *The History of the Northern Rhodesian Police.*

The Orders & Medals Research Society

Formed for the benefit of collectors and active researchers

Founded in 1942 the Orders & Medals Research Society (OMRS) aims to promote a general interest in orders, decorations and medals as well as to assist members in pursuing their research. The Society also aims to publish any information that may be of benefit to members.

Subscribers to the Society enjoy the advantage of a quarterly journal offering informative articles and advise on medals and military history.

Numerous branches are located nationwide holding regular meetings and discussion groups. Once a year an annual convention is held in London marking the highlight of the researchers' and medal collectors' year.

 **For further details, please contact
The Membership Secretary at
PO Box 248, Snettisham, Kings Lynn PE31 7TA**

Societies
for medal
collectors

Listed here are some of the many societies around the world that cater for the medal collector or those interested in military history. The details given are mostly the private addresses or telephone numbers of the membership secretaries to whom all correspondence should be sent. *We would appreciate information from other Societies who would like their details included in the next YEARBOOK.*

Association de Collectionneurs de Décorations et Médailles (MEDEC) (Paasbloemstraat 81, B-2170 Merksem, Belgium).

Austrian Orders Research Society (Salesianergasse 9, A-1037 Wien, Postfach 20, Austria)

Birmingham Medal Society (10 Edward Street, Milverton, Leamington Spa CV32 6AX. Tel: 01926 332884).

Bund Deutscher Ordenssammler e.v. (Postfach 1370, D-95012 Hof, Germany).

The Crimean War Research Society (4 Castle Estate, Ripponden, West Yorkshire HX6 4JY).

Crown Imperial (history, traditions, regalia, insignia) (B. Sutton, The Old Smithy, 35 Liverpool Rd, Buckley, Flintshire CH7 3LH).

French Medal Collectors' Society (Symboles et Traditions, 6 Rue Guersain, F.75006, Paris)

Indian Military Historical Society (A. N. McLenaghan, 33 High Street, Tilbrook, Huntingdon, Cambs PE18).

Life Saving Awards Research Society (Jim Lees, PO Box 248 (LSARS), Snettisham, King's Lynn, Norfolk PE31 7TA. Tel: 01485 541279).

London Medal Club (Jim Lees, 020 8560 7648).

Medal Society of Ireland (1 The Hill, Stillorgan, Co. Dublin, Ireland).

Mid-Western Orders & Medals Society (MIDOMS) (5847 Gilbert Avenue, La Grange, IL 60525, USA).

Military Collector's Club of Canada (MCCofC) (PO Box 64009, RPO Morse Place, Winnipeg, MB, R2K 4K2, Canada).

Military Medal Society of South Africa (1 Jacqueline Avenue, Northcliff 2195, South Africa).

Naval Historical Collectors and Research Association (1 Old Fire Station Court, Nailsea, Bristol BS48 4SE).

Orders & Medals Society of America (OMSA) (PO Box 198, San Ramon, CA 94583, USA).

Orders & Medals Research Society (OMRS) (PO Box 248, Snettisham, King's Lynn, Norfolk PE31 7NW).

ditto, Australia Branch (Sydney) (PO Box 484, Lane Cove, NSW 2066, Australia).

ditto, Canada Branch (Ottawa) (17 Ella Street, Ottawa, Ontario, Canada K1S 2S3).

ditto, Canada Branch (Toronto) (273 Corner Ridge Road, Aurora, Ontario, Canada L4G 6L6).

ditto, Hong Kong Branch (Flat 23, 11/F Mt Nicholson Gap, 103 Mt Nicholson Road, Hong Kong).

ditto, New Zealand Branch (Wellington) (54 Lohia Street, Khandallah, Wellington, New Zealand. Tel: 64 4 479 1622).

ditto, Northern Branch (Manchester) (7 St Michael's Avenue, Great Lever, Bolton, Lancs BL3 2LP. Tel/Fax: 01204 524011).

ditto, Scottish Branch (21 Hartington Place, Edinburgh EH10 4LF).

ditto, Sussex Branch (9 Merryfield Drive, Horsham, West Sussex RH12 2AA).

ditto, Cotswold Branch (Cheltenham) (22 Suffolk Road, Cheltenham, Glos GL50 2AQ).

ditto, Northumbrian Branch (41 Ashdown Avenue, Durham DH1 1DB).

ditto, Salisbury Branch (tel. 01722 716605).

ditto, Kent Branch (tel. 01634 725854).

ditto, Medal Ribbon Branch (tel. temporarily 01485 541279).

ditto, Miniature Medals Branch (54 Priory Bridge Road, Taunton, Somerset TA1 1QB, tel. 01823 259675).

Ordenshistorik Selskab (Falkoneralle 79, DK 2000 Frederiksberg, Denmark).

Société Suisse de Phaleristique (Box 1, CH-1137 Yens, Switzerland).

Stockport Militaria Collectors Society, Stockport Armoury (tel: 01709 557622).

Victorian Military Society (20 Priory Road, Newbury, Berks RG14 7QN).

West of England Medal Club (Exeter) (Otterburn Farm, Halwill, Beaworthy, Devon EX21 5UG).

Professional
directory

On the following pages are the names and addresses of auctioneers, dealers, booksellers and fair organisers, all of whom will be of assistance to the medal collector. Most are full time and many have retail shops and the collector is usually welcome during normal business hours. Some have extensive stocks of medals whilst others include medals in a more diverse inventory. A number of dealers are part time or work from small premises or from home and appointments are necessary as many keep their stock in the bank for security. Telephone numbers have been included where known and it is always sensible to make contact before travelling any distance.

AUCTIONEERS

The following hold regular medal auctions or feature medals in general numismatic or militaria sales.

Baldwin's Auctions
11 Adelphi Terrace, London WC2N 6BJ. Tel: 02079309808 (fax: 02079309450), email: auctions@baldwin.sh, www.baldwin.sh. *Specialist auctioneers of coins and medals.*

Bloomsbury Auctions
24 Maddox Street, London W1S 1PP. Tel: 0207 4959 494, email: rupert@bloomsburyauctions.com. *Medals, coins, books and prints.*

Bonhams (Glendining's)
Montepelier Street, London SW7 1HH, 101 New Bond Street, London W1S 1SR. Tel: 020 7493 2445 (fax: 020 7491 9181), www.bonhams.com. *Auctioneers and valuers of medals. Approximately four sales per year.*

Bosleys
The White House, Marlow, Bucks SL7 1AH. Tel: 01628 488188 (fax: 01628 488111) www.bosleys.co.uk. *Specialist auctioneers of medals and militaria.*

A. F. Brock & Co LTD
269 London Road, Hazel Grove, Stockport, Cheshire, SK7 4PL. Tel: 0161 456 5050, tel/fax: 0161 456 5112, email: info@afbrock.co.uk, www.afbrock.co.uk. *Specialist in the sale by auction of coins, medals, banknotes, stamps, jewellery and collectables.*

City Coins
PO Box 156, Sea Point, 8060, Cape Town, South Africa. Tel: 0027 21 425 2639 (fax: 0027 21 425 3939), email: auctions@citycoins.co.za, www.citycoins.com. *Postal medal auctions.*

Corbitts
5 Mosley Street, Newcastle Upon Tyne, NE1 1YE. Tel: 0191 2327268 (fax: 0191 2614130). *Regular sales of coins, medals and stamps.*

Dix Noonan Webb
16 Bolton Street, Piccadilly, London W1J 8BQ. Tel: 020 7016 1700 (fax: 020 7016 1799), email: medals@dnw.co.uk www.dnw.co.uk. *Auctioneers and valuers. Regular auctions of medals.*

Downie's
11 & 12 Block Arcade, 98–100 Elizabeth Street, Melbourne, Vic 3000, Australia. Tel: 0061 3 9654 4935 (fax: 0061 3 9654 3787), www.downies.com. *Sales with emphasis on Australian and UK medals.*

Edinburgh Coin Shop
11 West Crosscauseway, Edinburgh EH8 9JW. Tel: 0131 668 2928 or 0131 667 9005 (fax: 0131 668 2926). *Regular postal auctions of medals.*

Floyd, Johnson & Paine Inc
PO Box 34679, Chicago, Il 60634, USA. Tel: (703) 461 9582 (fax: 703 461 3059), email: FJP4Floyd@aol.com, www.FJPauction.com. *Medals and militaria.*

Jeffrey Hoare Auctions Inc.
319 Springbank Dr., London, Ontario, Canada, N6J 1G6. Tel: (519) 473 7491 (fax: (519) 473 1541), www.jeffreyhoare.on.ca. *Regular sales of medals and militaria.*

Alec Kaplan
PO Box 28913, Sandringham 2131, Johannesburg, South Africa. Fax: 0027 11 640 3427, email: rhodesia@wol.co.za. *Regular sales of medals and militaria.*

Lockdales
37 Upper Orwell Street, Ipswich IP4 1HP. Tel: 01473 218588, www.lockdales.com. *Regular sales of medals, coins, collectables. Call for venue details.*

Medal Auctions
PO Box 7997, Maldon, Essex, CM9 8WR. www.medalauctions.com. *Eight sales of medals and related items per year.*

Morton & Eden
45 Maddox Street, London W1S 2PE. Tel: 020 7493 5344 (fax: 020 7495 6325), email: info@mortonandeden.com. *Advisory service and auctioneers of medals and coins.*

Spink & Son Ltd
69 Southampton Row, Bloomsbury, London WC1B 4ET. Tel: 020 7563 4049/4053 (fax: 020 7563 4068), email: info@spink.com, www.spink.com. *Auctioneers and valuers. Regular sales of medals.*

Thomson Roddick & Medcalf
Coleridge House, Shaddongate, Carlisle CA2 5TU. Tel: 0151 264 0842, email: auctions@thomsonroddick.com. *Regular auctions of orders and medals.*

Wallis & Wallis
West Street Auction Galleries, Lewes, Sussex BN7 2NJ. Tel: 01273 480208 (fax: 01273 476562), email: auctions@wallisandwallis.co.uk, www.wallisandwallis.co.uk. *Regular sales of militaria, arms, armour and medals.*

Ware Militaria Auction
Hertford Rugby Club Function Rooms, Hoe Lane, Ware, Herts (venue only). Tel: 01920 871901, mobile: 0774 7860746, email: martin@ware-militaria-auction.com, www.ware-militaria-auction.com. *Quality militaria including medals, weapons, badges, insignia etc*

Warwick & Warwick
Chalon House, Scar Bank, Millers Road, Warwick CV34 5DB. Tel: 01926 499031 (fax: 01926 491906), email: richard.beale@warwickandwarwick.com, www.warwickandwarwick.com. *Regular sales of Orders, Decorations and other collectables.*

INTERNET AUCTIONS

Speedbid www.speedbid.com
Bidwyze www.bidwyze.com
www.bid2u.com

DEALERS

1st Class Medal Service

PO Box 449, Warboys, Huntingdon, Cambs, PE28 2WW. Tel: 01487 824104, email: tony@1stclassmedalservice. co.uk, www.1stclassmedalservice.co.uk. Medals mounted for wear and display. Medals, badges and militaria.

A.A. Medals

33 Arkley Road, Birmingham, B28 9PL. Email: bs@bid2u. com. www.bid2u.com. All British medals. Free lists by email or post.

Ackley Unlimited

PO Box 82144, Portland, Oregon, USA 97282-0144. Tel: (503) 659 4681, email: aunltd@aol.com. Orders, medals and decorations. Free quarterly lists on request.

Michael Autengruber

Schillstrasse 7B, D-63067 Offenbach, Germany. Tel: (69) 88 69 25 (evenings). Orders, medals, literature. Catalogues $US3 (Europe), $US6 (elsewhere).

Award Productions Ltd

PO Box 300, Shrewsbury, SY5 6WP. Tel: 01952 510053 (fax: 01952 510765), www.awardmedals.com. Suppliers of unofficial medals for veterans.

Bonus Eventus

Aartshertoginnestratt 27, 8400 Oostende, Belgium. Tel: (059) 801696. Medals and miniature medals.

Bostock Militaria

"Pinewoods", 15 Waller Close, Leek Wootton, Nr Warwick CV35 7QG. Tel: 01926 856381 (fax: 01926 856 381), email: bostockmilitaria@aol.com, www. bostockmedals.co.uk. British orders, medals and decorations. S.A.E. for free current lists. Callers welcome by appointment.

Paul Boulden

Parade Antiques Market, 17 The Parade, The Barbican, Plymouth, Devon. Tel: 01752 221443 (fax: 01589 632686). Medals and militaria. 6 lists p.a. (£3, £6 overseas).

British Military Badges

The Castle Armoury, 18 Castle Street, Dover, Kent CT16 1PW. 12pp list of British Military Badges. UK & BFPOs £2, Europe £2.40, Elsewhere £3.

David Brookes

PO Box 322, Rochester, Kent, England ME1 1LX. Tel: 01634 840296, email: dave@wharfinger.u-net.com. Dealing in Military Medals, Photographs and Ephemera.

Jim Bullock Militaria

PO Box 217, Romsey, SO51 5XL. Tel/fax: 01794 516455, email: jimbullockmilitaria.com, www.jimbullockmilitaria. com. Quality medals and militaria, medal framing and mounting.

Philip Burman

Blackborough End, Middleton, King's Lynn, Norfolk PE32 1SE. Tel: 01553 840350, www.military-medals. co.uk. Large and varied stock of orders, medals and decorations. Send large S.A.E. for lists, issued 6 times a year.

Chelsea Military Antique

Unit N13/14, Antiquarius, 131–141 King's Road, London SW3 4PW. Tel: 020 7352 0308, email: richard@chelseamilitaria.com, www.chelseamilitaria. com. Medals and militaria. Monday–Saturday, 10am–6pm.

Chester Militaria

6 Chirk Close, Newton, Chester CH2 1SF. Tel: 01244 344268. Medals and militaria.

Coldstream Military Antiques

The White House, Marlow, Bucks SL7 1AH. Tel: 01628 488188 (fax: 01628 488111). Medals, badges, insignia.

Collector's Lair

#205 - 15132 Stony Plain Road, Edmonton, Alberta, Canada T5P 3X8. Tel: (403) 486 2907. Medals, badges.

Norman W. Collett

PO Box 235, London SE23 1NS. Tel/fax: (020) 8291 1435, www.medalsonline.co.uk. British medals and decorations, mainly groups, with an accent on researchable recipients. Medals.

J. Collins Medal Limited

17 Queens Road, Warsash, Hampshire SO31 9JY. Tel/fax: 01489 582222. email: jcollinsmedals.co.uk, www.jcollinsmedals.co.uk. Naval, Miliary, and Airforce Research Service.

Colonial Coins and Medals

218 Adelaide Street, Brisbane, QLD 4001, Australia. Tel: 61 7 3229 3949 (fax: 61 7 3229 3945), email: coinshop@bigpond.net.au, www. coinmedalshop.com.au. British, Commonwealth orders decorations and medals. Also regular auctions.

Command Post of Militaria

1306 Government Street, Victoria, British Columbia, Canada V8W 1Y8. Tel: (250) 383 4421. Medals, badges and uniforms.

Conglomerate Coins & Medals

GPO Box 2831, Brisbane, Queensland, Australia 4001. Retail: Level 3, 276 Edward Street, Brisbane, QLD. Tel: (07) 3221 1217 (fax: 07 3221 9711, email: alforgan@powerup.com.au. Medals and medallions.

Peter R. Cotrel

7 Stanton Road, Bournemouth, Dorset BH10 5DS. Mail order only—callers by appointment. Tel: 01202 388367. British, American and general foreign medals and decorations. Medal albums etc.

Jamie Cross

PO Box 73, Newmarket, Suffolk CB8 8RY. Specialist in Third Reich medals, badges and decorations.

C. J. & A. J. Dixon Ltd

23 Prospect Street, Bridlington, East Yorkshire YO15 2AE. Tel: 01262 676877 (fax: 01262 606600), email: chris@dixonsmedals.co.uk, www.dixonsmedals.co.uk. British and world orders, medals and decorations. 4 large lists a year £12 (UK), £16 (overseas).

D.M.D. Services

6 Beehive Way, Reigate, Surrey RH2 8DY. Tel: 01737 240080. Victorian campaign medals and decorations.

Frank Draskovic

PO Box 803, Monterey Park, CA 91754, USA. Email: fdraskovic@ hotmail.com. *Worldwide orders and medals, especially European and Far Eastern.*

Edinburgh Coin Shop (Hiram T. D. Brown)

11 West Crosscauseway, Edinburgh EH8 9JW. Tel: 0131 668 2928 (fax: 0131 668 2926). British medals and decorations. Four lists a year and postal auctions.

Elite-Collections.Com

PO Box 56, Pontypridd CF37 2YL, South Wales. www. elite-collections.com. 30 page catalogue of British medals. Annual Subscription (10 issues) £5 (UK), Free on E-mail.

E-Medals.ca

Bought-Sold-Traded. E-mail: info@emedals.ca, www. emedals.ca.

First Light Militaria

P.O. Box 4984, Poole, Dorset, BH16 6WA. Email: info@firstlight-militaria.co.uk, www.firstlight-militaria. co.uk.. Buying and selling medals and decorations.

G. A. Medal Services

PO Box 374, Winchester SO23 7QX. Tel/fax: 01962 888427, email: gamedals@btinternet.com. Medal framing, mounting and research work.

Andy Garrett

Unit 9, Brackley Antique Cellar, Draymans Walk, Brackley, Northants NN13 6BE. British and foreign medals, groups and collections, badges and militaria.

Gateway Militaria

Box 24049, 13 - 1853 Grant Avenue, Winnipeg, Manitoba, Canada R3N 1ZO. Tel: (204) 489 3884 (fax: 204 489 9118). Medals and badges.

GB Military Antiques

Shop 17/18 The Mall Antiques Arcade, 359 Upper Street, Islington, London N1 OPD. Tel: 0207-351-5357, email: info@gbmilitaria.com, www.gbmilitaria.com. British medals, awards and militaria. Specialising in Wants lists, medal mounting and medal replacement service.

Glance Back

17 Upper Church Street, Chepstow, Gwent NP6 5EX. Tel: 01291 626562. Large stock of Medals, badges and military books.

Gordons Medals Ltd

Grays Antiques Centre, Davies Mews, Davies Street, London W1K 5AB. Tel: 020 7495 0900 (fax: 020 7495 0115), email: sales@cocollector.co.uk, www.cocollector.co.uk. Monday–Friday, 10.30am–6pm. Campaign medals, militaria, German and Third Reich. Catalogues £6 (UK), £12 (overseas air).

Louis E. Grimshaw

612 Fay Street, R.R. #1 Kingston, Ontario, Canada K7L 4VI. Tel: (613) 549 2500. Military antiques and collectables, including medals. Catalogues of arms, medals and militaria . Single copies $C5 (Canada), $US4 (USA), $US6 (elsewhere).

Great War Medals

22 Selborne Road, Southgate, London N14 7DH. Mainly WW1 medals and books. 36 page catalogue of medals and decorations, £7.50 (UK), £11 (overseas).

W. D. Grissom

PO Box 12001, Suite 216, Chula Vista, California, USA 91912. American medals. Free lists.

A.D. Hamilton & Co

7 St. Vincent Place, Glasgow G1 2DW. Tel: 0141 2215423 (fax: 01412486019), email: jefffineman@hotmail.com, www.adhamilton.co.uk . Buying and selling Medals, miliataria, badges, coins and banknotes.

Harpers

P.O Box 7745, Brentwood, CM13 3WZ. Tel: 01277 812 052, email: info@harpershome137@freeserve.co.uk, www.harpers-online.com. Orders, medals and military antiques.

Hilton Medals (H&B)

PO Box 82, Warrington, WA5 2FP. Tel: 01925 727035. Mobile: 07714174188, email: hiltonmedal@aol.com, www.hiltonmedals.co.uk. Featuring British gallantry Medals and campaign medals with a wide selection of WWI.

Holdich International

7 Whitcomb Street, London WC2H 7HA. Tel: 020 79301979/07774133493 (fax: 020 79301152), www.rdhmedals.com. Medals and Militaria. Medals mounted for wear.

Intramark Limited

Windsor Lodge, 56 Windsor Street, Burbage, Leic., LE10 2EF. Tel: 01455 612400 (fax: 01455 612483), email: intramark@btclick.com. Manufacturers of miniature medals, medal brooch bars & medal ribbon bars, medals ribbons etc.

Alec Kaplan

PO Box 28913, Sandringham 2131, Johannesburg, South Africa. Fax: 0027 11 640 3427, email: rhodesia@wol.co.za. Please write, fax or email for free catalogue.

Liverpool Medal Company

42 Bury Business Centre, Kay Street, Bury Lancs BL9 6BU. Tel: 0161 763 4610 (fax: 0161 763 4963), www.liverpoolmedals.com. British and world orders, medals, decorations. Plus miniatures & related books.

Lyme Valley Medals Limited

P.O.Box 2404, Stoke on Trent DT7 4WQ. Email: enquiries@Lvmedals.co.uk, www.Lvmedals.co.uk.

Giuseppe Miceli Coin & Medal Centre

204 Bants Lane, Duston, Northampton NN5 6AH. Tel: 01604 581 533. Medals, militaria etc. Free list.

Military Antiques

PO Box 318, Bromley, BR1 2UX. Tel: 07939 252 206, Email: enquiries@militaryantiques.co.uk, www.militaryantiques.co.uk. British campaign and gallantry medals.

Monarch Medals

PO Box 161, Sandwich, Kennt, CT13 9YB. Tel: 07834 624614, email: mark@monarchmedals.com. www.monarchmedals.com. Website contact only. Dealing in British Orders, Decorations and Medals.

Peter Morris

PO Box 223, Bromley, Kent BR1 4EQ. Retail premises Bromley North BR Station. Tel: 020 8313 3410 (fax: 020 8466 8502), email: info@petermorris.co.uk, www.petermorris.co.uk. Buying & Selling of Medals, Militaria, Coins & Banknotes.

MSM Awards

8 Price Tce, Matamata, 2271, New Zealand. Tel: (NZ) 647 888 9055 (fax: (NZ) 647 888 6560), email: Veteran88@Hotmail.com. Commemorative medals. Supplier of medal ribbons. Also medal remounting services.

Neate Militaria and Antiques

PO Box 3794, Preston St. Mary, Sudbury CO10 9PX. Tel: 01787 248168 (fax: 01787 248363), email: gary@neatemedals.co.uk, www.neatemedals.co.uk. Serious buyers of all Medals.

Detlev Niemann

Ballindamm 9, V Floor, 20095 Hamburg 1, Germany. Tel: 0049 40 3252 5354 (fax: 0049 40 3252 5454), email: Detlev-Niemann@t-online.de, www.Detlev-Niemann.de. Specialist in German orders, decorations, militaria, etc. Catalogue subscription £20 for 4 issues.

Nordheide-Versand

Nordheid-Versand Kai Winkler, Fachenfelderweg 67, D-21220 Seevetal. Tel: (0 41 05) 8 43 84 (fax: (0 41 05) 8 27 88), www.nordheideversand.de. Medals, awards, award-documents, miniatures, pins, uniforms etc.

North West Medal

PO Box 21070, 640 River Street, Thunder Bay, ON, P7A 8A7 Canada. Email: nwmedal@tbaytel.net, www.northwestmedal.com.

Pieces of History

PO Box 4470, Cave Creek, AZ 85331, USA. Tel: (602) 488 1377 (fax: 602 488 1316). Worldwide medals badges, patches, accessories etc. Lists available.

Pride of Place

Tel: 01980 670161. Email: raynewell@medalsframing.fsnet.co.uk, www.medalsframing.co.uk. Medal Framing and medal mounting service.

Q & C Militaria

22 Suffolk Road, Cheltenham, Gloucestershire GL50 2AQ. Tel/fax: 01242 519815, www.qcmilitaria.com. British and Commonwealth orders, medals, decorations and miltaria.

R & M International

PO Box 6278, Bellevue, Washington, USA. 98008-0278. www.randminternational.com. Well-illustrated 64 page lists of medals and decorations of the world, $US2.50.

Barbara Radman

Westfield House, 2G Westfield Road, Witney, Oxon OX8 5JG. Tel: 01993 772705. British and Foreign orders, medals and decorations. Specialist in Serbia, Montenegro, Russian and Baltic States.

Royal Insignia

Medal House, 57 Yishun Industrial Park A, Singapore 768730. Tel (65) 6487 7777 (fax: 65 6756 0366), email info@medals.com.sg, www.medals.com.sg. Manufacturers of orders and medals.

SBL Medals

30 Moor Farm Avenue, Mosborough, Sheffield S20 5JP. Tel/Ans: 0114 2481545, email: info@sblmedals.co.uk, www.sblmedals.co.uk. British military medals and decorations.

S. E. Sewell

PO Box 149, Stowmarket, IP14 4WD. Tel: 01449 782185, mobile: 07739 071822. Tel/Fax: 01449 782185, email: sewellmedals@hotmail.com, www.sewellmedals.co.uk. A wide variety of medals, mainly British.

E. C. Snaith & Son Ltd

20 Vale Street, Denbigh, Denbighshire LL16 3BE. Tel: 01745 812218 (fax: 01745 816367). Wholesalers to the Medal Trade.

Southern Medals

16 Broom Grove, Knebworth, Herts SG3 6BQ. 32 page lists of British and Commonwealth medals and decorations. £6 (UK), £9 (overseas).

Spink & Son Ltd

69 Southampton Row, Bloomsbury, London WC1B 4ET. Tel: 020 7563 4049 (fax: 020 7563 4068), email: info@spink.com, www.spink.com. Medal dealers and auctioneers.

Sunset Militaria

Dinedor Cross, Herefordshire HR2 6PF. Tel: 01432 870420 (fax: 01432 870309). Military research and world medal ribbons. SAE for list.

Jeremy Tenniswood

36 St Botolphs Street, Colchester, Essex CO2 7EA. Tel: 01206 368787 (fax: 01206 367836), www.militaria.co.uk. Orders, medals, decorations and militaria and related books.

T. M. Medals Ltd

Tel: 01908 337954, email: sales@tmmedals.co.uk, www.tmmedals.co.uk. Specialists in South African campaign medals and militaria. Items for sale on-line.

Toye, Kenning & Spencer Ltd

Regalia House, Newtown Road, Bedworth, Warwickshire CV12 8QR. Tel: 01247 6848800 (fax: 01247 6643018), www.toye.com. Manufacturers of miniature medals, medal ribbons, badges, etc.

Treasure Bunker Militaria Shop

21 King Street, The Trongate, Glasgow G1 5QZ. Tel/fax: 0141 552 4651, email: info@treasure bunker.com, www.treasurebunker.com Medals, badges, uniforms etc. From Waterloo to World War II.

Matthew Tredwen

PO Box 318, Bromley, BR1 2UX. Tel: 07939 252 206, Email: enquiries@militaryantiques.co.uk, www.militaryantiques.co.uk. British campaign and gallantry medals.

Ulric of England

PO Box 55, Chruch Stretton, Shropshire, SY6 6WR. Tel: 01694 781354 (fax: 01694 781372), www.britishmilitarymedals.com. All British military medals, particularly Waterloo medals.

Eugene G. Ursual

PO Box 788, Kemptville, Ontario, Canada, KOG 1JO. Tel: (613) 258 5999 (fax: 613 258 9118), e-mail: egu@magma.ca, www.medalsofwar.com. Medals, orders, decorations, miniatures and militaria. 10 lists a year $17 (Canada), $20 (USA), $25 (overseas).

Vernon

Box 1560MN, Wildomar, California, USA 92595. Canadian-related material.

Victorianmedals.com

PO Box 478, Grimsby, DN32 9WR. Tel: 07821 702299, email: duncan@victorianmedals.com. www.victorianmedals.com. Specialising in 19th century British and Imperial campaign medals.

Fred S. Walland

17 Gyllyngdune Gardens, Seven Kings, Essex IG3 9HH. Tel: 020 8590 4389 (fax: 020 8599 9923). Orders, medals and decorations. Auction/medal lists £7.50 (UK and BFPO only).

Stephen Wheeler

Retail Outlet: 20 Cecil Court, Leicester Square, London WC2N 4HE. London Military Market, Angel Arcade, Camden Passage on Saturdays; Jubilee Antiques Market, Covent Garden, Stand 111, Mondays. Tel: 0208 4642068 or 07778 848555. Specialist in British & Foreign Orders and Decorations.

Worcestershire Medal Service Ltd

56 Broad Street, Sidemoor, Bromsgrove B61 8LL. Tel: 0845 6582001 UK local rate (fax: 01527 576798). Email: wms@worcmedals.com. www.worcmedals.com. Specialists in Medals and medal mounting, storage cases, display cases, miniature medals, blazer badges and replacement medals.

I. S. Wright

208 Sturt Street, Ballarat, 3350 Australia. Tel: 61 3 5333 3476 (fax: 61 3 5331 6426). Email: ausnumis@netconnect.com.au. A range of military collectables from all countries of the world. .

Yeovil Collectors Centre

16 Hendford, Yeovil, Somerset BA20 1TE. Tel: 01935 433739. Medals, badges, militiaria etc. Occasional lists issued.

Carston Zeige

Carsten Zeige, Dammtorstr. 29 D–20354, Hamburg, Germany. Tel:+49 40 3571 3636. Email: info@zeige.com. www.zeige.com. German and Foreign. Catalogue subscription $35, for 5 issues.

BOOKSELLERS/DEALERS

In addition to the names listed below, it should be noted that a number of the medal dealers listed above regularly or occasionally include books on their medal lists.

Ian Allan
4 Watling Drive, Hinckley, Leics LE10 3EY. Tel: 01455 233747 (fax: 01455 233737). Publishers of Military Titles.
Website: www.ianallansuperstore.com.
E-mail: midlandbooks@compuserve.com.

Andrew Burroughs
24 St. Martins, Stamford, Lincolnshire PE9 2LJ. Tel: 01780 51363. Military history. Lists available.

Buffo Books
32, Tadfield Road, Romsey, hants SO51 5AJ. Tel: 01794 517149. Military and aviation only.

Andrew Burroughs
32, St Martins, Stamford, Lincs PE90 2LJ. Tel: 01780 751363. Military and naval, particularly WWII.

Buttercross Books
2 The Paddock, Bingham, Nottingham NG13 8HQ. Tel/fax: 0115 9 837147. Napoleonic era and First World War. Lists available.

Caliver Books
816/818 London Road, Leigh-on-Sea, Essex SS9 3NH. Tel/fax: 01702 73986. Military history up to 1900. Shop and mail order. Lists available.

Chelifer Books
Todd Close, Curthwaite, Wigton, Cumbria CA7 8BE. General military history, including unit histories. Lists available.

The Collector
36 The Colonnade, Piece Hall, Halifax, West Yorks HX1 1RS. Military, naval and aviation history: all periods.

Q. M. Dabney & Company
PO Box 42026-MH, Washington, DC 20015, USA. Military books of all periods. Lists $US1 each.

Peter de Lotz
20 Downside Crescent, Hampstead, London NW3 2AP. Tel: 020 7794 5709 (fax: 020 7284 3058). Military, naval and aviation history, with emphasis on regimental and divisional histories.

Tom Donovan Military Books
52 Willow Road, Hampstead, London NW3 1TP. Tel: 020 7431 2474 (fax: 020 7431 8314). Printed works, documentation and manuscript material relating to the British Military Services. Regular lists.

Francis Edwards
13 Great Newport Street, Charing Cross Road, London WC2H 4JA. Tel: 020 7379 7669 (fax: 020 7836 5977). All aspects of military history. Lists available.

Empire Books
61 Broad Lane, Rochdale, Lancs OL16 4PL. Tel: 01706 666678. Military, naval and aviaton. Special interest Australian forces, Vietnam and Colonial wars.

Chris Evans Books
Unit 6, Jervoise Drive, Birmingham B31 2XU. Tel/fax: 0121 477 6700. General military history. Lists available.

Falconwood Transport and Military Bookshop.
5 Falconwood Parade, The Green, Welling, Kent DA16 2PL. Tel: 020 8303 8291. Military, naval and aviation history.

Kenneth Fergusson
The Book Room, The Post Office, Twyning, Tewkesbury, Glos GL20 6DF. Tel: 01684 295855. Military and aviation history.

Ken Ford Military Books
93 Nutshalling Avenue, Rownhams, Southampton SO1 8AY. Tel: 023 8073 9437. British Colonial Wars.

John Gaunt
21 Harvey Road, Bedford MK41 9LF. Tel: 01234 217686. Numismatic books including medal reference works.

GM Services
98 Junction Road, Andover, Hampshire SP10 3JA. Tel/fax: 01264 362048. Postal auctions of military books.

Tony Gilbert Antique Books
101 Whipps Cross Road, Leytonstone, London E11 1NW. Tel: 020 8530 7472. Military, naval and aviation history.

Martin Gladman
235 Nether Street, Finchley, London N3 1NT. Tel: 020 8343 3023. Military, naval and aviation history.

G. L. Green.
18 Aldenham Avenue, Radlett, Herts WD7 8HX. Tel: 01923 857077. Naval and maritime history.

George Harris
Heathview, Habberley Road, Bewdley, Worcs DY12 1JH. Tel: 01299 402413. Napoleonic, Victorian campaigns and the First World War.

Hersant's Military Books
17 The Drive, High Barnet, Herts EN5 4JG. Tel/fax: 020 8440 6816. General military history. Lists available by period.

Michael Hicks Beach
99 York Mansions, London SW11 4BN. Tel: 020 7622 2270. British and Imperial military history.

Jade Publishing Ltd
5 Leefields Close, Uppermill, Oldham, Lancs OL3 6LA. Tel: 01475 870944. British and imperial military books.

Jerboa-Redcap Books
PO Box 1058, Highstown, N.J. 08520, USA. Tel: (609) 443 3817. British military books (all services), including collectables. Catalogues $US2.

Keegan's Bookshop
Merchant's Place, Reading RG1 1DT. Tel/fax: 01734 587253. Secondhand booksellers with good stock of military titles. Shop in town centre. Parking nearby.

King's Shilling Military History Books
15 Bodiam Avenue, Bexhill-on-Sea, East Sussex TN40 2LS. Tel: 01424 217156 All aspects of military history.

Roger Knowles
26 Church Road, Norton Canes, Cannock, Staffs WS11
3PD. Tel: 01543 279313. Military history

John Lewcock
6 Chewells Lane, Haddenham, Ely, Cambs CB6 3SS.
Tel: 01353 741152. Naval history.

Liverpool Medal Company Ltd
42 Bury Business Centre, Kay Street, Bury, Lancs BL9
6BU. Tel: 0161 763 4610/4612 (fax: 0161 763 4963).
Medal dealers, but publish an occasional separate
book catalogue.

London Pride
14E Fort Lee Road, Bogota, NJ 07603, USA. Tel: 201
525-1828 (fax: 201 525-0815). General military books.

Ian Lynn
258 Upper Fant Road, Maidstone, Kent ME16 8BX.
Tel: 01622 728525. Military history.

Marcet Books
4a Nelson Road, Greenwich, London SE10 9JB. Tel:
020 8853 5408. Naval history.

G. & D. I. Marrin & Sons
149 Sandgate Road, Folkestone, Kent CT20 2DA.
Tel: 01303 253016 (fax: 01303 850956). Specialises in
material relating to the First World War.

McLaren Books
91 West Clyde Street, Helensburgh, Dunbartonshire
G84 8BB. Tel: 01436 676453. Naval history.

Midland Counties Publications
Unit 3, Maizefield, Hinckley, Leicestershire LE10 1YF.
Tel: 01455 233747. Aviation books.

Military Bookman
29 East 93rd Street, New York, NY 10128, USA. Tel:
(212) 348 1280. Large stock of military history relating
to all services worldwide and all periods.

Military Bookworm
PO Box 235, London SE23 1NS. Tel/fax: (020) 8291
1435. Regimental and divisional histories, campaign
histories, biographies, school registers, army lists, etc.
Website: www.militarybookworm.co.uk.

Military History Bookshop
2 Broadway, London N11 3DU. Tel/fax: 020 8368 8568.
Lists, subscription £2.50 (4 issues).

Military Parade Bookshop
The Parade, Marlborough, Wilts SN8 1NE. Tel: 01672
515470 (fax: 01980 630 150). Wide ranging new and
secondhand books. Lists available.

Motor Books
St Martins Court, London WC2N 4AL. Tel: 020 7836
5376 (fax: 020 7497 2539). Comprehensive stock of
military books in print.

Military & Naval History
54 Regis Road, Tettenhall, Wolverhampton WV6
8RW. Tel: 01902 756402. British Military history. Lists
available.

Pen & Sword Books Ltd.
47 Church Street, Barnsley, S. Yorks S70 2AS. Tel:
01226 734555 (fax: 01226 734438), www.pen-and-
sword.co.uk. Military titles.

Savannah Publications
90 Dartmouth Road, Forest Hill, London SE23
3HZ. Tel: 020 8244 4350 (fax: 020 8244 2448). E-mail:

savpub@dircon.co.uk. Publisher and distributor of
works of reference relating to British Army, Navy
and RAF history/medals/biography and service
histories/genealogy. Free catalogues.
Website: www.savannah-publications.com.

Anthony J. Simmonds
23 Nelson Road, Greenwich, London SE10 9JB. Tel:
020 8853 1727. Naval and maritime history. Occasional
catalogues.

Andrew Skinner
42 Earlspark Avenue, Newlands, Glasgow G43
2HW. Tel: 0141 632 4903 (fax: 0141 632 8453). General
military history stock with special emphasis on
Scotland. Monthly lists.

Frank Smith Maritime Aviation Books
98/100 Heaton Road, Newcastle upon Tyne. Tel: 0191
265 6333. Naval, maritime and aviation history.

Spink & Son Ltd (Christie's International)
69 Southampton Row, Bloomsbury, London WC1B
4ET. Tel: 020 7563 4000 (fax: 020 7563 4066). Specialist
Book Department.
E-mail: info@spinkandson.com.
www.spink-online.com.

Tasmedals
8 Orana Place, Taroona, Tas 7053, Australia. Tel: 613
6227 8825 (fax: 613 6227 9898).

THCL Books
185 Lammack Road, Blackburn, Lancs BB1 8LH.
Military book specialist and publishers of collectors'
cards of medal heroes. Lists available.

Stephen Tilston
37 Bennett Park, Blackheath, London SE3 9RA. Tel/
fax: 020 8318 9181. General stock, but specialising in
the First World War. Lists available.

Token Publishing Ltd.
Orchard House, Duchy Road, Heathpark, Honiton,
Devon EX14 1YD. Tel: 01404 46972 (fax: 01404 44788).
E-mail: info@tokenpublishing.com.
Website: www.tokenpublishing.com.
Publishers of *Medal News* and *Coin News* and related
titles.

Ken Trotman Ltd.
Unit 11, 135 Ditton Walk, Cambridge CB5 8QD. Tel:
01223 211030 (fax: 01223 212317). Large, wide-ranging
stock. Lists available: 3 per year.

Brian Turner Military Books
1132 London Road, Leigh-on-Sea, Essex SS9 2AJ. Tel/
fax: 01702 78771. Printed works and documentation
relating to military, naval and aviation history,
specialising in the WWI.

Robin Turner
30 Great Norwood Street, Cheltenham, Glos. GL50
2BH. Tel: 01242 234303. Military, specialising in the
Napoleonic period.

Twin Pillars Books
145 Russell St. Kettering, Northamptonshire
NN16 0EW

Mark Weber
35 Elvaston Place, London SW7 5NW. Tel: 020 7225
2506 (fax: 020 7581 8233). Specialises in official
war histories and books by and about Sir Winston
Churchill.

Ray Westlake Military Books
53 Claremont, Malpas, Newport, South Wales NP9 6PL. Tel: 01633 854135 (fax: 01633 821860). General military books.

Terence Wise
Pantiles, Garth Lane, Knighton, Powys LD7 1HH. Military history especially regimental and divisional histories. Lists available.

Woodford Books
The Lodge, Well Street, Docking, King's Lynn, Norfolk PE31 8LQ. Tel: 01485 518700. Medal and military books, photograph albums, letters, ephemera.

Woolcott Books
Kingston House, Higher Kingston, Nr Dorchester, Dorset DT2 8QE. Tel: 0135 267773 (fax: 01305 848218). Military and colonial history, specialising in India, Africa and 19th century campaigns.

World War Books
Oaklands, Camden Park, Tunbridge Wells, Kent TN2 5AE. Tel: 01892 538465. Military, naval and aviation books and documents, particularly First World War, regimental histories, maps, diaries and photographs. Lists available.

World War II Books
PO Box 55, Woking, Surrey GU22 8HP. Tel: 01483 722880 (fax: 0483 721548). Second World War military history. 12 lists per year.

R.J. Wyatt.
33 Sturges Road, Wokingham, Berks RG11 2HG. Tel: 01734 780325. All aspects of British military history, with an emphasis on the First and Second World Wars, Volunteers, and the Territorial Army.

AUCTIONEERS/DEALERS/BOOKSELLERS

If your details listed above are incorrect, or if we have omitted to include you in this listing please advise us without delay to ensure that our database is up-dated in time for the next edition of the MEDAL YEARBOOK.

Details are included entirely free
Telephone: 01404 46972 or fax: 01404 44788

Those Who Dared

Gallantry awards to the British SAS and attached SBS Units 1941–1946

The special Air Service was born in the Western Desert of North Africa 1941. Soon the Unit grew from a small Detachment to a full Regiment and finally a Brigade. At the end of the War the SAS and SBS were disbanded before their exploits could be recorded and it is only recently that this information has come to light. This volume is the record of Gallantry Awards to the SAS and attached SBS Units 1941–1946 and is the only compilation of such awards of its kind. Essential reading for the medal collector or anyone interested in special forces.

And all for just £12.95 (plus £2.00 p&p)

TO ORDER CALL 01404 44166

TOKEN PUBLISHING LTD, ORCHARD HOUSE, DUCHY ROAD, HEATHPARK, HONITON, EX14 1YD

FAIRS

Many fairs are held regularly and organised by professionals, in addition a number of societies organise fairs for the public (Victorian Military Society, Aldershot Militaria Society, etc.). The dates are usually well advertised in MEDAL NEWS and other publications, however, times and venues are liable to change so it is advisable in every instance to telephone the organisers beforehand. Listed below are the major fair organisers and the events known to us.

Aldershot Militaria and Medal Fair
Princes Hall, Princes Way, Aldershot, Hants. Mark Carter. Tel: 01753 534777.

Bolton Militaria Fair
Horwich Leisure Centre, Victoria Road, Bolton. Northern Arms Fairs. Tel: 01423 780940 or 0113 2716180.

Britannia Medal Fair
Victory Services Club, 63-79 Seymour Street, Marble Arch, London W2. Six p.a. Britannia Enterprises, 12 Endlebury Road, North Chingford, London E4 6QF. Tel: 020 8529 6322. or 020 8590 4389

Bromley Medal and Militaria Fair
Civic Centre, Kentish Way, Bromley, Kent. Ray Brough. Tel: 07714 094009.

Cheshunt Militaria Fair
Wolsey Hall, Windmill Lane, Cheshunt, Herts. Hands Militaria Fairs. Tel/fax: 01892 730233.

Chessington Militaria Fair
Community Sports College, Garrison Lane, Chessington, Surrey. Hands Militaria Fairs. Tel/fax: 01892 730233.

Collectors' Market
London Bridge Main Line Station, London SE1. Every Saturday. Over 60 stands comprising medals, badges and militaria. Fax: 020 8398 8065.

Combined Services Collectors Fair
The Halton Gallery, Royal Airforce Museum, Graham Park Way, Hendon NW9. Contact: Alan McDonald, 5 Windsor Drive, East Barnet, EN4 8UE. Tel/fax: 0208 441 4557 or 07960 033914

Durham Militaria Fair
County Hall, Aykley Heads, Durham City. Northern Arms Fairs. Tel: 01423 780940 or 0113 2716180.

Farnham Militaria Fair
The Maltings, Bridge Square, Farnham, Surrey. Hands Militaria Fairs. Tel/fax: 01892 730233.

Guildford Militaria Fair
Guildford Civic, London Road, Guildford. Hands Militaria Fairs. Tel/fax: 01892 730233.

Ipswich Medal and Militaria Fair
Kesgrave Community Centre, Bell Lane, Kesgrave, Ipswich. Tel: 01449 780236.

Leeds Militaria Fair
Pudsey Civic Hall, Leeds. Northern Arms Fairs. Tel: 01423 780940 or 0113 2716180.

Liverpool Militaria Fair
The Village Hotel, Whiston, Liverpool. Northern Arms Fairs. Tel: 01423 780940 or 0113 2716180.

London Arms Fairs
The Paragon Hotel, Lillie Road, London SW6. 4 shows p.a. Douglas Fryer. Tel: 01273 475 959.

London Military Market—Islington
Angel Arcade, Camden Passage, Islington, London N1. Every Saturday, 8am–2pm. Over 35 stands. Tel: 01628 822503 or 01455 556971.

Macclesfield Militaria & Medal Fair
The Senior Citizens Hall, Duke Street Car Park, off Roe Street, Town Centre. Dave Cooper. Tel: 01538 703354 (eves/weekends) or 01538 702738 (office hours).

Midhurst Militaria Fair
The Grange Leisure Centre, Bepton Road. Hands Militaria Fairs. Tel/fax: 01892 730233.

Newcastle-upon-Tyne Militaria Fair
Park Hotel, Grand Parade, Tynemouth. Northern Arms Fairs. Tel: 01423 780940 or 0113 2716180.

OMRS Annual Convention
New Connaught Rooms, Great Queen Street, London WC2. Contact: OMRS Membership Secretary, PO Box 248, Snettisham, King's Lynn, Norfolk PE31 7TA. OMRS members and pre-registered guests only.

Stockport Arms Fair
The Armoury Hall (TA), Greek Street, Stockport. For details Tel: 0161 485 6908.

Stratford Upon Avon Militaria & Medal Fair
Leisure Centre. Mark Carter. Tel: 01753 534777.

Victorian Military Fair
Victorian Military Society, 20 Priory Road, Newbury, Berks RG14 7QN. Tel: 01635 48628.

Wakefield Militaria and Medal Fair
Outwood Memorial Hall, Outwood, Wakefield, W. Yorks. Tel 01925 727035.

Watford Arms, Militaria and Medal Fair
Bushey Hall School, London Road, Bushey, Herts. Sovereign Fairs. Tel: 01438 811657 or 01923 448903.

West Country Militaria and Medal Fair
Yate Leisure Centre, Kennedy Way, Yate, near Chipping Sodbury, Bristol. Mark Carter. Tel: 01753 534777.

York Coin & Medal Fair
Mezzanine level and First Floor, Knavesmire Stand, York Racecourse, York. Tel: 01793 513431 or 01425 534777.

Military, Aviation & Naval Book Fair, York
Novotel, Fishergate, York. Northern Arms Fairs. Tel: 01763 248400. Organised by the Provincial Booksellers Fairs Association. Held twice yearly.

For free entry into this directory simply email your details to carol@tokenpublishing.com

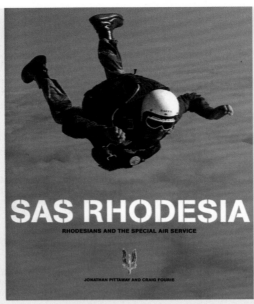

SAS RHODESIA

Museums and Collections

The majority of the museums listed below are the regimental museums of the British Army, Militia, Yeomanry and Territorials, but we have included other museums pertaining to the Royal Navy, the Royal Marines and the Royal Air Force where medals form a significant part of the collections. So, too, the museums of the police forces, fire brigades, Red Cross, Royal National Lifeboat Institution and similar bodies have been included where relevant. Readers should also bear in mind that many general museums in our towns and cities boast fine collections of military medals pertaining to their local regiments. We have included those of which we are aware. The date of foundation is shown in brackets after the name.

Some service museums have been undergoing refits, relocations and amalgamations. We would welcome further information from readers about these changes and about other general museums in their areas with a good coverage of medals to local regiments.

Space prevents us from going into details regarding the scope of individual museum holdings. We give the postal address, telephone number, and the name of the curator wherever possible, also the hours of opening and admission charges (where applicable) at the time of going to press. Where two charges are listed, the first denotes the full adult price and the second the concessionary charge (OAPs, students and children). Where three charges are given the first is the full adult price, the second the OAP concession and the third the children's charge. It is always sensible, particularly before travelling long distances to visit a museum or collection, to telephone and check that the published details are still correct.

Some museums may have libraries holding archival material; this should be checked out and the conditions for use ascertained as such holdings will not have the resources to answer detailed research enquiries.

Where museums are devoted to one particular regimental/service/unit or whatever, they are listed by title in alphabetical order. This may not always accord with the exact official name of the museum which is given on the address line. The well-known national museums are listed alphabetically by name. More general museums which include medal collections are listed by the name of the town. If you cannot see the name of the museum you require at first glance, it may be worth searching through the full list, as some museums escape neat classification and would require extensive cross-referencing to do them full justice.

Aberdeen Maritime Museum (1984)
Provost Ross's House, Shiprow, Aberdeen. 01224 5857888. Monday–Saturday: 10am-5pm. Free.

Airborne Forces Museum (1969)
Browning Barracks, Aldershot, Hants GU11 2BU. 01252 349619. Monday–Friday: 10am-4.30pm (last admission 3.45pm). Saturday, Sunday, Bank Holidays: 10am-4pm. Closed: Christmas and New Year. £3/£1. Tina Pittock and Ann Brown.

Aldershot Military Museum (1984)
Queen's Avenue, Aldershot, Hants GU11 2LG. 01252 314598. Daily, March–October: 10am-5pm, November–February: 10am-4.30pm. Closed: Christmas and New Year. £2/£1. Ian Maine.

Argyll and Sutherland Highlanders Regimental Museum (1945)
Stirling Castle, Stirling FK8 1EH. 01786-475165. Fax: 01786-446038. Daily, Easter–September: 9.30am-5pm, October–Easter: 10am-4.15pm.

Army Chaplaincy Museum
Amport House, the Armed Forces Chaplaincy Centre, Hants. 01980 618083. David Blake.

Army Medical Services Museum
Keogh Barracks, Ash Vale, Aldershot, GU2 5RQ. Civilian number: 01252 868612, Military number: 94229 5212, Fax: 01252 868832, Fax Military number: 94229 5332. Email: museum@keogh72.freeserve.co.uk.

Army Physical Training Corps Museum (1949)
Army School of Physical Training, Queen's Avenue, Aldershot, Hants GU11 2LB. 01252 347131. Fax: 01252 340785. Monday–Thursday: 9am-12.30pm and 2pm-4.30pm. Fri : 9am-12.30pm. Weekends by appointment. Closed: August, and two weeks each at Easter and Christmas. Free. A. A. Forbes and J. Pearson.

Army Transport Museum (1983)
Flemingate, Beverley, Humberside HU17 0NG. 01482 860445. Daily, 10am-5pm. Closed: 24-26 December. £2.50/£1.50. David Dawson.

Arundel Toy and Military Museum (1978)
Dolls House, 23 High Street, Arundel, West Sussex.
01903 507446/882908. Daily, June–August: 10.30am-
5pm. Otherwise open on Bank Holidays and
weekends in winter. £1.25/90p.

Aylmer Military Collection
Nunwell House, Brading, Isle of Wight PO36 0JQ.
01983 407240. July–September: Monday–Wednesday,
1pm-5pm. Otherwise by appointment. £4/£3.50/£1
(children accompanied by adults). J. A. Aylmer.

Ayrshire Yeomanry Museum
Rozelle House, Monument Road, Alloway by Ayr KA7
4NQ. 01292 264091. Monday–Saturday: 10am-5pm.
Sundays: April–October, 2-5pm.

Bangor, Museum
Ffordd Gwynedd, Bangor, Gwynedd, LL57 1DT. 01248
353368. Tuesday–Friday: 12.30pm-4.30pm, Saturday:
10.30am-4.30pm. 50p. Includes medals and militaria of
the Welsh regiments. Pat West.

**Bedfordshire and Hertfordshire Regimental
Museum**
Luton Museum, Wardown Park, Luton, Beds LU2
7HA. Tuesday–Saturday: 10am-5pm. Sunday: 1pm-
5pm.

Black Watch Museum (1924)
Balhousie Castle, Perth PH1 5HR. 0131 310 8530. Fax:
01738 643245. May–September: Monday–Saturday,
10am-4.30pm. October–April: Monday-Friday, 10am-
3.30pm. Free. Major J. W. Proctor, MBE.

100th Bomb Group Memorial Museum (1978)
Common Road, Dickleburgh, near Diss, Norfolk.
0379 740708. Medals and memorabilia of the Eighth
Air Force and 100th Bomb Group. May–September:
Saturday, Sunday and Wednesday, 10am-5pm.
October–April: weekends only, 10am-4.30pm. Free. S.
P. Hurry.

**Border Regiment and King's Own Royal Border
Regiment Museum (1932)**
Queen Mary's Tower, The Castle, Carlisle, Cumbria
CA3 8UR. 01228 532774. Fax: 01228 521275. Email:
RHQ@kingsownborder.demon.co.uk. Open daily.
April–September: 9.30am to 6pm, October: 10am-
5pm, November–March: 10am-5pm. Closed: 24-26
December & 1 January. Admission included in entry
charge to the Castle. £3.50/£1.80/£2.70. Curator:
Stuart Eastwood.

British in India Museum (1972)
Newtown Street, Colne, Lancs BB8 0JJ. 01282 613129/
870215. April–September (inclusive): Monday–Friday
(except Tuesday), 1pm-5pm. Saturday: 11am-5pm.
Sunday: closed. Closed Bank Holiday Mondays 9–23
July, 8–15 September. Prior to April and after the end
of September. Please phone 0976 665320 for opening
times. £3.00/50p.

British Red Cross Museum and Archives (1984) 9
Grosvenor Crescent, London, SW1X 7EJ. 020 7235
5454. Monday–Friday, 9.30am-4.30pm. Free, by
appointment. Nicola Bleasby.

Bygones
Fore Street, St Marychurch, Torquay, Devon TQ1 4PR.
01803 326108. Daily (except Christmas Day). Summer:
10am-10pm. Winter: 10am-4pm.

Caenarfon Air Museum
Caernarfon Airport, Dinas Dinlle, Caernarfon,
Gwynedd LL54 5TP. March–November: 9.30am-
5.30pm. £2.50/£1.50.

**Cambridge, Scott Polar Research Institute Museum
(1920)**
Lensfield Road, Cambridge CB2 1ER. 01223 336540.
Monday–Friday: 2.30pm-4pm. The Library and
archives (the latter by appointment only) are open
9am-1pm and 2pm-5.30pm, Monday–Friday. Free.
Robert Headland.

**Cameronians (Scottish Rifles) Regimental Museum
(1928)**
Mote Hill, off Muir Street, Hamilton, Lanarkshire ML3
6BY. 01698 428688. Monday–Wednesday, Friday–
Saturday: 10am-1pm and 2pm-5pm. Free. Terry
McKenzie.

Castle and Regimental Museum
The Castle, Monmouth, NP25 3BS. 01600 772175.
April–October: 2pm-5pm, daily. November–March:
Saturdays and Sundays, 2pm-4pm. Free.

Cheshire Military Museum (1972)
The Castle, Chester CH1 2DN. 01244 327617. Daily,
10am-5pm. £2/£1. Major Nigel Hine.

City of London Police Museum (1964)
37 Wood Street, London EC2P 2NQ. 020 7601
2705/2455. Fax: 020 7601 2747 Free, by written
appointment only. Roger Appleby.

Coldstream Museum
12 Market Square, Coldstream. TD12 4BD. 01890
882630. Open April to end September: Monday–
Saturday, 10am-4pm and Sunday 2-4pm. October:
Monday–Saturday 1-4pm.

Devonshire Regiment Museum
Wyvern Barracks, Barrack Road, Exeter, Devon EX2
6AE. Monday–Friday: 10am-4.30pm. Closed: Bank
Holidays. Lieutenant Colonel D.R. Roberts.

Devon & Dorsets Museum (1927)
The Keep, Bridport Road, Dorchester, Dorset DT1
1RN. 01305 264066. Tuesday–Saturday: October-
March. Monday-Saturday: April-September. 9.30am-
5pm. Sundays: July–August and Bank Holidays,
10am-4pm. £3.00/£2.00. Lt Col (Retd) R.A. Leonard.

Dingwall Museum (1975)
Town Hall, High Street, Dingwall, Rossshire IV15
9RY. 01349 865366. May–September: Monday–
Saturday, 10am-4:30pm. Otherwise by appointment
only. Includes medals and militaria of the Seaforth
Highlanders, and items pertaining to Major General
Sir Hector Macdonald ("Fighting Mac") Ian Macleod.

**Duke of Cornwall's Light Infantry Regimental
Museum (1925)**
The Keep, Bodmin, Cornwall PL31 1EG. 01208 72810.
Monday–Friday, 9am-5pm. £2.50/50p. Major T. W.
Stipling.

Duke of Wellington's Regiment Museum (1960)
Bankfield Museum, Boothtown Road, Halifax HX3
6HQ. 01422 352334/354823. Tuesday–Saturday: 10am-
5pm. Sunday: 2.30pm-5pm. Free. John Spencer.

Durham Light Infantry Museum (1969)
Aykley Heads, Durham DH1 5TU. 0191 384 2214.
Open every day except Christmas Day. Summer:
10am-5pm. Winter: 10am-4pm. £2.50/£1.25. Stephen
D. Shannon.

Essex Regiment Museum (1938)
Oaklands Park, Moulsham Street, Chelmsford, Essex
CM2 9AQ. 01245-615100. Fax: 01245-262428. Email:
pompadour@chelmsfordbc.gov.uk. Monday–Saturday:
10am-5pm. Sunday: 2pm-5pm (winter, 1pm-4pm).
Free. Ian Hook BA.

Firepower! Museum of the Royal Artillery.
Firepower, Royal Artillery Museums Ltd, Old
Laboratory Office, Royal Arsenal (West), Woolwich,
London SE18 6ST. 020 8855 7755. Daily (except
Christmas Day). £6.50/£5.50/£4.50. Library and
Archive available via appointment with Librarian on
0208-312-7125, various charges apply.

Fleet Air Arm Museum (1964)
RNAS Yeovilton, Somerset BA22 8HT. 01935 840565.
Daily, 10am–5.30pm (summer), and 10am-4.30pm
(winter). Open all year except 24, 25 & 26 December.
£8.50/£5.75/£6.75. Graham Mottram.

Fusiliers Museum of Northumberland
The Abbot's Tower, Alnwick Castle, Alnwick, NE66
1NG. 01665 602152. Easter–October: 11am-5pm, daily.
Malcolm Sunter.

Glasgow Art Gallery and Museum (1854)
Kelvingrove, Glasgow G3 8AG. 0141 287 2699.
Includes medals of the Glasgow Yeomanry, Highland
Light Infantry and regiments associated with the city.
Closed from 29th June 2003 to February 2006.

Gordon Highlanders' Regimental Museum (1961)
St Lukes, Viewfield Road, Aberdeen AB15
7XH. 01224 311200. Fax: 01224 319323. Email:
museum@gordonhighlanders.com. Website: www.
gordonhighlanders.com. April–October: Tuesday–
Saturday, 10.30am-4.30pm (closed Mondays).
November–March: by appointment only. Sarah
Malone.

Green Howards Regimental Museum
Trinity Church Square, Richmond, Yorkshire DL10
4QN. 01748 822133. Fax 01748 826561. Contact
museum for opening times. Admission charges apply.

Guards Museum (1988)
Wellington Barracks, London SW1E 6HQ. 0171
414 3271. Daily (except Friday): 10am-4pm. £2/£1.
Captain David Horn.

Gurkha Museum (1974)
Peninsular Barracks, Romsey Road, Winchester, Hants
SO23 8TS. 01962 842832. Tuesday–Saturday: 10am-
5pm. £1.50/75p. Major G Davies.

Hawkinge, Kent, Battle of Britain Museum (1969)
Hawkinge, Kent CT18 7AG. 0130 389 3140. Easter–end
of May: 11am-4pm. July–September: 10am-5pm.
£2.50/£2 £1.50. Mike Llewellyn.

Hertford Regiment Museum
At the Hertford Museum at 8 Bull Plain, Hertford
SG14 1DJ. 01992 582686. Fax: 01992 534797.

Hitchin Museum
Paynes Park, Hitchin, Herts SG5 1EH. 01462 434476.
Monday–Saturday: 10am-5pm. Closed: Wednesdays,
Sundays and Bank holidays. Free.

Honourable Artillery Company Museum
Armoury House, City Road, London EC1 2BQ.
Apply in writing for a visit.

Hornsea Folk Museum (1978)
Burn's Farm, 11 Newbegin, Hornsea, East Yorkshire
HU18 1BP. 01964 533443. Easter weekend, 1 May–30
September: Monday–Saturday, 11am-5pm and Sunday
2pm-5pm. £1.50/£1. E. Yorkshire Regt, E. Riding Yeo.,
Royal Artillery, The Home Front. Dr J. E. S. Walker.

Imperial War Museum (1917)
Lambeth Road, London SE1 6HZ. 020 7416 5320. Daily,
10am-6pm. Free.

Imperial War Museum (1976)
Duxford, Cambridge CB2 4QR. 01223 835000. Daily,
March–October: 10am-6pm and October–March:
10am-4pm. £8.50/£6.50. Children under 16 free.

Inns of Court and City Yeomanry Museum (1947)
10 Stone Buildings, Lincoln's Inn, London WC2A 3TG.
0171 405 8112. Monday–Friday, 10am-4pm. Free. Major
R. J. B. Gentry.

Intelligence Corps Museum
Defence Intelligence and Security Centre, Chicksands,
Nr Shefford, Beds SG17 5PR. 01462 752297. Monday–
Friday: 10am-3.30pm. Appointment necessary. Free.
Major A. J. Edwards.

Kent and Sharpshooters Yeomanry Museum
Hever Castle, Tonbridge, Kent TN8 7NG. 1 March–30
November: 12pm-5pm, daily. Winter (GMT): 11am-
4pm. Boris Mollo.

**King's Own Royal Regiment (Lancaster) Museum
(1929)**
City Museum, Market Square, Lancaster LA1
1HT. 01524 64637. Fax: 01524 841692. Email:
kingsownmuseum@iname.com. Monday–Saturday,
10am-5pm. Free. Curator: Peter Donnelly BA AMA.

**King's Own Scottish Borderers Regimental Museum
(1954)**
Berwick Barracks, The Parade, Berwick-upon-Tweed
TD15 1DG. 01289 307426. Fax: 01289 331928. Monday–
Saturday: 9.30am-4.30pm (winter). Closed: Easter,
Christmas, New Year and certain other holidays. £3/
£2.30/£1.50. Lieut. Colonel C. G. O. Hogg DL.

**King's Own Yorkshire Light Infantry Regimental
Museum (1932)**
Museum and Art Gallery, Chequer Road, Doncaster,
South Yorkshire DN1 2AE. 01302 734293. Email:
museum@doncaster.gov.uk
Monday–Saturday: 10am-5pm. Sunday: 2pm-5pm.
Free. Major C. M. J. Deedes.

King's Regiment Museum (1930)
City Soldiers, Museum of Liverpool Life, Mann Island, Liverpool L3 4AA. 0151 478 4080. Daily, 10am-5pm. £3/£1.50. Simon Jones.

15th/19th King's Royal Hussars (Light Dragoons)/ Northumberland Hussars
Tyne & Wear Museums, Discovery Museum, Blandford Square, Newcastle-upon-Tyne NE1 4JA. 0191 232 6789. Monday–Saturday: 10am-5pm. Sunday: 2pm-5pm. Ralph Thompson.

King's Royal Hussars Museum in Winchester (1980)
Home Headquarters (South): Peninsula Barracks, Romsey Road, Winchester. 01962 828541. Tuesday–Friday: 10am-4pm. Weekends and Bank Holidays: 12pm-4pm. Free. Major P. J. C. Beresford, Regimental Secretary.

Lancashire Fusiliers Regimental Museum (1933)
Wellington Barracks, Bury, Lanc BL8 2PL. 0161 764 2208. Monday–Saturday (closed Wednesday): 9.30am-4.30pm. 50p/25p.

Light Infantry Museum (1990)
Peninsular Barracks, Romsey Road, Winchester. 01962 828530. Tuesday–Saturday: 10am-5pm. Sunday: 12pm-4pm. £1.50/75p. Patrick Kirby.

Liverpool Scottish Regimental Museum
Botanic Road, Wavertree, Liverpool. 0151-645-5717. By appointment. Mr D. Reeves, Hon. Curator.

London Fire Brigade Museum (1967)
94A Southwark Bridge Road, London SE1 0EG. 020 7587 2894. Fax: 020 7587 2878. Email: museum@london-fire.gov.uk. Monday–Friday: 9am-4.30pm. £3 per person or for groups over ten people £2. Tour by appointment only. Esther Mann.

London Scottish Regimental Museum (1935)
Regimental Headquarters, 95 Horseferry Road, London SW1P 2DX. 0171 630 1639. Free, by appointment only.

Manchesters Museum (1987)
Town Hall, Ashton–under–Lyne, Lancs. 0161 342 3078 or 0161 343 1978. Monday–Saturday: 10am-4pm. Free. Dr Alan Wilson.

Metropolitan Police Historical Museum (1949)
c/o Territorial Policing Headquarters, Finance and Resources, 4th Floor, Victoria Embankment, London SW1 2JL. 0208-305-1676 or 0208-305-2824. Fax: 0208-293-6692. By appointment only. Ray Seal M.A.

Military Miniatures Museum (1978)
13 Cheveling Road, Old Heath, Colchester, Essex CO2 8DL. 01206 794473. Daily, 9am-5pm. Free, by appointment only. Anthony Debski.

Monmouth, The Castle and Regimental Museum (1989)
The Castle, Monmouth, Gwent NP5 3BS. 01600 772175/712935. Summer: daily, 2pm-5pm. Winter: weekends, 2pm-5pm. Other times by appointment. Free. Dr Eric Old.

The Muckleburgh Collection
Weybourne, Norfolk. 01263 588210. Daily (February–November): 10am-5pm. £5.50/£3/£4.50. Christine Swettenham.

Museum of Army Chaplaincy (1949)
Amport House, Amport, Andover, Hants. SP11 8BG. 01264 773144 or 01264 773401. Monday–Friday (by appointment only): 9am-5pm. Free. Curator: David Blake.

Museum of Lancashire
Stanley Street, Preston, Lancs PR1 4YP. 01772 534075. Houses the collections of the 14th/20th King's Hussars; Duke of Lancaster's own yeomanry; and a selection of Queen's Lancashire Regiment. 10.30am-5pm daily (except Thursday, Sunday and Bank Holidays). £2. Entrance for children is free. Stephen Bull.

National Army Museum (1960)
Royal Hospital Road, Chelsea, London SW3 4HT. 020 7730 0717. Fax: 020 7823 6573. E-mail: www. info@national-army-museum.ac.uk. (Closed: 1 January, Good Friday, Early May Bank Holiday and 24–26 December). Daily, 10am-5.30pm. Free. Ian G. Robertson.

National Maritime Museum (1934)
Romney Road, Greenwich, London SE10 9NF. 020 8858 4422. Fax: 020 8312 6632. Summer: Monday–Saturday, 10am-6pm and Sunday, 12pm-5pm. Winter: Monday–Saturday, 10am-5pm and Sunday, 2pm-5pm. Free. Director: Roy Clare.

National Museum of Ireland (1877)
Kildare Street, Dublin 2, Republic of Ireland. 01 618811. Tuesday–Saturday: 10am-5pm. Sunday: 2pm-5pm. Includes medals of the former Irish regiments. Free.

National War Museum of Scotland
The Castle, Edinburgh. 0131 247 4408 ext 2201. Email: e.philip@nms.ac.uk (enquiries). April–November: 9.45am-5.30pm. December–March: 9.45am-4.30pm. Free (but entrance fee to the castle). Edith Philip.

Newark Air Museum (1968)
Winthrop Airfield, Newark-on-Trent NG24 2NY. 01636 707170. Open daily except Christmas Eve/Day & Boxing Day. April–September: weekdays, 10am-5pm/ weekends and Bank Holidays, 10am-6pm. October–March: 10am-5pm, daily . November–February: 10am-4pm, daily . £4.00/£2.50. Mike Smith.

Northamptonshire Regimental Museum
Abington Park Museum, Abington, Northampton NN1 5LW. 01604 838110. Tuesday–Sunday and Bank Holiday Mondays: 1pm-5pm (November–February: 1pm-4pm). Free. Mrs J.A. Minchinton.

Order of St. John of Jerusalem Museum
St. John's Gate, St. John's Lane, Clerkenwell, London EC1M 4DA. 0171 253 6644. Tuesday–Friday: 10am-5pm. Saturday: 10am-4pm. Pamela Willis.

Oxfordshire & Buckinghamshire Light Infantry
TA Centre, Slade Park, Headington. Oxford OX3 7JL. 01865 716060. Monday–Friday: 10am-4pm. Free.

Polish Institute and Sikorski Museum
20 Princes Gate, London SW7 1QA. 0171 589 9249.
Monday–Friday: 2pm-4pm.

Prince of Wales's Own 9th /12th Lancers Regimental Museum (1972)
City Museum and Art Gallery, The Strand, Derby DE1
1BS. 01332 716659. Monday: 11am–5pm. Tuesday–
Saturday: 10am-5pm. Sunday and Bank Holidays:
2pm-5pm. Free. Angela Tarnowski.

Prince of Wales's Own Regiment of Yorkshire Museum
3A Tower Street York YO1 9SB. 01904 662790.
Monday–Saturday and Bank Holidays: 9.30am-
4.30pm. Closed between Christmas and New Year's
Day. Includes medals of The West Yorkshire and The
East Yorkshire Regiments, and The Prince of Wales's
Own Regiment of Yorkshire. £2/£1. Lieutenant
Colonel T. C. E. Vines.

Princess of Wales's Royal Regiment and Queen's Regiment Museum (1987)
5 Keep Yard, Dover Castle, Kent CT16 1HU. 01304
240121. E-mail: www.pwrrqueensmuseum@tinyworld.
co.uk. Summer: 10am-6pm, daily. Winter: 10am-4pm.
Major J. C. Rogerson.

Queen's Dragoon Guards Regimental Museum
Cardiff Castle, Cardiff, South Glamorgan CF1 2RB.
01222 222253. March, April and October: 10am-5pm,
daily. May–September: 10am- 6pm. November–
February: 10am-4.30pm. £3/£2/£1.50. Gareth Gill.

Queen's Lancashire Regiment (1929) Incorporating
East Lancashire Regiment, South Lancashire Regiment
(Prince of Wales's Volunteers), Loyal Regiment (North
Lancashire) Lancashire Regiment.
Fulwood Barracks, Preston, Lancs PR2 8AA. 01772 260
362. Tuesdays–Thursdays or by appointment. 9.30am-
4.30pm. Free. Lt Col M. J. Glover MA, AMA.

The Queen's Own Highlanders Collection
Fort George, Ardersier, Inverness, IV2 7TD. 01463
224380. Monday–Friday: April–September, 10am-
6pm/October–March, 10am-4pm. Free.

Queen's Own Royal West Kent Regimental Museum (1961)
St Faith's Street, Maidstone, Kent ME14 1LH. 01622
602842. Monday–Saturday: 10am-5.15pm. Sunday:
11am-4pm. Free. Colonel H.B.H. Waring, OBE.

Queen's Royal Lancers
Belvoir Castle, nr Grantham, Lincs, NG31 6BR.
March–September: daily, 11am-5pm (except Mondays
and Fridays). £5/£4/£3, family ticket £14. Captain
(Retd) J. M. Holtby.

Queen's Royal Surrey Regimental Museum (1979)
Clandon Park, Guildford, Surrey GU4 7RQ. 01483
223419. April–October. Closed: Monday, Friday,
Saturday. 12-5pm.

Royal Air Force Museum (1963)
Grahame Park Way, Hendon, London NW9 5LL.
020 8205 2266. Fax: 020 8200 1751. Email: andrew.
cormack@rafmuseum.org. Daily, 10am-6pm. Free. Dr
M. A. Fopp. Medal queries: A. Cormack FSA.

Royal Air Force Regiment Museum (1965)
Royal Air Force Regiment Depot, Royal Air Force
Honington, Bury St Edmunds, Suffolk IP31 1EE. 01359
269561. Initially by appointment. Ask for Museum
Director/staff.

Royal Armoured Corps Museum (1939), The Tank Museum (1923)
Bovington, Wareham, Dorset BH20 6JG. 01929 405096
(Library). Email: commerciala@tankmuseum.co.uk.
Website: www.tankmuseum.co.uk. Daily, 10am-5pm.
Closed: Christmas. Charges apply: please phone for
details. Colonel (Retd) John Woodward.

Royal Armouries Museum (1996)
Armouries Drive, Leeds LS10 1LT. 0113-220-1999.
Daily (except Christmas Day). 10am-5pm. Free.

Royal Devon Yeomanry (1845)
Museum of North Devon, The Square, Barnstaple,
Devon EX32 8LN. 01271 346747. Tuesday–Saturday:
10am-4.30pm. Alison Mills.

Royal East Kent Regiment, Third Foot (The Buffs) Museum (1961)
Royal Museum and Art Gallery, High Street,
Canterbury, Kent CT1 2RA. 01277 452747. Monday–
Saturday: 10am-5pm. Closed: Good Friday and
Christmas week. Free. Enquiries to National Army
Museum which now owns the collection on 0207 730
0717.

Royal Electrical and Mechanical Engineers Museum of Technology. (1958)
Isaac Newton Road, Arborfield, Berkshire, RG2 9NJ.
0118 976 3375. See website for changes and opening
details: www.rememuseum.org.uk. Monday–
Friday: 9am-12.30pm and 2pm-4pm. Weekends by
appointment. Closed: Bank Holidays. Free. Lt Col.
I.W.J. Cleasby, M.B.E..

Royal Engineers Museum
Prince Arthur Road,Gillingham, Kent, ME4 4UG.
01634 406397. All year: Tuesday–Friday, 10am-5pm,
(closed Monday) . Saturday, Sunday and Bank
Holidays 11.30am-5pm. £5/£2.50 for concessions.
Angela McLennan.

Royal Fusiliers Museum (1962)
HM Tower of London, EC3N 4AB. 0171 488 5612.
Daily, 9.30am-4.30pm. 25p. Maj. B. C. Bowes-Crick.

Royal Gloucester, Berkshire, Wiltshire (Salisbury) Museum (1982)
The Wardrobe, 58 The Close, Salisbury, Wilts SP1 2EX.
01722 414 536. Royal Berkshire, Wiltshire and Duke
of Edinburgh's Royal Regiments. See Gloucestershire
Regiments Museum for Gloucestershire Regiment.
See website for charges and opening details: www.
thewardrobe.org.uk David Chilton.

Royal Green Jackets Museum
Peninsula Barracks, Romsey Road, Winchester. 01962
828549. Monday–Saturday: 10am-5pm. Sunday: 12pm-
4pm. £2/£1.

Royal Hampshire Regimental Museum (1933)
Serle's House, Southgate Street, Winchester, Hants
SO23 9EG. 01962 863658. All year: Monday–Friday
11am-3.30pm. Weekends/Bank holidays: April–
October only, 12pm-4pm. Free. Lt–Col. H. D. H.
Keatinge.

Royal Highland Fusiliers Regimental Museum (1960)
518 Sauchiehall Street, Glasgow G2 3LW. 0141 332
0961. Monday–Thursday: 9am-4.30pm. Friday: 9am-
4pm. Free. W. Shaw, MBE.

Royal Hospital Chelsea
Royal Hospital Road, Chelsea, London SW3 4SR. 020
7881 5203. Email: curator@chelsea-pensioners.org.
uk. Monday–Saturday: 10am-12pm and 2pm-4pm.
Sundays (April–September only): 2pm-4pm. Closed
on Public Holidays. Further details on website: www.
chelsea-pensioners.org.uk. Free.

**13th/18th Royal Hussars (Queen Mary's Own)
Regiment (1957) and The Light Dragoons**
Cannon Hall Museum, Cawthorne, Barnsley, South
Yorkshire S75 4AT. 01226 790270. April–October:
Wednesday–Friday, 10:30am-5pm. Saturday and
Sunday: 12-5pm (Last admission at 4:15pm).
November, December and March: Sunday only, 12pm-
4pm. January and February: Closed. Free.

**Royal Inniskilling Fusiliers Regimental Musuem
(1938)**
The Castle, Enniskillen, Co. Fermanagh, N. Ireland
BT74 7HL. 028 6632 3142. Website: www.inniskilling.
com. Monday: 2pm-3pm. Tuesday–Friday: 10am-
5pm. Saturday: 2pm-5pm (May–September). Sunday:
2pm–5pm (July & August). Open Bank Holidays
except Christmas, Boxing & New Year's Day. £2 /£1 .
Maj. Jack Dunlop.

Royal Irish Fusiliers
Sovereign's House, The Mall, Armagh BT61 9DL. 028
37 522911. Website: www.rirfus-museum.freeserve.
co.uk. Weekdays and Bank Holidays: 10am-12.30pm
and 1.30pm-4.00pm. Ms Amanda Moreno.

Royal Irish Regiment Museum (1993)
Regimental Headquarters, Royal Irish Regiment, St
Patrick's Barracks, Ballymena, BFPO 808, Northern
Ireland. 028 25661 383. Email: hqrirish@royalirishreg
iment.co.uk. Website: www.royalirishregiment.co.uk.
Wednesday and Saturday: 2pm-5pm. Other days by
arrangement. £2/£1. Capt Mark Hegan.

Royal Leicestershire Regiment Museum (1969)
New Walk Museum, New Walk, Leicester, LE1 7EA.
April–September: Monday–Saturday, 10am-5pm and
Sunday, 1pm-5pm. October–March: close at 4pm. Free.

Royal Lincolnshire Regimental Museum (1985)
Burton Road, Lincoln LN1 3LY. 01522 528448.
May–September: daily, 10am-5.30pm. October–April:
Monday–Saturday, 10am-5.30pm. Sunday, 2pm-
5.30pm. £2/£1.20. Family ticket £5.20.

Royal Logistic Corps Museum (1995)
Princess Royal Barracks, Deepcut, near Camberley
Surrey GU16 6RW. 01252 340871. Tuesday–Friday:
9am-4pm. Saturday: 10am-3pm (Easter–end
September only). Closed: Sundays and Public
Holidays. Free. Major D.F. Hazel.

Royal Marines Museum (1956)
Southsea, Hants PO4 9PX. 02392 819385. Whitsun–
September: 9.30am-5pm. Winter: 9.30am-4.30pm.
£2.50/£1.50/ £1.25. Col. K. N. Wilkins, OBE.

Royal Military Police Museum (1979)
Rousillon Barracks, Broyle Road, Chichester, West
Sussex PO19 4BN. 01243 534225. April–September:
Tuesday–Friday, 10.30am-12.30pm and 1.30pm-
4.30pm. Weekends, 2pm-6pm. October–March:
Tuesday–Friday, 10.30am-12.30pm and 1.30pm-
4.30pm. Closed: January. Free. Lt-Col. Maurice Squier.

**Royal National Lifeboat Institution
Museum (1937)**
Grand Parade, Eastbourne, East Sussex BN21 4BY.
01323 730717. April–December: 9.30am-5pm, daily.
January–March: Monday–Friday, 9.30am-5pm. Free. J.
M. Shearer.

Royal National Lifeboat Institution Museum (1969)
Pen-y-Cae, Barmouth, Gwynedd. Free. Easter–
October: 10.30am-6.30pm, daily.

Royal Naval Museum (1911)
HM Naval Base, Portsmouth PO1 3NH. 02392 727562.
Daily, 10am-4.30pm. Closed: Christmas day and
Boxing day. £4.50. Dr H.C McMurray OBE.

Royal Navy Submarine Museum
Haslar Jetty Road, Gosport, Hampshire, PO12 2AS.
Mr Bob Mealings. 02392 510354 Ext. 227. Fax: 02392
511349. Email: curator@rnsubmus.co.uk 10am-5.30pm,
(April–October), 10.00am-4.30pm (November–March).
£4/£2.75. Family entry £11.

Royal Norfolk Regimental Museum (1945)
Shirehall, Market Avenue, Norwich NR1 3JQ. 01603
223649. Monday–Saturday: 10am-5pm. Sunday: 2pm-
5pm. 80p/40p. Kate Thaxton.

Royal Observer Corps' Museum
Newhaven Fort, Newhaven, East Sussex. 01273
517622.

**The Royal Regiment of Fusiliers Museum (Royal
Warwickshire)**
St John's House, Warwick CV34 4NF. 01926 491653.
Email: areasecretary@rrfmuseumwarwick.demon.
co.uk. Website: www.warwickfusiliers.co.uk. 10am-
5pm: Tuesday–Saturday and Bank Holidays. 2.30pm-
5pm: Sunday (May–September). Free. Maj. R.G. Mills.

Royal Scots Regimental Museum (1951)
The Castle, Edinburgh EH1 2YT. 0131 310 5016.
April–September: Monday–Sunday, 9am-5.30pm.
October–March: Monday–Friday, 9.30am-4pm. Free.
Lieutenant Colonel R. P. Mason.

Royal Signals Museum
Blandford Camp, Blandford, Dorset DT11 8RH. 01258
482248. E-mail: www.info@royalsignalsmuseum.com.
Monday–Friday: 10am-5pm. Weekend: (February–
November only) 10am-4pm. Family ticket £12. Colonel
C. J. Walters.

Royal Sussex Regimental Museum (1930) also the 4th Queen's Own Hussars; 8th King's Royal Irish Hussars; Queen's Royal Irish Hussars Museums
Redoubt Fortress, Royal Parade, Eastbourne, East Sussex BN21 4BP. 01323 410300. April–October. Other times by appointment. £1.50/£1. B. R. Burns.

Royal Ulster Constabulary Museum (1983)
Brooklyn, Knock Road, Belfast BT5 6LE. (028) 90 650222 Ext 22499. Monday–Friday: 9am-5pm. Free. Hugh Forrester.

Royal Ulster Rifles Museum (1935)
5 Waring Street, Belfast BT1 2EW. 028 9023 2086. Website: www.rurmuseum.tripod.com. Monday–Friday: 10am-12.30pm and 2pm-4pm. (Friday 3pm). £1. Major R. J. Walker.

Royal Welch Fusiliers Museum (1955)
Caernarfon Castle, Gwynedd LL55 2AY. 01286 673362. Fax: 01286 677042. Open daily (except 1 January and 24–26 December) from 9.30am (11am Sundays in winter). Closes 6pm (summer), 5pm (spring/autumn), 4 pm (winter). Peter Crocker.

St Helier, Elizabeth Castle and Militia Museum
St Helier, Jersey, Channel Islands. 01534 23971. April–October: 10am-5pm, daily. £2/£1.

The Sandhurst Collection, RMAS
The Sandhurst Cadet Through the Years. Old College, Camberley, Surrey GU15 4NP. 01276 412489. Free, by appointment only. Peter Thwaites.

School of Infantry and Small Arms School Corps Weapons Museum (1953)
School of Infantry, Warminster, BA12 0DJ. 01985 842487. Daily, 9am-4.30pm. Free. Lieut-Colonel Tug Wilson, MBE.

Sherwood Foresters Regimental Museum (1923)
The Castle, Nottingham. 0115 946 5415. Daily: 10am-5pm (except Friday, November–February when 1pm-5pm). Closed: Christmas Day and Boxing Day. £1.50/80p.

Shropshire Regimental Museum (1985)
The Castle, Shrewsbury, SY1 2AT. 01743 358516. April–September 30: Tuesday–Saturday, 10am-5pm. Sundays and Mondays, 10am-4pm. Open Tuesday–Saturday, 10am-5pm from October–March. Winter closure: December–January. £3/£1. Peter Duckers.

Soldiers of Gloucestershire Museum
Custom House, Gloucester Docks, Gloucester GL1 2HE. 01452 522682. Medals of the Gloucestershire Regiment Royal Gloucestershire Hussars. Open all year round. Closed Mondays in winter 10am-5pm. Entrance charge.

Somerset Military Museum (1974)
Somerset County Museum, Taunton Castle, Taunton, Somerset TA1 1AA. 01823 320201. Tuesday–Saturday: 10am-5pm. Free. Lieutenant Colonel David Eliot.

South Nottinghamshire Hussars Museum (1974)
TA Centre, Hucknall Lane, Bulwell, Nottingham NG6 8AB. 0115 9272251. Free, by appointment only. Curator Gill Aldridge.

South Wales Borderers and Monmouthshire Regimental Museum (1934)
The Barracks, Brecon, Powys LD3 7EB. 01874 613310. Email: wb@rrw.org.uk. October–March: Monday–Friday, 9am-5pm. April–September: 9am-5pm, daily. £3, under 16s free.

South Wales Police Museum (1950)
Police Headquarters, Cowbridge Road, Bridgend, CF31 3SU. 01656 655555 ext 28057. Monday–Thursday: 9am-5pm. Friday: 9am-4.30pm by appointment. Out of hours visits can usually be accommodated if notice is given. Free. Julia Mason.

Staffordshire Regimental Museum (1962)
Whittington Barracks, Lichfield, Staffs WS14 9PY. 0121 311 3240/3229. All year: Tuesday–Friday, 10am-4pm. April–October: Saturday, Sunday, Bank Holidays, 12.30pm-4.30pm. Closed: Christmas & New Year. Archives and school parties by appointment. £2/£1. Family ticket £5. Major E. Green.

Suffolk Regimental Museum (1967)
The Keep, Gibraltar Barracks, Bury St Edmunds, Suffolk IP33 1HF. 01284 752394. Weekdays: 10am-12pm and 2pm-4pm. Free. Major A. G. B. Cobbold.

Sussex & Surrey Yeomanry Museum (1993)
Newhaven Fort, Newhaven, East Sussex. 01273 611055. April–October, other times by appointment. Hon. curator Keith Fuller.

Tangmere, Military Aviation Museum (1992)
Tangmere, near Chichester, West Sussex PO20 6ES. 01243 775223. February–November: 11am-5.30pm, daily. £3/50p. Andy Saunders.

The Tank Museum (1923), Royal Armoured Corps Museum (1939)
Bovington, Wareham, Dorset BH20 6JG. 01929 405096 (Library). Email: commerciala@tankmuseum.co.uk. Website: www.tankmuseum.co.uk. Daily, 10am-5pm. Closed at Christmas. Charges apply, please phone for details. Colonel (Retd) John Woodward.

Towneley Hall Art Gallery and Museum (1902)
Burnley, Lancs BB11 3RQ. 01282 424213. Monday–Thursday: 10am-5pm. Closed: Friday. Saturday and Sunday, 12pm-5pm. Small collection including two VCs, other unique items seen by appointment. Free. Susan Bourne.

Welch Regiment Museum (1927)
The Black and Barbican Towers, Cardiff Castle, Cardiff, South Glamorgan CF1 2RB. 01222 229367. Daily: 10am-6pm (April–October), 10am-4.30pm (November–March). £2/£1. Lieut. Bryn Owen, RN.

Wellington Museum
Apsley House, 149 Piccadilly, Hyde Park Corner, London W1J 7NT. 0207 499 5676. Tuesday–Sunday: 11am-5pm. Free to under 18s/over 60s; otherwise £4.40/£3. Alicia Robinson.

West Midlands Police Museum (1991)
Sparkhill Police Station, 641 Stratford Road, Birming
ham B11 6EA. Free, by apppointment only.

Woodbridge, 390th Bomb Group Memorial Air Museum (1981)
Parham Airfield, Parham, Woodbridge, Suffolk. 01359
51209. Sundays and Bank Holidays: 11am-6pm. Free.

Worcestershire Regimental Museum (1925)
City Museum and Art Gallery, Foregate Street,
Worcester. WR1 1DT.01905 25371. Monday–Friday:
9.30am-5.30pm. Saturday: 9.30am-5pm. Free. Major
David Reeve. Archives: 01905 354359, by appointment.

York, Divisional Kohima Museum (1991)
Imphal Barracks, Fulford Road, York YO1 4AY. 01904
662381. Free, by appointment only.

York and Lancaster Regimental Museum (1947)
Brian O'Malley Central Library and Art Gallery,
Walker Place, Rotherham, Yorkshire S65 1JH. 01709
382 121 ext 3625. Tuesday–Saturday: 10am-5pm. Free.
Don Scott.

York, Yorkshire Air Museum and Allied Air Forces Memorial (1984)
Halifax Way, Elvington, York YO4 5AU. 01904 605595.
Monday–Friday: 10.30am-4pm. Weekends: 10.30am-
5pm. £2.50/£1.50. Peter Douthwaithe.

Details printed in this directory are correct at time of going to press, however, before setting off on a long journey it is advisable to check with the museum direct as regards current opening hours etc. Curators—if any information is not correct please call 01404 46972.

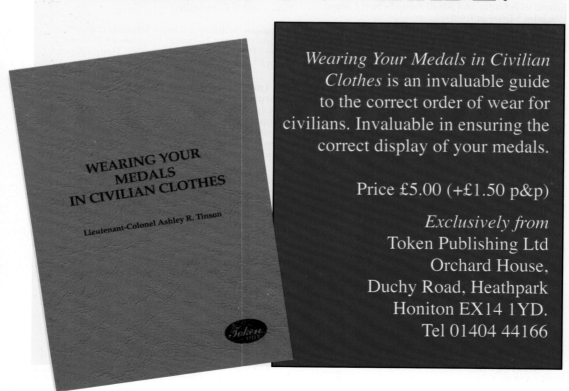

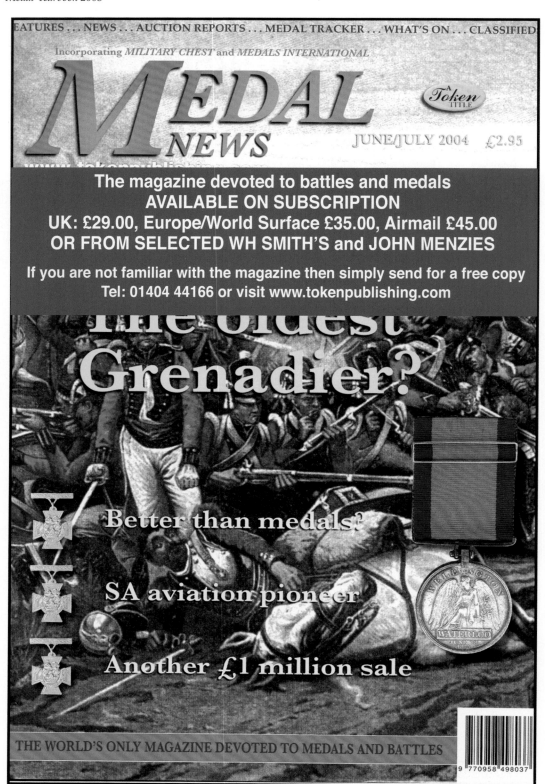

MEDAL RIBBONS

In this section we feature the *majority* of the ribbons for the medals included in the main sections of the book. Where the same ribbon is used for more than one medal, only one is illustrated here.

24. Victoria Cross

24. Victoria Cross, Navy to 1918

25. New Zealand Cross

26. George Cross

27. Distinguished Service Order

28/29. Imperial Service Order/Medal

30. Indian Order of Merit (military)

30. Indian Order of Merit (civil)

30A. Conspicuous Gallantry Cross

31. Royal Red Cross

32. Distinguished Service Cross

33. Military Cross

34. Distinguished Flying Cross pre-1919

34. Distinguished Flying Cross post-1919

35. Air Force Cross pre-1919

35. Air Force Cross post-1919

36. Order of British India (1st Class, ii)

36. Order of British India (2nd Class, ii)

36. Order of British India (1st Class, post-1939)

36. Order of British India (2nd class, post-1939)

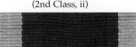

37. Order of Burma

38. Kaiser-i-Hind

39. Albert Medal (original 1st Class, Sea)

39. Albert Medal (1st Class, Sea)

39. Albert Medal (2nd Class, Sea)

39. Albert Medal (original 1st Class, Land)

39. Albert Medal (1st Class, Land)

39. Albert Medal (2nd Class, Land)

40. SA Queen's Medal for Bravery

41/42. Distinguished Conduct Medal

43. DCM (KAR and WAFF)

461

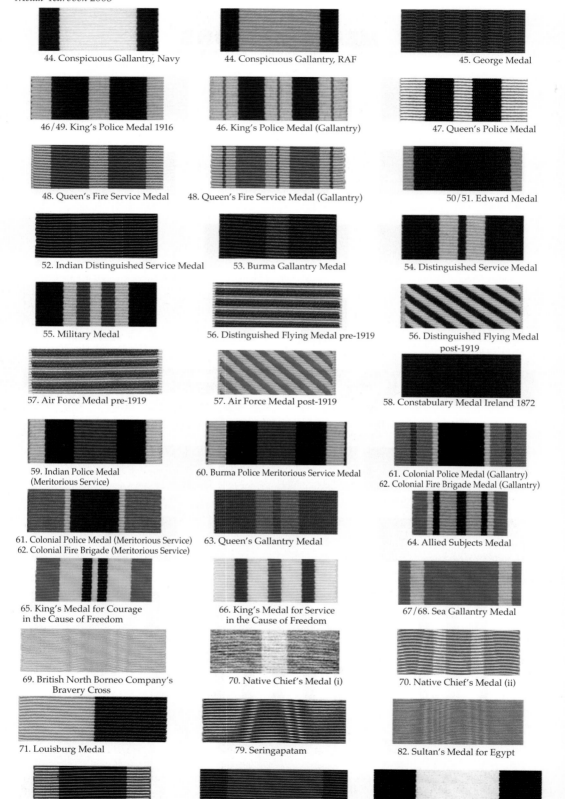

44. Conspicuous Gallantry, Navy

44. Conspicuous Gallantry, RAF

45. George Medal

46/49. King's Police Medal 1916

46. King's Police Medal (Gallantry)

47. Queen's Police Medal

48. Queen's Fire Service Medal

48. Queen's Fire Service Medal (Gallantry)

50/51. Edward Medal

52. Indian Distinguished Service Medal

53. Burma Gallantry Medal

54. Distinguished Service Medal

55. Military Medal

56. Distinguished Flying Medal pre-1919

56. Distinguished Flying Medal post-1919

57. Air Force Medal pre-1919

57. Air Force Medal post-1919

58. Constabulary Medal Ireland 1872

59. Indian Police Medal (Meritorious Service)

60. Burma Police Meritorious Service Medal

61. Colonial Police Medal (Gallantry)
62. Colonial Fire Brigade Medal (Gallantry)

61. Colonial Police Medal (Meritorious Service)
62. Colonial Fire Brigade (Meritorious Service)

63. Queen's Gallantry Medal

64. Allied Subjects Medal

65. King's Medal for Courage in the Cause of Freedom

66. King's Medal for Service in the Cause of Freedom

67/68. Sea Gallantry Medal

69. British North Borneo Company's Bravery Cross

70. Native Chief's Medal (i)

70. Native Chief's Medal (ii)

71. Louisburg Medal

79. Seringapatam

82. Sultan's Medal for Egypt

87. Bagur and Palamos Medal

91. Burma Medal

93. Naval Gold medal

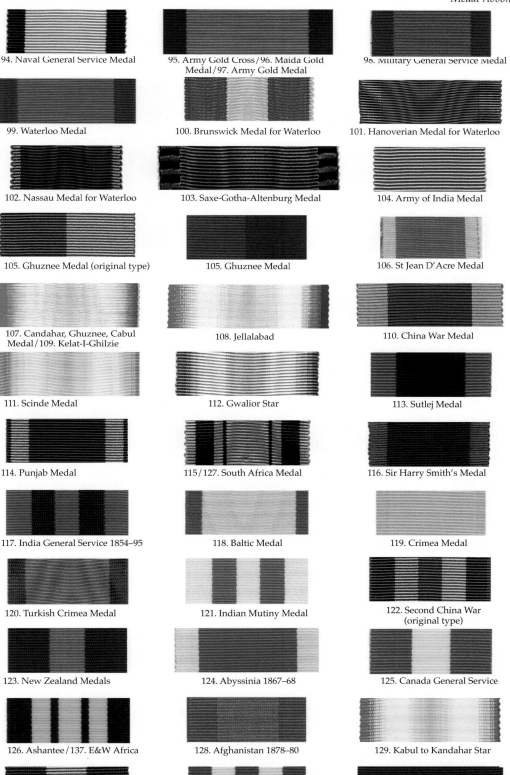

94. Naval General Service Medal

95. Army Gold Cross / 96. Maida Gold Medal / 97. Army Gold Medal

98. Military General Service Medal

99. Waterloo Medal

100. Brunswick Medal for Waterloo

101. Hanoverian Medal for Waterloo

102. Nassau Medal for Waterloo

103. Saxe-Gotha-Altenburg Medal

104. Army of India Medal

105. Ghuznee Medal (original type)

105. Ghuznee Medal

106. St Jean D'Acre Medal

107. Candahar, Ghuznee, Cabul Medal / 109. Kelat-I-Ghilzie

108. Jellalabad

110. China War Medal

111. Scinde Medal

112. Gwalior Star

113. Sutlej Medal

114. Punjab Medal

115/127. South Africa Medal

116. Sir Harry Smith's Medal

117. India General Service 1854–95

118. Baltic Medal

119. Crimea Medal

120. Turkish Crimea Medal

121. Indian Mutiny Medal

122. Second China War (original type)

123. New Zealand Medals

124. Abyssinia 1867–68

125. Canada General Service

126. Ashantee / 137. E&W Africa

128. Afghanistan 1878–80

129. Kabul to Kandahar Star

130. Cape of Good Hope GSM

131. Egypt Medal

132. Khedive's Star
133. Gordon's Khartoum Star

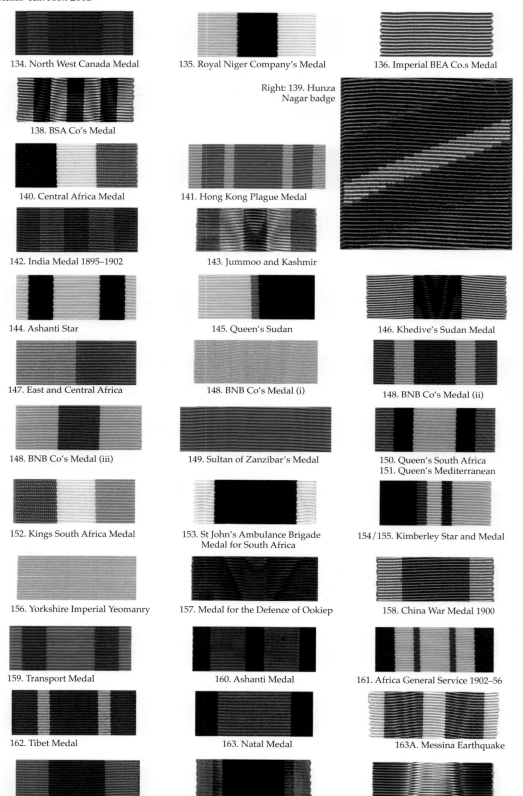

134. North West Canada Medal

135. Royal Niger Company's Medal

136. Imperial BEA Co.s Medal

138. BSA Co's Medal

Right: 139. Hunza Nagar badge

140. Central Africa Medal

141. Hong Kong Plague Medal

142. India Medal 1895–1902

143. Jummoo and Kashmir

144. Ashanti Star

145. Queen's Sudan

146. Khedive's Sudan Medal

147. East and Central Africa

148. BNB Co's Medal (i)

148. BNB Co's Medal (ii)

148. BNB Co's Medal (iii)

149. Sultan of Zanzibar's Medal

150. Queen's South Africa
151. Queen's Mediterranean

152. Kings South Africa Medal

153. St John's Ambulance Brigade Medal for South Africa

154/155. Kimberley Star and Medal

156. Yorkshire Imperial Yeomanry

157. Medal for the Defence of Ookiep

158. China War Medal 1900

159. Transport Medal

160. Ashanti Medal

161. Africa General Service 1902–56

162. Tibet Medal

163. Natal Medal

163A. Messina Earthquake

164. India General Service 1908–35

165. Khedive's Sudan 1910

166/167. 1914/1914–15 Star

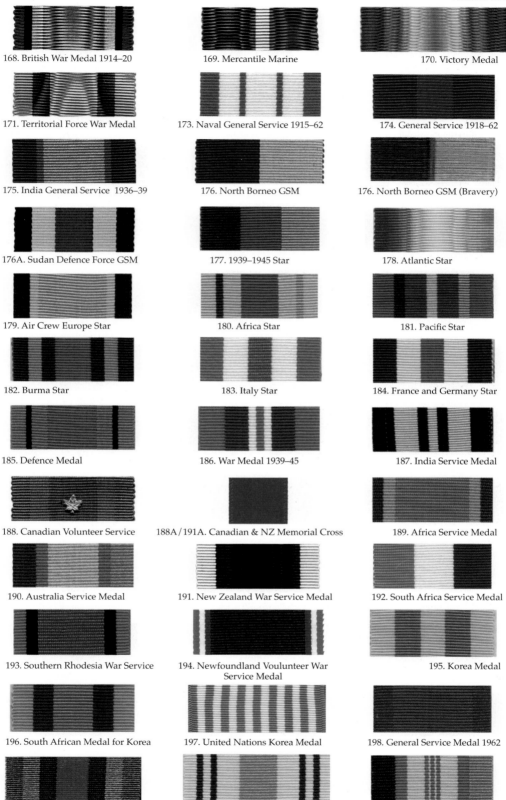

168. British War Medal 1914–20

169. Mercantile Marine

170. Victory Medal

171. Territorial Force War Medal

173. Naval General Service 1915–62

174. General Service 1918–62

175. India General Service 1936–39

176. North Borneo GSM

176. North Borneo GSM (Bravery)

176A. Sudan Defence Force GSM

177. 1939–1945 Star

178. Atlantic Star

179. Air Crew Europe Star

180. Africa Star

181. Pacific Star

182. Burma Star

183. Italy Star

184. France and Germany Star

185. Defence Medal

186. War Medal 1939–45

187. India Service Medal

188. Canadian Volunteer Service

188A/191A. Canadian & NZ Memorial Cross

189. Africa Service Medal

190. Australia Service Medal

191. New Zealand War Service Medal

192. South Africa Service Medal

193. Southern Rhodesia War Service

194. Newfoundland Voulunteer War Service Medal

195. Korea Medal

196. South African Medal for Korea

197. United Nations Korea Medal

198. General Service Medal 1962

198A. Operational Service Medal

199. UN Emergency Force Medal

200. Vietnam Medal

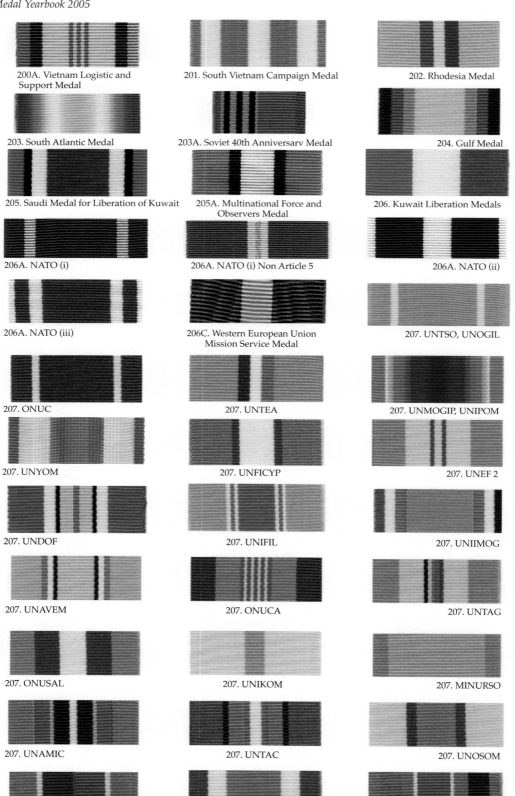

200A. Vietnam Logistic and Support Medal

201. South Vietnam Campaign Medal

202. Rhodesia Medal

203. South Atlantic Medal

203A. Soviet 40th Anniversarv Medal

204. Gulf Medal

205. Saudi Medal for Liberation of Kuwait

205A. Multinational Force and Observers Medal

206. Kuwait Liberation Medals

206A. NATO (i)

206A. NATO (i) Non Article 5

206A. NATO (ii)

206A. NATO (iii)

206C. Western European Union Mission Service Medal

207. UNTSO, UNOGIL

207. ONUC

207. UNTEA

207. UNMOGIP, UNIPOM

207. UNYOM

207. UNFICYP

207. UNEF 2

207. UNDOF

207. UNIFIL

207. UNIIMOG

207. UNAVEM

207. ONUCA

207. UNTAG

207. ONUSAL

207. UNIKOM

207. MINURSO

207. UNAMIC

207. UNTAC

207. UNOSOM

207. UNMIH, UNSMIH

207. UNIMOZ, ONUMOZ

207. UNPROFOR, UNCRO

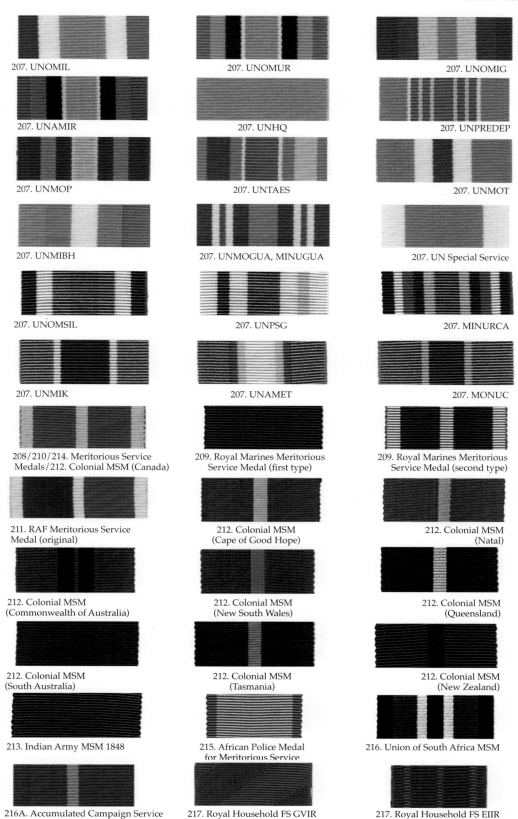

207. UNOMIL

207. UNOMUR

207. UNOMIG

207. UNAMIR

207. UNHQ

207. UNPREDEP

207. UNMOP

207. UNTAES

207. UNMOT

207. UNMIBH

207. UNMOGUA, MINUGUA

207. UN Special Service

207. UNOMSIL

207. UNPSG

207. MINURCA

207. UNMIK

207. UNAMET

207. MONUC

208/210/214. Meritorious Service
Medals/212. Colonial MSM (Canada)

209. Royal Marines Meritorious
Service Medal (first type)

209. Royal Marines Meritorious
Service Medal (second type)

211. RAF Meritorious Service
Medal (original)

212. Colonial MSM
(Cape of Good Hope)

212. Colonial MSM
(Natal)

212. Colonial MSM
(Commonwealth of Australia)

212. Colonial MSM
(New South Wales)

212. Colonial MSM
(Queensland)

212. Colonial MSM
(South Australia)

212. Colonial MSM
(Tasmania)

212. Colonial MSM
(New Zealand)

213. Indian Army MSM 1848

215. African Police Medal
for Meritorious Service

216. Union of South Africa MSM

216A. Accumulated Campaign Service

217. Royal Household FS GVIR

217. Royal Household FS EIIR

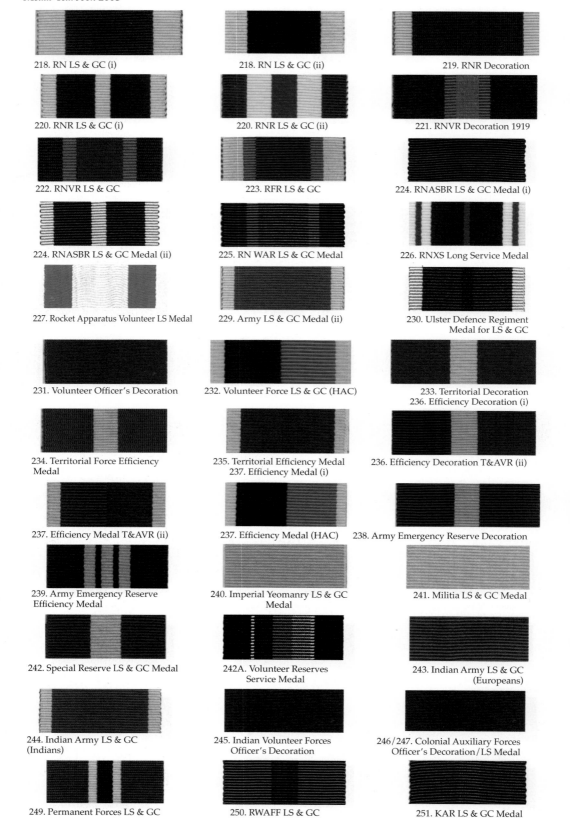

218. RN LS & GC (i)

218. RN LS & GC (ii)

219. RNR Decoration

220. RNR LS & GC (i)

220. RNR LS & GC (ii)

221. RNVR Decoration 1919

222. RNVR LS & GC

223. RFR LS & GC

224. RNASBR LS & GC Medal (i)

224. RNASBR LS & GC Medal (ii)

225. RN WAR LS & GC Medal

226. RNXS Long Service Medal

227. Rocket Apparatus Volunteer LS Medal

229. Army LS & GC Medal (ii)

230. Ulster Defence Regiment Medal for LS & GC

231. Volunteer Officer's Decoration

232. Volunteer Force LS & GC (HAC)

233. Territorial Decoration
236. Efficiency Decoration (i)

234. Territorial Force Efficiency Medal

235. Territorial Efficiency Medal
237. Efficiency Medal (i)

236. Efficiency Decoration T&AVR (ii)

237. Efficiency Medal T&AVR (ii)

237. Efficiency Medal (HAC)

238. Army Emergency Reserve Decoration

239. Army Emergency Reserve Efficiency Medal

240. Imperial Yeomanry LS & GC Medal

241. Militia LS & GC Medal

242. Special Reserve LS & GC Medal

242A. Volunteer Reserves Service Medal

243. Indian Army LS & GC (Europeans)

244. Indian Army LS & GC (Indians)

245. Indian Volunteer Forces Officer's Decoration

246/247. Colonial Auxiliary Forces Officer's Decoration/LS Medal

249. Permanent Forces LS & GC

250. RWAFF LS & GC

251. KAR LS & GC Medal

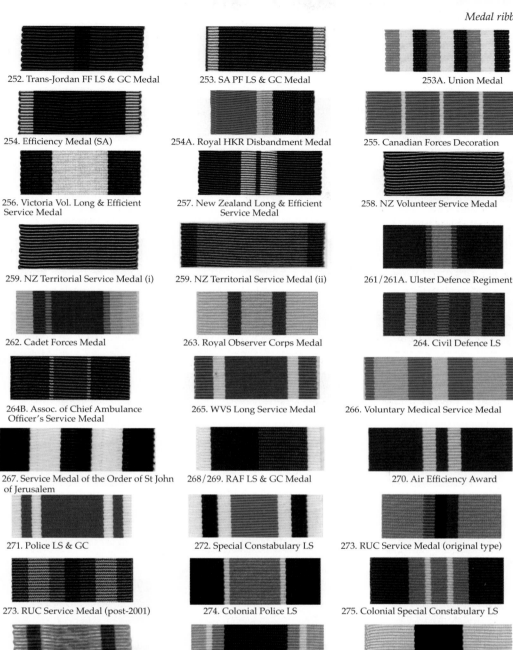

252. Trans-Jordan FF LS & GC Medal

253. SA PF LS & GC Medal

253A. Union Medal

254. Efficiency Medal (SA)

254A. Royal HKR Disbandment Medal

255. Canadian Forces Decoration

256. Victoria Vol. Long & Efficient Service Medal

257. New Zealand Long & Efficient Service Medal

258. NZ Volunteer Service Medal

259. NZ Territorial Service Medal (i)

259. NZ Territorial Service Medal (ii)

261/261A. Ulster Defence Regiment

262. Cadet Forces Medal

263. Royal Observer Corps Medal

264. Civil Defence LS

264B. Assoc. of Chief Ambulance Officer's Service Medal

265. WVS Long Service Medal

266. Voluntary Medical Service Medal

267. Service Medal of the Order of St John of Jerusalem

268/269. RAF LS & GC Medal

270. Air Efficiency Award

271. Police LS & GC

272. Special Constabulary LS

273. RUC Service Medal (original type)

273. RUC Service Medal (post-2001)

274. Colonial Police LS

275. Colonial Special Constabulary LS

277. Ceylon Police LS & GC Medal (I)

278. Ceylon Police LS & GC Medal (II)

279. Cyprus MP LS & GC Medal

280. HK Police Medal for Merit (1st Class)

280. HK Police Medal for Merit (2nd Class)

280. HK Police Medal for Merit (3rd Class)

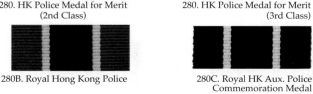

280. HK Police Medal for Merit (4th Class)

280B. Royal Hong Kong Police

280C. Royal HK Aux. Police Commemoration Medal

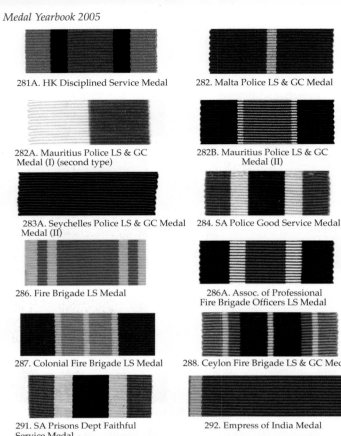

281A. HK Disciplined Service Medal

282. Malta Police LS & GC Medal

282A. Mauritius Police LS & GC

282A. Mauritius Police LS & GC Medal (I) (second type)

282B. Mauritius Police LS & GC Medal (II)

282. NZ Police LS & GC Medal (Second type)

283A. Seychelles Police LS & GC Medal (II)

284. SA Police Good Service Medal

285. SA Railways & Harbour Police LS & GC Medal (&290)

286. Fire Brigade LS Medal

286A. Assoc. of Professional Fire Brigade Officers LS Medal

286B. British Fire Services Assoc. Medal

287. Colonial Fire Brigade LS Medal

288. Ceylon Fire Brigade LS & GC Medal

289. Colonial Prison Service LS Medal

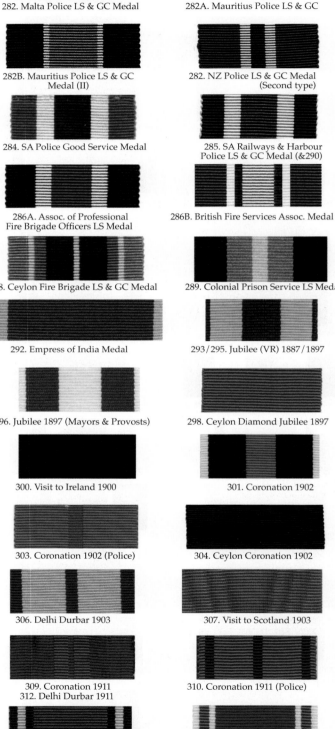

291. SA Prisons Dept Faithful Service Medal

292. Empress of India Medal

293/295. Jubilee (VR) 1887/1897

294/297. Jubilee (Police) 1887/1897

296. Jubilee 1897 (Mayors & Provosts)

298. Ceylon Diamond Jubilee 1897

299. HK Diamond Jubilee Medal

300. Visit to Ireland 1900

301. Coronation 1902

302. Coronation 1902 (Mayors & Provosts)

303. Coronation 1902 (Police)

304. Ceylon Coronation 1902

305. HK Coronation 1902

306. Delhi Durbar 1903

307. Visit to Scotland 1903

308. Visit to Ireland 1903

309. Coronation 1911
312. Delhi Durbar 1911

310. Coronation 1911 (Police)

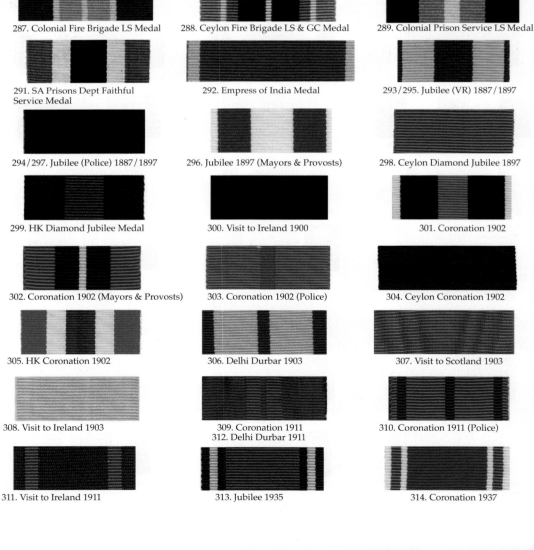

311. Visit to Ireland 1911

313. Jubilee 1935

314. Coronation 1937

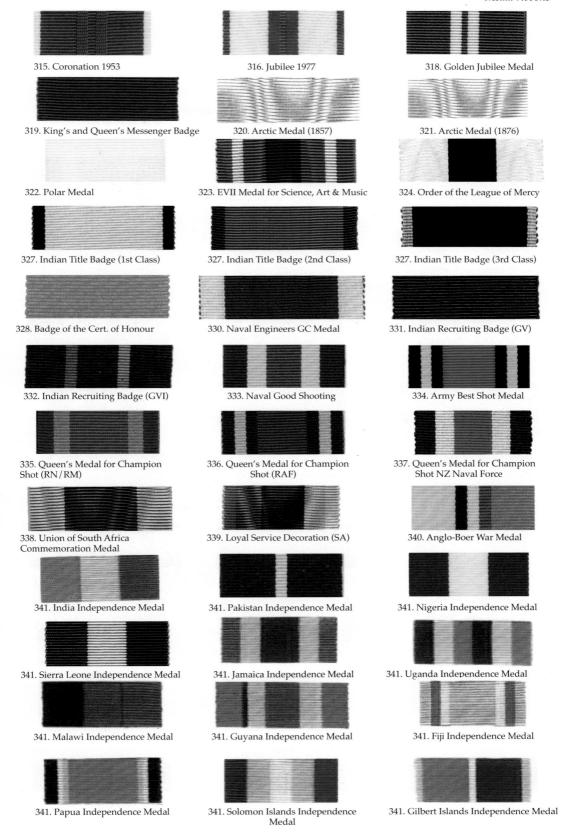

315. Coronation 1953

316. Jubilee 1977

318. Golden Jubilee Medal

319. King's and Queen's Messenger Badge

320. Arctic Medal (1857)

321. Arctic Medal (1876)

322. Polar Medal

323. EVII Medal for Science, Art & Music

324. Order of the League of Mercy

327. Indian Title Badge (1st Class)

327. Indian Title Badge (2nd Class)

327. Indian Title Badge (3rd Class)

328. Badge of the Cert. of Honour

330. Naval Engineers GC Medal

331. Indian Recruiting Badge (GV)

332. Indian Recruiting Badge (GVI)

333. Naval Good Shooting

334. Army Best Shot Medal

335. Queen's Medal for Champion Shot (RN/RM)

336. Queen's Medal for Champion Shot (RAF)

337. Queen's Medal for Champion Shot NZ Naval Force

338. Union of South Africa Commemoration Medal

339. Loyal Service Decoration (SA)

340. Anglo-Boer War Medal

341. India Independence Medal

341. Pakistan Independence Medal

341. Nigeria Independence Medal

341. Sierra Leone Independence Medal

341. Jamaica Independence Medal

341. Uganda Independence Medal

341. Malawi Independence Medal

341. Guyana Independence Medal

341. Fiji Independence Medal

341. Papua Independence Medal

341. Solomon Islands Independence Medal

341. Gilbert Islands Independence Medal

341. Ellice Islands Independence Medal

341. Zimbabwe Independence Medal

341. Vanuatu Independence Medal

341. SwazilandIndependence Medal

341. St. Christopher Independence Medal

341. Ghana Independence Medal

341. Kenya Independence Medal

342. Malta GC Anniversary Commemorative Medal

350. Shanghi Municipal Police (Specials) LS Medal

351. Shanghai Municipal Council Emergency Medal

352. Automobile Association Service Cross

353. Automobile Association Service Medal

L1. Royal Humane Society (1921)

L1. Stanhope Gold Medal

L3. Hundred of Salford Humane

L4. RNLI Medal

L5. SPLF Medal

L6. Lloyd's Medal for Saving Life at sea

L7. Liverpool S&H Society's Marine Medals

L8. SF&MRB Society Medal

L9. Tayleur Fund Medal

L12. Lifesaving Medal of the Order of St John (Original)

L12. Lifesaving Medal of the Order of St John (1888 on)

L12. Lifesaving Medal of the Order of St John (1950–1953)

L12. Lifesaving Medal of the Order of St John (1954 on)

L14. Liverpool Shipwreck and Humane Society's Fire Medal

L15. Liverpool Shipwreck and Humane Society's Swimming Medal

L17. Lloyd's Medal for Meritorious Service

L18. Liverpool Shipwreck and Humane Society's General Medal

L22. Tynemouth Medal

L23. Drummond Castle Medal

L28. Boys' Brigade Cross for Heroism

L29. Boys' Life Brigade Medal

L31. RSPCA Lifesaving Medal (Silver)

L32. Scout Association
Gallantry Medal (bronze)

L32. Scout Association
Gallantry Medal (silver)

L32. Scout Association
Gallantry Medal (gilt)

L33. CQD Medal

L34. Carpathia and Titanic Medal

L35. Lloyd's Medal for Services to Lloyds

L36. Order of Industrial Heroism

L37. Corporation of Glasgow
Bravery Medal

L38. RSPCA Margaret Wheatley Cross

L39. Lloyd's Medal for Bravery at Sea

* * * **STOP PRESS** * * * **STOP PRESS** * * * **STOP PRESS** * * * **STOP PRESS** * * *

198A. Operational Service Medal,
Sierra Leone

198A. Operational Service Medal,
Afghanistan

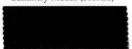

207A. International Conference on the
former Yugoslavia Medal

206A. NATO Service Medal
Eagle Assist

206A. NATO Service Medal
Active Endeavour

AUSTRALIAN MEDAL RIBBONS

A1. Victoria Cross for Australia

A2. Cross of Valour

A3. Order of Australia (General)
A15. Medal of the Order of Australia (General)

A3. Order of Australia (Military)
A15. Medal of the Order of Australia (Military)

A4. Star of Gallantry

A5. Star of Courage

A6. Distinguished Service Cross

A7. Conspicuous Service Cross

A8. Nursing Service Cross

A9. Medal for Gallantry

A10. Bravery Medal

A11. Distinguished Service Medal

A12. Public Service Medal

A13. Australian Police Medal

A14. Australian Fire Service Medal

A16. Conspicuous Service Medal

A17. Antarctic Medal

A21. Australian Active Service Medal 1975

A22. Australian Service Medal 1975

A23. Police Overseas Service Medal

A24. Defence Force Service Medal

A25. Reserve Force Decoration

A26. Reserve Force Medal

A26A. Defence Long Service Medal

A27. National Medal

A28. Champion Shots Medal

A29. Civilian Service Medal 1939–1945

A30. Australian Active Service Medal
1945–1975

A31. Australian Service Medal 1945–1975

A37. Gallipoli Medal

A38. Armistice Rememberance Medal

A49A. Humanitarian Overseas Service Medal

A50. Cadet Forces Service Medal

A51. Emergency Service Medal

A52. Ambulance Service Medal

A53. Australian Sports Medal

A54. Centenary Medal

A55. Anniversary National Service Medal

A56. A.C.T. Community Policing Medal

NEW ZEALAND MEDAL RIBBONS

NZ1. Victoria Cross for New Zealand

NZ2. New Zealand Cross

NZ4. NZ Order of Merit

NZ5. NZ Gallantry Star

NZ6/12. Queen's Service Order & Medal

NZ7. Gallantry Decoration

NZ8. Bavery Star

NZ9. Bravery Decoration

NZ10. Gallantry Medal

NZ11. Bavery Medal

NZ13. Operational Service Medal

NZ14. GSM 2002 Afghanistan (primary)

NZ14. GSM 2002 Afghanistan (secondary)

NZ14. GSM 2002 (Solomon Islands)

NZ15. NZ Service Medal 1946-49

NZ16. NZ General Service Medal (Warlike Operations)

NZ17. NZ General Service Medal (Peacekeeping Operations)

NZ18. East Timor Medal

NZ19. Special Service Medal

NZ20. NZ 1990 Commemoration Medal

NZ21. NZ Meritorious Service Medal

NZ22. Armed Forces Award

NZ23. RNZN Long Service Medal

NZ24. NZ Army LS & GC Medal

NZ25. RNZAF Long Service Medal

NZ26. Police LS & GC Medal

NZ27. Fire Brigades LS & GC Medal

NZ28. NZ Prison Service Medal

NZ29. NZ Suffrage Centennial Medal

NZ30. NZ Enforcement LS Medal

CANADIAN NATIONAL MEDAL RIBBONS

C1. Victoria Cross for Canada

C2. Cross of Valour

C3. Order of Canada

C4. Order of Military Merit

C5. Order of Merit of the Police Forces

C6. L'Ordre National Du Québec

C7. Saskatchewan Order of Merit

C8. Order of Ontario

C9. Order of British Columbia

C10. Alberta Order of Excellence

C11. Order of Prince Edward Island Medal of Merit

C12. Order of Manitoba

C12a. Order of New Brunswick

C12b. Order of Nova Scotia

C13. Star of Military Valour

C14. Star of Courage

C15. Meritorious Service Cross (Military Division)

C15. Meritorious Service Cross (Civil Division)

C16. Medal of Military Valour

C17. Medal of Bravery

C18. Meritorious Service Medal (Military Division)

C18. Meritorious Service Medal (Civil Division)

C20. Gulf and Kuwait Medal

C21. Somalia Medal

C22. South-West Asia Service Medal

C23. General Campaign Star

C24. General Service Medal

C25. Special Service Medal

C26. Canadian Peacekeeping Service Medal

C27. Canadian Centennial Medal

C28. Queen Elizabeth II's Silver Jubilee
Medal (Canada)

C29. 125th Anniversary of the
Confederation of Canada Medal

C30. Canadian Forces Decoration

C31. Queen Elizabeth II's Golden
Jubilee Medal (Canada)

C32. Royal Canadian Mounted Police
Long Service Medal

C33. Police Exemplary Service Medal

C34. Fire Services Exemplary Service
Medal

C35. Corrections Exemplary Service
Medal

C36. Canadian Coast Guard
Exemplary Service Medal

C37. Emergency Medical Services
Exemplary Service Medal

C38. Queen's Medal for Champion Shot
in Canada

C44. Commissionaires Long Service
Medal

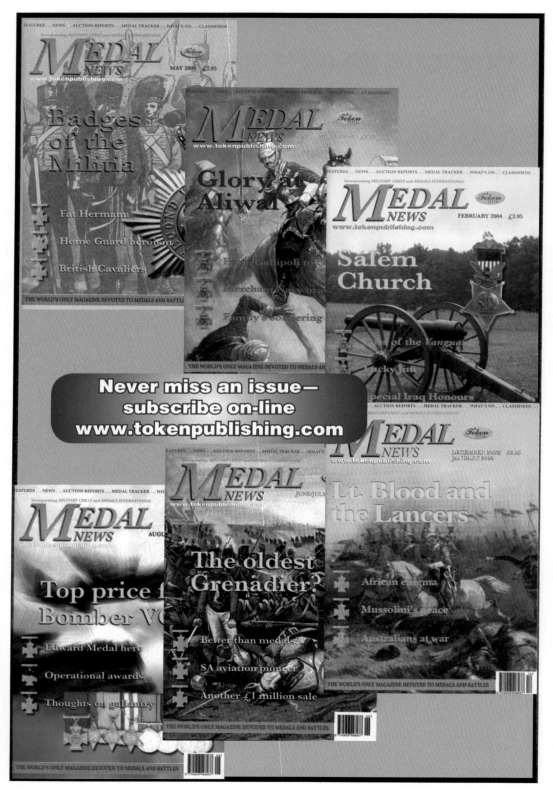

Never miss an issue—
subscribe on-line
www.tokenpublishing.com

INDEX TO MEDAL NEWS

Here we include the complete **Cumulative Subject Index** to the parent magazine MEDAL NEWS, commencing with the March 1989 issue, when it became a separate publication.

MEDAL NEWS was born in 1981 from the amalgamation of *Medals International* and *Coins & Medals*, into the popular title *Coin & Medal News*. However, the success of this magazine and the continuing growth of both the coin and the medal collecting hobbies prompted the separation of the two sections in March 1989. Since then both *Coin News* and MEDAL NEWS have grown from strength to strength and today are the hobby's leading publications, not only in the UK but MEDAL NEWS is the *only* independent magazine in the world devoted to the collecting and study of medals. Most later issues of MEDAL NEWS are still available, price £5—please enquire whether we have the issue you require (if not then photocopies of articles can be supplied at £5 per article).

NOTES

References are indicated **year, month: page,** for example 9004.18 means April 1990 issue, page 18; 9306.24 means June/July 1993 issue, page 24.

Each year runs from February to December. For example the year 1990 includes the December 1990/January 1991 issue (n.b. there are 10 issues per annum).

Names of ships are indicated in italics.

Names of people have been included where they appear to be the major subject of an article or where more than trivial information is included.

Abbreviations used:
(cr)   Indicates the inclusion of a full or partial casualty list.
(mr)   Indicates the inclusion of a medal roll.
(nr)   Indicates nominal roll.
(i)   Indicates that the reference gives information rather than the object itself. For example it tells you where to find a medal roll rather than reproducing the roll itself.
(p)   Indicates that the reference is to a picture of a person or object where little or no other information is given.
(mp)   Same as (p) except that the picture is of medals.
(br)   Indicates Book Review.

A

13 Stationary Hospital Pinetown Bridge 0310.31-32
17th Foot, William Caine 0311.14-16
19th Hussars, Col. J. C. Hanford-Flood 0308.21-22
19th Regiment of Foot, Pte Richard Davis in the Crimea – 0302.16-17
41 Independent Commando RM Korea 1950-52 0306.35-36
47 Royal Marine Commando 1943-46 (mr) 0304.16-18
£1million sale Dix Noonan Webb 0308.11
AA medal 9710.6
'A Crown of Life' Dianne Graves (br) 0011.35
'A Gazetteer of the Second Anglo-Boer War 1899-1902' Huw M. Jones & Meurig G. M Jones (br) 0004.34
'A Master Mariner's Log' Captain Richard Beard MBE (br) 0108.35
'A musket for the King, the trial and tribulations of a National Serviceman 1949 to 1951' L S Ives (br) 0306.51
'A Noble Crusade: the History of the Eight Army 1941-45' Richard Doherty (br) 0006.35
Abercrombie, John, Surgeon: Army of India Medal (mp) 9412.08
Abor 0303.29
Aboukir, and the *l'Orient* 0110.14-16
'Above the Trenches' (br) 9610.22
'Absent Minded Beggars', Will Bennett (br), 0002.36
Abyssinia (1868): 18th Bombay Native Infantry 9502.14
Abyssinia Medal (1867-68): naming 9003.22
Acasta: sunk 1940 9402.20-21
Accumulated Campaign Service Medal 9404.10
Ada: rescue (1875) 9403.18-19
Adams Allan Percy, Capt GSM 1918-1962 S. Persia 9910.18
Adamson, John (ed) and Lt Col H.B. Vaughan 'St George and the Chinese Dragon' (br) 0201.51
Aden (1857) 9010.12
Adkin, Mark 'The Waterloo Companion: The Complete Guide to History's Most Famous Land Battle' (br) 0202.34

Adolf Friedrich Cross (Germany) 8910.13
AE-1 (RAN submarine) (cr) 9306.12-13
AE-2 (RAN submarine) (nr) 9306.12-13
'Adventures in the Rifle Brigade in the Peninsula, France and the Netherlands from 1809: Capt John Kincade (br) 9807.29
'Air Force Records For Family Historians' William Spencer (br) 0008.35
Afghanistan, Maiwand. Saving The Guns 1880 0209.14-15
Afghanistan Medal
    92/Highlanders 9311.15
    naming 9003.23, 9004.18
Afghanistan, Operational Honours for 0303.15
Afghanistan Order of the Sun (mp) 9602.26
Afghan War (1842) medals 9003.22
Africa General Service Medal 1902-56 supplementary civilian awards (mr) 0009.26-27
Africa General Service Medal
    abbreviations 8905.26, 8906.24
    KRRC Somaliland (1903-04) (mr) 9006.14-17
    naming 9004.18
African Distinguished Conduct Medal 9008.15
African rating titles RN 9106.17
Africa Star
    Eisenhower, Dwight D., Gen. 9609.13, 9611.26, 9612.31
    entitlement 9504.10
    ribbon 8908.26
Ailsby, C. 'Allied Combat Medals of WWII' (br) 8911.07
Ainwick, Duke's School Old Boys 0111.22
Airborne Forces: Museum 9708.28-29
Air Crew Europe Star: ribbon 8908.26
Air France Disasters, Bahrain June 12 and 14 1950 0006.24-25
Air Force Cross 9105.13-17, 9511.16-17
    Air Training Plan WWII (mr) 9112.16-17

B

tropical helmet 9405.22-23
Life Saving Medallion to E.F Openshaw 0004.28
Life Saving Awards Research Society (i) 9103.05, 9403.19
Life Saving Medal (US) (mp) 9509.09
Lifford, A.H.A: WWI & Police medals 9604.25
Light Brigade, Troop-Sergeant William Bentley at Balaclava 0101.27-28
Light Cavalry: badges 9410.23
Light Dragoons
  at Waterloo 0401.33-35
  badges 9305.25, 9306.22
    arm 9004.24
Light Infantry
  85th 8910.20
  Albert Shako plates 9103.11-12
  Brigade badges 9709.27-28
Li Wo: WWII 8910.23, 9308.12-13, 9309.26
Lily, Cross of the (France): miniature (mp) 9509.09
Limb, Sue & Cordingley, P. 'Captain Oates - Soldier and Explorer' (br)
  9512.18
Lincolnshire Regiment: badges 9909.35-36
Lincolnshire Yeomanry: badges 9804.26-27
Lindall, H., Gnr, I Troop RHA (mp) 9602.08
Lindop, Lt 80/Foot: Ntombe River (1879) 8906.15-17
59/ Line Infantry Regiment (France)
  Crimea 9508.15
  Italian Campaign 9508.16-17
Lindsay, Captain Lionel Arthur 0005.30-31
Liprandi: Balaclava (Crimea) 8908.15-18
Lister, Frederick G., Capt 26 BNI: N.E. Frontier 9405.10-12
Litherland, A 'Standard Catalogue of Brit Orders Decorations & Medals'
  (br) 9104.25
Littlewood, Sydney C.T., RFC: Knight's Batchelor badge 9311.20
Liverpool Irish
  badges 9610.20-21
  piper's badge 9003.25
Liverpool Pals
  badge WWI 9012.22
  Memorial Fund 9409.05
Liverpool Scottish
  badges 9610.20-21
  piper's badge 9003.25
Livery Companies of the City of London in the Boer War 0305.32
Lizard: & *Goeben/Breslau* WWI 9302.18-19
Llewellyn, Margaret: RNLI Medal 8905.20
Llewellyn, Martha: RNLI Medal 8905.20
Lloyd, Henry, DSO (obit) 0108.09
Lloyd, T., F/Sgt 550 Squad (1944) 9410.15-16
Lloyd's War Medal for Bravery at Sea 9012.11-12
Loader, Roy, AB *Crane* 8912.12, 20, 9003.26
Lobb, Michael J., Capt, Corps of Royal Engineers: Queen's Gallantry
  Medal (1995) 9602.16
Local Defence Volunteers: badges 9105.24-25
Lodge, Gnr Isaac VC. Saving the Gun's at Sanna's Post 1900
  0208.25-26
Loewenhardt, Erich German Air Force: Blue Max 9411.12-13
Lombard, Fleur, firefighter: posthumous QGM 9807.06
London, City of, Imperial Volunteers 1900 0006.27-29
London & North Western Railway 'Pals' unit: WWI 9606.14
47 London Division: gallantry awards WWI 9302.20
London Fire Brigade; Station Officer E.W.R. Morgan GM, KPFSM
  (G), BEM; 0301.42-43
London Gazette, January 24 1946 Military Medal supplement 0005.28-29
London Gazette: PRO copies 9206.15
London Irish Rifles
  piper's badge 9003.25
  Territorial Force War Medal (1914-19) 9502.24
    (mr) 9408.13
London Medal Club Inception 0004.07
London Regt
  (1992) 9205.26
  badges 9110.26-27, 9111.26-27
London Rifle Brigade: badges 9605.20-21
London to Australia flight (1919-20) 9509.16-17, 22
London Yeomanry badges 9804.26-27
  City of London (Rough Riders): badges 9804.26-27 and 9805.27-28
  2nd County of London Yeomanry (Westminster Dragoons): badges
    9805.27-28
  3rd County of London Yeomanry (Sharpshooters): badges 9805.27-28
  4th County of London Yeomanry:badges 9805.27-28
  London Yeomanry and Territorials: badges 9805.27-28
London Welsh: badge WWI 9012.22
'Long Cecil'—siege of Kimberley 9908.24-26
Long & Efficient Service Medal (Victoria 1881-1902) 9610.16-17
Long Service and Good Conduct, Peoples, Joe. 0311.28-30
Long Service and Good Conduct Medals—Australia 0211.16-17
Long Service and Good Conduct Medals in the Victorian Army 0010.18-19
Long Service & Good Conduct Medal (RAF, GV): research file 9805.29
Long Service & Good Conduct Medal
  Army; ribbon 9503.25
  future development 9606.11, 26
  naming 9004.18-19
  RAF; ribbon 9604.26
Long Service & Good Conduct Medal (West African) 9008.15
Long service: 50 Years in Uniform, Pt Arthur Carter KSLI and
  Herefordshire Regt 9901.21

LSGC, 1st Class Sergeant Instructor Samuel Lambourne 0303.30-31
Long Tan, battle of (Vietnam): awards to Australians 9602.11-12
Longbottom, Brian V. Ldg Elec Mech *Voyager*: BEM 9404.17
Lonsdale Battalion: badge WWI 9012.22
Lord, Cliff & Birtles, David 'The Armed Forces of Aden 1839-1967' (br)
  0008.35
Lord Heneage, HMT: 9007.15-16
Lord Howe Island, Royal Australian Air Force Catalinas on 0003.35
Lord Strathconas's Horse, QSAs to (mr) 0206.19-20
Lord Wakefield of Hythe Commemorative Medal (mp) 9306.09
l'Orient and Aboukir, 0101.14-16
Lorne Scots: badge 9106.27
Lothians & Berwickshire Yeomanry: badge 9209.24-25
Lothians & Border Horse
  badges 9209.25
    piper's 9003.25
Lovat, Lord: death 9504.05
Lovat Scouts: badge 9210.24-25
Love, Frank, CERA RN: *Peterel* (Yangtse River) 9509.13-14
Love, Joseph R., RM: Tel-el-kebir (1882) 9406.12-13
Love, R.W. 'Diary of Admiral Sir B. Ramsay' (br) 9406.25
Lowland Brigade:bages 9708.25-26
Lowland Regiments: badges 9509.20-21, 9510.22-23, 9511.22-23
Loyal Britons of Westminster Medal 9006.26
Loyal Briton Volunteers Medal 9006.26
Loyal North Lancashire Regt
  at Maktau 0109.32-35
  badges 9612.27
  tropical helmet badge 9405.23
Loyal Nottingham Volunteers: shoulder-belt plates 9109.26-27
Loyal Regt: Musician badge 9403.25
Loyal Regiment, the, badges of 0311.23-24
Loyal Service Medal (Roumania) (p) 9210.27
Lucas-tooth Shield 9410.27
Lucknow 9003.20
  & *Shannon* 9302.12
  Eldridge, James QM Sgt 10/Bengal Light Cavalry: murdered 1857
    9901.22-23
'Lucky Girl Goodbye' Renate Greenshields (br) 0106.51
Lumsden, Frederick W., Maj RM: VC WWI 9603.18-19
Luneberg garrison: Ntombe River (1879) 8906.15-18
Lunt, James ' Jai Sixth (br) 9511.19
Luscombe, George, RMLI (18810 8903.14
Lushai (1889-92): KRRC (mr) 9312.15-18
Lusitania 9006.10-12, 9008.25-26, 9010.28
  Medal (Manx) 9006.10-12
Lutkin, William, Capt *Darvel*: MBE (1942) 9504.12-13
Lynas, Gilbert 82nd Foot 0208.19-20
Lynmouth Flood Disaster 1952 0208.16-17

M

Macalister, James: *Noreen Mary* WWII 9011.11-12
McCrae, John: Medals to be sold 9710.10
McCrae, John: Medal sale results (world record) 9801.09
McCrery N. 'The Vanished Battalion' (br) 9303.22-23
McCudden, J.T.B. (p) 9004.28
McDermott, Edgar J., PO *Voyager*: Queen's Commend. 9404.17
McDermott, Philip 'For Distinguished Conduct. . .register of DCM' (br)
  9409.24
McFarlane, Sgt W.J Yorkshire Regiment Long Service 0108.23
McGoogan, J. HMAS *Australia*, Duelling with the Kamikaze 0201.32-34
McIntosh Capt Angus, Maurice Geudji, and Flying Sgt Charles
    Corder—Beaufighter Crew 0201.36-37
MacArthur, Gen. Douglas and the Congressional Medal of Honour
  0101.19-20
MacDonald, John, 1/Bengal Fusiliers 9005.28
MacDonald, L. '1915 The Death of Innocence' (br) 9405.25
MacDonald, William, Col Sgt 1/Seaforth High 8912.19
MacDonald, William, Col Sgt 72/ Highlanders 8903.12-13
McDonnell, Thomas, Lt (p) 9408.09
MacDougall, D., Capt RAF: *Glowworm* explosion 9203.15-17
MacFarlane, John, Sgt 10 Squadron: MM WWII 9402.22
McFarlane, Vic, 12 Squadron: MM WWII 9402.21-22
MacGregor, John Lt Col VC: 9709.29
McGuigan, Sgt 1/ Argyll & Sutherland Highlanders: Palestine 9506.25
McHugh, Stephen, Sgt Parachute Regt: MC (1994) 9602.17
McIntosh Colin Alexander – Mid-air collision survivor 0310.22-24
McIntosh, G., Pte 6/Gordon High: Ypres VC 9411.15
McIntosh, John Cowe, Lt AIAF: London to Australia flight (1919-20)
  9509.17, 22
McIntyre, C. 'Monuments of War' (br) 9012.23
McIntyre, William: 4 with that name (1806-1933) 9405.21
Mackay, Dr James 'Soldiering on St Kilda' (br) 0209.35
McKay, David 93/ Highlanders VC memorial dedicated 9902.7
McKay, Robert 42/Highlanders 9109.20-21
McKinlay, PO Ronald DCM (obit) 0309.07
Mackinlay, G 'True Courage: The DCM to Australians' (br) 9302.23
McKenzie, Albert Edward VC 0005.11
McKinley, PO: CGM group (p) 9006.08
Mackinnon, W.H., Gen Sir (p) 9302.09
McLauchlan, Don, Lt Cdr: notice of death 9602.05
McLean, N.L.D., Lt Col Royal Scots Greys/SOE 9102.20
McPhail, H. 'Wilfred Owen Poet and Soldier' (br) 9405.24-25
MacPherson, A, FO 228 Squad: DFC *Kensington Court* (1939) 9410.12-13

West Yorkshire Medal Society 9510.26, 9512.26
West Yorkshire Regt
  badges 9512.22-23
    Leeds Pals WWI 9012.22
    Territorial Battn 9108.25
'Wet Review' Medallion (1881) 9412.16-17
Weymouth: *Konigsberg* (1914-15) (mr) 9205.18-19
Whale studies 1925 & 1939
  Polar Medal (1904) 8904.11-13
  Polar Medal (1904) (mr) 8905.15-18
Wharmby, Mike, Lt Col: OBE citation 9509.12
'Where Right and Glory Lead: The battle of Ludy's Lane' (br) Graves,
  Donald E. 9906.24
White, A.S. 'Bibliography of Regt Histories of Brit Army (br) 8911.18-19
'White Dragon—The Royal Welch Fusiliers in Bosnia' (br) 9810.26
White Lt Geoffrey Silver Star 0310.18
'White Knees, Brown Knees' Douglas J. Findlay (br) 0310.33
White, Osric H., Flt Sgt RNZAF: CGM(F) WWII 9609.14-15
White Russian awards (mri) 9111.04
White, WO George DCM (obit) 0301.09
'Who Downed the Aces in WWI' (br) 9612.32
Whyte, Mrs: RNLI Medal 8905.20-21
Wickenby, RAF, war memorial 8909.23
Wicks P/O B.J. Battle of Britain 0009.16-19
Wilfred Owen Society 9008.05
Wilhelm Ernst War Cross (Germany) 8911.20
Wilhelm's Cross (Germany) 8912.14
Wilkes, Peter DCM (obit) 0305.06
Wilkins, George H., Sir (1888-1958): antarctic flights 8906.24
Wilkins, George H.: Sir (Photo of plane) 8904.11
Wilkinson, Thomas, T/Lt RNR: *Li Wo* 9308.12-13
William Scoresby
  antarctic voyages 8904.11-13,8905.15-18 (nr) 8906.24
Williams, D. ' Black Cats at War. Story of 56/ (London) Div TA 1939-45'
  (br) 9509.07
Williams, E.G.'On Parade for Himmler' (br) 9408.25
Williams, John S. MBE, DCMLt-Col Chairman Gallantry Medallists
  League 0001.30-31
Williams Lt Col J. S. (obit) 0203.08
Williams, Robert Ralph OBE; heroes of the Albert Medal 0211.33
Williamson, H.J. 'Roll of Honour RFC & RAF 1914-18' (br) 9305.22
Williamson, Howard 'The Collectors and Researchers guide to the
  Great War' 0401.51
Willis, Flt Sgt: MM WWII 9402.21
Willits, W.E., Sgt 228 Sqad: DFM *Kensington Court* (1939) 9410.12-13
Wilmot-Allistone, Lt Alfred Barron; World War I POW 0301.44-45
Wilson, Eric VC 9904.25-26
Wilson, Heather 'Blue Bonnets, Boers and Biscuits. the Diary of Private
  William Fessey, DCM serving in the King's Own Scottish Borderers
  During the Boer War ' (br) 9905.26
Wilson, Field Marshal Sir Henry. Murder of 0301.41
Wilson J.M., W.H. Fevyer, and J. Cribb 'The Order of Industrial Heroism'
  (br) 0102.34
Wilson, John, Sgt. RE.: MSM Waziristan 8908.19-21
Wilson, John R. Ldg Sick Berth Att. *Voyager*: BEM 9404.17
Wilson, Noel, F.O. RAAF, GM (Timor WWII) 9502.18-19
Wilson, Trevor & Prior, Robert 'Passchendale-the untold story' (br)
  9704.32
Wiltshire Regt: Givenchy (1915) 9204.15-16
Wiltshire, Sydney GC (obit) 0311.06
Wimberley, C.N.C., Maj 71 Native Field Hosp: Gyantse Fort (1904)
  9404.20-21
Windsor Castle Co: badge 9105.25
Wingate, Orde, Maj Gen (p) 9604.07
Wingate, Reginald, Gen Sir 9305.08
'Wings Aflame' Stokes,D (br) 9908.37
Winston: Robert W. *Melbourne*; Queen's Commend. 9404.18
Winter War: Finland 9705.18-19
Winter, Charles Francis 9804.15-17
Wireless Observation Group WWI 9208.13
Wireless Operators WWI 9009.27
Wisnom, William, Capt: Tayleur Fund Medal 9403.18-19
'Without Hesitation, The story of Christopher Cox' Mary Hallett (br)
0306.51
Witte, R. C., 'Fringes of the Fleet and the Distinguished Service Cross'
  (br) 9711.31
Wittebergen (1900) bar to QSA 8908.27
Woman of the Bedchamber badge, Queen Alexandra (mp) 8905.09
Women's Army Auxiliary Corps: badge 9212.24-25
Women's Auxiliary Defence Service Medals (Finland) (i) 9502.06
Women, Bravery Awards to 0008.17
Women's Forage Corps: badge 9212.25
Women's Legion: badge 9212.25
Women, Orders and Medals of Modern Russia awarded to 0310.29-30
Women's Voluntary Service Medal (1961): ribbon
8909.26
Wood, Alan C and Treadwell, Terry C. 'German Knights of the Air 1914-
  1918' (br) 9711.31
Wood, Wilfred, Pte Northumberland Fus.: Railwayman VC WWI 9606.15,
  17
Wooden, Lt Charles VC 0305.24-25
Woodgate, E.R.P, Maj Gen Sir: Spion Kop (1900) 9408.14-17

Wooding, Ernest A., RCNVR: Albert Medal WWII 9405.18-19
Woodward, H.J., Able Seaman (p) 9306.11
Woolls-Sampson, Maj ILH: Elandslaagte (1899) 9510.15
Worcestershire Regt
  badges
    Musician 9403.24
    pouch & valise 9411.22-23
World War I *see* names of battles
WW1, saving the Guns at Le Cateau; 0401.24-25
  surviving British veterans awarded French Legion of Honour 9901.06
  Medal fakes and forgeries 0303.09
  Medal fakes and forgeries Part II 0304.09
, Church Army in 0304.13
, Silver War Badge 0310.34
  CD-ROM project 9603.25
  demobilisation papers 9404.25
  80th anniversary commemorations 9811.15
  Desert Mounted Corps 8905.25
  German awards 8908.09-10
  records 9206.14-15
  records release 9803.29 & 9909.28
  records, Army Officers' 9911.35
  Soccer Truce, death of Bertie Belsted 0110.08
World War II British Recipients of Soviet Decorations 0106.48-49
World War II, Caterpillar Club, Neville Anderson 0101.24-25
World Wide Web Collecting 0005.18-19
Worledge, cyril, Sgt RAF: DFM WWII 9609.15
Worth, Geoffrey P., PO [I]Voyager[i]: BEM 9404.17
'Wotsit': PRO Dog National Charity Lifesaver Award 9504.05
Wray, Air Commodore Arthur DSO, MC, DFC, AFC 0208.23
Wren, William – volunteering in World War I 0204.18-19
Wright R. and Rawnsey C.F.'Night Fighter'(br) 9908.37
Wusthoff, K, Lt German Air Force: Blue Max 9411.12-13
Wyatt (?Wylie), Lt RA (Port Natal) 8912.15
Wynn, K.G. 'Men of the Battle of Britain Supp Vol' (br) 9208.26
Wyon, William: medal designs 9102.24

Y

Yangtse River: *Peterel* 9509.13-14
Yarra Borderers (1912-18): badge 9005.25
Yatternick, F/OE 550 Squad (1944) 9410.15-16
Yellow Ribbon Medal (Japan) 9311.19
Yellow Ribbon Merit Medal (Japan) 9002.26
Yeomanry: arm badges 9004.24
Yeomanry badges
  Bedfordshire 9801.27
  Berkshire 9801.27
  Berkshire and Westminster Dragoons 9801.28
  Royal Buckinghamshire Hussars 9801.28
  Cheshire (Earl of Chester's) 9801.28
  Derbyshire 9802.26
  Royal North Devon 9802.26
  Queen's Own Dorset 9802.26
  Queen's Own Dorset and West Somerset 9802.27
  Essex 9802.27
  Royal Gloucestershire 9802.26
  Hampshire Carabiniers 9803.26-27
  Herefordshire 9803.26-27
  Hertfordshire and Bedfordshire 9803.26-27
  Inns of Court and City 9803.26-27
  Royal East Kent 9803.26-27
  West Kent (Queen's Own) 9803.26-27
  Kent and County 9803.26-27
  King's Colonials 9803.26-27
    Welsh 9704.25-26
  King Edward's Horse 9804.26-27
  Duke of Lancaster's Own 9804.26-27
  Lancashire Hussars 9804.26-27
  Leicesteshire (Prince Albert's Own) 9804.26-27
  Leicesteshire and Derbyshire (Prince Albert's Own) 9804.26-27
  Lincolnshire 9804.26-27
  London 9804.26-27
  City of London (Rough Riders) 9804.26-27 and 9805.27-28
  2nd County of London (Westminster Dragoons) 9805.27-28
  3rd County of London (Sharpshooters) 9805.27-28
  4th County of London 9805.27-28
  London and Territorials 9805.27-28
  Royal Mercian and Lancastrian 9805.27-28
  Middlesex (Duke of Cambridge's Hussars) 9805.27-28
  Norfolk (King's Own Royal Regt.) 9807.25-26
  Northamptonshire 9807.25-26
  Northumberland Hussars 9807.25-26
  Nottinghamshire (Sherwood Rangers) 9807.25-26
  South Nottinghamshire Hussars 9807.25-26
  Queen's Own Oxfordshire Hussars 9807.25-26
  Queen's Own 9807.25-26
  Royal 9807.25-26
  Shropshire 9808.27-28
  North Somerset 9808.27-28
  North Somerset and Bristol 9808.27-28
  West Somerset 9808.27-28

Index
of medals

AUSTRALIA

CANADA

NEW ZEALAND

SOUTH AFRICA

NOTES

351. SHANGHAI MUNICIPAL COUNCIL EMERGENCY MEDAL

Instituted: 1937.
Ribbon: 38mm bright red, having a broad white central stripe bordered black and yellow edges separated from the red by thin black stripes.
Metal: Bronze.
Size: 40mm.
Description: An eight-pointed star with ring suspension. (Obverse) a central medallion superimposed on the radiate star with the triple-shield arms of the Municipality surrounded by a collar inscribed SHANGHAI MUNICIPAL COUNCIL. (Reverse) a laurel wreath enclosing the words FOR SERVICES RENDERED - AUGUST 12 TO NOVEMBER 12 1937.
Comments: *Awarded to members of the Police, Volunteer Corps, Fire Brigade and civilians for services during the emergency of August-November 1937 when fighting between the Chinese and Japanese in and around Shanghai threatened to encroach on the International Settlement. Issued unnamed, but accompanied by a certificate bearing the name and unit of the recipient. Examples have been seen with the recipient's name engraved on the reverse.*

VALUE: £150–180   *Miniature*   £60–80

351A. CHINESE MARITIME CUSTOMS SERVICE FINANCIAL MEDAL

Obverse

Instituted:
Ribbon: Green, with yellow stripes.
Metal: Gold, silver or bronze according to class.
Size:
Description: An eight-pointed radiate star suspended by a plain ring, having an oval medallion on the obverse inscribed in Chinese and depicting a Chinese junk; (reverse) a horseshoe scroll inscribed THE CHINESE MARITIME CUSTOMS MEDAL with FINANCIAL across the foot. The recipient's name was engraved in the centre.
Comments: *The Chinese Maritime Customs Service was operated and largely staffed at the higher levels by British personnel from 1854 till 1950. Medals were awarded for five years' service or shorter service of exceptional merit and were granted in three classes, each of three grades, making nine variations in all, distinguished by the respective metals, and awarded according to the rank of the recipient.*

VALUE: —   *Miniature*   £90–100

351B. CHINESE MARITIME CUSTOMS SERVICE MERITORIOUS SERVICE MEDAL

Reverse

Instituted:
Ribbon: Green with yellow stripes.
Metal: Gold, silver or bronze according to grade.
Size:
Description: As above, but FOR MERITORIOUS SERVICE in the tablet on the reverse.
Comments: *Awarded for 25 years continuous service, according to the rank of the recipient, but later awards in silver or gold could be made on promotion to a higher rank, or for exceptional service, notably from 1931 onwards, following the outbreak of hostilities with Japan.*

VALUE: —

352. AUTOMOBILE ASSOCIATION SERVICE CROSS

Date: 1956.
Ribbon: Yellow with three narrow black stripes.
Metal: Silver.
Size: 36mm.
Description: A silver cross flory terminating in scrolls, with the AA emblem surmounted in the centre.
Comments: *Established in commemoration of the Association's Golden Jubilee, the Cross is the highest award to AA patrolmen and other uniformed members of staff for conspicuous acts of bravery involving an imminent risk of personal injury whilst on duty in uniform, or whilst engaged in an action related to duty. To date only 15 crosses have been awarded. A monetary reward accompanies the Cross.*

VALUE: Rare

353. AUTOMOBILE ASSOCIATION SERVICE MEDAL

Date: 1956.
Ribbon: Half yellow, half black.
Metal: Silver.
Size: 36mm.
Description: A circular medal in the form of the AA badge with wings sprouting from the top and flanking a claw and ring suspension. (Obverse) AA superimposed on a wheel, with the inscription AUTOMOBILE ASSOCIATION/SERVICE MEDAL round the circumference; (reverse) details of the award.
Clasp: A silver-gilt and red enamel clasp inscribed 192064 (ie. 20 years good driving, 1964) has been reported.
Comments: *Like the Cross, the Medal of the Association was instituted in commemoration of the Association's Golden Jubilee. The medal is awarded to members of the uniformed staff for courageous or outstanding initiative and devotion to duty. To date, only 60 medals have been awarded, including four in 1997, mainly for life-saving and bravery in accidents. A monetary reward accompanies the Medal. A Service Citation is also awarded for lesser acts, a total of 63 having been bestowed so far.*

VALUE: Rare

354. SUFFRAGETTE MEDAL

Instituted: 1909.
Campaign: Votes for women.
Ribbon: Three equal stripes of purple, silver and green.
Metal: Silver.
Size: 20mm.
Clasps: Prison bars surmounted by a broad arrow, or an enamelled bar in the WSPU colours.
Description: A small silver medal suspended by a ring from a bar with scrolled finials, engraved with the date of the award. A similarly scrolled brooch bar at the top of the ribbon is inscribed FOR VALOUR. The plain medal is engraved HUNGER STRIKE in various styles and hallmarked.
Comments: *This medal was awarded by the Women's Social and Political Union (WSPU) to those militant Suffragettes who were imprisoned for various acts of violence and who went on hunger strike while in prison. At first they were forcibly fed under the most barbaric conditions, as a result of which several died. The government then introduced the Cat and Mouse Act, whereby hunger strikers at the point of death were released, but were then re-arrested and returned to prison when they had recovered sufficiently from their ordeal. Bars were awarded in respect of subsequent periods of imprisonment and hunger strike.*

VALUE: £3500–£4000 (unboxed)
£5000–£6000 (in personally inscribed case)